The Irish Theatre Series 10
*Edited by* Robert Hogan, James Kilroy, Richard Burnham *and* Liam Miller

The Modern Irish Drama, *a documentary history*
IV: The Rise of the Realists, 1910–1915

The Modern Irish Drama
*a documentary history* IV

# The Rise of the Realists,
1910-1915
by Robert Hogan, Richard Burnham
and Daniel P. Poteet

The Dolmen Press

Humanities Press Inc.

*Set in Times Roman type and printed*
*and published in the Republic of Ireland*
*by The Dolmen Press Limited*
*North Richmond Industrial Estate, North Richmond Street, Dublin 1*

*Published in the United States of America and in Canada*
*by Humanities Press Inc.,*
*171 First Avenue, Atlantic Highlands, N.J. 07716*

*First published 1979*

ISBN 0 85105 350 5: The Dolmen Press
ISBN 0 391 01118 9: Humanities Press Inc.

BRITISH LIBRARY CATALOGUING IN PUBLICATION DATA

Hogan, Robert, b. *1930*
    The modern Irish drama.—(The Irish theatre
series; 10).
    4: The rise of the realists
    1. Theater — Ireland — History
    I. Title   II. Kilroy, James
    III. Burnham, Richard   IV. Poteet, Daniel P
    V. Rise of the realists   VI. Series
    792'.09415        PN2601

ISBN 0-85105-350-5

# Contents

Personally, I believe that when the history of this time is written, it will be found that Irish imagination to-day has begun to express itself in plays, precisely as Irish imagination expressed itself fifty years ago in songs and ballads.

W. B. YEATS, 1911

# Acknowledgements

Stephen Fay, for quotations from manuscripts of F. J. Fay.

Nevin Griffith, for quotations from *Sinn Féin*, and writings of Arthur Griffith.

*The Irish Independent*, for quotations from *The Freeman's Journal* and *The Irish Daily Independent* and *The Weekly Freeman's Journal*.

*The Irish Times* for quotations from *The Daily Express, The Dublin Evening Mail* and *The Irish Times*.

Gerald MacDermott, for quotations from the journals of Joseph Holloway.

J. C. Medley, for quotations from published works of George Moore.

*The Sunday Times.*

Oliver Weldon, for quotations from *In Clay and in Bronze* by Brinsley MacNamara.

Simon Campbell, for quotations from unpublished writings of Joseph Campbell.

Mrs. Eimar O'Duffy and Miss Rosalind O'Duffy, for quotations from *Printer's Errors* by Eimar O'Duffy.

The Estate of Ria Mooney and Proscenium Press for quotations from *Players and Painted Stage*, by Ria Mooney and edited by Val Mulkerns.

National Library of Ireland, for quotations from manuscript collections.

Michael Yeats, for quotations from published and unpublished works by W. B. Yeats.

Due to the postal strike in Ireland in 1979, we may not have contacted all holders of copyright material. If so, our apologies and assurance that the omission of proper acknowledgement was unintentional.

# Introduction

This volume, like the previous three of this history, attempts to ascertain the facts and to recreate the flavour of theatre in Ireland. The basic method of this history is to tell the story mainly in the words of those authors, actors and audiences who lived it. For this volume, we have again assiduously combed through all of the evidence which we could discover or obtain access to — in newspapers, in journals, in published and unpublished documents, correspondence and memoirs, even in fictional recreations, and in one instance in an interview with a still surviving participant.

We have, perhaps, more in this volume than in the previous ones, allowed our own critical comments to intrude. In the first volumes, many of the plays discussed were classic pieces by W. B. Yeats, J. M. Synge, Lady Gregory and a handful of other writers whose work is so well known and thoroughly discussed that any brief critical remarks would have seemed merely impertinent. In the years here under review, 1910 through 1915, the number of new Irish plays has much increased, but many of them have remained unpublished or have been long out of print. Consequently, we have resorted to contemporary plot summaries and sometimes to our own evaluations when the contemporary criticism seemed too scant, too caustic or too enthusiastic.

This period in Ireland, from the beginning of 1910 to the end of 1915, saw the stirrings of social and political disturbances that were to erupt with terrible and lasting impact in Easter week of 1916. Chiefly, there was a great labour struggle that began in the autumn of 1913 and that disrupted the city of Dublin for months, and there was also the far-reaching impact of the Great War which disrupted all of Europe for four years. In the small world of the theatre, significant events were also occurring, and new trends were becoming clarified. The Abbey Theatre became finally disassociated from its English benefactor, Miss Horniman, and found it necessary to tour frequently in England and for long periods in America. The tumultuous events of the early touring in America are recounted in an Appendix.

The quality of Abbey Theatre productions remained generally high, with capable producers such as Lennox Robinson and A. Patrick Wilson, and with a still intact company of brilliant performers such as Arthur Sinclair, J. M. Kerrigan, Fred O'Donovan and, often, Sara Allgood. The nature of the Abbey plays, however, had begun to change. Synge was dead, Yeats was doing little new work, Lady Gregory's new work was falling off in quality, and

George Fitzmaurice was to join the British army. The notable new dramatists were Lennox Robinson, T. C. Murray and R. J. Ray from Cork and St. John Ervine from Belfast. All of these writers were basically realistic in manner, and their prose melodramas began to supersede the earlier poetic fantasies and began, indeed, to seem the typical kind of Abbey play.

Occasional dramatists appeared who could possibly have stemmed this realistic trend. However, Daniel Corkery of the Cork Dramatic Society in his intermittent writing for the stage never long settled down to one particular dramatic manner. Eimar O'Duffy wrote some early satiric fantasies for Edward Martyn's Irish Theatre in Hardwicke Street, but was never quite in sympathy with the ideals of the group and turned his highly individual talents primarily to fiction. Gerald MacNamara was for years a principal author and actor for the Ulster Theatre, but many of his plays were short and very few were ever published—not even his very popular satire on the Abbey drama whose title gave a new phrase to the language, *The Mist That Does Be On the Bog*.

Pure entertainments, sometimes of considerable quality, continued to appear, but perhaps the most talented of such entertainers, George A. Birmingham, after much initial success, found that his second play caused a riot in Westport far more violent than the Dublin row over Synge's *Playboy*. That incident may well have been part of the reason why this prolific clergyman then ceased to write for the stage.

In these bustling years, the Ulster Theatre, the Independent Theatre of Count Markievicz and the Irish Theatre of Edward Martyn, as well as the newly formed second Abbey Company in Dublin, occasionally rivalled and even occasionally surpassed the efforts of the often absent Abbey Players. There has been a tendency to pay scant attention to the years between the last play of Synge and the first play of Seán O'Casey, but those dozen or so years were in actuality rich, vigorous and highly fruitful for the Irish drama.

It is with much regret that I have worked on this volume of *The Modern Irish Drama* without the genial and knowledgeable collaboration of Professor James Kilroy, my partner on the previous three volumes. However, for *The Rise of the Realists*, I have been highly fortunate in securing the eminently necessary collaboration of Professors Daniel P. Poteet and Richard Burnham. In the following pages, Professor Poteet has done much work on the year of 1911, on the original version of the year 1912, and on the Abbey tours in America. However, when I succeeded in losing the only typescript of the research for the year 1912 and could not bring

10

myself to start anew on it, Professor Burnham took the matter in hand and has succeeded in discovering much more than was in the original version.

ROBERT HOGAN

Dublin
August, 1978

# 1910

## THE CROSS IMAGE
### A National Drama

SCENE: *The outside of Michael O'Slatterley's public house. The Widow Flynn's cottage to be seen in the distance across the valley to the left. To the right the Atlantic. Seated on an upturned soapbox is a blowsey rascal, reputed to be a butcher, and named Burke. A filthy slattern with a red nose squats on the ground close by. She is the local Postmistress.*

BURKE: (*After a silence*) 'Tis meself now has just sold a sheep that died av a faver to feed the polis.

POSTMISTRESS: An' I'm just after coming frum lookin' into the letters an' parcels that come into the office.

BURKE: (*After a silence*) We're a witty people.

POSTMISTRESS: 'Tis a pity the world knows nothing uv us.

BURKE: An' us artistic.

POSTMISTRESS: Sure, 'tis meself has a fine cravin' for the realistic dhrama.

(*Enter O'Slatterley, very drunk indeed.*)

O'SLATTERLEY: The tap o' the mornin' to yez, bedad — I beg your pardon — God save all here. (*Hiccups loudly and falls headforemost through his own door and remains prone, his feet alone showing.*)

BURKE: He must be tired drunk.

POSTMISTRESS: 'Tis expected ov him. Sure, you wouldn't have him not amuse the gentry.

(*Enter Philly, a dirty nondescript, staggering.*)

PHILLY: (*Calling*) Molleen Pike. Polleen (*Hiccup*) Mike.

(*Molleen O'Slatterley appears at the door, standing on the body of her father. She is a well-looking girl, but we are given to understand that she is not in a cleanly condition.*)

MOLLEEN: Oh, ye are there now, an' ye dragging my fayther off to a wake, an' lavin' me in the darkness av the night — observe my diction.

PHILLY: Oh, but 'twas a wake — the regular thing (*Hiccup*); twelve men under the table head (*Hiccup*) drunk, an' twelve lyin' on th' (*Hiccup*) stones, dead (*Laughter*) drunk (*Hiccup*).

POSTMISTRESS: An' did ye not play cards on the dead man's chest?

PHILLY: We did not.

BURKE: Nor stick the end av a lighted rush in his mout'?

PHILLY: (*Shocked*) We did not.

13

MOLLEEN: Thin it wouldn't have gone down. I'm glad we didn't stage it.

(*O'Slatterley moves his feet in a very comic manner.*)

MOLLEEN: Where's me fayther?

BURKE: Av he was a dog he would bite ye.

MOLLEEN: (*Looking down*) 'Tis himself surely. (*Remains standing upon him.*)

(*Enter Polyanthus Hivvy, looking back into the wings in a very funny manner and carrying a parcel. He is recognisable as the comic lodger of the London music halls.*)

POLYANTHUS: I'm the new deputy-inspector.

BURKE: Another looney. Man, but aren't we all imbeciles in this countryside widout bringing you out of Carlow?

POLYANTHUS: But look at me characters! There's not a man in all Carlow that has a notion of truth. Read 'em. (*Hands letters to Postmistress.*) All lies.

POSTMISTRESS: Thanks. I've read 'em.

PHILLY: Let's all go an' catch jackdaws — that seems an essentially Irish (*suddenly recollects himself and hiccups*) idee.

(*Nobody takes any notice. Enter Twisty Barn, walking very slowly. He is, of course, considerably crazed.*)

TWISTY: Sure, 'tis one av these natural potes I am ye've heard about, for 'tis meself that knows the wonders of the night an' all that — an' stars — an' me lonely wandering in the dark lanes listenin' to the abandoned youths and girls kissing one another and making a noise like a rabbit, and me jealous because I daren't speak to one at all, but just wonder on lonesome in the darkness of the night.

MOLLEEN: Here, I said that.

TWISTY: Oh, it's an everyday phrase.

(*Burke yawns; so does Postmistress.*)

TWISTY: Sure, now, 'tis queer you looking bored and me after killing me da.

(*They all gather round with laborious excitement. O'Slatterley rises slowly and with difficulty.*)

MOLLEEN: Av ye have your da slain I'll marry ye; av ye haven't, I won't.

TWISTY: I split him to the middle with the edge of a loy.

MOLLEEN: You're the playboy of the western world, and a true type of the young manhood in your generation in this land, surely. I'll marry you. Here, come inside, an' I'll see to your feet and make a bed.

(*Enter Widow Flynn who appears sane and respectable, but at once repudiates the suggestion.*)

14

WIDOW: Oh, here's a man, a stranger man, and me having murdered himself is wanting one badly.

MOLLEEN: Go away. He's mine, I tell ye.

O'SLATTERLEY: (*Lurches forward and seizing Twisty and also his daughter, draws them together and leans heavily upon them*) 'Tis the will of God. (*Laughter.*) A single man is only a (*Hiccup*) jackass in his own (*Hiccup*) house. May I have many (*Hiccup*) grandchildren, though I don't see at all (*Hiccup*) what good that'll (*Hiccup*) do me.

   (*Enter Old Barn, a tramp, crawling on his hands and knees.*)

TWISTY: Me da.

MOLLEEN: Thin ye didn't kill him. I won't marry so.

TWISTY: I did me best. He kep alive to vex me.

WIDOW: Isn't he the walking terror, an' a liar, surely.

TWISTY: Av I did not, I will. (*Kicks his father on the head. Old Barn dies at once.*) Now, will ye marry me?

BURKE: There's all the difference between proving ye did a queer thing an' doing that same.

MOLLEEN: I won't marry ye, Twisty Barn.

O'SLATTERLEY: 'Tis the will of God. (*Laughter.*)

   (*Enter Gerringcop, a ragged stonecutter, carrying a block of marble.*)

GERRINGCOP: A couple of whales have come ashore on the beach, and the priest himself tells me to make a statoo out of this because of that.

POLYANTHUS: I wish I'd stayed in Carlow. They're all as bad as meself in this same place.

BURKE: (*Pointing dramatically at Polyanthus*) There's the wan man now to make a statoo of.

POLYANTHUS: I will not then.

   (*Enter Mountainy Man, perfectly insane.*)

MOUNTAINY MAN: No. You must take it to Dr. Dumpshay.

ALL: Of course. How could we be forgetting Dr. Dumpshay?

FEMALE ASCENDANCY DRAWL FROM THE STALLS: How delightfully Irish.

MALE ASCENDANCY DRAWL FROM THE STALLS: Yaws. Yaws.

   (*Enter Muskerry with his boots undone.*)

MUSKERRY: Here I am, beggared by my own children, according to the custom of the country.

   (*Enter a large crowd of old men and women haggling in a very sordid strain over their daughter's marriage fortune. They go to the right of the scene, and keep up a low continuous hum. Enter a large crowd of lunatics and imbeciles who form a group to the left. Enter Ellen McCarthy and Brian O'Connor.*)

15

MOLLEEN: Oh, ye did leave, Ellen. I thought ye would.

ELLEN: Yes, Brian came looking for copy for a novel, and as a sheep had died and the tea wouldn't boil, I thought I'd better cut it. Dublin people like you to be miserable, you know.

BRIAN: Yes, she's finished off one wretched affair by leaving Dempsey, and she's begun another by coming with me. God knows what I'm going to do with her in the suburbs.

O'SLATTERLEY: 'Tis the will of God.

BURKE: Ye had some fine notions of paytriotism I am given to understand, madam, wance.

ELLEN: Oh, yes, but one mustn't be altogether patriotic; it isn't artistic, you know.

*(By this time everybody is speaking with a London accent. Enter two distinctly Cockney burglars, one emphatically named Jim, and the other, therefore, named Bill. They both look very mystical.)*

BILL: Sai, Jim, wot'll yew dew wen yer gits ter ther glitterin' bloomin' gite?

JIM: *(With acute mysticism)* THEY.

BILL: Jim. I sai, Jim, 'ere's a bloomin' pagint.

*(They scrutinise the concourse of Irish types.)*

JIM: Taint a pagint. It's the Irish National Drama. They've got a prospectus in the 'Doily Mile'.

CURTAIN[1]

This broad satiric skit amused the readers of the 9 July issue of Arthur Griffith's Republican paper, *Sinn Féin*. Although the skit emphasises Synge's *Playboy of the Western World*, the plays of W. B. Yeats, Lady Gregory, Padraic Colum, Lennox Robinson, and even Lord Dunsany come in for a few knocks; and the reference in the last line to 'The Doily Mile' is a pointed barb at the attempts of Yeats and Lady Gregory to raise English money for the Abbey Theatre in London, now that Miss Horniman's support had virtually ended.

It was predictable that satiric attacks would be directed against the Abbey Theatre by such publications as *Sinn Féin* and *The Leader*. The Republicans had been for the last six or seven years growing ever more disenchanted with the Irish National Theatre Society. A patriotic parable like *Kathleen ni Houlihan* was a most acceptable kind of national drama, and so perhaps was even Lady Gregory's more tentative *The Rising of the Moon*. But the plays of John Synge were another matter entirely. In 1903, Synge's *In the Shadow of the Glen* had seemed to be a false and perverse defamation of Irish character and life. This feeling was reinforced

16

by *The Well of the Saints*, and in 1907 the production of *The Playboy* had exacerbated popular feeling enough to produce spontaneous disruptions of its performance.

To some extent, this dislike of Synge's plays was softened by Synge's own personal diffidence, and to some extent by his premature death in 1909. Nevertheless, the distrust and the intermittent dislike of the Abbey Theatre was most fostered by the continued production of the Synge plays. This distrust was not confined to ardent Republicans, but shared by a majority of the theatre's basically middle-class patrons. Neither W. J. Lawrence nor Joseph Holloway was deeply interested in politics, but their violent opposition to *The Playboy* was an accurate symptom of the feelings of the ordinary member of the Abbey Theatre audience.

To the mind of a Lawrence or a Holloway, the villain of the piece was not really Synge; Synge had been unfortunately exposed to morbid foreign influences, but basically he had a gentle and diffident innocence. He was the introspective artist who was utterly astonished at the effect of his plays. No, the villain of the piece was the aristocratic and enigmatic Yeats. And yet even here, an ardent dislike had to be tempered by a grudging admiration: for, no matter what their narrow critical biases, Lawrence and Holloway were basically compelled by their utter devotion to and their complete love of the theatre. To them, Yeats's sacrileges had to be — although unwillingly — balanced by Yeats's enormous virtues. And this ambivalent feeling about Yeats on the part of Lawrence and Holloway is a microcosm of the fascinating love-hate relationship between the Abbey Theatre and the bulk of its audience.

By 1910, the idea of the Abbey Theatre play had grown up in the mind of the audience. Such a play took for its subject the Irish peasant, and presented him really as a modern version of the ape-like Paddy who once appeared in the pages of *Punch*. This was a character filthy, drunken, immoral, blasphemous and foul-mouthed, and most typified by Christy Mahon or, worse, his father. The Irish peasant woman was equally squalid in her habits, enormously more strident in her conversation, totally amoral in her sexual predilections, and most typified by Pegeen Mike. However, by 1910 other plays in the Abbey repertoire were reinforcing this view. Even Lady Gregory's quaint little comedies had now congealed into a kind of formula; and her recent and thinner plays seemed to start from some utterly ludicrous idea that presented the peasant as a bumpkin, fool or idiot. And, following the death of Synge, the best of the new writers also tended to treat of peasant life, and to treat it most roughly. The realistic plays of Lennox Robinson, Padraic Colum, T. C. Murray and R. J. Ray had none of the extravagant language of Synge and Lady Gregory, but they had a similar view of the Irish peasant as grasping, mean, malicious, treacherous, uncouth, and basically stupid. The whimsical conceits of Synge and the charming Kiltartan of Lady Gregory seemed now replaced by a dialogue punctuated by 'damns' and emphasised with 'bloodys'.

And yet the plays of Colum and Robinson and Murray and Ray did have some power, did have some truth, did have some worth. Consequently, the mind of the ordinary theatregoer in the Abbey pit was in something of a schizophrenic state in 1910.

*　　*　　*

In 1910 the Abbey staged eight new plays, two revisions of earlier work, one translation, and one Irish play previously produced by the Theatre of Ireland. The first new play was John Millington Synge's posthumous *Deirdre of the Sorrows* which opened on 13 January. Synge had not completed the play when he died the previous March, but the theatre, according to a programme note, decided to produce it with only minor alterations.

> Mr. Synge began writing this play about two years before his death, but it was often put aside because of illness, and was left at the last unfinished. He had brought in a new character, Owen, and had meant to make more use of him, and he would have enriched and elaborated the dialogue, working it over and over again according to his custom. We are giving it as he left it, putting in not more than a half-dozen words and taking out here and there a sentence that did not explain itself.[2]

Synge's death and memories of the controversies surrounding his earlier plays produced a first-night atmosphere charged with excitement. But, as in the *Blanco Posnet* production of 1909, the actual performance was something of an anti-climax. The ubiquitous Joseph Holloway was, as always, there, and his reaction was exactly that of the many people who had violently opposed *The Playboy of the Western World*, but who had rather liked J. M. Synge.

> His idea seems to have been to wrest the legend from its exalted plane and breathe the commonplaces of everyday life into it — in fact, to vulgarise the beautiful legend. That he succeeded in doing this is only too true. His characters of Lavarcham . . . , of Owen a half-witted servant, and of an Old Woman might have stepped out of any of his latter-day peasant plays; the ruck of muck was in their speech. As a stage play, I fear Synge's *Deirdre of the Sorrows* is of little

18

worth. Up to a certain point, the last act is dramatic, but there it is allowed to fizzle out drearily in ineffective anti-climaxes, and the final curtain comes as a relief to all in front, even to Synge's most ardent worshippers. . . .

When the play was over and done, Seumas O'Sullivan said, as many of us chattered in the vestibule, that "There was nothing incomplete about it. The people in the play were human beings at all events and not merely inanimate Kings and Queens!" I grant that the loftiness of the theme was trailed in the mud if that's what he meant by "human beings", but the treatment took the grandeur and poetry out of the tale. . . .

All seemed afraid to express themselves freely or candidly on the play when it was over, but that the general impression was not favourable could easily be felt. Were the play an undoubted success, nothing could keep back the hymns of praise. It is only when failure is close at hand that silence holds thoughts in check.[3]

Most accounts report that the reaction to the play was enthusiastic, but others report that the entire production was depressing and even soporific. The reasons for this discrepancy were probably these: the ill-feeling about Synge's earlier work was still rawly evident, but it was counter-balanced by the sobering fact that the playwright was dead, and even that his death may have been hastened by the 1907 riots. In any event, *Deirdre* did not offer much to fight about. If its psychology was thought to be a de-meaningly modern treatment of the legend, its production by Yeats and Máire O'Neill was utterly, even a little boringly, reverent.

The reactions of the Irish critics ranged predictably along party lines. The ascendancy paper, *The Irish Times*, was gushingly admiring; Arthur Griffith's Republican paper, *Sinn Féin*, was highly critical. But Synge was dead, and even the violent W. J. Lawrence was a bit muted in his condemnation. As Lawrence wrote in *The Stage*:

The truth is that, by some curious process of divination, Synge arrived at a delicate appreciation of the colour and mystery of life without gaining any knowledge of the light which gave birth to the colour, or of the spirit lurking behind the mystery. Lacking informative power, his art had no health in it, could only deal with the beauty of externals, of decay. Roses he grew in abundance, but all are rooted in a charnel house.[4]

Yet Synge was dead, and what could be praised without loss of face was praised most highly, and so the acting of the title role by

Synge's fiancée, Máire O'Neill, was described by every Irish critic as 'a triumph . . . a remarkable triumph . . . a wonderful triumph . . . an exquisite embodiment . . . her greatest success.'

Perhaps what one needs in this case is the unemotional comment of the outsider. During the summer, on the theatre's second English tour of the year, the London critics saw the play, and Ashley Dukes wrote in *The New Age*:

> . . . *Deirdre of the Sorrows* moves haltingly upon the border-land between intention and achievement, in a dramatic half-world of blurred outlines. It was clearly meant to be a great tragedy, but it is not a great tragedy, and if the rewriting of it was to have been concerned, as Mr. Yeats suggests, mainly with the enrichment and elaboration of its dialogue, it would still have failed. Embroidery of phrase is a good servant but a poor master. It can easily strangle drama.[5]

In *The Sunday Times*, J. T. Grein wrote:

> It must be said in regretful candour that in spite of the goodwill which everybody bears to the Irish National Theatre, each renewed annual visit is accompanied by some disappointment. Some years ago, when we made the acquaintance of these players, their work filled us with enthusiasm. We realised the absence of craft, but we were moved to great admiration of the intuition and the zeal which left its impress on the work of every individual actor. They were amateurs — people, we understood, who left their trade to devote their spare time to the national cause of art, but as they had no ulterior motives they worked with a will in the spirit of crusaders. With the perpetuation of the Irish Theatre, with the constant change of management, and the travelling, it cannot be gainsaid that the *ensemble* has suffered deterioration. In other words, the amateurishness has become more glaring and enthusiasm has, at least outwardly, become damped under the stress of routine. For light work, such as in the delightful little pieces by Lady Gregory which are racy of the soil and of the time, the company is still well equipped. But when tragedy is touched, which demands profound introspection, and power of declamation, we observe that there is absence of individuality and especially of stage management.
>
> In the production, for instance, of the late Mr. Synge's last play, *Deirdre of the Sorrows*, there occurred lapses of stage direction which moved the most seriously inclined audience in the world to a faint titter. And on the whole one felt that

the task overwhelmed the efforts. For it is a mistake frequently found with amateurs, that whenever tragedy is performed they believe it to be their duty to abandon their natural voice and to preach in often sepulchral tones. This was the rule, not the exception, with the Irish players, save one or two, notably Miss Sara Allgood, whose creations of maternity are always remarkable, and Miss Máire O'Neill, whose obvious want of training is covered by the charm and the pathos which emanate from her personality. There is the making of a fine actress in Miss O'Neill, since she has the qualities peculiar to the Irish race — emotion, sweetness of voice, depth of feeling. On the other hand, she has not been taught to realise the fulness of her power: thus the figure of Deirdre, which, despite its attractiveness, is fraught with vigour, becomes shadow-like instead of dominant. . . . If tragedy in the higher sense of the word is to form a constant part of their programme, the actors should be trained for their work under competent guidance. If this cannot be obtained, well, then, let the players continue to regale us with those pleasant little episodes of Irish humour such as *Hyacinth Halvey*, which are within their province by their birthright, and not beyond their forces.[6]

But perhaps the most devastating comment upon the Irish actors was the critique by William Archer:

Most of them are professional actors, inasmuch as they have for years made acting the business of their lives. Some of them, too, are quite admirable comedians, and can portray Irish character with remarkable humour and discretion. Nevertheless, their general style is one of imperfect accomplishment. They have made an art of artlessness. They either cannot, or will not, attain that ease and freedom on the stage which is the mark of the actor — even of the bad actor — as distinguished from the amateur. After all these years, for example, they still share with the Wiltshire villagers [the Wiltshire Village Players, a group of English amateurs] a curious wooliness and indecision of attack. They seldom make an exit, but wander on and wander off. In the American phrase, they "happen along". There is no crispness, no accent, in their movements. And, again like the Wiltshire villagers, they tend all to speak in one cadence. Speech will follow speech in the same rhythm, each character unconsciously repeating the tune sung by his predecessor. Now, for a certain class of pieces, and especially for plays of peasant life, this little touch

21

of helplessness — for that, rather than artlessness, is the exact word — comes in far from inaptly. The air of hesitation, almost of depreciation, strikes us as a pleasant change after the metallic self-confidence of the ordinary actor, who sometimes imposes himself upon the public by mere aggressiveness of attack. But it is one thing to find helplessness pleasing up to a certain point, and quite another thing to declare it, in itself, preferable to accomplishment This peasant acting — for so it may be called, though I believe the Irish actors are, for the most part, townsfolk — this peasant acting has very real charms of raciness, sincerity, inartificiality. But it is an art which is possible only within very narrow limits; and though it is right that, in judging it, we should take these limits into account, it is neither right nor reasonable to speak as though they were positive advantages, and the conditions of all sound art.

It so happened that at the late J. M. Synge's play, *Deirdre of the Sorrows*, I was placed where I could barely hear one word in three of the dialogue. . . . It was not merely the difficulty of hearing that had spread a veil between me and the poet's work; it was the total absence of light and shade in the performance. The acting was far from being without merit. On the contrary, Miss Máire O'Neill's Deirdre was singularly beautiful, distinguished, and tragic. But even Miss O'Neill had to subdue herself to the general dimness, if I may so phrase it, of the whole picture. Only on reading did I discover that Mr. Synge had conceived Deirdre as a wilful, imperious creature, not without a spice of the devil in her. Miss O'Neill had not the freedom, had not the confidence, to indicate the transitions and put in the highlights. She seemed to be moving harmoniously through a melancholy, monotonous dream. And this was the tone of the whole performance. The general woolliness of touch and sameness of cadence left all outlines indistinct. It was impossible to see the characters clearly, or to realise in any detail the process of emotion. In the early days of Maeterlinck, the Théâtre de l'Oeuvre (if I remember rightly) used to act his works behind a gauze screen; and such a screen the Irish players carry round with them in their artless methods. . . . There was one point where one of the performers — Miss Sara Allgood, I think — tore the veil, and said something, of no great importance, with spontaneity and force. The burst of applause which followed was not so much a testimony of admiration as an irrepressible movement of relief.[7]

22

On 3 February the Abbey staged a revised version of Lennox Robinson's *The Cross Roads*, first produced the previous April. The consensus was that Robinson's revision improved the work. *The Freeman's Journal* described the changes:

> In its original form the play consisted of a prologue and two acts. In the prologue the heroine, in a farewell meeting with her fellow-members of the Erin Club in Dublin, before her departure to become a reformer in West Cork, expresses her opinions on the fruitlessness of debate at the club, and talks of the great things she will do for the community when she returns to Ballygurteen. The prologue was a weak spot in what was otherwise a drama of exceptional strength. In the revised version the prologue is omitted altogether, and so much of the dialogue as is necessary to complete the play is introduced at other points. There has been some bracing up of the play in other parts also. The failure of Ellen M'Carthy was left unaccounted for in the original, unless one accepted the theory of some adverse fate overtaking her. In the new version the matter is not left in doubt. In the scene between Ellen and Brian O'Connor, before Ellen's marriage, Brian, in his endeavour to persuade her to marry him, warns her of the evil consequences of opposing nature; and again when he meets her, when the "great black curse" has fallen on her, he reminds her of his warning of the danger of turning love from its proper course. The play in its new form is more intensely dramatic than the original version.[8]

A week later, on 10 February, the Abbey offered another revision. This was Yeats's *The Green Helmet*, an adaptation in ballad metre of *The Golden Helmet*. In *The Irish Independent*, J. H. Cox wrote:

> May I say that in this new form Mr. Yeats the poet rather conceals Mr. Yeats the dramatist? His "sense of theatre" was more in the original. For instance, in the beginning it took one a couple of minutes to get the drift of the talk, whereas it is a sound old theatrical proverb that not for a moment should the audience be left groping. But after all the poetry is the thing. And on this score the best I can say of the artists is that they did not commit the English crime of dragging the verses. A fault most incident to the actorial passion for clearness and realism was peculiarly noticeable in Mr. O'Donovan. He persistently carried his pauses into the middle of each line, thereby utterly destroying the lyrical effect. In this excess of

23

matter-of-fact realism, Mr. Sinclair was almost equally egregious. So the opening duologue between these two passed off, one may say, in prose. Not till Mr. Kerrigan arrived did the ear catch the measure and cadence of the verse. Really, when the subject is fanciful and legendary . . . the author's music should be given a chance.[9]

The reviewer for *The Leader* complained that the Abbey playwrights were continually tinkering with their work. 'They are always chopping up and changing some of the pieces at the Abbey.' he groused. '*The Green Helmet* was once *The Golden Helmet* — its next appearance may be under the name of the Grey Mullet.' [10] However, Padraic Colum in *The Manchester Guardian* called it a 'brilliant satire on Irish quarrelsomeness', and then added:

> *The Green Helmet* is thrilling in its rapidity, its suggestion, its triumphant verse. Mr. Yeats has discovered a dramatic medium. Rhymed verse has, of course, been used before in English drama, but rhymed verse in the ballad metre seems certainly an innovation. The verse is crisp, brilliant, and effective. This ballad verse is suitable only for a certain kind of drama, for drama near to comedy, working itself out in rapid action. *The Green Helmet* is probably the most effective stage piece that Mr. Yeats has written.[11]

A few days later G. H. Mair followed up Colum's review with another article in *The Manchester Guardian*, praising the play and describing the theatre:

> You leave O'Connell Bridge and go along the riverside; then you turn up a dark and mean street — one of those sombre streets that you find everywhere off the main thoroughfares of Dublin — and you are before its door. There is not much light about it and no façade to the pavement; and when you enter you walk through a rather gloomy hall hung with pictures and past a small cafe into the auditorium that is just as unpretentious. There is only one tier or gallery or circle, and the hall (it is rather a hall than a theatre) is neither high nor deep. The curtained stage is of pocket-handkerchief dimensions. . . .
>
> At the Abbey Theatre the association of authors and actors is closer than in any English-speaking company since Elizabethan days, and than it has been anywhere, I fancy, since the days of Molière. Mr. Yeats and Lady Gregory superintend closely all the performances and the rehearsals; it is (under the providence of Miss Horniman till September next and,

I hope, afterwards) their theatre. They move backwards and forwards behind the scenes and in front. Mr. Yeats occupies himself with problems of staging and lighting, busy with ceaseless experiment in new effects, in the artistic grouping of the actors, in the symbolism of their dress and gestures, in the intonation of their lines. Afterwards in their comfortable green-room (for in Dublin that almost discarded feature of theatrical architecture still exists) you may hear them, as I did, discussing, actors and authors together, how such and such a thing should be said, what was the precise meaning of this or that passage in *The Playboy*, what is the effect on the audience of a new trick of speech or a new gesture, and all the thousand and one subtleties that make up the fascination of the stage. And I am sure it is this fruitful co-operation and comradeship that makes the theatre what it is.

. . . A stranger could not hope to see in it [*The Green Helmet*] all that Mr. Colum, with his passionate pre-occupation with Ireland, sees, and I confess that its aspects as a satire on Irish quarrelsomeness did not occur to me. But at whatever its shaft was directed, it had an artistic appeal of a novel and arresting kind. . . . The stage setting, as always in the Irish company's poetical plays, was of a piece with the verse. One remembers the wonderful copper and green tones of the ship and its burden in *The Shadowy Waters*. Here green — a luminous, indescribable sea-green — and red were the notes on which the colour-scheme was built up till the pale and torch-lit darkness in which the climax came. Though the tiny stage was crowded with figures, there was never any sense of crowding. And when the declamation and the singing ended (it was beautiful singing, that of the women surging at the door, for Miss Allgood and her companions have beautiful voices) and the stranger had laughed his last and disclosed the riddle of his wager and the curtain fell you leant back in your seat with the even pleasure that comes of seeing something noble well done.

The night ended . . . with *The Playboy of the Western World*, on which we have all had our say and nothing fresh can be written now. Let it suffice that the acting seemed more surely inspired than ever and that we sat (many of us, I am sure, with the words of it running in our head in advance of the players, we knew it so well) wondering, as always, at the poetic figure of the shiftless fugitive Mr. O'Donovan has given us, and spellbound by the strange and entrancing fascination of Miss Máire O'Neill.[12]

25

Mair himself felt that fascination more than most, and in 1911 he was to marry Máire O'Neill.

The next two new plays were both by Lady Gregory. *Mirandolina*, her adaptation and translation of Goldoni's *La Locandiera*, had its premiere on 24 February; *The Travelling Man*, a one-act miracle play, had its premiere on 3 March. Neither made much of an impression on the critics. Of *Mirandolina, The Freeman's Journal* thought that the plot needed more work, and that Lady Gregory should take more liberties with her original. *The Irish Times* thought that the piece was entertaining but not as good as Lady Gregory's adaptations of Molière. Practically every critic, however, regarded the play as a fine vehicle for Máire O'Neill who played the frivolous innkeeper of Lady Gregory's title. None of the reviewers particularly liked *The Travelling Man*, and Jack Point of *The Evening Herald* thought that it was beyond redemption:

> Little fault can be found with Lady Gregory's one-act miracle play . . . except, possibly, that the central idea is a mistake. A "travelling man" is, I take it, a euphemistic way of describing a tramp, be he beggar, pedlar, or tinker, but almost invariably an undesirable who would be more likely to rob a poorbox than perform a miracle. And so when the mother — whom he has conducted safely to a cottage, where she is given food, rest and shelter — fails to recognise her benefactor until she afterwards hears he was walked over the neighbouring river, her mistake is perfectly natural. It will be observed that there is a certain similarity to *The Passing of the Third Floor Back*. That play was only saved from being objectionable by the admirable — and, if one may say so, reverential — acting of Forbes Robertson in the name part, and to my mind *The Travelling Man* is much inferior both to it and many of Lady Gregory's other plays.[13]

And with that conclusion, most critics would have to agree.

For three weeks in April the theatre was on tour in Belfast, Leeds and Manchester, but they produced a new play in Dublin on 5 May, Padraic Colum's three-act *Thomas Muskerry*. In its revised version, the play strikes one as almost masterly, but even this early version aroused a heated debate about whether it was a 'great' play or merely a morbid one. In these years any debate about an Irish play was usually argued from a purely aesthetic view or a purely nationalistic one. So *Thomas Muskerry* on the one, aesthetic hand was compared to *King Lear* and *Old Goriot*; on the other, nationalistic hand it seemed, as usual, a denigration of the Irish character. Colum did, unlike Synge, mainly escape charges of immorality, although the eagle-eyed Jacques did write in *The Irish Independent*:

> Really, I fail to find any good reason for this play. It provides hours of unrelieved dulness, serves up alleged humour that in third-rate pantomime would draw guffaws from stall Johnnies, and dialogue that is coloured with coarseness. The realism is gross. The author holds the door wide open and compels you to look inside. He insists on the details of scenes with a lack of reticence that is unnecessary, nauseous, in-artistic. It sins against good taste. It is intolerable.[14]

To this, Colum's friend Thomas Kettle, replied:

> What one . . . might ask is whether gloom is an unusual thing to find in an Irish workhouse? Let "Jacques" read again the Report of the Poor Law Commission; let him pay an hour's visit to any of our Workhouses and watch the pageant of misery shuffling by in that ugly brown uniform which degrades poverty below the level of crime; let him study the mass of problems, social, moral, and economic, which will be forced upon him by such a vision of destitution, and one might challenge him to leave the place with a light heart. Is it a sin against "good taste" to write a "gloomy" play or poem? If that be so, we shall all turn with great relief from *Thomas Muskerry* to the bright optimism of *Oedipus Rex*, the pleasant humour of Dante's *Inferno*, and the sparkling comedy of *Hamlet*.[15]

Of the many lengthy contemporary commentaries upon the play certainly one of the most thoughtful was that of Imaal in a paper usually hostile to the Abbey, D. P. Moran's *The Leader*:

> The plot of the play need not be rehearsed here. . . . As a plot it is not specially striking, no more than is that of Balzac's *Goriot*. The striking merit of Mr. Colum's play is that all of the characters are genuine characters; given these people, and certain antecedent circumstances, the plot is bound to result, being indeed the natural channel for the action of those characters to run through. One profound critic said that Mr. Colum's new drama was a collection of characters rather than a play; had the gentleman eyes he would have seen that a collection of such characters, brought together under given circumstances, is bound to result in dramatic action. Mr. Colum's play is strictly natural, and is not worked by the aid

27

of any *deus ex machina* : the characters make the play out of the natural clashing of their own passions and interests. . . .

That the play vividly recalls the theme of *Lear* and *Goriot* is too obvious to mention — were it not that the other critics seem not to have yet seen the resemblance. Three out of the four were pre-occupied with their resentment against the play, while *The Freeman* writer wanders off into matters about Nietzsche, and a preface of Mr. Colum's which he declares full of literary heresies. Not only is there a likeness in the theme, there are even resemblances in the treatment. The old Workhouse Master, like the ancient British King, holds on to power until his mind has, to say the least of it, become weakened. Even when he does retire he retains some of his old authoritativeness, and his behaviour towards Felix Tournour in the second act recalls Lear's attitude towards one of his daughter's men, just as the insolence of Tournour towards Muskerry recalls the insolence of the underling to Lear. Lear and Goriot have each a pair of undutiful daughters, while Thomas Muskerry has but one; the place of the second, however, is amply filled by a grand-daughter, and, to fill the cup, a grandson. Muskerry several times tells his daughter that he has always placed himself at her service and that of her family, just as Lear and Goriot have ever been at the service of their dutiless daughters. In Balzac's novel the old man's daughters "drain him dry as hay"; in Mr. Colum's play, the Crillys follow the same policy, so far as their power lies. Goriot dies friendless, cared for only by strangers; Muskerry dies the same way, the last kindness he receives being from a blind man and a poor boy. Muskerry's daughter has all the harshness of a Goneril or a Regan, while she and her detestable minx of a daughter are just as hard and grasping as the termagants to whom Lear gave so much, and who took the little he had left. Indeed the theme of *Thomas Muskerry* is so frankly that of Lear and Goriot that one marvels at the obtuse opacity of the critics who never took in the resemblance, or saw the parallel.[16]

Nevertheless, many criticisms were made of Colum's gloomy and sordid picture of Irish life, and of the indelicacy of his language. The poetess Ella Young defended the play against these charges by saying:

I am one of the several people who think *Thomas Muskerry* a great play, an achievement — not only the greatest play Padraig Colm has written, but the greatest play that has ever been written by an Irishman. It is subtle-minded and modern, and the people in it are people one could find in any little decaying Irish town, but as I watched the drama unfold, my mind went back to the Greeks: for this play is concerned with Fate and the struggle of man with Destiny — the subject of Greek tragedy. To the Greek mind it seemed that the struggle ended in the defeat of man: the Celtic mind, looking, it may be, deeper, sees a different ending, for in *Thomas Muskerry* the end is liberation, attainment, not defeat. Perhaps I ought not to claim this as a Celtic, but rather term it a modern point of view. . . .

When the curtain rings up on *Thomas Muskerry* we see a man who has shut himself in on all sides by conventions and petty habits and small authorities. His mind is like the little commonplace office which he has made as comfortable for himself as the nest is for the wren. There is, however, in him something that stirs and struggles; that wearies of the little office and the comfortable maxims; something that shows him, in a sudden flash of insight, how the grasping brother who robbed Miles Gorman of land and home gave him instead the freedom of the road.

With the stirring, with the self-assertion of this intangible something—this untamable intimate self of Thomas Muskerry — comes the self-assertion of Destiny in the shape of the grasping daughter with her husband and children; the incapable, inexorable family. They prevent him escaping to the country. They shut him in the workhouse, but yet they give him the chance of doing the one great deed of his life when he breaks from them and fronts the Guardians with the confession of his mistake about the tons of coal. They, finally, throw up the last heart-breaking barrier over which he leaps to freedom — for Thomas Muskerry escapes; he finds the freedom of wider roads than Miles Gorman ever travelled. Miles has said a prayer for him, "God be good to Thomas Muskerry." It was the last appeal, a pathetic, triumphant assertion of the untamable prisoner that was Thomas Muskerry's soul. . . .

I have set out, with perhaps unnecessary fulness, what seems to several people to whom I have spoken and to myself, the dramatic idea of the play, because I have heard it said that the play has no dramatic idea. With regard to the construction of the play, the dialogue, the situations, I can only say that they seemed worthy of the idea they embodied, and as good as the best work of Ibsen.[17]

29

This appreciation appeared in the 9 July issue of *Sinn Féin*; in the next week's issue a correspondent called 'X' launched a long, vigorous attack against it, in an article called 'Muskerryism'. The gist of the article was the old argument that defaming the Irish character was pandering to an English audience. The most telling paragraph, however, was the final one:

> Mr. Colum has not drawn men, and the pity of it is that, unlike his colleagues, he could draw them. Miss Young has described him as subtle-minded. He is much greater — he is peasant-minded. He is the only literary man in Ireland since Carleton who has got the wonderful mind which nine-tenths of our writers write about and nine-tenths never even vaguely understand — the mind of the man on the soil, in which all the virtues and vices of the indestructible Celtic race still dwell. Carleton, easily a greater man than Walter Scott, misused his gift. He played down to England. Since his time Ireland produced no man who could express that mind until it produced Colum. Just as we were trembling at the wonder, lo, the interpreter set off after the gods of other peoples, and his greatest praise now is to be compared with Ibsen. . . .[18]

To this charge Colum himself immediately replied:

> I have no desire to prolong the controversy which has arisen in *Sinn Féin* around my play, but you have put into your articles statements which I resent to the point of challenging. "Mr. Colum is an Irishman who . . . submits his plays to the judgment of the English public. . . .' I have never written an Irish play for an English audience. *Thomas Muskerry* was written for an Irish audience. It was produced in London as it might have been produced in the Shetland Islands. I did not spend twopence in discovering what the London papers wrote about my play. In connection with the London production the document that had the most interest for me was the royalty account. I have given my play to an Irish theatre. They are at liberty to produce it in London, New York, or Paris. I do not put myself under geasa to write for a London or New York theatre, but I assure you, my dear "X", that any play written by me for a non-Irish theatre will have no connection with Ireland.
>
> Now that the pencil is in my hand I may as well bring your impressions of Ibsen into line with reality. In the passage I have quoted you imply that Ibsen wrote in a language which is to Norway what Irish is to Ireland. In Norway there are

two literary languages—the "Landsmaal", derived from ancient Norse, a local and popular language and a literary language known to the whole of Scandinavia — Norway, Sweden, and Denmark. I might make a point by describing this language as Danish. It is sufficient that Ibsen did not write in the language peculiar to Norway — the "Landsmaal". His plays were produced in Christiana, but they were published in Copenhagen. As a literary man he did not look to Christiana for recognition; he looked to Copenhagen. I have by me a French book on Ibsen (*Ibsen, 1828–1906* par Ossip-Laurie), which contains some of the dramatist's letters. The only reference which he makes to Norwegian criticism is in terms of contempt. But he hopes for the approval of Danish men of letters, Brandes, Schandorf, Clemens Petersen. *Peer Gynt* is the most Norse of Ibsen's dramas. Ibsen is most anxious to have Petersen's opinion on the dramatic poem. When Petersen, writing in a Danish journal, slighted *Peer Gynt*, Ibsen writes one of the most passionate protests ever wrung from an artist by an unjust judgment. "Clemens Petersen has a great responsibility because God has confided to him a high mission," Ibsen writes to Bjornson. Please do not forget that Ibsen left his country. For twenty-seven years he remained away from a society he hated and satirised — the provincial society of Norway.

Ibsen imitated no one you say. Like every other artist, Ibsen derived his convention from a preceding artist. He reached his own through the conventions of the French playwrights, Scribe and Sardou. Ibsen had produced a half a dozen plays before *A Doll's House*. The English critic, William Archer, notices the break with the Sardou convention in the last scene of this play. I am proud to say that I once disciplined myself by writing in Ibsen's form.

*Thomas Muskerry* is not an imitation of any of Ibsen's plays. When people speak of a play as being like Ibsen they are usually thinking of characters and of an atmosphere rather than of a method of dramatic construction. But this atmosphere and these chraacters belong to modern analysis. Were Ibsen an influence with me I could have constructed a play that would have no soliloquies and no casual characters, the action of which would be complete in a definite time and without change of scene. I have written a play, each act of which is an episode having its own milieu. You imply that the characters in my play are feeble people. But the tragedy of the play is due to the impotence of old age. As a matter of

31

fact the central character is not inert; he is moving towards something, he is struggling against what thwarts his egotistic purpose. He has more initiative than Goriot in the novel in which Balzac relates a parallel tragedy. I could make a point by assuring the readers of this open letter that Crofton Crilly and Albert Crilly are at least as masculine as Tesman in *Hedda Gabler* or Hyalmar in *The Wild Duck*. I say boldly that Crofton Crilly and Albert Crilly are common types. You will find father and son in every Irish town. Then say you, "England is largely justified in keeping Ireland under her iron rule." I am concerned with human facts not with political inferences.

I am well aware that your able article is not solely directed against my play. Inspired by a good political motive it is directed against a group of dramatists. You speak very unnecessarily of the thief and the prostitute, and you suggest that no country would accept as national any work that had either degraded being for a central figure. I know that for me the Russian soul is incarnated in the prostitute Maslova of Tolstoy's *Resurrection*. Through her Tolstoy shows the inviolateness, the power of regeneration, the essential purity that is in the human soul. . . . But as I write I remember that for Russians their great novelist is no Tolstoy or Tourgenieff but Dostoyevsky, and I know that the characters in Dostoyevsky's novels are criminals and convicts. Set the gaol beside the thief and the prostitute and then acknowledge that a large part of Spain's glory is due to a novelist writing about a feeble-minded man, who read foolish books and who set out on a series of foolish adventures.

Remember, "X", that the phrase you use, "There but for the grace of God, go we", was not said by a dramatist. The dramatist knows that no chasm as wide as the grace of God divides him from the feeble, the foolish, and the degraded.

One word more, "X". You suggest that if I wrote a national play it would be skilfully kept from the stage. Let us be open about this. The directors of the Abbey Theatre are well-known people. I no more believe they would suppress a play for the reasons you imply than that the Editor of *Sinn Féin* would take a Castle appointment.[19]

There was a good deal more controversy about the play and although *Thomas Muskerry* occasioned no riot, it was certainly the most debated drama of the year. Colum continued to write plays intermittently throughout his long career, but with the possible exception of *The Grasshopper* which was an Irish adaptation of a German original, none of his later, more or less experimental work seems of the same remarkable quality as *Thomas Muskerry*. Colum remained full of energy and still prolific, but the extraordinary strength of *Muskerry* he never again equalled. Perhaps the reason may be partly that he had an alert and inquisitive mind which was intrigued by a Dunsany-like Middle-East,[20] by the folklore of Hawaii, and even late in life by the Japanese Nōh drama. Perhaps the reason was partly that he was soon to move to America, and the necessity of earning a living would force him to turn his pen to many tasks other than the writing of plays. Perhaps he merely had to live in too many places and do too many things to continue the superb exploration of rural Ireland that he had attempted in his first three long plays.

On 19 May the Abbey gave the first production to another even more unpopular play. This was Lennox Robinson's *Harvest*, a three-act play which might be described as a problem play about peasants. The piece received an extremely bad press which it did not entirely deserve. Although *Harvest* has dated badly and would not bear revival, it marked a definite advance over Robinson's previous work, and the vehemence of the attacks upon it had less to do with its intrinsic merits than with the author's unflattering treatment of his subject. The tersest dismissal of the play came from Jacques in *The Irish Independent*:

> To speak my mind about the stuff that was put on the stage of the Abbey Theatre last night by Mr. S. L. Robinson would be nauseating to me; a waste of space in this paper; and beneficial to none except those to whom public notice is as drink to the droughty.[21]

The correspondent for *The Evening Telegraph* was almost rabid in his denunciations:

> Not since the precious *Playboy* was thrust down the throats of the Dublin public by the D.M.P. and the Divisional Magistrates has anything so objectionable as the evil-smelling *Harvest* of Mr. Robinson been presented at the Abbey Theatre. Those who had seen his *Cross Roads* had reason to hope for a play healthy in tone, clean in treatment, Irish and National in sentiment and atmosphere. These are all the things *Harvest* is not. It out-Synges Synge. It gives us all the suggestiveness of the malodorous problem play without any intelligible problem. It is clever of its kind. It is intellectual — so are many things that are intolerable, some that are unspeak-

33

able. But as a product of what is alleged to be an Irish National Theatre it is repellent, repulsive, abhorrent. The last Act especially is a mere seething pot of vice, filth, meanness, dishonour, dishonesty, depravity and duplicity.

In all the peasant family of the Hurleys there is not one ordinarily decent individual, if we except the daughter-in-law, who is, of course, not a peasant, but the daughter of a colonel who has married beneath her. As in *The Playboy*, the blackness is unrelieved by a ray of light. Not a breath of fresh air even momentarily sweetens the stench of this stirred-up cesspool.

The father does not understand the elementary principles of honesty. The farmer, Maurice, is in ecstasies at the revelation of his "Da's" depravity.

The son in England recants his religion, if he or his family ever had any.

The son who is a solicitor in the West would not give a £5 note to save his father from the workhouse. He needed it all to buy a motor car.

The son who is a chemist's assistant attacks his own wife in a scene of exceptional repulsiveness because she will not invite an abandoned woman to live with them.

Lastly, the daughter is a creature of shame, open, brazen, unblushing, flaunting her vice and taunting her old teacher — why or wherefore who can say? — with being responsible for this "harvest" of sin and shame.

It is all a horrid miasma, and one leaves the theatre with a feeling of sickly loathing and a bad taste in one's mouth. The man of decent instincts who brought sister, wife, or sweetheart to the Abbey last night must have felt decidedly uncomfortable.[22]

The above was an unsolicited commentary sent to *The Evening Telegraph*, but the ordinary correspondent for the paper quite agreed with it, and accused Robinson of whirling his audience 'through a breathless three acts of cold, gratuitous, intellectual horror'. One of the few just resumés appeared in *The Irish Times*:

Since Mr. S. L. Robinson gave us *The Clancy Name* he has travelled far in his art. *The Cross Roads* marked his progress, and now *Harvest*, which was played last evening at the Abbey Theatre, is another milestone to show his advance. His latest effort is not likely to meet with approval in all quarters, as there are elements in it that may shock the susceptibilities of some of the habitués of the Abbey. It is not a play of the usual peasant type; though dealing with rural life it touches other problems. . . . The play is full of interest throughout. There are many striking situations which are vigorous and effective. The dialogue is clever, but the language occasionally is inclined to be coarse and smacks more of *Blanco Posnet* than an Irish peasant. There is some very plain speaking not often found in plays of this type, but on the whole it adds to the strength of the work, whose moral may be said to point to the evil of unwise education. Characterisation is one of the strongest features of the play, the characters being clearly defined and well developed.[23]

On 29 September a new play was produced at the Abbey by a new writer, and with a new young actor in the cast. The new play was *The Casting Out of Martin Whelan*, a realistic piece about rural Cork. The new writer was a young Cork journalist, Robert J. Brophy, who used the pseudonym of R. J. Ray. The new actor was a young man from County Westmeath, John Weldon, who used the stage name of Brinsley MacNamara.

Brinsley MacNamara was to play for a season or two with the Abbey company, and even to accompany the group on its first American tour. He was never, however, more than a promising actor, and he soon turned his attention to writing. There was a good deal of verse published in various Irish periodicals, and some short stories, and then, in 1918, a harsh realistic novel, *The Valley of the Squinting Windows*, which aroused great anger in his native town and caused his father to be boycotted in his job of schoolmaster. Something of his bitterness about this controversy MacNamara wrote into his first Abbey play, *The Rebellion in Ballycullen* in 1919. Throughout the 1920s and 1930s he was regarded as a very considerable novelist, and his plays during those years were prominent in the Abbey repertoire. In one of his rather sombre novels, however, he cast a comic eye back on his young years as an Abbey actor; in the following excerpt from that novel, *In Clay and In Bronze*, read for the Tower Theatre, the Abbey; for Seán O'Hanlon, J. Crawford Neil; for Mr. Lawlor, Seán Barlow; for Leonard Thompson, Lennox Robinson; for Barney Shaw's cowboy play, GBS's *The Shewing Up of Blanco Posnet*; for 'a certain person', Yeats; for Albert Donohoe, Arthur Sinclair; for a minor poet, Padraic Colum; and, of course, for *The End of Edward Corrigan*, Ray's *The Casting Out of Martin Whelan*, in which MacNamara played his first Abbey role.

Now he was standing before a little theatre whose name was vaguely familiar. Then he remembered there had been books of the plays that had been performed here among the batches of books his father had brought home with him from Dublin from time to time. Yet were these almost the only books he had been unable to read. In fact they had puzzled him exceedingly. Their characters were peasants like himself, whose woes and torments were his daily round. However could a man bring himself to write of such when he could be thinking instead of the beauty of the world and of dark-eyed girls with ribbons in their hair? . . . Yet, as he stood watching now, he saw rich and grand-looking people drive up to the door of this place. He saw women with bare, gleaming shoulders, and men in evening dress with stiff white fronts which shone beneath the lamps at the entrance to the theatre.

Martin went around the corner and entered the pit. His eyes were immediately held by the continual movement of well-dressed people coming into the stalls of the theatre. . . . Dublin was certainly a place of wonder. The lights were suddenly switched off, after the orchestra had played the overture, and he was looking at a scene out of the life he knew. He felt a sudden interest. The words of the characters in the play came to him as had the words of his mother and sister in his own home. And there was a girl in the play who, through the situation in which she was placed, grew to have a certain nobility in keeping with that of the heroines in some of the books he had read. And yet as she stood there, personified by a great actress, on the centre of the stage in her white apron with the bands across her shoulders, she was not at all unlike Lucy Flynn. And the man was like himself, but he did not marry the girl, and this was the first time he had seen such an ending to any piece of writing. . . .

He grew critical of the acting at the Tower Theatre. There he saw men work their artistic medium to a nicety as a means of creating laughter or gloom. He listened to the character in each succeeding play, and knew that theirs surely was not the speech of the peasant. It had the ring of the peasant's speech, and retained its turn of beauty, but it was not the speech of the men who went into Glannidan every evening and remained drinking in the gloom of the pubs. . . . He listened to their humour, but it was the humour which comes from flights of the mind and the humour he had known in Glannanea was something which came most often from a petty satisfaction of some low spite when one man got the better of another through the exercise of a little animal cunning. It was seldom that anyone laughed in Glannidan, but they were always grinning.

36

He saw the tragedies wherein one man or woman was made to possess a little nobility of soul and he felt that this was really a lie for in that part of Ireland that he knew he had never experienced such a thing. . . . He laughed loudly when O'Hanlon told him that there were people who believed that the Tower has been too hard on Ireland. . . .

From his enthusiasm for the Tower Theatre and its plays the present expedition had emerged. He had made a careful study of the way in which Irish peasants were portrayed at the Tower until the fancy had grown on him that he could play such parts probably better than these actors. And seeing that they relied upon their very lack of technical accomplishment for the best part of their reputation his lack of working knowledge of the theatre could not prove a very serious handicap. So, just as the darkness was beginning to creep in around Dublin, he turned his steps towards the Tower Theatre. . . .

The stage door was opened by a lady who might be one of the actresses, he thought, so nervous did her imperious manner make him. Martin was left to close the door. Half afraid he moved very slowly down a short stairway. The darkness of the place seemed to hold gloomy foreshadowings of this new and mysterious kind of life into which he was deliberately walking. His nostrils were assailed by a cave-like smell, and he saw what he took to be stage properties suspended from the roof, and miscellaneous things which made attempts to reach them from the ground like stalagmites and stalactites.

Martin made an enquiry for the stage manager, whom he considered to be the proper man to see, and soon that person appeared switching on the light as he came. In the sudden light he appeared spectral. His head was little and oldish, but he had the light body of a boy. He began to evince a kind of mechanical stage smile as Martin set out to recognise in him the stage manager of the Tower Theatre. He said his name was Mr. Lawlor. There was a kind of condescension in his tones as he chose certain moments in which to speak.

"So you wish to become a member of the Tower Company?"

"Yes."

"Well, then, you must see Mr. Leonard Thompson, who has all to do with the artistic side of the management. Come this way!"

Together they ascended the steep, straight stairs to the office. The mind of Martin was really agitated so near was he now to the presence of one whom he had always taken to be a

37

very great man. Mr. Leonard Thompson, playwright and manager of the Tower Theatre, was seated at his desk. To Martin he appeared as another young, old man. When he rose from his chair he looked most wondrously tall and spare of build. His eyebrows grew in a peculiar way which seemed to give him an expression of constant and intense surprise. This, combined with a certain delicate and apologetic method of movement, communicated the impression that he was surprised by the very fact of his own existence. Mr. Lawlor introduced Martin to Mr. Leonard Thompson and then very silently slipped out of the office upon his rubber heels, and Mr. Thompson displayed an air of excessive boredom as he waited for Martin to make known his business.

"I have called to know if you could find a job for me in the Tower Theatre?"

Mr. Thompson continued remote as he glanced over some type-written sheets in his hand.

"A job!" he at last plucked up courage to question, "a job as an actor?"

"Yes, a job as an actor," affirmed Martin.

By way of comment or reply Mr. Thompson made an unaccountable noise which Martin imagined must be his clever although curious conception of laughter. Then he said:

"You are probably aware that we here are different from other theatres."

Martin nodded and said that he was aware of this.

"Our players," proceeded the manager, "fit so perfectly into our plays. As a matter of fact they are specially constructed for the plays and the plays specially constructed for them. Take the case of a certain person for example, who writes by far the most of the plays we produce here. He is quite unable to write a line of his lines without a constant manipulation in his mind of the character who is destined to deliver it — I mean the line. From the very moment of its conception the dramatically contrived personality of the character is identified with the established personality of the player. Furthermore, a physical correspondence is instituted. If the player possesses a lisp it must be shown that as a result of a black curse or some other piece of fatalism the corresponding character in the play was born lisping; if he be small the stature of the character must be reduced to correspond. You may marvel at the detail of this person for he is marvellously attentive to detail. The most interesting arrangement, invented by him and perfected by me is one of the secrets of our phenomenal success as an Art Theatre. I assure you we have gone one better than the Greeks. They were frightfully keen on the unities of place and time: we pin our faith to the unity of identity. This is, as I have already explained, the artistic mergence of the player's personality in the personality of the character he is supposed to embody. ~. .

"Now, Duignan" (the sudden familiarity was amazing) "I look upon you as splendid material for a peasant player. That Irish face of yours with the addition of some artificial side-whiskers would make you in London or anywhere the typical Irishman — the Irish Paddy so dear to the political cartoonist of my childhood days. Also you have the agricultural, uncouth swing, and the rich, melancholy Celtic voice changing to a perfectly natural and vulgar brogue. In fact, so far as the Tower Theatre is concerned, you are 'the business'. . . .

"We have here the manuscript of a new play which we intend to produce in a few weeks' time. It is a Cork play, and you know what Cork plays are."

Martin said he knew.

"Well, in this play, *The End of Edward Corrigan*, a certain part occurs, that of a heavy, loutish drunkard, which would suit you better than any man I ever knew."

Martin smiled because of the compliment, and the anticipation.

"I admire your eagerness to take up this part, but we observe a certain slight formality here in the Tower. It is an examination in the reading of this test as we call it, about which a certain person is most particular."

Martin looked at the typewritten sheet which Mr. Thompson handed to him. It appeared just like the well-known "Advice to Playwrights submitting plays to the Tower Theatre", and was a list of phrases prevalent in Tower Theatre plays.

"Now you must read these phrases aloud for me, giving particular attention to the intonation," said Mr. Thompson, with a kind of aged concern strangely alien in so young a man.

Martin, in his eagerness, at once began to read:

"And she a woman with a big tongue on her a yard long, that does be always prattling."

"It's what I do be always thinking, lady of the house, if only you'd let a man in to stop along with you."

"It's a quare world, and a dark night, surely. God help us all!"

"It's what I do be thinking, and it's what I do be saying."

39

"Would you say him now to be in any way cracked or wrong in the head?"

"No bloody fear!"

"Ah indade I'm not. A'm going for a wee dandher down Sandy Row."

"For I have sucked its sorrows' sap out of the moon."

"Say, kid, this is a rotten town."

"All those gods whom their swarthy servant, Time, hath not yet slain."

"That will do," said the manager. "Your rendering is in every way uniquely perfect. Allow me to congratulate you already as a worker in our midst." . . .

He was rapidly surprising even Mr. Leonard Thompson.

"I say, Duignan, the way you let these 'blasts' and 'bloodys' out of your mouth is simply magnificent. Your performance as a porter drunkard is unique. Hitherto the drunkards of the stage were supposed to have produced their condition with wine or whiskey, but you are the first porter drunkard. That's right, allow yourself to dribble a little, as if you were about to vomit, and as you make your big exit lurch forward a little so as to communicate to the audience the effect of vomit which takes place just outside the door. That will be awfully good, and ought to please a certain person immensely. For a writer of peasant romance he has a surprising grasp of the essentials of realism. Do you know what he said to me the other day?"

Mr. Leonard Thompson here laughed one of his long, peculiar laughs.

"We were rehearsing Barney Shaw's cowboy play, you know, when he said:

'I don't doubt but that Albert Donohoe and the rest of them will make up all right in this curious little lapse of poor old Shaw's. They will be gotten-up according to the best ideas of the cinema in the togs that are supposed to be fashionable with those supposed cowboys in those supposed parts of America. Of course no such thing really exists, and I don't see why we should make this move to emulate the picture palace. We who have maintained a continuous procession of strange peasants across this stage should endeavour to give a unique reading. The cowboy represents the romance of America; the Tower peasant is our romance. To institute a combination of both might well be considered a stroke of genius. What would you say now to making our cinema-clad actors spit out as they take their places in the jury box?' " . . .

40

Just then the door of the Green Room opened and a tall, dark man came into the midst of the little crowd. He surveyed the accustomed scene, with a lifted, almost grandiose expression. . . . His hands were solemnly knotted behind him. . . .

Then entered the others whom George Moore might have written about very cleverly in *Hail and Farewell*. First came a certain person followed eagerly by a member of the Bureaucracy in Ireland, a minor poet and an American journalist. . . . The minor poet was a mere caricature in his verse as in his person of the tall, dark man. He now began to read a scrap of verse he had recently written on the back of an envelope, and the other considering all Dublin verse to be a sincere flattery of himself listened passively, the noise of the thing sounding in the mystical distance. . . . The minor poet's lines had the effect of lifting him out of his dark humour and he laughed heartily as the American journalist manifested himself, notebook in hand. He was one of the almost innumerable Americans who had written books on the Tower Theatre. This was how such books came to be written. A little hard-faced, insignificant-looking man occurred like this in the most inoffensive, apologetic way. He went prying about with a notebook in his hand, listening as it were at keyholes with the note-book in his hand. One scarcely noticed the little man at it until in his surprising American way he came into the possession of more knowledge of the institution than anybody connected with the Tower Theatre. Then the book appeared, a detailed compendium giving the inner history of every single play. It threw a powerful searchlight upon the activities of everyone connected with literature in Ireland, and the funny little man made a lot of money out of it. . . .

The member of the Bureaucracy and the minor poet drifted back to a certain person. The poet began to beg of him to accept a play for the Tower. He put the poet off with a joke, but it was not so funny although the reasons for the subconscious rivalry were perfectly obvious. Both were peasant romanticists. He might have been successful had he been a Cork realist. . . .[24]

The Corkman R. J. Ray contributed several realistic plays to the Abbey repertoire, and as he appeared at about the same time as two other notable Cork dramatists, Lennox Robinson and T. C. Murray, it was perhaps inevitable that Yeats should discern a school of Cork realists. But although Yeats took considerable pains with Ray's work, Ray never became as able or even as popular as Robinson or Murray; and to this date none of his plays has been published. On the occasion of his first play he received a distinctly mixed press. The most appreciative review appeared, as usual, in *The Irish Times*:

We have patiently waited for a play that gives us the truth about Ireland from the political standpoint. It was bound to come, and we have got it at last. Mr. R. J. Ray gives us a very faithful picture of rural life in Ireland in his play, *The Casting Out of Martin Whelan*. . . . It is not alone in title that the play has a Shavian flavour — for it naturally recalls to us *The Shewing Up of Blanco Posnet* — but the handling of the subject, too, recalls Shaw, inasmuch as the author is able to see his subject from both sides. We have no sooner laughed than we are laughed at. But the play is not all laughter. It has a very serious side, and it is its seriousness that makes it successful. While we enjoy a witticism — and there is much humour in the work — we are set a-thinking, for it brings us up against facts. Presumably, the object of the play is to show the antipathy of the peasant for informers, but the moral to be drawn is that there is no real public opinion in Ireland. People are too much governed by local circumstances and personal interests to give serious thought to serious things. We hear what the people say, but we never hear what the people think.

Mr. Ray in his picture, which he paints with wonderful realism, keeps the people in the background, but sets out at full length a few figures, which are at once recognized as those of the local bosses who dominate the people.

The action of the play takes place thirty years ago in the village of Ballintrosnan. Everybody is talking of electing to Parliament Martin Whelan, an Australian-Irishman, who has become popular chiefly because he has given a cup for a hurling competition. He does not, however, understand the people, and from what he sees detects in them a moral warp, but struggles against his feelings. He is inclined to be too plain-spoken, and expresses his feelings too sincerely. The only person who understands him is Ellen Barton, who has been educated abroad, and who also sees things as they are. Things are going fairly well with Whelan until he incurs the displeasure of the "leaders" by assisting to save from malicious burning the hayrick of a "grabber". On top of this the people learn that he is the grandson of Tim McGrath, an informer, who sent to the gallows a man who shot a land-

42

owner. Opinion chances at once. He cannot understand the reason of the change, even though he helped the grabber to save his hay and his mother's father secured the execution of a murderer. In the local league rooms a meeting is being held. The president and the secretary are drafting resolutions. There is one resolution proposing the demolition of a pump, but as the president's son is interested in it the resolution is torn up. Other resolutions are suggested, but as they are likely to affect the interests of the members they too go by the board. Whelan forces himself upon the meeting, and insists on getting particulars of the murder, an attitude which the leaders of the people hardly understand. They talk grandiloquently about his bad blood, but evade his questions. He appeals to Mrs. Barton, who has suddenly come in, but she says she has no more to say, although she has said nothing. He is cast out, and would leave the locality in disgust.

But there remains at least one honest soul — Ellen Barton. He goes to her father's cottage, though he has been told not to darken its door. He asks her to marry him, so that they might live their lives in Ballintrosnan. Ellen knows that he is ambitious, but she also knows that if she marries him his ambitions will be killed, and that in times and places unexpected he may have hurled at him the taunt that he is the descendant of Tim McGrath. While Ellen is making clear her answer, her father who has come to hate Whelan, enters. There is a violent scene, and Ellen, who does not wish to leave her father, nor to crush Whelan's ambitions, in reply to Whelan's questions, says she believes his grandfather was an informer, though in her heart she does not believe so. Whelan goes away, declaring that though Ellen is dear to him, the memory of his mother is dearer still.

This is the story of *The Casting Out of Martin Whelan*. The story itself is of little consequence, but the moral it conveys is of vital importance. Freedom of thought, freedom of speech, freedom of action, are not permissable in rural Ireland. The people have their opinions, but are afraid to express them. They are held back by men who talk of sunbursts, with a wolfdog and a bunch of shamrocks, of the people's rights, without consulting the people, and of the nation's wrongs, though they know not what a true nation is. The play is an excellent political sermon, whose text is taken from life as we find it in Ireland. We would have it played in every town and village in Ireland, but we fear the voice of the people, as we now listen to it through false trumpets, would

43

be raised against it. The author is to be complimented on his courage. The play was cordially received, and was performed to the accompaniment of continuous applause. . . . There was not a weak spot in the cast. The acting was natural and sincere. There was no exaggeration of the characters, for the artistes were too familiar with the parts to overdo them. It is not easy to discriminate where there is such all-round merit. In giving special praise to Mr. J. M. Kerrigan, who played to like the part of Peter Barton, a farmer of the past generation; to Mr. Fred O'Donovan, who has one of his best parts in Martin Whelan, and to Miss Máire O'Neill, who had in Ellen Barton a part that fitted her perfectly, we are but endorsing the verdict of the audience. . . .[25]

However, W. J. Lawrence had some reservations:

Special pleading in drama is hedged in with all sorts of difficulties and dangers. No thesis play can be written without a certain arbitrariness of plot which will inevitably at some crucial moment, shatter to pieces the psychology of one or other of the principal characters. The result, at best, will be but sublimated melodrama. It is perhaps no reproach to Mr. Ray that he has been unable to avoid this pitfall. Much may be forgiven to a promising young dramatist of original turn of mind and steadily progressive technique, who, as in this instance, is capable of conceiving a wholly new embroilment in Irish peasant drama. Nothing but lack of definition in the drawing of the principal female character and a consequently ineffective last act has prevented Mr. Ray from giving us . . . a notably fine play.[26]

And the critic of *The Leader* was definitely caustic:

In so far as *The Casting Out of Martin Whelan* is light peasant comedy it is excellent: where the play becomes, or is alleged to become, serious, it goes off. The first act was first class: the next developed into some cheap "prose-poetry" stuff, and the third went flat. Whilst waiting for the curtain to rise, we enjoyed the usual distractions. W. B. appeared like an apparition for a moment at the left-hand corner door, and dissolved from view — like a snow-flake on the river, etc. He wanted, no doubt, to break himself gently to the audience. The up and down the little stairs performance came along in due time: another lean and tall young man like W. B.'s double also sprinted up and down the little stairs: perhaps if the latter cannot write poetry he wants to show that he

44

can sprint. By the way, it would appear that long hair is gone out of fashion in poetic circles: the outward and visible symbol of poetry now apparently consists in the manner in which you carry your hands. . . .

And now to return to Mr. Ray's play. Mr. J. M. Kerrigan, as an old farmer, in our opinion comes out of it best; Mr. Sinclair, as a pig-buyer, next. Mr. O'Donovan had a part which unsuited him; indeed, he had a part that would probably unsuit anyone. Mr. J. A. O'Rourke played the village idiot to the life. Mr. MacNamara, who appears to be a new recruit for the Abbey, played the drunken man with a realism that one had to admire as a piece of acting, and it was so good that it excited disgust which one feels in the presence of a real drunk; the acting of Mr. Fred Harford was like a pebble in the heel of one's boot all the time. The women characters had not much chance to distinguish themselves.

The comic dialogue and the fun were good. . . . The amusing parts of the play were decidedly amusing; for the rest, it was poor stuff and flat.[27]

On 7 October Ray wrote his own reactions to some of the reviews to the Abbey's secretary, W. A. Henderson:

> *The Leader* man contrived to be funny with rudeness; much better he had been dramatically critical with soundness. . . . He does not realise that he possesses a large share of the conventional mind, and the conventional mind, watching Abbey theatre drama, is suggestive of satiric comedy. . . .
>
> I read the critique in *The Stage*. Like the curate's egg, mentioned in *Punch* once upon a time, "it is good in parts". . . . I don't appreciate the remarks about Ellen Barton. Miss O'Neill played splendidly. But it appears I deprived her of "all brogue". Further, "there was nothing of the free, impulsive nature of the Irish peasant girl" about Miss O'Neill. I wish the critic would live in Ballintrosnan, or some such locality for six months, and study the "Irish peasant girl" at first hand. I guarantee he'll be surprised, hardly agreeably. . . .[28]

On 27 October the Abbey introduced to Dublin the work of another Cork playwright, T. C. Murray, who was to be for the next quarter of a century perhaps the most solid craftsman of the serious realistic play that the theatre has produced. At this time Murray was a schoolteacher in County Cork, and his two-act *Birthright* was a study of West Cork peasantry. Its basic subject is a family quarrel about the ownership of land. Like many of the

45

later Murray plays, *Birthright* proceeds through a careful, leisurely exposition, through a slow tightening of tension, to a final explosive culmination. The seriousness of Murray's attitude and the soundness of his technique resulted usually in an absorbing and convincing piece of theatre. Although his plays were to deal with strong themes for Ireland — the overwhelming greed for land, spoiled vocations, clerical interference in schools, and even incest — the audiences were never tempted to protest against the blackness of his picture. His work did not seem to distort, to exaggerate, or to exploit, but to investigate fairly and humanely; and he was rewarded by twenty-five years of absorbed interest and attention.

Although some real flaws were noted in this early version of *Birthright*, the general opinions were that the play was 'a very good illustration of the excellence of the work that is being done at the Abbey Theatre', 'a noteworthy addition to its repertory', and 'the strongest play that has been staged by the Abbey people'. After the considerable opposition to the recently staged realistic plays of Colum, Robinson and Ray, this highly approving reaction to Murray was welcome indeed. The particular criticisms of *Birthright* as well as the general approval can be noted in the critique of *The Freeman's Journal*:

> It is a pity that we should have to mete out an adverse criticism to this play. But we cannot but regard this ending as a serious blunder. If Mr. Murray had shown the same skill in the handling of his catastrophe as he does in the handling of his crisis, he would have made Shane kill his brother when the passion was at its height in the last scene, and not when the passion had partly died down. Mr. Murray may retort, and with some justice, perhaps, that to do so would have been an obvious and commonplace treatment of the action. But he cannot escape the verdict, from the dramatic point of view, of insufficient motive for the actual killing of Hugh in the play. . . . [Shane's] killing of his brother in these circumstances constitutes what Aristotle would call "an improbable possibility". And what is more to the purpose, it turns what should have been a tragic ending into a melodramatic ending. . . . The main thing, however, is that he has given us a work of high merit. His construction, despite a few flaws — and we think that the two separate awakenings of the household is one — shows him a careful workman who has the root of the matter in him. And we may say the same thing about his dialogue and his characterisation. On the whole the play is a triumph for Mr. Murray, and the treatment of the theme is

46

full of nerve and power. We hope that every one who is interested in the production of serious work in Ireland will go to this play.

We would like to single out for praise the work done by Miss Eileen O'Doherty as Maura Morrissey, the mother in the play. Miss O'Doherty made a study of her part, which, although the word seems out of harmony with so subdued a character, we must call brilliant. . . .[29]

These were most sound remarks about the play's construction. Jacques in *The Irish Independent* had some other criticisms:

There are other faults in the work. They are Abbey Theatre faults. There is too much of "the-mist-that-does-be-on-the-bog" about the dialogue, and there is the irritating weakness of depicting character by making that character reveal itself in repeated forceful expressions that offend the ear. The art of suggestion is missing. The language colouring is laid on in harsh, ugly streaks in places. The author thereby depicts too much and leaves too little to the imagination of his audience. And that is about all I can say against the play. Mr. Murray can take his place in the front rank of Abbey Theatre dramatists. . . .

In *Birthright* he has given us one character at least that is perhaps the most real and most beautiful conception ever portrayed on the Abbey Theatre stage. This is Maura Morrissey, the brow-beaten wife and misunderstood mother. Miss O'Doherty, who filled the part last night, has found her role at last. She has never done anything better. Indeed, the acting all round was almost faultless. . . .[30]

In the light of these friendly criticisms Murray revised the play, and it remained for some years one of the most frequently revived pieces in the Abbey repertoire.

On 10 November Lady Gregory's new one-act play, *The Full Moon*, was first produced. 'C', probably Padraic Colum, wrote in *The Manchester Guardian* practically the only appreciative remarks about the new piece which he thought 'has character and situation, burlesque and horseplay. It has more, for it is a complete comedy. It has poetry and wisdom also.' [31] In *The Irish Independent*, however, Jacques was utterly dismissive:

At the Abbey Theatre last night a lunatic piece in one act was rehearsed by the players to the intense amusement of many in the large audience. . . .

47

> *The Full Moon* may convey a message. Is there no other
> way of conveying it? Even a music-hall knockabout farce, a
> circus or a penny gaff can make for laughter without appeal
> to the unspeakable tragedy of the mad-house. If the thing is
> intended as a contribution to our Irish dramatic literature, it
> fills one with sorrow for our dramatic literature. . . .[32]

Although Jacques was unnecessarily churlish, the other commentators basically agreed with him. The critic of *The Freeman's
Journal* felt regret at Lady Gregory's lack of judgment in allowing
the play to be staged. And even the sympathetic *Irish Times*, in a
rather sound critique, concluded that the piece 'could hardly be
regarded as a valuable addition of the Abbey repertoire':

> It is an unsatisfactory comedy, inasmuch as it is too mystic
> and its motive too elusive for the ordinary intellect. The
> strange mutterings of Connaught peasants, prompted by fears
> of being bitten by a mad dog when the moon is full, do not
> in themselves provide adequate material for even a one-act
> comedy, though they would, doubtless, be read with keen
> pleasure. The comedy lacks incident. The fun is provoked by
> a discussion amongst a crowd of peasants assembled in a shed
> at the railway station. Hyacinth Halvey, a familiar character,
> this time appears as the priest's boy, endeavouring, as usual,
> to live up to his reputation. He is waiting to meet the priest
> at the train, but hearing that there is to be a fair at Caragh
> on the morrow, decides to join the train, as he wants to be
> there with the boys. Cracked Mary and Davideen, a crazy
> pair, are in the crowd, and as they listen to the talk about the
> effects of hydrophobia, laugh to themselves at the madness
> of the people who are supposed to be sane. The moon is up,
> and the peasants are afraid to face it lest it do them harm, but
> Cracked Mary and Davideen go out to greet it, and as they
> go they sing. Halvey begins to talk strangely, and the others
> immediately conclude that he is mad, and proceed to tie him
> up. He hears the whistle of the train, and sets up a loud
> barking, as if he were the dog itself. The people become
> terrified, and fall over each other in their panic as Halvey
> dashes off and boards the train for Caragh. The *motif* of the
> play is not very clear, but now and again the dialogue sparkles
> with original humour and brilliant repartee, and the author,
> by her picturesque descriptions, imparts a saving grace to the
> piece. Compared with some of her well-known plays, *The Full
> Moon* is a mere trifle. It, however, gives Miss Máire O'Neill
> a further chance of displaying her versatility. Her portrait of

Cracked Mary is one of the best studies she has given us. Into this difficult role she imparts a degree of emotional feeling which makes her performance almost true to life. The characters, apart from that of Cracked Mary and Davideen, are the usual types which seem to be inseparable from the general run of Abbey plays. Needless to say, they were capably personated.[33]

On 24 November the Abbey staged its first production of Seumas O'Kelly's pathetic drama, *The Shuiler's Child*. The play had previously been staged by the Theatre of Ireland, and Máire Nic Shiubhlaigh had been much admired as the Shuiler. Now Máire Nic Shiubhlaigh had rejoined the Abbey company, and the piece was apparently seen as a vehicle for her, and of course it was also an appropriate addition to the theatre's peasant repertoire.

The last new Abbey play of the year was another short comedy by Lady Gregory, *Coats*, a pleasant if innocuous little play about how the editors of two country newspapers mistakenly switch coats and the revelations that ensue when they search the pockets. The piece was thought by all of the critics to be even more inconsequential than *The Full Moon*, and almost completely, if a little unjustly, ignored.

Apart from an occasional play by Yeats, the repertoire of the Abbey seemed now to have a certain sameness to it. Lady Gregory's short peasant comedies seemed ever more trifling and silly, and the significant new plays were strong, dark, peasant dramas. As An Philibín wrote in *The National Student*:

> Thus, in practically direct sequence, we have been given *The Cross Roads, Thomas Muskerry, Harvest, The Casting Out of Martin Whelan*, plays the power of which no one may deny; but also eminently depressing. It remains to state that *Birthright* is temperamentally in close agreement with its predecessors.[34]

Perhaps the best way to sum up this section is another short, satiric skit, *At the Abbey Theatre*, which was published by 'H. F.' in *Sinn Féin* for 14 May:

*(Grandfather, Grandson, and Grand-daughter)*
OLD GENT: *(Whispering)* I can't see the programme; forgot my glasses. What did you say this thing is called?
BOY: *The Pot of Broth*, grandpa.
OLD GENT: *Plot of Froth*, did you say?
BOY: No. *Pot of Broth*, by Mr. Yeats, the poet.

49

OLD GENT: *Bit of Froth? Pot of Froth?*

BOY: (*Loudly*) Not *Pot of Froth*! Broth, Broth!

OLD GENT: Don't shout, boy. Froth, Froth, yes. I've often heard of Yeats's Froth — this is some of it, is it?

GIRL: Mr. Yeats wrote that, grandpa, to show how easy it is to fool the Irish with a lot of talk and a few conjuror's tricks.

BOY: Don't be silly. Yeats never thought of any such thing.

OLD GENT: Sh! I want to listen.

GIRL: Then what did he write it for?

BOY: Someone gave him the idea.

OLD GENT: Stop that chatter, you two.

(*Whispers of "Hush, hush."*)

(*Curtain falls.*)

OLD GENT: Is that all?

BOY: That's all.

GIRL: Yes, that's all.

OLD GENT: Now we'll have something good. Padraic Colum, Yeats's disciple. Often heard of him. Good suggestive title. *Thomas Muskerry. Thomas Muskerry.*

(*Curtain rises.*)

(*Curtain falls.*)

BOY: Why doesn't Colum write in Irish?

GIRL: He hasn't got any.

BOY: Then why doesn't he write Irish plays?

GIRL: This is an Irish play; he says so himself.

BOY: Does he call that rotten crowd Irish?

GIRL: They're country people, can't you see?

BOY: No, I don't, and I don't want to see country people if they're like that. I don't wonder decent people are leaving the country if that's what it's like.

OLD GENT: Great play this. Colum's a great man. This is the sort of play that's wanted to stop all the nonsense that's being talked about the Irish people and their National ideals. Divil an ideal in this play that I can see. It's like Ibsen but for that. Ibsen'd be forcing his ideals on you one way or another all the time. The state of his country, his social problems, anything to make you feel uncomfortable. Colum knows better than to do that. Colum's people are as well done in their way as Ibsen's, but they might be of any nationality, except that Colum has, with his genius, made them Irish. So they are, so they are, a sordid, inefficient, incompetent, inhuman lot. Great touch to make the

50

only decent one in the play a blind man. Colum has learned a lot from Yeats. Clever of Yeats to catch Colum. Yeats'll mould him — Yeats'll mould him.

*(Curtain rises.)*

*(Curtain falls.)*

OLD GENT: *(Turning a beaming face round on the young people)* Great play; greater acting. Don't let me hear any more of your high falutin' nonsense about the nobility of the Irish character. Colum has painted them true. Colum knows them; he has no illusions about them. Listen to the way that chit speaks to her mother and talk to me of the love of the Irish children for their parents. Look at that shifty, snivelling wretch speaking to the bottle to restore his manhood. Listen to him cursing the town for his own shortcomings instead of cursing himself for being a curse to the town. Colum knows them. See how he makes the smartest chap show his common sense by wanting to clear out of the place to get on in the world.

BOY: Ah, stop, grandpa.

OLD GENT: "All slop," did you say? "All slop," indeed it's nothing of the sort; it's a great play.

GIRL: It's because Mr. Colum wrote it in English that it's horrid.

BOY: If he must write in English, why can't he use it only as every decent Irishman should, to try and effect something for Ireland. Here he's got a theatre at his disposal, and as fine a set of actors as you'd get anywhere, and a crowd that varies each night to listen to him. Why, the most obscure person working in the Gaelic League, if it's only addressing circulars, is doing more real work for Ireland than all the psychological studies dramatised in the best English that ever was written.

GIRL: The nastiest thing, to my mind, in the whole thing is that he's picked a plot about money, on purpose, so as to bring out all the worst side of the people. Sure, everyone's beastly about money everywhere in the whole world — even savages — and Colum makes it seem as if it were peculiar to Ireland and Irish people alone.

OLD GENT: Colum knows 'em; Colum knows 'em.

BOY: As we are we see.

OLD GENT: Eng! What's that you say?

BOY: Sh! The curtain's going up.

*(Curtain rises.)*

*(Curtain falls.)*

51

BOY: Is that the end? For goodness sake let's get out of this quick. I'm sick, sick, deadly sick. I can't breathe.

GIRL: I feel queer myself; but, listen to grandpa.

OLD GENT: Great play, great play, that'll take the enthusiasm out of them. Bit melancholy, perhaps. But nothing from beginning to end to make you feel uncomfortable about problems, political or social, or even responsible for the workhouse system, or that you are connected even remotely with these detestable Irish people. Blest if I didn't think that was going to be the object of the play. I'll come to the Abbey again. Great men, Colum and Yeats; great men. They're on our side; on our side. We have nothing to fear from either of them.

BOY: Oh, it's a rotten theatre, a rotten play, and a rottener house with their rotten applause. I'll go to the Tivoli tomorrow night.

*(Exit.)*[35]

\*     \*     \*

Early in May King Edward VII died, and this event caused great difficulty for the Abbey Theatre. At the time the new young manager of the theatre was Lennox Robinson; and in a letter written some months later to Yeats he explained exactly what happened:

Abbey Theatre, Dublin
31st Jan. 1911

Dear Mr. Yeats,
You have asked me to tell you exactly what happened on May 7th last. I read in the morning papers of the King's death but I never thought of the effect it would have on the theatres and places of amusement. However, about 11.15 our secretary came to my rooms and told me that he heard that the other theatres in Dublin were closing and asked me what we should do. I knew that the Abbey Theatre had been carried on from the beginning as a purely artistic venture, I knew that its policy was to ignore politics, and I though that if we closed we would be throwing ourselves definitely on one political side and that we should remain open, taking no notice of a circumstance that had no significance to the arts. However, I decided to leave the matter to Lady Gregory and went to Nassau Street Post Office and wired to her as follows:
"Theatres closing here. What am I to do? I think we should remain open but leave decision to you."

52

This was handed in ten minutes before twelve (Irish time). I then went to the theatre and waited for a reply. None came, and I decided to go on with the matinee. Lady Gregory's answer desiring the theatre to be closed came in the course of the afternoon — in the interval before the last act of the play we were performing. It was too late to stop the matinee then, and the good audience encouraged me to think that little criticism would be passed on our having remained open. It was too late to put notices in the evening papers cancelling the night performance, and if there was any crime in having played we had already committed it.

Yours sincerely,

S. L. ROBINSON[36]

Because of a dawdling messenger boy, Lady Gregory did not receive Robinson's query until the middle of the afternoon. She immediately wired back, 'Should close through courtesy.' Robinson then telegraphed her, 'Playing matinee, think too late to stop night show, but wire if you think otherwise.' This last wire was received at Coole between six and seven in the evening, by which time it probably was too late to stop the evening performance. That evening in the theatre, Robinson wrote a letter to Lady Gregory:

I hope you do not think I did wrong about playing the matinee. It was rather a problem to know what to do. Whether we opened or closed we would be blamed and all my inclinations were towards opening, so when I did not hear from you I went on with the performance. We are, I suppose, the only place open to-night, but then we are the only place which calls itself "national", and after all no one need come to us who doesn't like. As a matter of fact we have a very good house to-night as you see by the return, and most people seemed to come in the certain expectation of finding us open. So I think we did right. Do you think the King's death will injure us in London?
I think I can safely say that *Thomas Muskerry* is a success. I was very anxious about it naturally, but it improves with every performance, and everyone speaks well of it. Unpleasant as all the characters are, it has the quality of gripping your attention. Kerrigan has made a wonderful thing out of Crofton Crilly — it is not Colum's Crilly, but it is a very good thing and supplies some humour which the play needed. . . .[37]

53

When Miss Horniman learned that the theatre had remained open, she was infuriated, and she wired Lady Gregory on 10 May, 'Opening last Saturday was disgraceful, performance on day of Funeral would be political and would stop subsidy automatically, Horniman.' Then on 11 May, Miss Horniman wired Lady Gregory again: 'Subsidy ceases now unless directors and Robinson express regret in Dublin press that decent example was not followed at Abbey.' On 12 May, Robinson wired Lady Gregory, 'Evening papers publishing paragraph from Horniman stating will withdraw subsidy unless we apologise, think our explanation should appear simultaneously.' Lady Gregory wired back, 'Keep back apology, waiting Yeats's assent.' [38]

On 13 May, *The Irish Times* carried Miss Horniman's letter, followed by a statement from Robinson:

> Sir, — When I heard that the Abbey Theatre, Dublin, was open on Saturday, May 7th, I was both disgusted and angry that the good example of the other theatres had not been followed. Unless proper regret is shown in the Press by the directors my subsidy to the National Theatre Society will cease immediately, instead of continuing until next November.
>
> Yours truly,
>
> A. E. F. HORNIMAN

The manager of the Abbey Theatre has issued the following statement:

*Harvest*, a play in three acts, by S. L. Robinson, will be produced for the first time next week in the Abbey Theatre on Thursday; it will also be played on Saturday afternoon and evening.

There will be no performance on Friday.

The directors and manager regret that owing to accident the theatre remained open on Saturday last. Lady Gregory, who was in the country, had wired immediately on receipt of the news of the King's death, and of a telegram asking for instructions, desiring it to be closed; but this was late in the day; the matinee had already been put on, and it was considered too late to stop the evening performance.[39]

This was more an explanation than an apology; in any event, it failed to satisfy Miss Horniman. On 16 May, W. A. Henderson wrote to Yeats:

Dear Mr. Yeats,

I received a letter from Miss Horniman this morning. Mr.

Robinson has asked me to send you a copy of it. It reads as follows:

London, May 15th/10

Dear Sir,

Thank you for sending me the papers. That insignificant addition to the ordinary paragraph in advance will not save the subsidy. Maybe the Directors feel able to afford this, but please remind them of the Royal Letters Patent. Without these being renewed, everyone employed at the Abbey will be out of work next Christmas; so this matter concerns you all personally. My telegram to you (sent also to Lady Gregory) gave a chance to ensure the renewal of the Patent which I sincerely hope will be taken in time.

Yours truly,

A. E. F. HORNIMAN

I have sent a copy of this to Lady Gregory.

Yours faithfully,

W. A. HENDERSON[40]

The Nationalist element in Ireland was not pleased at the theatre's response either. An article on the incident by F. Sheehy Skeffington in the 21 May *Irish Nation* was entitled 'The Revival of Flunkeyism'; and an article on the same day by Arthur Griffith in *Sinn Féin* was entitled 'Bootlickers'. In August, Miss Horniman received an M.A. from Manchester University, and an interview given on that occasion indicated that her anger was still at boiling point:

Am I resuming my association with the Abbey Theatre, Dublin? No! I am not. You know — in fact, *The Referee* stated — *why* I withdrew my subsidy from that (to me) deeply interesting venture. So I will not go into further details concerning the reasons for my withdrawal in case I should again drop into politics. And Irish politics, as you may have noticed, are so contentious. Yes; in every Irish party.

It was I who first suggested that the National Dramatic Society in Dublin should play in a theatre of its own and not in halls. I not only suggested but I *made* the Abbey Theatre, and I worked terribly hard to set it going. I wrote three hundred letters all different with my own hand in ten days for the company when on tour. In all sorts of other ways I assisted to keep it going, besides providing the subsidy.

I shall hand over to the directorate the lease of the Abbey Theatre, which includes a house and a shop, all my property in Dublin. They have to give me £1,000, which is far less than I paid for the actual property.

It is evident the Irish "patriots" don't like me because I'm English. I'm proud of being English. . . .[41]

The affair arose at a particularly difficult moment. Yeats and Lady Gregory had been for some time involved in complicated negotiations with Miss Horniman about the disposal of the theatre at the expiration of the patent period. Although this affair did not upset the basic agreement by which £1,000 would be paid to Miss Horniman for the theatre, it did cause Miss Horniman to refuse to pay the final £400 of subsidy, half of which was due on 1 June and half on 1 September. The question of the subsidy payments was finally put into the hands of an independent arbiter, C. P. Scott of *The Manchester Guardian*; and he did not reach a decision until 1911. The non-payment of the subsidy was a serious matter indeed for the theatre, which from 31 July 1907 to 30 September 1910 had sustained a net loss of £623 17s. 8d.[42]; nevertheless, despite Miss Horniman's unreasonableness, she had poured a great deal of money into the theatre, and it could not have existed as it was in 1910 without her aid. One does wish that Yeats and Lady Gregory, despite the provocation, had acted more graciously.

The situation of the theatre was summed up by Yeats in a 'Private and Confidential' document entitled 'Samhain, 1910':

We have carried on the dramatic movement in Ireland for ten years, and since 1902 with an Irish Company, trained in the expression of Irish character and emotion. Since Christmas 1904 this Company has played in the Abbey Theatre, where an audience has been gradually drawn together. During the first two or three years this audience increased very slowly but during the last year it has grown rapidly and we seem to be on the edge of prosperity. During the twelve months ending with August 31, the close of our financial year, our receipts from performances in Dublin have much more than doubled, and our receipts from English tours more than trebled what they were in the previous year, whilst our Irish tours on which we lost money at the first, bring now a considerable portion of our income. We are almost independent of Miss Horniman's subsidy, which is £800 a year and the free use of the Abbey Theatre, for we have saved more than £800 during the last twelve months, and should during the next twelve months earn enough to cover also what Miss Horniman spends on the theatre's upkeep. In fact all the laborious building up, the slow amassing of a large repertory of Irish plays, the training of actors, the making of a reputation with the general public has been accomplished or all but accomplished, and without taking longer than is necessary in a work of our kind, and there is little need to make the Abbey Theatre a permanent part of Irish life and a powerful educational influence for those that are to come after us.

Miss Horniman's generous subsidy comes to an end with our Patent at the end of 1910, and if we are to apply for a new Patent the leases must be bought from Miss Horniman.[43] She writes offering us the group of buildings which contain the Abbey Theatre, its dressing rooms and scene dock, and a shop let at a high rent, for the sum she paid for them, £1,428. Part is freehold but the greater part is held under leases, and it is necessary that these leases should be renewed in November of the present year. She spent a large sum upon buildings, dressing rooms, a scene dock, &c., and in turning the shabby old Mechanics' Institute Theatre into the Abbey Theatre, and upon furniture, but for that she makes no charge. In fact she offers us a very considerable property at a very small price.

We are unable to accept this offer or to go on with our work without more capital. During the first years of our work, we were unable to put anything out of our receipts to capital, but we have now some £1,200, practically all accumulated during the last twelve months with the exception of a sum of £250 given by Miss Horniman for touring purposes. By the close of 1910 this should have grown to something over £2,000. We need, however, in addition to what will buy out Miss Horniman, enough money to permit of tours to new places, where we may possible lose money at first, and an increase of staff[44]; some thousands indeed. The chief immediate expense of the buildings must be the hiring of some experienced man to take over the general management, arrangement of tours and so forth.

For many years now Lady Gregory and I, helped by the late Mr. Synge as far as his health allowed, have taken a great deal of the work and the whole of the responsibility. We have done this unpaid, and this and the expense it entailed were only made possible in my own case by the success of a lecture tour in America. Our proper work, for we are writers, has been neglected more and more that we might do what a paid manager could have done better; and now that the business of the theatre is growing more complex and more absorbing it is growing beyond our powers. We cannot carry it on without help after the close of the Patent period, and another expense will be the paying of authors. We did not pay them while we considered our actors insufficiently paid, but from this on we shall give a percentage to all authors except to Lady Gregory and to myself, who wish for the present to give our plays for nothing.

We do not know whether this money will come from one person or from many, or not at all. We ourselves shall be ready to accept much or little according to circumstances. If some clever and courageous man[45] with ideas of his own should wish to carry on our work, we should be well content to be but writers again. On the other hand we are ready to go on advising authors and selecting plays. In fact we will after the re-organisation, if this seems desirable, accept any arrangement provided it leaves the Theatre intellectual and courageous.[46] We would sooner it came to an end than see the tradition we have created give place to one less worthy. At any rate, the work we began in 1898[47] and promised to carry on for but three years will have lasted for upwards of half a score, and should the Abbey Theatre come to an end it will leave behind it a great number of plays, some of them already recognised as a permanent part of Irish literature.[48]

On 16 June, *The Times* of London carried a letter from Yeats and Lady Gregory, appealing for funds to help carry on the work of the theatre. The letter explained that about £1,900 had been saved, enough to take over the theatre and to pay for a new patent, but that a sum of £5,000 was needed to maintain the theatre at its full strength. Toward that endowment of £5,000 the sum of £2,000 had already been given:

But should we receive no more than this £2,000 we shall still go on for as long as we can, but we shall be crippled, and not able to carry out plans for the strengthening and widening of our work, and we shall have, as in the year past, to give up to the actual business of the theatre so great a part of our own time as to interfere with our personal and creative work. We feel we have almost pushed the ball up the hill. We shall be grateful to any friends of our enterprise who will help us to keep it from rolling down again.[49]

The London friends of Yeats and Lady Gregory rallied round, and there were meetings held, interviews given, and letters written. For instance:

In connection with the appeal for funds for the Irish National Theatre, Dublin, recently published, a drawing room meeting was held yesterday by Lady Gregory at the house of Sir Hugh P. Lane, 100 Cheyne Walk, Chelsea. Among those present were Lady Falmouth, Lady Wantage, Lady Alice Shaw Stewart, the Hon. Mrs. Norman Grosvenor, Lady Mond, Lady Lindley, Lady Lewis, Mrs. George Cornwallis West, Mrs. Winston Churchill, Mrs. Colefax, Mrs. John Leslie, Mrs. Leverton Harris, Mrs. McGlyn, Mrs. Belloc Lowndes, Miss Una Birch, Sir Ian Hamilton, Sir Edward Ward, Sir Hugh Lane, General Lawson, Mr. Henry Tonks, M.P.; Mr. P. Wilson Steer, Mr. G. Bernard Shaw, Mr. Spender, Mr. Ford Madox Hueffer, and Mr. Austin Harrison. During the afternoon Miss Sara Allgood, Miss Máire O'Neill, and Mr. O'Rourke of the Abbey Theatre Company, played *The Gaol Gate* on a stage erected in the hall, and after the play the guests were addressed by Mr. Ford Madox Hueffer,[50] Mr. W. B. Yeats, and Mr. Bernard Shaw, who appealed for subscriptions towards the endowment fund of the Abbey Theatre.[51]

Naturally, the appeal for English support did not delight the Irish nationalist press, but Yeats and Lady Gregory had long realised that Irish money alone would not support the theatre. Of course Ireland was not ignored in the campaign for the Endowment Fund. On 27 October, for instance, there was a glittering social gathering at Pembroke House in Dublin. The purpose was, as *The Irish Times* put it:

to discuss and call attention to the affairs of the Irish Literary Theatre. Many *habitués* of the Abbey Theatre were present. Lady Walker, who very kindly gave her home and entertained the guests for the occasion, was assisted by Lady Lyttelton, Mr. Philip Hanson, Right Hon. W. F. Bailey, and other supporters of the Abbey Theatre in making the meeting a success. Mr. Philip Hanson and Mr. Edmund Bourke, who are acting as treasurers and trustees of the Abbey Theatre Endowment Fund, have already received promises of subscriptions from many present, in addition to the £2,000 received. . . .

The Lord Chancellor read the following letter which he had received from His Excellency the Lord Lieutenant:

Viceregal Lodge, 27th October
My Dear Lord Chancellor, — Will you kindly accept and convey to the meeting the assurance of the hearty good wishes

which Lady Aberdeen and I desire to offer for the success of the movement for the promotion and encouragement of the distinctive aims and operations of the Abbey Theatre. — I remain very sincerely yours,

ABERDEEN.

Lady Gregory said that for the first time in twelve years' work they had come to beg. It was now twelve years since Mr. Yeats and she thought of having plays by Irishmen performed in Ireland, plays that were not quite suited for the commercial theatre. They asked some friends to guarantee £300, and this was done. Among those friends were Mr. Justice Ross, Mr. Commissioner Bailey, Mr. Martyn, Lord Dufferin, Mr. Aubrey de Vere, and Mr. Lecky. That £300 was never called on, owing to the generosity of Mr. Edward Martyn. That carried them over a few years, and they became more ambitious, and wanted to have Irish plays performed by Irish actors. Then, with the help of Mr. William Fay, they began to have plays in halls without any capital. In this way they made a little money, and started with a small capital. Some of the plays were performed in London, and created interest among those who saw them. Miss Horniman then built the Abbey Theatre, and gave it to them with a generous annual subsidy for the period of the patent, which would expire in December next. During the last few years they had been able to put by some money, and had now £1,900. This sum they wanted to take over the leases of the Abbey Theatre. Their business advisers told them that £5,000 would enable them to keep their theatre as they wished — vigorous, intellectual, and courageous — for another half a dozen years. They wished to extend the scope of their work. They wanted now to be allowed to play Elizabethan works, the plays of Shakespeare. At the present they could only stage a play of Shakespeare as "a foreign masterpiece". (Laughter.) The managerial work had become so heavy that Mr. Yeats and she had to give up some of the personal work that they had been doing and put it on to their new manager's young shoulders. The speakers at the Theatre Royal on Wednesday had all taken for granted that, when a theatre performed what they called high class work, it could not succeed without an endowment. She agreed and she disagreed. She did not think that it could be done in England, for there they did things in a larger way. In the Abbey Theatre they did things so simply that she thought it would pay in a few years. Indeed, she thought that it would

60

be self-supporting if they could get twenty more persons in the stalls every night, and they hoped to have them in a very short time. Mr. Martin Harvey's reasons for their supporting the Shakespeare Memorial National Theatre were that the object was a worthy one, that the trustees would not misappropriate the money, and that their consciences would be set at rest in having read such a memorial. She thought that they might adopt those reasons in the case of the Abbey Theatre. That it was worthy of support was proved by the great kindness of the Lord Chancellor and Lady Walker. (Applause.) She did not think that their trustees would misappropriate the money — (laughter) — and she thought that they would have a good conscience as to dramatic work in Ireland, because she spoke from experience. (Applause.)

Mr. Birrell said that he was a very poor substitute for the Eloquent Dempsy. (Laughter.) Nevertheless, he had the greatest possible pleasure in moving that the Abbey Theatre, seeking as it did to foster Irish National drama, was worthy of public support, and that a subscription list should be opened with the object of securing its continuance and independence. . . .

Mr. Justice Ross seconded the resolution. . . . He was in the Abbey Theatre with some English friends when there were something like twenty policemen there to maintain order. He impressed on his friends that such a thing was rare. But the managers of the Abbey Theatre withstood the storm of truculence. The courage of Lady Gregory and Mr. Yeats kept the theatre open in spite of these people, and made them listen. Now these people were ready to support the theatre. As to the large theatres in Dublin opposing the patent of the Abbey Theatre, he thought that they owed a great deal to the Abbey Theatre. People would now listen to plays that they would not listen to before they were performed in the Abbey. People had found ideas in the theatre. It was a benefit, not merely to the capital of Ireland, but to the whole Irish race. (Hear, hear.) These plays had been performed in England, in the great centres of thought there, Oxford and Cambridge, where men came and appreciated the great intellectual treat that was put before them. (Applause.) This was a great advantage to Ireland. They indeed owed a great deal to the courage of that heroic woman, Lady Gregory — (applause) — and he hoped that her services would never be forgotten, for greater services had never been done to Ireland than by her. In Mr. Yeats they had a great poet. (Hear, hear.) His reputation was established, not alone in Ireland, but in England

61

and in America. It was, indeed, fortunate that the rays of his genius should shine on the Abbey Theatre. They had to lament the loss of that genius, Mr. Synge, to the Abbey Theatre. That theatre was a centre of light all over Ireland, and in supporting it they were showing that they were determined that the light should not be put out. (Applause.)

The resolution was passed.

Mr. Philip Hanson, M.A., announced that up to Wednesday morning, out of the £5,000 required for the endowment of the Abbey Theatre, £2,169 had been subscribed. The subscribers included many people in England who were interested in the movement, and also Viscount Iveagh, Lord Dunsany, and the Chief Secretary for Ireland. On the previous day £318 had been promised, and the names of the last subscribers included Lord and Lady Ardilaun, Mr. T. M. Healy, M.P., and Mr. L. Waldron. . . .

Lady Gregory announced that Mr. Telford had promised on behalf of the other theatres in Dublin, that they would not oppose the renewal of the licence of the Abbey Theatre. This was, perhaps, the best subscription that they had received.[52]

On 21 November, there was an afternoon entertainment at the theatre in aid of the Endowment Fund, and *The Irish Times* reported:

Yesterday afternoon Lady Gregory held a most enjoyable "At Home" at the Abbey Theatre, the many visitors present including supporters of the theatre in Dublin, personal friends and many guests from the other side. Lady Lyttelton, who frequently brings large parties to the Abbey, was present, wearing a beautiful long seal coat and black toque; Lady Plunkett wore black, with beautiful sables, small black toque, with silver cord; Lady Ardilaun was in black, with black velvet hat, green ostrich feathers. . . . Tea was served in the theatre before the performance of *Hyacinth Halvey*, one of Lady Gregory's best known plays, but which, to many present, was played for the first time. During the evening Mr. W. B. Yeats made known the present condition of the Abbey funds, and the reasons for the appeal for help.

During the afternoon a discussion took place with reference to the position of the Abbey Theatre.

Mr. W. B. Yeats said with regard to the fund which they hoped to start in connection with the Abbey Theatre, they had now got £2,800, but they had been advised by their business advisers to ask for £5,000. The theatre was not yet paying. It was a laborious work. Possibly the most celebrated theatre in the world was the Moscow Art Theatre, which was established ten years ago, and was not yet paying. The Abbey Theatre would be paying if they could keep their rate of expenditure at what it had been up to the last two or three years. They had had steadily increasing audiences. In the twelve months which closed last May they had taken three times as much as during any previous twelve months. They had reached a point at which success — and fairly rapid success — had been attained. The expenditure was always increasing in a theatre. The heating apparatus was not very satisfactory, and many things had to be done before they would feel that the theatre was quite efficient. They had appealed to lovers of theatrical art to give them their assistance, and a great deal of generous assistance had been given them. In England, the Playgoers' Clubs in Leeds, Liverpool, and Manchester were raising subscriptions for them, and he was to address a meeting in Manchester shortly in aid of the funds of the theatre. The Court Theatre in London had offered them the use of that building free for a week in aid of their funds (applause). He told them this to show that they were looked upon as being of something more than local importance. It was considered by students of the stage in many places that the work they were doing was an important part of the attempts now being made to re-model the modern theatre and make it more intellectual and vivid than for some generations. The most direct help they could give was to contribute to the funds. They calculated some time ago that if they had twenty more stalls a night they would no longer have the need of any fund. Saturday night after Saturday night they turned away people in the pit, but the stalls were empty. He wished that people would not only come to the popular plays, but also the experimental plays. If they were to create a vigorous, intellectual theatre, they must have variety in the work, and be continually experimenting. They wanted an intellectual, inquiring audience in Dublin, who would be interested in an experiment because it was an experiment, and so widen the borders of the stage. A theatre such as that must keep producing new plays. He would be glad of any suggestions from those present. (Applause.)

Mr. Justice Madden said it had been suggested to him that they should charge 4s. for the first two or three rows of the stalls. It was a suggestion worth consideration.

Mr. Yeats replied that they were the chilliest rows —

(laughter) — at least they were at present.

Lady Gregory remarked that those present would be greatly assisting if they would give their patronage to a lecture by Mr. Yeats on Tuesday week at the Royal Hibernian Academy, entitled "Personality in Contemporary Poetry", which was in aid of their funds. A good attendance would be very much appreciated.

A gentleman suggested that a Playgoers Club should be formed in Dublin.

Mr. Yeats said that the suggestion was a good one. Such clubs were doing remarkable work in the big English towns, and they had considerable influence on theatrical managers. They also had an effect in some measure on theatrical criticism. Mr. Yeats went on to speak of the theatrical criticism in Dublin, and inferred that it was not of a sufficiently technical character. He knew a reporter, he said, who told him he would probably have to go to a wedding, and from there to a political meeting, and afterwards to do a criticism of a play at the theatre.[53]

On a Saturday afternoon late in November, the Solicitor General, in the Library of Dublin Castle, sat to hear an application by Lady Gregory and Yeats for a Patent for the Abbey Theatre. Mr. J. Day appeared for the applicants, reviewed the assistance which Miss Horniman had given to the theatre, and spoke of the recent plans about the Endowment Fund. He then concluded that

> The memorandum agreed to by all parties provided that the new patent should be for twenty-one years, and should authorise the production of all acknowledged masterpieces of dramatic literature of the eighteenth century and earlier. Subject as above, the new patent should substantially embody all the restrictions of the old one.

There were no disagreements; however, Mr. Dudley White, appearing for the Theatre of Ireland, pointed out that his clients had no habitation and that its objects were similar to those of the Abbey Theatre:

> Mr. Edward Martyn and Mr. George Russell, etc., were completely in intellectual sympathy with the Abbey Theatre.[54] There ought to be a provision in the patent that the Theatre of Ireland should have the right to get eighteen days in the year to produce their plays in the Abbey, and get 40 per cent of the receipts.

Mr. Day said the application was most audacious, and Miss Horniman was so much opposed to this Theatre of Ireland that she would not allow them to use their theatre on any terms.

The Solicitor General said Mr. White's clients wanted to have all the advantages of this theatre without paying for it.

Mr. George Nesbitt was examined on behalf of the Theatre of Ireland, and said none of the actors were paid; they were all amateurs. They did not differ in any way from the Abbey Theatre, except that they performed plays in Irish. He did not object to the patent, but he asked that eighteen days should be reserved for the Theatre of Ireland during the year.

The Solicitor General said he could not hold out any hope of any such obligation being enforced on any theatre.

Mr. P. Cahill, optician, Wellington Quay, asked if Mr. Yeats would put on objectionable plays like *The Playboy of the Western World*.

The Solicitor General said that every patent contained a provision that no play should be produced which would be objectionable to the public. He thought nothing would prevent him making a favourable report to the Lord Lieutenant. The Irish public were under a deep debt of gratitude to Miss Horniman, and also to Lady Gregory, who had taken up the same disinterested attitude.

The proceedings then concluded.[55]

And so finally the theatre came into the hands of the Directors.

\*   \*   \*

Yeats lectured frequently during the year on the subject of the theatre. On 8 February, in the rooms of the United Arts Club in Lincoln Place, he spoke on 'The Tragic Theatre'. As *The Irish Times* reported:

Mr. Yeats, in the course of his address, said that he hated the contemporary theatre, because it was unreal, and that largely for technical reasons. The existing theatre was superficial, and pretended to represent something which it did not really represent. It represented a hypocritical morality, which was substituted for all sincere thinking. Against that temple of the false gods there was now a war proceeding, the leaders of which were seeking to substitute for the old conventional types characters true to life. But these new leaders were met by the difficulty of having to compete with the present-day

65

theatrical paint-pot effects. In their plays there was none of that insincerity, but a perfect play, with characters in it which were extraordinarily simple. He believed that the war would be carried to ultimate victory by the writers of realistic comedy — because comedy was the spirit of life. The changes which they were seeking to bring about were those which were intended to get rid of external things on the stage, and to create something which suggests the idea intended. Hence the real tragic art was indifferent to the external effect, which was never the same twice. It delighted in wonderful words, eloquent and resonant speech, because by that means it was able to represent the mind itself apart from external conditions. They in Ireland who were deeply interested in those matters had set out to try and create an art of tragedy which would delineate the passions of the soul, and that was what they had created. They had also created a comedy which shared with tragedy the scorn of external effects of all that the eye sees. It did not represent life as most people saw it but as it was recreated under spiritual influences. True comedy, like true tragedy, was founded upon a theory which was perfectly honest. The present prevailing stage views were founded upon a philosophy not created by the perceptions of simple men, but which had been created by the stress of artificial conditions, and, above all, under the stress of terror. That was the reason why they felt that those conventional characters should be driven off the stage. Mr. Yeats, proceeding, said that one thing which was necessary was freedom in literature.[56]

On 3 March, Yeats addressed the Ard Craobh of the Gaelic League at 25 Rutland Square, on the subject of 'The Theatre and Ireland'.

Dr. D. Hyde introduced the lecturer, and said Mr. Yeats had done more for Ireland than many of those who were present (applause). When other people were talking in Ireland — and a great nation of talkers we were — Mr. Yeats was working, and Ireland would never forget it to him. Mr. Yeats had given us a theatre of our own — a delightful bijou theatre, in which we saw the work of Irish artistes produced there week after week and month after month, and he had given us a body of Irish actors who were able to play as well as any actors that he (Dr. Hyde) had ever seen anywhere.

Mr. Yeats said the thing that was destroying the theatre in Ireland was the substitution of humanitarianism for artistic feeling. The business of art was the exposition of human nature in itself, making us delight in personality, in character, in emotion, in human life, when it is not troubled or persecuted by anything artificial. These things were being crushed away by all kinds of special interests. One man would spend his life in making money: another man would spend his life on a mathematical problem. Human nature should not be merely endured: it should keep its delight, its energy, and its simplicity. He believed that the countryman in Ireland, as the countryman who has kept his simplicity anywhere in the world, had kept his delight in human nature. In proof of this assertion the lecturer related a story, which, he said, had been told him by a Galway shepherd, about a certain Colonel Martin, whose wife was unfaithful to him. Colonel Martin discovered his wife in the company of a wealthy neighbour. There were two revolvers on a table, but Colonel Martin did not like to take an advantage of an unarmed man. He took other proceedings, and obtained two kegs of gold from the wealthy neighbour. He ordered his man, Tom, to put the kegs on an ass's back, and he went through the streets of Galway distributing the money amongst the poor. The wealthy man had men at every corner ready to attack Colonel Martin, but he could not attack a man who had been so good to the poor. At the end there was no money left, and the man, Tom, said his master would be in want before he died. And he was. He earned a livelihood by picking seaweed. That showed how the people delighted in a striking personality. It showed the mysterious love of that mysterious thing, human nature. When they could get free from the daily newspapers, from the rubbish, and get down to this rich soil, there could be a great artistic movement. Of course, in Ireland, he had no doubt, it would be in the Gaelic language; but that was not the question he was now considering. The National movement, in the expression which it had found at present, was destructive of imagination. The very form of propaganda which had spread all over this country destroyed the substance of thought and the substance of feeling, and it did it for perfectly demonstrable reasons. It began with the Young Ireland movement. There they had got a movement of most brilliant journalists. They had to represent to the minds of the people something which they could think of as Ireland; and when a group of people were organised about a conception the result must be commonplace. It was necessary for a National move-ment to have these conceptions. This conception was something upon which a great number of people must agree. They had to form a very commonplace conception, and that conception had stood in the way of all original creation in Ireland, and must for some time. The people were held together for practical purposes — not by what they loved, but by what they hated. "We all love different things and differently," said Mr. Yeats, "but we can all hate the same thing." There was hatred of England, he continued. With that one perhaps he had no reason to quarrel. But this hatred which was meant to be hatred of England had come to be hatred of Ireland. Was not the inspiring force of the orator hatred of some man? That had an utterly sterilising effect, for literature was created out of love. Every good thing was created out of love. Nothing was created out of hatred. Then there was the obstacle of perpetual apologetics. We carried on a lifelong argument which had for its subject the virtues and the rights of Ireland and the wrongs of England, and so on. We got into an unnatural way of seeing everything. He was alawys attacking propaganda. The propaganda he meant was that upon which men had to agree. He did not mean that which man had made out of his own life. They should distrust all organised thought — thought that was made not for its own sake, but that they might get men to agree upon it for some practical purpose. He admitted that a great deal of that thought was necessary. The beginning of success in literature was distrust in journalism. Ireland was the only country where a young man of seventeen dreams of becoming a journalist, where in other countries he would dream of being a poet, a pirate, or a soldier. If they wanted the people to learn Gaelic, if they wanted them to read it, if they wanted to produce something great to excite their interest in it, they should get people to find out the artistic conception. Learning Gaelic would not do it. One of the things that Synge feared was that Ireland was going to be denationalised, that Ireland was going to be de-Irished by English Victorian commonplace literature being translated into the Gaelic tongue and spread through Ireland. They had their little papers talking utilitarianism week after week. For the first time in the name of Ireland English influence was spreading through Irish, and not the nobler influence that was being crushed down there by the example of its own greatest men.

On the motion of Mr. P. H. Pearse, B.A., B.L., seconded by Lord Dunsany, a vote of thanks was passed to Mr. Yeats for his lecture.[57]

There was a good deal of criticism of this speech from all sides — from George Moore and *The Irish Times*, to Arthur Griffith and *An Claidheamh Soluis*.[58] But, regardless of what he said, Yeats was always good copy.

On 11 March, Yeats lectured in London on 'Mr. Synge and his Work', but the criticism of this occasion was largely directed to Bernard Shaw who commented on Yeats's speech.

Mr. W. B. Yeats, in the last of his course of lectures on the Irish Literary Movement delivered at No. 1 Old Burlington Street last evening, devoted himself in the main to the work of the late Mr. Synge, Mr. George Bernard Shaw being in the chair. Having referred to the work of Lady Gregory in the movement to keep alive the Homeric thought that still lingers in the home of the Western Gael, he said that while today men in Ireland were being occupied with politics and with such questions as the virtue of the Irish people they, the artists, were solely absorbed in the study of human life as a whole. Synge, he said, when he met him first in Paris had his fiddle with him and had learned Irish before setting out on his wanderings. His poems then were melancholy and he suggested to him that if he thought his path was plain he ought to go to the Aran Islands, which the poet afterwards did, being driven therefrom to seek greater loneliness in the Blaskets, where he was for a time completely isolated. One of the results of this experience was *The Playboy*. In this, Mr. Yeats said, there was shown the yearning of the unusual, where there was soon a whole district glorifying a young fool who was supposed to have killed his father.

Mr. Yeats, having referred at some length to the incidents which in the Abbey Theatre had followed upon the production of this play, suggested that the opposition to the play had entirely disappeared. Mr. Synge he described as a man incapable of a political idea. Though he knew him most intimately, he was not aware of his ideas on any political question. He did not think he read any modern books, but he was wanted in modern Catholic Ireland.

Mr. Shaw invited a discussion — would Lady Gregory lead off?

Lady Gregory said no. They were more interested in hearing what Mr. Shaw himself had to say.

Mr. Shaw declared that to anyone who understood true poetry what Mr. Yeats said was commonplace. That there was the reason that to the general mind Mr. Yeats made the impression of remoteness (laughter). It was to be noted that

Synge began his career by wandering all over the world and did not become conscious of Ireland before he got out of Ireland. As to the "movement", it might have begun anywhere in any country, and it existed everywhere. An artist saw everything. Some painters made lovely women. A great painter like Rembrandt painted even old ones. Nobody wanted mean or cowardly Irishmen. What was wanted was a particular sort of Irishmen, like the painter who wanted his women with a skin like a visiting card. But there actually were mean and cowardly Irishmen. But in Ireland they still had a strong sense of religion and honour — things which were not met with in England (laughter). When he spoke of religion, he spoke in the larger sense — the sense in which Mr. Yeats had been speaking. England had been ruthlessly commercised. That, of course, was a thing they could not very well help; but the consequence was, that since the essence of commercialism was to buy cheap and to sell dear, and since it was entirely incompatible with religion and honour, that had to attach themselves to what was looked upon with contempt in Ireland, namely, morality, which meant doing what everyone else did, for no better reason than that everybody else did it (laughter and applause). From one end of the Bible to the other there was not to be found the word "morality". There was the word "Pharisee", and Bunyan had something about the Town of Morality. Bunyan could not foresee that in the twentieth century they would all be living in this Town of Morality. Ireland could take care of itself. They in England were in a far more perilous state; but when they made an effort to save themselves, they would find that there was just as much genius here as there was in Ireland (laughter and applause).[59]

According to another account:

Mr. Bernard Shaw said in politics in Ireland a fantastic person was imposed on them called the Irishman, who was all nonsense. They had in Ireland the dirty Irishman, the mean Irishman, the cowardly Irishman, just as these types existed in every other country. Ireland had this advantage over England, that in Ireland they had still a strong sense of religion and of honour, but in England and America these had disappeared before the commercial spirit of the age, which was entirely incompatible with either religion or honour.

They had instead what was called morality — a word that was never once mentioned in the Bible, and was never alluded to there except in terms of reprobation. Ireland was well able to take care of herself, and England was more advanced towards a perilous state of damnation than Ireland was.[60]

Arthur Griffith, whose sense of humour was succumbing to his patriotism, had some uncomplimentary reflections about Shaw and his opinions:

> The stage Irishman, after passing through the incarnation of Paddy Whack, the Drunken Dragoon, the Cursing Tinker, and the Boy who Killed his Da, is now at the expert hands of England's chartered jester, Mr. Bernard Shaw, going to assume a new guise. He is to be a religious and honourable person, ignorant of the Sin of Commerce. The lady who lived at Leith — the lady very stylish, man, who yet in spite of all her teeth, fell dead in love with a harum-scarum-devil-may-carum, ranting, roaring Irishman, can now rest in peace. The new stage Irishman does not roar or rant or mention the devil. His voice is vaseline and his blood is mud. The British public in a sentimental mood wants piety and sawdust in its puppets. So enter Mr. Bernard Shaw, leading the Pious Fool, successor to the Popular Parricide. . . . Mr. Shaw lives by the British public, and therefore must please the British public. He tickles it and teases it, but he never insults or outrages its tradition. . . . It is a tradition of the British public that whilst the Irish are a clever people they are wholly impracticable, and Mr. Shaw wrote *John Bull's Other Island* to show the British public it was quite right. He is the cleverest flatterer England has ever hired, and now that the British public desires to drop the tear of virtue in its theatre stalls, Mr. Shaw produces the Religious, Honourable and wholly Uncommercial Irishman. . . . In view of the advent of the Pious Fool in succession to the Denegerate, as the type of Ireland, we look back with some respect to the drunken roysterers of Maginn and Lever. They had the saving quality of being masculine.[61]

On 23, 24, and 25 May, the Abbey company played at the New Theatre, Cambridge, and Yeats gave a long interview:

> "The side of our work with which we have achieved our greatest successes," said Mr. Yeats to our representative, "is undoubtedly the peasant comedy and tragedy. We have placed upon the stage for the first time the real Irish Life as opposed to the traditional. The dialect of Lever and of Lover was a composite thing, and displayed a very limited understanding of the peasant mind. The proper understanding of the peasant

71

mind only arose with an understanding of Gaelic.

"These peasant plays," he continued, "are not primarily studies of peasant life. Synge's plays, for instance, contain a philosophy of life just as truly as do the lyrics of Shelley. They express the ideas of the man in the symbolism of the peasant world he had studied so deeply and knew so well. His was not photographic art; it was symbolic. He used the Irish peasant as a means of expression, just as the painter uses the colours on his palette. His plays are the complete expression of his own soul.

"Lady Gregory's comedy is equally personal, but in a different manner. Both writers studied their symbols profoundly. Lady Gregory, I believe, wrote down over two hundred thousand words of peasant speech before she wrote a line of her dialogue. Synge, of course, lived in the cottages of the people as one of themselves.

"That part of our movement represented by Lady Gregory, Synge and myself, is individualistic. We aim at expressing ourselves, they in dialect, myself in verse. But there is a new movement arising that is representative of the social life and the economic conditions of Ireland. We have just produced in Dublin, for instance, and we shall stage it in London, a play by Patrick Colum, in which one sees what one often sees in Ireland, a man whose whole life is a struggle to get free from his duty to his family. The hero, Thomas Muskerry, a Workhouse master, is a sort of King Lear of the Workhouse. Then we have *Harvest*, by S. L. Robinson, a powerful play, in which is shown the struggle of the farming classes to bring up their children in the professions, thereby ruining their farms. We have produced another play which is a study of the moral conditions left behind by the agrarian war, the fear of public opinion and the like — *The White Feather*, by Ray. These men are the historians of their times, in a way that we are not.

"It is, of course, the poetical drama in which I am most interested, though until lately we have been unable to do very much in that direction because we have concentrated on our peasant work. *Deirdre* has lately been played in Dublin, however, and I am now going back with excitement to this work — and with scenery that will give me real pleasure. Mr. Gordon Craig, after years of study, has at last created a method for the staging of poetical drama which suggests everything and represents nothing."

Asked for some descriptions of this creation, Mr. Yeats said that the invention was Mr. Craig's patent, of which he had secured the Irish rights, and he could not enter into detail. "One sees upon the stage," said Mr. Yeats, "a vast Cyclopean place, where one can have the light and shade of Nature for the first time upon the stage. At last one escapes from all the meretriciousness, from the bad landscape painting, from the stage lighting which throws a shadow which in no way agrees with the painted shadow. At last we shall have a stage where there is solemnity and beauty, and where for all that, the verse is free to suggest what picture it will without having to compete with some second-rate painter."

Up to the present, Mr. Yeats explained, they had worked on the lines he explained to the interviewer five years ago, when he criticised customary stage methods with great severity. They worked by suggestion rather than by representation. An inside scene they presented as faithfully as their purse permitted. There it was possible to attain realism. But a landscape painted in the the ordinary stage manner, he contended, must always be meretricious and vulgar. "The moment an actor stands near to your painted forest or your mountain, you perceive he is standing against a flat surface." Far better, he argued, to suggest a scene upon a canvas, whose vertical flatness one accepts and uses, as the decorator of pottery accepts the roundness of a bowl or jug for the flatness of a plate.

A woodland scene might be represented, he explained, by a recurring pattern, or painted ground. Or there was the comparative realism of the Japanese print. This kind of decoration not only gave them a scenic art — which would be true art because peculiar to the stage — but it would give the imagination liberty, and without returning to the bareness of the Elizabethan stage. "Mr. Robert Gregory . . . has designed some beautiful scenes for us on these lines," added Mr. Yeats.

In conclusion, Mr. Yeats expressed himself as more than satisfied with the success the movement had achieved. . . .[62]

In July, Yeats was interviewed about his new play which Mrs. Patrick Campbell was contemplating producing:

"For more than a year past," said Mr. Yeats, "I have been helped much by Mr. Craig's inventions, which have provided me, so to speak, with an instrument by which I can construct my play in model, and enact my drama as on a chessboard while I compose it."

73

Mr. Yeats pointed out a miniature model of the Abbey Theatre in Dublin, on which, by the help of puppets, the scenes of his play might be arranged, and the various figures grouped and moved as in an actual drama.

With regard to the literary form of his new play, Mr. Yeats explained that it was to be a poetic drama, with much rhymed verse running through the more vivid parts of the dialogue. "I believe," he said, "that a movement in favour of the revival of poetic drama is now passing over Europe, a drama which will impress its audience through the medium of poetic suggestion rather than through wealth of scenic effect."

"May we expect your new play to be distinctly Irish in character?" asked our representative.

"*The Player Queen*, which is the title of the play," said Mr. Yeats, "will be a comedy of mediaeval or Renaissance life, and will not be distinctly Irish in character, nor, indeed, will it reflect the thought of any particular nationality, though, as is but natural, it will probably bear upon it the impression which much pondering upon Ireland must give to the work of any Irishman. One of the great difficulties at present in producing any poetic drama is to find the players; at present the number of actors capable of speaking verse upon the stage might be numbered upon one's fingers. . . ." [63]

In the middle of November, Yeats gave a series of lectures at the Memorial Hall in Manchester. The last lecture, on 14 November, was reported by *The Manchester Guardian*:

Mr. Yeats said he was trying in these lectures simply to give expression to some of the things he had thought and felt, as an artist, about beauty and truth and the meaning of human life. The artist, said Mr. Yeats, had no concern with morality, politics, humanitarianism, or philanthropy — all these had interest for him as a man, but as an artist his task was simply to pursue reality and set down the vision which revealed to him the meaning of life. This was the source of all great art, and he must resist the temptation which lured him away from it. In England men had been led away from art by the zeal of the reformer, because the artist absorbed in his vision had few friends, but let him once take up a cause and he gained a multitude of supporters. In Ireland the temptation was not reform, but national politics; all the dissensions in the Irish movement had come from the disturbance which the collective will wrought in the individual soul, leading it astray from the narrow path of personal vision.

Irish national politics dated from the Young Ireland movement, when Thomas Davis and his friends had created by
journalism a national ideal which was to take the place of
national institutions. The images they had created of the
ideal peasant and the charming colleen had spread wherever
their race was to be found, creating something like a world-
wide national consciousness, in which abstract virtues had
taken the place of realities. Out of this consciousness arose the
Gaelic movement; but by this time an industrial class had
arisen, the first their country had ever seen, and having neither
leisure nor a traditional culture, its leaders were banded
together only by political hatred and suspicion, so that their
journalism was altering for the worse the imagination of the
people. Passion in public life without culture was ignoble;
the man with no culture could do routine work without doing
any harm, but the moment he touched the artist's work of
expressing emotion he injured everyone he reached.

In similar plight, said Mr. Yeats, America and England
could turn to education, to the treasures of the library, but
Ireland had no national literature to which to turn. It was
for this cause that Lady Gregory and he himself had gone to
the folk-life of Ireland, for there only was the great imaginative
tradition of the people to be found. In the imagination of the
peasant lived the old Ireland of chivalry and nobility, which
was a name of enchantment throughout Europe, but unless
its imagination and generosity could be called back, it lay at
the door of death. It was because they knew this that the
Gaelic League went to the cottage for the ancient legends, the
imagination of the peasants and their attitude towards the
world, an outlook personal, individual, and therefore sincere.
The Irish countryman never remembered a hero for anything
good he had done, but for something artistic about the man;
he had the personal view of the Homeric Greek and an
imagination to be touched by the beauty of physical things,
as of the woman for whom "men would be drowning themselves, swimming of rivers to get a sight of her." But besides
an attitude towards life which was sincere, they got a language
wonderfully expressive, a speech to be compared only with
that of the England of Shakespeare — "The most beautiful
form of English now spoken on earth."

It had been their dream to bring the imagination of the
country back into the life of the town, not only its heroism
and legend, but its wonderful comedy and humours of speech.
Their success, so far as they had succeeded, was due to the

accident of his discovering J. M. Synge in Paris. When Scotland thought herself very religious and correct the mysterious caprice which decided these matters sent them Burns to celebrate everything that Scotland thought abominable. "Synge," said Mr. Yeats, "was Ireland's Burns. Ireland was absorbed in politics, as Scotland in religion, and Synge was the only man I ever met who was absolutely incapable of political thought. He had been all over Europe, flying from organised life; he had lived amongst the poor without taking the slightest interest in poverty, yet he loved the poor, for he found their lives more artistic and beautiful than our lives." Happiness came to Synge in the Aran Islands, where he escaped "the nullity of the rich and the squalor of the poor", where he found a traditional courtesy and people living in the face of the great realities, death, childhood, and the affections. Living in the presence of death his vision came to him; he paid the Irish people the greatest compliment of the artist by making them a symbol of his own life and himself speaking through their lips. Noble art was always passionate art, and in Synge's passion asceticism, stoicism and ecstasy all came together. . . .[64]

On the next day, 15 November, Yeats was in Liverpool, addressing the Liverpool Playgoers' Society on the Irish dramatic movement.

Mr. Yeats began by explaining his view of the function of the artist. "If," he said, "you can really keep your mind simply fixed on reality, say to yourself, 'I will express human nature for its own sake; I will give my vision of the world for the sake of the reality that is in front of me' — if you can keep to that and have the gift of expression, you become in the end a great artist." In England, social zeal lures the artist away from his reality; in Ireland, it is the subordination of the artistic vision to the necessities of the national propaganda that is the temptation. Mr. Yeats explained that while Ireland was once led by a few educated men, there has now grown up a middle class who have great zeal and self-sacrifice, but little culture. Irish politics are exceedingly emotional. It is, he declared, "a matter of life and death to the soul of Ireland" to bring this influence of art to the country, and to get it Mr. Yeats and his friends have gone to the Irish peasant for this culture as English people go to their written literature, and as Ibsen and his contemporaries went to the peasant at the beginning of their movement. They were bringing the culture of the peasant into the towns.

"We find in the peasant," he said, "visions of human life for the sake of human life, the vision of beauty for the sake of beauty. His thoughts are not organised. He is not a reformer. All the collective opinions created by young Ireland and those that came after have left him untouched. He sees to-day as he saw centuries ago, and he preserves to-day the old legends, the old songs, and above all he has his beautiful dialect of the English and his rich Gaelic tongue. The Gaelic League went to him for his dialect. We went to him for his dialect of English, for his songs and legends and his attitude to the world. We found there once more the solitary man, and we found again that God never shows himself but to the solitary man, whether on Sinai, or Patmos, or in the study. We escaped the gregarious man, the good citizen, the perpetual pre-occupation of politics, and we get down to a vision and an imagination that seemed to us as old as the world." The primitive Homeric imagination and simplicity of the peasant of the West of Ireland Mr. Yeats illustrated by haunting stories. The peasant, he said, forgets the good a man did, but remembers always the fine, the heroic quality in him. "He looks on man with the true eyes of the artist." From the unwritten literature the new Irish poets and dramatists have drawn their materials and their inspiration.

They are, Mr. Yeats told his audience, writing in the English dialect of the West, which is no patois but a pure dialect three centuries old, a dialect with the vocabulary of Sir Thomas Malory and the Bible. Reference was made in passing to Lady Gregory's translation of these Irish stories which led to the foundation of the Abbey Theatre in Dublin. The theatre movement began with a little group of shopboys, artisans and clerks, all amateurs, but the theatre is now practically paying, though Mr. Yeats drew an amusing picture of its early troubles, of the riots that took place, either through the use on the stage of plain, homely words, or because it was considered unpatriotic to represent Irish character as anything but creditable. The theatre, he said, has now won a victory for reality. Part of Mr. Yeats's lecture, and not the least fascinating part, was given up to an appreciation of J. M. Synge, and he read extracts from the poet's plays, notably *Deirdre of the Sorrows*, which, said Mr. Yeats, contains "the most beautiful writing of all contemporary drama".

Synge had used the dialect holding that "you cannot have noble drama without a vehement, powerful and beautiful speech". He was quite opposed to what we call realism on the

77

stage, yet "the more human nature the greater the art". Mr. Yeats had nothing to say against the politician, the moralist, or the humanitarian. He admires them in the citizen, but not in the artist. "The great artist differs from the sentimentalist in this," he said, "that he sees all the dreams of beauty men have had, but he sees reality as it is, and never disguises to himself what reality is." "It has been part of the whole movement," he continued, "to bring back the vivid speech of the people, because when you get a nation given over to abstract ideas the first thing that dies is language. You cannot imagine how dead and formal a thing is the language taught in our Catholic schools in Ireland. You have a beautiful literary speech which we use in Ireland with difficulty because it is full of your own history and your own moods." In Ireland to-day there is a healthy dramatic movement, a number of young dramatists at work, one writing of working class life in Belfast, others writing of the country people round Cork. Others there are of promise who may be going to be realists. Whatever they are going to be," added Mr. Yeats in conclusion, "they will not be shaped by us, but by the general consciousness of Ireland as she is." [65]

\* \* \*

The two other principal companies in Dublin which staged Irish plays were the Theatre of Ireland and the Independent Dramatic Company. Both companies were at best only semi-professional, and the quality of their productions seldom rivalled that of the Abbey company. Nevertheless, each group did stage a few productions of new plays; some of the plays were rather good; and many of the people connected with each group were very interesting indeed.

The Theatre of Ireland was basically composed of members of the Irish National Theatre Society who had split away from the parent group. The original members of the Theatre of Ireland were mainly the more patriotic members of the Irish National Theatre Society, and included Padraic Colum, Máire Nic Shiubhlaigh and her brother Frank, Máire Garvey and others. But, although the original split was along the lines of Art versus Nationalism, it is undeniable that clashes of personality—particularly with Willie Fay and W. B. Yeats — had also been important. In any event, the plays of the group were not particularly patriotic, and Seumas O'Kelly and James Stephens both wrote good work for the group.

78

In 1910, the Theatre of Ireland staged two programmes, both at the Molesworth Hall. On 18, 19 and 20 February, the group revived Charles Macklin's eighteenth-century comedy, *The True Born Irishman*. According to several reports there were good audiences, and many of the quips in the play seemed to have an amusing contemporary political relevance. On the same evening was produced a one-act tragedy by Kathleen Fitzpatrick called *Expiation*. Of it *The Irish Nation* reported:

> *Expiation* deals with the love which a wife has for her husband — a murderer. He has confessed himself to be such and expects that in consequence she will leave him. But she does not. Their love is all the world to her. It is a dramatic little piece, well constructed and boldly sketched . . . Mr. Carré was the husband and Miss Nora Fitzpatrick the wife. It was a new experience to see Miss Fitzpatrick in such a part, as previously she had been associated with Northern farce. She played with feeling and restraint. Some Northern mannerisms at times, however, were evident.[66]

In Easter Week, the theatre again produced a double bill. The opening one-act was *The Home-Coming* by Seumas O'Kelly, and *The Irish Times* summarised its plot thus:

> The scene is laid in a farmhouse from which a family named Ford had formerly been evicted, and was now being restored after a prolonged absence. There are public rejoicings, and, though the head of the family does not survive to enjoy "the long-expected day", his son and widow are reinstated amidst a good deal of ceremony. The widow, greatly affected by the appearance of scenes from which she has long been banished, becomes reminiscent. She recounts the deeds of her departed husband; tells how he was the first to stir up resistance against the evicting tyrant, and in the midst of her triumphant narration she herself is stricken with illness and suddenly expires. The moral of the play is by no means clear, but its dialogue was good, and the manner in which it was presented was entirely satisfactory.[67]

Arthur Griffith wrote in *Sinn Féin* that the play was

> . . . specially noticeable for the fact that it gives Máire Nic Shiubhlaigh a splendid opportunity to exhibit her great elocutionary genius. As Mrs. Ford, she held her audience spellbound in her speech to her son, recalling her early life, and her husband's stubborn resistance to the harsh laws under

79

which they had been evicted years before. The little play is a peculiar mixture of joy and sorrow, joy at returning to the old home, and sorrow with the memory the return brings. The final scene is an impressive blending of the rejoicing of the neighbours and the sorrow of the Ford family. Una Nic Shiubhlaigh as Agnes Dealy acted with much grace and dignity. John Connolly and Charles Power, as Donogh Ford and Hugh Dealy, both played with great restraint and feeling.[68]

The second play, by J. O'E, was a more curious matter altogether. As Griffith wrote:

> The second play, *The Spurious Sovereign, or Nailed to the Counter*, is described as "a burlesque melodrama", but there is much more burlesque than melodrama. The story is well connected, and carries a certain interest, but the author has apparently been more anxious to give his actors an opportunity to exercise their own individuality in playing than to give character to any of the parts. The play is a wild parody of the historic and romantic melodrama of the Lewis Waller and Martin Harvey type, and sometimes descends even further. A number of the parts are easily recognisable as satires on some English Dublin favourites and their method of stagecraft. All the parts are admirably filled, and the costumes which are very slightly burlesqued look splendid.
>
> Una Nic Shiubhlaigh plays the boy part of Kropotkin as "Little Lord Fauntleroy", the stage child, with splendid childishness, and in the prison scene where "Kroppy" is confined prior to his execution, she scored a grand success. Luke Killeen as Prince Robert, the soft, innocent, easily-fooled elder brother, deserves a special word. Seaghan Mac Murchada, the pirate captain, Prince William the usurper, acted with care and scored on every point, never over-acting and always interesting. P. Mac Shiubhlaigh as the A. B. pirate makes the house shriek with laughter in his tragic speeches and asides to the audience. Stephen James as the Icelander is apparently introduced to burlesque the attempts made in modern drama to give local colour to a scene by bringing on unnecessary characters, but in this case the local colour is used up to its full extent much to the delight of the audience.[69]

The 'Stephen James' who played the Icelander was the poet and novelist James Stephens.

Count Markievicz engaged the Abbey for three days in the middle of April for two plays produced by his Independent Dramatic Company. On 14 April, the company produced for the first time the Count's patriotic Irish melodrama, *The Memory of the Dead*. *The Irish Times* reviewed the proceedings with considerable kindness:

Count Markievicz's dramatic excursions have been so enterprising in the past that it was no surprise to find him tackling an Irish historical subject. *The Memory of the Dead* — a romantic drama of '98 — was produced for the first time at the Abbey Theatre last night, and was well received by an audience volatile in its enthusiasms. The play opens with preparations for rising and joining with the French allies; the second act occurs at the period of defeat, and the third takes place twelve months later, when the mournful aftermath of the revolution is going on. The author has marshalled his plot well about the incidents of the rising; his point of view, as may be imagined, is that of the insurgents, and the scene is laid mainly in a Streamstown home, where the spirit of insurgency has been fostered. There is a slight love interest at first, but we are soon in the midst of action. Colonel Charort, an officer in General Humbert's army, finds his way to the Streamstown home, and, seeing that the occupants are friendly, he seeks guidance across the mountains towards Donegal. All the men of the place, except the crippled old farmer, have gone out to fight, and the farmer's daughter, Norah, the wife of one who has gone forth, offers herself as guide. On their journey she meets her husband, who, then, leaving her to nurse a wounded comrade, James M'Gowan, takes the French officer on his further course. No more is heard of him for a year, until into the Streamstown farmhouse wanders a wretched figure of a man, who is not at first recognised as the husband of the desolate wife — Dermot O'Dowd. He learns that his disappearance has been accounted by most of his friends, though not by his faithful wife, as treachery to the cause for which he went out to fight. His identity is not revealed to the household until he falls, shot by soldiers who have tracked him here, for it turns out that under an assumed name he has undergone tortures, has refused to betray any information, and has escaped while under condemnation to be executed. His wife's trust in his faithfulness is justified by his end, and, over his dead body she declaims her resolution to bring up their child in the same creed as had animated Dermot O'Dowd It is an effective climax, and the last oration, like many other passages in a similar high-pitched key, was well delivered by Countess Markievicz, who took the part of Norah. Mr. J. M. Carré did well as the French officer, and Mr. George Nesbitt and Mr. Edward Keegan also acted with ease and confidence. Other parts were taken by Mr. Seaghan Connolly, Mr. P. MacCartan, Mr. M. Carolan, Mr. Mervyn Colomb, and Miss Honor Lavelle. . . .[70]

On the next evening the company presented the first and, apparently, the only production of a four-act comedy by the Count, entitled *Mary. The Irish Times* summarized the play thus:

> Mary, who has deserted her husband under circumstances which give rise to very uncharitable comments, returns to him in a casual manner after an absence of four years; but she does not care to live under his roof. She had been married to him against her will, and she is too romantically inclined to submit to domestic despotism. The husband is denominated a philosopher. He is in reality a vapid, expressionless character, and if any justification could be found for desertion of a husband by his wife, such an instance as the present would supply it. Mary, however, does not prove to be so black as she has been painted, and at the fall of the curtain she re-assumes her white wings. The male characters are Brown, Green, White, Black, Smythe, etc., a respectable sprinkling of wives being introduced. What the exact *motif* is was not apparent to the audience, but as the dialogue was often rather good, a certain amount of laughter was provoked. The principal artists were very efficient. Miss Mary O'Hea as Mrs. White, and Mr. George Nesbitt as Mr. Brown meriting especial praise.[71]

In the week of 23 May, the company appeared at the Gaiety in a somewhat revised version of *The Memory of the Dead*, and this was preceded by a farcical curtain raiser, *Home Sweet Home*, written by Nora Fitzpatrick and the Count.

Two Irish operas were produced during the year. On 29 March, the Dublin Amateur Operatic Society produced Signor Esposito's one-act opera, *The Tinker and the Fairy*, based on the play by Douglas Hyde. Of it, *The Irish Times* wrote:

> Dr. Esposito's original compositions are numerous and varied. An Irish symphony, a cantata, an Irish suite, and a string quartet all gained prizes in the composers' competition of the Feis Ceoil. He has written fine songs; his three Ballades for pianoforte are among the best compositions of the type written within recent years; his Sonata for violin and piano-

forte is a masterly work. Many other compositions, besides his excellent arrangements of Irish melodies, have been published. Nor is *The Tinker and the Fairy* his first operetta, for seven or eight years ago there was produced in London *The Postbag*, a setting of a libretto by Mr. A. P. Graves.

*The Tinker and the Fairy* has been on the stocks for some time, for it must be over two years since the Students' Musical Union at the Royal Academy of Music, arranged a programme consisting entirely of Dr. Esposito's work, and including the fairy music from this operetta. And now that it has been produced, it would not be fair to the composer to pretend that last night's performance was all that the music deserved. Miss Edwards (probably owing to nervousness) was not completely in control of her voice, and in any case she made too free a use of the *parlato*. Her "farewells' at the end were far too vigorous, both for dramatic and musical sense. Her voice should have been very soft and distant, blending gently with the background of fairy voices. Mr. Browner sang splendidly, but his voice was not a suitable blend with the soprano, as was obvious in the duet, "Thou hast banished age and care". Mr. Collins in his brief part was excellent. The chorus of female voices, in the fairy music, might have been still softer; in particular the first soprano part wanted toning down.

In spite of these minor defects, the merit of Dr. Esposito's work was quite evident. . . . He has not made it so elaborate as to get out of proportion with the subject, and, quite appropriately, the music is pleasant rather than deep. The composer's skill in orchestration is shown in the variety of the score, a quality which keeps alive the interest of the setting, and fills in the outline of the picture with attractive colours. There is not much originality of melodic invention, the charm of the music being mostly in the weaving of orchestral threads. The fairy music, allotted to a harp and three violins in the distance, accompanying a very beautiful succession of sixths in the triple voice part, is a particularly charming portion of the score. To associate with the entrance of the tinker the breezy rhythm of an Irish dance is another excellent touch; for the rest, the most striking passages were mainly those in which broad *cantabile* strains carried the music along, as in the passage commencing "Leave a world where all grows old". Dr. Esposito's work delighted the audience, which summoned him and the two principals several times before the curtain.[72]

In *Sinn Féin*, Arthur Griffith did not think that Signor Esposito had caught either the humorous or the ethereal spirit of the play in his music. Griffith also criticised the costuming, noting that the tinker was dressed in immaculate riding breeches and that the fairy's commonplace white gown was too 'palpably real and earthly'.

During the week of 16 May, the opera *Eithne*, with music by Robert O'Dwyer and libretto by Rev. Thomas O'Kelly, was revived. The principal singers were Joseph O'Mara and William Dever. On this occasion, *The Irish Times* was rather critical:

> Mr. Robert O'Dwyer's music is a very elaborate piece of work. Extravagant claims have been made for it as being purely Celtic in character, as embodying a purely national style. The music is too self-conscious for that. Mr. O'Dwyer rarely loses himself; he is very plainly conscious of two influences — on the one hand, what he knows of Wagner; on the other hand, what he knows of the modes and cadences of ancient Irish music. This at first thought seems a strange combination, and it is not surprising that in a first work of this magnitude the composer should not have been entirely successful in welding the two elements into one composite style. At the same time, there is no need to set down the combination as an unworkable one. . . . The weakness of his music in many parts of *Eithne* largely arises from too close an adherence to many of the most blatant mannerisms of Wagner, sometimes involving ugliness not justified by dramatic effect.[73]

There was a good deal of amateur activity during the year, and the production by amateurs of quite a few new plays. A particularly interesting performance was given early in February by Patrick Pearse's pupils at St. Enda's school of his one-act *Iosagán* and of Padraic Colum's *The Destruction of the Hostel*. On 9 April, Pearse's pupils presented these two plays at the Abbey, and on the same occasion they also staged Hyde's *An Naomh ar Iarraidh* and O'Grady's *The Coming of Fionn*. The effective simplicity of the productions was much admired, and *An Claideamh Soluis* reported:

> The visit of the Sgoil Eanna Boys to the Abbey on Saturday was a success in every sense. They had the pleasure of acting before a good house, and they were fortunate enough on this, their first appearance in public, to get through a long programme of four plays with only a few trivial hitches. The acting of the boys from the Gaedhealtacht in the Irish plays

was higher than anything yet achieved even by adult actors in Irish plays in Dublin. Padraic O Conaire, who took the principal part in *Iosagán* and in *An Naomh ar Iarraidh*, has the knowledge and the sympathy necessary for the proper interpretation of the Gaelic character, and he possesses the stage gift to a degree that is surprising in one so young and in an amateur. Mr. Pearse holds that acting should play a large part in school life, and he is right. Few things that we know of give the young mind such sympathy and tolerance for the humble, the poor, and the wronged, or teaches it the nobility and courage that are greater than all things else in education.[74]

In May the Irish Theatrical Club at 40 Upper Sackville Street produced two plays by Mary Costello, *The Coming of Aideen* and *The Gods at Play*; the Leinster Stage Society produced four plays at the Abbey, two by M. B. Pearse, *The Message* and *Over the Stile*, as well as O'Grady's *The Transformation of Fionn* and a Napoleon play by A. McGloughlin called *The Countess of Strasbourg*; and the Students' Union of the Metropolitan School of Art produced five plays at the Abbey, including the first production of Thomas King Moylan's *Naboclish*. None of these productions was of great merit, although Moylan's play did achieve some subsequent popularity among amateurs. *The Irish Times* wrote of it:

> It was described as "a practical joke in two acts", and it has the merit of being worthy of the description. Mr. Moylan has written a really clever skit on the self-sufficient type of Englishman who imagines he knows more about Ireland than the Irish themselves, and is too stupid to realise his own ignorance. This Saxon "week-ender" falls by mistake amongst the witty peasantry of Clare, who make a hare of him — all for the sake of obliging the stranger with "useful" information about secret societies and the like. Mr. Moylan displays undoubted dramatic ability, and it is to be hoped that his play will be added to the repertoire of the Abbey Company.[75]

Early in August the Gaelic League during its Oireachtas produced five plays at the Round Room. About the plays submitted for the drama competition in 1910, the judges, headed by Thomas MacDonagh, issued this preliminary report:

> In the three-act competition the only play selected for production is *An Snaidhm*, by Alfonso Labhraidh [*The Knot*, by Alphonsus Lowry], of Bootle, Liverpool, whose work received

high commendation from the judges. It is considered one of the best comedies of its length yet written in Irish. It is witty, surprising, piquant, and the characterization is very good throughout, the situations and openings of the acts and the curtains being well managed. Its production has been entrusted to the Keating Branch, and, with good acting, it can hardly fail to be successful.

The adjudicators could not see their way to recommend that any of the other plays sent in should be staged, but as the Committee was anxious that the competition should be carried out, they were submitted to two additional adjudicators, but with the same result. The following may be stated as some of the chief faults found with them:

Acts too short. Long soliloquies, which are unnatural at best. Killing of a man on the stage by choking. Too many asides. Burlesque incidents and conduct of the people inconsistent. Third act in one case may, according to author, be omitted! Wearisome, long details. Purposeless talk. Conventional, long-winded, uninteresting, incongruous language. Modern phrases in the mouths of Red Branch warriors. A series of tirades. No dramatic unity between the acts. Several of the efforts were very good as stories, but were not drama.

The Committee regret also that in the bilingual drama competition it was only possible to select one play for production, viz., *Oighreacht Roisín*, by Padraig O Seaghda [*The Inheritance of Roisín*, by Patrick O'Shea], of Colmdaniel, Co. Kerry. This play is fairly well constructed, the language, form, and general idea being good. The Colmcille Branch have been asked to undertake its production.[76]

In order that a second evening of drama be provided, the Committee selected three previously produced works, including two bilingual plays by W. P. Ryan, *The Queen's Visit* (*Cuaird na Bainroghna*) and *The Teacher from Tír na nOg* (*An tOíde as Tír na nOg*), and *Aine agus Caoimhín* (*Annie and Kevin*), a new one-act play by Tomás Mac Domhnaill, produced at short notice by the Theatre of Ireland. None of these plays was felt by the Gaelic League committee to be of major merit; however, partly in response to a resentful letter sent in by an unsuccessful playwright, a series of papers on the drama by Padraic Colum began to appear in the League's magazine, *An Claidheamh Soluis*. Although many plays had now been written and produced for the Gaelic League's annual competition, the standards still remained obstinately low.

On 10 and 11 October, a group called the New Ireland Dramatic

Society presented at the Molesworth Hall a revival of James Gregan's *Teig Corcoran's Courtship* and two new plays. One was a romantic drama by Joseph Ford called *The Bailiff of Kilmore*, and the other was an historical drama, *The Call to Arms*, by Peter Kearney who was to write Ireland's national anthem, 'The Soldier's Song'.

Beginning on St. Stephen's Day, the Pioneer Dramatic Society gave possibly the first production of George J. Hurson's four-act patriotic melodrama, *A Daughter of Ireland*, at St. Francis Xavier's Hall.

One might sum up the amateur dramatic movement in 1910 as more active than excellent.

*     *     *

1910 was just about the last year that the commercial theatres, the Theatre Royal and the Gaiety, could book the most notable London successes and the best of the English actor-managers. But in this year the Dublin playgoer could have seen F. R. Benson, Martin Harvey, Lewis Waller, H. B. Irving and, in his famous roles of Shylock and Svengali, Beerbohm Tree. On 12 May, at the Theatre Royal, Tree also appeared in *The O'Flynn*, a recent stage-Irish concoction by Justin Huntley MacCarthy. Of the production, the somewhat bemused reviewer of *The Irish Times* wrote:

> We certainly did believe that the Abbey Theatre had killed this sort of thing, and we do not even now believe that any other actor than Sir Herbert Tree could have successfully resuscitated the character [of the Stage Irishman]. The whole play is so much apart from reality that anything like a real Irishman would have been utterly out of place. We accept Sir Herbert Tree's Irishman for what it is in its place, and we acknowledge that it is good fun.
>
> Sometimes it is rather petty fun — not the sort of thing that one would have expected Sir Herbert Tree to rely on, even though he, alone perhaps among living actors, has the power to carry it through. To come down a chimney in the midst of a shower of loose bricks — that is how the O'Flynn makes his first entrance — is not the class of "business' with which a distinguished actor might be expected to commend a play to us; yet *The O'Flynn* is frequently at that level. . . .
>
> Sir Herbert Tree romps through his part with the greatest gusto, ever the dashing, volatile, debonair, gallant. We do not see why he should have a brogue, except as an added touch of romance; but there it is, and we felicitate Sir Herbert Tree

on his success in it. . . . Mr. W. G. Fay was Sir Herbert Tree's principal aider and abettor in the humorous element of the piece; he was quitely droll in his old inimitable style. . . .

The audience cheered enthusiastically at the close of the play, and called for a speech. Sir Herbert Tree, coming before the footlights, raised a laugh at the outset by remarking that he was "less nervous now". Continuing, he thanked the audience heartily for the great warmth of their reception of *The O'Flynn*. "I know," he said, "we are excused for having brought it before you, and I am glad you have received with so much enthusiasm Mr. Fay, who has done so much to teach me what little I know of the Irish brogue." There were renewed cheers as the curtain again fell.[77]

The Dublin playgoer could also have seen at the Gaiety such new plays as Sutro's *The Walls of Jerico*, Somerset Maugham's *Smith*, and Miss Horniman's company in Shaw, Bennett, Galsworthy and Rutherford Mayne's *The Troth*. *The Private Secretary*, now in its twenty-sixth year of touring, added a week's performances at the Gaiety to its already more than 16,000 performances. The D'Oyly Carte company appeared at the theatre, as also did the J. W. Whitbread company in the old Boucicault standbys.

At the Royal, the Dublin playgoer could have seen Harry Lauder, Little Tich, and even John L. Sullivan giving his 'celebrated monologue' in his booming voice and, despite his white hairs, fighting three exhibition rounds with Jake Kilrain. There were also a couple of Conan Doyle melodramas, *The Speckled Band* and *The House of Temperley*. The chief attraction of the latter play was a boxing match, about which *The Irish Times* enthusiastically remarked, 'Nothing like it has been seen on the stage since the chariot race in *Ben Hur*. The Johnson-Jeffries pictures pale into insignificance before it. . . . The audience watched its progress with feverish anxiety, and when the knock-out blow was given, staid and stolid folk could hardly restrain a cheer.' There also occurred at the Royal a symptomatic religious disturbance during a performance on 11 October of *Sir Walter Raleigh* by William Devereux. The ascendancy paper, *The Irish Times* thought the disturbance insignificant and hardly 'likely to enhance our reputation for liberality or sound judgment'. But *The Weekly Freeman's Journal* took it all more seriously:

A scene of an almost unprecedented kind took place during the performance, and a great portion of the later stages developed into dumb show in consequence of the determined opposition of a large section of the audience. . . . This play deals with the particular period of Elizabeth, "the Virgin Queen", and Mary Stuart, and its purpose, if it has any purpose at all, would seem to be the promulgation of polemical discussion as to the methods of the so-called plots against the life of Elizabeth — in other words, the Babbington plot — to point to Queen Mary as the murderess that unhappy lady was represented to be, and to give a sadly mistaken view of the episodes associated with the name of Fotheringay Castle. That purpose, and that alone, would seem to have been the genesis of the play, and in that light the thing is an outrageous libel. . . .

During the third act, in the Tower of London, the episode being the marriage of Raleigh and Elizabeth Throgmorton, an occupant of the front row of the dress circle, stood up and cried out, "I protest against this as an insult to the Catholic faith." This followed references to the Inquisition. Immediately a large number of the audience stood up and sang "Faith of our Fathers", and for quite a long time — almost to the end of the play — it was a case of dumb show, for no one could hear what was being said on the stage. Up to that point there was perfect peace and quiet. . . .

After the scene at the theatre a number of the audience proceeded to Foster Place, where a meeting was held. Some hundreds attended, including many members of the Ancient Order of Hibernians, Board of Erin. Mr. P. J. Medlar presided, and speeches were delivered objecting to the production in a Catholic city of a play which was objected to as being anti-Catholic in tone.[78]

The Empire and Tivoli theatres continued their usual variety entertainments, and the Queen's productions did not rise above the level of *Nick Carter, Detective* or *King of the Wild West*, which starred Young Buffalo and featured acting ponies and dancing Indians.

\* \* \*

For the week of 7 March, the Ulster Literary Theatre appeared at the Grand Opera House in Belfast. On Monday evening they presented their most popular plays, Gerald MacNamara's *The Mist That Does Be on the Bog* and Rutherford Mayne's *The Drone*. On Tuesday they presented a new three-act play by Mayne, *The Captain of the Hosts*. Of the production *The Northern Whig* wrote:

*Captain of the Hosts* . . . is the most ambitious bit of work Rutherford Mayne has yet attempted, and, except *Suzanne and the Sovereigns*, the biggest undertaking the Ulster Literary Theatre has tackled. Their other pieces have been more in the nature of studies, little segments of life seen at a new angle, elaborated with the patient skill of the man who carves cherrystones. This is on a different plane and a bigger scale, not a mere appetising mouthful, but a dish that one can get one's teeth into. . . .

Though his [Mayne's] rustic flute may have lost its "happy country tone", it has not lost its power of making music. His gift of observation does not desert him when he leaves the cottage for the red-brick suburban villa; his city types, from prize-fighters to religious frauds, are the real thing; and a strong dash of satire gives a welcome touch of tartness to the humour. He has got hold of a good central idea, though it is a difficult one to express dramatically, and it tends to evaporate in words instead of becoming crystallised in action. . . .

The curtain goes up on Neil Gallina, a dabbler in literature, who has taken to whisky to hearten himself in face of the sentence of death which the doctor who examined him for consumption has pronounced. Incidentally he finds relief in the company of light-hearted medical students and a pugilist and his backer, admirable comedy figures, who vanish all too soon from the stage. As the result of a drunken spree, Neil falls under the spell of Barbara, who helps her father in some mysterious evangelical mission work, the exact nature of which is never properly explained. He convinces himself that it is the father who has transformed him, and becomes a rousing speaker at mission meetings. In the meantime Barbara has come to realise that she has an individuality of her own, which is being stifled in an uncongenial atmosphere. She tells Neil that the services mean less than nothing to her, that if she was not a coward she would break free, and, spurred on by a hypocritical assistant of her father, lays a trap for the new convert, telling him she is going to leave the mission for a year. As one expects, Neil finds that with Barbara's departure, his enthusiasm oozes away, and he returns to his husks, to the whisky bottle and the pugilists; and when the repentant girl comes back to urge him to resist the temptation for her sake, not for the sake of the doctrine her father preaches, she finds it is too late; death has a grip on him; the captain of the hosts is stronger than her love.

It is plain, even from that bald outline, that the play has sound ideas in it; the conflict of the two personalities with the grim shadow of fate lurking in the background, is full of possibilities. But in the handling one feels that the author has not been wholly successful in bringing what he had to express across the footlights. Neil is good all round; a tragic figure, he captures the audience from the first. Barbara, however, lurks too much in the shadows. One sees what she is intended to be, one feels the magnetism she is supposed to exert; but she is more a mouthpiece for theories than a living figure whose words give a glimpse of her soul. . . . If the author's hand is not as sure in this portrait as it should be, he makes up for it by the reality of the minor characters. They are in his best comedy vein, and one will not readily forget the inimitable gardener with his project for a little mission tent of his own, the medical student, the pugilist, or the irreverent red-headed carpenter.

While the acting had not the balance and finish that one admires so much in *The Drone*, it showed genuine ability, though a few more performances are necessary to bring it up to concert pitch. Mr. Ross Canmer scored a triumph as Neil Gallina. Consumptives on the stage are not attractive, but Mr. Canmer did not essay an experiment in the horrible. It was the restrained naturalness of his acting that gave it the grim intensity the part requires. Miss Seveen Canmer had the most difficult task of all as Barbara. It was not her fault that the author has set so much of it in one key, and presented the girl always in a state of lyrical exaltation. In her big scenes, Miss Canmer displayed emotional force, but one would have liked to have seen Barbara occasionally as she must have been in ordinary, everyday life. . . .[79]

On Wednesday evening the company repeated *The Drone* and, as it was the occasion of the Samuel Ferguson centenary, gave a dramatic reading of Ferguson's poem, *The Naming of Cuchullain*. Joseph Campbell's sonorous reading of the role of Cathbad was very generally admired.

In November, the company returned to the Opera House for a revival of *Suzanne and the Sovereigns* which again, despite some raggedness in the acting and some necessity for the prompter, was greeted with delight.

*　　*　　*

The Cork Dramatic Society was still a much more amateurish organisation than its older counterpart in Belfast, the Ulster Literary Theatre. The productions of the Cork group were simple, at times almost primitive, and they were still staged in a small hall,

The Dun in Queen Street. Nevertheless, the Cork group mounted more productions and more new plays in 1910 than did the Ulster group.

The first Cork production of the year was on 11, 12 and 13 May when two new one-act plays — *The Burden*, a tragedy by E. K. Worthington, and *Struck*, a comedy by Con O'Leary — were presented. *The Cork Constitution* remarked that, while each play

> indicated dramatic talent in the authors, neither can be regarded as an advance upon plays which have been previously performed at this theatre. One does not desire to be severely critical but this Society has made something of a local reputation, and ought not alone live up to it, but improve upon it.[80]

*The Cork Tatler* agreed that 'neither was in any way comparable to the former productions of the Society', and then went on to describe *The Burden*:

> An old fiddler, straying through the fields, benighted, takes shelter by a fairy hill, and hears the fairy music; at daybreak he finds his way to a neighbouring public-house and tells his adventures to a group of peasants, miners and fishermen, who ply him with drink and then drag him off that he may try the power of this fairy tune on an old bed-ridden woman nearby, for he has told them that the tune has magic powers of healing in it. But he may play it only twice — the third time he plays it the fairies have warned him that he will die. On his return after playing the tune for the second time to the old woman, he, for no very obvious reason, plays it again and expires. To make such a story dramatic in any real sense calls for powers of fancy and imagination of which no traces are to be found in the present work. . . . There are in the play some touches in the portrayal of one of the characters not without shrewd suggestions of psychological detail that seem to point to this latter aim as that which appealed to the author, but there is no trace of imaginative unity in the conception: the author shows no sign of having in the least conceived what the thoughts or the feelings of the old man would be, nor did he get any assistance from the actor of the part; while the literary skill necessary for the construction and expression of such a piece of work was altogether absent. The dialect in which it is written is obviously studied and lacking any trace of spontaneity or naturalness.

The comedy, *Struck*, was a rather smart piece of mimicry, with a pardonable touch of caricature of the speech and manners of a certain class. As a monologue it might amuse for five minutes, but much more is needed for the most primitive comedy; there is in it neither character or action in the dramatic sense, nor ideas in the intellectual sense. It is all talk, or rather mimicry of talk, and cheap and rather vulgar mimicry at that.

The actors have not advanced, and this second [third, actually] experiment seems to prove that no advance is possible under the present conditions. The stage is too small, too near the audience to allow of any illusion on the one side or any ease at the other.[81]

On 2, 3 and 4 November, the Society presented two more plays — a revised version of Daniel Corkery's three-act *The Embers*, which had been the Society's first production in May of 1909; and the first production of a hero-play in one act, *The Last Warriors of Coole*, by T. J. MacSwiney. Of the new play, *The Cork Constitution* wrote:

*The Last Warriors of Coole* is in verse, and is a really commendable piece of work, indicating promise in the author. He seems to have written slowly and studiously, for the verse beautifully embodies the central idea. Many lines are of much beauty of phrase, and there is more than one striking descriptive passage. What amazes the spectator, who follows the play studiously, is the wonderful atmosphere produced by the stage-setting, the players and the words. One becomes interested, and then absorbed in thought as the idea is unfolded, until there is fully realised "Crimal's deathless hope and Fionn's saving of his people". If space permitted, a good deal could be written about the play, but it must be sufficient to state that it was a success, as it certainly deserved to be. . . . It was very well staged in dresses and scenery.[82]

This was Terence MacSwiney's first play for the theatre, but he and Daniel Corkery were to be its most prolific writers. In 1920, after MacSwiney had died in Brixton Prison from his famous hunger strike, Corkery described him as a young writer:

Music with him was, I think, the supreme art; he would listen to it with reverential awe; but literature was the one art he practised. At that time he thought that his life's work was to write books—for Ireland; and once he had taken his degree

93

he threw himself into the work with great zest. His preparation for the writing of drama was very characteristic of his earnest spirit. He began by reading, re-reading in some cases, all the standard works of criticism he could lay hands on. The only copy of Aristotle's *Poetics* I ever read I had on loan from him; Lessing's *Laocoon* he also read; modern criticism as well, and of course he kept fully in touch with the literature of the Irish renaissance. Shaw's dramatic technique he admired very much, but Shaw's philosophy we never discussed — it was so far apart from Irish life. He also read Molière and the other French classics; and both Shaw's technique in the matter of stage directions, and that of the French, as in the unfamiliar use of the word "scene" to denote a change in the number of characters on the stage, left their trace on his work. Most noticeably so in the one play he published, *The Revolutionist*. Ibsen and Maeterlinck he also read. The *Mary Magdalen* I read was his. Of Molière and Ibsen he had full sets — very fine editions. Synge he did not like; but then Synge's outlook on life and his own were frankly opposite.[83]

On 27, 28 and 29 December, the Society revived Corkery's *The Hermit and the King* and Robinson's *The Lesson of his Life*, and also produced for the first time MacSwiney's one-act tragedy, *The Holocaust. The Cork Constitution* wrote of it:

It deals with not an unusual incident in Irish life — indeed it might be said of humble life in communities not Irish. The scene is laid in a humble home, cold and unprovided for. The last offspring of a heart-broken mother and a father, who has striven hard to get work, is lying on her death-bed. The mother alone with it affords all the comfort she can, and her last hours of sorrow are broken into by the priest, who tenders her monetary assistance to provide the necessary nourishment and warmth for her dying child. She goes off and the doctor arrives — a young man of the world who regards the child's death as inevitable — and after some worldly conversation with the priest, he leaves to attend to other patients. Then enters the husband, desperate and at variance with the world. He argues with the priest, when his wife arrives and asks him to assist her in making the home more comfortable than it was. Then the tragedy ends with the unexpected death of the child. All the parts were filled with exceptional credit to the members of the Society, and the audience testified their appreciation by hearty applause.[84]

Imaal of *The Leader* was also at the performance: 'a poignant little etching of the problem of slum life — of unemployment, underfeeding, joylessness, and unregarded misery. . . . I think the best performance was that of Miss D. Gilley as Polly Mahony. She showed sympathy with the part, and feeling without exaggeration. . . .' [85]

# 1911

This year saw the final severance of Miss Horniman's connection with the Abbey Theatre. That severance did not come without a complex and sometimes acrimonious dispute over Miss Horniman's final monetary obligation to the theatre, a dispute resolved by the binding legal arbitration of the matter by C. P. Scott of *The Manchester Guardian*. The curious may read the small mountain of correspondence and documents in the case, in the National Library of Ireland (principally in Ms. 13,068), but, for our part, the business was such a depressing conclusion to a collaboration begun in such hope and good will, that it is best tersely summarised in the following Press report:

It may be remembered that Miss A. E. F. Horniman, the generous English lady who created a home for Irish drama at the Abbey and secured a six-year patent for the theatre, and subsidised for that period to the extent of £13,000, withdrew the subsidy on account of the theatre opening on the day of the late English King's death, with some months of the six years yet to run.

When the new patent was granted, again Miss Horniman proved her generosity by agreeing to hand over the entire property for the sum of £1,000 to the new patentee; but the new patentee, in paying that sum, wished to deduct the amount due according to the subsidy from the time of withdrawal at the late King's death till the expiration of the six years.

This Miss Horniman refused to accept, but agreed to leave it to arbitration. The arbitrator has just decided in favour of the new patentee; and Miss Horniman writes as follows — "I should like it to be known by all that I have paid the £400 because of the decision of the arbitration. There would have been no Abbey at all if my condition as to 'no politics' had not been tacitly accepted by the directors."

It was because in her opinion what she regarded as an unwritten condition of the agreement was broken that she proposed to stop the £400, which under the arbitration she has now paid.

Lately the members of the company presented her with a little token of their esteem, and Miss Horniman asks to give her thanks to the givers of the beautiful silver cup and illuminated address, and adds — "It is well that I should have a sign that there is some good feeling in regard to my efforts in Dublin." [1]

On this same day, letters crossed in the mail between Miss Horniman's solicitors and the Abbey directors. Yeats and Lady Gregory wrote:

> Dear Miss Horniman,
> We have just had Mr. Scott's award. We wish at once to say that remembering all your generosity in the past it was never our intention to press the legal point against you. If with all the facts before you you still cannot accept the integrity of our action, we cannot accept the money and the matter is at an end.
>
> Yours sincerely,<br>W. B. YEATS<br>A. GREGORY[2]

At the same time, Dendy and Patterson of Manchester, Miss Horniman's solicitors, wrote in part to the Directors:

> . . . our client wishes us to make it clear that if this money is paid it is solely because she accepts the Arbitrator's award, and that she still holds that there was an agreement as to "no politics", that the agreement was broken, and that she should not have been called upon to pay the money.
> We cannot help thinking that Miss Horniman is being very badly used.[3]

A few days later, Yeats wrote to D. F. Moore, a partner in Whitney and Moore of 46 Kildare Street, Dublin, who were the theatre's solicitors:

> Please write at once to Dendy and Patterson and say that as Miss Horniman does not accept the justice of Mr. Scott's award we cannot accept the money. We have Mr. Bailey's full approval, and Lady Gregory has seen this letter.
>
> Yours very truly,<br>W. B. YEATS[4]

On 5 January, the Abbey staged its first production of Douglas Hyde's *Nativity Play*, in an English translation by Lady Gregory. At the end of 1904, as readers of the second volume of this history may remember, a number of clerics had succeeded in quashing a performance of this play in Kilkenny. That incident, however, should be regarded as a symptom of the moral tenor of the time, rather than as an indication of any intrinsic irreverence in Hyde's short and simple play. Now, seven years later in Dublin, the play occasioned no protest at all. On the contrary, a typical reaction was that of J. H. C. in *The Irish Independent*:

> Profaned by every charlatan and soiled by all ignoble use, the stage reverted last night to its original purpose. The Abbey Company, interpreting the spirit of the season, presented a "mystery" play based on the simple and pathetic narrative of the Nativity. . . .
>
> It is slight. It is exceedingly short. Yet it serves to give precision and graphic impression to the first chapter of the story that transformed the world.
>
> As produced, the piece was a translation by Lady Gregory from the Irish of Dr. Douglas Hyde. The gifted translator has clothed it in English of quasi-Biblical sonority, lapsing now and then into Anglo-Irish idiom.
>
> The setting was wisely harmonised to the spectator's preconceived idea of the scene, being a replica of a well-known illustration of the Crib. . . .[5]

A more thoughtful critique from *The Irish Times* did not place the play, because of its subject matter, above criticism:

> *The Nativity Play* is a short piece, lasting, indeed, only about a quarter of an hour in performance. It was played in the straightforward, unaffected manner which is frequently a merit in the Abbey Company, but which at the same time sometimes, as to some extent in this case, results in the loss of an effective climax. . . .
>
> The play presents the very scene of the Nativity. A wattled enclosure in the centre represents the stable; through the chinks the flickering light from within strays mysteriously into the darkness that precedes the dawn. Two women meet outside, and in hushed voices tell of the strange things that have befallen them and occasioned their visit to the grotto. Unto each had the man and woman travelling up to Jerusalem appealed for refreshment and assistance; and afterwards miraculous signs had convicted each of failure to fulfil the calls of human charity. In repentance they follow into Bethlehem. Thereto come also the three wise Kings from the East, led by the wondrous star, and from the West three shepherds, led by a cloud of birds. At their approach the stable door is opened, and within are seen Saint Joseph and Mary Mother. The wise men and the shepherds present their offering unto Him whom

they call King of the World. Hearing this title, the two women who have been listening in the shadow, are struck with a great fear. "Let us go hence, and hide ourselves in a scarp of the rocks or a hole of the earth." As they turn, however, the voice of Mary Mother calls softly to them, bidding them approach in repentance and in joy, and hearken to the angels' song, which now comes softly on the air, and while the first faint light of dawn strikes the face of the hill. The women mutely respond, and as the curtain closes on the kneeling group words of assurance and comfort fall from the Virgin's lips. The profound impressiveness of the little piece, worthy of a Maeterlinck, was such that the applause of the audience— a necessary expression of appreciation — seemed an unfortunate disturbance of the mood of the moment.

At first thought one wondered whether anything had been gained by staging the piece — whether it was not eminently a thing to be read. On reflection, however, one was glad to have heard the gentle words softly pronounced in the musical accents of the Abbey players; one was glad to have seen this simple and reverent realisation of the scene. Mr. Robert Gregory's design for the scene, effectively supports the mood of the play, and will remain associated in the minds of many with every future recollection of the Nativity story. The employment of simple lighting effects has not been despised, and the soft rendering of a strain of Gounod's "Nazareth" helps to place the audience in the requisite frame of mind at the outset. Opinions will differ as to Lady Gregory's translation; there are some who think that her inversion of sentences and some artificialities of expression that belong neither to literary English nor to the speech of peasantry anywhere that we know have been overdone, and tend to detract rather than to lift, as she doubtless intended, out of the commonplace. . . .[6]

This tolerant reception of *The Nativity Play* was, as it turned out, no reason for optimism, for early in April the production of Padraic Pearse's *Passion Play* by his St. Enda's students evoked some clerical opposition.

Yeats was at this time greatly influenced by the scenic theories of Gordon Craig, a topic which is fully explored in Liam Miller's *The Noble Drama of W. B. Yeats*. In 1910, Yeats had, according to Craig's specifications, a number of tall screens which could be arranged on the stage in innumerable ways to fit the requirements of various types of plays. Craig's screens were used for the first time on 12 January for the first production of Lady Gregory's *The Deliverer* and for a revival of Yeats's *The Hour Glass*. (Lady Gregory's *The Full Moon* was produced on the same evening in a conventional set.) Before the production, on 9 January, Yeats explained the new theory of staging to *The Evening Telegraph*:

Mr. Yeats informed our representative that Mr. Craig is a son of Ellen Terry, the famous actress, and stated that he is the greatest stage inventor in Europe. The scenery, he said, differs entirely from the old style of scenery, and consists chiefly of portable screens, by means of which beautiful decorative effects can be obtained, the working of the screens being based on certain mathematical proportions by which the stage manager can make walls, pillars, etc. — a palace almost in a moment, a palace of great cyclopean proportions, and which can be changed again almost in a moment into a room with long corridors, and be changed again into a third and very different scene just as quickly.

But the old kind of scenery, said our representative, can nowadays be changed very quickly.

Mr. Yeats paused for a moment and thought, and walking up and down in front of the proscenium, stated the advantages of Mr. Craig's conception as follows:

"The primary value of Mr. Craig's invention is that it enables one to use light in a more natural and more beautiful way than ever before. We get rid of all the top hamper of the stage — all the hanging ropes and scenes which prevent the free play of light. It is now possible to substitute in the shading of one scene real light and shadow for painted light and shadow. Continually, in the contemporary theatre, the painted shadow is out of relation to the direction of the light, and what is more to the point, one loses the extraordinary beauty of delicate light and shade. This means, however, an abolition of realism, for it makes scene-painting, which is, of course, a matter of painted light and shade, impossible. One enters into a world of decorative effects which give the actor a renewed importance. There is less to compete against him, for there is less detail, though there is more beauty." [7]

On the same day, Yeats also spoke to a reporter from *The Evening Mail*:

One of the infirmities of the Abbey premises is the lack of depth of the stage, which has imposed limitations on the management in the presentation of plays which require a certain amount of pictorial illustration to harmonise with the poetical colour and surroundings in which the theme is set. Thanks to generosity, which has come from a quarter which enhances the value of the gift, this difficulty will be no longer felt, or, at all events, will be minimised almost to vanishing point. . . .

Mr. Yeats spoke in enthusiastic terms of the possibilities of the new scenic accessories, which he explained had been offered to the Abbey Theatre by Mr. Gordon Craig, the well-known son of Miss Ellen Terry, who was their monitor. Mr. Craig, as Mr. Yeats pointed out, had been reared up in the atmosphere of the Lyceum Theatre, as it was under the regime of the late Sir Henry Irving, for whom one of the features of every production of note was the realistic scenery. Never before had such a dominant and comprehensive spirit of taste controlled such work, or accomplished its work so effectually in appealing to the appreciation of the public.

"Growing up in such a world," continued Mr. Yeats, whose words will best explain the subject in hand, "Mr. Craig said it was necessary to invent decorative and ideal scenery for poetical work. He has been working at his scheme for years, and was chosen a year or so ago to produce a full *Hamlet* without excisions for the Art Theatre in Moscow, referred to by the *Times* . . . as the foremost theatre of Europe. He invented for the Art Theatre in Moscow a new system of scenery. By an arrangement of screens he can create upon the stage in a moment a great pillared palace. He can change that in a moment to a square room, and that again into a corridor. By his clever and unique arrangement he has succeeded in getting rid of the top hamper of the stage — the hanging mass of ropes and scenes, which enables him for the first time to use light and shade, natural and beautiful. In every art, if it is a genuine art, the artist works in those elements which are peculiar to it. If we are to get a beautiful art of stage decoration we must recognise that what makes the art of stage decoration different, let us say, from easel painting, is that the stage decorator has real light and shade and figures that move. It is necessary to get rid of painted light and shade, and to put in their places real light and shade. This means the abolition of realism in most of its effects, for these depend on painted light and shade, which, by the bye, is not so realistic, for, if one looks carefully, one finds that it contradicts the actual lighting. One gives the actor much greater importance. A mass of fussy details is swept away, and one gets

102

more beauty. I should say that the screen or queues are arranged in certain mathematical proportions, and give curious effects of grandeur."

Mr. Yeats further explained that Mr. Gordon Craig had patented his method, but out of his sympathy for the Abbey Theatre, he had given the management permission to use his invention. They intended, said Mr. Yeats, to use it for the first time on next Thursday night in a new play of Lady Gregory's, entitled *The Deliverer*, the scene of which was laid in ancient Egypt in front of a vast pillared palace. "On the same evening, there will be a revival," considered Mr. Yeats, "of my *Hour Glass*. For this Mr. Craig has himself painted the scene and designed costumes." [8]

Immediately before the performance, another reporter 'had a chat of ten minues with Mr. Yeats in regard to the new system of scenery':

"Continually, in the contemporary theatre, the painted shadow is out of relation to the direction of the light, and, what is more to the point, one loses the extraordinary beauty of delicate light and shade.

"This means, however, an abolition of realism, for it makes scene-painting, which is, of course, a matter of painted light and shade, impossible. One enters into a world of decorative effects, which give the actor a renewed importance. There is less to compete against him, for there is less detail, though there is more beauty."

In reply to a question as to the present position of the theatre, Mr. Yeats stated that Lady Gregory and himself now felt great responsibility. They were practically owners of the theatre, and they had their own company. They had already created a folk theatre, which had won great fame, but there was plenty more work to do. They had begun with the peasantry, because in every country the peasantry preserves in a more acute, obvious, and decisive way the characteristics of the country than any other class. They are little touched by alien influence. This was seen by both . . . Ibsen and Bjornson. They said that to understand the peasant you must know the Sagas, and to understand the Sagas you must know the peasant. But the Abbey Theatre did not propose to stop at the peasant, and proposed to give plays, either romantic and poetical drama, like Ibsen's *Brand*, or studies of the small seaboard towns of Norway, like *The Enemy of the People* and *The Pillars of Society*."

In Ireland also, Mr. Yeats went on, will come in time a school of good writers studying the problems of the day.

"Already we have had sent to us a remarkable work, a study of artisan life in Belfast.[9] If we can, we shall touch all Irish life, and from time to time we shall give work seeking merely the expression of beauty, for our theme is not only what the eye looks at in Ireland, but what the Irish mind imagines.

"Personally," he went on again, "I believe that when the history of this time is written it will be found that Irish imagination to-day has begun to express itself in plays, precisely as Irish imagination expressed itself fifty years ago in songs and ballads." [10]

However, after seeing the plays, the reporter's own view was that:

Somehow or other the new scheme of scenery did not work out according to specification; some people in the audience said, in fact, that it was nothing short of a fiasco. It was certainly a failure in *The Deliverer*, but it was in one scene a success in *The Hour Glass*, and bore out to some extent Mr. Yeats's theories about light.

Yet it must be said that, so far as Mr. Gordon Craig's ideas are concerned, they did not impress the large audience which tonight gathered at the Abbey Theatre.[11]

In any event, Yeats's preliminary puffing had invested the experiment with a portentousness that called forth some criticism of a finer quality than usual from the Irish Press. *The Freeman's Journal* wrote:

. . . Lady Gregory has not, we think, added much to her reputation as a dramatist by this play. The action after the slaying of the overseer halts and the construction is weak. The author fails to reach the height of emotion which is needed at the end.

Part of her failure must be ascribed to the dialect in which she has written the play. Why does Lady Gregory insist on giving us Kiltartan dialect in every conceivable circumstance? She should surely know that, admirably as it is suited to the treatment of some themes, there are subjects which lie entirely beyond its scope and moods which its use not only cannot realise, but actually destroy. If any one thing ought to have convinced Lady Gregory of its entire inadequacy, it ought to have been the fact that the setting of the play was Mr. Gordon

104

Craig's. It is one of the cardinal theories of Mr. Gordon Craig that any presentation on a stage should be a unity in which the spoken words and the acting and the setting and the colour should combine and blend to form a harmony of mood. The entire disparity between the Kiltartan dialect, destitute of all emotional colour, and the vastness of the scene, with its temple-pillars and amber lighting, and the Egyptian costumes of the officers and the king's heir, could not fail to destroy the very object for which Mr. Gordon Craig's system has been introduced. The matter becomes worse when one has to listen to such riotous colloquialisms as "schemin' michers", "the bell", and "too much gab you have", with the recollection in one's mind of the dignity of the words of the Story in Exodus.

It is difficult to pass judgment on the new system of stage-setting, so hard is it to rid oneself of the tyranny of custom and to enter a world where a totally different set of canons prevails. Mr. Gordon Craig aims at large effects and at giving a setting which suggests rather than depicts. The system which he employs seeks to achieve its aim by the use of a series of screens the full height of the proscenium, which fold and open according to the pleasure of the scene-designer. The screens are arranged according to a mathematical pattern, and are destitute of any painted design. Painting interferes, according to the theories of Mr. Craig, with the proper lighting effects. The setting of Lady Gregory's play was extremely simple. The screens were placed slantwise across the stage and were folded so as to suggest pillars. The lighting was from the top and the sides. One did not get, however, the sense of space which was intended by the artist. Possibly this is the fault of the construction of the theatre, the proscenium being so close to the auditorium, but it seemed to be in some measure due to the arrangement of the background. The lighting again was difficult to judge, partly because of the play, and partly because one was wandering in "Worlds not realised". If one may venture, in one's ignorance, to question why was there so much amber and so little white light? There was white light in *The Hour Glass* — the setting of which, by the way, was entirely beautiful and convincing — when the Angel enters, and perhaps in that we may have the answer to our question. It must be borne in mind in criticising Mr. Gordon Craig's work that he is not merely a reformer in scene mounting; he preaches an entirely new theory of the theatre. Far from pretending that his scenery can be employed in every play, Mr. Craig would banish from the stage to the study, almost every work which we call a play, and would substitute an entirely new art-form based on all the conditions — and not merely on some — of the theatre. Lady Gregory's play, written as it is, was perhaps a severe trial to which to subject a stage-setting which aims at creating a mood. In Mr. Yeats's Morality the setting did achieve, better even than the simplicity of the older setting, what it aimed at. The light effects with sombre and heightened tones according to the change in mood invested the play with a new beauty.

The acting of Mr. Kerrigan as the King's Nurseling did much to save Lady Gregory's play from the baldness of the dialect. Mr. Kerrigan has an emotional quality in his work which renders even the most crude dialogue beautiful in its effect. Miss Máire O'Neill as the Angel in the Morality fulfilled the whole intention which lies at the root of Mr. Craig's theory of the relation of the actor to the play. Her work was singularly delicate and lovely. We notice the appearance of a boy actor, Felix Hughes, who played the Child in *The Hour Glass* with a simplicity which marks him out as an actor with promise.[12]

*The Irish Times* began its critique with some obvious but necessary strictures:

> ... Mr. Yeats in a curtain speech during an interval last night, claimed it [the new system of staging] as marking "what the newspapers call an epoch". The Abbey Theatre, one may observe in passing, will gain less by rhetoric than by an attention to the small points of management which are calculated to make the theatre attractive to the public. Punctuality in commencing the performance, and less tedious intervals, would make the endowment fund go a good deal further than it promises to go under present conditions. Mr. Gordon Craig's scenic invention is, according to the programme note, to enable *Hamlet* to be played in full in reasonable time. We hope it will enable the Abbey Theatre Company to shorten its intervals, and make an evening at the theatre a brighter experience.
>
> If the introduction of Mr. Gordon Craig's system does not mark "what the newspapers call an epoch", it has, nevertheless, many striking points of merit, and constitutes a great improvement on the old staging. Mr. Yeats has spoken of Mr. Craig's "invention", and there is apparently a patent in connection with the system. But what is valuable in the new scheme does not arise so much from any "invention" as from

the application of genius to the methods and details of staging. There is, in the first place, a reduction of the stage furniture to its simplest elements, so that the figures of the players stand out more prominently against the primitive background, and attention is concentrated on the human and truly expressive elements of the drama. There is next a careful design and adjustment of the simple elements of staging which still further tends to secure that effect. Lastly, there is a similar care in regard to the supplementary elements — lighting arrangements and costuming. The success of these aims is the work of a genius of an individual producer, who combines with artistic and thoughtful ideas on the principles of staging, an unusual ability to deal with the mechanical problems involved in giving effect to those principles. A system will work itself out in varying and numberless cases; but the fulfilment of Mr. Gordon Craig's ideas will be according to the measure of the ability of the individual producer to deal with each new piece as it comes up for treatment. It may be noted too, that the main points in the methods of staging employed last night were put into practice years ago by Mr. Martin Harvey. The principles preached by Mr. Craig were acted on to some extent by Mr. Harvey in his production of *Great Possessions*; but they were more thoroughly carried out in his unjustly neglected *Hamlet*. It may be remembered that the scenery there used by Mr. Harvey was simple; it gave a sense of space, and it threw the movement of the drama through the human agents into strong relief. Furthermore, it was so designed that rapid changes were effected, enabling the presentation of a far larger portion of the play than is usual. In all these points it exactly tallied with Mr. Gordon Craig's arrangements.

The main point, however, is the fact that the new settings are far better than the old. The benefits of Mr. Craig's advice and assistance were more evident in *The Hour Glass* than in Lady Gregory's new piece. Indeed, we gathered that he was not so directly responsible for the latter. *The Hour Glass* is vastly more impressive with the new arrangements. The scenery, it may be explained, is a mere arrangement of neutral-tinted screens, the only "properties" being the Wise Man's seat (built of the same neutral-tinted material), the Wise Man's illuminated book, bell and the hour glass. The arrangement of the screens is designed with perfection, to permit of the most effective exits, entrances, and groupings of the characters, and also to admit of those variations in the lighting of the stage which supplied as powerful an aid to the expression of the emotional progress of the play as that afforded by incidental music in many productions. There is no attempt in Mr. Craig's scheme at realism; the new arrangements served to strip away everything that could distract from the emotional and dramatic unfolding, and to underline the most significant elements of the play. Those are the aims governing Mr. Craig's methods. With regard to the details of the play under treatment, the ingenuity of the particular designs employed secured the most impressive effects in the appearances of the Angel, and in the groupings on the stage, which, with the new costumes designed by Mr. Craig, were always picturesque. The figure of the Wise Man (Mr. Arthur Sinclair), in his dark and gracefully hanging robe, constantly afforded the same delight to the eye (as it appeared in relief against the plain light background), as one finds in Whistler's figure studies in relief against a white ground. There was many an effective picture on the same lines in the course of Lady Gregory's play, *The Deliverer*, in which the scenery consists of several square pillars, with a plain background, ranging obliquely across the stage. The only "properties" here are a few baskets in one corner, but the costuming is bright, and looks well against the plain surroundings. Detailed notice of the play itself must be deferred; suffice it now to say that its central figure is Moses. with an interesting variant, however, from the Bible story. We have the slaying of the Egyptian; but in the play, Moses is himself slain immediately afterwards by those whom he would have delivered. The place of such a play in the Irish dramatic movement is not very clear, unless it is intended as a political parable for Irish consumption. . . .[13]

The experiment was of such general interest that *The Irish Times* devoted a leading article to it:

Mr. Craig's designs do not supplant schemes of stage decoration that could be in the least accused of over-elaboration. In the very last new production at the Abbey — the translation of Dr. Douglas Hyde's Nativity Play — the stage setting was notable for its impressive simplicity. The aim which governs Craig's plans may be said to have been part of the Abbey creed from the start. All along the best of the serious plays produced in the movement have been marked by an effort to discard accessories and to throw dramatic motives into relief. Perhaps this led to carelessness in regard to setting, for these were occasions when the attention of the spectator, instead of being turned from the scenery, was occupied by its dinginess.

Mr. Craig's designs have, in practice, no pretensions, and for that reason do not disclose any shortcomings. To that extent they are an improvement in actuality upon the former practice of the Abbey, but follow the same intention. Those who support the Abbey ideals will not need, therefore, to examine themselves as to the theory of the thing. Their interest will be directed to the practical working-out of the guiding ideas. The comparison of the old and the new in relation to Mr. Yeats's *The Hour Glass* was favourable to the new. It will be instructive now to observe what others among the familiar plays will be selected for treatment in the fresh manner. Most of the comedies and some of the "peasant" plays, in which realism is the keynote, will, no doubt, be unsuitable for it.

Since a much greater responsibility is cast on the playing by the reduction of other features of production, it is encouraging to observe that the acting of the company appeared to be fully equal to the new requirements. The varied training associated with the "stock" company system has combined with the high ideals animating the members to bring them to an advanced position in their art. It is further obvious that the new methods of staging will subject not only the acting, but the plays themselves to more exacting scrutiny. Perhaps it was for this reason that what there is of dramatic value in Lady Gregory's new play, *The Deliverer*, is obscured by the incongruity of her curiosities of dialect with the Egyptian setting of the play, and by one or two other absurdities. There are elements in her play which cannot stand before a people with so keen a sense of the ridiculous as that which Irish audiences boast. In the new prominence given to the play itself they are mercilessly exposed. The play is imbued with something of whimsicality; but this is a more treacherous colouring in which to work on the stage than in books. The exposure of weakness which is likely to ensue from the application of Mr. Craig's ideas to production may hardly work in some individual cases, but the survival of only the fittest will tend to strengthen the movement. . . .[14]

Perhaps, after so many solemn remarks, the discussion of the Craig screens should be concluded by the irreverent Jacques:

Well, I'm not going to pretend that I noticed any of the effects that the programme says were for the first time made "possible". . . .

The new method of decoration was employed in Mr. Yeats's morality play, *The Hour Glass*, and I must confess I preferred the old setting to the new one. As an effort of literature *The Hour Glass*, like most things Mr. Yeats has written, is fine and noteworthy. When weighted with the pretentiousness of acted drama, as it was last night, it proves cold and uninteresting.

We also had in last night's bill two one-act pieces by Lady Gregory. One was *The Full Moon*, which I fondly hoped had waned in the old year. The other was *The Deliverer*, produced now for the first time. It is in the author's latest style, a style that makes me ask is it simply genius or something in the air?[15]

The Craig screens were used intermittently at the Abbey for many years — indeed, they were available for use until the Abbey fire of 1951, although they had by that time been reduced in size to fit the smaller stage of the Peacock. They did not, however, inaugurate any consistently applied new methods of staging and did not come into general use. The staging of most Abbey plays continued in the realistic tradition, and this was appropriate enough, as most Abbey plays were themselves realistic.

However, the next new Abbey play was *King Argimines and the Unknown Warrior*, a typical excursion by Lord Dunsany into the country of his own highly individual imagination. Most commentators thought that the company misunderstood this play and performed the latter part of it in quite the wrong spirit on its initial performance of 26 January. *The Freeman's Journal*, for instance, reported:

> There is something of the beauty of a mood of Maeterlinck in this play. Lord Dunsany is master of a language rich with imagery and romance, and he has used it so beautifully that the comparison is not a strained one. Nor is the dramatic value of the play lessened — as that of Maeterlinck's so often is — by the fact that his world is a dream-world, and his theme the theme of a wonder-tale. The first act halts a little in action, particularly in the commencement, where the dialogues might, we think, having regard to the length of the play, be shortened. But the second act is full of action, and the denouement is strongly written, though it suffered somewhat at the hands of the actors. This inequality is not, however, all to the advantage of the second act, which, although it has an Eastern imagery and beauty, which reminds one somewhat of the Book of Daniel, cannot compare with the lofty simplicity of the treatment of Act 1, a treatment which gives it some of the elemental strength of a Saga. The author is to be congratulated on making a dramatic success out of materials

which he has used with mastery in his tales — the piece has some suggestion of his wonder-tale, *The Sword of Welleran* — and which one would have been disposed to think could not have been made effective with a dramatic, as they unquestionably are with a narrative treatment.

The acting was not satisfying. Mr. Fred O'Donovan as Argimines, and Mr. Kerrigan as Zarb, are exceptions, but the rest of the company disappointed us somewhat. Mr. O'Donovan's work — Mr. Kerrigan had not a very important part — was admirable. He interpreted the character of Argimenes with a strength which never became unrestrained, and which gave exactly the note in which the part was written. But the same cannot be said of Mr. Sinclair's study of the character of King Darniak. The part, although there is not very much action in it, is an important one, and Mr. Sinclair, unfortunately, contrived to make it a dissonance, instead of a harmony, with the mood of the play. The King is drowsed when the prophet is foreshadowing his doom. The whole motive of the play demands that we should get in the scene a sense of overhanging fate. It is written in strong irony. Mr. Sinclair missed this entirely, and imparted an element of comedy to his part, instead of one of tragedy. The result was to tune his audience to an entirely wrong mood, and to almost spoil the climax. The fault, most probably, lies at the door of the management. The part demanded subtlety of acting, and Mr. Sinclair — admirable in work of another genre, is not a subtle actor. We are not satisfied with Miss Máire O'Neill as Queen Cahafru, nor with Miss Allgood as Queen Atharlia — what wonderful names Lord Dunsany imagines! Both were at fault in giving a note of slightly overdone levity to their lines. It demanded, no doubt, a severe study of their part to find exactly the right note to give the chatter of the Queens during the prophet's speech. Their acting is generally so excellent that they will, doubtless, find that right note at their next performance. The actors were not quite good at the denouement either. Here again was a severe strain, and it is perhaps not quite just to criticise overmuch their first performance. We think, however, that they failed to rise to the dignity of the climax when Argimenes ascends the throne. These things will be easily set right; the main thing is that the play was an achievement.[16]

W. J. Lawrence, in *The Stage*, echoed these criticisms and added some others about the staging:

The acting honours of the evening, however, undoubtedly went to Mr. Fred O'Donovan, whose intensity of style and unkemptness of appearance as the enslaved monarch produced the proper atmosphere of *bizarrerie*. That this was not maintained throughout the play was due partly to the mis-casting of one of the principal characters and partly to the defective staging of the last act. Hitherto specific lines of business have not been strictly followed by the members of the Abbey stock company. One and all have appeared indifferently in poetic play or farce. But it is growing perilous to put Mr. Arthur Sinclair into a wholly serious character, as the patrons of the Abbey have come to look upon him as the routine low comedian of the theatre, and generally settle themselves down for a laugh when he appears. This disposition on their part, combined with the absurd grouping and costuming of the characters at the opening of the last act, conspired to turn the latter half of the fantasy into a farce, and thus to destroy the whole atmosphere the author had been sedulously striving to create. Owing to the cramped aspect of the tiny Abbey stage, the Court scene with the King and his four consorts looking supremely uncomfortable in their preposterously large and clumsy crowns and seated almost cheek by jowl with the impassive idol, smacked at the outset of uproarious burlesque and recalled memories of *Bombastes Furioso* and of the side-splitting Court scene in the burletta of *Tom Thumb*. One expects much better staging than this now that the Abbey directorate has openly flouted the scenic methods of the traditional stage, and has called in the services of Mr. Gordon Craig to amend them. At present we cannot see that the Abbey scheme of mounting has benefitted much by his counsels. In the first act of the new play a cut tree drop was placed so close to the back cloth that ugly parallel shadows were thrown on the distant hills. . . .[17]

Although one of the best-known Irish writers of his day, Lord Dunsany was rarely Irish in his subject matter. Perhaps partly for that reason, few of his many plays were staged by the Abbey. He was much more successful as a playwright in England and particularly in America, where his short pieces were for years extremely popular in the Little Theatre movement.

On 2 February, the Abbey revived Yeats's *Deirdre* on a bill with Lennox Robinson's *Crossroads* and Lady Gregory's *Coats*. The main interest of the evening was probably the acting of Máire O'Neill. As *The Irish Times* wrote:

112

The production of two such plays as *The Crossroads* and
*Deirdre* on the same evening gives Miss O'Neill an opportunity
of showing the remarkable range of power that she possesses.
The contrast is extraordinary between two such characters as
Mrs. McCarthy, the shrewd old country woman from Skib-
bereen, and the beautiful, poetic legendary queen, Deirdre. It
is doubtful whether any other living actress would have so
adequately filled parts so strangely different in every respect.
Mr. Yeats's *Deirdre* has frequently been performed by the
Abbey Theatre Company within the last few years. Its
reputation as a poetic drama full of beauty of language and
idea, has been well established. It is to be doubted, however,
whether it has ever previously been given so fine an interpretation as the present. The name part is taken by Miss Máire
O'Neill. Those who have watched the steady yet rapid progress
in dramatic power of this young actress during the last couple
of years expected much, but few anticipated a performance
of such wonderful beauty and dramatic intensity as that which
she gave last night. As the play proceeded — as the tragedy
developed — Miss O'Neill showed her complete grasp of the
situation. Never for a moment did she falter. She was Deirdre,
and for the moment there could have been no other Deirdre.
Her voice, of wonderful power and beauty of tone, was kept
under perfect restraint. There was no wild declamation — no
tearing of the passion to tatters. There seemed to be no acting.
It was all real, vital, intense. At times the tragedy of the
position became almost unendurable. Mood changed with
mood. The stage was full of Deirdre. There seemed to be no
one else there that counted. The sorrow, the horror, the
pathetic beauty of the trapped queen, gripped the imagination.
The Abbey Theatre have found in Miss Máire O'Neill a great
Irish tragic actress.[18]

Yeats's revived interest in the staging of plays was evident in
some further reflections about the speaking of dramatic verse. For
instance, early in February:

In an interview on his forthcoming Causerie at the Little
Theatre, London, Mr. W. B. Yeats said:
"In the Abbey Theatre, Dublin, I had intended, side by
side with these Irish plays, to try and reach the Irish people
by a revival of the art of the Minstrel. The three great forms
of poetry — narrative, dramatic and lyric — have arisen and
taken their shape from the reciter, the player and the singer.
Why should we not bring these artists back once more to the

113

science of literature? In Ireland we have got the player once more to speak vivid, persuasive and powerful words, for that is the one principle that unites the art of Synge, the art of Lady Gregory, and my own art of verse — the verse drama. It should not be difficult to find singers who will have the beauty of the words for their pre-occupation; perhaps even it may not be impossible to create what no longer exists, to the accompaniment of very simple notes, played upon some stringed instrument — narrative verse. But in Ireland we have not been able to do much of these two arts, though we have found no great difficulty in getting a song sung when it is part of the play, so that the words carry little like a speech. We have not been able to do very much because a theatre is always in a hurry. But in England some friends of mine have taken up the thought, and on the 16th in London, I shall introduce to my audience not merely Miss Florence Farr, whose art of speaking to the psalter many of them know, but Miss Hilda Taylor, whose art is nearer to singing. She sings lyrics of my own, and of other people, as some country woman sings some old folk song, and yet without losing what they have of modern and subjective feeling. At least, so it seems to my ears, which are always delighted by her." [19]

*The Times* briefly reported the 'causerie':

Mr. W. B. Yeats gave a *causerie* at the Little Theatre on "Ireland and the Arts of Speech", in which he said that in the West of Ireland there still survived a remnant of the great popular culture founded on song or spoken traditional literature, once existing all over the world. In England, pre-eminently the land of that miserable thing, the printed book, members of a class now perfectly satisfied with a brass band and a gramophone, had once their lyric competitions in which the words were the important thing. The language of Western Ireland used by Mr. Synge, for instance, in his translations from Villon and Petrarch, was no *patois*, but had as much right to exist as our own common dialect. It was Tudor in vocabulary, Gaelic in idiom. The Irish Theatre, primarily a folk theatre, expressing the imaginative life of the people, had found good players, but without the minstrel and singer they could not give back to literature its old power over men's hearts.[20]

Another journal reported some rather more specific statements:

"Among the things that I most abhor," said Mr. Yeats, "is the tragic drawing-room recitation. The intensity of emotion

114

alike in audience and speaker necessary to the tragic spirit is a thing that cannot be manufactured in a moment. It needs the most careful art to get the right mood, the right atmosphere. At an evening party it is possible that a little story might be deftly told, an appropriate poem recited. But the tragic fragment, hurled unexpectedly by someone standing in the middle of the carpet to a circle of people who are pausing ill at ease in the midst of trivial gossip as they stand or sit around the wall, is meaningless and abominable. If it has any meaning at all, it can only mean that one member of the company has suddenly gone raving mad."

This was, as it happened, just one among many random thoughts which Mr. Yeats cast off throughout the afternoon, as he strolled at leisure about a dimly-lit stage, stopping every now and then to call the attention of an audience of evidently whole-hearted disciples to some point that struck him for the moment in an agreeable ramble through ideas.

One great foe of the "art of speech" was, he considered, the tendency to humanitarianism — the desire to have some practical effect, to do some practical good. This interfered with the pure expression of emotion. Another deadly foe was music. "We poets," he said, "are being crushed out of existence by the brass band and the gramophone. In the modern lyric the words are of secondary importance. Sometimes they cannot even be heard. How can true poetry be written to music for the sake of which the word 'love' must be drawled out with fifteen o's?" [21]

On 16 February, Yeats's early play, *The Land of Heart's Desire*, received its first production by the Abbey company. Ria Mooney, who was to become one of the most notable of Abbey Theatre actresses and producers, was at this time a little girl and a member of Madame Rock's Dancing Academy, and was considered for the role of the Faery. As she later wrote about the experience:

When I was about eight years old, I remember standing with my moon-like face pressed against the window of my father's shop in Baggot Street looking with intense interest at the passers-by, and noting the occasional odd-looking person who, I was invariably told, was from the Abbey Theatre and who would be on his way to the Arts Club in Upper Fitzwilliam Street. The very tall aristocratic man was a poet named Yeats; he always walked with his hands behind his back, and his head held high. The equally tall man who also walked with his hands behind his back, but with his gaze directed downwards, was another poet known as "Æ". His real name was George Russell, and he too was from the Abbey Theatre. Grown-ups said that though he had tried to start the first co-operative society in Ireland, he was more interested in writing. The little man with the big hat and the long cloak that reached the ground was James Stephens. He wrote books about fairies and leprechauns, they told me, which did not surprise me, because he looked like a gnome himself. Neither was I surprised to learn he also belonged to the group that came from the Abbey. The tall thin man who often walked with Yeats was named Lennox Robinson. The two slim figures who never seemed to smile were brother and sister, Robert and Dorothy Lynd. He was a writer and she was an actress — from the Abbey!

I came to the conclusion that only odd-looking people belonged to this theatre. I had a sneaking desire to be like them, but not at the expense of being attached to that strange place. My vanity would have been flattered by being considered different from the average person, as those men and women seemed to be — if only their Abbey Theatre had in some way been connected with singing and dancing.

It was a short time after this that I paid my first visit to the theatre, which I was told was owned by the poet called Yeats and a woman named Lady Gregory. The directors were about to present a play by their poet founder called *The Land of Heart's Desire*, and they wanted a child for the principal part. Someone must have told Joseph Sandes,[22] the drama critic of *The Irish Independent*, who had always been very kind to me in his reviews whenever I had appeared before him in song or dance as a pupil of Madame Rock's Dancing Academy, which I had been attending for some years. It seems he had suggested to someone at the Abbey that I might be suitable. As I was not aware that my mother even knew of the Abbey Theatre's existence until then, I was very surprised to hear some years ago from the relative who had been her bridesmaid, that the ambition of her life was to see me an Abbey actress. I can, therefore, imagine how eagerly she must have packed me off with my father to Abbey Street. The Fays had left, and I do not know who auditioned me, but as he was as small in stature as Frank Fay, it may have been Norreys Connell.[23]

The building my father brought me to on Marlborough Street was faced with blocks of granite in square shaped pieces. There were two windows consisting of small panes of white glass into which were inset panes of green-coloured glass

116

representing a tree with spreading branches. When we entered the vestibule, it was partitioned by what must originally have been a dividing wall, only half of which remained. This wall was painted cream like the other walls, and the lower half was panelled in black-panelled wood. The colour-scheme was black and cream or black and brown. At the other side of this dividing wall there was a counter and to the left of this another counter. There were portraits everywhere, and over the fireplace in this part of the vestibule was one of a lady. I was told that this was Lady Gregory, one of the founders of the theatre, and that the portrait had been painted by the father of the other founder, W. B. Yeats.

My father made some enquiries at the box-office, which was in the hall opposite the entrance, and when a man came through a small door in the same wall, we were shown again on to Marlborough Street through the main door by which we had entered. This door was painted black on the lower half with plain glass, and above it again panels above there was a glass canopy edged with a border of wrought-iron, also painted black. The canopy was supported by two black iron pillars. Stretching across, and a yard or two from the two windows was a railing, also painted black. We were directed to turn right after leaving the main building, pass Whyte's China store, and turn right again into Abbey Street; here, we found ourselves beside a high wall into which were set stone steps leading to two doors. There were many windows. We went through the furthest door.

"This used to be the entrance to 'The Mechanics' ", said my father. Inside, we climbed a flight of stone steps which led to a large room where a number of people were rehearsing.

When they broke up, the little man who had been giving them instructions came towards us and asked my father if he knew the meaning of "cussedness". When told it was quite a common Dublin expression meaning obstinacy, the little man returned to those who were waiting for him, and having told them the meaning of the word they left, and he came back to ask me to read the play. When I had finished reading the part of "The Faery Child", he told me that I had read the lines very well indeed, but to go out to the mountains and "listen to the wind", and then come back to him in a few days and read to him again, "like the wind sighing through the trees". I thought he was a little mad, but it was only what I expected to find in that dull building. I had no desire to go back. I need not have worried. When my mother read the play she

117

was horrified to think of her darling daughter having any part in such a pagan work.[24]

An adult, Máire O'Neill, was ultimately selected to play the Faery Child in this production, which was reviewed rather intelligently by *The Freeman's Journal*:

> Mr. Yeats's material is suited to the creation of a poem, but not to the making of an acted play. He contrives his denouement by introducing a child of Tír na nOg who spirits away the soul of Máire Bruin, the dreamer. The child comes in and dances and coaxes the priest to hide the crucifix, and then weaves her spells over Máire. At the end of the play we see Máire lying dead. We have not here the elements of tragedy because of the supernatural machinery. And if we leave the symbolism out of mind — as we are bound to do in judging of the work as drama — what have we? We are arrived at a confusion of values. Death is a note of tragedy if we take the realistic values as our standard. The death here is a note of exultation in the terms of the symbolic values of the play. So that we have the girl dead through the agency of the fiend, and sorrow in the minds of her husband and of the priest and of the parents, at the same time that the symbolism which underlies the play, requires us to see her released from dullness and free in the kingdom of her dreams. The actual values, and the symbolic values, are at a contradiction. . . . In *Kathleen Ni Houlihan* you can separate the play as an incident from the play as a symbol. And there is no clash of values when the two aspects are taken together. In the play you must keep the symbolism in mind all the time as a key by which to understand the incident. The differences makes *Kathleen Ni Houlihan* a work of convincing dramatic value, and this play a work which is meant more for the study than the stage. Nevertheless, plays that are not, in the accurate sense of the term, acting plays, have a fitness in a literary theatre, and Mr. Yeats's play, because it is so beautiful and has passages of such exquisite lyric value, had its fitness on the Abbey stage last night. Indeed, if it were only to let us see such delicate and wistful acting as that of Miss Máire O'Neill in the part of the Child of Faery, we would have willingly pardoned a much less dramatically strong piece on the stage. Miss O'Neill had a strange and dreamlike quality in her voice which set her apart in the relief which it was necessary to get as a contrast to the mundane scheme of the peasant household. . . .

118

And there was an elfin strangeness in her dancing when she is weaving spells for Máire and scattering primroses to keep back the priest from undoing her magic. . . .[25]

On the same programme was a revised version of T. C. Murray's *Birthright*, which in this form was to be one of the most popular Abbey plays of its day. Of the revision *The Daily Express* remarked:

> The outstanding feature of the usual triple bill presented at the Abbey Theatre this week is the production in somewhat remodelled form of Mr. T. C. Murray's *Birthright*, which, a few months ago, on its first presentation, introduced patrons of the Abbey to a new author whose work showed qualities of a high order. Since its withdrawal at the conclusion of its brief run, the author has recast and partly rewritten the second act, with the result that its dramatic action has been intensified and its final tragedy emphasised. Last night it was seen for the first time in its new form, and was received with very enthusiastic approval, the actors being recalled again and again at the end of the final act. The principal alteration made in the play is at the very end in the substitution of a murder for the suggestion of one. In the earlier version of the story, which has been so recently told that it need not be repeated, the ending was indicated by the sound of a gunshot heard from the back; as presented last night we had the final scene of passion and hate which terminates the smouldering feud between the two peasant brothers given in full view of the public, and accentuated with a realism which for a moment terrified at least a section of the audience. There is a fierce dramatic thrill in the last few moments of furious dialogue which leads up to the two young men closing in deadly handigrips; an accident lent its aid to art last night when in the whirl of swaying forms the kitchen table occupying the centre of the scene was with its contents sent crashing over the footlights into the orchestra, adding sound to fury in true melodramatic style. But Mr. Murray's play is something far better than mere melodrama. Eliminating the tragic note which is unfortunately too frequently dominant in the work of our young Irish writers for the stage, it is a vivid picture, in which the characters are strongly and vividly drawn, but yet with a perfect truth. There are many Morrissey families in the country in which the same canker is eating its way slowly and surely towards tragedy of a more subdued kind. . . .[26]

The Abbey staged no new plays until the end of March, but early in the month a revival of Fitzmaurice's *The Pie-Dish* occasioned an interesting letter to *The Irish Times*:

> Sir, Visitors to the Abbey Theatre last week had a rather strange experience in watching *The Pie-Dish*, which some of us will not soon forget. A death scene was before our eyes, whilst roars of laughter were falling upon our ears. It was gruesome. I have not a word of criticism for the actors. Mr. Arthur Sinclair's acting was beyond all praise. It was realistic in the extreme, so tragic that many eyes were turned away. But his prayers were received with outbursts of hilarity, and the agonising utterances of the women were punctuated with loud shouts of laughter. What the actors thought of it all I do not know, but some of the audience will not soon forget the hideous incongruity of the whole scene. Had an Irish tragedy been received after this fashion in England we would have waxed indignant at the coarse obtuseness of the Saxon, but what can we say when such scenes occur in the Abbey? — Yours, etc.
>
> W. HILLOX[27]

There has been a deal of speculation about why Fitzmaurice's very individual plays were not more welcomed at the Abbey, and Austin Clarke has even suggested that the reason was Yeats's jealousy of Fitzmaurice. That surmise seems farfetched, and, in fact, *The Country Dressmaker* was constantly revived and one of the theatre's most popular pieces for nearly twenty years. However, it should be borne in mind that the *Dressmaker* was a fairly conventional comedy that was rather broadly played. It offered no problems of interpretation to either players or audience. But Fitzmaurice's one-acts — *The Pie-Dish*, *The Magic Glasses*, and the extraordinary *Dandy Dolls* — were most unconventional plays. The two reactions which Hillox noted to the ending of *The Pie-Dish*, the comic and the tragic, were to a conventional notion of theatre mutually exclusive. However, the strength of the play is not that one reaction is wrong and the other right, but that both simultaneously are valid and, if the play is to be done well, necessary. It was not until the days of O'Casey, in the middle 1920s, that the Abbey was to discover that both reactions could legitimately and simultaneously arise from one scene. Consequently, the fact that some of these apparently muddled plays were, nevertheless, staged by the Abbey is, if anything, much to the theatre's credit.

The most important new play of the year was probably *Mixed Marriage*, which was first produced on 30 March. It was a four-act piece on a new subject by a new writer. The new subject was religious tension between Catholic and Protestant in the North of Ireland, and the new writer was St. John Ervine. The subject is still of vital interest to Ireland, and the best work of its author is still strong and fresh. If Ervine, who was to become one of the most distinguished Irishmen of letters, never quite attained the stature of Shaw, or even Synge or O'Casey, he was easily the equal of Robinson or Murray or Paul Vincent Carroll. On the occasion of this production, *The Pall Mall Gazette* remarked:

> Who is St. John G. Ervine? Nobody knows. Yet his play drew the biggest audience to the Abbey Theatre to-night that was ever seen there. Why? Well, possibly because the subject was one that had a close connection with the Irish politics of the day.
>
> The play has, however, nothing whatever to do with politics. Yet it dives deep into religious life in this country. In the fourth and final act the heroine is shot dead in a Belfast riot. The tragedy, according to all laws of the drama, seems to be more or less inevitable. "What is the moral?" I said to a very distinguished Irishman who happened to be sitting beside me. "Is it that there is no solution of the religious question in the North of Ireland?"
>
> "That," he said, "seems to be the moral of the play." [28]

Or, as J. H. Cox remarked in *The Irish Independent*:

> May we not call it a study in atavism? Mr. Ervine proves to us that prejudice is stronger than reason; that whatever a man may try to be, he reverts sooner or later to his primitive self; that inborn hatreds outlive conciliatory speeches and the clasping of hands; and that however impartially the individual may view things in the abstract, all his old passions will sway him as soon as a problem comes home to him personally, or as soon as he enters the crowd.[29]

The most successful Abbey plays have nearly always been conventional comedies or realistic dramas. As Ervine's seriously intentioned play had elements of both, and also as he was criticising the Protestant inhabitants of far-away Belfast, the Dublin audience took the play to its heart. Unlike Fitzmaurice, Ervine made his laughter subsidiary to his tragedy, rather than co-equal with it. Although Ervine's laugh lines had their satiric point, they served primarily as comic relief to a serious plat. As *The Irish Times* wrote, 'Even as we approach the more tragic moments, we are presented with a sally which serves to intensify the seriousness of the sentences that follow.' [30] We are not, however, presented with lines which, as in Fitzmaurice and O'Casey, seem overtly to undercut the basic thrust of the plot.

The upshot was that *Mixed Marriage* was a readily apprehensible play which, as *The Irish Times* wrote:

> . . . reflects in a vivid and novel manner the thoughts of our own age and our own country. It is in itself a justification of the existence of the Abbey Theatre. Many, no doubt, have long been impatient with the apparant want of considerable result from the movement initiated by Mr. Yeats; and have wondered whether we were ever to have more than fragments on the Abbey stage. Here, now, is a play that can stand by itself in the programme, and at the same time one that cuts right into a throbbing question which is of the gravest importance to every person in this country. . . . No author who has had to bow his acknowledgments from the Abbey stage has been more warmly acclaimed than Mr. St. John G. Ervine.[31]

For all of its still not dissipated merits, *Mixed Marriage* was early work and had faults. *The Freeman's Journal*, for the most part, very soundly noted them:

> In his anxiety, however, to state his case, Mr. Ervine has hardly bestowed sufficient care upon the medium he has chosen for the expression of his ideas. He has given us a satisfactory piece of propagandist work, but he has not given us a satisfactory play. In his first act, for example, instead of stating his problem in terms of drama, he has stated it in terms of rhetoric. We learn that there is a strike, that the father of the family is on the side of the strikers, and that his son is with him. We learn, too, that he is a bigot, and this his son is not. But we have absolutely no action. We might for all the world be listening to one of the lengthy stage directions of one of Mr. Bernard Shaw's plays with part of the preface expressing his political views thrown in. The dialogue is good, to be sure, and flashing with the sparks of Mr. Ervine's flints and steels, but that is not sufficient if the act is to be possessed of any dramatic value. The second act is little better. We have a repetition of Mr. Rainey's, the father's, views on Catholics and of Mr. Rainey's objections to them, which is quite needless and tiresome. And so far as the development of the plot goes, we learn — what we suspected all the time — that Hugh is going to marry Nora, and that Mrs. Rainey approves. The only merit of the act is the scene

in which old Rainey is won over by one of the strike leaders to use his power to prevent religious strife breaking the scene. We would suggest to Mr. Ervine that he should make his play a three-act instead of a four-act one. . . .

The construction of Act 3 is far better. Here we have not merely action but conflict. We have the conflict on the one hand between the old man's hatred of the marriage and his promise to allay religious bitterness, and on the other hand we have a conflict of far greater importance stated by the Catholic strike leader when he appeals to Nora to give up Hugh because her marriage will wreck the work of peace to which they have all set their hands. Mr. Ervine hardly works out this conflict between the Idea and the Woman as strongly as he might have. We are not prepared for the fact that the catastrophe depends on it, and that is to our mind a serious defect. . . .

Mr. Ervine puzzles us in the fourth act. It is not quite clear why the rioters should attack Rainey's house. . . . We think too that he might very well get rid of the bad habit of the silent curtain, which, we fear, he has learned from Mr. Shaw, and which he employs in the first two acts. A minor blemish in the play is that the dialogue up to the third act is so sparkling as to be more suitable for comedy than for tragedy. The effect is to tune his audience to the wrong note. It is a pity that a play so full of ideas and so excellent in characterisation — the characterisation of Mrs. Rainey is a masterly piece of work — should be spoiled by defects of construction. . . .[32]

Francis Sheehy-Skeffington was even more critical:

The construction of *Mixed Marriage* is very bad. The first two acts are useless; nothing happens, and the characters saunter aimlessly on and off the stage as Mr. Ervine requires, without due motivation. Much of the last act is unintelligible; why the mob is attacking Rainey's house, and why Hugh and Nora are there after having been turned out in the previous act, are points left unexplained. Throughout there is no economy in the dialogue. Every situation is prolonged until its effect is destroyed; every idea is bored into the audience by dint of unending reiteration. Nevertheless, the first-night audience was hugely delighted with the play; and the reason is clear. Ireland is just now full of discussion on the question of mixed marriage; but the rival sects, while attacking each other hammer and tongs, are agreed on one thing — that mixed marriages are undesirable. Enter to them both, Mr. Ervine, calmly assuming that the religious notions of both sides are of course mere superstitions, and that the social desirability of mixed marriages is incontestable! His audacity took by storm a public which had heard every aspect of the question but this. It is most amusing to observe the critics of the Irish political Press trying to steer round this point in their notices of the play.[33]

Perhaps the most critical commentator of all was the usually gentle Padraic Colum:

> The construction of the play is imperfect, and the dialogue is without literary distinction. One has a suspicion that the dramatist has unlearned his craft from Mr. Shaw and the new London dramatists. The play does not proceed by situation, and in the first, second and third acts the curtain falls before the author gives us any finality in the scene. Were it not for a few scenes in which the women reveal some wisdom and tenderness, *Mixed Marriage* would lose little by being rendered on the cinematograph. Mr. St. John Ervine has the power of creating character. John Rainey, with his distrust of the Papists and his belief in unreflecting action, is real. Perhaps Mr. Ervine tends to make Mrs. Rainey a type rather than an individual. Through the two women largeness is given to the play. They are outside of theological and business interests created by the men. The living impulse of human love is the reality for the women. The parts of John Rainey and Mrs. Rainey were well played by Mr. Arthur Sinclair and Miss Máire O'Neill, and Miss Mary Walker's rendering of the part of Nora Murray pleased the house. The Dublin players were embarrassed by the Ulster accent, which they endeavoured to reproduce. . . .[34]

These strong criticisms were just, but the equally strong merits of the play made it apparent to the enthusiastic Abbey audiences that an important new writer had appeared.

For the week of 3 April, the Abbey company appeared at Kelly's Theatre in Liverpool. They were back in Dublin on Easter Monday, and played every weekday night for the next two weeks. The company then went on an extended tour in England, appearing in such large towns as Manchester and Liverpool but also in many smaller ones such as Stratford, Scarborough, Leeds, Bradford, Harrogate, Sheffield, Bury St. Edmund's, Oxford and Cambridge, before concluding the tour with three weeks at the Royal Court

Theatre in London. Some glimpses of the company on tour may be gained from these letters of Kerrigan to Henderson:

Albert Hall, Leeds
[May 10th, 1911]

Dear "Hendy"

. . . I saw some of the Dublin papers with letters re *Playboy* — it must be a wonderful play to arouse so much controversy. It was received well at Stratford despite the rumours to the contrary. Of course it worried a few old ladies & gentlemen, but the majority of the audience enjoyed it. The English are an extraordinary people. Synge's "blasphemy" annoys; Shakespeare's passes unnoticed. At *Henry V*, Fluellen swore by "Chesus Christ" half a dozen times, & the Irishman while he was on the stage seemed to say nothing but *Christ*, *Bastards* & *Whoreson*. What would happen if we went that far?

Sally Allgood is still at Stratford. She was operated on this week I believe for inflammation of some of the internal organs. Her sister, Mrs. Callender, is nursing her.

Scarborough proved an awful fiasco. The last night wasn't too bad though. The idea of bringing us to a place with a population of about 3,000. . . . Unless something drastic is done I'm afraid our days in the land are numbered. Poor Robinson is hopeless.

By the way that letter signed "Another Irishman", I suppose the work of Holloway, illustrates what Shaw calls our national genius for treachery. This is an awful hole. Miss O'Neill & Miss Nic Shiubhlaigh are poor substitutes for Sally Allgood, but things may improve.

Bye Bye for awhile,

Yours,

J. M. KERRIGAN

Grand Opera House, Harrogate
May 16th, 1911

Dear "Hendy"

Thanks for letter & paper — it seems as though *The Playboy* ye shall always have with you. Leeds improved immensely towards the end, & the audiences were most enthusiastic. We had a splendid house here last night. The plays were received magnificently. Judging by the way *The Rising of the Moon* went, quite a goodly portion were Irish. . . .

125

When Holloway's died (that the day may be far I hope) it will be found that the word "Playboy" will be engraved on his heart. . . . I wrote again to Yeats & told him I'd stop no longer in the company if he refused to improve my position. Miss O'Neill was very bad in all her sister's parts. Her Feemy Evans was the limit. . . .

Robinson in an interview said Shaw would not live, that he only wrote for his day. Hard on GBS after taking Lennox under his wing. . . .

Best wishes,

Yours,

J. M. KERRIGAN[35]

The company opened at the Royal Court on 5 June, and shortly after that Yeats was interviewed:

"We are now doing well in Ireland," said Mr. Yeats. "Last year at the Abbey Theatre we were able — for the first time since we have been on our own resources — to cover all expenses, even to clear a small profit. The popular support we have always had in Dublin in our democratic audiences; but the difficulty has been to fill the more expensive seats in the house, hitherto sparsely occupied. Now we are getting all classes. People are willing to pay for the better places, which means that the theatre is more or less full in all parts."

"Splendid! And what about the supply of writers?"

"New native dramatists are coming forward with plays of a high standard. Why," added Mr. Yeats, with almost a note of triumph, "we have three new realist-dramatists from County Cork — men who are studying the conditions and problems of our national life."

"But," I interrupted (having Brieux's work in mind), "are not you — poet and idealist — opposed by nature to the drama of realism? The 'salutary' or tractarian drama, I mean, as opposed to the purely imaginative?"

And Mr. Yeats explained. "I do not think the play that displays argument is the best, nor the best that its writer can probably do. Logic in art should be hidden up as bones are hidden by flesh. But I look upon realistic drama as a phase in the evolution of national drama in every country. You have waves of it. And so we are delighted to get plays setting forth the clash of interests and of thought at work to-day.

"Every temperament, you know, leans, or drifts ultimately,

126

either towards politics or religion — to Parliament or the cloister; and both tendencies are seen in contrast in the work of Brieux and Synge. Meanwhile, the artist sits by the wayside," he ended, parabolically.

"Ah, Synge! Is there a new Synge on the Irish horizon?"

"I fear not. His temperament was unique.

"Who are our realists? R. J. Ray, Lennox Robinson (our author-manager), and St. John G. Ervine, who wrote a play dealing with the conditions of labour in Belfast that proved our greatest financial success. But there are others. T. C. Murray, for instance, and George Fitzmaurice, author of *The Pie-Dish*. Some of the plays sent in this year are marked by a wilder note."

As regards women playwrights, besides Lady Gregory's work, two one-act plays by Miss Letts have been successfully produced in Ireland. When I asked in which English towns the Irish players had been best understood and appreciated, Mr. Yeats plumped for Manchester, Oxford, Cambridge and Liverpool.

"Are we to see any new plays of yours this season?" I queried. And then came a vitally interesting item of news about Mr. Gordon Craig, whom Mr. Yeats spoke of as "the greatest inventor of artistic stage effects in Europe."

"No," he said. "I have acquired from Mr. Gordon Craig the right to use (in Ireland) his wonderful new scenic system of folding screens, built to mathematical proportions to fit into numbered squares on the stage floor; and I do not want to stage any of my verse-dramas without them. Gordon Craig knows how to copy nothing, and to suggest all; and by the use of his screens, which are of many sizes, and run on castors, you can create an entirely beautiful scene full of suggestion (not realistic), and build up vast Cyclopean buildings. The costumes of the players should show a corresponding dignity of design and line to harmonise with this staging, which has a fine severity. . . .

"Have you used the screens yet?"

"Yes, in Dublin, as a setting for *The Hour Glass*, and the result aroused great enthusiasm. My screens are of plain ivory tone. The lighting is effected through a transparent roof — getting rid of everything above the stage. By this method you can use your shadows, and bring into play moving figures and changing lights, elements of beauty lacking in an ordinary stage setting, where the light is only painted and the figures do not move." [36]

On this visit to London, the plays and players were generally very well received, and one critic even went so far as to say, 'That a playwright should set out to write a play like *The Pie-Dish* is in itself a justification of the Irish movement." [37] Robert Lynd wrote in *The Daily News and Leader*:

> The apotheosis of Synge has, no doubt, done much towards sending the crowd to the Irish plays. There have been other causes, however. The Irish plays have become in recent years broader in interest, bolder in action, more human and passionate in characterisation. There has never been any question as to their art, but they used to seem a little remote from common life. The newer plays — the plays of Mr. Padraic Colum, Mr. Lennox Robinson, Mr. T. C. Murray and others — take all contemporary life for their province, and give us an eager and imaginative social drama which achieves something of the Ibsen ideal of making the spectator "feel that he was going through a piece of real experience." [38]

The critic of *The Academy* had some specific remarks about the acting of Sinclair in *The Pie-Dish* and of O'Donovan in *The Playboy*:

> . . . The something more is given, not by Mr. Fitzmaurice in the matter of the play, but by Mr. Arthur Sinclair in the matter of the acting. We have seldom seen a piece of acting so extraordinary as the death of Leum Donohue in the hands of Mr. Arthur Sinclair. Simple, unstrained, unrhetorical in speech and gesture, the writhing of the body, the twisting of the limbs, and the slow, unhasting, agonised stumble of speech, as in paroxysms of pain the old man besought God or devil for time in which to finish his piedish gripped the soul with attention. But it was not in the play; it was Mr. Sinclair. . . .
>
> To clear all initial fault-finding, it should perhaps be said here that Mr. Fred O'Donovan was not the best of Christy Mahons. We have not seen him in this part before, and we consequently puzzled not a little at the energy he put into his words and actions at times . . . he missed thereby that quiet, unobtrusive, rythmical beauty . . . he missed that winsome wonder and slowly expanding musical flower of speech that is Christy's essential beauty. It was he who was chiefly responsible for the farcical element in the play. . . .[39]

Two weeks later, the same critic had some more specific remarks:

> . . . a warmth of praise must be accorded to Mr. Arthur Sinclair as Scapin. We have already had occasion to refer to

128

the splendid comedy powers of this really fine actor; but in *Les Fourberies de Scapin* it is not too much to say that the play is himself, and that he is the play. In no one point does he fail to swell out the humour of Scapin to the full; and yet he never once exaggerated.

The same night there was given Synge's *In the Shadow of the Glen.* Not altogether do we agree with Miss Máire O'Neill's interpretation of the part of Nora Burke. Very rightly she has laid emphasis on the hardness of Nora's disposition; but we would draw her attention to the fact that there is something more than hardness mixed up in her character. . . . She . . . was a woman with the great hunger of loneliness in her soul. This phase of Nora's character Miss O'Neill is somewhat apt to neglect. Nevertheless, the performance was a haunting one. It was played gravely, at least more gravely than was *The Playboy,* to its unutterable advantage. For we do not want to make farce out of so great a soul as J. M. Synge.

On Wednesday was given the first production in London of *The Casting Out of Martin Whelan*, a play in three acts by R. J. Ray. It was a strange and puzzling performance. Full of many fine moments as it was, and with a central idea that was well conceived, we had seldom seen any play that failed as this did. That the conclusion was weak was one thing; but it was far more than weak; in its weakness it puzzled and perplexed, as though it had narrowly, however absolutely, missed excellence. . . .

On the following evening came *Harvest*, by Mr. Lennox Robinson; and it did not take long to discover that the author had a very sceptical, if not a very cynical, regard toward those things that the ordinary Irish dramatist cherishes. In country faith and innocence he has little hope; and at education he openly scoffs. Indeed, it would be difficult to find in what he does believe — a state of mind it is to be hoped he will outgrow with a little more experience of life. Indeed, there are evidences enough throughout the play that Mr. Robinson's experience of life has been very superficial. . . .[40]

The London engagement did not conclude without awkward incident. On 26 June, *The Evening Telegraph* reported:

An incident not reported in the Press happened at the Court on Coronation night, when *The Playboy of the Western World* was on the bill. Not content with swathing the greater part of the auditorium with Union Jacks and covering the remainder with gilt cardboard prayers for "our gracious King", the management instructed the band to play the English National Anthem during the first interval. No sooner had the band struck up than vigorous hissing arose from all parts of the house, and the gallery, by way of counterblast, began singing "God Save Ireland" — probably the first time it was ever rendered in a London theatre.

All Irish-Irelanders who take an interest in the renascence of Irish drama will hear with regret of Miss Máire nic Shiubhlaigh's resignation from the Abbey company. She has been compelled to adopt this course, I understand, owing to a series of irritating incidents which culminated during the London visit. True as it is, it seems hardly credible that the pioneer actress of the national movement, the actress whose "wan disquieting beauty" and spiritual artistry Mr. A. B. Walkley, of *The Times* raved over when the company first visited London in 1903, has been kept in the background, practically doing nothing but walking on as an auxiliary. . . .

Surprise succeeds surprise, and I have kept the bonne bouche of my budget to the last. Patrons of the Abbey will learn with some astonishment that they will see very little more of the Irish National Theatre Society Company this year. Beyond a few performances in Horse Show Week, and a special command night when Sir Wilfred Laurier, the Canadian Premier, will attend, the company will act no more in Dublin until 1912. The fact is the appeal to the Garrison for funds to subsidise the Abbey has met with very inadequate response, and an immediate tour in America "to raise the wind" has consequently been deemed imperative. All arrangements have been made, and the company will sail for Boston (where they open early in September). A tour of at least three months' duration will follow. To my mind there are more unlikely things than this American campaign will lead to the temporary break-up of the organisation.[41]

Two days later *The Evening Telegraph* was able to give Yeats's refutation of some of the above charges:

Our London correspondent wires:

Mr. W. B. Yeats communicated to me last night an emphatic denial of the series of statements concerning the Abbey Theatre company contributed to Monday's issue of *The Evening Telegraph* by "A Well Informed London Correspondent".

Mr. Yeats says it is absolutely untrue to say that "not

130

content with swathing the greater part of the auditorium in Union Jacks and covering the remainder with gilt cardboard prayers for our 'Gracious King', the management . . . instructed the band to play the English National Anthem during the first interval."

Mr. Yeats states that not one Union Jack was displayed; nor one gilt cardboard; nor was any demonstration whatever of the kind made either by the directors of the Abbey or the management of the Court Theatre.

It is true the orchestra played "God Save the King". They did so, Mr. Yeats says, entirely of their own initiative, and without any suggestion from the directors of the Abbey Company or any knowledge on their part.

Regarding the statement that the company is about to visit America in order to "raise the wind" because "the appeal to the Garrison in Dublin for funds to subsidise the Abbey has met with very inadequate response," Mr. Yeats states that ever since the Abbey Theatre movement was founded the directors have had an American tour in contemplation. It has always been their view that the company could not claim to be a truly National company unless it played before the great Irish population in America as well as the Irish at home, and consequently, so far from being any departure from the ideal which they have set before them, the projected trip is merely a fulfillment of that idea.

The statement that Miss Máire Nic Shiubhlaigh is resigning from the company Mr. Yeats also declares to be untrue.[42]

Shortly after the return of the company from London, Lennox Robinson, the company's manager, was interviewed:

"Yes, we are back in Dublin again after our tour in England, the longest and most successful we have yet undertaken."

"What places did you do best in?"

"We drew our best audiences in Sheffield, Oxford, Cambridge, and London. In the latter place our audiences week by week grew larger and larger until we ended by having full houses every night."

"I believe there was some trouble in connection with your performances in Stratford-on-Avon?"

"No, it is an exaggeration to say that we had any trouble. The audiences in Stratford-on-Avon, I fancy, are accustomed to very little except Shakespearian work, and Shakespeare, as played to-day, seems rather far from reality. Our plays, with their intimacy and realistic acting, took large audiences in Stratford-on-Avon by surprise. One man, after seeing *The Shadow of the Glen*, told me that he had the uncomfortable feeling of a person spying on a private domestic scene, and I think there were many others who felt like him; but when they got accustomed to the plays, they received them with great enthusiasm. They listened to the first act of *The Playboy of the Western World* in dead silence, but once they had grasped the idea, and once they got accustomed to the style and treatment they were unanimous in their applause, or perhaps I should say almost unanimous, for two gentlemen and their wives walked out at its conclusion saying something about its blasphemy and bad language. I saw the same people thoroughly enjoying *Henry V* the next evening!"

"You are going to America, I believe?"

"Yes; we are really going to America in the autumn. We have been thinking of going for some years, and we have now signed a contract with Messrs. Liebler for a three months' tour, beginning in September. We start at Boston, and will probably go later to New York and Philadelphia. I am sure that the plays will prove a great success out there."

"What plays are you bringing?"

"We have made a list of about twenty-four of our best plays, but possibly we will not act more than half of these."

"We shall miss you very much from Dublin during the autumn."

"Oh! Dublin will not be left altogether destitute. During our absence the Abbey School of Acting will continue as usual. Mr. Nugent Monck, who studied his art under Mr. Poel, and has himself produced much Elizabethan and Shakespearian work, as well as certain old morality and mystery plays, and modern work by Ibsen and others, will take charge of the school until the company's return in January. We shall probably make certain experimental productions in the Abbey, drawing players from the pupils. Miss Nic Shiubhlaigh, whose capacity in romantic work has been so much admired, will remain in Ireland to assist in these productions. It is the wish of the management of the Abbey Theatre to give as complete a theatrical education as possible, and in future, during the absence on tour of the Abbey Company, we hope to arrange such teaching in Shakespearian and modern work as will enable the company on its return to concentrate on the teaching of folk-drama mainly. Mr. Nugent Monck has been selected to begin this new scheme because of his training under Mr.

Poel, whose ideals resemble so closely those of the Abbey Theatre itself, but Mr. Monck's Irish blood has been a secondary recommendation." [43]

During July and August, Sinclair arranged a tour of English music halls for himself, Kerrigan, O'Rourke and Sara Allgood in several of the theatre's short plays. The theatre proper re-opened in Dublin during Horse Show week; and then, in preparation for the forthcoming tour to America, played almost nightly in a varied repertory of the popular plays.

The evening of 4 September, however, was a special complimentary performance for W. A. Henderson, who was severing his connection with the theatre. On this occasion there were songs, recitations, orchestral selections, and the production of two one-act plays which were not to be included in the Abbey repertoire. One, *Falsely True*, by Johanna Redmond, had already been presented commercially in London; the other, *The Love Charm*, was a farce written by William Boyle for Sinclair to play in the music-halls. *The Irish Times* called it 'an impossible farce' and 'a mere trifle' hardly worthy of the author of *The Eloquent Dempsy*; and *The Daily Express* in almost the same words echoed that opinion.[44] A few days later Boyle wrote, rather typically, to Henderson:

> ... I'm not the least annoyed that the audience couldn't stand my little bit of a joke. The nonsense of "The Tivoli" won't do at "The Abbey" — that's clear. . . . I've had my share, and more than my share of flattery. It's a poor heart that never accepts a word of dispraise. *The Love Charm* is rubbish — I know that as well as any one in Dublin — and it is devoid of humour. But I have been to Music Halls a bit, & I find that humour is not desired in such places.
>
> Please remember *Falsely True* was not a success at "The Palace".
>
> Yours very truly,
>
> W. BOYLE[45]

On 8 September, the penultimate night at the Abbey, Yeats's *Deirdre* was on the programme, and he took the opportunity to talk of what Dublin might expect from the theatre while the company was abroad:

> We feel that we must seem to many of you to be neglecting our principal work by going so far from Dublin and for so long a time, for on Wednesday next we leave Queenstown for America. From the very start of our theatre we have desired

to take our plays to Irish America. Some seven years ago I lectured to a great school of Irish boys in a religious house in California. As I went to that house I passed under palms and all kinds of semi-tropical vegetation, and yet those boys were reading the same Young Ireland poets, and thinking almost the same thoughts that young Catholic boys would have thought in Dublin. The Irish imagination keeps certain of its qualities wherever it is, and if we are to give it, as we hope, a new voice and a new memory we shall have to make many journeys. But while our company is away the school of dramatic art, lately founded at the Abbey Theatre, will carry on its work. We have placed at the head of it for this autumn Mr. Nugent Monck, an Irishman of imagination and energy, who has learnt his art of the stage under Mr. Poel, of the Elizabethan Stage Society. We do not seek to establish in Dublin a rival to Mr. Tree's school. Our object is to train players to express the mind, and to copy the life of Ireland. Mr. Monck, with the help of his pupils, and probably some professional players, will give certain productions at the Abbey Theatre — perhaps a classical play, probably some old interludes and mysteries, as well as reviving a play or two from our repertory. We hope that in the course of time we shall have trained in this way a second company which will play at the Abbey when the main company is away, and we shall not greatly regret if we train also some rivals to ourselves.[46]

On 12 September, the company left Dublin for Queenstown and thence by boat to America. In Dublin, on 30 September, the following paragraph appeared in the Press:

It will be of interest to many people to know that classes for dramatic training will be held in the Abbey Theatre each evening, except Saturday, from 10th October until 19th December, when Mr. Nugent Monck, who has been specially engaged to conduct these classes, will give lessons in elocution, deportment and gesture, acting and rehearsing, and part singing. Those wishing to join the classes should apply at once to the Secretary, Abbey Theatre, for particulars.[47]

(One of the more talented people who applied was a young Galway man, Michael Conniffe, who, as early as 1902, had appeared in Dublin with the Tawin Village Players in Tomás O hAodha's *Seaghan na Sguab*, and who was to be connected with the professional stage until 1919. His memories of his life as an actor appear in Appendix II.)

134

Yeats had accompanied the Abbey to America, but he returned in late October, and was asked about future plans at the Abbey.

. . . Mr. Yeats referred to the Dramatic School which has been conducted at the theatre during the company's absence, and which is attended by some sixty students. He stated that they will give some performances. The repertory will probably include some old English mystery plays and possibly a play or two in Irish. "We are trying to train our players mainly for the representation of Irish life and Irish emotions, but we cannot do so without a certain amount of classical work of other countries. As far as possible we shall select this classical work, because of its bearing upon something being written in the country. For instance, we have always played a certain amount of Molière at the Abbey, because of its relation to the work of Synge and Lady Gregory. If we decide to play these old mystery plays, it is because it seems to us that the religious drama should find a home in Ireland.

"Our players while in America will rehearse work for use in Dublin, so that they will be able to open here at once with new work. We have a fine new play by Mr. T. C. Murray and another by Mr. Boyle. The company on its return will play continuously, not as in the past, only three nights a week." [48]

On 16 November there was a pupils' performance — as distinguished from a public performance — of the medieval morality play, *The Interlude of Youth*, of Douglas Hyde's *The Marriage* in Lady Gregory's English translation, and of Synge's *In the Shadow of the Glen*. What was billed as the first public performance of the School of Acting occurred on 23, 24 and 25 November, when *The Interlude of Youth* was repeated on a programme with the medieval mystery play, *The Second Shepherd's Play*. Between the two items on the programme, Nugent Monck gave a lecture which had its interesting moments.

In an interval in the performance a lecture on "The Rise of the Mystery Play" was given by Mr. Nugent Monck, director of the school. . . . Bright and chatty as it was, it provoked what might have been a regrettable scene. Mr. Monck was describing *The Second Shepherd's Play* about to be produced, and was emphasising the fact that all the shepherds in it were characteristically Yorkshire shepherds. He went on — "I have no doubt there were Yorkshiremen of that day who got up and protested that it was an insult to draw Yorkshiremen like that."

135

Immediately a gentleman sitting in the front of the pit said loudly — "Better not introduce that."

Another gentleman at the back of the stalls rose and turned towards the interrupter saying — "You must not make a disturbance."

The first gentleman retorted — "I will do so if I please."

Some ladies in the stalls cried "Put him out", and there was a movement from several directions, apparently in obedience to the suggestion, but it died away before the interrupter was reached.

Meanwhile the lecturer proceeded with hardly a pause, and the incident ended. . . .[49]

The irascible interrupter was W. J. Lawrence, the Dublin correspondent for *The Stage*, and subsequently an eminent theatrical historian, whose vitriolic detestation of *The Playboy* was still smouldering up to the 1920s.[50]

The plays themselves were received with interest:

Coming to the performance, not only were the plays unusual, there were several accompanying innovations. Broad steps led up from each side of the front of the stage, by which the players made their entrances and exits, passing close to the audience. The stage was lighted from the balcony by a lamp, just as a bioscope screen is. By the withdrawal of a curtain between two pillars midway on the stage it was possible to have a second smaller scene for the purposes of the second play, though the actors in the first scene remained sleeping in the foreground. All this was not only ingenious, but effective. The lighting was particularly good. Perhaps a less brilliant draw-curtain might have been provided, at least for the second play. . . .[51]

On 30 November and 1 and 2 December, the School of Acting presented a quadruple bill consisting of Hyde's *The Marriage* and *The Nativity Play*, and of Lady Gregory's *Dervorgilla* and *The Workhouse Ward*. On this occasion Monck was assisted in the production of the plays by Máire O'Neill, who had not wanted to accompany the Abbey to America because she had been married on 15 July to G. H. Mair, an English journalist who wrote for *The Manchester Guardian*. On 7, 8 and 9 December, the School of Acting produced again *The Interlude of Youth* and *In the Shadow of the Glen* (with this time Máire O'Neill as Nora Burke), and the first Dublin production of Rutherford Mayne's *Red Turf* which had just received its premiere in Belfast by the Ulster

Literary Theatre. Even the presence of Máire O'Neill in the cast did not help the reception of *Red Turf*, which Jack Point described in *The Evening Herald* as 'nothing more than a squalid row in a Galway kitchen between two farmers over a strip of bog".[52] Jacques in *The Irish Independent* was even more caustic:

> In one of the plays in the repertoire of the Abbey Theatre, Mildred, a character, says — "There's an open fire and a big pot hanging over it . . . and there's turf! It's just like a scene in the Abbey Theatre." But if Mildred wants to be up to date she will have to add to the things that remind her of a scene in the Abbey Theatre. She will say — "Oh, my! do you hear that dreadful man. He has said 'bloody' and 'blasted' three times in as many minutes. And that boy there called a woman a horrible name. And just listen to the woman the way she shrieks and rages and jeers at her husband. And oh, dear! oh, dear! isn't it dreadful how her husband blasphemes. Really the people here in Ireland don't seem to be able to utter a sentence without shouting it and using words like 'bloody', 'blasted', 'damn', 'hell', and invoking the Sacred Name. . . . It's just like a scene in the Abbey Theatre."
>
> The thing I saw last night was that — just like a scene in the Abbey Theatre. It was called *Red Turf*. . . . But what a pity that Mr. Rutherford Mayne should have lent his name to this by-product of Abbey theatricality. It is unworthy of the author of *The Drone*. It is not literature — it relies on curses and swear words to give distinction to a dull dreary dialogue. It is not art, for it is the mission of art not only to represent but inspire beautiful thoughts. It is a wretched attempt at drama — the only dramatic incident was the explosion of a cartridge, and that happened off the stage. It is a piece that as a music-hall sketch might win the applause of a cross-Channel audience. To me it was fifteen minutes of preposterous piffle. *Red Turf* is redolent rubbish. . . .[53]

On 14, 15 and 16 December, the School of Acting again performed *The Second Shepherd's Play* and also a revised version of Yeats's *Countess Cathleen*, with Máire O'Neill in the title role. When the play was published in 1912, Yeats described its new staging:

> Now at last I have made a complete revision to make it suitable for performance at the Abbey Theatre. The first two scenes are almost wholly new, and throughout the play I have added or left out such passages as a stage experience of some

years showed me encumbered the action; the play in its first form having been written before I knew anything of the theatre. . . . The new end is particularly suited to the Abbey stage, where the stage platform can be brought out in front of the proscenium and have a flight of steps at one side up which the Angel comes, crossing towards the back of the stage at the opposite side. The principal lighting is from two arc lights in the balcony which throw their lights into the faces of the players, making footlights unnecessary. The room at Shemus Rua's house is suggested by a great grey curtain — a colour which becomes full of rich tints under the stream of light from the arcs. The two or more arches in the third scene permit the use of a gauze. The short front scene before the last is just long enough when played with incidental music to allow the scene set behind it to be changed.[54]

The reviewers treated the production kindly. Jacques remarked about 'the all-round excellence of the performers' who 'were a very creditable advertisement for the Abbey School of Acting'. His only real strictures were against 'unnecessary excrescenses. Last night a face and head and tweed cap waggled about left wing in the Mediaeval Forest scene.'[55] The remarks of *The Irish Times* indicate that the row over this play in 1899 was nearly forgotten and, if *The Playboy* had not quite yet been accepted, at least *The Countess Cathleen* had.

> We may say at once that the play, as now rewritten by Mr. Yeats and presented at the Abbey, contains no incident to which exception could be taken. . . .
> With the artistic presentation of this subject we have no fault to find; the play is written with all the grace that we should expect of Mr. Yeats; the sacrifice of the Countess Cathleen is beautifully conveyed; the dialogue contains some charming imagery. It is the subject itself with which we are not quite satisfied. Here, as in Monna Vanna, a great sacrifice is shown. It is a sacrifice that involves the doing of evil that good may come. We are not quite clear whether Mr. Yeats condones this act. It is, of course, here an act removed from the region of possibility; this is covered by the use of the word "miraculous". The play must, therefore, be considered as the outcome of the intellectual speculation of an uncommon mind.
> Mr. Yeats has certainly found an impressive subject, yet its very impressiveness rather awakens criticism. We feel that he has rather abused his ingenuity, that his delightful fancy had been better employed. But in saying this we must not be

138

taken as condeming his play. . . . The audience last evening were evidently very pleased, and applauded heartily. . . .[56]

The hiring of Nugent Monck, the kind of plays that he produced, and the simplicity with which they were produced all obviously reflect Yeats's idea of theatre. The productions of the School of Acting were received with interest and respect, but not really with delight and enthusiasm. For a typical reaction, consider the following letter to the Press:

Sir, — Dublin playgoers have recently been made aware, through the medium of an uncontradicted statement in a contemporary that the play, *Eleanor's Enterprise*, was, by request, submitted to the managers of the Abbey Theatre, and declined by them on the ground that the members of the Abbey Company were unfitted to undertake *roles* representing men and women of the upper classes. It is notorious that they rejected *John Bull's Other Island*, because they were unable to fill the part of Broadbent. Now, of course, in each of these cases, the refusal may have been merely a polite variant of the formula, "The Editor regrets", given (with every right) because the management believed the plays unsuitable; on the other hand, it may have conveyed the sincere and considered opinion of the directors. If this latter be the case, Dublin audiences have some reason to ask: why is it?

Personally, I think the pronouncement quite unjust to the players. But supposing, for the sake of argument, that it is true they are incompetent to undertake *roles* such as those in question, is it not time that this state of things were altered? There is in connection with the Abbey Theatre a School of Acting, the pupils of which have just shown us that, as far as it goes, it is doing good work; but I venture to suggest that it does not go far enough. Many of us delight in the plays produced at the Abbey, and have consistently supported them; but we are now tolerably familiar with the kind of thing we must expect when we go there, and should like to know whether it is always to be the same. I maintain that it ought not. I maintain that the directors are keeping their scope too narrow; and keeping their genuinely talented players working in a rut; and that, from this point of view, the Abbey repertory wants reforming.

It is generally understood that the desire of the Abbey people, both directors and players, is to give representations of Irish life; but as a matter of fact they represent only a fraction of it. Their peasants and their ancient kings are as a rule admirable; but Ireland is not inhabited exclusively by peasants and ancient kings nor yet by workhouse paupers, fratricides, nor even parricide *manques*. That there are such people and such classes is, no doubt, true; but there are also certain classes with a little money, a fair share of leisure, and a considerable amount of education; and I see no reason why they should be ignored or treated as unrepresentative of Irish life. . . . Let the directors include the study of such parts in the curriculum of the Abbey School of Acting.

Yours, etc.,

FIDDLESTICK[57]

Nevertheless, as Lady Gregory remarked during *The Playboy* row, it was the fiddler who called the tune. We may take the productions of the School of Acting as, if not Yeats's attempts to call the tune, at least as his attempt to teach a new tune. But, as Fiddlestick's letter makes apparent, what the audience really preferred was an adroitly performed old tune, melodic, comfortable, familiar.

\*    \*    \*

In late April the Abbey had staged a few performances of *The Playboy*, and still there were some protests in the Press. Victor O'D. Power, a prolific writer of popular fiction and plays, wrote in *The Evening Telegraph* that, '*The Playboy of the Western World* is a peculiarly dull and stupid farrago of "literary" garbage, beneath serious criticism of any kind were it garbage only, instead of offensive garbage.'[58] Later in the month, the journalist Fred Ryan, who had been the first secretary of the Irish National Theatre Society and who had written its first realistic social play, *The Laying of the Foundations*, discussed the matter more seriously:

The revival of the discussion of *The Playboy of the Western World* and the . . . canvassing of its merits and demerits may make interesting a brief account of the inner history of this curious episode in the fortunes of the Abbey Theatre — a history which has hitherto never been published. . . .

Early in 1903 Mr. Yeats discovered Mr. Synge, who had written a playlet called *In the Shadow of the Glen*, which greatly took Mr. Yeats's fancy. It was, as most Dublin play-goers know by this time, a rather gruesome "bizarre" affair, and it struck the keynote of almost all Mr. Synge's subsequent work. . . .

Now, at that stage in the history of the National Theatre, as it was then called, the central piece, and, as one might say, the standing dish, was the peasant play. Nothing was at all "in the movement", outside poetic drama, which did not involve the half-door, and the dresser, and the turf fire. The peasant was held up as the essential figure in all racy drama. The mere town dweller, the city clerk or business man, or even the country shopkeeper, all these were excrescenes on Irish life. No one who had not a half-door counted. The peasant was on the pedestal. And often, or generally, he was a quaint kind of peasant, rather a sort of tramp, a strolling fiddler or ballad-monger, who earned his living "goin' the roads". To judge by the presentation of Irish life as it appeared on the stage of the National Theatre, Ireland was peopled by a race of Bohemians, full of dreams and visions, able to turn at a moment's notice, or on the occasion of the slightest domestic quarrel, to the life of "the roads", where, apparently there was always abundance and liberty. The people of Ireland, in fact, seemed to live by taking in each other's ballads. . . .

In addition to these circumstances these peasant characters spoke a strange and charming dialect, full of quaint images and melodious turns of phrase. If any critic, greatly daring, ventured to suggest that the picture was idealised, he merely revealed thereby his boorishness in the realms of Art. If he mildly remarked that he did not constantly hear these splendid phrases on peasant lips, that in fact the people of Ireland were not nearly so dreamy, so fantastic, he was silenced at once as a city-bred ignoramus. . . .

The sober truth, no doubt, is that the whole type was largely the creation of Mr. Yeats, Mr. Colum, and the rest. He was an invention of the charming fancy of poets. As the French say, the thing was "de la litterature". But whether a literary invention or not, it was a triumphant success. The Abbey peasant, with his splendid mouthfulls, passed through England, leaving a track of conquest behind. Like Bret Harte's stories of the early mining camps, why trouble about the truth when fiction was so picturesque? . . .

Then came Mr. Synge's *Playboy*. And from its production may be dated the second phase in the strange history of the Abbey peasant. Mr. Synge was a very companionable and modest personality. Nothing can be more unlike the truth than to picture him as a gloomy recluse, plotting how best he could malign the Irish character. He simply never thought at all of the effect of his plays, and was unconscious of the slightest party motive. But his art, as has been said, was harsh and odd. . . . Everyone remembers the outburst on the first per-

141

formance. That outburst was entirely spontaneous and unpremeditated, and came from an audience favourably disposed to the Abbey Theatre movement on the whole. It entirely bewildered and nonplussed Mr. Synge himself. He had really no doctrine or point of view to expound, and he had nothing of Mr. Yeats's sense for a splendid "reclamé". He had simply written a play after his manner, and had discovered a hornet's nest about his ears. . . . I met him one of the days whilst the battle was at its fiercest, and he smiled over the whole affair. He had no "views" about the "freedom of the theatre" or anything else; he had merely written his play.

The production of *The Playboy of the Western World*, however, marked the death of the old dreamy and moongazing Abbey peasant; by way of reaction, and by way of justifying Synge's harsh pictures, the peasant was henceforth damned. Till then he had been almost too good and simple for nature's daily food. Now he became a moral monster. . . . As a result, every peasant play now swarmed with a selfish, bitter, cursing rabble. If you did not sprinkle your dialogue with coarse and brutal expressions, you were mealy-mouthed and week-kneed. . . . He [the peasant] generally begrudged his father and mother a crust; his sister went light-heartedly on the streets; he sometimes killed his brother. . . .

There is, however, an important difference to note. With Synge his plays were written without malice or afterthought. The other plays were written to justify an attitude. The peasant suffered for the sins of the audience. And the whole trouble arises from the fact that neither the original tramp-peasant, nor the Synge peasant, nor the post-Synge peasant is really observed or drawn from life. All of these were invented by literary men. They smell of oil, and are constructed of paper and ink. Like romance of the Dumas school or Mr. Anthony Hope's *Prisoner of Zenda* stories, such work may or may not be amusing, but it is not a counterpart of anything that ever lived. The Synge peasant, of course, never was, on sea or land. That is now frankly admitted, and *The Playboy* is given as half farce. . . . Writers like Mr. Boyle, for instance, have observed their characters, with the result that plays like *The Building Fund* or *The Mineral Workers* are throbbing with life. Mr. St. John G. Ervine, in his play the other day, *Mixed Marriage*, has observed, and his Belfast artisan's home is admitted all round to be a triumph of portraiture. But then these authors have the gift for painting what they have seen. Mr. Boyle knows Irish country life. Mr. Ervine knows Belfast.

That is the difference. It is only the rarest genius, if indeed it be open to any, faithfully to write a play of a life he has not lived.[59]

A few days later, Padraic Colum entered the discussion.

Art is autobiography. Under the necessity for expression, the artist records the lover, the soldier, the misanthrope, the sage, the saint and the madman, as he discovers them in his own personality. Michael Angelo's statues, Shakespeare's plays, Wagner's operas, are autobiography. This autobiography is the more true because it is indeliberate. Perhaps a tale of love wakes the lover in him there, and he will be able to write his *Romeo and Juliet*. Out of an experience of ecstasy and waste he writes his *Antony and Cleopatra*. His thoughts have been uplifted, lonely and austere, and so he can mould the head of his Moses, and make the lineaments of the Father in Heaven. His *Siegfried* arises out of a tremendous egoism, vigorous nature, triumphant passion.

Here the man in the audience may put in a word and ask what this has to do with the Irish peasant on the stage of the Abbey Theatre. I must ask permission to be garrulous again.

Says the Eastern proverb — "A man is more like his own time than his own father." The dramatist is the child of his time and locality. The less powerful the personality of the dramatist the more he reflects the opinions and sentiments of his epoch. As he progresses towards self-realisation they become more exceptional — that is to say, his sentiments and opinions become more universal and his characters more typically human.

As the dramatist, so are his creations. They are like his time, place and people. For the sake of more vital expression he is compelled to think in terms of the lives he knows. If he aims at verisimilitude he can write with exactness of manners, customs and characters that he knows intimately. He observes life because he is curious about it. He looks — not with the eyes, but through the eyes. He sees with the brain.

A man who happens to be a playwright is walking through the country. He comes to a neglected house in a desolate place. He finds there an old man who is a miser, and a young woman who is the miser's wife. The lonely lives of the two infect his imagination. The playwright has known the bitterness that comes from the want of money, the tyranny of a fixed idea, the suspicions of an embittered old age. The play about the miser grows up in his mind. The greater the dramatist the

143

more exceptional will the character be as regards the life that you and I have imagined. But the miser on the stage will not be more wonderful than the miser in life. The miser on the stage — Is he an Irish peasant? you will ask. Let us leave the word "peasant" out of account. The miser on the stage and the miser in the house are not identical; no two things in nature are identical. But they are alike, as lives with like potentialities influenced by a like environment. He is a peasant in so far as his creator might have been a peasant.

If I were asked which of the Abbey Theatre plays — Synge plays, post-Synge plays, pre-Synge plays — approximated to the reality of peasant life, I would say that the play that had the most vitality in conception and execution. There are charming peasants and harsh peasants, good peasants and bad peasants. The one trait common to all peasants is life. Let a dramatist endow his characters with life, and no matter how extravagant they appear on the stage we will discover their originals in the life around us.[60]

Early in June, Ryan replied:

To come to particulars in the case of the Abbey peasant, at least in the post-Synge plays, the case is not that vicious and even repulsive types of character are portrayed; it is that scarcely anything but these are shown. Three or four instances I will give. In *The Well of the Saints*, the old pair, Martin Doul and his wife, who have their sight restored to them, are morally repulsive in their harshness and bitterness. The absence of kindliness, or even common decency, is abnormal; they are almost moral freaks. Such demented selfishness borders on lunacy. . . . I come to *Harvest*, by Mr. Robinson. In it there was scarcely a decent character, except the old school-master, and he was a fool. The people, again, were abnormal; but it was, again, abnormal ugliness. Or take, even, Mr. Colum's own *Thomas Muskerry*. The old man in it was treated with a bitter lack of the slightest shade of filial affection by his daughter, who brutally regarded him as a mere creature to exploit. . . . I am not saying that each and every one of these characters could not be matched in real life. My argument is that the combination of them in such disproportionate numbers gives as false a view of the real life of the people as if one were to pick out half a dozen Dublin lunatics and exhibit them as typical of the intelligence of the metropolis. . . .

What the Irish dramatists have to realise, if I may be so bold as to say so, is that Ireland is throbbing with plenty of real and interesting issues, out of which drama can be made, without wandering into lonely valleys or "desolate places" to discover some extraordinary exception, or some rare and incomprehensible emotion, which has little or no relation to the life of the country as a whole.[61]

*　　*　　*

The Theatre of Ireland mounted three productions during the year. The first, on 20 and 21 February, of *The Storm* by the Russian Ostrovsky, caused some initial difficulty when several Dublin theatres charged that the Molesworth Hall was not properly licensed for theatrical production. The difficulty was overcome, but the production by Fred Morrow, assisted by Count Markievicz, seems otherwise unnotable. The Molesworth Hall had never been particularly suitable for the staging of plays, and fortunately in November the Theatre of Ireland was able to discover a new venue:

> The Theatre of Ireland announces that, through the kindness of a sympathiser, it has at last secured a permanent home, and that all future performances of the Society will take place at The Hall, Hardwicke Street (near Rutland Square). The staging and lighting arrangements having almost reached completion, the inaugural performances will take place on November 17th and 18th, on which occasion the Society will repeat its most successful performance, *The Turn of the Road*, by Rutherford Mayne, preceded by a new comedy, *The Marriage of Julia Elizabeth*, by James Stephens.[62]

When the Theatre of Ireland opened in late November in the Hardwicke Street Hall, a correspondent for *The Irish Times* described the somewhat spartan accommodations:

> The old hall which the company has secured used formerly to be a schoolhouse; it would be hardly possible to imagine any barer, simpler place wherein to act; beside it, indeed, the Abbey Theatre is luxurious.
> You mount three steps from the deserted street and pass through the doorway straight into the theatre. One cannot even be asked to take off one's hat, for there is nowhere to put it!
> The hall has a bare floor, and simple rows of the commonest chairs. The stage has but one luxury, a fine velvet curtain; otherwise it is as simple as Shakespeare's stage. No footlights, no curtain bell, practically no scenery. With three loud knocks

145

from inside, the curtain rose — knocks like those opening the C Minor Symphony, and which we know Beethoven meant to represent "Fate knocking at the door".[63]

The account in *The Stage* was a bit more complimentary:

> After having long enjoyed a name, the Theatre of Ireland at last possesses a local habitation. . . . Thanks to the generosity of Count Plunkett in giving them the use of a quaint eighteenth-century building, once upon a time used as a Jesuit chapel, they now enter upon a new era of their existence. In this old hall a dainty little theatre has been construced under the superintendence of Mr. Fred Morrow, an elder brother of Mr. Norman Morrow, the well-known artist, who has also painted the scenery and devised a scheme of lighting which obviates the necessity of the long-beloved but now much abused footlights. In point of mysteriousness of approach, selectness of public, and the dim religious lighting of its tiny auditorium, the new Hardwicke Street Theatre recalls the Grand Guignol in Paris. But there all resemblance ends, for no element of morbidity enters into the attraction provided by the Theatre of Ireland. After the conventional three knocks which the society has long adopted from the French stage, the tableaux curtains rose at the first performance of *The Marriage of Julia Elizabeth*, a sparking little comedietta of lower middle-class Dublin life from the pen of Mr. James Stephens, the well-known novelist and poet. Informed by a pretty wit and evincing touches of a tricky Gilbert-like humour, this little piece, which forms the maiden dramatic effort of its author, was capitally acted and favourably received. . . .[64]

Stephens's genuinely droll play has never had the popularity that many short Abbey plays of no greater pretensions to merit have enjoyed, and one might wish that the piece had been presented at the Abbey where it would have commanded the talents of actors such as Sinclair, Kerrigan, O'Donovan or Morgan who would certainly have done it more justice. On this occasion, despite the able Fred Jeffs in the cast, *The Irish Times* could dismiss it as 'only funny. Not one thought lifts it above the merest and lowest match-making, and the match-making of Fairview or Oxmanstown is not picturesque.'[65]

On 18 and 19 December, the Theatre of Ireland presented a novel programme consisting of Jane Barlow's play in two scenes, *A Bunch of Lavender*, and of Watty Cox's comedy in two scenes, *The Widow Dempsey's Funeral*, adapted for the modern stage by

J. Crawford Neil of the National Library. *The Irish Times* treated the productions with some gentleness:

> In Jane Barlow's play we have a picture of unrighteous pride meeting with melodramatic retribution. The Widow O'Neill had a son, who was the apple of her eye, whose attainments were the pride of her heart. Unfortunately he was foolish enough to fall in love with a girl whom the widow considered just good enough to be a kitchen maid. He married the girl in spite of parental anger, as was only proper in such a young man. The couple were turned out into the harsh world, there to meet with early death. Naturally, we see Murtagh Regan, the girl's grandfather, incensed at the Widow O'Neill's hardness of heart. With appropriate sentiment he comes to the widow's garden for flowers to lay upon his granddaughter's grave. When the widow orders him forth, he puts a solmen curse upon the family and the flowers, and goes his way. Ten years after we find that the widow's sternness has not prevented her becoming superstitious. Her daughter Eileen, her sole remaining joy, is now about to marry Lance FitzAlleyne, a stalwart young man. The couple are seen in the garden. At intervals this happy conversation is interrupted by Mephistophelian laughter on the other side of the wall. We feel certain that they will never marry. Then FitzAlleyne leaves, wearing a bunch of lavender, the present of his sweetheart. Remembering Regan's curse, the widow sends after him to recover the lavender. It is brought back before many moments, with the news that FitzAlleyne is dead; he has been struck by lightning while sheltering with the lavender under a tree. The shock of this deprives Eileen of her reason. Thus is the widow punished for her pride.

While appreciating the author's ingenuity, we must confess to feeling a little unconvinced by her play. Certainly we felt that a tragedy in some form was approaching with the sureness of fate; but we were not quite prepared for the manner of it. Apart from this, however, the play was interesting; the dialogue in some parts showed a happy wit, though it would be improved by a more sparing use of inverted locutions.

Of the actors whose names did not appear upon the programme, the best was probably the young lady who took the part of Eileen.[66]

*The Widow Dempsey's Funeral*, the second play performed, is of a very different order from *A Bunch of Lavender*. It has been adapted to the requirements of the modern stage by Mr.

147

J. Crawford Neil, of the National Library of Ireland. Though rather trifling in subject, it abounds in humour, and its subject has a certain interest at the present day. In this comedy the keen wit of Watty Cox holds up to ridicule the love of gaudy display of a worthy greengrocer of Patrick Street in old Dublin. The most notable feature of the acting was the appearance of the well-known humorist, Mr. Fred Jeffs, in one of the parts. He was so eminently successful that we venture to hope he will be seen in such a role frequently in the future. . . .[67]

Jane Barlow (1857–1917) wrote popular poems and sketches of Irish life, none of great literary merit; Watty, or Walter, Cox (1770–1837) was an early nineteenth-century humorist and journalist. There was a certain curiosity value to the production of their work, but W. J. Lawrence was undoubtedly correct in his summation of the dramatic value:

> It is regrettable that little save disappointment awaited the audience which assembled on Monday evening to witness Miss Jane Barlow's maiden dramatic effort. Beyond a delicate sense of characterisation, the gifted author of *Bogland Studies* fails to show the possession of even elementary dramatic qualities. . . .
>
> Although styled a comedy in the programme, *The Widow Dempsey's Funeral* has no dramatic quality, and Mr. Crawford Neil, who has exerted his skill to adapt it for representation, has not been able to endow it with any. This defect arises primarily from the fact that it was not designed by its author for stage performance. Written and published as a pamphlet in Dublin in 1820 by the once famous humorist, Watty Cox, it is merely a social satire arranged somewhat amorphously in dialogue. . . .[68]

\* \* \*

A couple of Irish plays were given their first productions in London during the year. One of them was *Falsely True*, a one-act by Johanna Redmond, purporting to be about an incident in the Robert Emmet Rising of 1803. The play first appeared on the variety bill of the Palace Theatre on 6 March. The small cast was composed of Sara Allgood, W. G. Fay and Fred O'Donovan, and the piece was directed by Fay. According to *The Pall Mall Gazette*, the play

> tells the story of a young Wicklow man who, after Emmet's rising, found himself in prison, and, to save a younger brother

148

turned informer. It sets forth his emotions, and those of his father and mother in a situation which, to an Irishman, is among the most tragic; and it ends with the lad leaving his home for no man knows where, until "the red stain on his hands" has been wiped away. There are only three characters, and it is over in twenty minutes; but after the opening scene, which is principally expository, it is written and played with a passion that carries all before it; and when the curtain had fallen last night it had to be raised again and again while the actors—and eventually the author—bowed their acknowledgements of the applause. . . . The whole thing was stamped with sincerity. . . .[69]

In actuality, *Falsely True* seems to have been a conventional patriotic melodrama, and the main reason for its production was undoubtedly that its author was the daughter of John Redmond, the leader of the Irish Parliamentary Party. About the acting, W. F. Casey wrote to Henderson, 'Sara Allgood and Fred O'Donovan were very good at the Palace, but Fay! I simply couldn't believe my eyes he was so bad.' [70]

The play was first produced in Dublin on 17 April at the Rotunda, with Edward Milroy, Honor Lavelle and P. Mac Shiubhlaigh. On that occasion, Jacques rather accurately summed up the play:

> A little story like that told in Miss Redmond's homely style would cause a tear-drop as you read it in the quiet of evening. When it is served up to us in theatrical guise it leaves us cold. I have no fault to find with it, because it is familiar and commonplace and undistinguished. As a play it is simple, intelligible and coherent. But it is not at all great, and never approaches greatness. The language is often soaring and sometimes cloudy. And the theme has been used by other writers for dramatic purposes to much better advantage.[71]

On 1 June, Lord Dunsany's *The Gods of the Mountain* was produced at the Haymarket as a curtain raiser to Rudolf Besier's *Lady Patricia*, which starred Mrs. Patrick Campbell. Dunsany's play had characters with such names as Oogno, Thahn, Ulf, Agmar and Slag, and obviously there was little Irish about it.

There was little Irish about George Moore's dramatisation of his novel, *Esther Waters*, of which the Stage Society gave a few performances, beginning on 11 December. *The Daily Chronicle* thought the play both dreary and badly done, and *The Academy* remarked that, 'We can only say that we are sorry that the Stage Society saw fit to produce a piece of work so uneconomical in treatment and so utterly insalubrious in idea. The thing might have been written by an American Yellow-press man under the influence of absinthe.' [72]

*     *     *

In Dublin, the Theatre Royal was in something of a transitional period. It still booked touring companies of straight plays, but it was coming more and more to rely on musicals, the music-halls, and even gimmicks. During the year, M. Roubaud's Parisian Company played a week of matinees, performing Labiche, Augier and Molière in French. H. B. Irving and Julia Neilson appeared, as did J. W. Whitbread's company in Irish melodramas, and George Edwardes's London companies in several frothy musicals. One of the last of the great sensation melodramas, *The Whip*, was produced in April, and enchanted its audience with rushing trains, wreckage, and a climactic horse race with real horses on a revolving platform. Prominent among the musical hall performers who appeared at the Royal were George Robey, Little Tich, Bransby Williams, Cecilia Loftus, and the American tramp juggler W. C. Fields, who appeared during a week in which he was rivalled by an exhibition of colour cinematography by the Irish Animated Picture Company at the Rotunda.[73] However, the most lowbrow items of the year at the Royal were Lipinski's Forty Dog Comedians and a marvellous machine called the Pulsocon which cured people of rheumatism, arthritis, sciatica, lumbago, deafness, and a multitude of other ailments.

The offerings of the Gaiety Theatre were a trifle better. Ellen Terry appeared for a matinee, Alexander Marsh's Company presented some Shakespeare, Mrs. Mouillot's Company presented some apparently still popular T. W. Robertson plays, and Mona Limerick and B. Iden Payne's Company appeared in Shaw and Ibsen. For the week of 20 March, Juan Bonaparte appeared as *The Real Napoleon*, of whom he was allegedly the great grandson. The Castellana Opera Company played for a week, as did the D'Oyly Carte, and there were various other offerings on the general level of *The Chocolate Soldier, When Knights Were Bold, Charley's Aunt*, and *Brewster's Millions*. However, for the week of 4 December, the Players' Club, a group of Dublin amateurs that gave sporadic performances under the direction of Flora MacDonnell, mounted the first production in the British Isles of Maeterlinck's *Monna Vanna*. The play had been banned in England by the Lord Chamberlain, and there were mild objections in the Dublin Press to its presentation.

In Mrs. Mouillet's season in the summer, there was one item of Irish interest, the production of another curtain raiser by Johanna Redmond. Entitled *The Best of a Bad Bargain*, it served mainly, one suspects, as a novel advertisement. However, as *The Irish Times* reported:

> Its subject is the mercenary motive that so often leads to marriage in rural Ireland, and its characters are the trio so often found in a short play of the kind — a woman and two men. Ben Brusnahan (Mr. Charles Macdona) is a lonely farmer well on in years. Mary Sheehan (Mrs. Mouillot) is the buxom widow of a farmer, and is "well provided for". Brusnahan and the widow discuss marriage, and consequently their property. Their alliance would necessitate the sale of the farm of one or of the other. Brusnahan thinks that the widow should sell hers, and come to live with him; the widow thinks that Brusnahan should sell his, and come to live with her. Neither will give way on this crucial point. But Brusnahan is not the widow's last hope of a second husband. Jerry O'Rourke (Mr. Arthur Eldred), a young blacksmith, has placed himself and £50 at her disposal. O'Rourke's youth and his money decide the widow in his favour; and Brusnahan is left to repent his obstinacy. Unfortunately — or, perhaps, fortunately — for the widow, O'Rourke has not got £50 at all, and he innocently applies to Brusnahan for it. The farmer resolves to sell his farm, and save the widow from the deceptive blacksmith. This he does most successfully, and to the utter discomfiture of his rival. The widow is horrified to learn that it was the intention of O'Rourke to bring her to live with his mother, and melts into tears. Needless to say, before many minutes have passed, she and Brusnahan resolve to make "The Best of a Bad Bargain".

Miss Redmond has certainly not minimised the coldness of these matrimonial calculations. But in this respect she shows only a praiseworthy desire to set forth impartially what she believes to be the truth, though it be somewhat unpleasant. Of the three characters in this play Brusnahan appears the only one actuated at any time by any slight degree of sentiment. At the beginning he is merely mercenary; the revelation of danger to the widow kindles sentiment, which is fanned by a little jealousy. As for the widow, she is allowed to possess sufficient vanity to dull her keenness in matrimonial bargaining. In O'Rourke we can find but the single motive of money. This blacksmith does not strengthen the plot so much as we

151

might expect. He is altogether a foolish young person, and the failure of his plan makes us wonder how he ever thought it out. The dialogue of the play is creditable, and here and there flashes of wit occur; but we venture to suggest that a little condensation would improve the first of the two scenes. Considered as a whole, the play is evidently the work of a thoughtful writer, and of one from whom we may expect more pretentious work; and it deserves no small measure of praise. It was well acted last evening, though such expletives as "sure" and "yerra' did not ring quite true when uttered by players unaccustomed to their use.[74]

For the week of 11 December, Count Markievicz's Independent Theatre took over the Gaiety. For the first night and three other performances during the week, they presented George A. Birmingham's new comedy, *Eleanor's Enterprise*, preceded by Gordon Campbell's curtain raiser, *Self Sacrifice*. On 12 December and for two other performances, they presented Count Markievicz's *Rival Stars*. *Eleanor's Enterprise* was the type of genial broad comedy that readers of Birmingham's novels had come to expect; and it was probably the most successful production and the most adroit play that the Independent Theatre Company had attempted. Nevertheless, as Jacques correctly pointed out, the play had been rejected by the Abbey:

Can it be possible that the Abbey Theatre directors have made another blunder? . . .

It was current gossip at the Gaiety Theatre last night that Rev. Mr. Hannay, better known by his pen-name, George Birmingham, had offered his three-act comedy, *Eleanor's Enterprise*, to the Abbey Theatre for presentation, and that the play was not accepted. I give the current gossip for what it is worth, with the remark that if the report be true the Abbey Theatre people have made a bigger blunder than when they rejected the Shaw work. The Abbey company could not play the *John Bull* piece — it was beyond them; they could play *Eleanor's Enterprise* — it seems as if made for them.

However, the George Birmingham play has fallen into good hands — very good hands indeed. The Independent Theatre Company gave the new dramatist — I think he is new in drama, though a very old and dear friend in fiction — a right hearty and successful send-off at the Gaiety last night. It did one good to hear a crowded stalls and circle echo with genuine unrestrained laughter.

152

The story is just the kind of entertainment we would expect from the author of *Spanish Gold* and *The Major's Niece*. The Doctor Reilly of the play is the Rev. Meldon of the novel, as ingenious and polished a prevaricator as ever came out of Westport. The inventive faculties on this occasion were exercised on behalf of the charming Eleanor Maxwell (Countess Constance de Markievicz), a Girton girl on a visit to her aunt, Lady Kilbarron (Miss Violet Mervyn). Eleanor's sympathies have been roused by the conditions of life of the cottagers on her uncle's estate. She wants to uplift them. She will go amongst them; live with them; show them how to cook cabbage, how to wash their babies, how to — well, she will show them things the Congested Districts Board never could show them. . . .

It's capital entertainment, this new play. No need to put out the stars, turn off the sun, and suspend the laws of nature because of it. Because it is not great, though it is very pleasant nonsense. Its dialogue is direct, fresh, and natural. It is its chief feature and its chief charm. The staging, too, was uncommon. The introduction of a real live donkey into Act 2 was risky. This actor wanted to add to the realism of last night's cottage scene, and there were fears at one time that he would create a discord by walking into the orchestra. The look he cast on Reilly during that gentleman's discursive plamash was one of the good things of the scene.

The acting was good. Countess Markievicz can win hearts on the stage, as she can off it. She was not even self-conscious in her duel with two policemen. . . . Miss Mervyn was fine in the last act, but best of all was the Mrs. Finnegan of Miss Helena Molony. This was a capital sketch, and was well balanced by the performance of Mr. J. Connolly as Paudeen Finnegan.

Mr. P. Quill, who gave us an amusing Doctor Reilly, betrayed his nationality when he spoke of "the idear". He appeared earlier in the night in a fantasy by Gordon Campbell (son of Mr. Campbell, K.C.) as a sloppy-eyed, long-haired post-impressionist type. The fantasy was entitled *Self-Sacrifice*. It was pure farce, but an attempt was made to present it as comedy. If it had any merit, it was not sent across the footlights.[75]

Jacques was much less delighted with the Count's new play:

A new play in three acts by Count Casimir Dunin Markievicz, entitled *Rival Stars* (first time on any stage), was

153

produced last night at the Gaiety Theatre, Dublin. The
audience (in places) was small, but select; the laughter (in
places) was explosive, and the applause (also in places) was
very hearty.
What it was all about I would not attempt to say. No doubt
the author and the members of the Independent Theatre
Company knew the whole story, which, as far as a mere outsider could gather, had reference to an English artist in Paris,
his wife, his wife's sister, a maid-servant from Tyrone, a
Jewish journalist who seemed to spend his time making
windy speeches and smoking cigarettes, and a crowd of gro-
tesquely dressed artists who enjoyed themselves to their hearts'
content. . . .[76]

A clearer view of the proceedings appeared in *The Irish Times*:

The productions of the Independent Theatre Company at
the Gaiety Theatre this week are remarkable for the high
quality of the acting. Last night the second of the two new
plays . . . was carried through to success very largely by the
acting. Madame Constance de Markievicz and Mr. Patrick
Quill added fresh laurels to those gained on Monday night;
Miss Violet Mervyn, having a fuller and more emotional part,
showed to still better advantage than before, while a newcomer in Mr. John Raeburn gave a thoroughly admirable
study of a part that presented little inspiration. Count Markievicz evidently wrote *Rival Stars* with great enjoyment, and
it was acted in the same spirit. Dramatically, the fault of the
piece is want of consistency. There is a basis of serious plot
on conventional lines; there is a great deal of adroit comedy
and of sheer fun-making; and there is an incident taken
directly from a popular musical comedy of the most flippant
kind. We all remember the Portuguese twins in *The Belle of
New York*. Count Markievicz is too full of spirits to work out
consistently his serious *motif*, which, however, offers him some
opportunities for introducing characteristic dialogue — Oscar
Wilde fashion — on social and art topics. The serious part
of the play deals with the over-productive subject of misunderstandings between husband and wife. The author shows
some skill in providing the right atmosphere for the subject . . .
in the strained excitement attending Robert Ellis's artist life
in Paris, things happened which bore a less tragical complexion
when a cold douche in the form of a solicitor coming to ne-
gotiate a separation allowance precipitated the heat-fog of
misunderstanding which had arisen between Robert Ellis and

Dagna. The scene of the whole story is laid in Ellis's studio in Paris. It is in filling in the colour that Count Markievicz finds opportunity for the expression of his high spirits. He is able to introduce some highly entertaining characters, as well as a riotous "chorus" of artists and models who maintain the Bohemian life with gusto. . . .[77]

Although the play was heartily applauded and the Count received a curtain call, the Birmingham play was far more entertaining, and it replaced *Rival Stars* for the last night of the run.

On 5 August, Frederick Mouillot died in Brighton, and *The Irish Times* reported:

Although Mr. Mouillot had been in ill-health for some time, his death was altogether unexpected. . . . Mr. Mouillot was born some forty-six years ago in Dublin. He was educated in Wesley College, and from the days of his youth the drama had an interest for him above all else. At the age of 17 he determined to follow the bent of his inclination; and he soon found an humble place in the ranks of the theatrical profession. . . . For several years he was the leading man in Miss Janet Steer's Company. . . . He entered into partnership with Mr. H. H. Morrell, a son of the late Sir Morrell Mackenzie, and he took part in the production of many plays. They were mostly musical comedies, some of which attained great popularity, such as *The Shop Girl*, *The Country Girl*, and *The Gaiety Girl*. . . . When he returned to Dublin for the purpose of founding the present Theatre Royal, he therefore came as no stranger, but as one who had an intimate knowledge of the ways and the wants of Dublin theatregoers. At the time of Mr. Mouillot's return, Dublin was not altogether ill-provided with theatres. There was the Gaiety, under excellent management, and the Leinster Hall, which was also used for theatrical performances after its re-building. But there was little doubt in the mind of Mr. Mouillot that love of the drama was sufficiently great in the people of his native city to warrant the erection of another theatre. The traditions of the old Theatre Royal were also in his thoughts. After consideration, he determined to make the venture, and set to work without delay. First he approached Mr. David Telford in the matter, and with the aid of that gentleman a syndicate was formed, the other members being Mr. David Allen, jun.; Mr. S. C. Allen, Dr. E. W. Harris, and the late Mr. J. F. Warden (of Belfast). The project quickly gained ground, and on the 13th

155

December, 1897, the present Theatre Royal was opened on the site of the Leinster Hall. Mr. Mouillot was appointed managing director, and this position he has filled with distinction ever since. . . . Mr. Mouillot's theatrical enterprises and theatrical interests increased in number year by year. He directed the management of no fewer than fourteen theatres in the provinces and in the suburbs of London, also was concerned in other ventures in the theatrical world, including a dramatic agency in London. Within recent years, too, the Dublin Theatre Company acquired the Gaiety Theatre. . . .[78]

The productions at Dublin's other commercial houses were not notable. The Queen's did, for the week of 13 November, present two Irish plays, but they were of small interest. The main item was a romantic play in the Boucicault manner, entitled *A Daughter of Ireland*, by a Northern writer, G. J. Hurson. Of it, *The Irish Times* remarked:

> The kind of Irish drama that is being played at the Queen's Theatre this week may not come up to the exacting standard of our modern dramatic school, but it will certainly give keen pleasure to lovers of the older school, in which men fight for the cause that is dear to them, and do not waste fine words over it. *A Daughter of Ireland* is fashioned rather after the Boucicault models than any other, but it contains less of the burlesque element that often spoils a robust Irish drama. Though the rebellion period has been almost exhausted as a well from which many a good drama sprang, the author in this instance has managed to make his handiwork appear near while preserving many of the well-worn features that characterise plays of that period. . . . There are some stirring incidents, some touching love scenes, and these, with an occasional sparkle of humour, serve to furnish an interesting drama. . . .[79]

The one-act curtain raiser, P. Kehoe's *When Wexford Rose*, was produced for the first time, and occasioned little comment.

\*     \*     \*

There was a good deal of amateur activity in Dublin, but little of lasting significance. The Leinster Stage Society, whose fortunes were directed by Willie Pearse, played at the Abbey on 23, 24, and 25 February. The pieces presented were the first productions of M. B. Pearse's adaptation of *The Cricket on the Hearth*, Morgan

O'Friel's *The Skull*, and revivals of James Cousins's *The Racing Lug* and of Æ's *Deirdre*. On 26 December, the Society again appeared at the Abbey for matinee and evening performances. *The Skull* and *The Racing Lug* were repeated, and there were first productions of M. B. Pearse's *The Good People* and Séamus O'Heran's unfinished *For a Lady's Sake*. Of the Pearse play, *The Irish Times* reported, 'It is a plea for an ancient race, our old friends the fairies, who seem to have fallen on evil days since the introduction of railway trains.' [80]

On 28 February, the Ui Breasail Amateur Dramatic Society appeared for one night at the Abbey in a programme of three one-acts, only one of which — Brian MacCarthy's *Down in Kerry* — appeared to have been of Irish interest. About it, *The Irish Times* remarked:

> It opened in a rather interesting manner, and seemed to promise well, but it was soon made apparent to the audience that its purpose was an advertisement for consumptive harms, and that the author's object was to proclaim the advantage of fresh air, wholesome living, and the virtues of the travelling educational "van". Health lessons are disagreeable at any time, but they seem particularly nauseous when conveyed through the medium of a play with so attractive a title.[81]

On 3 April, an announcement appeared in the Press that created some consternation:

> The announcement that the boy actors of St. Enda's College, assisted by the students of the new sister college of St. Ita's, are to perform a Passion Play in Dublin this week has created much interest. The play is in three acts — the Garden of Gethsemane, "Behold the Man", and On the side of Calvary. Mr. Pearse, the headmaster of St. Enda's, who has arranged the play for the stage, explains that all of the speeches put into the mouths of the characters are taken from one or other of the Gospels, with the exception of certain words in the last act, attributed to the holy women by a very ancient Irish tradition.[82]

A few days later, the following letter appeared in *The Irish Times*:

> Sir, — In your issue of Monday there appeared a notice of a public performance of the Passion Play in the Abbey Theatre on Friday and Saturday next. As this play depicts the most solemn and sacred scenes in connection with Our Divine Redeemer's life and passion, I write on behalf of many in our

157

city who hope that the authorities will not permit such sacred scenes to be put upon the stage of the theatre. It is surely unedifying and improper for any persons to take into their mouths such solemn words as were uttered by Our Saviour in the Garden of Gethsemane, and to reproduce them upon the stage of a playhouse or theatre.

I trust the Dublin public of all religious denominations will utter their voice in public protest against such action, and will show their disapproval of it by their absence from such a representation. — Yours, etc.,

F. R. GOFF, CLK.[83]

To this, Pearse replied:

Sir, — The letter of the Rev. F. R. Goff in your issue of yesterday shows an attitude of mind very different from that which has characterised the bulk of Christendom in all the believing ages and countries. The suggestion that it is "unedifying and improper" for any persons to take into their mouth the words of Christ in Gethsemane and to reproduce the scenes of the Passion on the stage will come with a shock to all who know the part that sacred drama played in the rich and beautiful Catholic life of the Middle Ages, and still plays in the life of certain Catholic countries. That which was not unedifying and improper when done by modern peasants, can surely not be unedifying and improper when done by our students. Our endeavour, whatever its crudenesses, will be sanctified by the faith and by the reverent spirit of our young players. A number of Catholic clergymen were present at a dress rehearsal to-night: they were not disedified. I do not think the Rev. Mr. Goff will be disedified if he comes to the actual performance. — Yours, etc.,

P. H. PEARSE.[84]

The play was performed at the Abbey on 7 and 8 April, without incident. As *The Irish Times* reported:

There was a large audience, to whom Mr. Pearse, at the outset, addressed the natural request that there should be no attempt at applause. The demeanour of the audience during the play betrayed no evidence that the susceptibilities of any member had been offended. Assuming, indeed, that those present had no objection to the principle of a Passion Play, it was not possible to realise how they could take objection to any detail of the production. The only point on which adverse criticism could fasten itself was a minute artistic imperfection, no more than a superfluous triviality — the sound of Pilate's horses approaching the palace, a slight excess of realism. With this small exception, the representation contained nothing that could needlessly offend. The beautiful, yet simple, scenery; the tableaux of figures garbed in costumes that fell in graceful lines; and were of colours bright and varied, yet soft; and the well-managed lighting effects, contributed to securing pictures full of solemn beauty. This is not the place to discuss the question whether the introduction of the person of Christ on the stage is indefensible; but if ever there was a case for a waiving of the objection, it exists in this production, which is as far divorced from secular suggestion as anything could be. The names of those taking part are not mentioned, and they are nearly all boys and youths, pupils of St. Enda's and St. Ita's Schools. There is, therefore, no room for personal glorification. The dialogue, which is in Irish, follows very closely, almost throughout the words of Scripture. In the first act Jesus is seen in the Garden of Gethsemane; the Agony is represented, the injunction to "watch and pray" is given to the sleep-o'ertaken disciples, the kiss of Judas is given, and Jesus is taken away by the guards. The second act presents the "Christ or Barabbas?" episode; and in the third act the final scene of Calvary is reverently and impressively given. We confess that we had not been prepared for so touching a performance.[85]

On 17, 19, and 21 April, the Pioneer Dramatic Society staged Hurson's *A Daughter of Ireland*, which they had already presented the previous Christmas. And on alternate nights, 18, 20, and 22 April, the group staged the first Dublin production of *The West's Awake; or The Dawn of Freedom* by Joseph M., or, as he later called himself, J. Malachi Muldoon.

During the week of 4 September, the Irish Theatre and National Stage Society gave a series of matinee performances at the Queen's, and produced for the first time Johanna Redmond's *Pro Patria*, Mary Costello's *The Coming of Aideen*, and J. Malachi Muldoon's *A Hospital Ward*. *The Irish Times* described the occasion:

In *Pro Patria* Miss Redmond has chosen for her material an incident in the insurrection of 1798. The action of *Pro Patria* takes place in a cottage in the Wicklow mountains, kept by Mrs. Kelly, the wife of a rebel, and her daughter, Sarah, and used as a resort by certain of the insurgents, including Michael Dwyer, the local rebel leader, and a follower of his named John, who is Sarah's lover.

159

While the two women are anxiously awaiting the return of the rebels a knock is heard, and a spy, disguised as an old woman, seeks shelter, and is admitted. In the meantime, the rebels return, and in the excitement of the moment the presence of the old woman is wholly forgotten. The spy overhears all the conversation, and, having obtained the necessary information, escapes unnoticed by anyone in the house. The climax is not long delayed; the house is surrounded by soldiers, and the rebels make their last stand. In the fight that ensues the leader, Michael Dwyer, is slightly wounded by a shot. In order to secure Dwyer's escape, his follower, John, who bears a striking personal resemblance to his leader, dons his cloak, while Dwyer is carried into another room. An English officer, bearing the warrant for the execution of Dwyer, enters, followed by some soldiers, and arrests John, who is disguised in his leader's cloak. The officer, unlike most English officers portrayed in plays dealing with '98, is not at all a hard-hearted individual, and concedes to Sarah's request not to search the other room, where she informs him her wounded lover is lying. The curtain falls on Sarah lamenting the fate of her lover. . . . Miss Mary Costello's play, *The Coming of Aideen*, an interesting comedy, full of sparkling dialogue, and the one-act drama entitled *A Hospital Ward*, by Mr. J. M. Muldoon, were also performed. . . .[86]

W. J. Lawrence, writing the *The Stage*, was considerably less tolerant:

If the Irish Theatre and National Stage Company desires to convince the Dublin public of its *raison d'être*, it will have to provide better fare. . . . There is a limit to human credibility even in the regions of the footlights, and Mr. J. Malachi Muldoon, in *A Hospital Ward*, has far exceeded it. . . .

Miss Redmond would be well advised if for the present she eschewed historical drama and devoted herself to the writing of modern Irish peasant comedy, for which she has many gifts. In dealing with sterner subjects her technical knowledge is as yet too weak. . . . The chief spoils of the performance fell to Miss Kathleen Drago, whose acting as Sarah had flashes of tragic power and only failed to reach a fine emotional climax because the author deserted her at a crucial moment. . . . We regret we cannot say much for the stage management of *Pro Patria*. At the opening of the play, where Sarah should place a lighted candle in the window as a beacon, there was no ledge or other convenience provided where she could rest it. The attendance was small and the interest evoked only lukewarm.[87]

*   *   *

In Belfast, the Ulster Literary Theatre presented three new plays, along with revivals of *The Drone* and *The Enthusiast*, during the week of 4 December at the Grand Opera House. The first of the new plays, *Charity*, was a one-act by Molly F. Scott of Waterford; and it was first presented on the opening Monday. *The Northern Whig* reported 'A packed house gave a rousing welcome to the Ulster players', and then went on to describe the new play:

> Though dealing with peasant life, it does so in a very different fashion from the other studies staged by the Theatre. They made their mark by their action and humour; in *Charity*, on the contrary, it is largely a question of atmosphere. The author, Miss M. F. Scott, is evidently a novice at playwriting. She misses many good chances that an old hand would have seized of tightening up the story and making it run smoothly and unbrokenly. The constant procession of visitors into the farmhouse, who act as a kind of chorus to the tragedy — for tragedy it is — becomes unwieldy to handle, and the characters crowd the stage unduly without giving the sense of life and movement that a crowd should have. Miss Scott has shirked the difficult business of explanation, so that one finds it hard to puzzle out exactly who everybody is, with the result that the thread of the story at times gets badly snarled. But when one has made these deductions, which are, after all, not crying sins in the work of a beginner, and will easily be remedied by practice, *Charity* remains a singularly appealing piece of work. The central idea of the peasant family who have slaved to the bone to put a son in the church, and discover after his death that his money, which might have set them on their feet, has been willed to "charity", has a fine touch of tragic irony, and is elaborated with convincing skill. Where a professional author would have seen a golden chance of tub-thumping and rhetoric, Miss Scott prefers the more artistic way of dramatic expression, and has the courage to draw no moral, but to lay the stress on the human aspect of the problem. It is not a piece that makes for brilliant acting; the company have to bend all their efforts towards getting the mood of the playwright across the footlights; and the more subdued they are, the better they will achieve this. The players last night showed a good grasp of essentials, but indistinct delivery in the first few moments

161

which really give the audience the clue to the author's idea marred the effect rather badly. Then the grouping was not happy, though this was probably due to inadvertence, and can be corrected without difficulty. But on the whole they caught the spirit of the play, and when it is repeated to-morrow evening they should be well into their stride without any suspicion of the jerkiness that one expects almost as a matter of course at a first performance. Mr. Arthur Malcom as Timothy Tracy was specially good, his rendering of the long-winded story was splendid, and his acting all round did more than that of anybody else to hold the play together. . . .[88]

On the next night, 5 December, the theatre gave the first productions of Rutherford Mayne's *Red Turf* and of William Paul's *The Jerrybuilders. The Northern Whig* thought much more highly of *Red Turf* than did the Dublin papers that reviewed a Theatre of Ireland performance of the play on 6 December.

> *Red Turf* . . . runs no longer than half an hour, but into that there is compressed more of the stuff of drama than would furnish forth half a dozen theatrical successes. In some ways it is the most striking thing Rutherford Mayne has done, and certainly it gives the company one of their biggest chances in the way of emotional acting. The author tried for the same style of effect in *The Troth*, but since then his handling has become surer, and he knows how to get the most out of his material. The story develops swiftly and inevitably, and there is an intensity that one missed in the earlier work. It deals with the grimmest side of Irish land-hunger, the passionate hate that possession of a piece of land can breed between neighbour and neighbour, and no concessions at all are made to the sugar-and-milk school. The sordid bitterness of *Red Turf* may irritate some people, but on others and on those who know Ireland best it will have a tonic effect. It lends itself to bravura acting, but the sensationalism is always within the bounds of possibility, and the company presented it in a fashion that made it ring true. One weak touch was Heffernan's bringing the gun as a present to the Burkes; it gave the secret away at once. The old man, splendidly rendered by Mr. J. M. Harding, has achieved his purpose when he has explained the feud between the families, and Burke's final speech to his wife shows that the murder was more than a blind impulse. The acting all round was exceptionally good: it had the right note of ferocity that the piece demands. As Mary Burke, the woman who rouses murder

162

in the man's heart and then tries to stave it off by a few mild words, Miss Josephine Mayne scored one of her biggest successes. She gripped her audience from the first, and, while always rising to a situation, kept herself well in hand throughout. The statuesque pose at the end is a thought too long; it would perhaps be better if she was drawn by some fatal fascination towards the door and only clasped her hands above her head when the shot rang out. The crooning, too, over the child seemed a false touch. A woman aflame with such rage would not have switched into another mood in a few seconds. . . .

If Rutherford Mayne's *Red Turf* is a study in scarlet, Mr. William Paul's *Jerrybuilders* is a symphony in grey. . . . *The Jerrybuilders* does possess style in a high degree; what impresses one in it is less the plot and the action than the accurate observation of detail, the insight into types, and the skill with which dramatic realism is used to give artistic impression to a side of life in which nine out of ten would fail to see any possibilities. Mr. Paul is a pioneer in his way, one of those who hold that city streets are as interesting as the open field and the "parlour house" as rich an emotional centre as the farm kitchen. . . . The first act in the frowsy lodgings is masterly, one of those happy jets of inspiration that all too rarely flood up in an author's mind. There is scarcely a weak touch in it, though the speeches here and there would bear pruning and the action might move a little more swiftly. But the characters are absolutely alive — Mary Crichton, who reminds one of Meredith's "falcon in a cage, condemned to do the flitting of the bat"; Ada Kelly, resigned to the monotonous grind of existence; Rowan, with his airy dreams; the inimitable Rev. Joseph M'Curdy, and that gem of a landlady, Miss Beggs. The whole act has a freshness that promises big things. Mr. Paul states his problem admirably. He can hardly be said to work it out with the same certainty. The second act — the best-mounted scene, by the way, the Theatre has ever staged — is not in tone with the first. One gets the idea that whereas in the first the characters made the play, in the second, clever as some of the handling is, the author is too obviously manipulating the pieces on the board to get a dramatic effect. His Mary Crichton is the best-planned and most ambitious study of a woman in any of the Ulster plays up to the present, but, though one can see what the author aims at, he has not quite realised it. This is due, not to lack of sympathy with her, but to over-partiality. We are made to see everything through her eyes, and yet she herself is never explained, and remains to the end "une femme incomprise". In the piece she wants to have her cake and eat it too, to play fast and loose with Rowan and sell herself to Grainger for position, and then in the country phrase "rue her bargain". Now, one imagines that Mr. Paul did not intend to convey this impression at all; if one reads between the lines his idea seems to be that the woman should not necessarily have been tied to either of the two men, that she should have been able to live her own life as she would have liked to live. The misfortune is that this does not come out in the written words, and Mary remains an enigma to the end. But, though the writing does not always do her justice, the acting did. Miss Eveleen Fitzgerald's interpretation of the part was a real triumph. She is the best recruit the Ulster players have enlisted for many a day, though recruit is not the right word for one who showed a veteran's command of her art. Some of the speeches she has to deliver are rather sermons than dialogue, but Miss Fitzgerald made them at once natural and impressive, and her treatment of the climax in the second act had a touch of genius. She is a wonderfully fine elocutionist, though one never thinks of elocution when she is speaking, and she uses gesture and action as they should be used — to drive home the words, never for their own sake. Those who care for a finished piece of acting will not miss Miss Eveleen Fitzgerald's performance this week. Miss Kathleen Lawrence as Ada Kelly, the shop girl, made a splendid partner to Miss Fitzgerald; she did so well what she had to do that one only regretted she did not appear in the second act. Miss Marion Crimmins's Eva was also good, and a capital study of a most offensive middle-class type, and one liked the finish of Miss Kelso's Eileen. As Miss Beggs, the landlady, Miss Mary Crothers ran her Kate in *The Drone* very close. If *The Jerrybuilders* shows nothing else, it shows that the actresses in the Ulster Literary Theatre are now able to give the actors a lead. The men were on this occasion rather out of it, though one must make an exception in favour of Mr. Gerald MacNamara's comedy parson, a wonderfully unctuous bit of work. . . .[89]

Earlier in the year, the professional actor Whitford Kane, who was most sympathetic to the Ulster Literary Theatre, arranged for a week's playing at Kelly's Theatre in Liverpool, with an added matinee at the Gaiety Theatre in Manchester. The actors, like those of the Irish National Theatre Society in 1903, were employed by day, and Kane had great difficulty in getting them away from their jobs. Not all of the women players had jobs, but there were other difficulties. As Marion Crimmins remarked, 'I got on because I wasn't very religious, and it wasn't a sin to play on the stage. Whitford Kane had gone round until he was dog-tired, asking all the different mothers. "Oh, no, they wouldn't allow their girls to go to Liverpool, a place they didn't know." ' [90]

The troop opened in Liverpool for the week of 8 May, playing *The Turn of the Road*, *The Enthusiast*, *The Drone*, and *The Troth*, and were well received. Nevertheless, Kane later wrote:

> Though most of the troupe were splendid in the peasant roles of the play, none of them had any sense of professional responsibility. It fell to me to see that no one strayed off for a walk just as the bus was ready to go into Liverpool, and again I had to be on the alert to see that no one escaped before we reached the theatre. I had a terrible time and felt like a hen with a flock of ducks.[91]

\*   \*   \*

In Cork, the Cork Dramatic Society appeared on four different occasions at the Dun Theatre and presented eight plays, half of which were new. On 19, 20, and 21 April, the company presented three one-acts. There was the first production of Daniel Corkery's comedy, *The Onus of Ownership*, and the first production of T. J. MacSwiney's comedy, *Manners Masketh Man*, as well as a revival of MacSwiney's hero play, *The Last Warriors of Coole*. *The Cork Constitution* did not think that the two new comedies marked any great advance:

> *Manners Masketh Man* is really a sketch in dramatic form. It is very well written, the dialogue is good, and the characters well drawn, but the piece never becomes a real, full-bodied one-act comedy.... The scene is laid in a drawingroom of the Brennans. Paddy Brennan, with his sisters, is going to a party. Paddy is young enough to be cynical superficially, and not old enough to be sensible with soundness. He pretends parties are a bore; also pretends to a fine candour, but at the psychological moment, in the presence of Sarah Mullins, a lady evidently, or, at any rate, apparently, of uncertain age, masks himself most completely. Convention conquers him, and one feels he is the young man convention will always conquer. The several

165

characters were, on the whole, well taken. The defects were a certain stiffness at some points, and emphasis, or want of it, at moments in the dialogue. Mr. MacSwiney should do better, and, in all probability, will, but perhaps it will take the trend of *The Last Warriors of Coole*. All the better, if it should.

Mr. Corkery is really an idealist, despite any proofs that may to the contrary be adduced, and one who has followed his work dramatic with interest felt a certain surprise in following *The Onus of Ownership*. That the author of that fine poetic play, *The Hermit* and the three-act play *The Embers* could turn, on a sudden, and write a one-act comedy on the lines of *The Onus of Ownership*, is really startling and, intellectually, uncanny. But the fact remains, and facts are stubborn things. There is uniform merit in Mr. Corkery's comedy. It is a clear-cut and well-conceived picture of a phase of city life. Jeremiah Farrell (Mr. C. B. Ronayne) is the owner of several houses in a poor street or lane of the city, and these houses are far from being in a satisfactory state of repair. Cunning and diplomacy are in the nature of Jeremiah, to whom, and his wife (Miss M. Moynihan), the audience are introduced of an evening when the rain is heavily falling. The fun then turns on the entrance of two tenants, Mrs. Casey, a widow (Miss D. Gilley), and Mrs. Dorgan, a widow (Miss B. Duggan); and there is increased merriment with the arrival of Paddy (Mr. T. O'Hea), brother-in-law to Mrs. Casey, Johnny-boy (Mr. J. Scannell), brother-in-law to Mrs. Dorgan, and Mikus (Mr. P. J. K. Lynch).

The picture would appear to be a true one. The brothers-in-law are to repair the houses, and they are stated to be trades-men; but they are not; one is a bird-catcher and the other a window-cleaner, and, of course, the tenants' houses are never well repaired. The author displays a fine ingenuity in giving contrast to the characters and breadth to the comedy. The dialogue is very well managed, some of the touches being very fine, and the skill in developing the scene as a whole is very considerable.[92]

On 18 and 19 May, the Society revived MacSwiney's *The Holocaust* and Robinson's *The Lesson of his Life*, and gave the first performance of Corkery's Extravaganza in one act, *The Epilogue*. No very adequate description of *The Epilogue* has so far come to light. Mrs. Brooke Hughes in *The Cork Tatler* remarked that 'neither critics nor audience understood it', and *The Cork Constitution* only remarked that:

It is a play dealing with the failure of a dramatic society, which the author is careful to mention, is not the Cork Society, but it is a strain on the audience to be convinced that Mr. Corkery had not his own society in his mind when writing the play. . . . The play was exceedingly well produced, the various characters finding ample representatives.[93]

On 6, 7, and 8 December, the Society repeated *The Onus of Ownership* and produced for the first time MacSwiney's three-act play, *The Wooing of Emer*. Of the new play, *The Cork Constitution* wrote:

It is written in heroic blank verse, with a fine rhythm and balance. There are lines of worth and beauty that are a delight to the ear, and there are whole passages in which description or feeling with thought, find expression in phrases that a poet alone could frame. The defect of the verse would appear to be a certain floridity, and an attenuation of an image or idea by an elaborate embroidery of words. But every poet's work has defects. A play in heroic blank verse is venturesomeness carried to extreme by any author, for, except the word-painting is of a high standard, the scenes well arranged, the action definite and with a forcible culmination, either subjective or objective, an audience is apt to become wearied. Well, Mr. MacSwiney's play has defects in these things, but at the same time its merits are conspicuous. But, to deal with the play, *The Wooing of Emer* belongs to the heroic period, and is written around Cuchullain. The tale is told in Miss Huel's book — how Cuchullain searched for a wife and could find none to please him; how a friend told him of Emer; how he went and saw her, and they loved one the other; how Forgal and Wily, her father, were opposed to the wooing, and Cuchullain goes away, promising when he had performed heroic deeds to return. And he did return, and despite Forgal carried off Emer, he (Forgal) being accidentally killed. In Mr. MacSwiney's play the first act is laid in the shadow of trees beyond the Dun of Forgal at a date after Cuchullain has become acquainted with Emer, and the second and third acts are within the ramparts of the dun. In the first act the author indicates the relations between Cuchullain and Emer, and what may possibly follow from them; in the second act there is shown the anxiety within the dun lest Cuchullain should return and take away Emer, and in the third act is shown his return, his departure with Emer, leaving Forgal broken-hearted. There are some fine and some impressive scenes in the play, but the end is hardly effective. The climax is too long open out and ends on a subjective rather than an objective note. Forgal the Wily in mood furious would make a better picture dramatic than Forgal does as presented. Again, there is a deal more in the play than the cast gets out of it. They do not in the main speak the blank verse as it should be spoken, and, of course, the staging left much to be desired. Adequately staged and well acted, the play would make, one should think, an instant success. At the same time the company deserves praise. The performance was far better than any amateur could give, and ought to improve if the play should be revived. In view of the many limitations, the Cork Dramatic Society are entitled to every praise for essaying a play of very embarrassing difficulties, due to the excellence of the heroic verse and the scenes which need artistic and elaborate staging.[94]

Later in the month, on 27 and 29 December, the play was revived by the Society; and on 26 and 28 December Corkery's *Embers* and Robinson's popular *The Lesson of his Life* were also revived.

# 1912

At the Abbey Theatre, 1912 began with the Number One company still on tour in the United States and with Nugent Monck's School of Acting continuing to give public performances of early English morality and miracle plays. On 4 January, Monck produced *The Annunciation* and *The Flight into Egypt*, but the houses were extremely small. *The Evening Telegraph* suggested why:

> It is doubtful if the revival of these plays and the production of them on the modern stage with charges for admission is exactly the sort of work for which the Abbey Theatre School of Acting is best fitted. Not that there was any want of reverential feeling in the performances last night. Quite the reverse. In the acting and in every detail of the production down to the burning of the incense in the theatre before the performance began, the aim of the company appeared to be to realise an atmosphere of sanctity in keeping with the Great Mysteries which the plays commemorated. But this is not what the public expects to find in a theatre which is so much identified with *The Playboy of the Western World*, *The Shadow of the Glen* and similar plays. The public do not go to the theatre to pray, least of all to the Abbey Theatre, and as these performances are given for the benefit of the public, which charges for admission, just like any other theatre, and not like a school, they are a waste of time except in so far as they may be useful for those engaged in them. The plays last night were produced to practically empty benches. It is a pity that it should be so, for the performances were of high merit, and deserved better. . . .[1]

W. J. Lawrence, however, believed that the second company, although they performed capably and even with distinction on occasion, often had small audiences because they were:

> Compelled to make various atonements for the sins of the first [company] in their notoriety-mongering with *The Playboy* in America. It was the only ready means that the Dublin public had of signifying its disapproval of that shameless campaign. But it was a thousand pities that any reason for abstention should have arisen, for several of Mr. Monck's productions were amongst the most delightful, both from a pictorial and dramatic standpoint, ever seen in the Abbey.[2]

W. B. Yeats wrote to Lady Gregory after he had seen Monck's production of the four early English morality, miracle and mystery plays. He was encouraged by what he had seen, especially Monck's performance:

> The general mass of the players are as simple as the old material but there is a certain percentage who have real acting power and who have picked up bad tricks or have a real tendency to trick in themselves. I think in some ways I may be useful to Monck in watching carefully from this point of view. The four mystery plays yesterday were lovely things to look at and Monck's own acting as St. Joseph was really very fine. It was like Frank Fay in *The Interior*. He came to play by an accident, he had cast one of the school for the part but found him shortly before the curtain was to go up making a joke of the part of the play to some of those about him. Monck insists on the work being taken very seriously and especially so in the case of these religious plays so he put the man out of the part and took it himself without rehearsal. It was much the best piece of acting he has done. One of the men was a really excellent 1st Shepherd but his performance was a stage convention. I got Colum to come in. I have commissioned him to go over all these plays and turn them into Irish plays. I mean that every shepherd or peasant is to be an Irish shepherd or peasant and that the old English is to go out. Scholars will probably be indignant but I think the audience will be glad of it. I feel too, that it is necessary in order to free the actors from every trace of trick.[3]

W. B. Yeats also provided Lady Gregory, then in America, with his reasons for the poor attendance:

> I cannot make out whether we have done ourselves good or harm with the mystery plays, we had very poor houses indeed last week, but we had the opera against us which drew a lot of our audience and the wet weather kept more of them away. There is no doubt about the enthusiasm of a good many people on the other hand. I hear of people — the sort of people who would go to the odd places — being shocked at the staging of religious subjects, there have been a good many priests but on Saturday a little group of priests left after the first play (*The Annunciation*). It is a lovely and reverent thing but I daresay St. Joseph shocked them when he says to Mary "I can see that you have taken up with some young man, and I do not blame you." It is a curious study of tenderness

and jealousy. Colum was delighted with that play and all the players said they brought St. Joseph and the religious story so near to one. (I heard this from others too. L.R.B.) He is modernising and Irishising them for us.[4]

On 11 January Monck produced Lady Gregory's one-act play *MacDaragh's Wife* for the first time at the Abbey. Like so many producers employed by Yeats and Lady Gregory, Monck was not entirely allowed to create his own production. Yeats, still under the influence of Gordon Craig, made several suggestions for the scenic arrangements in *MacDaragh's Wife*:

I am taking the dialect work from to-morrow. With the possible exception of *McDaragh's Wife*, with which Monck has gone some distance while I was away. The scenic arrangement was mainly mine in the first instance. I suggested the big double door at the back which opens to show the crowd and I don't remember whether I or somebody else invented the idea of the forge, but it has great pictorial value. The two women sit talking over the fire which one of them stirs from time to time. I am wrong, when the play starts one of them is on a stool looking out of the door. I felt that in a play like this where there is no action you require change of picture to symbolize the change of mood. One gets two fine pictures at the end, the men coming in through the lighted door-way. Then they bring out the coffin which is covered with a cloth or with the "middling clean sheet" or something. The others all kneel. There is this picture for some of McDaragh's final words. Then they raise it to carry it out. I think too, we will got more out of the sound of the pipes from having the great lighted door to suggest distance and mystery.[5]

Not only did Yeats tell Monck how to stage *MacDaragh's Wife*, but he also told Lady Gregory how to rewrite her play in order to improve its structure and, at the same time, make it more dramatic:

We had the Dress Rehearsal of *McDaragh's Wife* last night and I want to give you my impressions while they are still fresh. . . . I feel that the opening conversation of the two women is a mistake. One wants to have the whole thing displayed in action like a child's story. I send you this suggested scenario. "One woman is more amiable than the other, she says that without giving any details that it is a hard thing that the woman in the next room should have none to follow her to the grave, someone passes, she says she will go out and ask them to go to the funeral, the other says it will be no use, the first woman goes out and comes in having met with a refusal, the second woman — who is sitting over the fire indifferently — says something scornful of the dead woman — some piece of gossip. Two more people pass and the same action takes place and on each refusal the second woman says something against the dead woman. At last the first woman gives it up, then they discusss McDaragh and how he will take the news. When he comes in the play is alright. I am not sure whether the passers by should say anything, a distant murmur of speech might be sufficient or it might be better perhaps to bring one of them in. I feel that the force is taken out of the play if we do not see the refusal of sympathy as plainly as we see the granting of it after the pipes are played. Now, as to our production, the scene is beautiful, the double doors of the forge are but half open at the beginning, one flap is shut I mean, we have got the light so that there is a perfect illusion of daylight outside shooting a ray into the house, at the part farthest from the door is the red glow of the forge, but if you think this irrelevant when you see it we could have any sort of a big fire on an open hearth, the essential thing is the big doors. The carrying out of the coffin on the men's shoulders and the gathering of the crowd in the light outside beyond the now opened door are most impressive. Mrs. Roberts is one of the old women, she is adequate; Miss Moloney is the other, she is full of admirable dignity and character though curiously enough she had seemed no good in the other rehearsals. McDaragh is not good, he feels his part, to some extent he knows what to do but his voice is not sufficiently flexible.[6]

The Dublin critics faulted both the play and the acting. *The Evening Telegraph*, for instance, remarked:

It is faulty in construction and in the production of it last night the players were unable to free themselves from its defects. Indeed, they rather added to its artificiality by omitting altogether the closing part of the play as given in the text published in America. . . . When he [MacDaragh] is told that she [MacDaragh's wife] is dead he goes into the room and returns in a moment, and in the presence of the unsympathetic hags delivers a whining speech about the good qualities of the wife he has lost. Here was a bit of defective construction. The place for this outburst was the death chamber and not the forge

172

with the two hags as the audience. But as there was no change of scenery, and as it would scarcely do to make the death chamber the scene of the play, there seems to be only one way of avoiding the artificial situation witnessed last night, and that is not to stage the play at all.[7]

W. J. Lawrence in *The Stage* wrote that Lady Gregory presented an undramatic theme, treated it in an epical way, and allowed her dialogue to ramble:

All these faults have prominent exemplification in *MacDaragh's Wife*, which neither in the ordinary dynamic sense nor in the rarer static sense can be considered drama. There is no unfolding, no development; all is talk and tediousness . . . possibly there may be some elements of drama in all this, but they certainly were not educed by the indirect, verbose, narrative method employed by the author.[8]

Lawrence also found the acting uninspired.

Unfortunately the acting was for the most part tame and spiritless, and only served to accentuate the weakness of the composition. There was a palpable lack of transitional power and variety about Mr. Philip Guiry's MacDaragh, and his acting was too commonplace to give the necessary indications of the eerie powers of the piper. Mrs. Roberts gave but a faint and shadowy outline of the First Hag and failed to rise to the occasion at the juncture where, for the cynical equivocations, the hag is half strangled by MacDaragh. There was more picturesqueness and surety of touch about the Second Hag of Miss Moloney, but unfortunately, after the long opening colloquy, she had little to say and nothing to do.[9]

The evening was not a total loss, for the acting of Violet McCarthy in Rutherford Mayne's one-act *Red Turf* was considerably admired. *The Evening Telegraph* wrote:

The part of Mary Burke, which was filled by Miss Máire O'Neill when the play was first performed in Dublin, was taken last night by Miss Violet McCarthy, a young actress who possesses qualities of grace of manner, sweetness of voice and declamatory power that should win for her a place on the stage equal to that now occupied by the lady whose place she filled last night. In fact it may be said she is another Máire O'Neill. . . . Miss McCarthy is a very clever artiste who can enter into the spirit of the part she has to play. . . .[10]

173

And Jacques wrote in *The Irish Independent*:

> Miss McCarthy, who, I understand, comes from Lismore, has a stage style of her own, in which perfect naturalness is the outstanding feature. There is ease and grace in her movements, and a complete absence of that what-will-I-do-with-my-hands embarrassment that labels the amateur. For twenty minutes or so she kept last night's piece going and never once was she at fault in word or gesture.[11]

On 18 January, the School of Acting revived Boyle's *The Building Fund*, and Lady Gregory's *Dervorgilla* and *The Rising of the Moon*. On this occasion the acting was more generally admired, and *The Irish Times* took particular notice of another young actress, who appeared in Boyle's play:

> . . . the success of the play depended on the performance of Nora Desmond, who gave a remarkable portraiture of the miserly old woman, Mrs. Grogan. In voice, action, and gesture she was the old woman to the manner born. Her study reminded one forcibly of a somewhat similar portrait by Miss Máire O'Neill in the *Riders to the Sea*, and in other respects too she resembled her. Her acting certainly gave promise of a distinguished future and it would hardly be surprising if Miss Desmond proved to be one of the leading ladies of the Abbey.[12]

During his tenure as head of the Abbey Theatre School, Nugent Monck helped train and develop other talented actors and actresses besides Nora Desmond. He possessed, according to W. B. Yeats, 'an organising genius', 'a gift for awakening devotion' and 'a curious influence on the character of those about him'. One of the actors in the Abbey Theatre School, a solicitor called Henry, told Yeats that Monck had helped to make a fellow student, Charles Power, into a more effective actor: simple and unpretentious, what he used not to be. Although Monck had the ability to speak sternly to his students without putting them against him, he did have his personal aversions as Yeats amusingly told Lady Gregory:

> A surprising thing has just happened at the Abbey, about two months ago a young man called Carter came and joined, he was very pretty and very effeminate looking. He told Monck that he sometimes went about in girl's clothes, that his family in order to make him manly had sent him to sea but that it was no good, he has run away and now they had consented to his going on the stage. Monck hated him with a sort of blind fury, and did everything to get rid of him because of his

174

feminine airs. I found that I had a shrinking from him, and noticed that the men generally shared it, at the same time I felt the pathos of the poor boy's life, for he was obviously always trying to ingratiate himself with everybody. He didn't re-join this term, he had an aunt and begged various members of the Company if they met his Aunt not to mention him. Last night in the Green Room a member of the Company told us all how he met the Aunt and the Aunt said "my niece tells me she has had such a pleasant time in the Abbey Company." The result was universal fury, the angriest of all was a young woman who said that he or she had tried to put his arms round her waist. I understand that he or she is now dancing as a woman in the Pantomime! He or she as a young woman would have been perfectly charming.[13]

On 20 January, an informative interview with Monck by J.P.M. appeared in *The Evening Telegraph*:

Having turned to him as a greyhound does a hare I asked him what he thought of the Abbey School of Acting? He at once became enthusiastic. There are, according to him, 65 members at least of the new school, all energetic and sincere, but not all geniuses. I suggest that maybe he had forgotten that he was working on virgin clay. He replied yes, but incidentally re-marked that there are many kinds of clay, some of which are plastic; there are others which are not. With regard to the Abbey School, he mentioned that he had found that the Irish School had wonderful adaptability. In England there were student actors wanting to know the why and the wherefore of every intonation and of every gesture. In Ireland it was differ-ent; the pupils he had met, immediately in most cases after the smallest hint fell absolutely into the parts, the acting might be good or bad, but it was natural, which was its great feature.

Then I suggested, "You had nothing to do with their training, Mr. Monck?" All I could get as an answer was, "I occasionally suggested new movements." To those who have seen the School of Acting, comment on Mr. Monck's remark is superfluous.

I asked him did he find any difficulty in training the School for the mystery plays and the up-to-date Abbey plays. He answered, "To a great extent no." They had a good idea from the far side of the footlights (of which we will deal later on) of the ordinary Abbey plays; in the morality and mystery plays, according to Mr. Monck, and the Dublin public will agree with him, training was wanting. In this he said that their

175

appreciation of the parts, whether from natural talent or from training, was wonderful.

He was getting so enthusiastic on the players that I had to side-track him by asking how he came across the "Abbey" first. He confessed that he staged *King Argimenes* for them at the Court Theatre, London, in last year. I awkwardly enough then asked: "Then you have been in the past a producer as well as an actor?" I got as a reply, "I am principally a producer; my acting you can judge for yourself." I next got him to talk of the Morality and Mystery plays. He had produced several. Mr. Poel practically started the movement with *Everyman*, but our (as we may now call him because he has Irish relations) Mr. Monck promptly followed with the three Chester plays. He then produced in Norwich and London *The Plays of Paradise*, and in London *The Song of Songs*, which were an artistic and also a financial success. He was now getting tired, and I was getting interested, so I stated that I did not believe in the revival of the Mystery plays.

As I expected, I had the sticking point and I stuck to it. His point was that at present in scenery and dress we overburden the play itself and the actors; it is absolutely necessary to go back to early times in order to counteract this growing tendency. He does not want the pre-Elizabethan drama without any adjuncts in the way of scenery to be the predominant feature on our stage. But as the pre-Raphaelite school went back to nature, he wants us to go back to the foundation of drama, and then as the pendulum always swings and then stops, we shall arrive at a happy medium. He was again getting anxious and tired (probably of me), so I said I did not agree with his system of lighting the stage. He promptly defended it. In this world as at present constituted, our lighting comes from on high, except when in the gloaming we sit over a fire. Mr. Monck, who is practical, even though poetical, ignores the gloaming, and wants the light from on high. He instanced as a proof of his theory the success of the lighting in Lady Gregory's new play, *McDaragh's Wife*. There you had an interior or dim and dark, but there was a brilliant burst of sunshine coming through the open door at the back of the stage. He said such an effect could not be produced by footlights. I had seen *McDaragh's Wife*, and had admired the setting, so I could not disagree.[14]

On 10 February, an article in *Sinn Féin* vigorously attacked the Abbey for calling itself a national theatre and yet failing to produce

176

plays in Irish.[15] Over the years this was to become a very familiar complaint; however, on this occasion, five days after the appearance of the article, on 15 February, the theatre did coincidentally produce a play in Irish. This was Douglas Hyde's *An Tincéar agus an tSídheóg* which in its English version, *The Tinker and the Fairy*, had been first produced in 1902 in George Moore's garden in Ely Place. This was the first time, however, that the Abbey had played in Irish, but as Yeats wrote to Lady Gregory, 'I think the play in Gaelic is good policy just now and I hear a good many Gaelic Leaguers are coming.' [16]

W. J. Lawrence said that in thirty years of experience he had 'never seen anything more beautiful in a theatre than his [Monck's] staging of the forest scene in . . . *The Tinker and the Fairy*'.[17] *The Evening Telegraph* also approved of Monck's staging which it said was 'an attempt . . . to reproduce an out-of-door atmosphere in harmony with the dialogue of the play. . . .' It said that 'the setting gave the audience the feeling that they were breathing the air of the woods.' [18]

*The Irish Times* stressed that particular mention should also be made of Michael Conniffe's performance in *The Tinker and the Fairy*, 'which was marked by splendid declamation and thorough conception of the part'.[19] Conniffe was a Galway peasant (as Yeats called him) whose fee and keep at the Abbey Theatre School were being paid for by another member of the school who believed in him. Several weeks prior to the opening of *The Tinker and the Fairy*, Yeats said that Conniffe had given a most amusing performance in the 11 January production of *The Workhouse Ward*. And, according to Yeats, the Abbey school was putting on *Spreading the News* for Conniffe's sake since 'his dialect was a wonderful thing and he was most observant and intelligent.' [20] After Yeats savoured Conniffe's performance in *Spreading the News* on 8 February, he said to Lady Gregory, 'I don't think we have a better Bartley Fallon, there was something delicate and touching about him.' [21] Later, on 18 March, after a rehearsal of W. B. Yeats's one-act farce *The Pot of Broth*, Yeats was again delighted with Conniffe's performance, as he told Lady Gregory: 'Conniffe is beautiful in it, better, I think, even than Fay, he makes it natural, real folk, and I really shouldn't mind it going back into Repertory for touring purposes. There is something curiously touching in his humour, and his business at the enchantment is full of new invention. He is incarnate fantasy.' [22]

Because the opening night performance of *The Tinker and the Fairy*, which played on a double bill with Lady Gregory's three-act comedy *The Canavans*, grossed £11, Yeats was ecstatic. It was

177

much the best house for a Thursday since the Abbey Theatre School began:

> Lady Lyttleton brought down nineteen people including the Duchess of Sutherland and I am told that a good many Gaelic Leaguers — Mrs. Salkeld says she knew about twenty — took places in the balcony instead of the pit to encourage us, at least I'm told so, the pit itself was very empty. We had the leading Gaelic people, but the test will be tomorrow when we will see if we can get the sixpenny people — *The Tinker* was very well done, and of course had a tremendous ovation at the end. Monck made a fine forest scene for it, by mixing up the cloth of *The Piper* with *Argimenes* trees. The Duchess of Sutherland seemed very much interested in it with a view to her Highland Theatre. . . .[23]

Despite the good attendance, not another Gaelic play was performed at the Abbey for twenty-six years. From time to time, individuals like Alice Milligan advocated the production of Gaelic plays despite the fact that such dramas, as she admitted, did 'not often attain to the dignity of being classed as literature. . . .'[24] P. S. O'Hegarty, however, did not believe that the Abbey should perform plays in Irish with only slight literary merit:

> Gaelic Leaguers who do not support the Abbey Players, either through prejudice or because they are not interested in drama, always root out one solitary reason for their hostility. "Why don't they play a play in Irish?" Now that leads naturally to other questions. For instance, are there any plays in Irish worth playing except Padraic O'Conaire's, and not even all of his? Has anybody ever submitted a play in Irish to them? Has the Gaelic League ever asked them to do a play in Irish, or ever helped them to organise an Irish side to their company? And above all, what encouragement have they had in their uphill upbuilding of drama in Ireland from the Gaelic League, and what support from Gaelic Leaguers?[25]

On 29 February, the School of Acting presented for the first time in Dublin the fifteenth-century morality play, *The Worlde and the Chylde*, more commonly known as *Mundus et Infans*.

The central idea of this old play recalls Shakespeare's well-known lines on the seven ages of man. The various stages of existence from childhood to old age are presented. When the erstwhile child has reached the stage of manhood he is led astray by Folly. By the time he has reached old age he finds himself forsaken by the world. The moral is sufficiently obvious, but it was effectively enforced by the old morality, which was well acted last night.[26]

W. J. Lawrence was less laudatory and thought that Monck had tampered too much with the original script:

Certain passages in Manhood's account of the sowing of his wild oats in Southwark no doubt demanded deletion through being a trifle too outspoken for these squeamish days. But, on the whole, one takes leave to think that a somewhat too liberal use has been made of the pruning knife. Most of the female characters, or to speak by the card (seeing that the old moral-ities were acted entirely by men) most of the characters now allotted to women, have been reduced to the level of walking-on parts. If in this respect our task of criticising the acting has been considerably lessened, it has also been rendered light by the obvious limitations of the play. Where the characters are mere abstractions, speaking in alliterative verse, and often making direct appeal to the audience, acting in the modern sense is hardly to be expected. Sensible elocution fulfills nearly all the demands. Looking very like an old-fashioned Hamlet in his sombre doublet and hose, Mr. Nugent Monck not only brought this desirable quality to bear on his assumption of Manhood, but he furthermore contrived to clothe the dry bones of the symbol with human flesh and blood, and to invest it with a measure of individuality. Agonised emotion was also infused into the abstraction when Manhood merged into Age, an abrupt transition indicated with much truth and force by this sterling young actor. Master Hughes, as the Chylde, spoke his lines capitally and showed the necessary effervescence without betraying any trace of that precocious prettiness which offends in the average child actor. Mr. Patrick Wilson, arrayed strikingly as a Franciscan friar, delivered his admonitions as Conscience with telling gravity and power; but Mr. Philip Guiry, as Folly, was much too serious and proved lacking in the necessary volatility and light-heeled grace usually asso-ciated with the type. . . .[27]

On 1 March, it was announced that Monck planned to leave the Abbey and return to England to pursue his acting career. The Abbey players returned from America on 12 March, and the School of Acting dissolved and became the Abbey's Second Company. The Second Company gave its inaugural performance on 19 March in Yeats's *A Pot of Broth* and Boyle's *The Mineral*

*Workers.* They played to very small houses, but that may have been because they were upstaged a few nights earlier by the first performance of the returned First Company.

On 14 March, only two days after their return from the United States, the Number One Company performed *In the Shadow of the Glen, Birthright* and *The Workhouse Ward* to a very large audience. Indeed, Jacques noted that there were no empty seats in the stalls and no spare room in the pit.[28] When Lady Gregory came onstage to announce a change in the programme, she received a great demonstration of welcome. Nevertheless, it would hardly have been an Abbey evening without criticism. It came, predictably, from Jacques:

> But while we did not renew acquaintance with all those interesting people who were under the fire of gun-metal watches and garden produce in New York, and were taken prisoners of war in Philadelphia, we hailed home many of them. It struck me that our old friends have picked up some bad habits — I mean bad stage habits — in America. For one thing neither Mr. Sinclair nor Mr. Kerrigan looked the parts in Synge's play. No Wicklow herd would wear his hair like Mr. Sinclair, and no tramp would be so polished as Mr. Kerrigan. In *The Birthright* again Mr. Fred O'Donovan's toilet was too carefully immaculate.
>
> However, we can forget everything but the acting of Miss Eileen O'Doherty as Mother Morrissey in *The Birthright* — a play that, in my opinion, is the greatest in the repertory of the Abbey Theatre. This opinion has been strengthened after seeing last night's performance. Nothing like the acting of Miss O'Doherty has been witnessed in Dublin for many years. It is not too much to say that the young artiste made the play. The awful silence that followed the curtain-fall was because of her and her tragedy. The vented cheers that followed the silence were for her too. We can give the go-by to many things produced by the Abbey people, but *Birthright* is not one of them.[29]

*The Freeman's Journal,* however, believed that most of the company had benefitted from the tour:

> The chief impression left, as a whole, by the performance was that the American experiences of the players had, if nothing else, very appreciably improved their art. Each and every member of the company seems somehow to be more word-perfect, and all have gained that confidence and assurance that they, to some degree, lacked before their departure.[30]

On 28 March, the First Company gave the premiere of William Boyle's three-act comedy, *Family Failing*, in which Arthur Sinclair scored a great personal success. As W. J. Lawrence wrote:

> If recurrent laughter and applause afford any criterion, the chief honours of the evening must be awarded to Mr. Arthur Sinclair for his delicately humorous and appreciative exposition of the inert but agile-minded Dominic. Rarely have we seen this excellent comedian in a part so well adapted to his powers.[31]

*The Irish Times* commented:

> Mr. Boyle's new play is a great success for Mr. Sinclair. There is hardly any play in the Abbey repertoire which depends so much on the efforts of one star actor as does this. . . . Mr. Sinclair, it is true, seems to revel in every word of his part, but for the other parts there appeared to be much talking without adequate point. Hence some dragging moments. Not, however, while Mr. Sinclair was on the stage. . . . Nothing funnier exists in the whole range of Abbey comedies than Mr. Sinclair as Dominic. . . . Mr. Sinclair, who has no more humorous "creation" to his credit, is himself the play. . . .[32]

And Padraic Colum, reviewing Boyle's play for *The Manchester Guardian*, said that 'In the acting the triumph goes to Mr. Arthur Sinclair. It will be long until we forget his laxity and helplessness, and then his devouring energy.'[33] Ironically, ten days before this performance, Yeats had considered punishing Sinclair. As Yeats told Lady Gregory, he was annoyed with Sinclair for gagging disgracefully in Boyle's *The Building Fund*:

> I don't want to speak to him about it at this moment but he should be told that he will not be allowed to play it again unless he gives an undertaking not to gag. Somebody else must be kept ready to take his place and he should be told that Boyle will have the reason explained to him of the change. I believe the whole question of gagging should be fought out on the Boyle play because he would be afraid of Boyle because of his music hall ambitions. He also gagged in *Workhouse Ward*, but has the excuse there — I'm sorry to say — of the coat not fitting which left him a pause which he would feel justified in filling up as he did with "This is a double-breasted coat. The man that wore it was very thin." But for the excuse I would suggest putting Conniffe in instead. By what I hear from the others Sinclair has become intolerable, for instance

he dislikes Miss Nesbitt, and when she is playing with him finds various ways of making himself offensive to her, interpolating offensive gags for the purpose. I saw him doing the same sort of thing with Pelly on Saturday, he kept interpolating "poor little Mike", and the unhappy Pelly is quite scared enough as it is. It's quite possible that I should simply tell him that he will be taken out of both plays for gagging and that Boyle will be told the reason. One could then let him back on his showing persistence or keep him out. There is a good deal to be said for allowing others to play some of our very popular parts, for good as Sinclair is, his popularity has been greatly made by his parts.[34]

Despite Sinclair's personal achievement in *Family Failing*, and his belief that the play was a great success, it was not given a good critical reception.[35] However, W. A. Henderson had prepared Boyle to expect damnation when he indicated that several of the Abbey players declared *Family Failing* not equal to Boyle's other plays, an opinion which Henderson endorsed after he saw the play performed. Boyle, too, had doubts, as he told Joseph Holloway:

What I feared myself was that the critics would say I was repeating myself, for truly "Dominic" is, though I did not notice this when writing the thing, a kind of mixture of "Shaun Grogan" and "Dempsy". Nobody, however, hints this.[36]

Boyle was upset because he suspected that some of Maria Donnelly's lines had been deleted without his knowledge by the Abbey:

None of the notices gives the least idea of the "Maria" I have conceived. I suspect some of her lines must have been cut out. Her part is almost as big as "Dominic's" and her emotional outbursts — her grumbling at her brothers and allowing no one else to do the same gives, to my mind, the best acting part I have written. Either I am grossly deceived in my character drawing or the "reading" is all wrong. I believed "Maria" would stand out very prominently as a feminine creation.[37]

It was the Abbey management, so Boyle believed, that was in part responsible for the poor critical reception of *Family Failing*:

Henderson somewhat hypocritically laments that I was not able to be present at the rehearsals. As if I would not have been able had I the least belief I would have been permitted! Clearly they did not wish me to be there on the first night or they would have told me when the play was to come on. If the piece had not been killed, I owe its escape, I am convinced, to the players rather than the management. I fancy I am the only author living who was denied the advantage of seeing his own piece rehearsed and picking up the dropped stitches in his knitting. Surely the Dublin critics might make a little allowance for this since they can't be ignorant of the Abbey's way of treating me.[38]

Frank Fay, however, had little sympathy with Boyle because he believed, as he said to Joseph Holloway, that Boyle allowed his principals to be purchased by the Abbey management:

I had heard a while ago about Boyle's new play. I cannot understand Boyle's having denounced *The Playboy* and left the Abbey Theatre, and then turning round, and when there is money to be got out of them, and selling his plays to an institution which in his opinion, is libelling the Irish people. Even recently he wrote an article on *The Playboy* in a Scotch paper against the *Playboy*. Boyle would not have got a look in the Irish National Theatre Sociey or, later, at the Abbey but for Will and I. We had to fight for him against almost the whole Society who didn't think his work "class" and didn't know a good acting play when they read it. Had Boyle not broken off the *Playboy*, but stood by Will and I, we'd have been in the Abbey still, because the popularity of his plays was a strong weapon in *our* hands to fight the Gregoryization of the theatre. The old lady was fiercely jealous of Boyle, and was greatly relieved by his succession. On the Monday after the production of the *Playboy*, I saw her in the morning and she said to me "that's a rotten branch gone".[39]

The play itself was not a great success. *The Irish Times* thought it too discursive, and Padraic Colum thought it too 'relaxed in structure. The play drifts along in dialogue and spasmodic action.'[40] W. J. Lawrence justly remarked that 'after an opening act of genuine comedy, the action descends to a farcical — almost ultra-farcical plane, and towards the end one detects a palpable forcing of the note.' [41] This judgment prompted Boyle to a defence:

I know it is not as good as "Dempsy" but it is a much better play than the "Min. Workers". I can see that the way in which Robinson "produced" it exaggerated its farcical aspect. I had nothing about fire irons being polished — never thought of such a thing — and as far as emery paper —!! [Lawrence in his review had said: 'Humorous, by the way, as is the situation at the opening of the third act, when he bustles about

183

cleaning everything and anything — the business of the scene is overdone. The imagination boggles on finding a small Irish farmer vigorously polishing up the fire-irons with emery paper!!'] Well, the Donnellys are not the sort of people would know even what it was. How little those Abbey people know of country life is apparent from their bringing in such "business". Then again I had nothing in my stage directions about a "stretcher bed". I had about a *bed chair* — one of those cheap iron things with gaudy cotton cushions round which a good deal of the "business" turned [Lawrence said that "old Robert willingly accepts a stretcher-bed in the parlour"] and I had in the first act a saddle and bridle hanging on the brick wall which the servant girl was to pull down (not the wall — the saddle and bridle) and run out with when she could not find a rope to pull the old cow out of the bog hole. It is farcical, no doubt, but I have seen it actually done in an emergency. But where's the use of talking? You Dubliners know more of farm life than the farmers. I made a play to amuse an audience legitimately, and they were amused — that's the main thing.[42]

Later in the year, however, Boyle rewrote the play for publication:

I have "patched up" *Family Failing* by largely rewriting Act II and mending all the rest of it and have sent it to Gill for printing. You think patching up is useless. I can tell you the whole of play writing is one continual business of patching, and I very much doubt that a good play has ever been written without mending again and again — especially in rehearsal. I am certain I have improved it. I have hacked off the beginning of this act and commence with Jos and Dominic resting after their day's exertions and Mrs. Carragher coming in with the things in her basket.[43]

On 11 April the Abbey produced for the first time Lennox Robinson's three-act play, *Patriots*, and most of the critics strongly admired it. In *The Evening Herald*, Jack Point said that *Patriots* 'is much the best of his works, and . . . truly a valuable addition to the Abbey repertoire'.[44] *The Daily Express* thought it 'one of the best plays that has seen the light in the Abbey Theatre for some time', and also thought it 'very cleverly conceived' and the dialogue without 'a word too much in it'.[45] Robinson himself echoed these sentiments thirty years later when, in his autobiography *Curtain Up*, he referred to the play's 'precise construction, the tightness of its dialogue. . . .'[46] J.P.M. in *The Evening Tele-*

*graph* also thought the play 'the best thing Mr. Robinson has done for the Abbey', but criticized the content:

> The physical force movement in this country is held up to a great deal of sympathy, and its advocate last night, James Nugent otherwise Fred O'Donovan, received loud applause. However, the movement which is generally referred to as the Parliamentary, did not get equal justice. Its prototypes were shown as having not the smallest symptom of backbone, and there was not one single member of what was referred to as the "League" — what League was left to guesswork — who could be said to represent the force and intellect of the Parliamentary Party as contrasted to the exceptionally well-drawn character of James Nugent, the physical force advocate. This was a cardinal fault in the play.
>
> Stress was laid, and decidedly too much stress in the writer's opinion, on what might be called the apathy of the provinces to virile nationalism to-day, but no explanation was properly given of the change which twenty years has brought in developing what may be called the Parliamentary machine. The period of twenty years is taken not from the writer's mind, but from the play itself.[47]

On 15 April, a Miss Byrne wrote to Yeats, who was in London, a quite vivid description of the play's reception:

> It is quite the best thing he has done — though now he says he feels that he could have done so much better — and I think one cannot help feeling that there is even better work to come from him yet. The effect on the audience was quite extraordinary, they never seemed to miss a point on either side, they listened with rapt attention like a class of well behaved school children eager to be taught and willing to hear all their faults with meekness, I never remember an audience quite like it, there was lots of laughter where there should be, and choking sobs the next moment, and on all sides I heard from the pit and when I moved in the stalls such things as "a wonderful play", "a marvellous piece of characterisation", "Not a word that is unnecessary, every speech tells", "so wonderfully well balanced", "a remarkable work", "what brains that man has". And the funny part is that no one could be sure what his politics were! The applause came in such bursts here and there that the players had to stop, particularly at the end of the Second Act, where James leaves his old friends finding they are no longer in sympathy with his ideas,

O'Donovan was splendid, I think it is the best part he has had, indeed they all acted it as if they *felt* it all, the only blot on it was poor Power, in one bit I liked him, but in most of it he was so very much "Power", full of artificiality and tricks, though honestly I believe that many of his tricks are natural to him, for the other morning I was writing for Mr. Robinson in his room, when Power came in and his manner was very much the same, he can never forget himself, and it is not a pleasant self! Miss Drago as the crippled girl was a wonderful study, but she did not speak at all distinctly at all times, and there were times when it was quite impossible to hear Sinclair, but this did not happen at all the performances, of course, I told Mr. Robinson, and I think he spoke about it.[48]

The disapproving opinions came, predictably, from Jacques, Holloway and Lawrence. Jacques, for instance, wrote:

After one act of it I thought I should go writing the heading differently — Patriots at the Abbey. The second act was no better, and the third! Ah well. There were no riots. There was tolerant laughter from the select stalls and loud applause from the deeply impressed pit. . . .

It is a theme out of which a deft dramatist who knew his powers and recognised his limitations might make an interesting play. What Mr. Lennox Robinson has produced is something that strives to be distinguished and remains always just commonplace. The Abbey players are wasted in it. Mr. F. Donovan as the central figure, has to throw speeches off his chest like to those delivered of old by the Boucicault heroes.[49]

Lawrence's review in *The Stage* was equally unflattering, but a sustained, informative and well-documented assault. He believed that the piece was weakened by discursiveness, tedious exposition and 'depicting the existence of a physical force party, so comparatively recent as the year of 1893, a flouting of fact that destroys the illusion of action for all save the most ignorant of Irishmen.'[50] A present-day critic would probably consider the play a worthy piece for its time, but hardly one that would bear revival.

On 15 April, Joseph Campbell's two-act play *Judgment* was performed by the second company, but only after much fuss and several lengthy letters between Yeats, Robinson and the author. As early as 26 July 1911, Yeats wrote Campbell to say that he, Lady Gregory, Robinson and another reader had read, but were perplexed by the play. Yeats felt it 'a most imaginative thing' with 'considerable dramatic power', but with 'a sudden failure of interest' toward the end:

One expects a third act to almost the last movement. One expects "the stranger" whose entrance is most imaginative to influence events more decidedly. . . . The play should close on the emotion the whole play builds up, a sense of obscurity and mystery of life and not conclude as it is. Accept your inconclusive end, insist on it, make a point of the collapse of interest. Life is like this. Make defeat a point of art.[51]

Despite his reservations Yeats held out hope for a production in the Spring. On 17 January 1912, after an interview with Yeats, Campbell sent the script to Nugent Monck to be produced by the School of Acting, but a few days later the play was returned with the statement, 'Mr. Monck has decided to leave the production of your play *Judgment* until the return of the Abbey Players from their tour in America, as it could need more experienced players than members of the school of acting.' [52] After the First Company returned from the United States, Campbell again wrote to Yeats about the play, but received a reply from Robinson who said, 'We do not think that the second company is experienced enough to play your play. There seems to be no possibility of getting to it before next Autumn, when we [the First Company] will be a whole season in Dublin and have more time.' [53] Two days later, Robinson wrote again to say that the Second Company would perform the play.[54] Campbell, now somewhat exasperated, remarked, 'in the time I have spent writing foolish letters and answering foolish replies I might have written quite a decent satire on the methods of the Abbey Directors!' He continued:

Well really I don't mind who does it, or if it is done at all. Your second company — I think — and you agree — is incompetent to do a play in which acting is required. They are all right going through a mystery or morality in which they have antique words to speak in a mildly beautiful way — but they never convey — at least to me — the feeling of sincerity. There is not a member of the second company with a spark of personality or intelligence except Mr. Conniffe. He has a voice worth money and a presence which grips both in comedy and tragedy.

I will consent to the production of *Judgment* by the second company on condition that my name is suppressed as author and that I am cast (anonymously) for the part of the "stranger" myself — without salary of course.[55]

'Campbell,' wrote Yeats to Lady Gregory, 'has been writing the most ill-bred letters.' [56]

In any event, neither Conniffe nor Campbell appeared in the play, and Campbell was actually barred from rehearsals. As Robinson said, 'I never let anyone attend my rehearsals. I have never found it a satisfactory plan. I think your play will go all right.' [57]

Robinson was wrong, for the play was generally slated. According to Lawrence in *The Stage*, excessive realism was the problem.

> Dramatic photographers overlook the fact that the fragrance of life, artistically speaking, lies not so much in life itself as in the philosophy to be extracted from it. That is why audiences resent being brought face to face with the naked verities in all their gross and palpitating ugliness.[58]

Lawrence also thought that the staging was unfortunate:

> Although the play is wholly and solely a slice from life, and as such devoid of all theatricality, the scene shows two rooms arranged after the approved method of conventional melodrama, with the partition down the middle. In the one room are assembled the women of the district praying round the corpse; in the other the men engaged in converse about the deceased. In a play of this order the arrangement impairs the illusion, and, in a small theatre like the Abbey, seriously hampers the action. As the view of the corpse is purely for spectacular effect, it would suffice if seen through an open door at the back.[59]

*The Irish Times* faulted the play for touching on the seamy side of life, and J. H. Cox in the *Independent* thought it marred throughout by desultory and uninteresting talk.[60] A hard, stark study of Donegal peasant life, *Judgment* was certainly a difficult play to do effectively, and it obviously was not done effectively. Nevertheless, it was a piece of some achievement, and perhaps if it had been done better Campbell might have been encouraged to write more for the stage.

In any event, Yeats returned the play to the author on 6 May, saying that the theatre surrendered all rights to it.[61] In an earlier letter, Yeats had remarked that he thought the play 'full of imagination and suggestion' but with no chance of 'success with an audience':

> We put it on, that you might see your work on the stage and so have the chance of learning your craft of dramatist. We look upon it as part of our duty to give dramatists this chance though it of necessity means a money loss. We put on the

188

play in fact not for the audience but for your sake. It was better to do it with a second company than wait on, in the remote chance that the first company would have time for it. You will yet do a fine play I believe.[62]

Shortly after, Campbell himself told the actor Whitford Kane that he might have the play for an American tour, but warned that it was 'a strong, unpleasant play' that 'won't be popular with ordinary audiences'. Campbell thought that the first act had been well received in Dublin, and might be performed by itself. He did offer to work on the second act if Kane wanted a complete play, and said of the second act, 'At first the ending was much stronger. Yeats asked me to change it, and I spoiled it!' [63]

Yeats did not see the production of *Judgment*, as he was in London arranging for a production of *The Workhouse Ward* at the Prince of Wales Theatre. That production with Michael Conniffe, Farrell Pelly and Sheila O'Sullivan did not go smoothly, for the stage manager at the Prince of Wales continually interfered with the actors. As Yeats reported:

The very first day he wanted me to tell them to have neither accent nor dialect during the first few minutes of the play. Now our art is the reverse of all this. We say first of all be old men and do not expect to please everybody. We begin with expression as in all the other arts and not with the public.[64]

The Prince of Wales's directors particularly objected to Conniffe's Galway accent which they thought a London audience would not understand. Although Yeats agreed that Conniffe's performance was lost in a large theatre before an audience that knew little of Ireland, he was delighted by Conniffe whom he found a fountain of humour. He also thought that the Abbey should have no further dealings with theatres in England unless an experienced individual with an understanding of the contemporary stage accompanied the players.

If Monck had been with us now he could have come over and rehearsed them [the Abbey's second company] and stood between them and the Stage Manager here, and on the very first night would have known if changes were necessary. We must never send these people out without some professional person ready to act in our interest. . . They will always require . . . one thoroughly experienced player to hold them together and as I think to represent us in dealing with the management of theatres. He should find substitutes if a player gets ill and so forth.[65]

189

In the meantime, the main Abbey company left Dublin at the end of April for an English tour that would take them to Belfast, Liverpool, Manchester, Glasgow and London. Everywhere they were received with great enthusiasm.[66] A typical comment was that of W. F. Casey, the popular Abbey dramatist who was now a London journalist and who was to become the editor of *The London Times*:

> Irish drama is the only drama of our time in which you will find romance. So far as I know there is not a single English dramatist — with the exception, perhaps, of John Masefield in whose work one gets romance. One gets sentiment, pathos, wit (sometimes), force, tragedy even, but never romance. The theatre in England seems to be bound helplessly by the manacle forged first by Oscar Wilde, and fastened more firmly on by Bernard Shaw — the manacle of cleverness. Every writer for the stage is obsessed with the notion that he must be clever at all costs. Now cleverness, when it is natural and when it is big enough, cleverness like Wilde's or Shaw's, is all very well, but it is also very rare. Unfortunately, shrill, small cleverness is exceedingly plentiful, and so poor London is surfeited with cleverness — and bored, bored. In our souls we are aching for something very different; consciously or merely instinctively, we want romance. London is tired of wit, however clever, that is self-conscious and given with a nod and a wink to see how we're taking it; she is tired of strong situations, however brilliantly contrived; wearily we ask for romance. The Irish Theatre is the only theatre in which it is to be found.[67]

Casey, like many others, believed that it was the unaffected simplicity and versatility of the Abbey Players which made them so special:

> The Abbey Theatre players are wonderful. Their most obvious quality, the secret no doubt of much of their power, is simplicity; but observe — if there be any need to point it out — that this simplicity in no way excludes subtlety or profundity. This simplicity of which I speak seems to come from a certain humbleness and devotion in the artist; it is characteristic of all great art, of whatever sort, for without it the art has a way of becoming too self-conscious, artificial, and bad. But to me the most astonishing thing about these players is their versatility. To the regular playgoer, accustomed to seeing his favourite actors and actresses doing much the same thing in quite the same way year after year, this versatility comes as a delightful revelation. Any one or two of the programmes

190

will illustrate it. The other night I saw one of the new plays —
*Patriots*. In the second act Mr. J. M. Kerrigan appeared as a
priest, a sincere man, a little disillusioned, with too much
generosity of mind for his own comfort; and in the last act
Mr. Kerrigan played the part of a mean, cynical, talkative old
caretaker of a country town hall. In each case he was perfect.
I am certain that no one, however observant, in the audience
could have told without reference to his programme that the
parts had been doubled by the same actor.

Or take Miss Sara Allgood. Last week as Kathleen ni
Houlihan she was thrilling and charming with her beautiful,
tragic voice, so that it rang afterwards, hauntingly, in one's
ears; this week you can see her, wonderfully different, as the
soured, unattractive, well-to-do shop-keeper who broods silently and hatefully over her wrongs, and then finally bursts out
to save her child. Or you can see her as Mrs. Broderick in
*The Jackdaw* — the most comical figure of tearful helplessness
imaginable. And so with the others. This wide range and their
simplicity and the romance of the plays are what make the
whole thing such a sheer joy.[68]

While the Abbey Players were in residence at the Royal Court
Theatre in London, they staged two premieres, T. C. Murray's
*Maurice Harte* and Lady Gregory's *The Bogie Men*. Murray's play
was originally called *The Levite*, and on 17 March he wrote about
it to Holloway:

I wonder have they rehearsed *The Levite* in America? I rewrote the second act since I sent the original ms. and Yeats
seems to think it in its present form a much stronger play than
*Birthright*. In one sense it will strike a new note on the Abbey
stage in as much as the atmosphere of the play is strikingly
Catholic. Yeats said he thought they would produce either
this or Robinson's new play soon after returning.[69]

The play, of course, did not receive its first production in Dublin,
and this disappointed Murray because:

The whole atmosphere of it is Catholic and Irish in its best
sense. . . . Four priests — three of them on the Dublin mission
— have read the ms. and have given it as their opinion — that
it is elevating and that it introduces for the first time perhaps
the note of Irish Catholic life on the Abbey stage.[70]

When *Maurice Harte* opened in London on 20 June, Lady Gregory
said that Murray 'was called for by the audience and had a tremendous reception. . . . It makes one feel repaid for so much

work.' [71] The play was to be one of Murray's most popular, but the initial press reaction was certainly mixed. E.F.S. in *The Westminster Gazette* thought the new piece a good deal poorer than *Birthright*:

> It seems to me that there is a serious fault in the way of repetition. The first act and the second, in a sense, are almost identical in chief scene and situation, the only difference being that in the earlier the catastrophe is averted, and when the catastrophe comes one feels it to be accidental rather than inevitable. In each act we are taken through the same series of emotional states in the same order; moreover, I doubt whether the subject justifies the author in harrowing our feelings with a catastrophe even worse than death. Finally, by way of fault-finding, I venture to suggest that it is a real weakness that the objection of Maurice to enter the priesthood is treated axiomatically. This objection and its foundations are the real basis of the play; yet we are left entirely ignorant whether his difficulty is on a point of dogma, or whether he feels himself too weak to withstand the instincts of the flesh, and therefore dare not undertake the calling.[72]

One of Murray's constant characteristics was the slow, meticulous build-up to the powerful climax. This early slowness seems to have been noticed in *Maurice Harte* by Murray's fellow Corkman, D. L. Kelleher:

> This play, in many ways more subtle than *Birthright*, suffers, however, from overlapping. Brilliant and intensely moving as it is, act one, wherein the young clerical student declares that he will not return to Maynooth, and yet, at last, unbends to his parents and his parish priest, might have been condensed into the exposition of act two. . . . Mr. Murray, in beating his play out into two acts, has demonstrated his details for the benefit of the less quick-witted amongst his audience.[73]

When Murray's climaxes finally did come, they erupted with powerful abruptness. Some critics thought the ending of *Maurice Harte* actually too abrupt,[74] but others, in what is really a considerable testimony to Murray, thought his ending really too painful for the stage.[75]

Almost all of the critics who saw the first London performance spoke of the skill of the Abbey Players. Murray, however, believed that his play 'was produced in a very imperfect state':

> With the exception of Sydney Morgan as the priest — a study which will delight Catholic Dublin — there was a lack of

subtlety — almost crudeness in the whole interpretation. More than once it was easy to see Sara Allgood prompting Sinclair and Eileen O'Doherty who were simply groping through the entire action![76]

Sara Allgood, however, in the role of the mother, was most strongly praised by all of the critics. Yeats, curiously enough, was not always impressed by Sara. A few months before *Maurice Harte*, he had written to Lady Gregory:

The utmost Miss Allgood can reach to, when not helped by observation is emotion as undistinguished as that of Longfellow's poetry. She acted my *Deirdre* as if it were an extract from *Evangeline*. There is nothing personal in her emotions, I shudder at the thought of her ever doing work of mine where there is any complexity of feelings. I don't think she will be good in *The Countess Cathleen* but she may get through it without destroying the play for the range of emotion is small, not very subtle, and she is never long enough on the stage to be monotonous. If she had tried to educate herself she might have got some tragic power in the sense that I am using the word. . . . I wish that Sally's ambitions had inspired you instead to write her some part which would display all her capacity where that is extraordinarily great — that is to say where it is confined within limits of sympathetic observation; if you could make a play like *Canavans* with a woman's part as prominent in it as the man's part is in *Canavans* and the subject matter of the same sort or a tragi-comedy which would no more draw on her creative powers than *Riders to the Sea*, you would make her fortune and the fortune of the Theatre. I am sorry to write all this but I don't want you to promise to her what I may have to greatly oppose, the taking of an oratorical or monotonous or commonplace Grania performance to England or America. Watching the members of the School has shown me more clearly than ever that the distinction always is between those who act from experience and those who act from observation. We may never get an actress with real emotional power but that makes it all the more necessary not to kill fine work by giving it to our people while they are not ready for it. Your *Grania* published in a book will attract some emotional actress in America or in England if we do not force the play into failure. Miss Allgood may do what she likes in Dublin but I feel at this moment as if I would rather give up the whole theatre than allow her to spoil your play anywhere else.[77]

Nevertheless, the Abbey Players were having an extremely successful London season. Murray described them as 'fashion's latest cult',[78] and Lady Gregory wrote John Quinn that 'Lloyd George has been twice and brought a party of six last time. Sir E. Grey and other Cabinet Ministers have been and smart society crowds in. I have twice had Duchesses in my box, very glad of a seat.' [79] *The Northern Whig*, in reporting on the theatre's popularity, also justly noted that the nature of the theatre's repertoire had changed:

London during the last few weeks is witnessing an Irish boom elsewhere than in the House of Commons. At the Court Theatre the Abbey Players, whose tour, it will be remembered, began in Belfast, have made the dramatic hit of the season, scoring an even greater success than during their six months' visit to the States. According to the paragraphists they have drawn to see them all sorts and conditions of notabilities, from Sir Edward Grey to Mr. Ben Tillett; in fact, not to have been at the Court is to label oneself as neither fashionable nor intellectual. One section of the community, however, while joining in the general welcome, is palpably ill at ease. Even to the casual reader the critical notices betray more than a hint of bewilderment; thickly peppered as they are with praise of the acting, one divines behind them a growing doubt as to the ends which the acting is meant to serve. The formulas that seemed so right a few years ago no longer apply; in face of plays like *Patriots*, *Thomas Muskerry*, and *Maurice Harte*, to describe the Irish school in the old terms as sounding "faint harmonics of weird elfish freakishness", or as "a shimmering oasis of fantasy in a desert of drab drama", is flatly absurd. The Theatre, it is not denied, is doing things, only they are the things nobody expected it to do. Instead of being "glamorous" and "mystical", the new writers are uncompromisingly realistic and practical, they are more interested in potato patches than fairy rings, and find inspiration in the facts of the present rather than in the high heroic memories of the past. To judge by the emphasis practically every London critic lays on the absence in the later plays of the poetic symbolism of Mr. Yeats or the coloured imagery of Synge, one feels that in their view the new school of dramatists has swerved from its true line of advance into a blind alley.[80]

Lady Gregory's *The Bogie Men*, the other new play produced in London, opened on 8 July, and both the play and the actors were slated. *The Referee* thought it 'an artless trifle',[81] and *The Pall Mall Gazette* thought:

> Lady Gregory's play was a disappointment. Its little joke did not quite come off. Mr. Kerrigan and Mr. O'Rourke were partly, no doubt, to blame; they were nervous and often indistinct. But no actors could have made the play as compact and clear as it should have been. The idea is capital but the working out of the idea is vague and ineffective. . . . After it is all over you think how funny it ought to have been. And it would have been extremely amusing if it had been worked with the neatness Lady Gregory usually puts into her work. As it was, the joke of it fell flat, and Mr. Kerrigan and Mr. O'Rourke were not really responsible for its flatness.[82]

Although Kerrigan and O'Rourke were obviously insufficiently rehearsed, *The Globe* thought that their acting showed up certain general inadequacies common to the Abbey Players:

> It is when the Irish players are called upon to present a work essentially undramatic and lacking in action that what is monotonous in their methods is made most apparent. These actors from the Abbey Theatre, Dublin, discard almost entirely the aid that gesture gives to the players' art, so that such a one-act play as *The Bogie Men* by Lady Gregory, given for the first time last night, resolves itself into little more than a dialogue, and one in which the suggestion of recitation rather than natural speech is emphasised. From what one could understand of *The Bogie Men* (and neither the writing nor the delivery was any too clear) Lady Gregory has given us another piece more literary in form than dramatic.[83]

According to Ann Saddlemyer, Lady Gregory herself was not happy with the play and in her copy made several textual alterations:

> Originally Taig forces Darby to leave the coach-shed while the two sweeps effect their transformation; she has simplified construction and production by keeping both characters on stage throughout. She also strengthens the dialogue by eliminating much of the talk between the two characters when they are at cross-purposes. Doubtless these alterations would have been further tested in performance before the creator was completely satisfied, but once again we can observe her determination to toughen pattern and eliminate any weakness or slowing-down of the action.[84]

On 11 July, at the Royal Court, the Abbey Players presented a new revision of Yeats's *The Countess Cathleen*. The production by Nugent Monck received generally mixed notices. For instance:

> The third scene in the hall of the Countess Cathleen was beautiful in colour and design; and the curtains used in the other scenes were simple and good, and the lighting effective. But there were several clumsy hitches which should have been avoided — the whispering and noise before the last scene, and the glare of light from the ground-floor box before the angel's entrance. Nor were the spirits who came to carry away the gold at the demons' bidding at all well managed.[85]

*The Pall Mall Gazette* noted that the present version in some ways did not improve on either the 1892 or the 1901 versions:

> . . . there are things we miss in the present version, especially the deafness of Oona and the scene in which Cathleen repeats to her the news of evil brought by the gardener and the herd; her speeches bring out the beauty of her character almost as much as when she says to the poet, Aleel:
>
> > God's procreant waters flowing about your mind,
> > Have made you more than kings or queens; and not you
> > But I am the empty pitcher.
>
> That love-scene was never a waste place, but Mr. Yeats has touched the old beauty with new colour, and has made it more beautiful. Her bidding him to go,
>
> > And silently, and do not turn your head;
> > Good-bye; but do not turn your head and look;
> > Above all else, I would not have you look.
>
> is a fresh inspiration, like the depth of feeling in her saying after she is alone —
>
> > I never spoke to him of his wounded hand
> > And he is gone.
>
> And the beauty of it made us all the more angry that the Countess Cathleen should turn from her poet-lover to her little chapel, because all her heart was possessed by the grief of others. What had she left to give them but gold and hope of a future life — she who could not take her present joy to heart?
>
> In the famine the peasants were selling their souls for money to demons who were disguised as merchants. The Countess gives them money to save their souls and at last

being robbed of her possessions, she, too, sells her soul to the demons for five hundred thousand crowns. It breaks her heart, and she dies. But the demons have not got her soul; for an angel tells her lover

The light beats down; the gates of pearl are wide,
And she is passing to the floor of peace,
And Mary of the seven times wounded heart
Has kissed her lips, and the long blessed hair
Has fallen on her face.

The entrance of that angel was a blot upon Mr. Nugent Monck's production. There was first a flame of light in the ground-floor box and some whispering, then she appeared, holding a feeble torch, and, mounting the steps from the stalls to the stage, she made her way across in a slanting line. The arrangement completely failed to gain any effect, and spoiled the last scene of the play. With the exception of this angel, and the capering spirits who come at the demon's bidding to carry off the money bags, the production was in the right spirit, and no doubt these defects will be immediately remedied.

The demons themselves were very well played by Mr. Hewetson and Mr. Kerrigan. And Mr. Patrick Murphy, as the first peasant to call them in from the woods, helped to make their entrance intensely weird and impressive. Indeed, the whole of Mr. Murphy's performance was keen and admirable. Miss Máire O'Neill returned to the company to play the Countess Cathleen, which she played at the first production of the play at the Abbey Theatre. She has a beautiful voice and fine feeling, but has not the emotional power or dignity of Miss Allgood. Mr. Fred O'Donovan was a great disappointment as Aleel, the poet. He did not appear to realise the meaning of what he said.[86]

When the theatre presented the new version in Dublin in September, Sara Allgood replaced Máire O'Neill as the Countess and was highly praised, but Fred O'Donovan's Aleel was still disliked.[87]

The Abbey Players returned to Dublin in the last week of August. Nugent Monck returned with them, to be associated with Robinson in the day-to-day management, which Yeats and Lady Gregory increasingly wished to avoid.

While the Players had been on tour, the theatre was redecorated, and Jacques remarked:

Black and white and bright gold predominate in the scheme of decoration — a suggestion, perhaps, that the Abbey has left

197

behind it its days of full mourning. And if the theatre is filled to overflowing at every performance as it was last night, we need not trouble to question the symbolic value of gold in the mural colouring.[88]

On 3 October, the Second Company appeared at the Abbey in *The Second Shepherd's Play* and *The Country Dressmaker*, but from 9 October through much of November they toured the provinces, visiting such places as Carlow, Maryborough, Tullamore, Kilkenny, Naas, Mullingar, Athlone and Galway. The company conducted a 'fit-up' tour in which they carried everything necessary to convert the ordinary platform of any hall into a fully equipped stage for each two-night stand. Mid-way through the tour, Yeats told Lady Gregory that he 'never thought the second company good enough for anything but very small parts in music halls. . . . I am against accepting an engagement until they are actually good enough. We cannot risk the reputation of the theatre.'[89] Nevertheless, the Second Company was frequently admired; and Michael Conniffe as Hyacinth Halvey, Nora Desmond as Kathleen Ni Houlihan and as Mrs. Grogan in *The Building Fund*, and H. E. Hutchinson as Shaun Grogan in *The Building Fund* were particularly noted.[90]

The provincial tour of the Second Company provided many rural Irishmen with their first view of the new Irish drama, and one correspondent for *The Irish Times* was as much interested in the reaction of the audience at Doneraile as he was in the plays being performed:

> How delighted these peasant folk were, their bright, fresh faces reflecting the joy in their hearts at seeing for the first time genuine Irish plays. They had, of course, probably seen in that hall travelling companies in some blood-curdling melodrama, but here was Irish life, their own life, presented to them in some of its various phases. In following the plays they showed that intellectual keenness which characterise their race. They did not miss a single point. They never laughed or applauded out of place. They responded to the call of the players like true playgoers. The casual visitor from Dublin became infected with their enthusiasm, and, although he had seen the plays often before, he followed with the audience every movement on the stage, and his ears, with theirs, were strained to catch every word. Seldom did he enjoy a performance more heartily. Players and audience were in perfect accord.[91]

According to *The Evening Telegraph*, however, the naturalness and quiet dignity of the Abbey's acting did not appeal to everyone in rural Ireland:

> While to persons of culture the Abbey style holds a charm that no other form of dramatic fare can quite equal, to other people, who may not be so well able to distinguish all its beauty, particularly in the provinces, where practically only the vilest and most rubbishy of rubbishy melodramas hold the field, the Abbey plays may seem quite tame and insipid after these "blood and murder" shockers.
>
> Now, so far as the Abbey plays and players are concerned there are both these sections to be found among provincial audiences. There are the people who come to the plays knowing all about their scope and meaning, before they do come; and then there is the larger section who come simply because it is some form of entertainment, and they want to be entertained. It is the latter section of the audience which provides the work of propaganda; it is trying to grip and hold their attention with a style of play and playing quite foreign to them that forms the most educative work the players can do.
>
> Let me give an example, if I may, to show what I mean. In one town the players followed that fiery gem, *The Kelly Gang*, which had been played the preceding week. Now the audience which went to see Ned Kelly knock spots off the Australian police the one week came back the next to see the Irish Players. It will be readily understood that some of them were not altogether pleased when they discovered that *Kathleen Ni Houlihan* was not quite after the style of *The Bad Girl of the Family*. The spirit of Ireland, so beautifully visualised by Yeats in his fine little play, was largely a puzzle to many of the audience, and they only appeared to get their good humour back again when *The Building Fund* came on, and they discovered that "Shaun Grogan" was a villain black enough to deserve hissing. *The Rising of the Moon*, delicate little work though it is, quite took their fancy, however, with the result that the great majority of those very people who were most puzzled by the elusive "Kathleen" came back the next night to see the other plays. . . .
>
> To all who have the higher ideals of the drama at heart this should be encouraging. Perhaps there is no place where the silliness and rottenness of the old school of plays and acting can be soon in a worse degree than that found in the Irish provinces. That being so, it is good to know then that

the Abbey second company are having such encouragement in their first propaganda tour with the new school of Irish drama. The audiences have been large, and, in most places, enthusiastic. The second night of the visit has also generally drawn more people than the first — a fact which speaks for itself.[92]

On 17 October, the First Company presented a new play in Dublin, St. John Ervine's *The Magnanimous Lover*. An excellent character study of religious hypocrisy in the North, the play was too strong for the palate of the South and was thoroughly deplored. In brief, the story tells how the unctuous Henry Hinde returns to Belfast, offering to make an honest woman out of the girl he had seduced some years earlier. The girl, Maggie Cather, a kind of Shavian new woman, has succeeded so far in raising their child and refuses to have anything to do with him. This, nowadays innocuous story evoked some ferocious responses. *The Irish Times* said that the play 'contains a great deal of language to which one listens with extreme discomfort', and contended that those Abbey plays which were textually the coarsest were often the weakest intellectually and morally.[93] Jack Point in *The Evening Herald* was unable to give samples of the play's dialogue, 'which in a decent newspaper, would mainly appear in the form of initials and dashes. . . .'[94] The ever-irascible Jacques provided one of his briefest and most vitriolic reviews:

#### CENSOR, PLEASE!

I visited the Abbey Theatre last night to do a notice of a new play by Mr. St. John G. Ervine, entitled *The Magnanimous Lover*. It was received with laughter, cheers, hisses and hooting. The thing is too foul for dramatic criticism, and I am NOT a sanitary inspector.[95]

It was, however, the Dublin theatre correspondent for *The Stage*, W. J. Lawrence, whose remarks seemed the most obsessively puritanical. His objection to Ervine's use of the word 'whore' resulted in his own refusal to use the word, substituting 'wanton' for it:

On more than one occasion we have found it necessary to protest in these columns against the disposition of Abbey Theatre realists to indulge in offensive diction of a wholly gratuitous order, and we regret now the necessity which demands a severer condemnation. Hitherto our strictures have been levelled at the use and abuse of a certain sanguinary

200

epithet common to the barrack-room and the street; but, ill in taste as is this adjective, it is not so gross to female ears as the old English vocable which Mr. St. John G. Ervine puts into the mouth of his principal female character in his new play. It is no excuse to say that Shakespeare makes Othello use the word in his great scene with Iago. No modern representative of the Moor since Edwin Forrest has ever dared to utter the phrase, and the usual custom has been to substitute the word "wanton". Had the first-night audience exercised its prerogative and vigorously hissed this breach of good taste, we should not have dwelt upon the point, but, unfortunately, ever since Mr. Yeats called in the police to eject legitimate protestants against *The Playboy* the Abbey audience has failed to exercise its functions and permitted judgment to go by default. This is a parlous state of things in a country where there is no censorship.[96]

After the publication of Lawrence's remarks, Ervine wrote him a letter:

You will find the word "whore" in the printed version of my play. You will also find it in the Bible. Am I to understand that you would walk out of church if the word were read during the lessons? May I add that a man who can suggest that the modern West End actor is a competent person to censor Shakespeare is very clearly . . . what shall I say? . . . a Dublin dramatic critic.[97]

Ervine, never a man to accept criticism meekly, also wrote a scathing letter to *The Irish Times* in which he replied to the other Dublin critics:

Not one of these gentlemen (for God made them, and they must be allowed to pass as men) has the common honesty to state why he considers my play to be a disgusting thing! Not one of them has enough decency left in him to state in what respect *The Magnanimous Lover* is unfit to be played. Do they complain of the word "bastard"? Then they must complain of *King John* and *The Tragedy of Lear*, and a dozen other Shakespearean plays. They must forbid their children to read the Bible, or to visit the North of Ireland (though I do not suppose that that will break their children's hearts), and they must carefully avoid all contact with real things and real persons. The word "bastard" is a word in frequent use in Belfast; it is heard there as frequently as the expression, "To Hell with the Pope!" It is an English word, and a good word, and a word that men and women are not afraid to hear uttered when it is spoken as seriously as it is spoken in my play.

I am isolated here from the currents of thought in Ireland, and my isolation enables me to write this of those who are left in my home: the struggle for political freedom has so absorbed the race that the Irish mind is still where the English mind was in 1800. The Dublin dramatic critics are the symbols of the decadence of Dublin: they are exhausted men, holding their fingers on their lips and whispering, "Oh, hush! Oh, hush!" You have a hundred years to make up in Ireland; your chief need is to pen your minds and to shut your mouths; to learn common sense, and to cease to play the fool. Wait, just you wait, you Dublin people, till Ireland has Home Rule, and we men from Ulster will put blood in your veins, and show you how to live. No wonder that my friends refuse to be governed by you; nor will they ever be governed by you! So soon as they can get quit of that typical Dublin man, Sir Edward Carson, they will take you in hand, and make men of you.[98]

Ervine's letter was, as William Boyle told Joseph Holloway, 'a real corker'. Boyle believed that Ervine was in a temper when he wrote his letter, and he said that Ervine was foolish to print his letter for the amusement of the public. According to Boyle, Ervine suggested that when Dublin applauded his first play, *Mixed Marriage*, it was discerning, but when it failed to praise his second play it was nowhere. Boyle was most disturbed by Ervine's tacit assumption that people had only gone to the Abbey to see *The Magnanimous Lover*. As he said to Holloway: ' . . . the sheer impudence of assuming that all the people who paid their money on those evenings paid it *solely* for his piece! My piece, of course, drew nobody.' [99]

Not everyone, however, objected to Ervine's play. One individual, who signed herself 'one of the audience', said in a letter to *The Irish Times* that she 'cannot recall a stronger or more powerful presentation of a bit of real life than this little one-act play'. She believed that it depicted 'with ruthless truth the injustice of our social life that would have one law for the man and another for the woman — an injustice that is largely responsible for the strength and violence of the feminist movement.' As she said, 'It would be interesting to know how many of the Dublin press notices were written by women. . . .' [100]

Lady Gregory was little surprised by the reception of Ervine's play. As she wrote John Quinn, she had 'thought it was likely to be attacked somewhere or other, probably by Protestants', and so she kept it back until Ervine had made his reputation with *Mixed Marriage*. She was convinced that the agitation was insincere and that the newspapers were being dishonest:

> They say there were hisses and boos, whereas there was only one boo the first night, and the second night, stirred by the papers there were two men hissing, but the audience put them down with applause. The attendance kept up well too in spite of the papers, but oh it was a long fight against insincerity and organised stupidity.[101]

On 21 November, Yeats's revised version of *The Hour Glass* and a new two-act comedy by Lady Gregory, *Damer's Gold*, were performed at the Abbey. Neither play was well received. *The Freeman's Journal* said that Yeats's new version 'left by no means a pleasant flavour behind it',[102] and Jacques thought that the new version did not establish characters with whom he could sympathise:

> One is pained with surprise that the author should assist to have his work boshed and bewildered as it is in the version we witnessed last night.
> The Fool in the first version we used to look upon with an eye of pity and love and reverence. He was simple and help-less, and so near to God and all things that belong to God — the fields, the birds, the beasts, the sun and moon and stars. The present Teigue is no longer such a loveable Fool. He is just a dolt, a clod. We would give him pennies to get rid of him and no pity.[103]

Jacques also criticized the acting and staging in Nugent Monck's production:

> The pupils in the old version made their entrances and exits with a show of spontaneity in their actions. Last night pupils came on and went off like automata. Their movements were drilled. Mr. Eric Gorman was the only one of the ten who disposed himself with naturalness.
> The Angel awakened no spiritual feeling. Her entrance from the darkened auditorium and her exit at the rear of the stage—her back being all the time towards us was ineffective.[104]

The most informed and devastating review was by W. J. Lawrence:

> Abbey playgoers are growing somewhat aweary of new ver-sions, both of plays that have been popularly accepted and

plays that have not. In their eyes it is futile to gild refined gold as it is to polish up pinchbeck. Paramount among Abbey dramatists not content to let well alone, is Mr. W. B. Yeats, whose unceasing revision is due to the obsessions of an unattainable ideal. Much may be forgiven to genius, but when a little classic of the Irish Literary Theatre like *The Hour Glass*, after being familiarised to the public by occasional performance over a period of ten years, and published among the author's collected works, is rewritten from a different standpoint and its primeval beauties marred, the time is ripe for protest. Practically nothing has been gained by remoulding the play in accordance with Mr. Nugent Monck's fanciful concepts of the old English interlude platform stage of the pre-theatrical era, and that despite the fact that the entry of the characters through a side door near the orchestra in the auditorium imparts to the whole a naïve, untheatrical air. While much of the original dialogue has been retained, its grave and dignified simplicity has been marred by mere verbal embroidery. Worst of all, an entirely new denouement (which has not even the merit of originality, as it is merely an echo of Adelaide Proctor's Story of a Lost Soul) utterly destroys the compelling irony of the old play's noble ending. . . .

In accordance with his own individual staging of the play, Mr. Nugent Monck gave a reading of the Wise Man entirely different from the readings of the three or four players who preceded him in the part. Seated throughout at a table on a dais, he obtained an effect of dignified stoicism by acting that was sculpturesque rather than vividly emotional. This undoubtedly proved telling by way of contrast to the tumultuous action of the pupils, but one is moved to inquire whether consummate repose is compatible with sustained mental agony. Beyond avouching for its competence, the rest of the acting calls for no comment. Much of the sculpturesque effect of Mr. Monck's acting, as if in alto relieve, was due to a highly artistic concentration of amber light projected from the front balcony. Apart from this, however, the staging of the play was gravely objectionable to the aesthetic eye. For no other purpose than that the angels should have a staircase to descend by at the close, the stage was unequally divided after the manner of a two-room scene in a crude melodrama, thus seriously cramping the main action. This ugly arrangement could easily be obviated by showing the angels through a back transparency.[105]

In the summer of 1976, *The Hour Glass* was effectively staged at the Project Arts Centre in Dublin by James Flannery, who has argued convincingly that the poetic version of 1912 was 'superior not only technically but above all in the expression of its tragic theme' to the earlier prose versions.[106]

No critic, either in 1912 or since, has had much praise for Lady Gregory's *Damer's Gold*. This was her third new play of 1912 and probably prompted Frank Fay to remark waspishly to Lawrence:

> I hope you have counted and will publish the number of times the pieces of that selfish old lady have been published. I viewed her entrance into our movement with distrust, from the first. . . . One of these days if someone doesn't do it, I shall count the number of times her pieces have been played up to the time we left. . . . Yeats and Gregory have grabbed the thing for themselves that was meant for the country.[107]

Lawrence himself said that *Damer's Gold* was dull, wordy, and insubstantial:

> If Lady Gregory's latest play gives a true portraiture of the Connaught peasant there must be profound observation at the base of Mr. George Moore's recent dictum that the Irish are not really humorous, but merely loquacious. Never, perhaps, on the stage did fine people talk so and to so little purpose. One could hardly see the fruit for leaves. The truth is that Lady Gregory's amusing, if at times far-fetched, imbroglio lacks a sufficiency of substance for the two-act form, and that she has striven to pad it out by emulating the verbal magic of John Millington Synge. But tropes and metaphors, however beautiful, become tedious to the listener unless they are thoroughly apposite and have driving power behind them. Consequently there were many dull moments in the new play, especially at the beginning, when the characters were long in coming to Hecuba. Inasmuch as she has drawn the character of a miser on somewhat new lines, Lady Gregory deserves commendation, but in avoiding the Scylla of conventionality she has fallen into the Charybdis of psychological inconsistency. In other respects our capacity for make-believe is now and again stretched to breaking-point.[108]

Nor did Lawrence think highly of the acting:

> Mr. Sinclair, in the strikingly drawn character of the miser, appeared somewhat flurried in the first act, and he accentuated the defective psychology of the type by adopting a finnicking suburban Dublin accent, utterly out of place in the mouth of

205

a Connaught peasant. But at least he differentiated well the various phases of emotion through which Damer is supposed to pass. Miss Sara Allgood gave a spirited rendering of the volatile Delia Hessian, and by the vivacity of her delivery got well over the stumbling blocks of the abounding tropes and metaphors. In any other hands this character would have proved ineffably tedious. Mr. U. Wright was excellent in a nonchalant interpretation of the lucky Simon; and Mr. Sydney Morgan and Mr. Kerrigan lent material aid to what must be deemed a fairly sound all-round performance.[109]

On December 20, Lady Gregory accompanied the First Abbey Company on another American tour, which was to continue until May, 1913. The company included Nugent Monck, Sara Allgood, Mona Beirne, M. J. Dolan, Kathleen Drago, H. E. Hutchinson, J. M. Kerrigan, Eithne Magee, Sydney J. Morgan, Eileen O'Doherty, Frederick O'Donovan and his wife, J. A. O'Rourke, Arthur Sinclair and Udolphus Wright. Lily Yeats wondered how America would react to Monck who was the company's manager as well as an actor. As she wrote to John Quinn, 'He puts all . . . into the middle ages — does it well but will act himself — is not good, and his English voice comes in as a strange thing . . . among the other voices.' [110] Lennox Robinson also had some reservations about Monck:

> Monck was asking me what he was to do in America and I told him — seeing about the salaries was one thing and he said he would — now he is getting at O'Donovan to do tours which isn't fair on O'Donovan who will have plenty to do with his acting if nothing else and really Monck won't have much to do. . . .[111]

On 26 December at the Abbey, the Second Company appeared in a new one-act play, *A Little Christmas Miracle* by E. Hamilton Moore. Most critics, probably because of the play's subject-matter, treated the piece gently, but it appears to have been fairly vapid. The play has not been published, and the manuscript is unavailable, but W. J. Lawrence reviewed it with some fullness:

> As the first work of a new Abbey playwright, this gave indications of sterling promise, albeit it introduced us once more to our old friend, the Long Arm of Coincidence. It was a daring experiment in a Catholic country to bring the Blessed Virgin on the stage as the *dea ex machina*, and if the outcome was not disastrous, it was because the logical issues were seriously shirked. In avoiding disaster all possibility of success

has been negatived, but the fault, as we shall see, lay with the producer, and not with the author.

It is a stormy Christmas Eve in a rude dwelling-house on the rock-bound coast of Ireland. The scene is dimly outlined by the glowing, gipsy fire, over which Bridget Cassidy cowers, and by the lantern which two wreckers, Daniel Byrne and Larry Sullivan, have placed in the window. The booming of signal guns is heard, and it soon becomes apparent that a labouring vessel is nearing her destination. But only Bridget Cassidy evinces any compassion for the helpless creatures on board. Embittered by his sufferings, and nursing a deep revenge, Michael O'Halloran gloats over the fact that the sailors are going to their doom. In a long and powerful speech he recalls how, years previously, a vessel from the Argentines had come ashore in a storm at that very same spot, how he had saved and sheltered the captain, and how the man he had snatched from the jaws of death had rewarded him by eloping with the apple of his eye, his only daughter. Left desolate, he had sworn an oath of deep revenge against the betrayer, never to be relaxed until the Mother of God came down and demanded his forgiveness. At this juncture Larry Sullivan enters bearing the body of a shipwrecked sailor, which he flings down by the glowing embers. Believing him to be dead, the wreckers proceed to search the sailor's pockets for booty, but the warmth slowly revives him, and he asks for news of his vessel. Not only is he captain of a merchantman trading from the Argentines, but Michael O'Halloran recognises in him the betrayer of his daughter. Just as O'Halloran is about to slay the exhausted and helpless man with his own clasp-knife, the barn-door suddenly opens, and a hooded woman enters bearing a child. This causes a momentary diversion. Welcomed by the good-hearted Bridget Cassidy, the Strange Woman lays down her infant boy in the rude bed and sings a brief lullaby. Then the emotional crisis is resumed. O'Halloran tells the Captain that his oath of revenge cannot be foregone unless his hand is stayed by the Mother of God. It is so stayed, for the Strange Woman, who stands by her sleeping child, suddenly divests herself of her hood and stands (suppositiously) revealed as the Blessed Virgin. And then, with the Virgin's delivery of a homily in verse to the awe-stricken group, the curtain slowly and ineffectively descends. Here we have a magnificent situation, which in the hands of a Reinhardt might be made to possess high spiritual power, bringing home to the heart the divinity of forgiveness. It is, of course, a moot point whether

207

it is the mission of the stage to inculcate such lessons in the manner indicated, but if the task is undertaken it should at least be carried through with complete moral courage. At the moment of divine revelation some striking physical trans-figuration of the Blessed Virgin should be indicated, either by a rapid change of costume or a flood of well-directed light. It was surely a mistake to preserve the semi-gloom of the scene until the fall of the curtain. Mr. Lennox Robinson's scheme of staging was here wholly at fault. . . .

Taken in the mass the second company of Abbey Players are little inferior in artistry and ensemble to the first company, and no serious fault can be found with the rendering of *A Little Christmas Miracle.* Beyond the fact that he made excessive demand on his powerful lungs, we have nothing but praise for Mr. Patrick Murphy's stirring exposition of the resolute and revengeful Michael O'Halloran. Mr. Murphy may be counselled to abate his temperamental boisterousness, which at all times and in all sorts of parts, rudely mars his sound histrionic capacity. Miss Helen Moloney's portrayal of the warm-hearted Bridget Cassidy proved of eminent service as affording the necessary highlight in a picture characterised by inspissated gloom. In the difficult and delicate *role* of the Strange Woman, Miss Nell Byrne brought her powers of imagination to bear with considerable effect, and struck the right note by maintaining the character throughout on a plane of ideality. If at the close it did not appear obvious exactly what the Strange Woman symbolised, the fault was not hers, but the producer's. In these matters the last word is not always with the player.[112]

Late in December, the intelligent but often astringent Ernest A. Boyd published a scathing attack on the Abbey:

The Abbey Theatre season has just closed, and the company has started upon one of these prolonged tours which now seem to be an established feature of the National Theatre. Some years ago these frequent absences would have awakened regret in those who felt themselves thus deprived of their only escape from imported drama of the "digestive" order. We have, however, now been accustomed to a different state of things. It is not so long since the Abbey Theatre favoured Dublin with only four weeks' performance in the course of ten months. Even then one of those flying visits was due to the influx of strangers in Dublin during Horse Show week. It is evident, therefore, that nationalism and patriotism, which were at one time the watchwords of the Irish dramatic movement, have been relegated to a position of secondary importance. When the public and resources of the Abbey Theatre were considerably more limited, it could afford to perform continuously in Dublin. Now that its audience has grown and its popularity has increased, frequent touring seems to have become a pecuniary necessity. So we arrive at the apparently paradoxical conclusion that, as the financial side of the enterprise improved, so the need grew for augmenting the receipts.

A survey of the past season's performances would suggest that perhaps other than material motives account for the prolonged absences of the Abbey Company from Dublin. Latterly the most pronounced feature of the Abbey Theatre programmes has been their lack of variety. The names of three of the more prominent dramatists have held almost uninterrupted sway. However meritorious the works in question may be, it is obvious that they cannot be performed for ever. Even the new audiences, which are not disposed to be critical, must eventually tire of the same dramatic fare. Instead, however, of varying the monotony, the management seem to prefer touring, which saves the trouble of renewing the repertoire, and gives the public time to forget. In the absence of enterprise, it becomes imperative that considerable intervals should elapse between one series of familiar plays and another. Thus, in confining its attention to certain popular plays calculated to draw good houses, the Abbey Theatre is in a fair way of removing entirely its *raison d'être*. The ordinary commercial theatre may safely be trusted to look after the question of long "runs"; a repertory theatre should aim at something better. It must make experiments, and even sacrifices, in the interests of dramatic art. Otherwise it may cease to exist.

An examination of the work of the Abbey Theatre during the last couple of years will show that very little has been done to justify its existence either as the home of repertory or as the seat of a national drama. There was a time when a stand was made against the demands of mediocrity. Nowadays popular approval seems to be the supreme test of the Irish dramatist. His play will be rejected or rarely performed unless it makes a direct appeal to the widest popularity. Not only is this the standard which regulates the performances in Dublin, but the popular judgment here decides what plays will be given in the United States. A play like *Thomas Muskerry*, for example, is rarely performed, although the author is probably the finest of the Irish dramatists since Synge. Unfortunately for his chances of immediate success. Padraic Colum will not write melodrama, his plays have a thesis, and, of course, do not stand the test of popularity. Like *The Land* and *The Fiddler's House*, *Thomas Muskerry* must be studied in the printed form, where it will soon be necessary to seek all that is best in Irish dramatic literature. As far as the Abbey Theatre is concerned, these plays have almost lapsed into oblivion. Yet there is a wealth of material upon which the National Theatre could draw. The names of Æ, George Moore, Edward Martyn, and others suggest a fine series of revivals of which there is a great need in the present stagnation. So long as this material is not utilised, it is useless to plead the dearth of new playwrights as an excuse for the monotonous mediocrity of recent Abbey Theatre performances.

The serious feature of this absence of enterprise in the present policy of the theatre is the deterioration which is resulting from it. Irish drama is rapidly becoming conventional English melodrama with a local setting. All that is drab and violent in Irish life is exploited with a view to "powerful" situations. Two of the dramatists whose work is most frequently seen vie with Mr. Walter Melville in the manufacture of artificial thrills. As a result, a change has taken place in the supporters of the Abbey Theatre. The new audience is as different from the old, as the latter was from the votaries of musical comedy. Those who supported a movement which aspired to the renovation of dramatic forms have almost withdrawn, now that the original ideals have been abandoned. Instead of trying to educate public taste, the Abbey Theatre has become its follower. It seems impossible that financial considerations have made this change necessary. If so, then the means will defeat the end, for, in the process of making money, all that is characteristic of the dramatic movement in Ireland is being lost. New dramatists have little to encourage them unless they are prepared to write down to the level of popular melodrama. The steps which have been taken to establish a repertory theatre in Dublin indicate the trend of public opinion. It is felt that the Abbey Theatre no longer serves the best interests of modern drama. The presence of an efficient repertory theatre may spur the directors to make some effort to retain their hold upon the intelligent public. The present policy must end in disaster. Unless good plays are produced and past successes revived, the Abbey Theatre will continue to decline until it is scarcely distinguishable from the ordinary commercial theatre. But before it reaches that stage,

210

it will, as the Irish National Theatre, have ceased to exist.[113]

Boyd's diatribe aroused several responses,[114] but the most authoritative was Lennox Robinson's:

Mr. Ernest A. Boyd has criticised at some length the general policy of the Irish National Theatre, and has in particular attacked the theatre's season which has just closed. He deplores the lack of variety of our programmes during that period, and he says that "the names of three of the more prominent dramatists have held almost uninterrupted sway."

May I, quite briefly, analyse our season's work? We gave 146 performances; we produced 32 plays; we gave examples of the work of 14 dramatists. Six of these plays were produced twice (I mean during two different weeks), one was produced three times, the other 22 got a single series of performances. During the same season the Liverpool Repertory Theatre produced 14 plays, and the Manchester Gaiety 12. We produced 32.

He accuses us of "confining our attention to plays that attract good houses". Can he or any other regular attendant of the Abbey Theatre honestly say that *The Piedish, Thomas Muskerry, The Countess Cathleen, The Piper, The Shadow of the Glen, The White Cockade, The Glittering Gate, The Hour Glass, The Unicorn from the Stars* are really popular, drawing plays? If we were really out just to make money, would we have produced all those plays since last August? Would we not have confined our attention to *The Playboy, Mixed Marriage*, Mr. Boyle's comedies and a few other plays? If during last season our weekly takings kept curiously level, may it not be because these once unpopular plays are finding an audience, and not because the plays themselves — because they draw large audiences — are deteriorating in quality? Certainly a play is not necessarily a good play because it is popular, but neither is it necessarily a bad one, and is not the vision a little distorted which sees in a full theatre and a popular play the germs of decay and death?

During the last two years we have produced 23 new plays; during the previous two years we produced 22, and previous to that again 21; so, at any rate, our average of production is not falling.

I do not know who the "three more prominent dramatists" can be. I thought, perhaps, they were Mr. W. B. Yeats, J. M. Synge, and Lady Gregory; but Mr. Boyd says these "prominent dramatists'" work "vies with Mr. Walter Melville in the

211

manufacture of artificial thrills". I do not think their bitterest enemy could accuse the three dramatists I have mentioned of supplying this form of entertainment. Can he mean Mr. St. John Ervine? His two plays have had three productions. Or Mr. Boyle? Two of his plays have been produced once. Or Mr. Fitzmaurice, with the same average? Or myself, with two productions of one of my plays? Or Lord Dunsany and Messrs. Casey, Colum, Norreys Connell, Shaw, who have each had one play produced once?

I think that Mr. Boyd is a very warm admirer of Mr. Colum's work, and that grief at finding only one of Mr. Colum's plays in our autumn programme has led him into exaggerated statements. At any rate, he will be glad to hear that *The Land* is one of the plays we put down for revival this spring. He will also be glad to hear that we suffered a small loss on our last reason's work in Dublin. He would, perhaps, be more glad if I could tell him we were bankrupt — though where Ireland's National Theatre would be then I do not know.[115]

Constance de Markievicz also said that Boyd's criticisms contained various mis-statements which resulted from his limited knowledge of the birth and growth of the Irish National Theatre movement:

Mr. Boyd says: "When the public and resources of the Abbey Theatre were considerably more limited it could afford to perform continuously in Dublin. Now that its audience has grown and its popularity has increased, frequent touring seems to have become a pecuniary necessity." Mr. Boyd is apparently not aware that the National Theatre Company were given the Abbey Theatre to play in free of rent by Miss Horniman, and not only this, but were given a generous subsidy yearly. Previous to this the company was practically an amateur company, consisting of a number of clever, busy young people, most of them working in the daytime, who willingly devoted their spare time to the art they loved. On Miss Horniman's generous gift they left the works they were engaged on and formed themselves into a professional company to develop the national dramatic art of the country.

It was only when Miss Horniman withdrew from the enterprise that the company were forced to consider ways and means. Surely Mr. Boyd would not wish to suggest that the actors and actresses of a repertory theatre need not be paid, that the theatre is free to them, and that light shines for their

212

performances at the bidding of a benevolent gas company, that advertisements appear, costumes are provided as it were by the touch of a magic wand?

This, alas! is not so. Even a repertory theatre cannot avoid the commercialism of having to pay for what it and its staff require, and of providing food and raiment for those whose life is given to the work.

The National Theatre Company cannot, in common fairness and truth, be called "a commercial theatre". A commercial theatre is a business concern run by an individual or a board of directors to make money. The balance sheet — duly audited — which appeared in all the papers a short time ago should surely prove to all that Lady Gregory and Mr. Yeats have not made fortunes out of the enterprise, but have generously given their time and talents to the work of building up Irish dramatic art.

Ireland is a small, poor country, and we have not a rich board of directors or a clique of rich amateurs who are willing to pay heavily to gratify their taste in drama. Our directors are supported by people who are comparatively poor. Dublin is not a big city, and the population of Ireland is small, consequently authors are rare.

Making a rough calculation from the balance sheet, the expenses of the theatre — without calculating the actors' salaries — are over £60 per week, and all expenses for the year some £9,000. Travelling expenses are only a little over £300. The takings are over £11,000. Anyone who frequents the theatre should be able to judge how much of that £11,000 is reaped in other lands to enable them to be with us at all.

The aim of our Irish Repertory Theatre is slightly different from the aim of those of other countries. In England and elsewhere they stand for the production of so-called literary plays that are appreciated by so few that no commercial manager would put them on, while our National Theatre Company have started on a much more arduous and difficult task. Their work is to create an Irish theatre. They began with nothing; no plays, no actors — nothing but their own brave hearts. Now they can already show us a splendid company of actors playing a fine repertory of plays in a nice little theatre. Many of the plays are good; some may be bad; but all are very Irish. The movement is still in its infancy. If it should fail, it will be we — the public — who are to blame. No theatrical movement can develop without the support of an enthusiastic public. It is we who must applaud the good plays

213

and fill the theatre, so that our company are relieved from the disagreeable necessity of going away to make their living and keep their theatre open.

They give us what they can; we must help them to give us more. All honour to Mr. Yeats and Lady Gregory and their little band of pioneer authors and actors, and all success to them in their uphill task.[116]

Joseph Holloway joined the fray with these statistics:

I thought it might be of interest to those taking part in the above discussion to know that the Abbey players (known as "Number One Company"), now touring in the United States, gave 93 performances at the Abbey Theatre in 1912, performing 30 pieces. Five of them were played for the first time in Dublin — viz. *Family Failing* (Boyle), *Patriots* (Robinson), *Maurice Harte* (Murray), *The Magnanimous Lover* (Ervine), and *Damer's Gold* (Lady Gregory). New versions of Yeats's *The Hour Glass* and *The Countess Cathleen* were given, and the Yeats-Gregory play, *The Unicorn from the Stars*, was revived. The plays in which the company appeared were: Lady Gregory's *The Workhouse Ward* (10 times), *The Rising of the Moon* (16), *Spreading the News* (4), *The Jackdaw* (7), *Coats* (12), *Hyacinth Halvey* (4), *The White Cockade* (4), *Damer's Gold* (4), *Kathleen ni Houlihan* (14), *The Pot of Broth* (4), and *The Hour Glass* (4), and Yeats-Gregory's *The Unicorn from the Stars* (2): J. M. Synge's *Riders to the Sea* (8), *In the Shadow of the Glen* (12), and *The Playboy of the Western World* (3); William Boyle's *Family Failing* (8), and *The Eloquent Dempsy* (8); T. C. Murray's *Birthright* (8), and *Maurice Harte* (8); Ervine's *Mixed Marriage* (10), and *The Magnanimous Lover* (4); Bernard Shaw's *The Shewing-Up of Blanco Posnet* (8); Lord Dunsany's *The Glittering Gate* (7); Lennox Robinson's *Patriots* (13); Casey's *The Man Who Missed the Tide* (4), and *The Suburban Groove* (4); George Fitzmaurice's *The Piedish* (4); Norreys Connell's *The Piper* (4); and Padraic Colum's *Thomas Muskerry* (4). The above list will show at a glance the plays produced, and the number of times each was given.[117]

The letters of Robinson, the Countess and Holloway were quickly replied to by Boyd, who hardly was one to shirk an argument.

The use of statistics is, I take it, the last resource of critics who are without argument. The figures quoted by Mr. Lennox Robinson sound very imposing, as also does Countess de

214

Markievicz's excursion into the realms of problematical book-keeping. As I heard her figures disputed, in her own presence, by an equally good authority, I shall not attempt to discuss her knowledge of the financial working of the Abbey Theatre. I am content to accept her statements, however, as they have no value, except in so far as they prove my original contention that money-making is responsible for the present policy of the theatre. Her restatement of the aims of the National Theatre should interest Mr. W. B. Yeats — particularly her sneer at "so-called literary plays" — with the implied argument that anything is good enough, provided it be "very Irish". He founded a theatre for the production of poetic and literary drama; it has become the home of a certain crude realism, which is rapidly degenerating into commonplace melodrama. The times have changed, and the champions of the Abbey Theatre with them.

The dangers of the statistical method in discussion are illustrated by a comparison of Mr. L. Robinson's letter with that of Mr. Holloway, which appeared in your issue of the 3rd inst. From the latter it appears that there were more performances of Lady Gregory's work last year than of Synge and Yeats together, while Messrs. Boyle and Murray had each four times as many performances as Padraic Colum. The interminable *Family Failing* was actually played eight times, as against three performances of *The Playboy*. These facts need no emphasis to prove that, as I said, popular taste is the usual standard, that the same names appear with monotonous regularity, and that the better the play the less it is performed. The plays which Mr. Robinson cites as proof of the contrary are mainly very short, and capable of being sandwiched in between the productions of the popular idols. On looking over the programmes for the past two years, I find that almost every week one or two plays of Lady Gregory's were produced, while the names of Boyle, Robinson, and Murray were seldom long in the background. Incidentally, of course, and particularly when sufficiently short, "so-called literary plays" were performed, as they did not interfere with the inevitable farces and melodramas. When this order is reversed, and more revivals are undertaken, such as that promised by Mr. Robinson, the Abbey Theatre will cease to owe its reputation to a glorious past.[118]

The Countess then accused Boyd of 'cheap sneers and tawdry sarcasm', and he accused her of evading the question, and the editor mercifully announced that, 'This correspondence is now closed.' [119]

* * *

Count Markievicz produced two new plays, Edward Martyn's *Grangecolman* and Eva Gore-Booth's *Unseen Kings*, for the Independent Theatre Company on 25 January at the Abbey. Martyn's play received mixed notices from the Dublin critics. *The Evening Telegraph* said that *Grangecolman* 'runs along merrily for the first two acts with some sparkling bits of dialogue here and there, and the climax is brought about effectively'. It also believed that 'the clash of the two women characters was well sustained throughout.' Like most of the Dublin papers, *The Evening Telegraph* praised the acting.

> Miss Edith Dodd gave a most telling representation of the bright, cheerful young secretary. It was an admirable piece of acting. The Countess Markievicz as Colman's daughter was also very good. Her study of the part was even better than her recent performances in other plays. The male characters were good, and that of Lucius Devlin was exceptionally so. Mr. P. Quill was a picture of laziness in the part. In make-up, manner, speech and action he did full justice to it.[120]

W. J. Lawrence did not believe that the Countess de Markievicz made Mrs. Devlin into a plausible character, and said 'that there were moments of stogyness in her acting'. He also faulted Martyn for being too influenced by Ibsen:

> Mr. Martyn is still cumbered by Henrik Ibsen. One has always felt that if he would give free play to his own personality and strive to express Irish life solely through that medium, and not in terms of the Norwegian master, he might write a highly interpretative and completely satisfying play. There are, indeed, inklings of revolt from the old glamour in *Grangecolman*; for while, on the one hand, Mr. Martyn's central character, Catharine Devlin, is one of those introspective Ibsen women who don't know exactly what they want and won't be happy till they get it, on the other, the teaching of the play is diametrically opposed to the spirit of the Scandinavian dramatist. In his ardent championship of the old-fashioned or womanly woman, Mr. Martyn throws a bombshell into the camp of the Suffragists. . . .[121]

How well Martyn understood Ibsen's dramaturgy is an open question, but there is no question of Martyn's admiration; for him Ibsen

was 'the most original as well as the greatest of dramatists.' [122]
Among the other critics, Jacques cursorily dismissed the play:

> Mr. Martyn was called and bowed his acknowledgments, and
> no doubt takes his work most seriously. I can't, and don't. If
> the three acts were boiled down to one, it might be worth
> while as a twenty minutes' sensation. In its present form it is
> tosh. The interpreters made the most of it.[123]

*Sinn Féin*, though not so quick to dismiss Martyn as a playwright,
nevertheless criticized him for excessive melodrama:

> Mr. Martyn's *Grangecolman* fails, like all Mr. Martyn's plays,
> save *The Heather Field*, in the catastrophe. In *Maeve*, in *The
> Enchanted Sea*, and now in *Grangecolman*, Mr. Martyn dis-
> sipates a good play into melodrama, and melodrama that
> suggests burlesque. The author of that fine play, *The Heather
> Field*, has, since he wrote the latter, seemed rather to cultivate
> the little defects in it than its excellences. The catastrophe of
> *The Heather Field* smelled of melodrama, but it left us im-
> pressed. The swinging rope with the heroine — if we can apply
> such a word to any of Mr. Martyn's women characters — at
> the end of *The Enchanted Sea* and the lady in the white sheet,
> with her face and breast besmeared with blood in *Grange-
> colman* do not impress us in the least. If we look sad at these
> bloody finales it is because it is sad to see how easily a good
> play can be spoiled by a clever man who lets a curious
> emotionalism obscure his vision of the slender line that divides
> the sublime from the ridiculous. We tire, too, of Mr. Martyn's
> weak men and strong women, not because they are weak men
> and strong women, but because they are what Miss Farquhar
> did not believe in — ghosts — ghosts of the people of *The
> Heather Field*. . . . Of a lesser man than Mr. Martyn we would
> write softer things, because we could not expect so much. But
> Mr. Martyn can do large things in drama, and does not do
> them because he lets a little devil compounded of perversity
> and sentimentality run away with him at the end.[124]

Eva Gore-Booth's *Unseen Kings*, which concerned itself with
the closing moments in Cuchulain's life, was also criticized by the
Dublin critics who did not deem it fit for the stage. *The Evening
Telegraph* said, 'it is a beautiful piece of composition to read or to
hear read, but it is the strain imposed on the audience by the stage
production does not give it a chance of being appreciated.' [125]
Jacques in *The Irish Independent* commented, 'we can find pleasure

in the poetry of this talented Irish lady when we read it far away from a theatre. It is not the same thing when given to us as it was last night.' [126] Only Lawrence managed to notice any notable good qualities about the performance:

Although there is rich ore (of a kind) in the old Gaelic Cuchulain Saga, no one has been able as yet to stamp it in the dramatic mint, and pass it as current coin. About the first to essay the task was Mr. W. B. Yeats, whose *On Baile's Strand* proved years ago to be one of the scrappiest and most ineffectual of his plays. It has never been revived. Viewed from a strictly dramatic (or shall we say orthodox) standpoint, Miss Gore-Booth is no more successful than her predecessors. Written in limpid, gentle-flowing verse, to whose beauty justice was done by all save one of the exponents, her play never quickens the pulse nor stirs the emotions. Thanks to the pleasant ripple of the verse, and a picturesque, reposeful staging which had nearly all the immobility of a tableaux, the whole had a sensuous charm akin to that possessed by Maeterlinck's *Pelléas et Mélisande*. Footlight presentations of this kind are mere opiates for the soul, leaving the mind untouched. . . .
In speaking of the acting one must concern oneself solely with the delivery of the verse, for in a play of this order subtle characterisation is out of the question. The keynote of the play was struck at the beginning by Mr. George Fitzgerald's delivery before the curtain in complete darkness of the prologue in which the symbolical title is finely elucidated. This was given with a bold sonority and fine intelligence, showing that in Mr. Fitzgerald we have the makings of a sound Shakespearean actor. Apart from this, no general scheme of delivery was followed. Some of the players treated Miss Gore-Booth's verse frankly as speech, but gave it its full musical qualities; and some, like Miss Violet Mervyn, intoned it with a truly sacerdotal impressiveness. At war with the two methods was that of Mr. Quill, who, in a part that admitted of none, was more intent on acting than on extracting the full poetic measure out of his lines. Unhappily, there was little melody in his voice, and he delivered his rhythmic quatrains as if they were the baldest of prose. Moreover, neither the music of the two songs, as set by Prof. Max Mayer, nor their rendering (competent as it was) by Miss Nettie Edwards and Miss Eileen Furlong, was in keeping with the dreamy atmosphere of the piece. The music was florid and declamatory, and the rendering

218

after the method of the old operatic convention. But these discords were only momentary, and the general effect was one of sensuous charm. To that the highly intelligent stage management of Count Markievicz largely contributed.[127]

On 19 February, the Independent Theatre Company, again at the Abbey, gave the first performance of *The Dangerous Age* by Mrs. O'Hara, better known as Norah Fitzpatrick. Jack Point in *The Evening Herald* called it 'a capital comedy sketch', and summarizes the marital mixups between a London barrister, his wife and a Suffragette called Matilda Strongbow:

> Burns, having come to the conclusion that the Suffragette is becoming rather amorous, thinks it is about time to get her out of the house. His wife, on the other hand, laughs at his fears, and points out that Matilda is engaged to an African missionary, and "makes up" as that mystical personage, which so upsets the Suffragette that she clears out right off.[128]

This confection occasioned 'much merriment' and 'several curtains and calls'.

By 1 July, the Theatre of Ireland had already mounted as many productions, five, as it had in the two previous years. However, only two of the productions were new, Thomas MacDonagh's one-act *Metempsychosis* and Victor O'D. Power's two-act *The Ordeal of David*. *Metempsychosis*, originally published in *The Irish Review* (February, 1912) before its performance on 18 April, received unanimously poor reviews. *The Freeman's Journal* said that it 'was a poor play, badly acted' and wondered 'whether it was written as a skit on transmigration or represented an effort at pose on the part of the author.' [129] Jacques in *The Irish Independent* also dismissed the play:

> *Metempsychosis, or A Mad World*, a play in one act by Thomas MacDonagh, may be a skit upon transmigration or some other kind of ation, but the people of the play never gave us a fair chance of judging what it was all about. One of the characters (Earl Winton-Winton de Winton of Castle Winton, near Drogheda) drew diagrams on a blackboard that suggested a proposition in Euclid, and delivered windy speeches. The Countess talked about orchids, and The Stranger about a small boat. Being only an ordinary person, I gave it up.[130]

As usual, W. J. Lawrence was the most detailed in his analysis. He contended that many young Irish playwrights like Thomas

MacDonagh, not only took themselves too seriously but also assumed that good literature necessarily made for good drama:

Mr. MacDonagh has fallen a victim to that miasma of preciosity which at present besets the new school of young Irish playwrights. Under its baneful influence they are more disposed to seek after the creation of literature than pulsating drama. The habit, in Dublin, of printing new plays as soon as they are acted, and sometimes beforehand, is establishing a type of dramatist whose appeal is primarily to the cool and critical reader, and only secondarily to the spectator in the pit. No great, or even healthy, national drama was ever produced under these conditions. There is no legitimate court of appeal beyond the theatre. One is moved to these reflections by the fact that Mr. MacDonagh has hit upon the material for a good theosophical skit only to destroy its pungency by taking himself and his subject a deal too seriously. It is mere midsummer madness to offer *Metempsychosis* as a picture of manners. . . . It will be readily seen from this outline of Mr. MacDonagh's play that the whole point and humour of the satire depend upon the drawing and the portrayal of the character of the stranger. Without an exaggerated foil to the character of the aristocratic theosophist, say, some sort of quaint being like Jacques Strop or the Curate in *The Private Secretary*, the whole thing falls to the ground. In not providing that foil, Mr. MacDonagh has shown his incapacity for dramatic contrast. No actor could have made the character of the Stranger effective on the lines mapped out. He is described by the author as "about thirty, timid, shy, awkward in company, opportunist in conversation, with no interest if anything but his present fad, enthusiastic when speaking of it, otherwise hesitating, and given to distraction". In faithfully depicting these idiosyncrasies, Mr. Robert Eaton only succeeded in unfairly convincing the audience of his amateurishness and of an uncertainty as to his lines. Needless to say, any characterisation whose faithful mirroring gives rise to this ambiguity argues of a lack of dramatic visualisation on the part of the author. So much for thinking of how one's play will read in the study, instead of how it will act. Somewhat appeased at first by the permeating artificiality of the peculiarly mad Pythagorean, Mr. Crawford Neill contrived, on warming to his work, to give a plausible interpretation of the well-defined character. His impersonation, however, was somewhat lacking in the necessary note of distinction. Miss Moira Walker, in the trifling role of the Countess, perfectly realised the author's concepts, and showed all the languor and boredom accompanied, of course, by a gentle courtesy, that marks the caste of Lady Clara Vere de Vere.[131]

Victor O'D. Power's *The Ordeal of David* was first performed on 1 July. *The Irish Times* commented on 'the excellence of the dialogue',[132] as did Jack Point in *The Evening Herald*, who also remarked the 'not particularly original' plot.[133] That plot was summarized by *The Evening Telegraph*:

> The scene is laid in the Skibbereen district, County Cork, and the plot is conversant with Irish peasant life and the domestic circle of a family group consisting of the Widow Mahony and her two sons David and Flurry. The former, who is of a philosophical and literary turn of mind, falls in love with Nonie Burke, a comely colleen. His mother denounces the girl in all the moods and tenses, and vehemently opposes the match. David, however, is firm in his protestations of attachment, but for prudential reasons does his love-making by proxy through his rollicking light-hearted brother. The result is that Flurry and Nonie embark to America on a runaway match. The disconsolate Davy lets his farm and goes to Wales as a miner. In the end, however, all winds up happily in the denouement, and everyone goes away pleased with the play and the players. The performance was loudly applauded, and the author called before the curtain.[134]

While he was writing plays for the Theatre of Ireland and editing *The Irish Review*, Thomas MacDonagh was also engaged with Count Plunkett in founding the Irish Theatre. In some letters to Frank Fay, MacDonagh indicated that he and Plunkett wished Fay to return to Dublin as the Irish Theatre's manager or actor manager:

> In the first place Mr. Plunkett and I are of the opinion that the new theatre should pay you £150 for the year. . . . with you here, we shall proceed to look for our players. . . . By principal actor I meant the right thing, what I know you will be, not a person who would go title role in all things or the like. . . . Really the theatre [in Hardwicke Street] is Plunkett's building. . . . It is Plunkett you have to thank for the offer of the theatre to you for teaching work. It was his suggestion.[135]

It was MacDonagh's desire not to duplicate Abbey work or to employ established actors:

I think we ought to surpass their acting. I think we shall manage to have worthy plays. About players, frankly I would prefer to have young unspoiled people. Men and women have young, spring-like enthusiasm for a thing like the drama only once in their lives. If they take the tide, as you did, they ripen to summer and autumn, if not — well, they cannot have a second spring. Maura Walker has been a dismal failure these past years. When you taught her she did good things. Then when left to herself she went off and off. I am sure it would be far easier work to begin with another girl of twenty such as she was ten years ago than to try to galvanize her into the same thing again. She is, I fear, incapable of the kind of young enthusiasm that we shall want. Her brother Frank is still worse than she, and brings an air of casualness with him. He has ruined thing after thing by not learning his lines. I honestly and sincerely assure you that I have no ill will or ill feeling towards a single member of these dramatic societies which have failed so, but I think we should not risk having to do unpleasant things, and it is always better not to bring in those whom you may have afterwards to put out. This whole thing may cost me personally some friends — I hope not, though — but I am not prepared to let my friends who have no business in this galley put any list on it. From what I have seen of them at work, I think that Fred Morrow, Seumas (Starkey), Connolly, and all the Walkers except Annie, who is with the Abbey, are hopeless in anything which demands punctuality and efficiency — anything by way of a theatre. They are all of us, and they will all be friends of our theatre, but I think they are incompetent for the work we have to do.[136]

MacDonagh told Fay that he, like Count Plunkett, did not want to be the Theatre of Ireland, because they were both disgusted with its inefficiency:

> We do not want to begin with a past. We are not against the Theatre of Ireland or against the Abbey, though I think we are necessary only because of the failure of those two in different directions.[137]

To entice Fay to join the new venture, MacDonagh was persuasive. He told Fay that as manager he would be autonomous and be able to conduct classes in acting and to have a reasonable amount of free time. Unfortunately Plunkett became ill, and so the formation of the new Irish Theatre was delayed and its first play not produced until November, 1914, by which time Frank Fay, for one reason

222

or another, was no longer interested in joining the new venture.

\* \* \*

Throughout 1912 in Ireland there was considerable activity among amateur theatre companies. Groups such as the Iona Players, the Pioneer Club, the Ringsend National Dramatic Association, the Aeolian Dramatic Club, the Leinster Stage Society, the Dublin University Dramatic Society, and the Metropolitan Players each managed to give at least one performance. However, the number of new and significant plays produced were few. Johanna Redmond's new one-act play, *Leap Year*, was performed in the Aughrim National School on 4 February by Miss Redmond and Mr. Murrough Barry O'Brien before an appreciative audience.[138] Miss Redmond's fifteen-minute comedietta was again performed on 18 March by the Pioneer Club at St. Francis Xavier Hall. This time, however, it enlarged its title to *Leap Year in the West* and was performed by Herbert Mack and Jennie Webb, who 'interpret a simple little episode in which jealousy over a simple flower causes the "bit of trouble" between the loving boy and girl. . . .' [139] The play, said *The Irish Independent*, was set:

> in the interior of a Roscommon cottage, and the story concerns the love affair of Mona Garry and Cathal Connor. Mona, while not a flirt, is a desperate teaser, and plagues the life out of poor Cathal who at length becomes so desperate that Mona relents and the curtain falls on a happy reconciliation.[140]

According to *The Evening Telegraph*, '. . . in the working out of what is really a very ephemeral but most natural complication the dialogue is racy of the soil, and captures the audience in such a way as to make everyone regret that the play is so almost bewilderingly brief.' [141]

On the same programme was a three-act historical drama, *O'Donnell's Cross* by Miss L. McManus, the author of popular fiction. This occasion appears not to have been the first production of the play, but *The Irish Times* admired the construction and the dialogue.[142]

Padraic Pearse's one-act morality play in Irish, *An Rí* (*The King*), was acted by the pupils of St. Enda's College, Rathfarnham, on 15 June. *An Rí* was, according to *The Evening Herald*, 'both in the matter of intelligent interpretation and in spectacular effect . . . highly creditable to the actors and to the master.' [143] *The Irish Times* approved of St. Enda's activities in the language movement, and said they were bearing valuable results. According to this paper, Pearse's pageant play, performed at St. Enda's annual garden party, was eminently suited to its environment:

No more fitting locale could be imagined for the performance of an historical episode, for the grounds of St. Enda's have been specially favoured by nature. In a secluded spot, sheltered by tall elms, the play was enacted, an ivied archway forming a perfect background to a natural stage. The youthful performers, in their traditional Gaelic dress, fitted into the scene as perfectly as if they were part of it. The play dealt with an historical episode in which a little boy wins freedom for the people after many failures by an unrighteous king. The play was admirably performed, the students showing a very intelligent conception of their work. They spoke their lines with delightful clearness, and they revealed a thorough knowledge of Irish pronunciation. There was music in their speech, and there was sturdy confidence in their acting. Needless to say, the large company that watched the play enjoyed it beyond measure.[144]

Only one other new play performed by an Irish amateur theatrical group was mentioned in the newspapers. However, this play, A. Patrick Wilson's *Victims*, a labour play in one act presented by the Irish Workers' Dramatic Club, was not discussed by the press. *Victims* was, one gathers from the programme, first performed on 26 December, had a cast of four characters, and was set in a tenement house.

Toward the end of 1912 many individuals believed that Dublin needed a repertory theatre to improve the quality of productions offered in the city. On 25 October, Joseph A. Keogh (later J. Augustus Keogh), the stage manager for Ben Iden Payne's company, wrote about the matter to *The Irish Times*:

A permanent repertory theatre in Dublin, built by the citizens, owned by the citizens, and run by the citizens, for the enjoyment and instruction of the citizens? I have often wondered if it would be possible to organise a body of influential and interested inhabitants of the city of Dublin into a committee that would have for their object the founding of such an institution in their city. What a boon it would be!

When that truly great benefactress of the drama, Miss Horniman, who, by the way, did so much for the Abbey Theatre Players, opened the Gaiety Theatre, Manchester, as a repertory theatre, her ideas were as follows:

(1) A repertory theatre with a regular change of pro-

224

gramme, not wedded to any one school of dramatists, but thoroughly catholic, embracing the finest writings of the best authors of all ages and nations, and with an especially widely open door to present-day British writers, known and unknown.

(2) A permanent stock company of picked, front rank actors and actresses.

(3) Efficient production.

(4) Popular prices, and all parts booked.

Needless to say, all these ideas have been carried out to the letter. The result is that Manchester enjoys the best of everything in the way of dramatic production. The Manchester Repertory Company is held in the highest esteem by all the dramatic authorities throughout the English-speaking world. Glasgow followed Manchester's example. Then Liverpool established her own Citizen's Theatre. Birmingham, Bristol, Sheffield, and Leeds have already the idea, and show signs of falling into line very shortly. Can Dublin support a repertory theatre? . . .

Dublin is the only city in the United Kingdom outside London where an opera company can stay for a five or six week's season, and show enough profit to make a return visit worth while. This speaks well for the musical and artistic taste of the city.

Are the people of Dublin to be for ever denied witnessing such plays as John Galsworthy's *Strife*, or *Justice*, or *The Pigeons*, Ibsen's *An Enemy of the People*, the plays of Arnold Bennett, St. John Hankin, or Granville Barker, simply because managers are afraid to tour them? I say that there is a very large audience for plays of this description in Dublin. I also contend that Dublin and cities of the same intellectual calibre suffer in consequence of the brainless lethargy of other places, which are either unable or unwilling to appreciate this class of play. The visits of Miss Horniman's Company to the Gaiety have always been successful, and only for this lady's enterprise Dublin would probably never have seen Galsworthy's *Silver Box*, or Shaw's *Widowers' Houses, Candida*, etc. The visits of Mr. Granville Barker's companies have always been highly successful. . . .

The theatre is a necessity; but to be effective it must be freed from the manacles of mere commercialism. The modern theatre has become a gigantic force, vital in its effects. It demands the attention of all thinking persons. The influence of the theatrical renaissance is far-reaching. The modern theatre is destined to become the most powerful educational

225

instrument the world has ever known. Our City Fathers are, I fear, a long way off thinking so; therefore, the chances of a municipal theatre being erected in Dublin are very much remote. However, Liverpool has a theatre such as I advocate for Dublin, and she would not have that but for the enterprise of her citizens.[145]

The considerable support, both in the editorial and correspondence columns of the paper,[146] indicates a dissatisfaction with the almost purely national repertoire of the Abbey. To some extent, the formation of the Theatre of Ireland in 1914, of the Dublin Drama League in 1918, and of the Dublin Gate Theatre in 1928, were all attempts to fill this need for a broader, world repertoire of plays.

Although the Gaiety Theatre had invited Flora MacDonnell's local company to perform Shaw's *John Bull's Other Island* in October, most of the productions in Dublin's commercial theatres were of the strictly lowbrow order that had prompted Keogh's proposal. For example, during the week of 22 April, the Theatre Royal presented the farce *Baby Mine*, and the advertisements for this production, which *The Irish Times* called 'utterly silly', invited audiences to laugh at the first act, scream at the second, and yell at the third. On the week of 4 May, the Queen's typically presented a play called *An American*, which it described as a genuine American melodrama of the cowboy order. During the week of 10 June, the Empire offered *Elizabeth and the Baby*, a sketch that involved a domestic misunderstanding over a gold mine and a racehorse. According to *The Irish Independent*, however, it was the domination of the music-hall that most threatened the life of legitimate drama in Dublin:

> If the Dublin public prefer ten or eleven turns of dancing, singing, juggling, and flying pictures to three acts of serious drama, or of intellectual comedy, neither preaching nor satirising will avail to change their tastes.[147]

\* \* \*

During 1912 the Abbey Players were not the only Irish company to perform in England. On 6 February The Ulster Players, an off-shoot of the Ulster Literary Theatre organized by the actor Whitford Kane, presented Rutherford Mayne's *The Drone* at the Royalty Theatre in London. According to *The Pall Mall Gazette*, the Ulster Players were 'one of the most interesting' repertory theatre groups 'now rekindling the native drama and reviving the art of acting in England, Ireland and Scotland'.[148] The performance

226

of the Ulster Players, said *The Pall Mall Gazette*, was 'delightfully acted', exciting 'burst after burst of the heaviest laughter . . . ,' and 'if we had not the spoken music with which Miss Máire O'Neill and Mr. Fred O'Donovan have so often enchanted us in the Dublin plays, we had something none the less racy and enjoyable.' [149] *The London Times* also noted that 'the speech of County Down is not so melodious as that of the region covered by the dramatists of the Abbey Theatre.' [150] *T.P.'s Weekly* even more specifically compared the Ulster Players with their Abbey Counterparts:

> The humour would be broader, the consciousness of the make-believe finer, and the self-analysis more biting and evident. And it is here that Mr. Rutherford Mayne scores as a dramatist of the first order. He gives the touch of canniness and seriousness to situations almost farcical which at once creates an atmosphere and gives you Ulster as apart from any other part of Ireland.[151]

During their London stay, the Ulster Players performance of *The Drone* was watched by the American manager William A. Brady, who subsequently arranged for the Ulster Players to visit the United States in December, 1912, where they played in Washington, Baltimore and New York.

While the Ulster Players were touring America, the Ulster Literary Theatre mounted some new productions in Belfast. A repertoire season at the Grand Opera House was now an annual event, and on the week of 9 December three new plays were performed. According to *The Northern Whig*, the attendance at the opening night was exceptionally good, and the bookings for the remaining performances promised to be even better: '. . . it is plain the Society is well out of the wood through which every amateur organization is forced to grope a painful way, and can rely on a solid measure of support for everything it brings forward.' [152] Nevertheless, as *The Northern Whig* suggested:

> . . . while it is good to have gained an audience, and better to have enlisted actors, for a society of the kind "the play is the thing". In that respect the Ulster Theatre has not quite fulfilled all hopes. The standard of earlier years has not been surpassed; in what may be called legitimate drama as distinct from fantastical burlesque we have as yet nothing to beat *The Enthusiast* or *The Drone*. Of course inspiration blows where it lists. As the hero of *The Drone* profoundly remarks, "You can't rush an inventor", and you certainly can't rush a

playwright. But plays a theatre must have, and if Ulster writers are slow in coming forward the Society should not hesitate to look further afield. Otherwise there is the danger of letting good acting material run to waste, and the still graver danger of being content with easily-won successes. Popular demand and box office necessities cannot be ignored, but out of seven performances in a year to give as the mainstay of four *The Turn of the Road*, which the actors have at their finger-tips, does not strike us as a masterstroke of policy.[153]

Of the two new plays staged on 9 December, *The Northern Whig* preferred Gerald MacNamara's *Thompson in Tír-na-n'Og*, which seemed better constructed than his previous pieces.

Where they rambled it goes straight to the mark, and its compactness and logical handling of topsy-turvy inventions are a delight to all who care for good craftsmanship. The idea on which the piece turns is a dramatic inspiration in itself; to shoot one of King William's generals at the Scarva sham fight into "Tír-na-n'Og", the Irish land of perpetual youth, and confront him with the heroes of the ancient legends, Cuchulain, Finn, Angus, Maev, and the rest, makes for inextinguishable laughter. To have such an idea is one thing; to work it out as Gerald MacNamara does is another. Satire, burlesque, and rough-and-tumble farce is mingled together in the little piece in the most delirious way, and for three-quarters of an hour last night the audience rocked and roared as one has seldom heard theatre-goers in these degenerate days. Yet never once does the author let his stuff run away with him; the game of cross-purposes between the unfortunate Thompson and his tormentors is played out with a touch of Gilbert's diabolical art in extracting the last drop of absurdity from a situation with an unmoved face. Towards the end a little pruning might be desirable, for the continuous harping on Gaelic threatens to become wearisome. But only the slightest pruning is needed. . . .[154]

Not only was MacNamara's ingenuity praised, but also the artistry of the players in the Ulster Literary Theatre was acknowledged:

Immense is the only word that describes Mr. J. M. Harding's Thompson. He has won laurels before, and deserved them, but this is his high-water mark, a bit of comedy acting of which one will long cherish the memory. The heroic figures from the cycles were excellent, and, though it is invidious to select names where all were good, one would like to mention

Mr. Jackson Grahame's High King, Mr. C. K. Ayre's sturdy Cuchulain, the coquettish Grania of Miss Eveleen Fitzgerald— an exceptionally clever bit of work — and the stately charm with which Miss Kathleen Lawrence played Maev.[155]

MacNamara's play was to become the second most popular piece in the Ulster repertoire, and was exceeded in performances only by Rutherford Mayne's *The Drone*.

The other new play staged by the Ulster Literary Theatre on 9 December, *Family Rights* by Miss M. F. Scott, was not well received by *The Northern Whig*:

> It is more like a piece of music-hall cross-talk than honest comedy. A slanging match between a couple of shrews may be quite legitimate if it has any ulterior significance than picturesque vituperation, but *Family Rights* has none. The plan is weak and the framework palpably machine-made, and, while the author proves she can write forcible dialogue, one can accept neither the fiction by which she brings her characters together nor the solution with which she ends it. Its main feature was the acting, and though this came easily enough to old hands, one must unreservedly compliment Miss Peggy McCurdy, a new recruit to the strength of the company. Her Mrs. Rooney was a triumph both of observation and acting. One has seldom seen on the stage this type of nagging woman hit off with the same skill. Miss McCurdy has it in her to go far, and one hopes that the Ulster Theatre will give her the chance of handling bigger and better stuff in the near future.[156]

*The Belfast Newsletter* reacted somewhat more favourably to *Family Rights*, a play that has yet to be published:

> In its range it is little more than a sketch, but it is well put together, and there are more genuinely humorous touches in than are to be found in many a four-act play that has had the advantage of being artfully boomed by people who know the value of advertisement. The material out of which it has been created is scanty enough, but it is skilfully handled, and in the circumstances it is rather a pity that the authoress could not have arranged for a more convincing ending. When Mrs. Fogarty and Mrs. Rooney fell out regarding the Christian name which has to be given to their grandson, the fun is fast and furious, for the women are very jealous of the honour of their respective families, and with the crescendo of passion provoked by their mutual recriminations some starting home truths are blurted out. The two husbands apparently accus-

229

tomed to explosions of this kind, stand idly by whilst the combatants bespatter each other with mud, and Miss Scott is only able to find her way out of the entanglement by allowing a neighbour to break in on the two women in order to announce the death of the child, who, the newcomer explains, had previously been christened and given the name of Patrick instead of Dan or John, as had been designed. It would have been better if the authoress could have discovered some other means of bringing out a truce. Neither of the grandmothers appeared to be very much affected last night on hearing the news of the child's death, and perhaps Miss Scott did not intend them to be, but the play would have left a more vivid impression if she could have managed to separate the pair of termagants in some other way. The acting was very good, although there were moments when the action and the dialogue could have been made more compact and impelling. One glaring fault was the low tone in which some of the artists spoke their lines. Mr. J. M. Harding, one of the most brilliant actors that the Ulster Literary Theatre has yet produced, was a striking exception to this rule. The need for clean enunciation is all the more pressing having regard to the fact that to many members of the audience the dialect is apt to sound somewhat strange and unfamiliar, much as they may admire it and sympathise with the efforts to keep it alive. Mr. Harding was very happy in the role of Dan Fogarty, who, one would judge from the eloquence with which he proposes the toast that starts the trouble between Mrs. Fogarty and Mrs. Rooney, is an ardent politician, revelling in the use of platitudes and in the sound of his own voice, but at bottom a simple, good-natured soul, resolved to follow the line of least resistance in domestic matters, even though he may have an exaggerated sense of his own importance when he is in the company of his male friends in the public house parlour. Mr. Harding's portrait of the old man was very subtle and forceful, and the comedy owed a great deal to the keen intuition which he displayed. Miss M. Crother's command of the dialect and her knowledge of the Ulster character enabled her to make Mrs. Fogarty a very life-like personage. Miss Peggy McCurdy was efficient as Mrs. Rooney, and the little that Mr. G. A. Charters had to do in the role of John Rooney was done with the utmost ability and judgment.[157]

On 10 December the Ulster Literary Theatre performed their third new play of the season, William Paul's *Sweeping the Country*, another work that has never been published. Paul's play received a mixed notice from *The Belfast Newsletter*:

It reveals defects of construction, and the dialogue is occasionally wanting in vigour and spontaneity, but there is some clever character drawing, and the humour is delightful in its freshness and homeliness. The portraits of James McKay, chairman of the Oldtown Urban Council, and a consummate trimmer; Mrs. McKay, an indolent-minded creature who solemnly avers that she does not take any interest in politics and has her knitting in her hand from morning till night; Arthur Vincent, the apostle of the Irish National Regeneration Alliance, who, to use a colloquialism, has the "gift of the gab" and a distressing habit of exercising it; Andy Cunningham, an old labourer, who has a passion for gossip and litigation, along with a large fund of mother-wit; Paddy Doyle, a youthful member of the United Irish League, who will not commit himself to anything until he has had a resolution passed in support of it by the all-important executive; and Albert Barr, who is on the other side of politics to Paddy and only agrees with him in differing from the artful McKay — all these portraits remind one of people whom one has met in real life; and a comedy presenting characters so real and well-contrasted could not possibly be dull. Mr. Paul is not yet thoroughly the master of his medium. His knowledge of stagecraft lands him into awkward predicaments, and it is only by a big effort that he succeeds in extracting himself. He can't get his creatures to move as naturally as he would like them, and sometimes they are awkward in their entrances and exits. Perhaps he has also tried to put too much into his play. At the opening things fall rather flat, and the experience is repeated at the opening of the second act, when the women are depended upon to sustain the flow of conversation. Mr. Paul's men are much more natural than his women, and we get more genuine fun out of them as the plot is developed. On no account would one have missed the mirth-provoking scene when James McKay plans that round-table conference for the purpose of discussing the preparations for the visit of Oldtown of the founder of the Irish National Regeneration Alliance, which, like so many other organisations that have sprung up in this country, is to break down faction and unite all parties on a common platform. Arthur Vincent, the advance agent, speaks eloquently of the aims and possibilities of the Alliance, and he appears to have gained a signal victory when in an unfor-

231

tunate moment he drags out of a handbag a bundle of posters, which are printed on green and orange-coloured paper in order that both parties may be placated. The posters announce a public meeting at which McKay has promised to preside. Paddy Doyle, a Nationalist, and Albert Barr, an Orangeman, have been called in for consultation, and they are for the moment captured by the glamour of Vincent's rhetoric, but the bills in green and orange recall them to their senses. They accuse Vincent of playing a trick on them, vehemently denounce McKay for his share in the conspiracy, and afterwards persuade the organisations they represent to pass resolutions violently condemning the Alliance and expressing disgust at the conduct of McKay in associating himself with it. In its performance by the members of the Ulster Literary Theatre at the Grand Opera House last night the play suffered as a result of the failure of one or two of the artists to memorise their lines. Mr. Gerald MacNamara, as James McKay, was the most flagrant offender, and he had repeatedly to have resort to the prompter. The chief honours of the evening went to Mr. Alan Whitley, whose Paddy Doyle was a masterpiece of stage portraiture. Mr. Whitley is a recent recruit to the Ulster Literary Theatre, but if he had been a veteran at the business he could not possibly have acquitted himself with greater distinction. His was the speech and the manner that one hears and sees on the streets, and his Paddy Doyle, a shrewd, dry-humoured customer, was astonishingly true to life. Mr. J. M. Harding was as quaint and intimate as ever in his admirable study of old Andy Cunningham, who is so staunch in his convictions that he declines to paste the green bills on the hoardings. Mr. John Field was very competent in the role of Albert Barr. Mr. Jackson Grahame was an alert and plausible Arthur Vincent. Miss Eveleen Fitzgerald is deserving of praise for her impersonation of Mrs. McKay. The other roles were filled by Miss Kathleen Lawrence (Molly McKay), Miss Mary Crothers (Mrs. Gray), and Mr. C. J. Abbey (Charlie Moore). Some of the speeches were very indistinctly heard last night, and one had a tantalising experience in trying to piece the words together.[158]

*     *     *

In 1912 the Cork Dramatic Society continued to attract young writers and perform their plays. On 10 April, before a large audience at the Dun Theatre in Queen Street, the Society staged

232

a new one-act comedy by D. P. Lucy, *The Passing of 'Miah*. It played on the same bill with two earlier pieces, Corkery's *The Hermit and the King* and Con O'Leary's *Struck*. Although it has remained unpublished, Lucy's play was to become one of the most popular Cork plays. *The Cork Examiner* described its plot:

> When the curtain rises one finds an ex-soldier (Morgan) discussing among other things a certain bank-robbery that has taken place in Cork — they wonder where the thief may be. When the police in fulfillment of their daily duty come on the scene we find their minds also on work of the bank robbery. Soon after, a gentleman who introduces himself as "Miah Duldoon", of the "Department", strolls into this electric air. By plausible lying he becomes intimate with the publican, and incidentally begins to wind himself into the affections of the daughter, much to the chagrin of Mr. Twomey, her old lover. Enmity arises between the two. Meanwhile Morgan discovers that the gent from the "Department" is none other than a certain Jim Kelly, a deserter from the "Munsters". The complications ensue. "Miah" is arrested on suspicion; he escapes, is hidden in a barrel, is discovered, and led triumphantly to the Barracks. There it is found that a telegram has arrived from Cork stating that the real bank robber has been arrested in the city. "Miah" returns in triumph. But Twomey is not so easily deceived. He has observed the collusion between Morgan and "Miah"; he bribes Morgan; comes at Miah's history, and soon afterwards informs him of the fact. "Miah" sees but one hope of escape — to put Twomey out of the way. As a fact he stuffs his neck and crop into the self-same barrel, as earlier in the play did a like service for himself. The turning of the tables on the ancient lover is all very good unexpected comedy. The police came a second time seeking "Miah" in the barrel — they find the lover. And the curtain comes down on Miah's absence; he has passed — and the contents of the publican's drama with him. From this outline it will be seen that the comedy is full of bustle. There are no dead moments. Yet since the characters remain true to themselves the play never degenerates into farce. The humour has a local touch and is never forced. The dialogue is concise — sometimes a single word conveying the thought. The play was well acted, even in the smallest detail. There was no halting of words or action.[159]

The Cork Society staged no further plays until 2 December when it revived *The Passing of 'Miah* and staged a new Corkery play,

*Israel's Incense. The Cork Constitution* had a number of reservations about the new piece:

It is not a play which can be judged, or at all judged, when one has seen it once only. Incident and action are almost wholly absent, and this because it is a play of ideas; that is the statement of the author, Mr. D. Corkery. One of its defects is that the idea is made to carry more than it will bear. It is over-burdened with thought — introspective and other. Mr. Corkery is a poet, and will be, perhaps, always a poet first and a dramatist afterwards. In his *Embers* the same fault is very noticeable. That play, even the re-written version, is prolonged and involved, and so too is *Israel's Incense*. It should make an appeal to the cultivated intellect and the rich imagination, but one thinks — may be mistakenly — that it would be much more enjoyed on the printed page than before the footlights. In book form one would not wish a line omitted, altered or changed for the prose is of the finest quality — full and resonant — and written with an attention to assonance somewhat rare nowadays; but in play form for the stage a good deal might with advantage be omitted and a good deal more altered. The setting is an ancient Ireland, and the central idea is concerned with Fohnam, a sculptor. In the prologue he is alone in the woods, and the author would have the audience understand he has come there to fathom his thoughts. He meets King Tethra and his followers and returns to Court, and from thence the ideas of Fohnam held sway, but finally his thought masters him and disaster follows upon all he does, and in the end all that remains to him of intellectual worth is of no moment. The play is very difficult to follow, and the fault lies with the author. But, withal, it has a rare dramatic beauty. The players were seen to great advantage. Mr. C. O'Leary was excellent as the King; Mr. J. Flynn stood out prominently as Keltar, the Keeper of the Annals, and so did Mr. P. J. K. Lynch as Fanla; Mr. T. O'Hea as the sculptor had a part peculiarly difficult and handled it excellently; Mr. J. Gilley was good as the King's Herald; Miss M. O'Connell did well as Alova (the Queen); Miss L. Desmond and Miss N. O'Brien were interesting as Singing Maidens; Mr. D. Breen wrote the songs in the piece; Mr. C. Foley was very clever as Connud, and the parts of Ivor, Mr. P. Mulcahy; Delbay, Mr. P. O'Connell; and a Sailor, Mr. C. Perrott, were well taken.[160]

*The Cork Free Press* thought that the play was as yet too much for the local players, and went on to remark:

Mr. Corkery writes beautiful stuff, realistic word-pictures, which, if one closed his eyes and listened merely to the actors, would intoxicate the auditor with its perfervid imagery — but this is not drama. No one will deny that Milton's *Paradise Lost* or Dante's *Inferno* is supreme art, but to cut these up into lengths and assign them to the different actors is not making a drama. The setting of *Israel's Incense* is old Irish, though the place is described as "Here or Elsewhere", or the time, "Yesterday or To-day". Why this vagueness, considering that the costumes, actors, and environment are obviously the first or second century of the Christian era? And why *Israel's Incense*? There is nothing whatever in the piece to suggest either incense or Hebrews. Fohnam, the sculptor, excellently played by Mr. T. O'Hea, is a visionary of the Hamlet type who achieves nothing because he is in advance of his age. He carves a statue of "Womanhood" which displeases the primitive people who surround him because she typifies the stern grief of the mother who gives her sons to the ravens in battle instead of having children playing round her knees. The sculptor's statue of "life" in the market-place also causes displeasure, because it is symbolical of a worker, not a fighter and a reveller, and so this dreamer falls foul of everybody, from the King downwards. He is beloved by the singing maiden, but spurns her, and makes love to the Queen, who at first favours but ultimately discards him. The whole action of the piece is a Greek tragedy, gloomy, relentless, and one must confess a bit disjointed. Plenty of pruning is necessary, for it is too much "words, words, words". The actors did their best and special mention must be made of Mr. P. J. K. Lynch as Fanla, the King's Counsellor, who, as usual, spoke his lines and acted in fine style.[161]

The play was evidently important to Corkery, for he seems to have revised it several times, and some years later it was presented at the Abbey under the title of *Fohnam the Sculptor*. To judge by the printed text, however, one must conclude that the piece was never worked into legitimate drama or effective poetry.

On 3 December, the Society staged a triple bill of one-act plays, which included Corkery's fairly successful comedy, *The Onus of Ownership*, as well as two new pieces, *The Crossing* by Con O'Leary and *Drift* by John F. Lyons. On this occasion the Society played on the much roomier stage of the Opera House, but once again the audience was small.

According to *The Cork Constitution*, O'Leary's *The Crossing*

235

was clever and merited a larger audience, but it was also highly derivative:

> The author of this play has come under the influence of Synge, and the dialogue has a good deal of the poetic beauty, richness of imagination, and flexible strength that makes the dramatic work of Synge memorable. All the characters are well drawn, and are alive in the best dramatic sense of the word. If the play were not so reminiscent, especially the character of the ballad singer; if it came clean from the intellect and imagination of the author it would be a near approach to a masterpiece; as it is, one must make large deductions. The scene is laid in the kitchen of a very poor lodging-house, kept by one William Fenton. Tramps, with other objectionable persons, lodge there in a casual way. One lodger is Mary the Roads, and a second is Mathew the Rhymer. Mary's son has been condemned to be hanged for murder, and around this fact the whole interest of the play centres. William Fenton has a brother, Thomas, who is far away and in some employment not known to William. Mary bemoans the fate of her son, and has the sympathy of the ballad singer, who has a ballad ready, and will sing it on the morning of the execution. There is breadth and power in the scene between her and the Rhymer and William, and the ballads give adequate atmosphere in a fascinating way. Then Thomas Fenton returns. He learns with dismay that his brother keeps a lodging house, and with greater dismay that the mother of the murderer is before him. The scene so shapes itself that the mother dies suddenly, and then Thomas Fenton makes the startling disclosure that he is the common hangman, and will execute her son in the morning. The dramatic surprise in the last incident is well conceived. Mr. J. Flynn was clever as Wm. Fenton; Miss M. O'Connell attained a high standard as Mary the Roads; Mr. P. J. K. Lynch will yet distinguish himself as an actor, for his Mathew the Rhymer was self-restrained and finished in all respects; Mr. T. O'Hea was good as Thomas Fenton. . . .[162]

The critic for the *Cork Free Press* called *The Crossing* 'a powerful and even painful play' and indicated that 'the only fault to be found with it is the rather stilted phraseology of some of the characters. One does not find tramps and wastrels terming a face a "visage", and so on. . . .' [163] The play was later produced by the Abbey.

The critic for the *Cork Free Press*, however, believed that the tragedy *Drift* by John F. Lyons was 'the most effective and most convincing' of the three one-act plays performed on 3 December:

Its theme was emigration and the sundering of ties and the breaking of hearts so common and so heart-rending a feature in Irish peasant life. The piece was most convincingly played, and made a deep impression, the author being called and warmly applauded. The acting all through was most natural and affecting, and Mr. Lyons is to be congratulated on a charmingly real and moving piece of work. Miss M. O'Connell was excellent as the aged and over-wrought mother; Miss L. Desmond made a pathetic "Mary", the self-sacrificing daughter; "Shaun" had a manly exponent in Mr. T. O'Hea; and Mr. P. J. K. Lynch gave a capital study of Donald O'Neill, while Ned Corcoran, the postman, was naturally portrayed by Mr. J. Flynn.[164]

*The Cork Constitution* did not, however, agree, remarking:

In part, at any rate, it appears to be in the wrong key; the love-making between Mary Downey and Donal O'Neill is an example at point. But the play is really clever. The scene shows a cottage interior, Mrs. Downey's husband (or is it?) has been in America twenty years; she laments him, and still more she laments the approaching departure of her son, Shaun, for America. He has a friend Donal O'Neill, who is also going to America. Donal is in love with Mary Downey. The whole play is so written as to secure the tragic note, as it really is, of the emigration question. Shaun goes; Donal goes. A letter comes from America; it tells of the death of Mrs. Downey's husband (?). The curtain falls on this climax. Mr. Lyons should do better work, and, no doubt, will. As. Mrs. Downey, Miss M. O'Connell was good, but the make-up was indifferent; she looked young — not old enough to be the mother of Mary.[165]

Another amateur group in Cork, the Dramatic Society of the I.C.I. C.Y.M.A., staged an evening of plays. On 21 and 22 November, in the Gregg Hall, South Mall, they produced *Blind* by R. Cooney, *Under a Delusion* by Dixon Child, and *The Dream Market* by J. Bernard MacCarthy. *The Cork Constitution* reported that the pieces were well acted and staged, but perhaps only *The Dream Market* is of interest, for this unpublished work was by a writer who was to become one of Ireland's most prolific playwrights. As *The Cork Constitution* described it:

237

This play is in two acts, and the author is Mr. J. Bernard MacCarthy, Crosshaven. While Mr. Cooney's play is concerned with conventional dramatic methods — and none the worse for that — Mr. MacCarthy adopts Abbey Theatre or repertory theatre methods, and the contrast was interesting and instructive. The play is concerned with one Allan Moore, who has literary tastes and is a dreamer. His mother, who is a widow, does not understand him, and what he writes she describes as "dream papers". Living with the widow is Kathleen Ryan; the widow has adopted her. She falls in love with Alan. There is an Iris Cairnham, who has a friend and lover, Captain Gainford. She is a flirt, a woman with a mercurial temperament, and she recklessly plays with the hearts of men. To the house of the widow came one day Iris and the Captain, who upbraids her for her behaviour to her men friends. The conversation so shapes itself that the Captain wagers with her that she cannot win the heart of Allan Moore. The terms of the wager are written. While the two are conversing, they are alone. When they leave, Iris leaves after her the written terms of the wager, and the paper is found by Kathleen Ryan. Allan enters, and she shows her jealousy of Iris. He assures her she need not be jealous, and she in turn expresses her opinion of Iris in harsh terms. Asked by him to prove what she says, she replies he ought to take her word, which he refuses to do. The affair of Iris and Allan proceeds, and Iris falls in love with him. He returns home at a late hour, and is followed by Iris. He upbraids her as a wanton flirt, and she convinces him she really loves him. Kathleen hears the declaration, sees the attitude of Allan, and goes out. When she returns they are gone, and the play ends as she burns the written wager in the flame of the candle. The play is full of real dramatic quality, and the author should yet do highly meritorious work as a playwright. He received a call upon the fall of the curtain and it was most richly deserved. As the widow Moore, Miss Dora Ingle was delightful; Miss Olive Brooke Hughes was excellent as Kathleen, and the emotional moments quite held the audience; Miss E. M. Bridges gave proof of genuine dramatic talent as Iris Cairnham; Mr. T. Horne very admirably painted the interesting character study, Allan Moore; Mr. F. W. Thompson stood out prominently in the cast as Captain Gainford. His acting was finished and of a high standard.[166]

238

# 1913

For Dublin, 1913 was probably most notable for the great labour dispute which began in Horse Show week, lasted well into 1914, and directly involved a third of the city's population. Now the Great Lockout is perhaps mainly known through James Plunkett's novel, *Strumpet City*, or through Seán O'Casey's plays, *Red Roses for Me* and *The Star Turns Red*. Then, it was a traumatic disruption of the city's life, and it involved, much to their credit, many of the city's intellectuals — Æ, Yeats, Shaw, Conal O'Riordan, the Count and Countess Markievicz, Maud Gonne, and an obscure Dublin working-man, Seán O'Casey.[1] This account, of course, is a theatrical rather than a social history, but the labour troubles did have an effect upon the theatre, as we shall see.

\* \* \*

The Abbey Theatre had an enormously busy and really rather brilliant year. For the first four months the First Company was still playing in America, but the Second Company was continuously active at home, giving a changing bill each week which included Hyde's *The Marriage*, Boyle's *The Building Fund* and *The Mineral Workers*, Mayne's *Red Turf*, Fitzmaurice's *The Country Dressmaker*, Synge's *Riders to the Sea* and *The Shadow of the Glen*, Lady Gregory's *Workhouse Ward*, *Dervorgilla*, *Hyacinth Halvey*, *The Rising of the Moon*, *The Gaol Gate*, and *Spreading the News*, Ray's *The Casting-Out of Martin Whelan*, Yeats's *Kathleen ni Houlihan* and *The Pot of Broth*, Murray's *Birthright*, and first productions of G. Sidney Paternoster's *The Dean of St. Patrick's*, Hauptmann's *Hannele*, Strindberg's *There are Crimes and Crimes* and *The Stronger*, John Guinan's *The Cuckoo's Nest*, Gertrude Robins's *The Home-Coming*, *Broken Faith* by Geraldine D. Cummins and Suzanne R. Day, and George Fitzmaurice's little masterpiece, *The Magic Glasses*.

The First Company returned in May to perform briefly at the Abbey, and then both companies combined their resources for six weeks at the Royal Court Theatre in London. Sinclair and a few of the other actors then toured the English music-halls, performing one-act plays for the remainder of the summer.

The Abbey re-opened early in September, and except for three days at the Curragh and a week in Liverpool, remained open for the rest of the year. Sometimes the theatre was open for its usual

Thursday, Friday, Saturday and Saturday matinee schedule; and sometimes it was open for six days with a Wednesday matinee also. In such instances, the Second Company would usually take one half of the week and the First Company the rest.

In the last four months of the year, the joint productions included Ervine's *The Magnanimous Lover*, Guinan's *The Cuckoo's Nest*, Ray's *The Casting-Out of Martin Whelan*, Hyde's *The Marriage*, Fitzmaurice's *The Country Dressmaker*, Boyle's *Family Failing*, Lady Gregory's *The Gaol Gate*, Tagore's *The Post Office*, Hauptmann's *Hannele*, Boyle's *The Building Fund*, Robinson's *Patriots*, Paternoster's *The Dean of St. Patrick's*, Yeats's *Kathleen ni Houlihan*, Lady Gregory's *The Canavans*, *The Second Shepherd's Play*, *Broken Faith* by Cummins and Day, Fitzmaurice's *The Magic Glasses*, Yeats's *On the King's Threshold*, Lady Gregory's *Damer's Gold*, Synge's *Riders to the Sea*, Boyle's *The Eloquent Dempsy*, Lady Gregory's *Spreading the News*, W. F. Casey's *The Suburban Groove*, Lady Gregory's *The Rising of the Moon*, Murray's *Birthright*, Lady Gregory's *Hyacinth Halvey*, Ervine's *Mixed Marriage*, O'Riordan's *The Piper*, Casey's *The Man Who Missed the Tide*, Lady Gregory's *Workhouse Ward*, Synge's *The Shadow of the Glen*, Lady Gregory's *Mac Darragh's Wife*, Boyle's *The Mineral Workers* and *The Building Fund*, and the first productions of T. C. Murray's *Sovereign Love*, Joseph Connolly's *The Mine Land*, Mrs. Bart Kennedy's *My Lord*, R. J. Ray's *The Gombeen Man*, Ervine's *The Critics*, Seumas O'Brien's *Duty*, and Séamus O'Kelly's *The Bribe*. In addition, the Abbey was rented during the year to the Ulster Players, to St. Enda's School, and to the Irish-speaking group. An Cluithcheóirí. 1913 is not generally regarded as a remarkable year for the Abbey, but with extended tours to America and London, with a constantly varied schedule from the theatre's repertoire of favourites, and with fourteen new productions, the theatre had never performed the function of a repertory company so thoroughly and excitingly.

In America, the First Company with Sara Allgood, Sinclair, Kerrigan and O'Donovan offered a generous selection from the theatre's repertoire, including *The Playboy, Riders to the Sea, Blanco Posnet, Kathleen ni Houlihan, The Countess Cathleen, The Rising of the Moon, Workhouse Ward, Mixed Marriage, The Magnanimous Lover, Maurice Harte, Patriots, The Building Fund* and other plays. The critics again greeted them with a chorus of praise for their simplicity and sincerity, and, except for a week of poor houses in Pittsburgh, the company played to large and appreciative audiences. For the month of January, the company was at the Fine Arts Theatre in Chicago, except for a matinee on

10 January in South Bend, Indiana, at Notre Dame University, where the audience was estimated at 1,700 people.

After Chicago, the company played a week in Montreal where there was some mild opposition to *The Playboy*. The United Irish League of Montreal labelled the play 'A vile misrepresentation of Irish life'. However, the performance occasioned only 'a little disaffection, which . . . was quickly repudiated and lost in the hearty applause given'.[2]

On 3 February the company opened for a week at the Nixon Theatre in Pittsburgh to good notices and poor houses. Then, on 10 February, the company began a very successful five week engagement at Wallack's Theatre in New York, during which time they went through most of their extensive repertoire. As the reviews on the tour had been overwhelmingly admiring, it might be interesting to note the lonely but probably valid criticisms of *The New York Globe* about the production of Robinson's *Patriots*:

> As for the acting it must be confessed that the Abbey Theatre players do not show up to advantage in a large house. Moreover, their style of acting is not suited to this type of play. What they need to cultivate — particularly the younger members of the company — is variety. Their habit of dropping the voice at the end of every sentence, and dividing the sentence into short-winded fragments gives an air of naturalness and freshness to the impersonation of peasants in rural communities. But when it comes to small-town, middle-class types, their method seems dull and monotonous. Many of their speeches were inaudible.[3]

After New York, the company went to Philadelphia where *The Playboy* was largely attended and well received. However, when the company then moved to Boston, the Mayor requested them not to stage *The Playboy*. Otherwise, the four weeks run at Boston's Plymouth Theatre was most successful, and on 24 March the company gave the first performance of Lady Gregory's *Galway Races*. This performance has been unnoted by historians, and the little play, at least in its Boston version, was never revived. From the Boston reviews, the play seems to have been a considerably rewritten version of Lady Gregory's early piece, *Twenty-Five*, and it was later to be rewritten as *On the Racecourse*. The Boston reviews were collected and summarized by Holloway:

> The Boston *Journal* of 25 March writes: "*Galway Races*, Lady Gregory's newest contribution to the series of plays of Irish life and character, is a collection of folk songs to which

241

a slight story has been tied. Miss Allgood, Mr. Kerrigan, and Mr. Doran played it well."

The Boston *Traveller* (25 March) says: "It is a quaint little piece, interspersed with melodious Irish songs."

The Boston *Evening Record* remarks: "Lady Gregory's little comedy of the *Galway Races* presenting the story of a wandering follower of the races, who collects a few coins by a gambling game; of his wife who sings songs to draw the crowds, and of the returning sweetheart, is slight. It gives Miss Allgood a part in which her youth and comeliness are manifest, and it serves as vehicle for a number of Irish folk songs pleasing in themselves, but rather forced into the scene. Miss Allgood, Mr. Kerrigan, and Mr. Doran acquitted themselves satisfactorily with little to do or say."

The critic of the Boston *Evening Telegraph* writes of the piece: "The truth is that there seems little to it but strong, handsome Miss Allgood, as ballad singer; Mr. Kerrigan, as a liquorish country-fair gambler, who had wed her, and a lean stranger who had loved the woman before he went away to seek his fortune — these three and a half-dozen delightful old folk tunes which they sang. The stranger gambled at the husband's wheel and lost his five golden sovereigns, yet whether out of love for the woman he could not wed, but could thus give comfort, no one could surely say.

"The husband hinted as much, but Lady Gregory who really knew all about it, left things very hazy. There was just a little patch of the rich sunlight of humanity flicking here and there across a morning of scraps by an Irish roadside. Yet even that was delightful in its way." [4]

On 21 April, the company gave a final matinee in New York before sailing for Ireland. The matinee was in aid of the Municipal Art Gallery Fund, and was attended by many prominent Irish Americans, including John Quinn, Finley Peter Dunne, and the Hon. W. Bourke Cockran who had on the first tour violently opposed *The Playboy*, but who now made a speech congratulating Ireland on the intellectual contribution it had made to the world through its plays and players.

The company then boarded the *Cymric* and arrived in Queenstown on 1 May, and proceeded immediately to Dublin.

> ... Mr. Arthur Sinclair said that the Company were all merry and bright. He should say, however, that an unfortunate accident occurred on the trip homewards to Lady Gregory. On Monday last Lady Gregory, while entering a companion-

way on board the *Cymric*, had her hand caught in an iron doorway, which swung to in a lurch of the vessel. He (Mr. Sinclair) was first to her assistance, and found her in a fainting condition. The injury, which was to her right hand, was so serious as to call for the attention of the ship's doctor. Lady Gregory sustained a severe shock, but he was glad to say that she was rapidly recovering from the effects of the injury. . . .

Mr. Sinclair mentioned that the only appearance the first company will make this season at the Abbey will be that arranged in aid of the Art Gallery. Later on, they will go to Oxford, Birmingham, London, where they will go into vaudeville next month, and they will enter upon a tour of the provinces, which will include appearances in Manchester, Brighton, Glasgow, and Newcastle-on-Tyne.

It was characteristic of Mr. J. M. Kerrigan that very soon after being welcomed home by his mother and the other members of his family, he should say: "I must now be off to take a view of my native city." He was taking the city's views, a process more agreeable to him perhaps than giving his views to the Press.[5]

The members of the company who arrived with Lady Gregory this afternoon were — Miss Allgood, Miss Mona O'Beirne, Miss Eithne Magee, Miss Kathleen Drago, Miss Eileen O'Doherty, Messrs. Arthur Sinclair, J. M. Kerrigan, Fred O'Donovan (and Mrs. O'Donovan), J. A. O'Rourke, S. Morgan, U. Wright, M. J. Dolan, Eugene Monk.[6]

Lady Gregory, whose arm is protected by a sling, left for her residence in Gort this evening, and Miss Allgood has gone to London.[7]

\*    \*    \*

When the First Company arrived back, the Second Company, led by Lennox Robinson, was playing in the South; and on 3 May Robinson wrote to Lady Gregory from Cork about an extraordinary reception given to *Hyacinth Halvey* in Mallow:

Dear Lady Gregory,

I was very glad to see from the papers that you had all got back safely. I hope your hand is better — it must have been horribly painful. You will be amused to hear there was almost a riot last night in Mallow over *Hyacinth Halvey* — of all plays! There was a very large and appreciative audience, but at the very beginning of *Hyacinth* some of the gallery apparently got it into their heads that the play was making fun of

243

the priest — or religion. "Looking at the pictures in the Lives of the Saints" was hissed. They hissed Hyacinth himself, and shouted "Is that Irish?" when he declares he'll commit some crime. Oh! it was quite like America and *The Playboy*. They got quieter then, but were ready to hiss at any moment. It was only a group in the gallery — one or two drunks I think — but it was a curious attitude to take up. *Hyacinth* always seemed so innocent. We did fairly well at Tralee. *Bunty*[8] had been the previous week and had cleaned out the town — if we have a good house at Mallow tonight I think we will just about come through the week without loss.

I will be in Dublin tomorrow night.

Yours sincerely,
LENNOX ROBINSON[9]

Under Robinson, the Second Company had been very busy, playing constantly and even presenting several new pieces. The first new production appeared on 24 January, and was an ambitious four-act drama by G. Sidney Paternoster entitled *The Dean of St. Patrick's*.[10] This was apparently the first play to be written about the powerful but dramatically enigmatic figure of Jonathan Swift. In later years the subject was taken up, with various degrees of success, by Arthur Power, Lord Longford, W. B. Yeats, Denis Johnston, Paul Vincent Carroll, Sybil Le Brocquy and Eugene McCabe. The central problem with Swift, which perhaps only Denis Johnston has solved with any dramatic effectiveness, is the nature of the Dean's relations with Stella and Vanessa. Certainly, some of the later dramatists who attacked the problem did so because, quite legitimately, the Dean spoke to something important to them. Thus, Yeats's Swift becomes a useful exemplar of his theory of history, and Carroll's Swift becomes a rather distorted surrogate for the author. In any event, G. Sidney Paternoster did not hesitate to depart from the known facts for his own purposes, and arranged an aborted marriage for Swift and Stella in St. Patrick's Cathedral. As *The Irish Times* summarized the plot:

In the first act (the rectory at Laracor, 1710) we have Swift's departure for London, after an avowal of love to Stella, and a reference to the mental complaint, the fears of which had hitherto kept him from that avowal. In the second act (1713) Swift is shown at the Van Homrigh's, and, in addition to the piquant passages with Vanessa, we have a vigorous introduction of political interest, concluding with Swift's relegation to the Deanery of St. Patrick's. The scene of the third

244

act is laid in the cathedral itself (1716), where Stella is seen awaiting the arrival of Swift and of the Archbishop to marry them. With much boldness, the author brings Vanessa on the scene, and there is a powerful passage between the two women, and then another between Swift and Vanessa. In the last act, Swift receives the news of Stella's death, and the fall of the curtain leaves him alone with his bitter reflections.[11]

The play has never been published, but probably the soundest evaluation of its merits was the review in *The Irish Citizen*:

> This four-act semi-historical play was produced last Thursday by the Abbey's second company. On two grounds it stands out for praise — firstly, it is a piece a long haleine, for it occupies easily the whole evening, unaided by the usual Gregorian after-piece, and it returns to the Abbey's earlier manner of historical plays. Excepting these points, however, the play is a "misfit", partly because it smells overmuch of the lamp and strains unduly after effect, and partly because, for good or ill, the Abbey caste is, with one or two exceptions, irrevocably wedded to "peasant" drama and by very reason of its exquisite fitness to folk-play, unsuited for eighteenth-century courts and deaneries. The Dean's glamour and genius are singularly unconvincing — it is very hard to take a genius for granted in a novel or on the stage; the patriot, the pamphleteer, the politician, are overlooked in the lover. Stella, whose wit and verve were as sharp as the Dean's own, is over-sentimentalised, while Vanessa emerges from Mr. Paternoster's crucible as a shrewish little minx. History is unduly tampered with, and in the last act melodrama is indulged in to make of the gloom of that lacerated heart more lurid, more falsely pathetic. Mr. Murphy made the best of the trying title role; his rendering was careful and studied, but hardly happy. Nell Byrne was a sweet and appealing heroine, but one missed the genius and humour of Swift's Stella of the cipher love-making language. Ann Coppinger was a hussy to the life, but not Vanessa. The minor characters were more successful, because less ambitious: Mrs. Dingley (Nora Desmond), the faithful Patrick (Michael Conniffe), supercilious Oxford (Charles Power) came nearer the scope of regular Abbey drama. In a theme more congenial to his talent and to that of his players, Mr. Paternoster may do better.[12]

On 20 February the Abbey produced Gerhardt Hauptmann's *Hannele*, and two weeks later, on 6 March, August Strindberg's

*There are Crimes and Crimes.* Hauptmann and Strindberg were known in Dublin only by reputation, and their reputations were like that, even still, of Ibsen — morally suspect. However, Robinson, having perhaps learned caution from the Miss Horniman controversy of 1910, chose two plays that were, even for Dublin, morally impeccable. Nevertheless, the *Times* critic still wrote wafflingly of *Hannele* that:

> On the Continent it was deemed over-religious, and in America it was condemned as being to a certain extent irreligious. It is easily understood, therefore, that the play does not lend itself readily to the ordinary canons of criticism. On people of a certain temperament it would jar excessively, while to others it might appeal with a deep religious fervour.[13]

Jack Point in *The Evening Herald* wrote in the same vein, comparing the play to *The Passing of the Third Floor Back*, and wondering if any 'particularly useful purpose will be served in this twentieth century by the impersonation of sacred personages.' [14] It is refreshing, then, to turn to the critique of S. Mac O in *The Irish Citizen*, which seems exactly on target:

> The performance of the German poet, Gerhardt Hauptmann, through the dream-play, *Hannele*, at the Abbey last week, was one of those occasions that reduce the critical fraternity to the mental state of the critics at the end of *Fanny's First Play*. They go to the theatre with the smug assumption that they are going to criticise the play; while the truth is that the play sits in judgment on their intelligence. They go away and write "Hannele is blasphemous," "Hannele is commonplace," "Hannele is glorious," "Hannele is unconvincing"; and all the time the play's not the thing! The only thing that matters is Hauptmann; the poet who takes in one hand the most sacred figure of Christian idealism, and in the other the product of a lop-sided Christian social realism, a suicide girl-waif; and, putting between these two some specimens of the proletariat, the middle class, and the overlords — a background of actuality to a foreground of dream and symbol — offers to us a mind poised and beautiful that touches humanity with the light of the spirit, and invests Godhead with something of humanity. Surely a rich gift to this age of intellectual prostitution.
>
> The acting of the play was good. Miss Lilian Jago as Hannele scored a decided success. Her grip and enunciation should carry her far. The other parts were all excellently

filled; but the part of the Stranger, though taken with great solemnity, would be much enhanced if the player was the possessor of a clear voice capable of inflexion. We congratule Mr. Lennox Robinson on the delightful mounting of the play. We regret we cannot congratulate Dublin on its dramatic taste: the audience for the first Dublin performance of a Continental masterpiece was pathetically small.[15]

Lilian Jago as Hannele was admired by all the critics, but when the play was revived in April *The Irish Citizen* critic

> . . . did not "enjoy" it half so much as on its first production. Perhaps that was because the delicacy of the play does not permit of faulty presentation, and faults were plentiful. The same actor played the Stranger, and spoke the lines very monotonously. The mother in the dream again chanted her speech. The drunken father was not improved by the change of actor. The gauze curtain, crumpled and illuminated in parts, worried the eye.
>
> With these blemishes removed, the performance would be excellent. Miss Jago as Hannele maintained her fine level as an actress. Notwithstanding a very evident sense that some of the actors were speaking memorised sentences, and were always remembering mannerisms of the first-company players, it was good to feel quite certain that the words would come all right. The pauper crowd was very much alive. . . .[16]

Of *There are Crimes and Crimes*, the *Times* critic remarked in the space of two sentences that it was (1) interesting, (2) fairly interesting, and (3) 'as boring as laboured sermons always are'. Perhaps this was because the play had 'a great deal of wearisome and twaddly conversation'. At any rate, he went on to say:

> The play, in short, abounds in illustrations of moral truth, graphically presented. As presented by the Abbey company, it was without offence — perhaps a desirable statement, in view of Strindberg's reputation. Shortened to some extent, it would be one of the most interesting things in the Abbey *repertoire*. There was much good acting in the production. Mr. Tomás Thornhill only needed to be a more mercurial sort of person, but a certain stiffness was to be excused in an actor of so little stage experience. "Tomás Thornhill", by the way, is the pseudonym of a gentleman who was probably well known to most of the audience.[17] Miss Elizabeth Young presented a very fascinating portrait of the brilliant Henriette. Her dresses alone were things of wonder. In her acting she

maintained a high degree of intensity. . . . The staging was excellent; for a drama of ideas — for all drama that can do without the support of mere auxiliary interests — the simple curtain settings, with the minimum of properties, are quite the best. Mr. Lennox Robinson's production was eminently satisfactory.[18]

Jack Point, imperceptive as usual, thought that 'The stage accessories were rather primitive', and that the piece was 'much ado about nothing'. He did concede that the production had some interest, inasmuch as 'several of our modern Irish plays are largely second-hand Strindberg stuff touched up a bit, naturally, with a trifle of green paint.' [19]

On 13 March, the Second Company presented for the first time John Guinan's three-act comedy, *The Cuckoo's Nest*. Jack Point, whom one must sometimes suspect of either insanity or drunkenness, has an incredible review, that maunders on at great length about the habits of cuckoos, before finally noting that there are no cuckoos in the play, except possibly one of the characters. About the only specific criticism in his long notice was that Farrell Pelly as a farm labourer should not have parted his hair in the middle and worn rings, but he vaguely intimated that the subject of matchmaking lacked novelty, none of the characters was lovable, and the dialogue was badly handled.[20] Actually, the interesting quality of Guinan's dialogue was the only point the rest of the critics could agree upon, and probably the only point of interest about the play today. The *Times* critic, for instance, wrote:

The merit of the play does not lie in its dramatic strength, for there are many necessary elements lacking. It is devoid of action, and the characterisation is rather weak — we can hardly expect perfection in a young playwright in his first play. Its greatest attribute is its picturesque diction, which seems to be modelled upon Synge's style. But though Mr. Guinan has the gift in an exceptional way, he has not yet acquired the art of cloaking his language and making it subsidiary to the character. No matter how fascinating the language — and Mr. Guinan's language is fascinating — unless there is life and movement in the play it will not stand much strain. The first act of *The Cuckoo's Nest* is, for instance, extremely good, but subsequently the play has a tendency to run down for want of sufficient motive power. Even the author's delightful phraseology does not save it. The bread is too thin for the butter.[21]

Actually, this play as well as Guinan's subsequent work has this same fault, a rich dialogue which talks about rather than dramatizes an overly elaborate plot. It was a fault that was to bedevil even more notable Irish dramatists such as George Fitzmaurice and M. J. Molloy. Probably the soundest comment on the play is again from *The Irish Citizen*:

> To those who remember the thrill of an Abbey First Night in the old days, these premieres always give a certain sensation: there is always the possibility of being privileged to preside at the birth of a masterpiece. But *The Cuckoo's Nest*, though a fair specimen of the average peasant play, encouraged no such hope. It is a comedy of intrigue; relying rather on comic juxtaposition and verbal entanglements than of play of character. The dialogue often sparkles, and again is almost as boring as would be the case in real life. It has the same dread facility that makes Lady Gregory's wittiest repartee dull, because one gets too plentiful a crop. The whole play needs compression, particularly the last act: it is a piece in which nothing happens, and there is much talk about it. The characters are left paired at the end exactly as was suspected from the beginning, save in one instance.[22]

Gertrude Robins's *The Home-Coming*, a one-act tragedy first produced on 10 April, utilised the old story of a grasping peasant couple who murder a rich visitor for his gold, only to find that the visitor was their long-absent son. George Lillo had used the story centuries before, and T. C. Murray was to use it several years later for his Abbey play, *The Blind Wolf*. Both Miss Robins and Murray placed their plays on the Continent rather than in the Irish countryside. As both short tragedies are rather *The Playboy* in reverse, we might plausibly surmise that both authors were understandably afraid of a patriotic protest. Nevertheless, both plays would probably have gained in strength and verisimilitude by an Irish setting. To Jack Point, the Galician setting of Miss Robins's play simply accentuated the threadbareness of the story, and he thought that 'Messrs. Guiry, Connolly, Pelly, and Miss Moloney did the best they could with such a play.'[23] *The Irish Citizen* thought the play merely grim, but 'Helen Moloney, on whom the burden of the representation fell, gave an admirable study. . . . The other parts were less satisfactorily filled, and the dialogue was often unconvincing.'[24]

On 17 April, the Second Company presented Strindberg's *The Stronger* as a curtain raiser to *The Mineral Workers*. Jack Point, after noting that the play was described as a comedy in one act, dryly added that he observed no act within in it, and that 'Strindberg had original ideas as to what constitutes humour.' He also noted that the play took place in a Paris restaurant where smoking was 'quite plainly permissible', and that 'From the caterer's point of view, the staging was on the plain side.' [25] Elizabeth Young spoke the play's monologue to Una O'Connor, and *The Irish Citizen* thought that she did it with 'excellent finesse'.[26]

The Second Company continued its remarkable productivity the next week when, on 24 April, there was a triple bill that included the first productions of *Broken Faith* by Suzanne R. Day and Geraldine Cummins, and also of George Fitzmaurice's wry masterpiece, *The Magic Glasses*. Miss Day and Miss Cummins were Cork ladies who continued, like Somerville and Ross, their writing partnership for several years. Indeed, in later life Geraldine Cummins wrote a biography of Edith Somerville, as well as several volumes of psychical research. At this time, both ladies were very active in the Munster Women's Franchise League, of which Miss Day was the Secretary. The Day and Cummins play has not been published, but in the contemporary review it received a good deal more attention than did *The Magic Glasses*. The most sympathetic review was, naturally, in the suffragette paper, *The Irish Citizen*. After noting that the house was sadly empty, the reviewer addressed himself to *Broken Faith*:

Here we have the familiar poor interior, where the harassed wife is hard put to it to place even a "dinner" of bread and tea before her husband, who comes in from work. The man, Michael Gara, a lazy, wretched, dispirited type, always complaining of bad luck, and without energy to seize a chance of work when it offers, is at last goaded by misery into crime. Then the despicable man and his doting old mother think it may be possible to throw the blame on the unhappy wife, and they both implore Bridget to confess to the crime; she actually consents to do so, and Michael is exulting in the prospects of a free life in America, when she asks him what about the children? Will he take them with him to the States? He callously refused to sling any such burden round his neck, and says the children can go to the workhouse till their mother comes out of jail. Instantly Bridget breaks her promise — the father may desert his children, but she will never do so; and the play ends with the arrest of Michael. It is a sordid tragedy, redeemed by the heroic character of the woman, as indeed we should expect to find in the work of a lady who adds no small share of dramatic ability to her well-known feminist and philanthropic activities.[27]

Actually, fuller summaries in other journals make it evident that there was considerable awkwardness in the handling of the plot, particularly in offstage incidents and characters.

Fitzmaurice's *Magic Glasses* received both much less space and much less gentle treatment. One reviewer simply said, 'It is a piece of unmitigated nonsense, capitally acted and productive of a good deal of amusement, but not worth detailed examination.' [28] Jack Point remarked merely 'a clever little joke, but it is distinctly funny.' [29] The best notice called the play 'an extraordinary farce' which 'in its quaint and rich vocabulary, keeps up the best tradition of the Abbey Theatre'. However, all of these notices were only a paragraph long, and even the admiring comments seemed to miss the point of the play. This reception was hardly lost on Fitzmaurice who wrote (in the only letter of his which has so far come to light) later in the year to Lady Gregory:

> Duagh
> Kilmorna
> 21 September 1913

Dear Madam,
    As I have already informed you I returned *The Dandy Dolls* to the theatre at the request of Mr. Yeats. The reasons you give for his rejecting it were such as he gave me himself, but I did not accept them as valid, nor the criticism in general which he was pleased to make on the play, inasmuch as he was utterly at sea as to the inner meaning and drift of the piece, and I wrote two letters to him explaining this. The second rejection, however, I took as final and I did not intend to bother further about getting it taken at the Abbey. Shortly afterwards I got a letter from the Abbey asking me to send on the play, stating that Mr. Yeats thought it and *The Magic Glasses* the best plays I had given them but that *The Dandy Dolls* could not be produced at that particular period — about Easter. If this was not an intimation that the play was accepted and would be played in due course, I don't know what to think.

> I am, Madam,
> Yours faithfully,
> GEO. FITZMAURICE.[30]

However, it was not until after Fitzmaurice's death, more than fifty years later, that the Abbey produced *The Dandy Dolls*.

On 30 June, during the season at the Royal Court in London, the Abbey gave the first production to R. J. Ray's *The Gombeen*

*Man*. Although Yeats does not seem particularly to have encouraged Fitzmaurice, he apparently took considerable time and pains with Ray. Yeats's first comment on the submitted manuscript was probably in July, 1911, when he wrote:

GOMBEENISM by R. J. Ray.
Fine, but some incoherence. One character threatens and does not perform. Must be read again and criticised to author in detail.[31]

On 13 October 1912, however, Ray had written to Yeats, apparently having gotten no further on with the play:

Dear Mr. Yeats:
I had a letter from Mr. Robinson this morning: he hopes, but his letter makes it appear rather doubtful, to give a performance of the *Martin Whelan* play at the Abbey Theatre before Christmas.
I take it for granted you would have a great deal to do with the arrangement of the Abbey programme from now to Christmas on, or any time, and you would confer a favour on me, and a big favour too, if you would let the *Whelan* play get through before Christmas. I think I have made it as good as I can make it, and I hope you will also think so.
There is the *Gombeenism* play: I am engaged on its revision, or rather re-writing, according to your suggestions. Well, about that play: I waited with patience — there were, to be sure, a few growls — for nearly fifteen months, and I shall have to wait a long time yet before I see it performed. And what I want to say is — but, really, I don't well know how to say it. I can only repeat if you will let the *Whelan* play get through before Christmas you will confer upon me a very big favour indeed. I trust you won't disappoint me.
Sincerely yours,
R. J. RAY.[32]

Yeats did see that the revised *Martin Whelan* play went on, and he also must have written immediately back to Ray, who then replied:

Williamsville, Sunday's Well, Cork
25 October 1912

Dear Mr. Yeats:
I send you *Gombeenism*, I think I might almost say, re-written.
It runs this way:

252

In this Act is *adumbrated* the evil intention of Stephen Kiniry
— that Mrs. Kiniry should be driven to drown herself. You
will find this at pages 5, 6, 11, 18, 19, 21, 22, 23, and others.
I also make clear that about his mere ill-treatment of Mrs.
Kiniry, the gombeen man does not care what the neighbours
think. You write in your criticism: "Let Richard Kiniry
threaten the revelation of a crime", and that is the note, in
large degree of the first Act.

In this Act the intention of Stephen Kiniry to drive Mrs.
Kiniry to drowning herself is made clear and strong. The
scene between Stephen Kiniry and his son, Richard, has been
re-written; other scenes in the Act have also been re-written
with object of giving marked definiteness to the drowning
idea. In regard to the idea that Mrs. Kiniry should in due
course have a child, that is a little more than adumbrated in
this Act. The scene between Stephen Kiniry and his wife has
been rewritten, and the child idea comes in this way: Mrs.
Kiniry is half afraid to tell her husband. You have this:
page 36.

STEPHEN KINIRY: Will you be telling me in two words what's
after bringing you here again?

MRS. KINIRY: 'Tis something is in my mind and heart all this
day, Stephen; something I'd like to say, and can't be sure I
ought to say.

And lower down, same page:

MRS. KINIRY: . . . When I was standing near the window
to-day I saw a poor woman singing in the street, and she
had a little baby at the breast and . . . Stephen . . . Stephen.
(*Draws back.*)

Lower down Stephen Kiniry accuses her of thinking of the
dead man and the dead child, and says it was a woman's wish
he might never hear the cry of a child in the house: then,

MRS. KINIRY (*wildly*): A woman said that, did she? . . . A
woman said that? (*With tense emotion.*) But suppose,
Stephen . . . suppose?

STEPHEN KINIRY (*Aroused and eager*) Suppose? . . . Good
God, do you mean — ?

But Mrs. Kiniry is afraid of him and afraid of herself and will not answer direct. You see, the mention of the child here in the second Act heightens the tragedy, for in the third Act she speaks out — but I will deal with that just now. In the closing scene between husband and wife in this Act, the drowning idea comes out clearly.

### ACT III.

In your criticism you write: "The main point is the last Act." This is now quite easily the most powerful Act in the play. At the outset Martin Shinnick arrives; there is mention of the drowning idea and murder; then the Naughtons and Connors arrive; then Richard Kiniry enters: he is now friendly; he says a good many things which indicate what the gombeen man has been doing to drive Mrs. Kiniry to drown herself. Then Mrs. Kiniry enters: the child is again mentioned. On pages 45 and 46 you will find this mention of the child idea; also pages that follow. Then enter Stephen Kiniry. He threatens Martin Shinnick with eviction from the farm: then Mrs. Kiniry declares herself. You wrote in the criticism: "She returns, speaks a few words to her father and goes into the inner room; or else Stephen Kiniry has come in with her," but you add, "I do not know what the machinery should be." Well, I saw only one way out, and that was to make Mrs. Kiniry speak out. Here I am on very delicate ground: it was quite clear to me the declaration should come in a passionate way, *Preceded by something else*, spring from that something, and the audience would have it humming in their ears before they knew where they were. I do not set out here what precedes the declaration, but this is the declaration: ". . . Stephen! Stephen! to save you and redeem you, for your joy or for your sorrow, the cry of a child — YOUR CHILD AND MINE — will be heard in the house, and the emptiness and the loneliness will be gone for ever! (*There is silence.*)

What follows looks simple to read, but it was the very devil to put together. You will see how all the characters go off except Stephen and Richard, his son. It is Mrs. Kiniry herself, before she goes "off" declares the child may be an idiot. It's not ingenious; it is perfectly natural why the words come from her. The last scene is between Stephen Kiniry and his son. I flatter myself you'll find it satisfactory.

I hope you will favour me with a reply at as early a date as possible about the play. I think there is not a single

obscurity in the play. However, you may still think changes
necessary.

Sincerely yours,

R. J. RAY[33]

On the occasion of the London opening of the play now called
*The Gombeen Man*, the London correspondent of *The Irish Times*
wrote:

> The scene is laid in a small village, and Stephen Kiniry, the
> gombeen man, is feared and hated by the whole community,
> including his one-armed dissolute son, Richard. Stephen has
> married as his second wife the daughter of Martin Shinnick,
> over whose farm he has a mortgage which he uses to compel
> the woman to marry him. She was a woman mourning a loving
> husband and a dead child. Stephen, finding that he is not to
> have a son, tries to drive her to madness and suicide. He
> beats her, and is always whispering to her of a lonely road,
> the dark waters of Avonmore, and a face floating in the night.
> The poor distracted creature, half dazed with fear, one night
> rushes out into the darkness. Her old father and the neigh-
> bours think that Stephen has succeeded in his hellish work,
> and come to accuse him, but she comes back. Before them
> all she tells Stephen that she is to be a mother, but Richard
> compels her to tell them also that she has been warned by a
> woman that her child would be the child of a foolish woman
> and grow up without sense if it lived. Horror-stricken to his
> soul, the wretched man finds that his wickedness has turned
> upon himself. The curtain falls with him, sitting alone in the
> dark with black despair brooding over him.
>
> The subject is a gloomy and even terrifying one, but the
> fine acting of the players made it real flesh and blood drama.
> From the opening moments the elements of tragedy began
> to reveal themselves, and prepared the audience for a sorrow-
> ful ending. The characters are skilfully and clearly drawn,
> and full justice is done to them by the acting. Mr. Arthur
> Sinclair has never acted better than he did as Stephen. Hard-
> hearted, cruel, even monstrous, he yet was able to show the
> intense longing of a man for a decent son to take the place of
> the drunken reprobate, Richard, the coming of whom would
> in all likelihood have changed his whole nature. That magni-
> ficent actress, Miss Sara Allgood, played Mrs. Kiniry with a
> fine restraint. It was a *rôle* that in the hands of an uncertain
> actress would have been dangerous and perhaps ridiculous.
> But not for a moment was it over-acted or unreal. Pathetic

and touching as Miss Allgood made it, the part went to the hearts of the audience at once. Mr. Fred O'Donovan was capital as the graceless son, while other *rôles* were well played by Mr. J. M. Kerrigan, as the gombeen man's scoundrelly clerk; Mr. S. J. Morgan, as Martin Shinnick; and Mr. Guiry and Miss Eileen O'Doherty as Mr. and Mrs. Naughton, victims of the gombeen man.

The drama was well received, and the company were called several times before the curtain.[34]

The play was not seen in Dublin until 11 November. Then the ordinary *Times* critic thought that it was 'extremely powerful and well constructed', and that 'Seldom has a play been so well acted at the Abbey Theatre.' [35] Jack Point, oppressed as was the *Times* critic by the play's gloom, thought that Ray had belied his promise and made the fundamental mistake 'of writing not a drama but an Abbey play'.[36] Although Jack Point lumbers on in his usual churlish way, one feels that some of his points — such as the similarity of the gombeen man to Bill Sykes and of his wife to Nancy — are palpable hits, and that the play must have verged frequently on ferocious melodrama. However, this must only be conjecture, for none of Ray's plays has been published.

On 12 July the Abbey players ended a six weeks tenure of the Royal Court, and Yeats was interviewed by the *London Evening News*:

A tall, graceful figure of a man with fine eager eyes, a wisp of iron grey hair tossed across his left brow, Mr. W. B. Yeats, the man from Sligo, poet and mystic, co-director with Lady Gregory of the Players, talks with a vivacity that is inspirational.

"The Irish Players return to Dublin after the most successful season we have had in London," he said. "Yes, we are going to run an American tour again, for this has now become a regular thing since we opened up there seven years ago. From New York we visit in turn, Boston, Chicago, Philadelphia, and other centres, as well as the two principal Canadian cities, where they are quite the vogue.

"As for myself, the son of the famous Major Pond has just arranged a lecture tour in America, when I shall speak on three subjects, 'The Theatre', 'Dramatic Art', and 'Contemporary Lyric Poets'."

When asked why none of the Yeats plays had appeared in the present repertoire, and what had become of the theory he had pleaded for so eloquently in *Samhain* (for the rhythmical utterance of blank verse), he answered: "Being verse my own plays demand a certain cast — and we find it difficult, owing to engagements, to get the right people together."

"And why is it you play Molièrean comedy in a translation? Surely the Irish drama is more suitable!"

"It may not be so popular with sophisticated London, but in Dublin, the audiences think it is fine. In Paris, the people there would say the same thing — feeling how fresh and artless it is after the pedantic, stiltish, and conventional mode of the Academie Française Company, which only succeeds in tiring them with Molière's work."

"Could we not, with advantage, adopt some of Gordon Craig's methods of staging?"

"His ideas are very beautiful, certainly, and we could use them, but the difficulty is Craig himself. He would only consent upon condition that he staged the play himself. This is not always convenient. You say that his theory seems to lead to one end — the final elimination of the actor. That, believe me, is one of Craig's paradoxes. He would put the actors out by the front door — but then he would let them in by the back." [37]

No new plays were produced until the autumn, when T. C. Murray's one-act, *Sovereign Love*, was done on 11 September. This play was a revision of Murray's first play, *The Wheel o' Fortune*, which had been done a few years earlier in Cork. Of his revision, Murray wrote:

I have been rather bored from people saying: "Why didn't you write a comedy? Life itself is such a gloomy affair, we want to forget its oppression in the theatre" — you know the stock argument. I determined to dodge the reproach, and so *The Wheel o' Fortune* worked into *Sovereign Love*, which, however, is only a tentative title. Some time ago I got a number of ex-pupils of mine to do *The Wheel o' Fortune*, and I learned such a lot during the rehearsals that I saw possibilities in it, and this was an added motive in setting me to work.[38]

The plot of the revised version is usual enough, and as Jack Point remarks:

It is sufficient to say that Donal Kearney, farmer, has two daughters, to wit, Ellen and Katty. Charles O'Donnell, another farmer, has a son David, and the drama turns on the endeavour to make matrimonial arrangements for the young man. The other man — there is, naturally, another man —

257

is Andy Hyde, a "returned Yank", who, like all returned Yanks, is supposed to be an eligible partner and possibly a millionaire.[39]

The review also makes the point that although 'Mr. T. C. Murray is generally admitted to be in the front rank of our present Irish dramatists . . . I am inclined to think that the author is more at home in what may for convenience be styled an Irish problem play . . . than in the domain of comedy.' That is a well-taken point, particularly if one compares *Sovereign Love* with other, more lively handlings of the subject — say Fitzmaurice's *'Twixt the Giltenans and the Carmodys* even. It was not really until the end of his long and distinguished dramatic career that Murray again turned to comedy, in his ill-fated *A Flutter of Wings* which the Gate ill-advisedly snapped up from the Abbey's reject pile.

On 2 October, the Abbey presented Joseph Connolly's three-act comedy, *The Mine Land*, which had previously won a prize in Belfast. The *Times* described the play as 'an eminently satisfactory piece of work', with a well-built and cohesive plot that contained no grotesque improbabilities. *The Irish Citizen* thought that the play was hardly a success: 'Great hopes were aroused by the first act, which is a capital study of Antrim farmhouse life; but the story fell rather flat in the remaining two acts. There is really not enough material for three acts. . . .'[40] Jack Point was more enthusiastic about the Second Company than he was about the play:

> Somebody not long ago remarked — and he had some grounds for his opinion — that at present the Abbey No. 2 Company is doing more for the Irish dramatic movement than the No. 1; that it is in fact doing the spade work, which is all-important in the laying of any foundation. It is interesting, even if the spectacle is pathetic, to watch attempts to revive a person who has been some considerable time under water by means of artificial respiration, and to bring out a sinking patient for a "mouthful of air" is undoubtedly a kindly if usually a futile act. Some of the work of the No. 1 Company is of this description, for sundry plays in their repertoire have been as dead as a door-nail for years, and any number of presentations will never make them acceptable. True, there are favourable notices, but with English criticism of Irish drama, as in English food ships, the element of charity plays an important part. Nowadays it is usually the No. 2 Company that has the trouble of making up a new drama, and which gives the Irish dramatist a chance. Last

258

night there was produced at the Abbey a new comedy by a new author, Mr. Joseph Connolly of Belfast. Plays with the scene laid in north-east Ireland are not often seen at the Abbey Theatre, though I can recollect one, something about a man who deserted his sweetheart, was "saved", and came back to make her honest — absolute rubbish in fact.[41] *The Mine Land* is not rubbish, but is a domestic comedy, clever in sundry respects. If the story is a little thin, the central idea is not a hackneyed one. Matta Lynn, a County Antrim farmer, and his wife, Jane, are visited by three members of the Geological Society. There is a gully on the farm which they want to inspect, as they are on the look-out for "ammonite". A certain Barney O'Hara, in love with Annie M'Kendry, becomes suspicious, and suggests that the geologists are really mining experts in search of a gold mine. Matta is warned against parting with any of this valuable land, but nearly sticks "the old Jew Liddell" for a couple of hundred. Liddell is, however, saved by Mrs. Lynn. It turns out there is no mine, and the love business between Barney and Annie terminates to the general satisfaction. The cast of ten was good, Miss Una O'Connor as the wife being an easy first with Mr. Morgan a good second. Miss Eithne Magee was the niece, and the Charlie McCrea of Mr. Seán Connolly was a good character study.[42]

Another one-act, this time with a rather thin plot, was first performed on 17 October, Mrs. Bart Kennedy's *My Lord. The Irish Citizen* called it

a slight piece in one act, dealing with the passing away of feudalism in Ireland. The dying lord, to his horror, finds that his tenants will no longer follow his behest and vote solid for his "nephew, the Captain". The power of O'Connell is stronger than fear or sentiment; the serfs are throwing off the chains. The possibilities latent in the idea were not, however, dramatically realised, and even the personality of Arthur Sinclair, as the dying lord, could not rescue the play from flatness. The other characters got no chances, one "tenant" being merely the replica of another.[43]

The *Times* agreed, remarking that 'the piece lacks dramatic strength, and bears the impress of the *litterateur* rather than that of the dramatist.' [44] Actually, the piece was very short, and more a sketch than a play. There was a slight novelty in the staging, for the stage picture was divided into two rooms, in both of which part of the action took place. However, this technique had been used in the middle of the nineteenth century by Boucicault and others, and was not enough to save the play.

An extremely witty play which has fortunately been printed is St. John Ervine's one-act, *The Critics*, first produced on 20 November. Ervine, smarting over the rough handling of his previous Abbey work, subtitled his little *jeu d'esprit* 'a little Morality for the Press'. Set in the foyer of the Abbey during a play which turns out to be *Hamlet*, *The Critics* assembles as dimwitted a quartet of dramatic critics as had been seen since *Fanny's First Play*. Their dialogue must have been particularly galling to the real Dublin drama critics, for it contained many actual quotations from the Dublin reviews of Ervine's earlier work. The *Times* critic sniffily remarked, 'Out of such conceptions it is easy to make one laugh, and Mr. Ervine can boast that he did that. Whether he was laughed more at than with is another question.' [45] Jack Point, perhaps the most notable Ervine-baiter, began his notice benignly but ended more characteristically:

> Last night *The Critics, or A New Play at the Abbey Theatre*, "A little bit of Morality for the Press", by the author of the absurd but *Magnanimous Lover*, was produced for the first time at the Abbey Theatre. I must confess that I went to see the show with some conviction that it would prove to be another sample of Ulster impertinence — of that colossal cheek which has played so important a part in making the success of many a man hailing from the much-discussed North-East corner of Ireland. It is only fair to say that, with many of the Pressmen, I really enjoyed the little skit, which to my mind, is much more clever than Mr. Ervine's more ambitious work. Of course the central idea is not a new one, and Mr. Ervine is not quite on the same plane as either Sheridan or Shaw, but at the same time he is to be congratulated on at least handling his subject — subjects if you will — in a different fashion than they are treated in *Fanny's First Play*. Having lent a hand in the demolition of *The Magnanimous Lover*, I can fairly claim to be partly responsible for last night's amusing sequel, which can do no harm to anybody. The dramatic critic who thinks *Hamlet* grossly improper and imagines Shakespeare to be a Corkman I am anxious to meet, but, meantime, would casually point out to Mr. Ervine that *Hamlet* is not recognised as perhaps the greatest of plays on account of certain language used by the distracted Ophelia. It is somewhat of a pity that Abbey

260

dramatists of promise are in such a hurry to make a reputation and create a sensation. It does not follow that because Synge achieved a big success with a play which suggests the partiality of the Irish people, and more especially the women of the West, for a criminal, that any "shocker" will succeed. The scene of *The Critics* is laid in the vestibule of the Abbey Theatre. There was, however, no suggestion of a vestibule about the stage except the portraits of Lady Gregory and Mr. George Russell, and the porter in uniform. No members of the audience, no cloakroom or attendants were to be seen, but, of course, this could be easily remedied. As for the alleged story of the play that can be easily told. One dramatic critic doesn't see the play at all; he gets his impressions from the man on the door. The three others do see a lot of it, but leave early on the ground that *Hamlet* is unfit to be presented before the daughters of Erin. But although this is trivial and sufficiently absurd, it is only fair to Mr. Ervine to say that much of the dialogue, especially at the start, is clever and amusing, and likely enough, if he only left social problems alone, he may yet write a real good comedy — and the Abbey wants a new one badly at present. The acting of the piece was very good indeed, Mr. Kerrigan being quite excellent, but Messrs. O'Donovan Morgan, Sinclair, and Hutchinson were very good indeed. After *The Critics*, *Mixed Marriage* by the same author was played. Having seen it before, it is scarcely necessary to say I didn't sit it out, but take it for granted that Messrs. Sinclair, Wright, Kerrigan, O'Rourke, and Misses Eithne Magee and Eileen O'Doherty did the best they could with it.[46]

A less crotchety judgment was that of 'Joan' in *The Irish Citizen*, who thought that the play was 'an exquisite and telling piece of satire'.[47]

In the middle of December, the Abbey staged two premieres in one week. On 16 December, Seumas O'Brien's one-act play, *Duty*, was first staged; and on 18 December, Séamus O'Kelly's *The Bribe* was done. *Duty* remained a popular piece for years, and on its first production *The Evening Herald* called it, 'One of the best little comedies produced so far at the Abbey Theatre.'[48] *The Irish Times* agreed, ranking it with *The Eloquent Dempsy, Mixed Marriage*, 'or any other of those plays which have made the reputation of the Abbey Players'.[49] That judgment has not held up over the years; however, the following plot summary will indicate that the piece was a harmless and adroit piece of fun:

261

The audience is introduced to the back kitchen of Mrs. Catter's public-house in a country village on a Sunday night. Only *bona fide* travellers, of course, are entitled to be on the premises, but two workingmen, Padna Sweeny and Mike Goggin, contrary to law, are seated at a table drinking tankards of porter, and making philosophical comments on the police, Government, law, and all things aflecting the all-important working man. Little they trouble themselves about the uneasy feeling of the hostess, who is trying to coax them to leave. A knock at the front door and Head Constable Mulligan enters, just as Padna and Mike have escaped into a back room. The Head Constable (Mr. Sinclair) struts about the apartment in all his portly majesty, and although duty weighs heavily upon him, he is not averse to a drop of something to warm him. Mrs. Cotter takes the hint, and the Head Constable takes the drink. While he is enjoying his potation and his pipe, Sergeant Dooley (Fred O'Donovan) knocks at the door and announces "Police". The Head Constable conceals himself in the coal-hole, and the sergeant, with some uncomplimentary references to his superior officer, goes through the same performance as the Head Constable. While the sergeant is resting and refreshing himself, Constable Huggins, on his round of duty, comes along and complains of "cramps". The hostess is again generous, but the constable must do his duty, and insists upon searching the coal-hole, where he finds his two superior officers, begrimed with coal dust and more or less under the influence of alcohol. The scene that ensues between the three guardians of the peace and of the law cannot be described. It must be seen in order to be thoroughly appreciated. Throughout the performance the audience screamed with laughter, so comic were the situations. Miss Una O'Connor was excellent as the landlady of the public-house. At the fall of the curtain the players were warmly applauded, and the author was called for, but he was not forthcoming. . . .[50]

On 18 December, Séamus O'Kelly's well-crafted, full-length play, *The Bribe*, was equally well received, but, like *Duty*, it has not outlived its day. Indeed, the only pieces by O'Kelly which have yet some vitality are the short, charming one-act, *Meadowsweet*, which was revived at the Peacock in 1969, and possibly *The Shuiler's Child*, largely for the Shuiler's brilliant closing speech and as a vehicle for two actresses. Initially, though, *The Bribe* was popular and several times revived. *The Irish Times'* reaction to it is typical:

Just now the Abbey Theatre is in its second springtime. It is bringing forth a succession of new plays by new authors, and these productions are destined to rank with the best of their predecessors. Following quickly upon *Duty*, which was played for the first time on Tuesday evening, and was a great success, comes *The Bribe*, which was received last evening with every mark of approval. Mr. Séamus O'Kelly has taken for the subject of his three-act play a commonplace incident in our Irish public life — the election of a dispensary doctor. He shows us how some Boards of Guardians are induced to vote, not for the best candidate, but for that one who has most influential friends, and who can buy the votes of the representatives of the rate-payers. To most people this is a subject that does not seem to be capable of making an absorbing stage play, but Mr. O'Kelly has made excellent use of his material, and has woven out of it a very interesting drama. . . . The Abbey first company interpreted the author's meaning with absolute accuracy. Mr. Arthur Sinclair, in the character of Kirwan, was not as comfortably fitted with a part as he invariably is. He seemed to be oppressed too much by the way in which he had compromised his honour, and he was slow and grave beyond the requirements of the part. Mr. Kerrigan was excellent as the guardian who stood up for all that is true and good and who boasted of the thickness of his "hide". . . .

At the close the actors were warmly applauded. The author was called for, and he bowed his acknowledgments from the stage.[51]

H.R.W. in *The Evening Mail* described the play even more warmly as 'a finely balanced work of art, which is not only strong in dramatic characterisation, but its progress is steady and continuous. Its dialogue is natural and true, and the conclusions of each act poetic and very impressive. . . . The author has created an atmosphere at once highly entertaining and powerfully dramatic. Such a play may be regarded as a human document and one of the most distinguished works in the Abbey repertoire.'[52] Unfortunately, to read the play now is to find it Galsworthy and water.

* * *

In a very strong Number One Company, the dominating male actor was Arthur Sinclair, although he was closely pressed by J. M. Kerrigan and Fred O'Donovan. The best appreciations of

Sinclair and Kerrigan that we have discovered were published in 1913 by W. A. Henderson who had been the theatre's secretary, and whose scrapbooks have proved a boon to scholars. On 26 April, in a Dublin paper, he wrote of Kerrigan:

The Abbey players return to Dublin next week. During the tour Mr. Kerrigan has notably added to his personal popularity and to his reputation as an actor, and has received many appreciative notices from first-class American critics. Lady Gregory evidently wrote her latest play, *Galway Races*, recently produced in Boston, to exploit the undoubted gifts of Miss Allgood and Mr. Kerrigan as singers of old Irish ballads. His interesting career may be briefly sketched.

J. M. Kerrigan is the most keenly intellectual, the most satirically humorous of the Abbey players. His conversation is characterised by shrewd observation, originality, and surprisingly apt phraseology. At times it degenerates into flippancy, and then he patters along gaily, pouring out in irrepressible haste jests and witticisms, nonsense and wisdom, sarcasms and lively criticisms. He has a store of strange and ludicrous anecdotes, and sings old Irish ballads with curious pathos and naïvete. He occasionally indulges in gagging, and now and then a sly impromptu sets the house in a roar. These clever impromptus have often been retained in the plays. Quick-witted, volatile, restless, he is a pleasant companion. He dearly loves a joke; for example, on a Treasury day, the following note was slipped into my hand. "I would feel obliged if you would let me have 10s — ten shillings, amount which I consider due to me for moral and intellectual damage through having to appear in a play in which I have not been rehearsed, and for having to do so in ill-fitting trousers. The former may injure my reputation as an actor, the latter wounds my vanity as a man. (Signed) J. M. Kerrigan."

Born not far from the Tolka, his father was a Co. Dublin man, his mother was one of the O'Briens of Clare. East and West were joined in his parents.

When his schooldays were ended, he served a short apprenticeship to journalism. It will be remembered that the talented and versatile Denis J. Downing, sportsman and journalist, the "Doctor Dick" of *The Evening Herald*, founded and established an office in Dame Street; here the youthful Kerrigan was installed as the junior of a staff of three. Funds were often low, and it is told that the two colleagues often tossed for what money was in the exchequer, there not being sufficient

264

for both. Kerrigan received here a preparatory training in a school of Bohemianism which no doubt influenced his life.

He was a fine athlete and an enthusiastic footballer. Swimming was hereditary, and when opportunity presents he indulges in sea bathing and boating. Last year he saved the life of a Dublin gentleman at New Brighton, who narrowly escaped drowning. This gentleman told me that he owed his life to Mr. Kerrigan who promptly came to his assistance.

In October 1906, Kerrigan called at the Abbey Theatre and had an interview with Mr. W. G. Fay. That interview determined his career. I heard W. G. Fay say to his brother that Kerrigan was a promising recruit. It must always be remembered that the two brothers Fay selected and trained all the Abbey Company. Their dramatic instincts were invariably true, and their judgments seldom at fault. I watched Kerrigan pass out that day; his face was radiant with joy, and his feet scarce touched the concrete floor. I knew that there was one perfectly happy man in the world. Once again it was my lot to see the reflex of a seraph's smile on a human countenance, and the same light-footed progress to the Abbey door. Mr. Yeats was about to attend some function, and he wanted his boots cleaned. A shoe black was sent for, and when the polishing was done the lad passed smiling to the door.

Later Mr. Yeats discovered that he had given him half a sovereign instead of a sixpence. Someone suggested following the cleaner, but Mr. Yeats generously said, "I have given it to him, let him have it." J. M. Kerrigan's first appearance on the Abbey stage was on 10 November 1906, in two small parts — a fisherman in *Riders to the Sea* and Robert in one of the Kiltartan Molière plays, *The Doctor in Spite of Himself*. A fortnight later he played Conchobar in Yeats's verse play, *Deirdre*, and his first press notice said: "Mr. Kerrigan in the character of Conchobar played an unpopular part very tolerably."

On that memorable Saturday night, 26 February 1907, when *The Playboy* was first produced, Kerrigan played the part of Jimmy Farrell. Having enthusiastic faith in the literary genius of Synge, and a high appreciation of the man himself, it has been a privilege and a pleasure to him to interpret Synge's characters. Later in the year he originated the important part of Patrick O'Connor in *The Country Dressmaker*.

When the Fays resigned in January 1908, Kerrigan had many notable parts assigned to him, and since then he has played in almost every play in the Abbey repertoire. When

265

he feels the part suits him, he acts it with marked intelligence, originality, and character. He is seldom at home in romantic or sentimental studies. A type which suits him admirably is the breezy, light-hearted individual, with a dash of wit and a smatter of dialect; his Martin Kelly in Casey's *The Man Who Missed the Tide* stands as a notable success. The dour, shrewd, stubborn peasant is perfectly portrayed by him; witness his Martin Hurley in *Harvest*, and Shane Morrissey in *Birthright*.

But his versatility, talent, and diversity as an actor are well established; the following impersonations, so variable yet so distinct, linger in the mind, and mark him as a creator of types — the ballad singer in *The Rising of the Moon*, the tramp in *In the Shadow of the Glen*, the burglar in *The Glittering Gate*, Dr. Bunbury, Strapper Kemp, Stephen J. O'Reilly, and Henry Hinde in *The Magnanimous Lover*. But his greatest triumphs are his unique characterisations of aged men.

Rumour has it that he hunts for his models down Santry way, among the loitering ancients of Ballybough, Clonliffe, and Drumcondra, but wherever he finds his material, he uses it with the genius of an artist. To select but two from his gallery — the Pauper in *Thomas Muskerry* and the Hallkeeper in *Patriots*. Both are faultlessly perfect creations, two petite studies of surprising truth and brilliancy. The actor is scarce five minutes on the stage, yet in the space he dispels illusion and creates an atmosphere.

The scenes might be detached from the plays, and still would be puissant to hold an audience. For the moment the stage has vanished; it is a workhouse ward; a muttering, servile old pauper stumps across it, and is gone. Again, a garrulous caretaker, with age-stiffened joints, is arranging chairs in a hall. He stops for a time to babble out grumblings and local gossiping. He mounts a chair and turns out the lights. That is all. Yet the subtle skill of the actor has vitalised for us scraps of real life. Every moment, every grimace, every intonation tells, and the scene is permanently etched into the mind. This is the Kerrigan quality at its highest, and it is studied artistic work of this kind that has given reputation to the Abbey Theatre, and made its style of acting remarkable throughout the world.[53]

Some weeks later, Henderson wrote a similarly evocative sketch of Sinclair:

On Sunday the Abbey Company goes a-roaming again, this time to Oxford, Birmingham, and a lengthy season in the

Court Theatre, London; then it will supply "turns" in that monster theatre of varieties, the London Coliseum. Arthur Sinclair will play leading parts in all of these engagements. After his success in the last American tour, a sketch of his career will be of interest to his Dublin admirers. Several ladies seeing Arthur Sinclair taking the air in Grafton Street have conveyed to me their impression that he was effeminate and conspicuously vain. On promenade he may appear so, his tight-fitting garments, his ample cravat, his raven locks parted across his forehead, his complexion, his peculiar gait as he swings a dandy cane, all suggest the stylish buck of past generations. But Arthur Sinclair, despite his out-of-door "make-up", is one of the most masculine of Abbey players. He has an iron will, determined and obstinate. No threat, or flattery, or persuasion will move him from his appointed path, or coerce him to do the thing he has made up his mind not to do. At times I have been tempted to nickname him Stonewall Sinclair. He is frankly, bluntly egotistical, and makes no pretence of disguising it. He loves to talk of himself, of his triumphs, of the parts he has played, of the laudations and applause showered on him, which he has undoubtedly deservedly earned. Now this is not strange or abnormal; all actors in common with most men and women who use their voices on platform, stage, or pulpit, whether they are players, singers, orators, or politicians, are more or less vain. Some have powers of suppression, others have not. Vanity and jealousy are dominating traits. . . . To his friends Sinclair boasts that he is the greatest Irish comedian on the boards, and there is no resisting his claim. As an exponent of flamboyant Irish character he stands beside Boucicault, Charles Sullivan, O'Grady and others, and he is greater than them, for he can impersonate character which they could not touch. How brutal he can be as Tom Dempsey, how priggish as Claude Callan, how disgustingly crapulous as Michael James, how severely stubborn as John Rainey, how blatantly hypocritical as Elder Daniel. The spectacle of the old man clutching his "Piedish" is a remarkable study in sheer imbecility; the sightless Martin Doul groping his way across the stage almost convinces an audience that the player is actually blind. These are a few random proofs of his marvellous versatility. It was written of his Scapin: "It is not too much to say that the play is himself and that he is the play", and this is true of many plays in which he has appeared. His rare gifts as a comedian have been noted and applauded by the greatest critics in England

and America, but his peculiar humour is best exemplified and most provocative of genuine hearty laughter, so persistent indeed that it often mars and impedes the progress of the play; nevertheless, an actor who can produce such hilarity merits high praise, and deserves the affection of his audience. The three dramatists whose plays are the best medium for his comedic genius are Boyle, Synge, and Lady Gregory. But his most characteristic triumphs have been in the comedies of William Boyle. His humour finds admirable scope in Shaun Grogan, Jeremiah Dempsy, Daniel Fogarty, and Dominic Donnelly. In all these he has created types which will be quoted and live long in the public memory. It is only fair to state that the first three characters were originally played by W. G. Fay, but Sinclair did not imitate his equally talented predecessor, but wrought out and individualised his own conceptions. These plays have demonstrated his skill and power in holding an audience through three acts; a fine test, as he is seldom off the stage during the whole play. One critic notes of *The Mineral Workers*, that "the interest of the play went in and out with Fogarty" when Sinclair was playing the part. So much for his acting; a few biographic details will serve to demonstrate his slow but sure progress towards the head of his profession.

Arthur Sinclair was born in Dublin, and was educated in Marlborough Street Training College. He was apprenticed to the Law, but office work was not to his liking, so on a day in the last months of 1904, he heard of the Irish National Theatre Society for the first time, and of a vacancy for an actor. He called on Frank Fay, who quickly espied his acting talent, and he was at once engaged. His first appearances on the stage were made on the opening night of the Abbey Theatre on 27 December 1904. He created the small parts of King Daire in *Baile's Strand* and James Ryan in *Spreading the News*. A few weeks later he played the cripple in the *King's Threshold* and a pupil in *The Hour Glass*. He was associated with Boyle's plays from the first, for he created Dan McSweeney in *The Building Fund*, and Captain MacNamara in *The Eloquent Dempsy*. His most notable success was King James in *The White Cockade* on 9 December 1905. Later on, on 9 March 1907, he originated the part of the Sergeant in *The Rising of the Moon*, a character which he has played with signal success over two hundred times to delighted audiences. It is no exaggeration that his acting popularised this play, and held it continuously on the stage for the past six years. After the secession of Fay in January 1908, he became the leading actor of the Abbey Company. In the September of the same year the late Captain Shawe-Taylor invited the company down to Galway to play in the Industrial Exhibition in that city. A large goods shed was fitted up as a theatre, and a small stage built on the top of several hundred tons of coal. There were no dressing rooms, and each time the actors had to change they were obliged to rush across, through crowds, to a house on the opposite side of the road. One night, after a performance of *Spreading the News*, an amusing incident occurred. At the close of the play, Sinclair as Bartley Fallon is handcuffed. Somehow the manacles jammed, and they could not be got off. Sinclair made a swift dash across the road with the handcuffs on, closely followed by Morgan in his part of a policeman. The people imagined that a prisoner was attempting an escape; a hue and cry was raised, and soon a dense crowd was around the two actors, from which they were extricated with much difficulty. Frequently we had to call to our aid our actor policeman, Sydney Morgan, to keep the crowd back, so intense was the desire to see the Irish plays in Galway at that time. On the last night of the engagement Miss Allgood and Sinclair were presented with handsome gold medals by the Exhibition Executive in recognition of their rank as Ireland's leading actress and actor. Sinclair has played in the "Halls" on his own account, and has had many offers from leading managers. Sir Beerbohm Tree first offered him the part in *The O'Flynn*, which W. G. Fay afterwards played, but his engagement prevented him accepting it. Sinclair has had an exceptionally brilliant career as an actor; he wrought hard, and concentrated all his energies and soul in his profession. He has provided genuine fun for thousands, and memories of nights of uproarious laughter are associated with his name. Truly it may be said of him that he added to the gaiety of nations.[54]

\* \* \*

The Abbey's season at the Royal Court aroused considerable discussion about the current merits both of the company and of the repertoire. Leading the attack was the popular novelist 'Rita'. What she said may be inferred by St. John Ervine's rejoinder:

> "Rita" attacks the Irish plays because, as she says, they are monotonous and depressing and concerned exclusively with peasant life, and with an ingenuity which I neither admire

nor envy she shows that if the people of Ireland are really as the Irish dramatists make them, they are totally unfit to govern themselves! It is an old saying and a true one that the less an imaginative writer dabbles in politics the better it is for that writer's reputation.

Much of what "Rita" says in her article is a repetition of much that is said of the Irish plays by Dublin critics. There is not any conspiracy on our part, organised or otherwise, to depict the "worst and most sordid traits of Irish life'. My personal acquaintance with my colleagues is limited to Mr. Lennox Robinson, whose play, *Patriots* is the finest political play that has been produced since Mr. Shaw wrote *John Bull's Other Island*; Mr. W. B. Yeats, whose plays cannot possibly be described as "sordid" or lacking in "heroic incidents", or concerned exclusively with peasants; Lady Gregory, who possesses more of the comic spirit in her little finger than the whole of the English dramatists possess in their whole bodies, and Mr. Padraic Colum, whose work is full of the delicacy and poetic feeling for which "Rita" longs.

Not one of these writers can be said to be like another in method or style. Mr. Robinson and myself are dubbed the realists of the Irish theatre, but our plays differ as completely as the most ardent individualists could desire, and it may help to dispel the ridiculous theory of a conspiracy if I say that both my Irish plays were written before I knew Mr. Robinson or had seen any of his work.

We are a scattered band, we Irish dramatists, working entirely in our own fashion, and using only the materials we find lying about us. My play deals with the Ulster people, the Orangemen from whom I come, while Mr. Robinson deals with the people of Cork, Lady Gregory's peasants belong to Galway, Mr. Colum's to the midlands of Ireland, and Mr. Yeats's people live in the past and in the imagination. Each of us tries to do what no English dramatist does, write out of our experience and knowledge. This is true of Irish drama, as it is untrue of English drama, that each person in the plays is a living being, observed and understood. If you ask me what is the dominant note of Irish drama, I reply in one word: Sincerity.

"Rita" complains that we do not write of the Irish aristocracy or of the Irish middle-class; but why in heaven's name should we? Has "Rita" ever seen an Irish aristocrat? If so, can she lay her hand on her heart and say that one of them is worth the trouble of studying for dramatic purposes? There

270

is not a lord in Ireland with the life in him that there is in a peasant.

So it is with the Irish middle class, which is as dull and empty as the middle class in England, which it imitates in everything. A peasant in Ireland differs from a peasant in England as thoroughly as an intelligent man differs from a fool; but a middle-class man in Ireland plays the sedulous ape to the middle class in this country; and the result is neither an Irishman nor an Englishman but a "perfect gentleman". The mind of the middle-class man in Ireland is shown most clearly in our lawyers, men of fictitious emotions and common, ugly, vulgar habits and thoughts: vulgar, that is to say, in the way in which a snob or a prig is vulgar because they are pretentious and unreal.

But apart from the emptiness of the Irish aristocracy and the commonness and vulgarity of the Irish middle class, there is a far greater reason why the Irish dramatist should be preoccupied by peasant concerns. It is that Ireland is a nation of peasants. All the vitality and colour in Ireland come from the peasants, all the vigour and clash of personalities and swift changes of nature come from poor tillers of the land, and where these things are there also is drama.

The moment a nation ceases to be national it ceases to be interesting; the moment a class ceases to be local, it ceases to be dramatic. When England was a nation it gave birth to Shakespeare; now that it is an empire it can only bring forth Kipling. The Irish peasant has remained national and local, and therefore literature can deal with him; but the Irish lord and the Irish middle-class man have been denationalised, and they have lost their souls in the process.

The dramatist is right when he takes the peasant as a protagonist of his dramas, for the peasant has courage and meanness, cowardice and nobility, humour and the lack of it, cruelty and gentleness, high feeling and low feeling, wit and dullness, generosity and greed, mingled in his nature; in all of which the stuff of drama is to be found.[55]

E. A. Baughan, of the London *Daily News*, thought that the Abbey plays were becoming 'quite mechanical'.

I am not in a position to know whether they do truthfully represent Irish peasantry, but I imagine not, because I note in these plays the love of the sensational and horrible which has a certain vogue in these days. Week after week I have gone to the Court Theatre, and have come away thoroughly depressed. What good is done (I have asked myself) in putting such brutal and ignorant types on the stage? They do not make fine drama, for you cannot make fine drama out of protagonists, who, judged from the ordinary standard of human beings are little better than imbeciles.[56]

The Court season occasioned, really for the first time in England, much criticism about the quality of the acting. John Palmer, in *The Saturday Review*, wrote of the players 'that the bloom is rubbed off their innocence, that America and the Coliseum have been bad for them'.[57] *The Manchester Guardian* thought that:

> The Abbey Theatre players . . . have lost something of their old simplicity, and are beginning to act like real West End performers. The worst offender, it appears, is Mr. Arthur Sinclair, a delicious comedian, who has acquired a number of unhappy mannerisms. Mr. Sinclair, always deliberate in his delivery, has become positively funereal in speech and conduct, and some of the pauses and stretches of silence which occur while he is on the stage are desolating. . . . And might not the Irish Players leave "gagging" to inferior actors?[58]

*The Pall Mall Gazette* answered the charge:

> Mr. Arthur Sinclair, it is true, occasionally speaks rather more slowly than is necessary; but one who has seen all his performances in London this season, and in several seasons previously, may perhaps be allowed rather positively to say that to describe them as "funereal" and "desolating" is to exaggerate grotesquely.
>
> As to the "gagging", this is really a very serious charge. . . . Inquiry in the proper quarter, however, will probably elicit the fact that nothing in the nature of promiscuous gagging can be laid at the doors of the Irish Players. Here and there in the plays of Mr. St. John Ervine, Mr. Lennox Robinson, and perhaps of other authors, a line or two have been inserted which are not found in the printed editions; but if in every instance the author has approved of these little additions, what more is there to be said?
>
> "A little discipline" is always a good thing; but the Abbey Theatre is in no need of it to save its acting from "decay". Such acting as London has seen on every other night during the past fortnight at the Court Theatre, not only from Miss Allgood and Mr. Sinclair, but from Mr. O'Donovan, Mr. Kerrigan, Mr. Morgan, Miss O'Doherty, Miss Magee, and

others, have been the very worst imitation of the beginnings of decay ever seen on the stage.[59]

Perhaps to complete the continuum of possibilities about the acting, E. A. Baughan's charge in *The Daily News and Leader* should be noted:

> When we looked on the Irish players as amateurs we even praised what was really a fault. Their naturalness was unconscious. They have now become sufficiently artists to strive consciously after naturalness, but it is the wrong kind of simplicity. They study to speak without being stagey, but their art is from the lips only. Over and over again during the past season I have noticed whole scenes let down because these players will not act. They are so obsessed with naturalness that they are no longer natural, and are not men and women who feel but men and women who only talk. There are exceptions, of course, and without wishing to be invidious I must praise Mr. Kerrigan and Mr. O'Donovan, both of whom do act as well as speak, but in general the style of acting is like the plays — under-developed.[60]

These three descriptions would seem to exhaust the range of possibilities. What the reality was the baffled historian can only surmise.

* * *

In 1913, the struggle between censoriousness and tolerance continued as usual. Still, it was a struggle, and it would be erroneous to cite merely the blatant instances of narrow-mindedness and to conclude that puritanism won all of the battles. For instance, *The Playboy* was by now grudgingly accepted, and when Norreys Connell's *The Piper*, which on its original production had threatened to cause an uproar of *Playboy* proportions, was revived in 1913, one critic could now say:

> *The Piper* was splendid and the house, a small one, eagerly rose to it. There was a whole happy half-hour of mixed comedy and tragedy. It is a gem. Its satire moves with dramatic earnestness. The Abbey stage has done nothing better of its kind. And the company know it. If their reputation depended upon nothing else, this would be sufficient.[61]

But, although Dublin had now assimilated older plays like *The Playboy* and *The Piper*, vehement reactions might still be expected for any unconventional new work. For instance, early in January,

273

John J. Rossiter made a speech to the Irish Theatrical Club in which he assailed a recent Abbey play which was probably Ervine's *The Magnanimous Lover*.

> . . . within the past few months, not to go further back, a drama which was supposed to convey a moral lesson by using blasphemy and filthy expressions, with a plot which no decent person could witness without feeling indignant at its being supposed to represent any phase of Irish society.
>
> "It was so shameful," he proceeded, "that some of the leading players of that establishment [the Abbey Theatre] told me they themselves declined to take the parts allotted to them. They felt they could not soil their mouths with the foul words of the play. Happily, the whole consensus of public opinion — the Dublin critics, the actors, the audience, and the public interested in such matters — so severely dealt with this drama that it will never, I hope, be resurrected from its well-deserved oblivion." [62]

But perhaps the most revealing symptom of prevailing public morality might be the following leading article in a Dublin newspaper:

> The arrival of Johnson, the negro boxer, in London, with a retinue made up of a white wife, a secretary, and a company of boxers, and his impedimenta, including two motor cars and twenty trunks, is in one sense a matter of no importance whatever. Nevertheless, it opens up a very big problem — the old colour question, which has been a menace in the United States for years. . . . The black man may be a champion boxer, none the less he is mentally and morally on a much lower plane than his white "brother". The experience of America is that when you scrape off the thin veneer of some generations of half-civilisation you will find the savage and brutal instincts of the barbarian. These instincts are only kept in check by the stern and almost brutal justice meted out to the perpetrators of hideous outrages. They explain the absolute insistence on the exclusion of the nigger from white society, and above all from the company of the wives and daughters of white men. . . . The mere circumstance that Mrs. Johnson is a white woman is looked on as a kind of outrage to the feelings of the ordinary citizen. Whether the management of the halls in question will think the extra advertisement sufficient warrant for continuing the engagement remains to be seen. Perhaps the hint that their licences will be opposed later on may weigh in the matter.[63]

In a few months, Jack Johnson and his wife were to appear, not quite without protest, at a Dublin music-hall.[64]

Synge's *Playboy*, although it had by now exhausted most of the overt rancour in Ireland, was still capable of causing protests among the expatriate Irish. For instance, on 27 November, the press reported:

> Synge's comedy, *The Playboy of the Western World*, was produced on Monday night for the first time in Liverpool by the Abbey Players at the Repertory Theatre, and (says *The Liverpool Daily Post and Mercury*), as has occurred in a number of other places, there was a demonstration against the play by a section of the audience.
>
> In consequence of this, little of the last two acts could be heard. After the performance a member of the company who had been with the players in America did not seem to take the demonstration very seriously.
>
> "It is unfortunate," the writer goes on, "that people who wish to consider such things on their merits as works of art should be prevented from doing so by others who have perhaps higher motives in view. It would have been kinder for those who objected on national, moral, or religious grounds to have walked out of the theatre; as it was, they remained to protest vigorously to the end, and although the actors held to their task manfully, not much of the last two acts was heard. The first act was received with unstinted laughter and applause; the reception of the second and third acts was decidedly mixed, but the verdict of a packed house was overwhelmingly favourable." [65]

During the week the controversy occasioned some letters to the press:

> Mr. Yeats wrote a letter to *The Times* from Stone Cottage, Colman's Hatch, Sussex, under Saturday's date: "Yesterday our manager received a message from the police asking that the play should not be produced at the Saturday matinee. If the police are to be allowed to suppress plays at their will a very serious issue has been raised affecting the reputation and financial interests of managers and dramatic authors. That for the first time a performance of *The Playboy* should have been prevented by the mob, reinforced by the police, matters little to the Irish players. It cannot be in the interest of the public that the police should be left under the temptation to suppress the victim to avoid the trouble of suppressing the more formidable malefactor. They might as well forbid a man,

whose watch had been stolen, to leave his house because of the indignation his complaint had caused among thieves, as forbid without process of law or public inquiry the production of a famous play which lies under no charge of immorality, and is held by most educated Irishmen to be a master work of the dramatic literature of Ireland."

To this charge the Head-Constable of Liverpool replies to an interviewer of the Liverpool *Evening Echo*, "It is absolutely wrong to suggest that there was any request on the part of the police that the play should not be produced at the Saturday matinee. No influence whatsoever was brought to bear on the management in this direction. The superintendent who was on duty expressed the opinion that there was a likelihood of trouble arising on Saturday if the performance of the play was repeated because he had noticed that the people who had been at the previous performances were booking seats for the Saturday afternoon. None of our men were inside the theatre, and we were quite prepared to deal with any disturbance outside. There was no disorder in the streets, and the people went quietly away."

Mr. Godfrey Edwards, manager of the Repertory Theatre, replied to Mr. Yeats in *The Times*: "Neither the manager of the Irish Players nor the management of the Theatre received any communication at all from the police requesting the withdrawal of this production. What did happen was that owing to the disturbance which had taken place, the police simply suggested that in order to prevent any further and perhaps more serious disorders, an alteration in the programme might be advisable for the Saturday matinee. Having succeeded in giving this play a fair hearing, the management decided, entirely upon their own responsibility, to alter the programme, and *The Playboy* was in no way suppressed by the action of the police, as suggested."

To this Mr. Yeats replied in *The Times* of yesterday: "Mr. Godfrey Edwards says in *The Times* of to-day that the police of Liverpool did not 'request' but 'simply suggested' the withdrawal of *The Playboy*, and the 'management' of the Repertory Theatre accepted the police 'suggestion' entirely upon their own responsibility. *The Playboy* has been played in many towns in America, in England, and in Ireland, and besides those, always increasing in number, who consider the play a classic. Others, resenting the sarcastic genius of its creator, have organised demonstrations; but nowhere outside Liverpool have the police 'made suggestions', which are a

276

precedent for mob law, and a menace to all playwrights who would serve their art and not their praise, and have enough imagination and power to be loved and hated." [66]

Yeats was apparently livid about the withdrawal of the play, and in December he demanded a full account of the matter from the theatre's new manager. That new manager, who had been appointed in September, was A. Patrick Wilson; and from Wilson's resumé (as well as from the letters he wrote to Yeats and Lady Gregory during the fracas), it would seem that he did not acquit himself badly.

Abbey Theatre, Dublin
21 December 1913

Dear Mr. Yeats,

Mr. Robinson asked me during the week to send a full statement of what exactly transpired in Liverpool before *The Playboy* was withdrawn but I am sorry I have been unable to give the matter proper attention until to-day.

In the first place I would explain that the actual management of the Repertory Theatre lies in the hands of Mr. Godfrey Edwards, the Managing Director, and Mr. T. J. Pigott, the Business Manager. Mr. Edwards occupies the position formerly held by Mr. Basil Dean. It was with these two gentlemen that I had to deal, and the row on Monday night sent both of them into a panic. I believe that the whole secret of their attitude lay in the fact that their theatre had been doing very bad business and they were afraid that the trouble would offend the public and result in even worse business for the future.

As you already know, they wanted the play taken off the bill for the remainder of the week, but this I absolutely refused to do and demanded adequate protection in order that the play would get a hearing on the Thursday night. During the interval between the Monday and Thursday there had been a full meeting of the Repertory Directorate and the message was conveyed to me through Edwards that they were willing to let the play go on and that adequate protection would be provided. This, in view of the attitude taken by me throughout, was making a virtue of a necessity if you like.

On the Thursday afternoon Edwards further informed me that the Chief of Police could not allow his men into the theatre but that he (the Chief) had suggested that a number of commissionaires should be hired to keep order. The commissionaires to the number of a dozen or so were hired and with their help I had every interrupter fired out of the building that night. I would here say that I got but little assistance from the local management in securing order, and I had to fight the rowdy element practically single-handed, but as I did eventually succeed in obtaining order for the last act I naturally thought that the back of the bother was broken for the week.

At the conclusion of the performance the first thing I did was to go round and warn the Players not to leave the theatre for a little as a threat was made to me in the gallery that some of the malcontents would wait for the company at the stage door and assault them. I found the company quite cheerful and all of my opinion that we had smashed the opposition. To think of taking it off on the Saturday afternoon no more crossed the minds of the players than it had done mine.

In consequence of going behind I was a little late in going to the office to square my returns, and when I got there I found Edwards and Pigott, together with Mr. J. J. Shute, the chairman of the Directors, waiting for me. They told me that Superintendent Smith, the chief superintendent of the Liverpool police force, had just been in, and had wanted the bill changed at the Saturday matinee. When I asked why he wanted any such thing, I was told that it was because of the trouble that had been given by the crowd in the street outside the theatre, and that the police feared an outbreak of factionism on the Saturday if the play was put on again. Vivid pictures were drawn for me by both Edwards and Shute of the wildness of religious bigotry in the city, and in the interests of public peace they thought the bill should be changed. I saw at once that I was up against a situation that required delicate handling for, quite apart from anything the police might have said, I realised that the most bitter opponents *The Playboy* had were the managers of the Repertory Theatre, and the visit of the police had given their opposition an amount of backbone which it had not before.

As a preliminary for anything I might have to do, I went out and asked Kerrigan and Wright to come into the office, which they did. The same story was repeated that the police wanted the bill changed owing to the fear of riots outside the theatre, and the same pious hope was expressed that the desires of the police would be complied with. I asked for time, at least till the following morning, to consider the matter, but was pressed for a decision that night. In giving my decision I never thought of the police for one minute. All that I felt

278

about them was that they had given Edwards and Company a handle which would be used for all it was worth. The question was as to whether I could fight the Liverpool management further without infringing the terms of our contract. I could have refused to allow the players to do anything but *The Playboy* at the matinee, but by doing so I believe that I would have laid myself open to a charge of breach of contract. Whatever I might have done in the matter of further opposing the Liverpool management's desire for a change of bill in the state of mind they were then in would probably have brought us into the law-courts and I could not risk that. Against my inclination altogether I agreed therefore that the bill be changed, and it was communicated to the press then and there. I will say that while I recognised quite well that the action of the police had been used for all it was worth by the Liverpool management to influence my decision, I did not for a moment question the truth of it. On the Friday I tried to get Chief Superintendent Smith on the telephone but failed, and owing to pressure of business between salaries and fixing up the return journey I had no time to visit the police office. On the Saturday, however, I obtained an interview with Superintendent Smith, and he admitted to me that he had suggested to Edwards that the bill should be changed. He admitted that the police, of course, had no power to stop the play, but as there were signs that there would be a good deal more trouble on the Saturday he thought it was as well that it had been taken off. Since I have seen the police version in the press, I have wondered if Edwards went to Smith in the first instance, or if Smith came to Edwards. I have a feeling now that Edwards got an expression of Superintendent Smith's private views after the performance in order to stiffen his own opposition to the play, and be in a stronger position to fight me. I cannot of course prove that, but in view of the correspondence in the press since, it seems rather like it. Kerrigan and Wright will bear out what I say in regard to what transpired in the office after the Thursday night.

I have little to add in addition to the foregoing except to say that I don't think the Liverpool Repertory Theatre will last much longer. I believe that a special meeting of shareholders has been called to consider the theatre's financial position during this week, and I will be much surprised if the place holds together as a practical concern till the end of this season.

In conclusion I will say that every action of mine that week in Liverpool, and it was a strenuous one, was taken in what I considered were the best interests of the company. It was with a very keen feeling of regret that I consented to the withdrawal of *The Playboy*, and I regret it still, but I believe yet, however, that if I had not consented the result would probably have been a lawsuit.

Yours faithfully,<br>A. PATRICK WILSON[67]

*    *    *

In March there was an exhibition of stage designs by Gordon Craig in the Central Hall, Westmoreland Street, Dublin, and Yeats delivered two lectures there. The first, on 'The Theatre and Beauty', was delivered on 18 March. Yeats was introduced by Count Markievicz, who said that Craig had done his best to banish vulgarity from the theatre.

Mr. W. B. Yeats, who was cordially received, said that he had always wondered why no one had written a history on vulgarity. They had books on every conceivable subject, but this was the one subject which had never been even given a definition. It was a subject that could be written in many volumes, and he supposed somewhere in the last chapter of the tenth volume would be given a final and complete definition of vulgarity. He would like to say what he would do in one chapter of that unwritten book. That chapter would be given to the theatre. They had vulgarity all around them. It was quite a modern thing. It did not enter the theatre of Sophocles or the theatre of Shakespeare, or the wonderful theatre of the fifth century in India — the most subtle of all the primary arts. The reason of it was that in olden days there were just well-educated men and wholly uneducated men. Those uneducated men had in their own homes beautiful poetry and ballads, and they learned them in their own way from their fathers. When the history of vulgarity was written it would be seen that there was something that made the men of to-day sing not "Barbara Allen", but some music-hall ditty. They wanted the history and psychology of that. He thought the psychology of it was the tendency all over the world to educate men whether they liked it or not, and when they had educated a man against his will he revenged himself by liking all the worst things. So all over the world the natural instinct and taste had been destroyed, and instead had been

280

put a very unreal taste, and so there had arisen the popular play, the insincere play, the play which did not make them think, but which enabled them to stop thinking. So, too, was it with the insincere novel. Those kind of ideas had gone all over the world, and in every European country there had spread this insincere literature. This insincere literature was able to pay great prices. The uneducated mob now paid the piper and exacted the tune, and all the art movements of to-day were attempts to recover control of the means of expression, the most powerful of which was the theatre, which was also the most debased, because nowhere else had the uneducated mob got so tight a grip. Theatres needed a vast audience to succeed. A book could be published and expenses paid if about two hundred copies were sold, but a play could not be staged without a great expenditure of money. Therefore, the theatre was the place where the half-educated had got the tightest grip. Besides, the theatre had its hold on the newspapers through advertisements and notices. They had a combination of the theatre of commerce and the newspapers supporting it. It was a vast vested interest of the ill-educated expressing itself in multitudes of copies day after day. Now and again there were intelligent criticisms in the Dublin papers. They showed that the writer had studied the work, but the ordinary critic could not write those articles. Ireland in this respect was not peculiar. It was upon that that they made their war, and one form of that war was the realistic play. The realistic play aroused an intelligent passion of reality, and until they had banished from the theatre the sentimental situation and replaced the ideals of the play of commerce by stern reality, they would not be able to get on to the stage a noble realism. He wanted now to discuss with them the sheer technique of the theatre of commerce, and to make them realise what an imperfect instrument was the theatre of commerce, which, notwithstanding all its vested interest and control of the Press, was already passing away. In Germany they were putting it aside altogether. In every art, if they were to succeed in it, they must discover what forms of expression were peculiar to it. If they tried to make the theatre compete with the painter working at his easel, they would make the theatre a meretricious thing, and that was what the theatre of commerce had done. He contended that if the theatre was to be a genuine thing, if the stage was to lose the meretriciousness, flashiness, and childishness that had made the word theatrical a by-word, it must use real light and shadow, it

281

must give the utmost importance to the movement of the actor, and it must use its own shape, perspective, and architecture. If they viewed Mr. Gordon Craig's models in the exhibition, they would realise the extraordinary beauty which was got by the very simple mechanism of screens. Mr. Gordon Craig, by his process of analysis, had brought the stage back to express those things which it alone could express better than art. Mr. Yeats, having referred in detail to the ideas as inculcated by Mr. Gordon Craig, said that he hoped to persuade Mr. Gordon Craig to add to his school of stage a school of oratory, and when that was done Mr. Craig would find that great literature did not alone belong to the study, but was pre-eminently a thing of the theatre, and that the theatre was the place for beauty that appealed to the eye, and for the beauty that appealed to the ear. (Applause.)

A hearty vote of thanks to Mr. Yeats brought the proceedings to a close.[68]

A few days later, in a lecture on 'The Poetry of Rabindranath Tagore', Yeats made some significant remarks on politics and the theatre:

If you organise, if you deal with the crowd, if you try deliberately to convert, you compromise. You no longer speak your own thoughts; you speak the things that you think will please other men. That is what made some of us here turn away from politics. I saw that when you are attempting to speak high things and sincere things, and at the same time carry on a political life, sooner or later you give up the sincere things and high things, and you speak expedient things. Do not think I am condemning politics. They are necessary to Ireland, and I have no doubt they are necessary for India; but my meaning is — different men for different tasks. For those whose business it is to express the soul in art, religion, or philosophy, they must have no other preoccupation. I saw all this years ago, at the beginning of this movement, and I wrote the *Countess Cathleen* to express it. I saw people selling their souls that they might save the souls of others.[69]

*     *     *

One great controversy, which began this year and was to last for many years, was that of the Hugh Lane pictures. That matter has been sufficiently discussed in many places, but it might be briefly noted that the initial difficulty in 1913 hinged upon the

282

building of a municipal gallery in Dublin to house Lane's projected gift. The most dramatic site proposed was a gallery to span the Liffey. Bernard Shaw, interviewed about the matter, remarked, 'Has Sir Hugh Lane ever smelt the Liffey?' [70] At any rate, Lady Gregory, who was Lane's aunt, was extremely interested in the project, and she involved the Abbey in a number of benefits in Ireland and abroad to raise money for a gallery. One typical indication of the theatre's involvement may be seen in the following account:

> The Abbey Theatre First Company, who have just returned to Ireland from a prolonged and extensive tour in America, appeared at the Abbey Theatre yesterday in two performances. These, their only performances in Dublin for the present, were given in aid of the fund for the erection of a Municipal Gallery of Modern Art, towards which the company have guaranteed £1,000. . . .
> The announcement had been made that at the evening performance the Mansion House Committee would present Lady Gregory with an address, thanking her for the generous subscription which she has secured for the Gallery in America. Lady Gregory was not well enough, however, to attend, and Miss Sara Allgood received the address on her behalf, and communicated a message from her in reply. The ceremony took place during the last interval. . . .
> Miss Sara Allgood received the address (together with a beautiful bouquet), and read a message from Lady Gregory, in which she said: "The Gallery is very near my heart, for besides the joy the pictures will be as a possession, I feel sure that, through their influence, we shall before long have a distinctive Irish school of painting, and of always remembering that at the St. Louis Exhibition we were the only country without one. I told some friends in America of our danger in losing these pictures, and they were in sympathy with us. For, while they are building their nation, we are rebuilding ours, and they look on Art as one of the great educators and endow it very lavishly. . . . I am very proud of the Abbey Company, with which I have been so closely associated, for their ready and spirited proposal to take upon themselves a guarantee that means a good deal of self-denial and a good deal of hard work. And I am very proud also of the great generosity and patience of my sister's son, Hugh Lane, for I was in no city of America where I did not hear his wonderful gift envied and he himself coveted as a citizen." (Applause.)

Mr. W. B. Yeats responded on behalf of the Abbey Players, whose generous support of the Art Gallery project the Lord Mayor had also referred to with gratitude. He read a portion of a speech made in America by Mr. Bourke Cockran, hailing the Abbey Players' work as a token of the intellectual re-creation of Ireland, and said that the speech showed that the Players in America had overcome opposition, and had had their justification and acceptance. It was only natural and right, Mr. Yeats went on to say, that in their success they should wish to do their part in creating in Dublin this great Gallery. "We workers of the theatre often feel — I think we all feel at times just a little sadly — how brief is our triumph, how soon it changes and is forgotten. In the time of Shakespeare the London players must have felt that their theatres were as permanent as the Thames and a great deal more entertaining: and to-day we are not certain about their shape or about their detail. This theatre of ours to-day will change and pass away; the time will come, perhaps, when people will dispute as to the shape of its galleries, perhaps as to the number of its galleries. But the collection of Sir Hugh Lane's will span the Liffey in those days, a permanent memorial of the taste and enthusiasm and generosity of one man, and the enthusiasm and generosity of those who helped him to do his work.

"But I am not afraid that this time will not be remembered. I have no doubt that all we here in Ireland to-day are living more or less in the eyes of an unborn public, that we are more or less playing our part before an audience, not like this small audience, but a great audience of the unborn; because this epoch in Ireland is one of supreme importance." Mr. Yeats referred to the Young Ireland movement of his early days, and to its spirit and its results, and went on to say that in the present epoch a more profound change still was taking place. There was an expression of nationality which was more lasting and penetrating than any that Young Ireland could give. Young Ireland was compelled by circumstances to give a political expression to its ideals. The present generation was the one in which they saw Irishmen learning to love the arts for their own sake. It would be remembered as the generation in which the Irish people became a modern people — in which they ascended upon their own thrones and received there the honour of men. (Applause.) Mr. Yeats concluded with an expression of thanks on behalf of the Abbey Players to the Lord Mayor for his references, and to the audience for their welcome to the company back from America.[71]

* * *

In November, Alfred Esmore made some interesting reflections about the Ulster Literary Theatre:

> Even the production and rehearsal of the plays are unique. Thus the playwright has ever before him the capabilities of the individual member to whom the role will be entrusted, and the incident and character is fashioned to wrap around him or her. Then, when put into rehearsal, every situation and gesture is subjected to severe criticism that it may be in perfect consonance with life as it really is. And when the public come to see the play, it is as if they were the actual fourth wall of the room wherein is transpiring real talk and action, so what must strike one, perhaps, as being the most admirable feature of the Ulster Theatre productions is the spontaneity and freshness with which all go through their work, and the absence of anything in the nature of posing or self-consciousness either in the acting or in the general spirit which pervades their theatre. In fact it was not until very recent years, and then only in conformity with the insistence of theatrical managements, that the names of the players were given on the bills.[72]

The Ulster Literary Theatre took over the Abbey on 31 January and 1 February, to present William Paul's two-act comedy, *Sweeping the Country*, and Gerald MacNamara's subsequently very popular one-act, *Thompson in Tír Na nOg*. Although Jack Point remarked in his usual, gratuitously surly fashion that he had recently criticised rather severely Ervine's *The Magnanimous Lover* as 'one of the worst plays ever produced in the Abbey Theatre', he, and his colleagues, were unanimous in their enjoyment of the current double bill from the North. *The Evening Mail* critic, for instance, wrote:

> From the Northern point of view Mr. Paul is, perhaps, remembered in his work called *The Jerrybuilders*, which has been described as the best attempt to handle a big human problem. In his latest attempt he goes farther afield, because he deals with a national question that concerns North, South, East, and West. How he deals with it can only be estimated by those who go to the Abbey Theatre — those who were there last night, and those who will patronise the matinee to-day and the evening performance. *Sweeping the Country* is an intensely interesting play from the Irish point of view.

285

The moral of it all seems to be that you cannot occupy a position creditably in Irish life unless you take a decided position, on one side or the other. The "trimmer" is barred and banned, and is never a delectable creature. You cannot sit on the fence. Choose your side in politics, act well your part — there all the honour lies! James McKay, J.P., Chairman of the Oldtown Urban Council, is not by any means an original creation. He might be aptly described as the "Mr. Facing-both-ways" of Bunyan's *Pilgrim's Progress*. But the idea is brought up to date, and we have a man who is in doubt whether to associate himself with the tenets of the United Irish League or the Loyal Orange Institution! The absurdity of this condition of things naturally impressed itself on the audience. Throughout the humour of the piece caught on at once, and evoked hearty merriment of a spontaneous character. In the part of McKay Mr. Gerald MacNamara played well, and did not betray any of that nervousness that was attributed to him on the occasion of its first production. Indeed it must be said that he is an actor of undoubted qualifications. One might even go further and say that if he is an amateur the profession could very easily take a lesson from his book.[73]

*The Irish Citizen* thought the play a kind of Northern *Eloquent Dempsy*, ill-constructed, with technical deficiencies, but entertaining in its 'admirable studies of Ulster character'.[74]

The critics thought that MacNamara's 'Thompson' was genuinely diverting. Jack Point, for instance, wrote:

The idea of suddenly transporting an individual from one age into another is by no means new, but it abounds with possibilities of which the author has made the most. Admission to Tír Na nOg is only to be had by those who distinguished themselves in Eirinn — you must have at least killed somebody. Thompson, of Scarva, a latter-day Orangeman, gets in by accident, and is a puzzle to the High King, Finn, Angus, Cuchulain, Grania, and the other occupants. No one can make him out, for one one knows his language. Angus gets over the difficulty by casting a spell over them all, himself included — they can speak English and nothing else. Thompson, whom they conjecture must be the son of Thomp, is brought before the Ard Righ, but still remains a puzzle. The task of discovering his right to admission is entrusted to Grania — a Gaelic Delilah. She succeeds, and Thompson is tried by a kind of court martial. The indictment against him is a formidable one. He has an English name, though he indignantly denies being an Englishman; he can't speak Gaelic; he has never killed anybody; he knows nothing of the history of Ireland prior to the Battle of the Boyne, and last and worst of all, he has fought with the peelers whom the High King describes as the Fianna of the present day. The result is a foregone one, but as there is nothing but peace and harmony in Tír na nOg and no executions are permitted, he is merely burned to ashes at the stake. Much of the dialogue, it may be observed, is written in the style of the high-class Abbey plays. It will be observed that good-humoured fun is made of all sorts of people — Orangemen, Gaels, Hibernians, Irish heroes and heroines, but everybody seemed to enjoy it.[75]

\* \* \*

In May, the Countess Plunkett made application for a licence for music, singing, and dancing in respect of the premises known as the Hardwicke Street Theatre, Hardwicke Street.

Mr. De Renzy, K.C. (instructed by Dr. O'Connell), who made the application, said it was on behalf of the Countess Plunkett. His lordship might be surprised to hear such an application on behalf of a lady like the Countess Plunkett. She, however, was engaged largely in charitable and philanthropic work in Dublin. The history of these premises which she has in Hardwicke Street was interesting. The first Jesuit Church in the city of Dublin was there, and afterwards, he understood, they were the original premises of Belvedere College. They subseqently became a national school, and then for some time they were derelict. The Countess Plunkett purchased the premises, and they were used in part as a guild for carrying on carpet manufacture and other useful work. He understood that a portion was used during the day for work done by the Dun Emer Art Guild. Her ladyship had a son who was largely interested in writing Irish plays and she was desirous that these plays, which were short, should be performed occasionally for her friends, partly for charity and partly for the amusement of people in the neighbourhood. It was necessary to comply with the law in order to use this place as a semi-private or semi-public theatre, and to get a licence to enable her to give entertainments involving music and singing. The Corporation officials had inspected the place, and it met with their requirements. The inspector made inquiries among the people of Hardwicke Street, and the univer-

287

sal opinion was in approval of it, and they thought it would be a benefit to the locality. Inquiries were also made of Rev. Fergus Greer, rector of the parish, and he expressed warm approval.[76]

This project was to grow into the Irish Theatre, of which Edward Martyn was the guiding spirit. Its first production did not, however, appear until 1914.

In May and in November of 1913, An Cluithcheóirí, a new group of Irish players, presented two programmes at the Abbey. D. P. Moran, who was by now caustically critical of the literary movement in English (in many cartoons, poems and squibs in *The Leader*, Yeats is always 'Pensioner Yeats', Æ is always 'the Hairy Fairy', and even George A. Birmingham is 'the bigot of Westport), was quite sympathetic; but, as his grasp of Irish was apparently not great, his helpful comments were a bit low-brow. He thought, for instance, that the translation of O'Kelly's *The Shuiler's Child*, produced in May, was 'talky and actionless', and suggested that the theatre should choose plays which emulated films and contained much more action. He thought Padraic O'Conaire's *Bairbre Ruadh*, also produced in May, was somewhat better than *The Shuiler's Child*, but still talky.[77] In November, An Cluithcheóirí rented the Abbey to produce *Fa Bhrigh na Mionn*, a translation of *Kathleen ni Houlihan*, and An Seabhac's *Dubhairt sé Dabhairt sé*. *The Leader* thought this a livelier programme, and even unbent enough to say that Yeats's play was his 'greatest claim to fame'.[78]

\*     \*     \*

At the end of 1913, one theatrical correspondent justly summed up the situation of the commercial theatre:

> The year 1913 has not been a very flourishing one for either music or the drama. Dramatically it has been unusually poor. This is accounted for in two ways—that the London managers are no longer touring the provinces or sending as many plays as usual on tour, and that the public taste is veering round to variety performances. . . .
>
> There can be no doubt that the picture palaces have affected the theatres to a considerable degree. . . . Within the area bound by Dame Street, Grafton Street, Sackville Street, and Mary Street, we have no less than eight or nine picture-houses — all doing excellent business, while the suburbs are well provided in this respect; and while music and the drama have been showing a decline in popularity during 1913, the

picture houses have been forging ahead. The great advantage of the picture houses is the convenience of the continuous performance, and they have always a great variety of subjects. Perhaps we have too much cowboy drama and many of the comedy pictures are coarse. . . .

The one form of theatrical art that seems still to hold its own in public regard is the musical comedy — a list of successful works in this category since *Faust Up to Date* would fill a couple of columns of this paper, and looking over the musical plays announced for future production in London, it does not appear that there are any signs of waning popularity. . . .[79]

The Theatre Royal and the Gaiety were both controlled by the Dublin Theatrical Company. In July, the company's chairman, David Telford, defended the offerings of the city's two major commercial theatres.

The charge made against us, Mr. Telford explained, was that of deliberately withholding plays for the sake of economy. Of course there isn't a word of truth in that, and the newspaper concerned generously withdrew that statement when the facts were put before it.

Economy is not in question, he went on, for that would be the very worst sort of economy, because any money that is made out of theatrical business is made on the big and expensive productions; and, as a matter of fact, we are paying far bigger terms now than were paid twenty or thirty years ago.

I will admit at once that it's more difficult to obtain really good plays now, with prominent actors in the cast, than it was some years ago; and the reasons are not far to seek. In the first place, the London theatres have multiplied so much in recent years that the managers do not find it so easy to let them as they used to, and hence they occupy them themselves with whatever plays they have, or with revivals. Then, again, when "stars" go on tour they seem to find it more profitable to go to America or the colonies; and I am sorry to say that when they appear in England and Scotland, and even in the metropolis of Ireland, they are not accorded the support they used to receive.

Furthermore, the geographical position of Dublin is making managers, on a short tour, more reluctant to come here, and sometimes the Press is not too kind to them when they do come. Do not take me as finding fault with the Press criticism, but I merely wish to point out to you some of the difficulties that theatrical proprietors have to deal with. A notable example of this was in the case of Pavlova who is, I think, a very great artiste. She cancelled her contract for a return visit owing to the adverse criticism of one of the Dublin morning papers.

Notwithstanding all this I assert that Dublin has got in the past and will continue to get in the future, if we can obtain it, every play that is worth having which goes on tour.

Can you give me some examples, Mr. Telford?

Well, I would like to mention some of the big theatrical people who have visited Dublin from time to time, and to tell you so far as I can ascertain, what their movements are, and why they are not all coming to Dublin this autumn.

Sir Herbert Tree is not touring this year. Laurence Irving would have toured with the *Typhoon* this year, and was to have visited Dublin, but finds he cannot get a consecutive tour, and has abandoned same until next year. Jas. Welch will tour with *O, I Say* after the London run, which will probably be next spring, and will visit Dublin; Sir George Alexander is doing a short tour of *Bella Donna*, and negotiations are going on at present regarding a visit to this city. Arthur Bourchier had fixed a date for a Dublin visit, but has intimated that he has now decided he will not leave London this autumn. A date was arranged for Dublin with Cyril Maude, but owing to his American contracts starting earlier than he had originally arranged he has been obliged to abandon his tour. Lewis Waller is at present touring America, and Fred Terry has been booked for Dublin, and will be here in September. We hoped for a farewell visit from Sir Johnston Forbes Robertson this autumn, but his American arrangements have interfered; he has, however, definitely promised to come next year.

I am sorry we won't have the Quinlan Opera next Christmas, as they will be in the colonies. During this autumn we will have a return visit of *The Chocolate Soldier* and of *Kismet*, and all the new musical pieces will be presented, viz., *Gipsy Love, Princess Caprice, The Girl on the Film*, and *O, O Delphine*.

You will see that we have been making every effort to get the big theatrical attractions, and we hope that those who do come will be generously supported; the purely dramatic attractions have not been supported in recent years as formerly, and I can only account for this by the change in the public taste to light opera, musical comedy, and variety entertainment.

In self-defence, the very best of the theatrical people have had to follow their patrons to the music halls, some of them temporarily, and I regret to say, a good many of them permanently.

"Do you think, then, that the public are to blame for a decline in theatrical attractions?"

Certainly. It's entirely a question of supply and demand. I am continually being told — by the best people, too — how much they appreciate the short, bright Hippodrome entertainments at present running at the Royal.

"Do your patrons appreciate the liberty to smoke which has recently been granted?"

Oh, yes; it has added enormously to the popularity of the Hippodrome season, and I may say we have had no complaints from anyone; the ladies do not seem to mind it a bit.

"It is rumoured that you intend to run Hippodrome all the year round at the Royal. Is there any truth in that?"

None whatever; and I see no indication of any such change — we must either present Hippodrome or close the theatre for six or eight months of the year. We must, of course, bring grand opera and such of the big spectacular plays as are available to the Royal, but with these exceptions it is our present intention to set the Gaiety apart exclusively for drama, comedy and light opera.

"Do you think that Dublin is as well catered for in amusements as the large English and Scotch cities, say Glasgow, Birmingham or Liverpool?"

I don't think it, I know it, and the prices here are cheaper than in any of the towns you have mentioned. I was rather amused to see Dublin mentioned in the Press the other day as a city without amusements when, as a matter of fact, every important theatre in the towns that you have mentioned is now closed, and Dublin alone is able to keep its premiere theatre open, and is providing amusements which are apparently appreciated by their patrons.

"You say that you do not see any immediate change in the popular taste for light amusement?"

Well, the king has set the example; it is only a short time ago that he had all the music-hall stars playing before him in the Palace in London, and I notice that when he was staying at Knowsley, Lord Derby organised a variety entertainment for his amusement. Then, the music-halls are made very attractive; the quality of the performance is improving wonderfully; they are well lighted, with comfortable seats and moderate prices; and my own personal view is that the more

291

people become accustomed to this light class of entertainment, the less they will feel inclined to sit out a three hours' play, sometimes of a very sombre nature. . . .

"I suppose London is almost entirely your source of supply?"

Practically. The Repertory Theatre in Manchester, conducted so ably by Miss Horniman, occasionally sends a company on tour, and they have been in the Gaiety on several occasions; then a band of talented and realistic actors and actresses in Dublin, known as "The Dublin Repertory Theatre", are producing plays at the Gaiety. And although the plays produced have been by distinguished authors, the productions have been everything that could be desired, and the acting has been excellent — still the amount of public support they received has, I regret to say, been very discouraging.

"It all comes back, then, to where we started. The public wants to be amused and not instructed?"

It looks like it, doesn't it? But all the same, we will continue to bring the best plays that can be obtained to Dublin, because I am glad to say there is still a good audience for a good play, when there is a big name in the cast, but not otherwise, so far as my experience goes.[80]

The chief Dublin venue for touring musical comedies from London was still the Theatre Royal, and during the year the theatre presented such confections as *The Dollar Princess, The Dancing Mistress, Princess Caprice, The Quaker Girl, The Girl on the Film, Hullo Rag-Time, Oh! Oh! Delphine* !!!, and Oscar Straus's *The Chocolate Soldier* which was loosely pilfered from Shaw's *Arms and the Man*. The few dramatic offerings of the Royal were not calculated to corrugate anyone's brow. Pauline Chase appeared in *Peter Pan*; J. Pitt Hardacre anachronistically produced *East Lynne*; one of the last of the actor-managers, Fred Terry, appeared in his hardy vehicle, *The Scarlet Pimpernel*; Vedrenne and Eadie presented Arnold Bennett's *Milestones*, while Vedrenne's old partner, Granville Barker and his wife, Lillah McCarthy, sent out an adaptation of Bennett's *Buried Alive*, called *The Great Adventure* — a distinct comedown from the heady days of the Royal Court venture. The Royal also welcomed music-hall productions, with bills headed notably by Marie Studholme, Little Tich and Bransby Williams, and not-so-notably by Barnold's Dogs and Monkeys. However, there were also two appearances by the Quinlan Opera Company, one for a period of four weeks, and another week in which they produced Wagner's Ring.

The Gaiety offered a similarly mixed bag, although its cultural
level was pitched slightly higher, and there were a few productions
of Irish interest. There were the usual musicals and the Christmas
panto, but there was also a couple of weeks of the D'Oyly Carte
and a week each for the Corinthian Opera Company and the
O'Mara Opera Company. There were the usual simplistic dramas
and light comedies of the season, such as *The Barrier* by Rex
Beach, 'America's Greatest Writer', or *A Royal Divorce* with the
Napoleon impersonator Juan Bonaparte, or Percy Hutchinson's
*Officer 666*, but there was also a curious production of *Jim the
Penman*, now regarded as a humorous anachronism, and there was
the perennial *Charley's Aunt* by Brandon Thomas's Company.
One item of Irish interest was produced on 25 and 28 February
during the two-week visit of the F. R. Benson Shakespearean
Company, and this was the first production (and apparently the
last) of Darrell Figgis's verse play, *Queen Tara*. Despite the title,
however, the play was not on an Irish subject, and it was not
particularly exciting. Jack Point in his review wrote:

> It would be not unreasonable to imagine that in a city
> which is assumed to be enthusiastic over everything connected
> with Art — including galleries — a new play written by a
> Dublin man, and produced by a company of the quality of
> the Benson combination, would require the unwelcome an-
> nouncement "House full" to be displayed at the Gaiety. It
> was otherwise last night when *Queen Tara*, a verse drama by
> Darrell Figgis, was put on for the first time. If, however, there
> was no difficulty in securing a seat there was no lack of
> appreciation by the audience, whose approval Mr. Figgis had
> to acknowledge, at the same time alluding to the admirable
> manner in which the Benson Company had performed his
> play. Nowadays plays in blank verse are rare enough, and
> possibly that supplies one explanation for "the house"; or
> mayhap there may have been an obsession that the drama
> had something to do with the historic hill of whose queens
> history is strangely silent. As a matter of fact, the action takes
> place in Illyricum, a country not to be found on the map of
> Europe, but from internal evidence it is a reasonable con-
> clusion that Mr. Figgis had, when he wrote his play, one of
> the belligerent Balkan States in mind, and that the assassi-
> nation business of the denouement is a more or less accurate
> reproduction of well-known historical events. At any rate,
> Serge and Peter, the names of the king's brothers-in-law, are
> sufficiently Slavonic to warrant the inference. As an example

of blank verse, *Queen Tara* shows that not only has its author made a fruitful study of Shakespeare, but has, moreover, acquired what may be irreverently described as the Shakespearean trick of handling the dialogue. This in itself is a rather notable achievement, but on the other hand the story, as it stands, scarcely affords sufficient possibilities — there are, in fact, very few "complications". I — not having read the play carefully — expected something would develop in Act II out of the entray of Hagen, Queen Tara's former lover, but there did not. Hagen does no more than kiss the Queen's hand and arouseth the passing jealousy of the king, and then disappears to return no more. At any rate, he serves one useful purpose, as he gives an opportunity to Miss Gladys Vanderzee, who takes the name part, of giving one of the best of the several finely written speeches in the play, that beginning:

> Dear love! I think indeed men are as hemp,
> Spun o'er the fingers, and by the craft of women,
> Bent to what shape we will.

Again, the assassination of the king, queen, and her brother, which is the crowning tragedy, is not over-well worked up to, and moreover, the final scene in which conspirators Brabo and Mark confess that the assassination of Julian was merely a bungle, and are duly arrested on the order of Antony, who appoints Peter king "subject to ratification by the Senate" is not particularly convincing. The only fault which Julian's subjects can find with him is that he married a woman — an adventuress, no doubt — who once "darned his socks". All things considered, ability to darn anybody's socks is no bad qualification even for a queen, and certainly is not a sufficient excuse for regicide. Nevertheless, although *Queen Tara* is hardly likely to create as much stir as the average musical comedy, its dialogue is very far indeed beyond the average of many plays that have proved to be a little gold mine. Mr. Figgis has already made a name in literature, and there is no apparent reason why, with a little more experience in the matter of construction, he should not make a reputation as a dramatist of ability.[81]

This was gentle treatment indeed, and H.R.W. was both more just and more specific in *The Evening Mail*:

> It is not a stage play; it is, like most of Shakespeare's plays, more suited to the study. A drama or tragedy written for the stage should have action, a steadily moving plot, and stirring

dialogue. This is the modern idea. Ibsen is even more advanced than this, for he does not relate a story, but acts a climax. The events leading up to this climax have taken place before the rise of the curtain. In one sense Mr. Figgis's play is formed on this basis, for matters are approaching a climax at the beginning of the first act, but what little action there is, is constantly delayed by fine speeches and soliloquies. When Tara receives the mysterious ring from a mysterious stranger which causes such alarm, Cathna, her maid, would in the ordinary way exclaim, "What's the matter?" Insted of which she says:

> Madam, what's this
> Has broken on you, and banished colour and blossom
> Out of your cheeks?

When Antony asks the king what new trouble has come upon him, he does not answer directly and to the point, but says:

> Trouble, Antony,
> It is the chief business of the world. That's nothing
> But they who find it, can tell their life,
> And say, this is a bolt the gods have thrown.

I point out these passages not to disparage the work as a literary drama but as a drama for the modern stage and as a reason for its lack of power to grip a modern audience. Mr. Figgis repeats himself occasionally and weakens his climaxes. Thus we have Brabo ending the first act by saying, "Let's go and have a flagon of wine", and the same character concludes a scene in the second act with the remark, "That demands a beaker of red wine." The character of Hagen, one which one might have reasonably expected to be one of singular strength and importance to the plot, turns out to be a mere incident, and quite unnecessary. Tara herself is vague and misty. Whether she was a woman with a past, a vile intriguer, a designing woman with vaulting ambition, or whether she was the innocent victim of slander and genuinely in love with the king is not satisfactorily explained. The king himself seems to have been a man of noble principles and high courage, but since he became, as he describes himself, "a love-sick bungler", he does not appear to have received, nor has he indeed merited, the love of his people.[82]

In other words, in *Queen Tara* Figgis is not so much exploring Yeats country, as he is lost in the land of Stephen Phillips.

Also at the Gaiety, B. Iden Payne's Company played the week of 17 November in Shaw's *Man and Superman*, and for the week of 20 May Alexander Marsh's Shakespearean Company appeared with Frank Fay in several minor roles. There was a week of charity performances starting on 1 December, in which several home-grown one-act plays by Mary Costello and Alice Maye Finny were performed.[83]

Much more interesting were the productions of the Dublin Repertory Theatre, which was an outgrowth of Count Markievicz's Independent Theatre. For its first season, the group engaged the Gaiety for the week of 21 April to present François Coppée's *For the Crown*, for the week of 12 May to present Shaw's *The Devil's Disciple*, for the week of 11 August to present Galsworthy's *Strife*, for the week of 6 October to present Shaw's *John Bull's Other Island*, for the week of 24 November to repeat *Strife*, and for the week of 8 December to present Galsworthy's *The Silver Box*. The leading spirits of the new group were originally Edward (or sometimes Evelyn) Ashley, and Count Markievicz. However, on 20 May, *The Evening Mail* reported:

> Last night at a dinner in the Dolphin Hotel Count Markievicz was presented with a gold match-box, suitably engraved, from some of his friends in Dublin, principally members of the Dublin Repertory Theatre.
>
> Count Markievicz has been for some time past very prominent in local theatrical affairs, and he recently devoted much of his time and experience to the establishment of the Dublin Repertory Theatre. In this undertaking his assistance was of the utmost value, and the successful launching of this enterprise is very largely due to his unrelenting efforts. His departure from Ireland for his annual visit to his native country, Poland, was considered a suitable occasion by some of his friends to show their appreciation of his work in connection with Irish dramatic affairs, and of his genial and vigorous personality.
>
> Count Markievicz will be absent from Dublin for a few months, and will return in good time to resume with his co-workers the direction of the repertory movement for the autumn and winter season.
>
> Mr. Jack Morrow presided, and after dinner, in a felicitious speech, referred to the many sterling qualities of the Count.
>
> In proposing his health, he said that he was sure it was the wish of all that the name of the Countess should be coupled with the toast.

The toast having been honoured with acclamation, Count Markievicz, in a characteristic speech, returned thanks. He said that he felt deeply the remarks of Mr. Morrow, and was particularly grateful to him for having coupled his wife's name with the toast. Since he came to Dublin, he said, his best friends had been amongst those whose interest lay in the drama, and in this connection he would like to say that he keenly appreciated the kindly sympathy which he had always received from the Gaiety Theatre and all connected with it, especially his old friend, Mr. Martin Murphy (applause). He thanked them all for their handsome present, and hoped to be back again in Dublin in a few months, when he would have the pleasure of seeing his old friends again (applause).

On the motion of Mr. Seumas O'Sullivan, Mr. Morrow vacated the chair, which was then taken by Mr. Frank Fay, who is now appearing at the Gaiety Theatre.

Mr. Seumas O'Sullivan in an eloquent speech proposed the health of the Chairman, and spoke in flattering terms of the good which Mr. Morrow and the Morrow family had done for Dublin from an artistic point of view.

He spoke of the Count as a man who had "tended to take some of the greyness from this old city of ours, wherein, without such men, we were sinking into a quagmire of the most undesirable virtues" (laughter and applause). . . .[84]

Despite this testimony of affection for the Count, all was not well with the Repertory Theatre, and a foreshadowing of the ensuing break between the Count and Ashley may be seen in a comment on this testimonial dinner by another member of the Repertory Theatre, S. W. Maddock:

. . . I think it right to say that an equally large share of credit is due to Mr. Evelyn Ashley, the other director of the Repertory Theatre, and to Miss Flora MacDonnell who produced the first play, both of whom have given us artistic productions from time to time during the past twelve years of plays by Ibsen, Maeterlinck, Shaw, etc., and who were primarily responsible for the establishment of the Repertory Theatre in Dublin. It seems peculiar to find no reference whatever made to the efforts of our own people, while, as usual, the foreigner is glorified as being the saviour of art amongst us.[85]

The surliness of Maddock's letter presaged what happened next. In the middle of November, some time after the Count's return

297

from Poland, his enlivening connection with the Irish theatre came to an end. Primarily, the reason was his wife's prominence in the cause of the workers during the Great Lockout. However, the Count's sympathies were entirely in agreement with his wife's, and in a vivid letter to the Press about the events of Bloody Sunday he himself had concluded, 'No human being could be silent after what I saw. These acts of uncalled for and inhuman cruelty must be punished.'

The specific theatrical dispute is detailed in an exchange of letters which the Count released to the press:

To the Editor of *The Irish Times*:

Sir, — I would thank you to publish the enclosed correspondence, which has passed between myself, as director of the Dublin Repertory Theatre, and Mr. Telford, the chairman of the Gaiety Theatre Company, and my co-director of the Repertory Theatre, Mr. Ashley. The correspondence sufficiently explains my reasons for severing my connection with the Repertory Theatre. Yours, etc.,

DUNIN MARKIEVICZ

United Arts Club, 44 St. Stephen's Green
Dublin, 12 November 1913

COPY

The Directors, Dublin Repertory Theatre
Gaiety Theatre, Dublin
26 September 1913

Dear Count,

I enclose you, as promised, copy of Mr. Telford's letter to me, and also copy of my reply thereto. I am exceedingly sorry to be compelled to take this course, but you must see plainly that Madame's attitude, however well-intentioned, has already done our movement very great injury, and to insist on her appearing on the stage, in view of what Telford says, is quite out of the question.

Yours faithfully,

A. E. ASHLEY

COPY

Trinity Chambers, 40 and 41 Dame Street
25 September 1913

Dear Mr. Ashley,

I had a conversation with Count Markievicz over the telephone this afternoon about staging *Eleanor's Enterprise.*

The last conversation we had on this subject, I was under the impression that it was definitely settled that it was not to be put on, but the Count now still wishes it, and he wishes Madame to play in it. Owing to the high feeling which prevails in the city at the present moment, and owing to the prominent part which the Countess has taken in the labour disputes, I honestly do not think that her appearance on the stage would be good for business, and although the Count agrees with me in this, he still presses that the piece should be produced before the end of the present year.

I am aware from the conversations we had on the subject that you feel very strongly about this matter, and also that if she insists on playing, a number of other artists will refuse to play. Under these circumstances, what do you suggest should be done? If the Count and you would consent, I would prefer to cancel the remaining dates, but if you will not agree to that, you must produce such plays as I approve of. I must confess I strongly disapprove of *Eleanor's Enterprise* in present circumstances, but the Count has pressed me so hard that I very reluctantly told him that, if he obtained your consent to the Countess playing, I might reconsider the matter.

Faithfully yours,

D. TELFORD.

COPY

26 September 1913

Dear Mr. Telford,

I am duly in receipt of your letter of the 25th inst., and quite agree with all you say as to the inadvisability of allowing *Eleanor's Enterprise* to go on, or of the Countess Markievicz appearing at all in our productions, and I have already expressed my opinion on the subject to both the Count and Countess. If the Count cannot see that his attitude and that of his wife is only calculated to do the Repertory Theatre movement irreparable injury, then I suggest the sooner he severs all connection with it the better.

I shall make arrangements for the production of other plays for November and December.

Yours faithfully,

A. E. ASHLEY

Surrey House, Leinster Road, Rathmines
October, 1913

Dear Sir,

Since our interview of the 14th inst. I have been considering my position as joint manager of the Dublin Repertory Theatre Company, and in view of the attitude adopted by Mr. Ashley and you with reference to your refusal to allow the production of *Eleanor's Enterprise*, as arranged, if Countess Markievicz is to play a part, I see no course open to me save to retire from the joint management of the Repertory Company.

Please cancel any engagements made by me, and understand that I can no longer be responsible in any way for the company. I am sending copies of all correspondence to the press.

Yours faithfully,<br>DUNIN MARKIEVICZ.

David Telford, Esq.
40 Dame Street, Dublin.

Surrey House, Leinster Road, Rathmines
October, 1913

Sir,

As I am convinced that your policy must be fatal to the interests of the Repertory Theatre movement, as well as insulting to the people of this city, I feel it is impossible for me to retain my position as co-director of the Dublin Repertory Theatre Company.

Your obedient servant,<br>DUNIN MARKIEVICZ

A. E. Ashley, Esq.[86]

Then, on 12 December, it was announced that:

Count Markievicz, who was prominent on the Larkinite side during the height of the Dublin crisis, has left the city, and is on his way to Russia. . . .

Prior to his departure from Dublin Count Markievicz was entertained by the Abbey Company, and a dinner was given in his honour by the Arts Club. . . .

The Count does not propose to make Dublin his home in the future, but he hopes to pay occasional visits.[87]

Except for a several weeks' run of the Christmas pantomime and a week's visit from the Rathmines and Rathgar Musical Society in *The Mikado*, the Queen's depended upon a weekly change of programme supplied by provincial English and, occasionally, Irish touring companies. As was the usual custom, these companies presented their plays twice a night. The plays continued to be either sensational or sentimental melodramas. However, the purist might sift them down into several particular topics. There were, for instance, romantic female dramas such as T. Edward's Company in *A Lad's Love*, T. Arthur Jones's Company in *When Other Lips*, T. Morton Powell's Company in *Two Little Vagabonds*, Herbert Fuller's Company in 'The Great Human Play', *A Noble Mother*, E. L. Garside's Company in *A Girl's Good Luck*, Richard A. Green's Company in *Breaking a Woman's Heart*, or Mr. and Mrs. F. G. Kimberley's Company in *The Path of Sorrow*. There were also cowboy dramas such as Travis Green's Company in *Queen of the Redskins* or George A. Street's Company in *The Cattle Thief*. Sometimes the cowboy motif was blended with sex, as in a number of Mormon plays such as Frank Bertram's Company in *Through Death Valley, or The Mormon Peril*, or Miss Winifred Maud's Company in *The Mormon and the Maid*. And sometimes there were just sex dramas such as Mr. and Mrs. Millane's Company in *A White Slave*, or Will H. Glaze's Company in another play of the same title. There were also dramas about drunkards, detectives, convicts, mill workers, mine workers, and even several about the plight of oppressed Russian serfs. Typical of the more sensational fare at the Queen's would have been the following production:

> Thrills and chills in equal parts; murder and tortures (various) ditto; a sprinkling of love-making and just enough humour to keep the murder scenes from growing monotonous — these are the component parts of the thrilling drama, *Through Death Valley, or The Mormon Peril*, which is staged by Mr. Frank Bertram's Company. . . . At least six of the characters meet death on the stage by shooting or stabbing, and the awful sufferings of a man tied to a tree and tortured by a rattlesnake, and the agonies of a party dying from thirst and want of food are successively portrayed. . . .[88]

Equally enthralling would have been *A Fool in Paradise*:

> Dorian, Earl of Notron, is the central figure, and in this part Mr. Cecil Gray gives some remarkable acting. Lured to the use of drugs by Natalie Winter, known as the Vampire

301

Woman, the young Earl becomes a wreck, still holding to a belief in the goodness of the creature who has destroyed him. Eventually driven mad by the revelation of her true character, Dorian is imprisoned by her in a secret cell. The extraordinary intensity which is evident during this scene spreads from the actor to the audience, and the whole house is enthralled by the realistic representation of a raving madman. . . .[89]

The Boucicault-Whitbread tradition of patriotic Irish melodrama was kept alive by Ira Allen's and P. J. Bourke's companies, both of which toured in the provinces and occasionally appeared in the Queen's. For instance, in 1913 Allen's company visited the Queen's for the week of 17 February with *The Bailiff of Ballyfoyle* and for the week of 21 July with *Father Murphy, or The Hero of Tullow* in which Peter Judge, who later under his stage name of F. J. McCormick was to become possibly the best of modern Irish actors, was a minor member of the cast. P. J. Bourke's Company also visited the Queen's twice during the year with his own plays: for the week of 17 March with *The Northern Insurgent* and for the week of 24 November in *In Dark '98*. That last play, a typical specimen of its genre, was reviewed like this:

> Judging from the warm appreciation bestowed on it at the two performances last night, *In Dark '98* is certain to have a very successful run at the Queen's Theatre this week. The play, which is an historical one in twelve scenes, deals with the '98 movement, and the actions of the more prominent of the United Irishmen are powerfully portrayed, while the intrigues of the English secret service are laid bare. The career of Wolfe Tone is splendidly staged, including his last great fight in Lough Swilly. From the first scene at Dunleary in 1795 to the last in the historic year of the Rebellion, the drama never flags in interest, and at times the incidents portrayed are of the most thrilling character. In the first act Miss Lily Roberts sang "My Irish Queen" in charming style. Produced by Mr. P. J. Bourke's No. 1 company of Irish Players, the drama is splendidly staged; and the various artistes enter thoroughly into the spirit of the patriotic production. The music for the piece has been specially written by Mr. F. L. Baynton, musical director of the theatre, and is highly appropriate.[90]

The Tivoli and the Empire continued their usual twice-nightly variety programmes, which occasionally included one-act plays of no greater merit than Frank Street in *The Gun Fighter*. The Empire

302

rose to a visit from Lupino Lane, but the usual offering was more on the level of the Tivoli's visit from Smaragda's Cats, 'the Acme of Animal Training'. Perhaps a typical example of this entertainment might be suggested by the following description of a performance at the Empire during the week of 13 October:

> Foremost on the programme is, of course, the name of Apollo, a great athlete and strong man, whose splendid feats of muscular prowess are creating a sensation wherever he goes. . . . But the next trial of strength was a startling exhibition. Apollo half reclined on the stage. A wooden platform with a hole for his head to protrude was placed on his chest and body. On this structure a piano carried by six men was placed, and the men also took up positions on the impromptu stage. A lively tune was played on the piano, and one of the gentlemen danced a jig. There was loud applause. The *pièce de résistance*, however, was Apollo's illustration of how a well-favoured man can permit a motor car to run over his prostrate body without causing any damage whatever to the person underneath the wheels. . . .[91]

The quality of music-hall humour was interestingly discussed by H.R.W. in his column in *The Evening Mail*:

> A thoughtful critic has been analysing the humour of the music-hall. He finds it generally confined within the following limits: (1) alcoholic excess, (2) personal deformity, e.g. policemen's feet, (3) conjugal infidelity, (4) studies of insect life, e.g. seaside lodgings, and (5) exaggerated metaphor, e.g. "giddy kipper". To which we may add the influence of mothers-in-law in the house, the birth of twins, girls at the seaside, and the inevitable gagging at the orchestra, with its allusion to the trombone as a "ham bone". We also have the distortions of national characteristics — the Jew as a mean skinflint, the Scot as devoid of humour, the Irishman who says "Begorra", and the Londoner who says "Wot o!" Truly, there is room for a new humorist on the music-hall stage.[92]

Finally, among the minor excitements of 1913 at the commercial theatres were an alleged bombing incident and an attempted suicide. On 10 May, a bomb was discovered in the women's lavatory of the Empire, and a note attached read: 'Votes for Women. No Property or Life Safe Until We Get It.' The whole affair was a curious one, and not the least curious aspect (which seems never to have been raised in Court or in the Press) was how the note was to have been read in the event the bomb exploded.

In any event, the Dublin suffragettes denied having anything to do with the matter and 'repudiated the suggestion that they would undertake any act dangerous to life'. A young lady attendant at the theatre was charged in the case, but the testimony at her trial was confused, and she was discharged. One would hazard the guess that the matter really stemmed from personal animosity among several lady employees of the theatre, that the bomb was never intended to go off, and that the suffragette note was a red herring.[93] On 4 August, a young man from Fairview attempted to commit suicide by jumping from the second circle of the Theatre Royal into the parterre 'under circumstances indicating derangement of mind'. That distance was about 25 feet, and the young man injured his right leg and abdomen, and was committed to the Richmond Asylum.[94]

\* \* \*

In June, a very belated footnote to the first production of a play in Irish was written by Alice Milligan:

> To the Editor of *The Weekly Freeman*:
>
> Sir — It is dangerous to start a newspaper correspondence on any subject, one never knows where it will end, and hoping to give some useful hints on stagecraft to the Gaelic League, I have aroused the ire of one Maelmuire, who reminds me that some fourteen years ago I insufficiently dressed and barbarously painted a stage army in a play at Letterkenny. The occasion was a starting point in Gaelic League history, as that on which the first bit of drama was acted in Irish, else I would let Maelmuire have the last word; but I feel bound to quote from an old poem of Mac Gilbride Mac Conmidhe a description of the Northern soldiery at the fatal Battle of Down.
>
> > Fine linen shirts upon the race of Con.
> > The Foreigners one mass of iron.
>
> Our army went clad in the simplest of garments, brown and yellow, to recall the crotal and saffron-dyed shirts of the ancient clansmen, but our Kings, Chieftains, Druids, and Saints were suitably and splendidly attired. At a second historical play, acted by the pupils of the Loreto Convent, under the direction of a reverend mother who was herself an artist, the properties were so substantially made and beautifully finished as to arouse the astonishment of a man from the Theatre Royal, Dublin, who came down to arrange the scenery.

Maelmuire refers to the Macroom actors who staged Father O'Leary's play; it was in fact that very band of actors who lamented to me the difficulty of staging *Maeve*, and I am strongly of opinion that the Gaelic League should prepare and hire out from headquarters well-designed costumes, simple scenery, and properties.

ALICE MILLIGAN[95]

A belated footnote to Synge's *Playboy* appeared in the Press in May:

> At Castlerea Petty Sessions, before Mr. E. Sanford Wills, John Kearney, an aged man of Cloondaharra, charged his son Tim Kearney with assaulting him. The old man explained to their worships that his son had repeatedly assaulted him, and on the 12th May had given him a black eye. He had to fly out of the house and take refuge in a neighbour's house. At the same time he appealed to their worships to give his son until Monday next, by which time he would probably have gone to America. It was the drink that ruined him.
>
> Mr. R. M. Rice said if the court granted the application they might be assisting this man to evade justice, and if he came back again he might kill this old man.
>
> Defendent was sentenced to fourteen days imprisonment.[96]

On 8 January, Johanna Redmond, John Redmond's daughter, who had had some success in London and Dublin with her patriotic one-act plays, married Max Green, Chairman of the Irish Prisons Board. On 12 January, the eagle-eyed Holloway noted that a figure from the distant past, Agnes Robertson, the divorced wife of Boucicault, was honoured by a dinner in the Hotel Cecil, London:

> She is frequently seen at first nights in London in late years, and rarely misses a piece produced by her son, Dion G. Boucicault, at the Duke of York's Theatre, where she always looks one of the most distinguished and charming persons present. . . .[97]

On 7 April, Frederick Ryan, who had been the first secretary of the Irish National Theatre Society and whose play, *The Laying of the Foundations*, had been its first realistic social drama, died. As *The Manchester Guardian* reported:

> In the death of Mr. Frederick Ryan Ireland has lost one of the ablest and most high-minded of journalists . . . for although he had been for some time the editor of *Egypt* in

305

London his connections with the Dublin Press were still maintained. He had not yet reached the age of forty, but his ideas were of the doctrinaire kind that found favour with Nationalists of a past generation, and in his hatred of compromise and power of putting the extreme claims of Ireland in dry, prosaic language he often reminded one of John O'Leary and the Fenian group. Irish Nationalism, in his opinion, was not sufficiently democratic, and in a little paper which he edited called *Dana*, he used to examine all modern Irish movements in the light of the first principles of a democrat and a rationalist, usually finding them wanting! I remember that he attacked Synge's *Well of the Saints* on the ground that Synge should have indicated more clearly his own disbelief in miracles and that he suspected the Gaelic League of clericalism. *Dana*, to which Mr. George Moore, Mr. Cunningham Graham, and a host of distinguished writers contributed, soon shared the common fate of all things that are rare. Afterwards Mr. Ryan went to Egypt. The experience did not turn him into an Imperialist, for he became editor of an Egyptian Nationalist paper now discontinued in Cairo, and he had just died in the house of Mr. Wilfrid Scawen Blunt.[98]

Canon Sheehan also died during the year, on 10 October.

Also in this year, James Cousins, whose close association with the dramatic movement had been severed about ten years earlier by Yeats, left Ireland for India. The initial announcement was made in late February in *The Irish Citizen*, the organ of the woman's suffrage movement in Ireland which Cousins had founded and edited. As *The Evening Mail* noted:

> Mr. Cousins, who is attached to the teaching staff of the High School, Dublin, is a prolific writer, and has written several volumes of poems that have established his reputation. His wife is the well-known militant suffragist who was yesterday released from Tullamore Jail.[99]

Later in the year, in May, there was a special presentation to Cousins and his wife.

> On Thursday, 29 May, the complimentary performance of two of Mr. Cousins's plays took place in the Hardwicke Street Theatre, which was crowded with friends and admirers of Mr. and Mrs. Cousins, desirous of paying them a final tribute of regard before they left Ireland. The two plays, representing widely different aspects of Mr. Cousins's genius, were enthus-

306

iastically received. *The Racin' Lug* is a study of the life of fisher-folk in a north of Ireland sea-coast village — a piece of real life, sympathetically interpreted. *The Sleep of the King* is a poetic allegory, an interpretation of Celtic story in terms of esoteric philosophy. In both, the special feature of the acting was the appearance of Miss Máire Nic Shiubhlaigh in the roles which she created on the first performance of the plays. Miss Honor Lavelle, Mr. Jack Morrow, Mr. Crawford Neil, and Mr. Mac Shiubhlaigh appeared in the other chief parts, while the scenery and staging were looked after by Mr. Jack Morrow and Mrs. Roberts. . . .

Mr. Padraic Colum said that Mr. and Mrs. Cousins had made comrades by scores in every field; and it was the experience of those comrades that the Cousins were always loyal to their ideals and to their friends. He desired to speak more particularly of Mr. Cousins as a poet and dramatist. His powers in this field had been exemplified by the two plays produced that night. *The Sleep of the King* had been produced with great dignity and beauty. *The Racin' Lug* was one of the plays dealing with the north of Ireland, of which they had too few, as compared with those dealing with other parts of Ireland. It was one of Mr. Cousins's distinctions that he had introduced to them in the south the humanity of the north; and on the other hand, to the north he had introduced Ireland's "inextinguishable dream". He was difficult to place among Irish writers. He had studied the philosophy behind the Irish myths; and he (the speaker) regarded him as having affinities less with Celtic poets than with the Celtic philosophers — with those philosophers of the ninth century whose interests were in all that was difficult, rare, and esoteric. Mr. Cousins carried on the tradition of Johns Scotus Erigena. Writing before Mr. Cousins had published any of his poems, Mr. Stopford Brooke had defined the task of Irish poetry in words that might fittingly be applied to Mr. Cousins's work. More than any other man, he had deliberately undertaken to show the powers which spiritually moved under the visible surface of human life. His wonderfully clear handling of difficult themes, his technical excellence, and his observation of nature, earned the admiration of all. Moreover, he was distinguished for those qualities without which the poet becomes a mere dilettante — for his hatred of injustice and his genuine patriotism. His wish to Mr. and Mrs. Cousins would be that they reach the highest achievement that belonged to their own spirit. . . .

Mr. Cousins said that he did not recognise himself in all the kind things that had been said about him. For whatever he had done, he threw the "blame" back on them. He and Mrs. Cousins had attempted to live up to the highest they could see and feel; and that was only possible through the association with many friends. They were leaving Ireland in search of something that would enable them to intensify their lives and their work, to come back as soon as possible, and then to remain as long as possible, and to give something a little richer than they had yet been able to give in whatever service might then be necessary for the upbuilding of the land and its people. He greatly appreciated what had been said about his sympathy with the people; he had always found an inspiration in intercourse with the unspoiled peasantry of the west. He spoke also of the necessity of food reform; with impurities in the body, one could never build up a healthy nation. . . .[100]

On this occasion a presentation of £77, which had been collected from friends, was made to the Cousins. Among the subscribers were Douglas Hyde, Æ, Cornelius Weygandt, Joseph Holloway, Dudley Digges, Vera Esposito, S. R. Day, and even W. B. Yeats who wrote:

> I did not wish to join the Committee, as I make it a rule to join no committee which I cannot attend. I have pleasure, however, in sending what I can for the presentation. I value Mr. Cousins very much.[101]

April saw the first production of a one-act play by Padraic Colum, but it was not done in Ireland. As Holloway reported:

> Sometime last year Padraic Colum wrote a one-act play entitled *The Betrayal*, and it was accepted by Arthur Sinclair for production at the Coliseum, London, last summer, but from one cause or another the four weeks' engagement passed but Colum's play remained unacted. This was a great disappointment for the young author, as he went on honeymoon to London to see his play produced.
>
> It was on last Monday week (7 April) at the Royal, Manchester, the play first came to life on the stage when given by B. Iden Payne's company, with Payne as producer. The only Irishman in the cast was the young Dublin actor, Joseph A. Keogh,[102] who filled the role of innkeeper, in whose house in a small town in the west of Ireland, about the year 1790, the action of the little drama takes place. There are only four

308

characters in the piece — viz., an agent, an innkeeper, a street ballad singer, and a bellman. The plot is what Ernest A. Boyd sees in all Abbey plays — melodrama!

An agrarian crime has been committed, and £100 reward is offered for information as to the murderer. The people all know who did the act, but none will inform. A land agent, who is also a magistrate, is at his wit's end to find out who did the deed, and questions without avail the innkeeper, when poor Peg, a ballad-singer, whose son has been condemned to death for deserting from the army, comes in and implores the agent to save the life of the lad. He promises to do so if she tells who committed the murder. This she refuses to do, and ultimately driven to desperation she slays her tempter with his own sword-cane, and going out among the people learns that her own son has turned informer to save his life!

Of such sensational material is the plot built up. *The Stage* says: "*The Betrayal* is a clever, if not entirely convincing little play"; "Bayard" in *The Sunday Chronicle* says: "The Irish drama is best interpreted by Irish players. I was reminded of this last week by a one-act piece called *The Betrayal*. The playlet deals with an episode of Irish life about 1790, when agrarian crime was rampant. It is a weird thing of half lights and undertones, with a brief lurid flare of tragedy at the end — a typical Abbey Street play. Such plays require, above all, atmosphere, and no one can impart it so well as the Abbey Street artistes. Under Saxon treatment *The Betrayal* is somewhat tedious in development, and the abrupt climax is obscure and unconvincing. Still, an audience unfamiliar with the Irish players' distinctiveness would find the piece interesting in some degree."

C.E.M. (Montague), the greatly-thought-of dramatic essayist of *The Manchester Guardian*, thinks "Padraic Colum, the Irish poet, no mean poet either, and also well up to the second rank of Abbey theatre dramatists . . . has done best when he has worked on the peasant life of central Ireland. . . . For *The Betrayal* he has gone to the western verge of his kingdom, and coming back, he has sat down to write on that part of his study where Victor Hugo comes easily to hand. *The Betrayal* is Hugoesque melodrama: it has the gathering pace, the rapid final, superior position of climax on climax, the capping of emotion with emotion and surprise with surprise, the daring bid for a tremendous curtain. . . . There was something about the whole play that kept down the temper-

309

ature of one's interest. We think it must have been a touch of chill in the dialogue, which was immensely better in some ways than that of most plays, but still had not all the freshness of life. . . . You may call it the broad touch, or you may call it a higher pressure of imaginative energy (of the special dramatic kind) to the square inch; whatever it be, it is the one thing the want of which seems to us to keep Mr. Colum from being as fine in a play as he is in his best lyrics.[103]

One contributor to the Cousins's presentation was the American critic Cornelius Weygandt, who in 1913 published one of the first academic treatises upon the Irish drama, *Irish Plays and Playwrights*. As an introductory survey, presaging a good deal of such subsequent academic journalism, the volume even today retains a deal of charm. A not untypical Irish reaction (and one which persists to the present day) was: 'Mr. Weygandt has chosen an interesting subject for his book, the title is attractive and calculated to attract the reader, but the contents are extremely disappointing. It is surprising how often one has to make the same comment upon American literary studies. . . .' [104]

\* \* \*

On 9 January, Charles Hawtrey produced and played the leading role in George A. Birmingham's second play, *General John Regan*, at the Apollo Theatre, London. It was one of the most successful plays of the London season and was generally pronounced a delightful romp. The distinguished J. T. Grein wrote of it in *The Financial News*:

> As an old and experienced playgoer, who knows every trick of the trade, I do not laugh easily, but yesterday I felt like a schoolboy out for a holiday. I laughed and perceived that I infected others, as others stirred my merriment.
>
> Maybe that humour was not on the highest plane, but it was certainly of the soil. It was Irish, and as a clever novelist next to me happily said, "Full of qualities and no virtues." [105]

Later in the year, this droll entertainment was produced in New York with Máire O'Neill, now Mrs. George H. Mair, heading the cast. Nobody could have prophesied that when it made its appearance in Ireland in 1914, it would evoke a more violent reaction than did even *The Playboy*.

# 1914

Late in June the Archduke Ferdinand was assassinated at Sarajevo, and by the first week of August most of Europe was at war. In Ireland, feeling ran high. The establishment and the middle-classes were solidly pro-British. After all, the Home Rule Bill had finally been passed by the British parliament, and its enactment was only deferred until the war was over. John Redmond, the head of the Irish Parliamentary Party, pledged the support of the Irish Volunteers, and before the war was over thousands of Irishmen had joined the British army.

But to the small patriotic vanguard in Ireland, Redmond's move was a sell-out. Traditionally the patriot had regarded England's distress as Ireland's opportunity; and so English propaganda about the plight of small nations, particularly Catholic Belgium, was received with sardonic scepticism by such men as Padraic Pearse, Roger Casement and James Connolly. Seán O'Casey, who had not yet begun to write plays, published some caustic anti-recruiting ballads. And on a Sunday, late in July, the Volunteers engineered an illegal landing of guns at Howth harbour. Then, later in the day, as an outgrowth of the gun-running, English troops fired into a crowd on Bachelor's Walk with devastating effect.

For Ireland, then, the turmoil that began with the labour war of 1913 was to continue. In one form or another it was to continue for ten years.

\*     \*     \*

The offerings of the commercial theatres in Dublin had been strongly criticised for several years. The war and also a disagreement with the Dublin Steamship Company about transporting stage sets from England only increased the poverty of the offerings of the commercial stage. The Theatre Royal was entirely given over to Hippodrome seasons and reviews. The most notable headliners during the year were Bransby Williams and Little Tich, and there was one home-produced review called *Irish, and Proud of It*. The Empire and the Tivoli continued, although less notably, the same policy. The Gaiety, however, managed several weeks of interest. In February, there was a visit of Leonard Boyne's company in the controversial *General John Regan* of George A. Birmingham; and when the furor had died down, there was a repeat visit in November. Edward Compton's Comedy Company appeared in March in various nineteenth-century favourites.[1] In May, the Dublin

Repertory Company revived Birmingham's *Eleanor's Enterprise*, in which Breffni O'Rourke and Una O'Connor were much admired. However, in Act II, they were supported by the introduction of various domestic animals on the stage, and one critic remarked that, 'The unrehearsed vagaries of hens, goats, etc., are apt, at times, to have a distressing influence on the players.' Late in September, Fred Terry and Julia Neilson played a week of *Sweet Nell of Old Drury* and *The Scarlet Pimpernel*; and in the middle of October Lewis Waller played a week of *Monsieur Beaucaire* and *The Other Side of Love*, the latter piece co-authored by Dion Clayton Calthrop, a descendant of Boucicault. For the last two weeks of November, the Moody-Manners Opera Company appeared in their usual repertoire of *Fra Diavolo, The Bohemian Girl, Satanella, The Lily of Killarney, The Daughter of the Regiment, Carmen*, and other pieces.

The Queen's continued its usual *mélange* of kitsch about misunderstood wives, white slaves, intrepid detectives, American Indians, Chinese fiends, French revolutionists, Australian bandits, and even Irish patriots. One is particularly piqued by the name of the villain in *The Gambler's Sweetheart* — Carlos Mendoza, the Mexican Snake. And one can only speculate about what the full-size British monoplane had to do with *Her Night of Temptation*. Perhaps more germane to *Her Fatal Marriage* was the curious incident of the villain, Zaco Malleto, apparently changing into a skeleton in full view of the audience. A typical example of the Irish melodramas at the Queen's was *For Ireland's Liberty*, written by P. J. Bourke and presented by his company during the week of 11 May. *The Irish Times* thought it a 'rollicking, martial melodrama', and described it thus:

> Its name is enough to indicate its style and character. The scene is laid in the County Sligo, and the period is the middle of the seventeenth century. The action opens in the spring of 1641 in an old churchyard on the banks of Lough Gill, when Gilbert Harrison, a Scottish Puritan settler and a soldier of the King, in his search for the Wild Rose of Lough Gill encounters many an Irish soldier, from Owen Roe O'Neill, the hero of Benburb, down to Shamus O'Toole, a big private in the Rory O'Moore Regiment. The play is a series of intrigues, skirmishes, imprisonments, and shootings. Kathleen Ni Cunin and her brave companion, Noreen O'Regan, suffer a great deal, the former from the unwelcome attentions of Gilbert Harrison, and the latter from other warlike adventurers whom she rejects. It is not all blood and thunder, however,

for there is an undercurrent of romantic sentiment interwoven with the political troubles, which greatly enhances the story. The scenery is very good, and historic places such as the Bridge of Finae, Dromahair Castle, and a street in Galway, are presented. The company are excellent actors, one and all. The part of the Wild Rose was admirably played by Miss Peggy Courtenay, who is already favourably known in Dublin. Miss Lily Roberts as Noreen acted and sang very nicely. There are over twenty members of the company. The audiences gave them a rousing reception, and the entire play went with great success. . . .[3]

In December, P. J. Bourke was presenting his patriotic melodrama, *In Dark '98*, at the Queen's, and his advertising posters aroused the displeasure of the authorities for their anti-British bias.

It is reported the military authorities in Dublin have ordered the immediate suppression of some of the posters extensively displayed throughout the city for some days past, advertising the production of Mr. P. J. Bourke's Irish Drama, *In Dark '98*, at the Queen's Theatre. It is said that the poster which most offended was one headed "Stop Press", dealing with the "Battle of Lough Swilly" at the time of the second French expedition to Ireland in 1798. The wording of this poster:

NEWS
STOP PRESS
GREAT NAVAL BATTLE AT LOUGH SWILLY
THE HOST FIGHTS THE
BRITISH FLEET ALONE
QUEEN'S THEATRE THIS WEEK.

Orders have been given, it is stated, that the copies of this poster, and also of the large coloured posters showing a battleship preparing for action, have to be either taken down from the hoardings or else obliterated.[4]

The cinema grew in popularity, and new picture-houses opened. The only film of vaguely Irish interest, however, was a three-part drama of Boucicault's *The Streets of New York*, presented during the week of 27 July at James Joyce's Volta.

\*     \*     \*

The great theatrical rumpus of 1914 was the astonishingly violent riot in Westport on 4 February, over the production of George A. Birmingham's *General John Regan*. This riot is virtually forgotten, as indeed is Birmingham's light comedy, but it was a

313

more ferocious affair than *The Playboy* riots of 1907 or *The Plough and the Stars* riot of 1926. Most Irishmen who saw the play in 1913 during its London run, or in 1914 in Ireland, thought that it was genuinely droll and basically innocuous. However, the fact that a riot could occur in Westport and minor disturbances in other provincial cities indicates that Irish morality, self-esteem and patriotism were smouldering coals that could flare up at any minute.

The matters at issue in the play were two: the character of the servant-girl in the hotel, who was seen as a female Handy Andy and, therefore, an insult to Irish womanhood; and the incident wherein the parish priest apparently accepts an invitation from the local hotel owner to step into his parlour and have a drink. These seem trivial enough matters, but in Westport they were enough to cause a riot in the theatre, an actor knocked unconscious, windows broken out of buildings, the author burnt in effigy, five baton charges by the police, and several persons seriously injured.

The play had been originally produced in 1913 in London by Charles Hawtrey, and was one of the successes of the season, running for over three hundred performances. It was subsequently produced in New York with Máire O'Neill, and in 1914 two separate companies brought the play to Ireland. The first was a provincial touring company of W. Payne Seddon who opened his tour on 26 January in Kilkenny. The second was Leonard Boyne's company which opened in the Gaiety, Dublin, on 16 February. A correspondent from Kilkenny remarked of the first Irish performance:

> Those who had seen the play produced in London noticed that it differed in some minor respects from the London version, the part of the parish priest being toned down so as to redeem it of what many regarded as an element of offensiveness, and one incident was omitted altogether. The humorous points in the dialogue were keenly relished by a crowded audience, and at the fall of the curtain some hissing was mingled with the applause.[5]

On 30 January, the play was produced at the Cinema Theatre in Galway, and a correspondent reported:

> The farcical comedy got an extremely mixed reception, and although the second act, in which the western priest appears so prominently, had after its reception in Kilkenny and Sligo been modified, portions of it were warmly resented and received with hoots and jeers from the middle and back of the hall.

When it was announced that the comedy would be repeated to-night, there was considerable hooting and hissing and some applause, and afterwards the play was discussed everywhere, and while some only expressed disappointment that it was not so screechingly funny as they had been led to believe from English reports, others roundly denounced the farce as a gross travesty of western life and an insult to the Catholic priesthood.

"Mary Ellen" aroused universal indignation, as she is regarded as a type not of a western peasant girl — the brightest in the world — but as a simpleton or imbecile.

*General John Regan* shows that while "G.A.B." has produced exaggerations of extreme types, he has entirely failed to grasp the most intimate personal relationships of the people.[6]

On 3 February, the play received a somewhat hostile reception at Castlebar, and on 4 February it opened in Westport. By the end of the evening, twenty young men had been arrested, and the best account of the events is the testimony at their trial in July:

An extraordinary amount of public interest was manifested in the trial, which began at the Summer Assizes in Castlebar to-day, of the twenty Westport young men who are charged with being participants in the riot which occurred in Westport on 4 February last, on the occasion of the production of the comedy, *General John Regan*.

When the cases were called, Mr. Hunes, K.C. (who, with Mr. Coll, appeared for the Crown) applied for an adjournment of the cases, grounding his demand upon an affidavit made by Mr. Hurst, County Inspector of the R.I.C., who stated that he understood that an extensive canvass of jurors had been made on behalf of the accused. Counsel said the case arose out of the production of the play known as *General John Regan*, about which his lordship had probably heard.

His lordship (the Lord Chief Baron) — Oh, I have heard of it, but I am happy to say I never saw it (laughter).

District Inspector Neylon, Westport, was examined and deposed that there was a good deal of sympathy with the defendants all over the country.

The Lord Chief Baron — There is a good deal of sympathy for the character of the priest, who, it is stated, was misrepresented in the play.

After a lengthened argument his lordship refused the Crown applications, and directed the trial to be proceeded with.

The twenty defendants when arraigned all pleaded not guilty. It was decided to first try a section of five of the ringleaders, and they were then placed in the dock, their names being Thomas Hughes, Michael Scott, Charles Hughes, Andrew Malony and Joseph Gill.

The first witness examined was District Inspector Neylon, Wexford, who deposed that on the night of 4 February a play called *General John Regan* was billed to be played in the Town Hall, Westport. In consequence of information received he and thirteen police went to the hall. When the play began there were about sixty people at the back of the hall, and they began to groan and tramp their feet, and continued this during the first act. In the second act a performer who represented "Father McCormack" came forward, and the crowd at the back rushed up and stormed the stage and assaulted the actors. It appeared to be an organised attack. The actor representing "Father McCormack" got bad treatment.

Witness took some of the police on the stage and tried to save the actors at the time, and the house was pandemonium, and the people who came to see the play left the hall as fast as they could, some of them shrieking. A number of broken chairs and forms were thrown at the police and the actors. "Father McCormack" was thrown down and some of his clothes torn off, and one section of the crowd was striking him as fast as they could, while more of them were dragging him through the wreckage towards the front of the stage. In the pit were standing over one hundred people who had their hands out, and were shouting, "Throw him down here." The actor at this stage appeared to be insensible, and witness put his arm around him and took him to the dressing-room. Then witness and the police had to go to the rescue of the other actors and bring them to a place of safety.

Witness saw Thomas Hughes strike one of the actors, and Scott was a general ringleader. The men in the pit made a second raid on the stage. They broke up chairs and forms and hurled them at the police. He called on the crowd several times to disperse, but they wouldn't do so. The electric light was turned off, and there was a regular fusilade of missiles flung at the police, witness having to hold up a chair in order to protect his face. Meantime the actors presented a very miserable appearance in the dressing-room, all the windows of which were broken and heavy stones lying all over the floor.

Witness left some police to protect the actors, and brought the remainder outside the hall, where there were over 700 people assembled at the Octagon. He saw the windows of a Mr. O'Callaghan's house broken, and then a Catholic clergy-

316

man came on the scene and asked the crowd to go home, stating to them that they had already done enough mischief. The actors were staying at Joyce's Hotel, which was then attacked, all the windows being broken. The police were stoned, and a baton charge was ordered, which had the effect of dispersing the crowd. Later on he had to order another baton charge at the Octagon, but it was only after four such charges that the crowd was dispersed. The police were assailed with stones and bottles. Witness received two blows on the head, the second of which stunned him. Shortly after he was again at the Octagon, and was staunching his wound when two men rushed at him. One of them caught him by the throat and tried to knock him down, and the other also joined in the attack. One of the men was arrested, but he had to be released owing to the attitude of the crowd. Witness after the attack was confined to bed for fifteen days, and was unfit for duty for three months, and at present he was only able to do partial duty.

In cross-examination witness said there were five baton charges in all, and he was the only policeman who received serious injuries. He heard that Gill was one of the men who attacked him. He struck Gill twice with his baton, but he did not see Gill lying on the ground, or hear him cry out, "Don't kill me." Witness didn't know if he was a delicate man, but he got delicate after that (laughter).

Mr. McDermott (defending) — He didn't get £500 compensation to cure his delicacy, as you did (laughter). Do you know that he has recently undergone a very serious operation in Dublin? Yes.

Corroborative evidence was given by Head-Constable Noonan, who in cross-examination stated that on the Sunday previous a notice was posted up warning the people not to attend the play, as "it ridiculed" priests and "was hunted off the stage in Kilkenny".

Sergeant Sheridan said he heard the crowds shouting "Down with Hannay" and portion of the attire of the clergyman was put on a stick and burned.

Constable Johnston deposed to hearing Scott say that "he would do six months for some of the police". In cross-examination witness denied seeing the District-Inspector baton Gill and knock him down.

Several witnesses were examined for the defence, and their evidence in general went to show that though most of the accused were present on the occasion none of them interfered

317

in any way with the police, who, it was alleged, behaved in a brutal and outrageous manner. Counsel for the Crown, addressing the jury, commented upon the manner in which the evidence for the prosecution had been received by the jury.

The Foreman — That is a poor reference to a lot of jurors.

His Lordship — Mr. Hynes is perfectly justified in saying it. We are not all blind. Charging the jury, His Lordship said there was abundance of evidence that there was an organised disturbance to stop the play, which amounted to a riot, and one of the counsel for the accused, Mr. Cox, admitted there was a riot. On the result of this trial would depend where the other fifteen accused would be tried.

His Lordship pointed out, in conclusion, that there was no direct evidence connecting Charles Hughes with the riot.

The jury, after twenty minutes' absence from the court, returned with a verdict of "Not Guilty"; and the accused were then discharged, the trial of the other fifteen defendants being adjourned to the next Assizes for the county.[7]

After the riot, Cannon Hannay, the author, was interviewed in Glasgow, and said that the reasons for the riot were 'A complete mystery to me.' He also mentionad that after the London production he had given a public lecture in Westport and told the story of the play to an audience which seemed delighted by it.[8]

After Westport, Payne Seddon's company toured the play in several other Irish towns to reactions which ranged from frequent applause to continual hissing by a few young men. In general, the press regarded the outbreak as silly; for instance, a leader in *The Irish Times* sardonically entitled 'The Western Athens', thought that the riot

> . . . shows that some of the inhabitants of Westport have not the humour to see a joke, the intelligence which would prevent them from behaving ridiculously, or the dignity which would enable them to keep their tempers. In Sligo and other towns the play had a cordial reception. We trust that, when it comes to the capital, Dublin will vindicate the common sense of Ireland.[9]

When Leonard Boyne's London Company brought the play to the Gaiety in Dublin during the week of 17 February, there was scattered hissing and booing on the opening night, but the week ended with overflowing houses, 'hearty laughter and unrestrained applause'.[10]

*       *       *

318

A particularly embattled defender of the public morality during these years was a young man, William Larkin, who frequently appeared in court, sometimes with his brother Francis, to explain various disturbances in places of public amusement, such as throwing bottles of ink at cinema screens and oranges at actresses, or objecting at the top of his voice. In early March, one judge in the Southern Police Court, ruling on Larkin's conduct at the Gaiety during a production of *Who's the Lady?*, was most sympathetic:

> Mr. Drury said that under the section under which the charge was brought he had power to fine the defendant, unless there were extenuating circumstances. Having regard to the comments on the play in the Press and the statements of the prisoner himself, he considered that in this case there were extenuating circumstances. And not only that, but he considered that the defendant had done a public service, and he would dismiss the case. . . .[11]

However, *The Irish Times* editorially pointed out that:

> If Mr. Drury's verdict were to establish a precedent, the right of individual protest might soon make all theatrical performances impossible, for there are few modern plays which somebody or other is not prepared to denounce as immoral or suggestive, or — in the last resort — an insult to Irish patriotism. . . . Mr. Drury's judgment threatens to let loose on society a horde of irresponsible tyrants of public taste and public morality. We have too many of these autocrats in Dublin at the present time.[12]

Larkin's point of view was that, 'But I suppose playgoing Dublin does not mind — anything in the shape of foreign garbage is good enough for it.'

Art and entertainment, morality and patriotism: the skirmishes went on, as they still go on today.

* * *

Early in January, the Abbey Theatre filled an engagement in Cork, and for the rest of the month the first and second companies divided the week at the home theatre, each playing for three days. On 29 January, the Second Company presented the first production of *David Mahony* by Victor O'D. Power, who wrote, 'I believe . . . its human note will carry it through. It certainly depicts West Cork rural life as I've known it by an intimate and daily and hourly personal experience through many a long and happy year!'[13] Although Power was new to the Abbey boards, he had written other plays, such as *The Banshee's Cry* and *The Perils of Sheila*, which were toured by the O'Brien and Ireland Company in the provinces. Mainly, however, he was an enormously prolific writer of popular fiction for such journals as *Ireland's Own*, *The Weekly Freeman's Journal*, and *The Weekly Independent*. *David Mahony* appears to have been an innocuous peasant comedy of intrigue, and Jack Point wrote of it:

> ... Mr. Power does not consider himself under any obligation to exploit the worst traits of the Irish peasant. In consequence, *David Mahony* belongs to the class of drama which George Bernard Shaw entitles "plays pleasant", even if Mr. Power had to bring in the inevitable stage villain, Flurry Mahony to wit. David is the Widow Mahony's good son who is practically tied to his masterful mother's apron strings. An attractive colleen, Norrie Burke, comes to stay with her Aunt Peggy — somewhere in the vicinity of the picturesque West Cork seaside village, Glantore — and falls in love with David, who, however, is painfully shy.
>
> Flurry, on the other hand, is a bit of a scapegrace, and when David entrusts him with the matrimonial negotiations Flurry proceeds to make love on his own account and succeeds to the extent that Miss Burke allows him to purchase two tickets for America. The plot, needless to say, is not particularly new, and all things considered, "The Courtship of Miles Standish" is distinctly ahead of *David Mahony*, but it serves. It is hardly necessary to add that Mr. Power has done the right thing in restraining Norrie — if she ever had the intention — from eloping and in sending the worthless Flurry, who, with other faults, is partial to strong drink, with his mother across the herring pond. So far as *David Mahony* presented opportunities, the play was well acted.[14]

On 5 February, the First Company sailed for Chicago on their third tour. They had an extremely rough crossing, and Sinclair wrote to a friend:

> On the Atlantic
> On board R.M.S. *Oceanic*
> Friday, 6 Feb. 1914
>
> Dear B. — This is our second day out and the boat is rocking dreadfully. There is a very heavy gale blowing. . . . Too rough to write further.

Sunday, 8 Feb. 1914

We are after passing through some dreadful seas. On Friday evening a frightful wave struck us, smashing deck chairs, stateroom windows, and injuring several passengers. One man lying in his bunk had his head split open. Dossy Wright had his shoulder fractured and was nearly washed overboard. The Captain of this boat is a brother of Captain Smith who went down with the *Titanic*.

Monday, 9 Feb. 1914

Another rough day. We were hoping to reach New York on Wednesday evening, but have had to slow down considerably, so shall probably be a day late. Too rough to write further.

Tuesday, 10 Feb. 1914

Another awful day. My nerves are all on edge. We do not expect to land before Friday. Very cheerful.

Wednesday, 11 Feb. 1914

Still dreadfully rough. We are only just crawling. If we get in on Friday we shall be lucky. We are due in New York to-day. We are over 700 miles from it yet — 760 to be accurate.

Thursday, 12 Feb. 1914

We are in a frightful snowstorm. The seas are awful to look at. Twenty-four hours overdue. The worst trip I ever remember.

Friday, 13 Feb. 1914

At last we are near our journey's end. The ship is covered with snow. We hope to land this evening. Good-bye.

ARTHUR[15]

Fred O'Donovan wrote an even more horrendous account:

I was sitting on the deck just coming on to dusk. There were very few people about, when I heard a woman shriek. Looking down the deck I saw the ship plunge into a tremendous sea. The officer on the bridge afterwards estimated it at 70 or 80 feet. With a terrific roar and crash the great mass of water fell on the deck, breaking the woodwork into atoms, and twisting the ironwork as if it were wire. Before I could do anything the water rushed down on me, and I, in my chair, was caught up as if I was a cork and dashed against the side rails, then hurled right along to the further side of the deck.

Everybody on deck at the time shared the same fate; we were completely submerged and thrown thirty or forty yards away from where we had been sitting. Then the ship lurched and the water began to flow off, leaving us lying in about three feet of water. One man was quite unconscious, and the women were hysterical. We had to wade along the decks knee deep to get inside, and when we did we found that the wave had smashed into the fore cabins and the water was pouring into the ship in tremendous volumes, and all hands were called to bail out. They were bailing out until 10 o'clock that night. One man was lying in his cabin when the wave smashed the four-inch plate glass window and cut his head open. Quantities of deck chairs were swept overboard, and but for the side rails holding fast I would have been at the bottom of the Atlantic. The crew say they never experienced a sea like it, and one or two more of its kind must have proved too much for the *Oceanic*. Mr. Wright had his back fractured and was nearly washed overboard.[16]

The *Oceanic* arrived in New York on 13 February, and *The New York Times* reported that, 'Her rigging and decks were covered with ice. On the bridge the frozen snow was a foot deep. The crow's nest on the foremast looked like a miniature cottage made of snow and ice which glittered in the electric light when she made fast at the pier.' The Captain stated that, 'It was the worst storm I have ever experienced at sea, and the longest passage the *Oceanic* has ever made since she entered the New York service fourteen years ago. The worst weather was from 4 o'clock yesterday morning until 5 in the afternoon, when the northwest gale blew at 80 miles per hour with squalls which reached a velocity of 100 miles per hour, accompanied by heavy snow. . . .' [17]

Despite the rigours of the journey, the company managed to open at the Fine Arts Theatre in Chicago on 17 February with *Sovereign Love* and *The Well of the Saints*. The company stayed in Chicago for a month, and was generally much admired, although one critic noted that they were getting careless in 'such routine matters as mnemonics and operating the curtain'.[18] Eileen O'Doherty was particularly singled out for being weak in her lines, and another critic, commenting on the production of *The Well of the Saints*, compared Eileen O'Doherty to Sara Allgood:

Instead of the fleshy Allgood, who was so valiant a gypsy of the road in the blind mate to Doul, lean, uncertain, little Doherty who is unequalled in original spinsters and wraithlike keeners, played the part of Mary in squeaky, inaccurate

322

plainness, without colour or vitality or character force. Sydney Morgan does Timmy with capital frankness and strength, and Eithne Magee has grown into a beauty with considerable charm, and much smartness of artistic aim.[19]

After a month's stay in Chicago, the company toured various midwestern and eastern states, doing mainly a succession of one-night stands in cities like Indianapolis, Milwaukee, Springfield, Urbana, Kalamazoo, Ann Arbor, Madison, Grand Rapids, and Buffalo. They also went into Canada, and concluded their tour in Toronto. When they returned to Dublin on 6 May, Arthur Sinclair said that this was the most successful tour yet, that they had visited twenty-two cities, and that their reception was most cordial.[20]

Back in Dublin, it was announced on 19 February that the Abbey Theatre School of Acting was opening for its spring session, and that Miss Carteen Sheddon from London would be the new teacher of voice production. She was described as a gold medallist of the London College of Music, for voice production and elocution.

On 13 March, some members of the old Second Company and some of the new Abbey students played in Edward McNulty's three-act play, *The Lord Mayor*, and in St. John Ervine's one-act comedy, *The Orangeman*. This occasion was the premiere of McNulty's play, but Ervine's had already been seen at the Birmingham Repertory Theatre. McNulty, who was new to the Abbey, wrote several other plays and some novels, but is best remembered as the boyhood friend of Bernard Shaw. The fullest account of the performances is that of H.R.W. in *The Evening Mail*:

> It is probably not to the advantage of any play to have it produced for the first time by a company which, for the most part, never appeared previously on the stage. The players themselves suffer no disadvantage, for in a new play they invite no comparison, and rather fix the standard of criticism; but the play itself is apt to suffer. This was not the case with Mr. St. John Ervine's bright satire, *The Orangeman*, which is short, and has but four characters, but Mr. McNulty's play, *The Lord Mayor*, was at a distinct disadvantage, having so few of the parts played by experienced actors. Much of the dialogue was hurried, giving a feeling of abruptness and often brusqueness, not in sympathy with its character. Every allowance must, however, be made for a first night with new players, and it must be said, at least, that in every instance there is great possibility of improvement. The chief interest was naturally centred on Mr. McNulty's comedy in three acts, *The Lord Mayor*.

The title suggests a subject which provides excellent opportunities for satire and good humour. It has the distinction of being the only Abbey play dealing with Dublin city life. I do not go so far as to say it is biographical; but one can trace in it a composite picture of some of the Lord Mayors familiar to us during the past ten or fifteen years. The first scene is laid in a solicitor's office, where there is being held a meeting of creditors of James O'Brien, an ex-ironmonger, who offers two shillings in the pound. It transpires that O'Brien finds himself in these sore straits through the social ambition of his wife, who induced him to aspire for civic honours. True, he became a member of the Corporation, and though he never raised his voice at the meetings, he attended committees with such unfailing regularity that he neglected his business, which gradually fell away until he found himself on the verge of bankruptcy. Now Gaffney, the solicitor, who had a liking for O'Brien's daughter, was a shrewd man, and conceived the idea of making O'Brien Lord Mayor, a scheme which, if successful, would release O'Brien from his financial embarrassment, and advance him in power and influence. But power and influence at the command of so weak a man as O'Brien would be useless unless exercised by Gaffney. With the help of some of the creditors who are also members of the Corporation, who naturally prefer twenty to two shillings in the pound, O'Brien is elected, owing to the fact that he has pledged himself not to receive the king on his proposed visit to Ireland. O'Brien, it is needless to state, is an illiterate man, and his speeches are written out for him by Kelly, Gaffney's clever clerk, and drummed into him by his daughter, Moira. O'Brien manages to get along fairly well despite the fact that he mixes up his after-dinner speeches with political speeches and addresses on character which he is supposed to deliver to the children of some convent school. Having felt secure for at least twelve months he is deminded by an emissary of the Lord Lieutenant that he must look to the future. He is asked to receive the king under a promise of a Baronetcy and a fixed salary as an Insurance Commissioner. This offer, under the urgent advice of his ambitious wife and that of the wire-pulling lawyer, he is inclined to accept, but ultimately declines.

Here we have material for excellent comedy, but I cannot say that Mr. McNulty has made the most of his opportunities. Much of the dialogue drags for want of crispness and point, and many of the incidents are rather more suitable to farce than pure comedy. The two charwomen, Mrs. Murphy and

Mrs. Moloney, though excusable in farce, are impossible in comedy. They form no essential feature in the story of the comedy, and yet they obtrude themselves at the most unexpected moments. Can it be reasonably supposed that a man of Gaffney's personality could not get rid of a couple of charwomen in his own office without the aid of his clerk? In the scene in the Lord Mayor's office, Gaffney is practically turned out of the room by the disreputable pair of viragoes. Another example of Mr. McNulty's weakness in construction is the character of Mr. Butterfield, who is said to be a member of the secret service. He is a man with an utter lack of diplomacy. He approaches the wife of the Lord Mayor with a view to influencing O'Brien to accept the Baronetcy in return for a surrender of his avowed principles. This he does with undiplomatic abruptness and brutal frankness. In the last scene this officer of the Secret Service reveals his mission to Gaffney, whom he never saw in his life before, and does not appear to regard it as unusual that a couple of charwomen enter the office of the Lord Mayor in the middle of a most private conversation.

In his dialogue the author makes good use of an excellent gift of keen satire on the method in which our Corporation meetings are conducted, but he is occasionally unnecessarily coarse in his language. Profane language is not unusual at the Abbey, and we are told by the author of *The Critics* that the stage manager has a habit of introducing imprecations which are not intended by the author, but I must confess I do not approve of anything which is dramatically superfluous. As examples of humour I do not think that the confusion of words such as "basin" for "basis", or "infernal" for "informal" are commendable. I do not think that there is anything laughable in a man saying, "there is a silver cloud in every lining", any more than in saying that "a turn will worm". This is musical comedy humour and not what we expect in the Abbey Theatre. I cannot help thinking that if Mr. McNulty's play were reduced to the limits of one or two acts it would be brighter and brisker, and the dialogue would not suffer by a judicious application of the blue pencil.

Of the actors the best were the Gaffney of Mr. Reginald Montgomery, the Kelly of Mr. Michael Hayes, the admirable sketches of the Charwomen by Miss Sheila O'Sullivan and Miss Maura O'Byrne, the fine picture of the "strong and silent" Lord Mayor by Mr. Seán O'Connolly, the ambitious Lady Mayoress by Miss Maureen Delany, and the carefully acted part of the daughter by Miss Cathleen MacCarthy. Mr. Michael Conniffe's study of Scanlon was also an admirable piece of work.

Mr. St. John Ervine's new one-act play, *The Orangeman*, is a refined and clever character study, representing the unconscious bigotry of the typical North of Ireland Orangeman, who seeks to impose his principles on his son, who has rather more liberal views than himself. A fine climax is reached when the son, who combines the fiery temperament of his father with the moderate principles of his mother, puts his foot with a vigorous kick through the drum which he is invited to beat in the Orange procession next day. This clever and humorous comedy was finely acted by Mr. A. Patrick Wilson (John McClurg), Miss Cathleen MacCarthy (Jessie McClurg), Mr. Seán Connolly (Andy Hameron), and Mr. Tomás O'Neill (Tom McClurg).[21]

*The Irish Times* admired the 'smart dialogue' and the droll charwomen in the McNulty play,[22] but Jack Point in *The Evening Herald* managed his usual digs at his *bête noir* Ervine and at Ulstermen in general:

It is generally admitted that the success of the Ulsterman is due to his "cheek" rather than to his ability. In a "game of Bluff" he can in fact hold his own against all comers. Mr. St. John Ervine, whose one-act play or, more properly, sketch, *The Orangeman* was produced at the Abbey last evening, is an Ulsterman — he has mentioned the fact in both the English and Irish press, and incidentally threw in some particulars about his religious opinions. Almost the only objection I have to *The Orangeman* is its title, which is calculated to create an erroneous impression. In most parts of Ireland the Orangeman is considered a rather stupid person, with an objectionable habit of throwing bolts and nuts; the Orangeman takes a different view, and probably considers himself entitled to be considered a "glorious, pious, and immortal" individual. This suggests that a play with such a title is likely to make trouble, but as a matter of fact there is little in Mr. Ervine's sketch to worry anybody. On the whole, it is as amusing as anything he has yet done, though the story is a trifle on the "thin" side.[23]

As an antidote to Jack Point's view, one might note the following Ervine letter which is anything but bumptious and abrasive. The play referred to early in the letter is very possibly *The Orangeman*; the tragedy referred to later is *John Ferguson*.

326

9 Arcade House,
Temple Fortune,
Hendon, N.W.
12 Jan: 1914

Dear Yeats,
   Your letter is a humiliating one, but I begin already to feel
that it is a purge. Every writer needs some sore thing to
happen to him — and I know well that I needed a humiliation
more than most men; for I was catching the journalist's trick
of writing easily: I was in that state when I was inclined to
fill up the gaps in my imagination with jokes. Please do not
think that I knew that when I sent the play to the Abbey:
it was your letter which had the effect of clarifying my sight.
If I had known what I know now, I should not have sent the
play to you. I will put it away for a while and perhaps I shall
be able to do something with it later. At the moment I am too
preoccupied by a tragedy for the Abbey to think of anything
else. There must not be any humour in a tragedy, even when
it is natural humour. The danger of writing in natural style,
as I do, is that the humorous things follow on the heels of
bitter and terrible things, and make laughter where there
should only be silence. I suppose a comedy is like a tree in
foliage, while a tragedy is as bare as the branches in winter.
I have been in the country for a short while this winter and
I know now, as I never knew before, that bare branches are
very beautiful. I suppose I was unaware of their beauty
because I had always before seen only the foliage.
   I hope you are very well. I am sorry that I was unable to
help Lady Gregory more effectually in finding a new manager
for the Abbey.

Sincerely,
ST. JOHN G. ERVINE[24]

On 2 April, the Abbey presented a triple bill which included the
first production of J. Bernard MacCarthy's one-act play, *Kinship*.
MacCarthy was a Cork postman who was to have a prolific, if not
very distinguished, writing career. The production was little noticed
in the press, and *The Irish Times* gave it short shrift:

> Another new playwright in the person of Mr. J. Bernard
> MacCarthy made his bow to the Abbey audience last evening
> in a one-act play, *Kinship*. While being rather crude in con-
> struction, the play shows promise from the point of view of
> characterisation, but on the whole, it does not carry conviction.
> Hugh Connell, in order to provide the necessaries of life for

327

his wife, who is dying, tries to persuade his brother, Mike, to turn informer, and thereby procure £50 "blood money". Mike finally agrees, but when he finds he has been tricked he kills his brother. The play is gruesome, and though the author tries once or twice to brighten it by a flash of humour, the general tone is one of depression. The acting, especially of Mr. Seán Connolly as Hugh, and of Mr. Shaun Joyce as Mike, was very creditable. It was a pity that the part of Bride Cassidy was not made more prominent by the author, if for nothing else than to give Miss Cathleen MacCarthy more scope for her talent. She is the happy possessor of a melodious voice, closely resembling that of Miss Máire O'Neill, and she will, doubtless, distinguish herself in more important parts.[25]

*The Irish Citizen* thought the play more glum that good:

> *Kinship* is a gloomy tragedy, resembling *Birthright*. . . . The only relief to the gloom of the play is the steadfast principle and endurance of the widow Connell, ably acted by Nora Shannon. . . . The new company is very much improved; but though the acting is in many respects excellent, they are still not quite at home on the stage. . . .[26]

In a good production, *Kinship* could appear quite strong, but it is a theatrical vehicle rather than dramatic literature. Consider, for instance, the conclusion:

> TWOMEY: I did not. I told no lies. But you did in order to have him give me up to the guards, so as to get some of the money. (*To Mike*) But, you dirty traitor, Bride Cassidy will never marry you now. Marry you, is it? She'd rather be dead, an' so would any other girl, than marry you with your hands filled with blood money. She'll spit on you and curse you to her dying day!
>
> MIKE: (*Turning fiercely to Hugh*) You blasted liar! 'Twas you made me do it.
> (*He rushes at him.*)
>
> WIDOW: (*Getting between them*) Don't, Mike, don't!
>
> HUGH: I — I told the truth.
>
> MIKE: You didn't, you damned cur. It's written on your face. I see all your treachery now. This was what you were plotting and scheming for, wasn't it? But you'll pay for it if ever a man did! (*Snatching up poker from hearth and rushing at Hugh.*)

WIDOW: Don't, Mike, don't . . . for the love o' heaven!

MIKE: (*Throwing his mother roughly aside*) By God! I'll make you suffer for your treachery!

HUGH: (*Trying to avoid onslaught*) Stop, Mike, stop!

MIKE: (*In a frenzy of blind rage*) Take that! (*He strikes his step-brother full on the forehead with the poker.*)
(*Hugh staggers and drops to the ground. The Sergeant has sprung forward but is too late to prevent the murderous blow. Mike, panting, gazes at the fallen figure.*)

WIDOW: (*Nearly hysterical*) Oh, God! Mike, what have you done? You've killed him. (*She kneels down by Hugh's side and tries to lift his head.*) Look up, Hugh, look up. . . . It's not dead you are . . . speak!
(*The Sergeant kneels down and examines the stricken man.*)

SERGEANT: (*Looking up startled*) Good God! He's dead!
(*Mike reels drunkenly, covering his face with his hands. The Sergeant gets up, advances towards him, and places a hand on his shoulder.*)

QUICK CURTAIN[27]

This dialogue is annotation for actors, rather than the language of tragedy. Some twenty years later, MacCarthy defended his practice in the Foreword to *The Man for Mannarue*. In replying to an American critic who had complained that there were no dashing Irish lovers in MacCarthy's work, MacCarthy remarked that the Irish were a practical race, and that the language of the people was basically prosaic:

> In rural communities everywhere land and livestock must always play an important part in matrimonial arrangements, and it must have been the same in grandmother's day . . . And the fierce struggle that land requires for its subjection is not congenial to the growth of a saccharine phraseology of love. . . . Take the letters read in an Irish breach of promise case — they are usually business-like documents with a stray word of affection at the end.[28]

During the week of 13 April, the Abbey presented six short plays, one of them a trifling new piece by the theatre's manager, A. Patrick Wilson. This was *The Cobbler*, and it was well received, even though *The Irish Citizen* thought it gave 'no scope for acting',[29] and *The Irish Times* thought 'it has little action, and its dialogue is not especially distinguished'.[30] *The Evening Mail* critic added that:

329

The piece is essentially simple, yet its very simplicity is its chief attraction. It is the story of a shoemaker who has, as his protege, a youth so clever at school as to gain the prize of a Bible. In this reward of learning and all that it betokens, the poor man places great store, and looks far beyond to the high place which his charge will in time fill as a Churchman. The vocation is not at all to the liking of the winner of this prize, and when it was found later in the river by a neighbour, and the explanation given that the zealous schoolboy had thrown it at the head of an adversary in reply to the taunt that he was qualifying to become a clergyman, and a manly encounter ensued, dire disappointment was experienced by the patron of the promising schoolboy. The principal part was taken by Mr. A. P. Wilson, who, as may be expected, entered thoroughly and naturally into its presentation. Miss Cathleen Mac-Carthy, as the village gossip, enhanced her reputation at the Abbey. The other principal parts were well sustained by Messrs. Seán Connolly, Tomás O'Neill, Arthur Shields, and Felix Hughes. The play was well received.[31]

J. Bernard MacCarthy's three-act play, *The Supplanter*, was first presented on 4 June, during the Abbey's visit to the Royal Court Theatre in London. The play met some opposition from the English censorship because of its use of the word 'bloody', which, however, Bernard Shaw had recently used to stunning and much publicised effect in his highly popular *Pygmalion*. When the play first appeared in Dublin on 3 September, *The Irish Times* thought it another sordid, crude melodrama of rural life, although Ann Coppinger in the comic role of the Widow Flynn was said to rank with Sara Allgood's best work.[32] A gentler, and probably sounder, view was Jack Point's:

The outline of the play is easily sketched. A farmer's widow, Mrs. Keegan, in whose kitchen the entire action takes place — needless to say, the kitchen is in Cork — has an industrious son, Phil, who has made the farm a success. The widow, widow-like, thinks she would like a second husband, and her choice falls upon a drunken wastrel John O'Connor — a sort of Hibernian Bill Sykes — and she marries him in spite of the protestations of her son. The marriage is bound to be an unhappy one, as O'Connor looks on the farm as a means to obtaining more drink than formerly. Indeed he brutally tells the lady so — he has married not her, but the farm. Act 2 is supposed to take place six months after Act 1, and Act 3 three months later still. Here we have Mr. MacCarthy's first mistake — the spreading of the action over nine months. The denouement is that O'Connor, who has stolen 30s. which somebody had after three years paid up to young Keegan, is shot by the latter while on his way to the village to spend a half-sovereign in drink. There are six characters in the cast, but only these three matter, for Ellie Cassidy, Pad Saunders, and the Widow Flynn, who supplies a little comic relief, have really little to do with the working out of the action. It is perfectly obvious that there is not enough in such a plot to make a three-act drama. If O'Connor was to be shot, he should have been wiped out at the end of Act 1 or early in Act 2. I imagine, however, apart from the *Birthright* finish, Mr. MacCarthy suffers from the usual obsession of the average Abbey playwright, that while an Irish peasant may safely be presented as a villain, under no circumstances should he be funny. There are, no doubt, Irish people built on the Bill Sykes model, but they are rare, and if repulsive rather uninteresting. The acting, on the whole, was good, and the dialogue, some of which was clever, was gone through all right. Act 3, where Keegan hides the money somewhere on the top of the dresser, I imagine, while the villain watches him through the partially opened door, is rather crude and melodramatic. And, by the way, Mr. Fred O'Donovan, who cleverly acts the part of Phil Keegan, is open to criticism on the score of his costume. In Act 1 we see this industrious peasant in a white shirt, riding-breeches, and leggings. In Act 2, six months later remember, he is still wearing the same shirt and breeches, and they also do duty in the final tragedy. The murder is committed with a gun, which is visible during the previous act. Now, when Keegan rushes in amid the groans of the people outside, reminiscent of *The Only Way*, his shirt is covered with blood. I don't recollect having ever shot a man, but I have shot many birds and sundry beasts, and I don't recollect ever getting a splash of blood. Bloodstains are always consequent on a struggle at close quarters, and are usually present when a knife or other sharp instrument is used. It is a matter of detail, no doubt, but it makes the finale a little absurd.[33]

Joan in *The Irish Citizen* commented upon the quality of the acting:

The waster [is] . . . powerfully portrayed by Sydney J. Morgan, who has had much success in "dour", ungrateful parts. . . . To Fred O'Donovan seems generally to fall the role of *jeune premier*, and he always plays with distinction, though one would wish for him sometimes a more virile part. The love interest is slight and perfunctory, as if the dramatist dragged it in to please his public. Eithne Magee did not succeed in giving sufficient tragic force to Eilie Cassidy. Ann Coppinger gave a vivid rendering of the gossiping Widow Flynn, who is like a chorus to the tragedy; and Kathleen Drago as Mrs. Keegan . . . gave a poignant study of that sore-beset woman, who pays to the uttermost for a mistake in judgment. Her voice has wonderful inflexions and vibrations that haunt, and her playing is always restrained and effective.[34]

On 27 August, the Abbey players returned to Dublin and presented for the first time the droll one-act play, *A Minute's Wait*, by Martin J. McHugh. This was to become a justifiably popular piece among amateurs and was years later filmed with Jimmy O'Dea. Although not much revived in recent years, it has basically the same plot as one of Seán O'Casey's last plays, *The Moon Shines on Kylenamoe*, and would certainly still stand up to some of the minor Lady Gregory plays. McHugh lived in the West of Ireland at this time and, like Victor O'D. Power, was mainly known as a prolific writer of light Irish fiction. He became acquainted with Joseph Holloway, and his many enormous letters to Holloway are hilariously boring. One of his daughters, Mary Frances McHugh, became a novelist of some interest. W. J. Lawrence described the occasion with his usual thoroughness:

Provocative of much laughter, *A Minute's Wait* turned out to be a right merry satire on the proverbial unpunctuality of the trains on the small branch lines in remoter Irish districts. The staging of the little play is a potent exemplification of the law of the fourth wall of the stage, as the audience are supposed to view the action from the belated train. Lacking better amusement, all the idlers of Dunfaile have strolled down to the station to see the last train depart. All sorts of humorous delays occur. The train is overcrowded and all the passengers can't get in because a newly varnished compartment has been locked and no key is obtainable. Just as affairs are straightened out, it is discovered that a goat and some cabbage plants have been left behind. Both have been locked at different times by different officials for safety in the first-class waiting room, the result being that space is economised on transit, the plants travelling inside the goat. The green flag is once more raised when Tom Kinsella and his wife arrive with a hamper of lobsters for the railway directors' dinner on their inspection

332

tour at Ballyscran. The guard again endeavours to start the train, but finds to his disgust that during heated discussion over Kinsella's lateness all the passangers have transferred themselves to the platform again. No sooner has he got them back into their places than a telephone message arrives from Ballyscran ordering two goods waggons to be attached to the train. Eventually, when the minute's wait has developed into close on an hour, the train is dispatched. Meanwhile, in the lulls between the hurly-burly a delicious little comedy is enacted. Mrs. Falsey, who is accompanied by her orphaned niece, Mary Ann McMahon, is returning home from marketing at Dunfaile, and while waiting at the station meets her old acquaintance Barney Domigan, who has brought his son Christy to the place to strike up a match for him with a supposedly well-to-do farmer's daughter. On learning how the land lies, Mrs. Falsey proves a true tactician, and by subtle insinuation, which ultimately develops into direct statement, shows Barney that his projected daughter-in-law's fortune exists only on paper. Happily for Domigan's peace of mind, she has a satisfying alternative policy to propound, and does it with splendid approach. Her niece Mary Ann has been left £350 in hard cash by her father; the money is in the bank, and she shows him the receipt. Already on the platform seat the young couple have been making sheeps' eyes at each other. A bargain is struck, and the Domigans go back with the subtle-minded aunt and her reticent niece.

Well received as were the little farce and its diffident author at the close, the acting left room for considerable improvement. The truth of the matter is that the Abbey Players do not always realise that different dramatic themes require different handling, especially in the matter of pace. Their slow, deliberate method of attack is destructive to the humours of farce and causes dragging. Mr. Sinclair was the chief offender in this respect, besides being considerably handicapped by ill-knowldege of his lines. A hesitating or groping farcical actor is a contradiction in terms. Apart, however, from this pervading slowness of pace, little fault was to be found, and some of the acting was admirable. Premier honours must be given to Mr. J. A. O'Rourke for his well-observed, richly comic embodiment of old Pat Morrissey, the much-worried porter. Miss Norah Desmond's inflexibility of manner, with its denotements of a steely intellectuality, was well adapted for the steady manœuvring of Mrs. Falsey. Mr. Philip Guiry as Christy Domigan was confined largely to stage business,

333

but contrived to heighten the illusion of the match-making episodes by remaining quietly in the picture. He might, however, with advantage, abandon the whisky-bottle incident, which is mere extravaganza. Mr. Fred O'Donovan, in a wonderful disguise, contrived to provoke much merriment by his long-winded remonstrances as Andy O'Rourke, the station-master; and Mr. Kerrigan, full of aplomb as ever, was quaintly humorous as the chronically belated lobster-catcher. Once the acting is speeded up and effected with a little more animation, *A Minute's Wait* will prove an acceptable addition to the Abbey repertory.[35]

On 9 September, the Abbey produced another short Ulster play, R. A. Christie's *The Dark Hour*. The daily reviewers, probably mistakenly, regarded the play as droll comedy along the lines of *Bunty Pulls the Strings*; and the piece was evidently played mainly for laughs, more or less as the Abbey came to play many pieces during the sojourn in the Queen's in the 1950s and '60s. Joan in *The Irish Citizen* wrote, 'The piece is slight, and the note of tragedy suddenly turned to farce (a characteristic apparently of Ulster stagecraft), rather jars from the artistic point of view.' [36] A more just view of the play was W. J. Lawrence's:

> Mr. Wilson's spirited policy at the Abbey of producing a rapid succession of new pieces has proved so efficacious in the arousal of interest and in the procuring of full houses that one is sorry to have to record a temporary set-back. For the qualified failure of *The Dark Hour* both the author and the players must bear their measure of blame. While indicating the possession of capacity for character-drawing, Mr. R. A. Christie is seriously lacking in dramatic visual-isation. Much whirring of his mechanism takes place before there is any material movement, a wastage of effort due to some extent to the employment of unnecessary cog-wheels. We are in William Thomas Finlay's farm-kitchen by the sea in County Down. A stiff nor'-easter has suddenly sprung up, and the good woman of the house is seriously concerned for the safety of her son, Samuel James, who has gone in a boat with old McDowell to a neighbouring island to buy sheep. Fearing that he will return, according to habit, in drink, she expresses her anxiety to her husband's father, old William Finlay, a grunting, cantankerous creature, who has a contempt for women, and gives her absolutely no sympathy. Paren-thetically, it may be said that the story is much confused by frequent mention of people who do not appear, and neither

dialogue nor programme gives the perplexed spectator any aid in working out the intricacies of the Finlay family-tree. When the storm is at its height, the farm kitchen is visited by Mary Davis, Samuel James's sweetheart, and by Rachel McDowell, the old wife, both distraught by the dangers which surround the occupants of the boat. To the plaints of one and all, old William Finlay has but a grim cynical rejoinder. With the coming of Wandering Danny and his eerie telling of the legend of the alienated St. Colmcille, how his spirit returns to Ireland on the storm, a solemn note is struck, which sufficiently indicates the author's intention at this juncture; an intention, however, which was largely nullified by the mistaken attitude of the players. Here, where a delicate note of pathos should have been struck, the outcome was laughter. Affairs reach (what should have been) an emotional crisis when Willie Davis rushes in to paralyse the weeping woman with the intelligence that a boat is being beaten in helplessly on the shore. On the heels of this comes the dread intimation that a party of men are carrying a body towards the house. The supposed corpse is brought in, and it turns out to be the helplessly intoxicated Samuel James, who had landed with old McDowell before the storm broke, and had laid down in a field to sleep off his potations.

Brilliant acting on the part of the Abbey players has often floated many a waterlogged craft into the haven of success, but in this case we have the other side of the picture. The play not only bore potent signs of insufficient rehearsal but, what is infinitely worse, of an almost general miscomprehension of the author's meaning. For the obtaining of the full effect of the shock of the comic crisis, it needs that the preceding scene of the weeping women should be played in a spirit of quiet, unexaggerated pathos, so that the audience might be affected and momentarily deceived. But the players chose at this juncture to play for the laugh, and got it — to the entire destruction of the culminating dramatic effect. Unfortunately, too, Mr. J. M. Kerrigan was seriously miscast as the grimly cantankerous old grandfather, into whose temperament he infused a genial note, making him a not unlovable being. Mr. A. Patrick Wilson or Mr. Sydney Morgan would have struck a less mellifluous note. As it was, Mr. Morgan did justice to the author's intentions by his forceful, impressive delivery of the St. Columcille legend, but the effect of the narrative was wholly destroyed by the discordant attitude assumed by the others. In the circumstances, ensemble went

335

wholly by the board. Miss Nora Desmond laboured hard to produce some effect with the strenuous character of Mrs. Finlay, but her efforts were discounted by the inappropriate likeableness of Mr. Kerrign's old grandfather, which placed the attributes of the domineering woman of the house in rather an unenviable light. Might it not be as well in future to permit Abbey playwrights to conduct their own rehearsals? Seeing that it has not been the custom, it is surprising that misconceptions have not more frequently occurred.[37]

On 23 September, the Abbey gave the first production of Con O'Leary's one-act play, *The Crossing*. O'Leary was born about 1890 in Munster; and his first play, a one-act work entitled *Struck*, had been produced by the Cork Dramatic Society in May, 1910. O'Leary became a successful London journalist, and in addition to a handful of plays wrote the autobiographical *An Exile's Bundle*, a chatty and charming guidebook titled *Wayfarer in Ireland*, and several novels, including *Passage West* and *Grand National*.

The Abbey had a crowded house on 23 September, partly because the other play on the bill was Boyle's popular *The Eloquent Dempsy* with Sinclair in the title role, and partly because the prices of most of the theatre's seats had been reduced. A high point of the acting in O'Leary's play was Kerrigan's rendering of two ballads. A low point was the tendency of the audience to laugh at Sinclair, even though he was in a serious role. This tendency can be observed over the years, no matter whether the actor was W. G. Fay, Arthur Sinclair, Barry Fitzgerald, or Harry Brogan.

*The Crossing* itself received mixed reviews. Jack Point thought that the characters were objectionable and that the play was gruesome, and Joan in *The Irish Citizen* thought it 'a slight curtain raiser of no special significance. . . . It harrows one to little purpose, and the juxtaposition of hangman and his victim's mother is rather too forced to be effective. There is not a relieving ray to break the morbid gleam throughout.'[38] However, W. J. Lawrence more tolerantly thought that O'Leary was promising and would 'do good work when he has amended his technique and discarded from his bench such obsolete tools as the soliloquy'.[39] *The Irish Times* wrote in a similar vein:

> *The Crossing*, despite its intense gloominess, has much to commend it from the dramatic standpoint. Its diction has a picturesque touch that is not unlike that associated with Synge's plays, while its construction is cleverly designed. Mary the Roads, hunted by the people because her son is a mur-

derer, seeks refuge in a lodging house, and bemoans her lot, but sings her son's praises. Matthew the Rhymes, a ballad singer, in her hearing rehearses a ballad which he is to sing on the morrow after the execution. Fenton, the lodging-house keeper, endeavours to turn them out lest his wealthy brother, who is coming home, might find them under his roof. The brother upbraids him for desecrating the home. Mary, hearing the chapel bell, thinks her son has been hanged, and falls dead. Instead of the ballad Matt sings a hymn, and Fenton's brother confesses that he is to be the hangman. The denouement is well concealed, and there is an effective curtain. Mr. O'Leary's career as a playwright will be followed with interest, but it is to be hoped that he will not continue to use hues so black as those he avails of in *The Crossing*. The piece was well acted, the honours being carried off by Miss Nora Desmond, who, as Mary, once again showed her remarkable aptitude for old-woman parts, and Mr. Kerrigan, whose portrait of the ballad singer was an effective study. Messrs. Sinclair and O'Donovan were also good.[40]

On 30 September, Wilson produced *The Prodigal*, a play in four acts by an Ulsterman, Walter Riddall, who died before the play opened. *The Irish Citizen* was so ecstatic in its review that one wishes the play had reached print:

> *The Prodigal* is admirable in every respect — in dialogue, in dramatic fitness, in keen and accurate observation of Northern human nature in all its phases . . . so dramatic in essence, so full of striking situations and telling juxtapositions, that no summary can do it justice. As an exposure of "cant", it is not to be surpassed by anything the Abbey yet produced. Its production adds another to the long roll of Abbey masterpieces, and shows that the theatre that produced *Riders to the Sea, Patriots, Kathleen ni Houlihan*, is full of new possibilities and promises of fresh growth. . . .[41]

*The Irish Times*, although less fulsome, thought the play proved 'eminently successful':

> *The Prodigal* is more of a comedy than a play proper, but it is comedy of original kind, and wonder is aroused as to whether the theme on which the humour is based is intended to point a moral. Strangely enough, the humour takes its rise from the portrayal of religious manifestations, or, as it transpires, lack of religion, and one scene is devoted to an open-air preaching episode. As the leading characters in this scene

337

inveigh chiefly against the smug and self-sufficient members of churches and chapels, no one's feelings are hurt. The play centres in one Stanley Walker, a gay young gentleman, whose late nights are a trouble to his family, particularly as his sister is engaged to a clergyman. When Stanley announces that he is "saved", matters look more promising, but hope is dashed to the ground by his connection with preachers whose creed consists of "dim glimpses of the obvious", and an intention to reform every other church and sect. This connection, however, lasts but for a day, for Stanley's new heroes expose the shallowness of their "religion", and matters resume their *status quo*. If, as a rake, Stanley's behaviour exasperates his correct but Philistine father, his behaviour as one of the "saved" is like a red rag to a bull. The scene in which he dares to suggest that his father is a worthy object of prayer is immensely funny, and shows Arthur Sinclair, in the part of Samuel Walker, at his best. J. M. Kerrigan gave an excellent study of Billy Bradley, the energetic street preacher, bursting with eagerness to get to the street corner and impress his forcible negations on the multitude. Fred O'Donovan made use of his opportunities in the character of the unhappy Stanley, earnest while converted, and effective when resuming his deplorable ways. In the part of his brother George, H. E. Hutchinson acted in that very natural, easy way which makes all his work convincing. Philip Guiry sustained the character of the Rev. Hugh Chapman with credit, and S. J. Morgan appeared in the new guise of John Evans, a mission worker. Without exception the female characters were ably portrayed. Nora Desmond made a tender mother, Sara Walker; and Eithne Magee acted brightly in the part of Helen, her daughter. Though a small one, the part of Lizzie Bradley was played in finished manner by Kathleen Drago, and Ann Coppinger gave an excellent presentation of the character of Maggie, an old family servant.

A word of praise must be added for the excellence of the make-up, a feature which is always in evidence at the Abbey Theatre. A stage device which might be given a temporary rest, though it proves distinctly helpful in imparting the true domestic atmosphere, is that of depicting the progress of tea or supper.[42]

On 13 October, the Abbey produced *The Cobweb*, a one-act melodrama about the 1798 period, by 'F. Jay', which was the pseudonym of F. J. Little of Dublin. This play seems really more appropriate for the Queen's than the Abbey, and one suspects that it was produced, not because it was greatly admired by Yeats or Lady Gregory, but because Wilson's policy was to stage as many moderately plausible new plays as possible. *The Evening Herald* dismissed the piece rather tersely:

> Our bookshelves are littered with the romances of '98. One more makes little matter. Mr. F. Jay has given us the one more — *The Cobweb*. It is a one-act play of the romantic tragedy order. Last night it got its first production at the Abbey Theatre.
>
> The scene is laid in Dublin Castle. There we see Under-Secretary Cooke receiving reports from his slimy spy. Thither comes Eustace Hyme, one of the United Irishmen leaders, presumably to woo his sweetheart, Kate Caraher, niece of Edward Cooke. Hyme in a quarrel the previous night ran his sword through his opponent. He is a murderer at large. Cooke uses this knowledge to force Hyme to turn informer. Thither also comes the notorious Leonard McNally, who needs no compulsion to betray his fellows. It would be wholly unfair to the author and the producers alike to make known the ending.
>
> The piece is new but very trifling. The subject is old but well-treated. Its greatest weakness is its verbosity. If Hyme said the things the author makes him say in the manner he said them last night, he reserved a more lingering end than that of the bullet. Mr. Sinclair gave a perfect study of the cynical yet very human under-secretary. It is a new role for him and one that suits him. The other players did not exactly help out as they might have done. But it is hard to do much with a work that offers only five minutes of intense emotion and those moments at the climax.[43]

Although *The Cobweb* is not an important play, its production offers a salutary lesson: when one regards a play through the eyes of a reviewer, past or present, intelligent or stupid, one is viewing through quite clouded spectacles. The most informed, perceptive and experienced reviewer sees only the end product. He can only dimly surmise how that product was attained, and often the faults or qualities that he attributes to an actor or director may be wildly wide of the target. As a case in point, here are some remarks of the most knowledgeable contemporary Irish critic, W. J. Lawrence, on the acting in *The Cobweb*:

> Careful as has been Mr. F. Jay's study of the period, *The Cobweb* is much too arbitrarily constructed to be considered

otherwise than on the plane of melodrama. As melodrama it called for vigorous acting, but this it seldom got, although the audience, to judge by the generous applause at the end, remarked no deficiencies. Much of this lack of impressiveness was due to the over-subdued style in which Mr. Sinclair portrayed the conflicting elements in Mr. Secretary Cooke's character. Highly artistic as was his acting in the scene where his niece pleads for the life of Walsh, the transition would have been all the more striking had his earlier colloquy with Hyme been given in more forceful fashion. . . . Mr. Philip Guiry conveyed with much naturalness and discrimination the agonised mind of the tempest-tossed young patriot, but his leave-taking of his lady-love lacked impressiveness, and his impersonation as a whole would gain by the infusion of a little more vigour and vehemence.[44]

In a letter, Arthur Sinclair took issue with Lawrence's criticisms:

Dear Mr. Lawrence,

Without taking exception to your criticism of *The Cobweb* in this week's *Stage*, I would like to say a few words in justification to myself.

The play, as you have very rightly described it, is pure melodrama. Well, the most melodramatic character in the piece is the hero, Eustace Hyme. Guiry, who played this part, was in my opinion very bad. At rehearsals I pointed out this fact to Wilson and suggested O'Donovan for the hero, but there was not time for the change. If Eustace Hyme had played his part as it should be played and flung his speeches at Cooke, then I, as Cooke, could have topped him, but Hyme did not do this; therefore, it would have been absurd for me to play the scene in any other way than what I did.

During the ten years I have been on the stage, I have learned a little, and one thing I know is that if you have a bad actor to play with, then it's nearly boodbye to your own show. I proved this sometime ago when I played with a member of the Second Company at the Coliseum in *The Workhouse Ward*. Another thing I have learned is that quietness is often a lot more effective than loudness even in melodrama, and if you were to read carefully through Cooke's lines, you would find that very few of them call for the melodramatic method.

When you take the above facts into consideration, you must admit that I did not do *too badly*. I never remember in the Abbey such silence during a serious play before, and I think this is a slight tribute to me, considering the hard struggle I have to fight against my reputation as a comedian.

In conclusion, I would like to add that I do not think it at all fair to criticise a play on a first night. Nobody can do justice to themselves. I am generally feeling for my lines. If you had seen the piece on, say, Saturday night, you might have written a different story.

Yours sincerely,

ARTHUR SINCLAIR[45]

It should be borne in mind that Sinclair was a notably egotistic actor, and that already he was beginning to play broadly[46]; nevertheless, his comments are a salutary reminder of the limitations of the critic. Also, Sinclair's charge that the critic should not review the play on the first night has been echoed by many theatre people through the years. Indeed, Lawrence tacitly admits the point by his frequently remarking that the Abbey players during these years are rarely at their best on opening nights.

On 20 October, the Abbey presented a new one-act play by W. P. Ryan, *The Jug of Sorrow*. Of it, Jacques wrote in *The Evening Herald*:

> It is distinctly encouraging to see the enterprise of the Abbey Theatre paying. The audience last night was as big as I can remember to have seen for years past. Something new each week has become a standing order, and the novelty last night was a comedy in one act by Mr. W. P. Ryan. . . . The worst that can be said of it is that it is cheap ware. It fell flat at times, but Mr. Kerrigan set it up again, and though it toppled dangerously it never fell to pieces.
>
> Mr. Ryan gives us the familiar country kitchen scene. It is Syve's house, but Peg, an old gossip and retainer, makes as much of the hearth as Syve. They barge each other and backbite their neighbours. And the neighbours — if Nora is a sample — spend their time backbiting each other. Nora has heard that her doting father is going to make her a stepdaughter, and to get even with the newcomer she removes the household crockery from the family dresser, leaving one solitary jug. Seumas called this his jug of sorrow.
>
> As the women in the piece are reminiscing viragos, so the men — with the exception of the priest — are ranting poets. Seumas exudes nonsense about wedding a Bride of Wisdom, and Donal woos his Nora in sloppy verse. The "comedy" comes in when Peg threatens to faint, begs a drop of whiskey, and gets the dregs of a kitchen bucket. The Jug of Sorrow

was very near a crash at this juncture.

If Mr. Ryan's sole purpose was to win a laugh he succeeded, thanks to Miss K. Drago, Ann Coppinger, and Eithne Magee, and Messrs. Kerrigan, Guiry, and Morgan.[47]

Despite the generally tolerant reception, the play seems to have been merely a theatrical entertainment; and even at an early revival one critic remarked that, 'It is a play that cannot afford much gratification to the literary admirers of the theatre. The acting was fair and the make-up wretched.'[48]

The first notable play about the Dublin working man was A. P. Wilson's *The Slough*, which he produced at the Abbey on 3 November. The subject was both original and topical, for a prominent part of the action was a labour dispute reminiscent of the Great Lockout which had ended inconclusively earlier in the year. Wilson had some qualifications for writing on such a topic, for under the pseudonym of 'Euchan' he was a prominent contributor to the weekly newspaper of the Irish Transport and General Workers Union, *The Irish Worker*. Indeed, he had engaged in its pages in a lengthy controversy with Seán O'Casey who was, in the early 1920s, to write the most notable plays about the Dublin slums.[49] Wilson's play has not been published, but a summary of its plot shows a family resemblance to O'Casey's *Juno and the Paycock* and, to some extent, to *The Plough and the Stars* and St. John Ervine's *Mixed Marriage*. The parallel with *Juno* is particularly strong: the father is a ne'er-do-well, a daughter loses her virtue, another daughter dies of consumption, and a young man is harmed by the social unrest. I do not know if O'Casey saw *The Slough*. Despite his dislike of Wilson, he would have been vitally interested in the subject-matter and particularly in the character of Jake Allen, a dramatic version of O'Casey's friend, the labour leader Jim Larkin. (This role, acted by Wilson himself, was thought by most reviewers to be weakly played, and unworthy of the flamboyant original.) However, I am not really suggesting that O'Casey was influenced by Wilson or Ervine or Oliver Gogarty's *Blight*; for when a dramatist uses a family as a microcosm of urban decay, similarities are simply inevitable.

*The Irish Times*, which thought the play 'an excellent piece of work', summarised it like this:

> Next to a war it is probable that nothing holds so much that is tragic and dramatic as a strike. *The Slough*, a new three-act play by A. Patrick Wilson, is a drama dealing, under a thin disguise, with the Dublin strike of last year, and the point of view is that of the "under-dog". The author does

not intrude his sympathies to the detriment of the play, which is not used to point a moral. Its tragedy is relieved by a good deal of humour, and its well-connected incidents in which many instances make the heart beat fast with excitement. Occasionally the characters use phrases and accents not usually associated with the stations of life they depict; but this may be excused on the ground that dockers are given to expressing their opinions in sentences far too short for the making of a play, and ventilate their grievances when they become too heavy to be borne in actions rather than words. The play opens with a scene representing a kitchen in a city tenement. On the bed lies Peter Hanlon, the proud and independent head of the household, indulging the "after five o'clock" Sabbath sleep. Overcrowding has spoilt the temper of the family, and amid their quarrelling a grey-haired mother slaves for the comfort of all, and tries to keep the peace. A pathetic figure is a young daughter with pale cheeks, and a cough which bespeaks her early decease. Murmurs of a strike are brought in by Margaret Kelly, a kindly neighbour, and their portent is confirmed by her son Edward and by Tom Robinson, sweetheart of Annie Hanlon, the consumptive, who works in a factory. The next scene — that of the committee room of the General Union — is extremely humorous, and terminates in an uproar as Peter Hanlon is fired out as a defaulter. In the last scene, back in the tenement, the failure of the strike is admitted, and attributed to lack of co-operation by the tradesmen. An attack is made by the strikers on the house; Peter Hanlon comes in with his head bleeding, and in the *mêlée* outside Tom Robinson is arrested. The blow proves fatal to Annie Hanlon, and as Margaret Kelly remarks, to pray "is the only thing for poor people like us to do". Jack Hanlon, the young son, has gone out of the squalor to begin a struggle for himself, and [another daughter, now a prostitute] is back on a visit from Liverpool, glorying in freedom from her former shop life.[50]

Jacques in *The Evening Herald* wrote:

There are two scenes in the play that put it away and beyond anything seen at the Abbey. They are the meeting in the Committee Room of the General Union and the final wrecking of Hanlon's windows. No one but a person endowed with a strong sense of the theatre could have achieved such downright realism. Excellent character bits, of contrasted kinds, adorn the drama.

343

The dialogue is three-quarters slang. In its way it is an education. But it is the workmanship of the new playwright that delights one by its dexterity. The story is told clearly, and moves hurriedly to its inevitable denouement. And yet wheels creak. The creaks are in the dialogue. I have yet to meet a mechanic who would talk about whirling belts that would whirl in a dance, and clanging wheels and bolts that would be the sweetest music if his sweetheart would marry him. These lovers converse in Wilde aphorisms about Gods of love and clouds of commercialism. One of the characters calls this talk pretty nonsense, and I leave it at that.

An admirable company played with sincerity and unusual skill. Miss Kathleen Drago's study of the dying girl was the most poignant thing she has yet done. She got a curtain of damp handerchiefs from the audience after many spasms of suppressed tears. The author himself carried the house by his impersonation of the strike leader, but his voice was not always articulate, a fault that was common to many of the players. Others who fitted splendidly into the whole scheme were Mr. O'Donovan, Miss Nora Desmond, Miss E. Magee, Miss M. O'Byrne, and Mr. Sinclair.

Despite its blemishes — they are few — *The Slough* is a powerful play. Few dramas as good have been seen here for years.[51]

*The Irish Citizen* was most enthusiastic also:

At the Abbey Theatre this week, Mr. A. Patrick Wilson scores a triple triumph — as manager, author, and actor. To take the Dublin strike of last year as the theme of a play, to fill the role of the strike leader oneself, and to produce the result to a Dublin audience, requires no little audacity; and Mr. Wilson on Tuesday night was obviously nervous and doubtful about his play's reception. He need not have been; though there is much that might be improved in detail, the whole effect is that of a vivid and realistic picture of Dublin's industrial warfare, and of the sufferings, above all, of the women. Most people will, in the first instance, be attracted to *The Slough* in order to see the Dublin strike leader on the stage. But the committee-room scene in Act II, where Jake Allen, a tempestuous but lovable personality, directs like a whirlwind the affairs of his "General Union", is not the best part of the play; it does not succeed in being as dramatic as the reality. The other two acts are cast in a Dublin tenement house; and these are full of life. It is a reflection on Dublin

dramatists that it has been left to a stranger (for Mr. Wilson
is no Dublin man) to use this splendid material for realistic
drama. The only previous use of it I recall is Miss Day's little
propagandist play, produced this year by the I.R.L.[52] Mr.
Wilson, however, is not propagandist; he simply unfolds
realities and leaves us to draw our own conclusions. He fails
to get the Dublin dialect correctly; his younger characters
particularly, have not the authentic note of the Dublin tenement; but this is a fault that would hardly be noticed outside
of Dublin; and in the essentials of character and motive he is
strictly true to life. His women are especially good: the worn
old mother, trying to keep together a family of squabbling
children and a drunken husband; the shrewd, kindly neighbour-
woman, who moralises on the strange "tiredness" that comes
over the men "after five o'clock of a Sunday"; the young
vixen, whose high spirits and abounding vitality turn only to
evil in a poisonous atmosphere, and who flings off the yoke
of industrial slavery for the "freedom" of the streets; the
gentle consumptive, who coughs out her life as the result of
factory work — these four constitute a vivid gallery of Dublin
types, and Maura O'Byrne, Nora Desmond, Eithne Magee,
and Kathleen Drago all added to their laurels in portraying
them. Miss Drago's presentation of the dying girl was specially
fine, and moved the house deeply. Among the men, Arthur
Sinclair's rendering of the porter-sodden "scab" will rank
with his best impersonations. It is unfortunate that the
audience always associates Mr. Sinclair with comedy, and
laughs even at his tragic moments; which must be very trying
to an actor who has repeatedly shown that he can fill serious
parts well. All the other actors were well up to their usual
high standard. It is heartening in these days of theatrical
depression, to find the Abbey audiences so steady and
appreciative.[53]

Historically and perhaps artistically, Wilson's *The Slough* seems
the most significant production of the year. A pity that one is not
able to speak more certainly, but the play was not published, and
I have not been able to discover thus far a manuscript.

On Boxing Day, the Abbey produced for the first time Richard
Brinsley Sheridan's classic burlesque, *The Critic*. The cast was,
like that of *The Slough*, very large, and minor roles were taken by
such subsequently eminent artists as Maureen Delany who played
the Justice's Lady, Arthur Shields who played the Constable, and
his brother Will (Barry Fitzgerald) who played the Second Sentinal.

The staging was undoubtedly a bit beyond the resources of the Abbey, but the evening was not unsuccessful. As *The Irish Times* noted:

> The playgoer who expects to find in Sheridan's *Critic* the scintillating wit and sparkling epigram which pervade *The Rivals* and *The School for Scandal* will be disappointed. With these two brilliant comedies *The Critic* will not stand comparison, as it is farce pure and simple, and considering that it was written but a few years after them, it might be expected that Sheridan would have done better with it, at least from the point of view of staging. It is, in fact, a very difficult play to stage, and on that account alone it was rather a daring experiment to produce it at the Abbey Theatre. Considering, however, the difficulties with which Mr. A. P. Wilson had to contend, the performances on Saturday, which were attended by large audiences, proved very successful. The eighteenth-century atmosphere was well reproduced, but occasional allusions to modern institutions came somewhat as a shock. These interpolations could easily be omitted. That was the only obvious fault in the presentation of the play. The acting was consistently good, and considering the length of the cast, there were very few weak spots. Mr. Puff, whose business has very much expanded since his day, found a capable exponent in Mr. Arthur Sinclair. . . . The performance was greatly enhanced by the fact that the Rafter brothers were the singers. Their singing was marked by much refinement, their rendering of "Simple Simon" being especially good. The setting and mounting of the play, considering the limitations of space, were excellent, and in this respect a special word of praise is due to Mr. J. F. Barlow. In *Kathleen ni Houlihan*, which preceded *The Critic*, Miss Desmond gave a striking study of the title role. . . .[54]

*The Irish Citizen* added some comments about the acting:

> J. M. Kerrigan was inimitable. . . . As Whiskerandos he acted an appallingly bad actor (a difficult task) with dogged woodenness. Ann Coppinger played up to him. There was never anything like her representation of Tilburina. Her faint, her madness, her use of handkerchief to dry her tears all added to the excellent fooling! Almost all the characters deserve praise. I single out especially Mr. Charles Power, who was very cleverly inane — his faint was also charmingly wooden! J. R. St. Rich, whose silent part suggested what Mr. James Larkin

might resemble if he tried to act "Napoleon on the Deck", and Mr. J. H. Dunne, who too, was brilliantly a wretched actor. . . . As Mr. Sneer, Mr. Guiry's poses were especially good. His sarcastic boredom was just right. Arthur Sinclair as Mr. Puff was the life of the piece. He was advertiser and author to the manner born. His gesticulations were especially delightful. . . .[54]

\*     \*     \*

On 1 May, the Ulster Players appeared in the Abbey in Gerald MacNamara's *The Mist that Does Be On the Bog* and in Lynn Doyle's four-act comedy, *Love and Land*. Lynn Doyle (originally a facetious 'Lynn C. Doyle') was the pseudonym of Leslie Montgomery, the author of the popular and droll *Ballygullion* stories of Northern village life. His play is precisely described by its title. Although one critic thought it 'weak in dramatic fibre' and another thought it hackneyed in its situation, it was generally enjoyed. Jack Point recounts its plot at some length:

> The time is the present and the place is the Co. Down. The piece is neither political nor sectarian, and except for a mention by the widow of a visit she and her intended had paid to Father So-and-So, religion does not come in at all — a marvellous thing for the North-East of Ireland. The names of the characters, however, suggest that they belong to Irish, not "Scots Irish" stock. Considered as a story, *Love and Land* is not very absorbing, but the plot is really the least meritorious matter in an undoubtedly clever piece. The dialogue is excellently written and it bristles with that peculiar form of humour we associate with the Northern province and many of the situations are both effective and amusing. It may be guessed from the title — which, by the way, could easily be bettered — that *Love and Land* is concerned with match-making. Anyone who knows rural Ireland — and in this matter North and South are not far removed — is aware that the girl is only an item among the articles knocked down to the bidder. Most important is the fortune, then perhaps, the girl, followed by the stock and the odds and ends — a hen has been known to upset the arrangements. It will be seen that it is really the hand of the man that is, so to say, up for auction, and this is the central idea of *Love and Land*. A certain Peter O'Hare is a fairly prosperous farmer with £600 in the bank, a farm, stock, and a house with a new gable end. Naturally such a prize, even if red-headed and a half idiot, is much sought after, and early

347

in the play we learn from the conversation between him and his neighbour Pat Murphy, that he is in the position of the donkey between the bundles of hay and that his affections are wavering between Mary O'Connor, daughter of a local publican, who possesses a terrible taste for tippling, and Rose Dorrian, daughter of a neighbouring farmer. Murphy, who, as he says himself, has all the disadvantages of being married without any of the advantages, has for housekeeper a wily widow, Mrs. Doherty, who is determined not to remain a widow long, and she too, has her eye on O'Hare, his goods and chattels. The action begins in Murphy's kitchen, then it shifts to O'Connor's public-house. O'Hare turns up, but gets a poor reception from the vivacious Mary. In his clumsy way he starts making love to her, and the matches in his pocket take fire and his trousers get burned. The sufferer retires to an inner room where he finds an old pair of the proprietor's. He leaves in a rage, carrying the burnt garment under his arm, and declares he will propose to the first girl he meets, who happens to be Rose Dorrian. There is a scene between O'Connor and his daughter, whom he upbraids for letting such a fine chance escape. She cries, and in a fit of temper declares she will marry anything. Rose arrives and mentions the proposal she has received, but meanwhile the swain has proposed to the barmaid, so O'Hare is in an awkward predicament. There are any number of complications and heated scenes — as they say of the Commons — between O'Connor and Dorrian but, to cut a long story short, the widow gets temporary possession of the coveted man and hurries him off to make arrangements on her own account. Then she comes back and in triumph with the document which settles Dorrian's place on herself. Her triumph is, however, shortlived, for a telegram arrives which Murphy opens. O'Hare is on his way to America, having disposed of all his effects. The denouement is highly diverting, but indeed, there was hearty laughter all through the play, and sundry curtains at the close.[55]

For the week of 14 December, the Ulster Players returned to Dublin, this time playing in the Gaiety in Rutherford Mayne's new comedy, *If!*, and in the three-act version of his *The Drone*, and in Gerald MacNamara's *Thompson in Tír na nOg*. *The Drone* and *Thompson* were the Ulster Players' most popular pieces. On this occasion, *The Evening Mail* called *The Drone* 'the work of a man who appreciates and has mastered all the practical difficulties of stage production. . . .' [56] And *The Irish Times* wrote that *Thompson* was 'one of the most amusing pieces that has ever been written in connection with the Irish dramatic movement.'[57] About the new play, *If!*, *The Irish Times* was more critical:

In Mr. Rutherford Mayne's latest comedy, *If!*, which was performed at the Gaiety Theatre last evening by the Ulster Players, there is excellent material, but it is not generally utilised to the best effect. The play is rather uneven, and it requires some judicious pruning before it can be regarded as finished. Mr. Mayne pokes much harmless fun at the people of Portahoy, a seaport in Ulster, which is in the throes of a political election. He depicts the fervour of the Orangemen of the town in their devotion to their cause and to Colonel Sylvester, an excitable gentleman, who is the Unionist candidate. The Colonel promises a sum of £2,000 to build an Orange hall if a free site is obtained. Tom, a waiter in the local hotel, is the fortunate owner of a desirable site, and though he is offered a substantial sum for his interests by a pottery syndicate, he is induced to hand it over to the Orangemen on the condition that Colonel Sylvester wins. Tom in his heart is very anxious for the Colonel's defeat, but despite the machinations of the "suffragettes" in poisoning the water supply and making many voters ill, the Colonel wins. The story is somewhat jagged, and at times it is tiresome, but there is much sparkling dialogue that saves the play. Mr. Mayne can draw his characters strongly, and he certainly shows his power of characterisation in Colonel Sylvester and Tom. The latter is a delightful study of a type that is not unfamiliar in commercial hotels in the country. The acting was highly creditable, the honours being borne by Mr. Rutherford Mayne, who made the part of Tom a dominant factor; and by Mr. Herbert Grant, who made the most of the exacting part of Higgs, a pottery expert. The characters of Strong and Mooney, the leading Orangemen, were splendidly taken by Messrs. Walter Kennedy and John Field. Joe, the boots, found a capable exponent in Mr. Joseph Roney. The female parts, which are not very important, were filled by Miss Rose McQuillan, Miss Kathleen Lawrence, Miss Josephine Mayne, and Miss Marion Crimmins.[58]

\* \* \*

On 2 November, the new Irish Theatre in Hardwicke Street opened its doors for the first time with a production of Edward Martyn's new five-act comedy, *The Dream Physician*. On the occasion, Jack Point reflected:

349

The number of Dublin theatrical ventures which have had a short and more or less merry existence is not small, but Mr. Edward Martyn, the moving spirit of the Irish Theatre, which gave its first performance last night, hopes to escape the rocks and quicksands on which these other ventures have perished. Mr. Martyn explains that while the Abbey drama is concerned with peasants and the lower middle class, the new theatrical company will be "for the production of native works dealing with the lives and problems of people more complex" than the Abbey types of character. The work of the Irish Theatre will not, however, be in opposition to that of the Abbey, but will in a manner supplement it. Furthermore, the management hope that by the organisation of talented amateurs for the production and study of native Irish drama, a school of young dramatists who will devote themselves to this particular department may be created. As there are still in Ireland other people than peasants, a theatre which only deals with peasants can only be, says Mr. Martyn, a folk theatre. And so while Mr. Yeats and Lady Gregory have at first chosen their plays among the lowly and unsophisticated, Mr. Martyn's selection is to be from the superior and refined.

The great question, he says, is: Will the amateurs respond to his invitation? Will they have any higher ambition than showing themselves off before admiring friends who will consider their least performance wonderful. The new Irish Theatre is, it seems, not intended to be run as a commercial venture. It will follow the successful example of the Abbey, and may also create for itself a "thinking audience".

After the numerous letters to emulate the commercial theatre, some sympathy may be hoped for among the more intelligent of Dublin amateurs. And so Mr. Martyn says they intend to go forward with the title he invented in '99, the Irish Literary Theatre. The managers or directors of the Irish Theatre are Messrs. Edward Martyn, Thomas MacDonagh, the poet; and Joseph Plunkett. Mr. John MacDonagh is the stage and general manager.

The first performance of the theatre attracted only an audience of moderate dimensions.[59]

*The Dream Physician* seems, for the most part, laboured, artificial and silly fooling, but it does have one amusing act in which Martyn pays back some scores to a thinly disguised George Moore, and even gives a few slaps to W. B. Yeats and the young James Joyce. On the whole, however, the play was, justly, not much liked, and

*The Irish Times* is sound enough in its strictures:

A strange medley is *The Dream Physician*, a new five-act play by Edward Martyn, produced last night at the Irish Theatre. The theme of the play, as set forth in the first three acts, is wildly improbable, and it was not made any more convincing by the casual way in which tragic episodes were treated. It cannot be described as anything more than trivial, and the question arises as to whether the first three acts were intended as anything more than a setting for the fourth, though indeed, they form a strange excuse for it. The fourth act holds a good deal of interest, and is also amusing. Compared with the succession of commonplace phrases which make up the others, its construction is clever, though not brilliant. In the third act is introduced a kind of futurist journalist, by name George Augustus Moon. The part is so grotesque that it is obviously a caricature of a well-known *litterateur*, and one suspects that the play is in some measure a return for lampoons upon celebrities in Irish art circles. Those in the know will enjoy the fun, for George Augustus shows himself well qualified to return the doubtful compliments showered upon him by one Beau Brummell, a remarkable exponent of the capabilities of the banjo, and advocate of a chorus of babies pinched when required to squeal. The part of Beau is very capably played by Mr. J. M. S. Carré, and Mr. John Mac-Donagh made the character of George Augustus very whimsical. Miss Una O'Connor was not able to do herself justice in a part so unreal as that of Audrey, and seemed to be overwhelmed by the superficial air borne by all the tragic situations. The part of Bridie Whelan is a small one, but was sustained with credit by Miss Helen Bronsky. The other characters lacked depth, and call for a good deal more careful study.[60]

*The Irish Citizen* added some sound criticism of the plot:

There are two distinct parts in the play, and they are not well blended. There is the tale of a wife who goes mad, thinks she has killed her husband, and cannot be brought to regard her living husband as anything but an imposter. There is also some rather heavy satire at the expense of Mr. George Moore — here Mr. Martyn is "getting his own back" — and some lighter satire of Mr. Yeats and certain devotees of "artistic" cults. The mad woman is finally cured by being brought into the presence of George Augustus Moon, whose antics are so

351

grotesque that she is easily induced to believe that she is in a dream, and that her belief that she has killed her husband is also part of the dream. But both parts of the play suffer by the juxtaposition. The satire is leaden-footed, and unlikely to cause more than passing amusement; while why Mr. Shane Leslie should be brought into the play — under the thin disguise of "Shane Lester" — is one of those things no one can understand.

Mr. Martyn always fails in portraying women; he appears to regard them as lesser beings, unimportant except as clogs on man's path to perfection. This play is not free from suggestions of such bias.

On the other hand, the acting was admirable, and shows what a large reserve of acting talent there is in Dublin outside the ranks of the Abbey company. . . .[61]

One must admire Edward Martyn. His dedication to the intellectual drama, and his constant attempts to found a Dublin version of the *Théâtre Libre* finally had an influence — most specifically in the founding of the Dublin Drama League in 1918 and, about ten years later, in the founding of the Gate Theatre. However, it must be said that his own attempts at drama were invariably awkward. One act of *The Dream Physician* is good fun, and there are some points of interest in *Maeve*, and *The Heather Field* is of historical importance. But finally, and unfortunately, his plays are simply singularly bad. Not one would bear revival, and even in their own day they practically always bored their audiences stiff.

By the end of the year, the Dublin Repertory Theatre had fallen on lean days, and their last performance of 1914 was in the small hall of the Little Theatre in Upper O'Connell Street. However, the play presented on this occasion was Shaw's *Mrs. Warren's Profession*, and this was the first public production of the play in the British Isles. The play dealt with prostitution and, of course, had some under the ban of the English censor. Evelyn Ashley, the producer of the Repertory Theatre, took advantage — as had Yeats and Lady Gregory in the *Blanco Posnet* affair — of the fact that Dublin had no legal censorship. As in the case of *Posnet*, there was a warning from Dublin Castle to the theatre. In this instance, the warning was that a penalty of £300 per performance might be inflicted. However, Ashley persisted, and the play was performed on 16 November. The women's rights magazine, *The Irish Citizen*, which would be expected to admire the play, gave it a qualified rave; the ever-moral Jacques of *The Evening Herald* gave it an equally predictable condemnation:

352

The public looked forward to a shindy. But there was none. The little theatre had every seat occupied. The performance was dull and very commonplace. But applause — for the players — was frequent and hearty. . . .

The play, in fact, belongs to the class commonly known as "advanced drama", and that is, possibly, the chief reason of its selection by the Dublin Repertory Theatre. Personally, I am entirely convinced that the drama renounces its chief privilege and glory when it waives its claim to be a popular art and is content to address itself to coteries, however "high browed". The theatre never has been, and never will be, a moral dissecting room. . . .

Within limitations, the production as such was creditable to the stage management. The prompter was a busy person at intervals. It was a pity to see two such clever actresses as Miss Flora MacDonnell and Miss Una O'Connor wasting their talents on the ungrateful parts of mother and daughter respectively. Mr. Carré, too, always a natural player, was obviously not always at his ease as the family friend. . . .[62]

On 27 March, a group of amateurs rented the Abbey to present *Candidates*, a three-act comedy by Cruise O'Brien, the well-known journalist, and *A Question of Honour*, a one-act drama by Annie J. Lloyd. The one-act was described as 'cast in a tragic vein' and hinged 'on the infatuation of a married woman for a young officer in a regiment stationed in India, and who, in a moment of pique, on hearing that her adored one's affections were fixed on another object, shoots herself — off the stage, of course.' [63] Several critics complained of being unable to hear the actors, particularly Mrs. T. Kirkwood Hackett, but one suspects that this is one of those plays which is better seen and not heard.

The plot of *Candidates* was summarised by *The Irish Times*:

Patrick Hennessey, who is a member of parliament for a rural Irish constituency, finds it necessary to fight for his long-secure seat against Sir Dighton Stinmut, the local magnate, who is being driven into politics by his ambitious wife. Both candidates seeking the support of Thomas Blake, who is the influential man of the district, find themselves up against Mrs. Blake, who sounds them discreetly on the woman suffrage question. She, however, being dissatisfied with both candidates, decides to run her husband, who is an anti-suffragist, as a suffragist against them. This leads to amusing situations which are made more amusing still by the witty dialogue which runs through them. Interwoven with the main plot is the love story of the son of the Blakes and the daughter of the Stinmuts. The characters in the play are all clearly drawn, and the acting was decidedly good, particularly that of Mrs. Katherine O'Brien as Mrs. Blake and that of the author as Sir Dighton Stinmut. The Patrick Hennessey, M.P., of Mr. F. Edwards was was somewhat overdone.[64]

One suspects, nevertheless, that the production was rather like the curate's egg, as one critic remarked that, 'Several of the male characters were somewhat overacted, and reminded one occasionally of the old-time stage Irishman.' [65] As both Cruise O'Brien and his wife were prominent supporters of the Suffrage movement, the most sympathetic account of the play appeared naturally in the suffrage magazine, *The Irish Citizen*, which thought 'the evening's entertainment a great success'.[66] The editor of the paper succeeding James Cousins was Mrs. O'Brien's brother-in-law Francis Sheehy-Skeffington, who on 24 and 25 April had a play produced at the Molesworth Hall. The occasion was the Daffodil Fete organised by the Irish Women's Franchise League, and on that same occasion was presented a number of Feminist Tableaux. Mrs. Cogley appeared as Sappho, Miss Maxwell as Florence Nightingale, Mrs. McDonagh as Maeve, Máire Nic Shiubhlaigh as Saint Brigid, 'John Brennan' as Anne Devlin, and Madame Markievicz as Joan of Arc in full armour. *The Irish Citizen* prints a charming picture of Joan handing a sword to 'The Suffrage Prisoner', impersonated by Miss Houston who is languishing in a gown adorned with fleurs-de-lis. Sheehy-Skeffington's play, *The Prodigal Daughter*, was reviewed at some length in *The Irish Citizen*:

It is, needless to say, an entirely suffragist production. Lily Considine, after learning nothing at the local national school at Ballymission, and less during four years in a Loreto convent, and being bored by a spell of philandering with clerks and such nonsuches, has her first real thrill when she breaks a Government window as her protest against the denial of votes to women. She feels that the vapidity of her life, and that of other women — she is even compulsorily emancipated from helping in her father's shop — is owing to the false views of life and silly education bestowed on them as political and economical nonentities. She further refuses to be a domestic drudge, and intends to dedicate her life and energies to the feminist cause. She breaks this news quite off-handedly to her family and parish priest on her return from the sequel to the window-breaking episode — a month's imprisonment. I must say they take it wonderfully well. There must have been culture somewhere in the air or in the national school, for they all express themselves moderately and with intelligence. The sister, who is married to the bibulous doctor of the district, is neatly suppressed for suggesting Lily is a disgrace, and the father positively hustled when he rashly undertakes to burn the "Votes for Women" flag rather than have it hang out over his shop-front.

The parish priest never once raises his stick or his voice, even when he is requested to preside at a suffrage meeting on the following Sunday in the Chapel Yard!

The author adopted the Shavian method of argument. The weak characters present the wrong views only to be successively bowled over like ninepins by the strong character, who shares the outlook of the author. The result is very good propaganda.

The different parts were played with humour and distinction, and the curtain fell after a most enjoyable half-hour or so, leaving us certain that the conversion of Ballymission is in excellent hands.[67]

On 19 and 20 May, another amateur group, the St. Mary's College Literary and Dramatic Society of Rathmines, rented the Abbey to present J. M. Barrie's *The Professor's Love Story* and the first production of a one-act play by the Dublin man H. B. O'Hanlon, *Her Second Chance*. O'Hanlon was to become something of a protege of Edward Martyn, and his early play was gently reviewed by *The Evening Herald*:

Considered as an initial attempt, *Her Second Chance* is deserving of much praise. The manufacture of a really good drama is a very difficult feat, very much like what the making of a watch used to be before the advent of up-to-date machinery. The difficulty lies in the construction and arrangement rather than the dialogue, and there is only one way to acquire the knack of plot building — that is by practice. It may, then, be guessed that the dialogue of *Her Second Chance* is the strong point. The characters are only three in number — Callaghan, a wild Irishman, in whose flat in London the action takes place, hour 1 a.m.; Sidney Wainford, a broken-down gentleman; and Sparkles, Callaghan's old and somewhat crusty retainer. It will be observed that at the very outset Mr. O'Hanlon handicapped himself severely when he included no "woman in the cast", although one will expect from the title of this curtain-raiser that the lady would develop in the course of the proceedings. At the same time the dialogue is distinctly

355

clever, and if I don't mistake, I may have an opportunity of writing an appreciation of a more ambitious effort by the same author.[68]

Around 1 July, Elizabeth Young played the title role in Æ's *Deirdre* in a performance in Miss Inglis's garden at 64 Upper Leeson Street. She was supported by W. Earle Grey as Naisi and Margaret Guinness as Lavarcam. Katherine Cruise O'Brien justly did not think *Deirdre* a theatrical piece: 'Æ fails to make an acting play because he loses himself in the beauty of his lines and forgets that the action drags. And in his management of the catastrophe, he fails altogether in tragic action.' [69] On 12 October, at the Abbey, an entertainment was given for the benefit of the Soldiers' and Sailors' Families' Association, and on the programme was the first and apparently only production of A. P. Wilson's one-act recruiting play, *A Call to Arms*. Despite Sinclair, O'Donovan, Nora Desmond and Eithne Magee in the cast, the play was regarded as 'not much more than a trifle, but it is amusing and was cleverly acted'.[70]

*　　*　　*

In rural districts, there were yet vestiges of a rudimentary folk drama that much predated and had nothing to do with the literary drama inaugurated by Yeats, Moore and Martyn in 1899. For instance, in Claremorris, late in February, a group of Straw Boys made the news:

> Riot and unlawful assembly to the disturbance of the peace and the terror of his Majesty's subjects were the charges which formed the subject of a Crown prosecution at the Swinford Petty Sessions to-day against six young fellows from the neighbourhood. . . . The accused, it was alleged, formed a party of straw boys, or what is more popularly known as "wholpers", and disported themselves by an excessive exercise of the caprice peculiar to the custom in rural parts of the country of celebrating marriage festivities.
>
> The complaint was that they exceeded the bounds within which their presence was usually tolerated on such occasions, and became violent and a menace to the comfort of the guests. The house in which the festivities were in celebration was Patrick O'Brien's, of Derryronayne, and while the guests were enjoying themselves, the defendants, who were disguised, arrived and forced their presence on the company. They were, it was alleged, armed with scythe blades, graips, and forks, which they used upon the police when the latter intervened

for the preservation of the peace. In the melee the police were assaulted, and Sergeant Clancy, who was the principal Crown witness, was unable to attend, he being under medical treatment for the injuries he received.

The accused after their arrest were taken before a magistrate and remanded to Petty Sessions with the substantial bails, themselves of £40 and two sureties for each of £20.

Constable Cox gave evidence that Sergeant Clancy and himself were present at the wedding house on duty on the night in question.The defendants turned up in disguise, armed with scythe blades, forks, and graips, and shovels. They danced outside, and demanded beer, and were supplied with a drink each. Two of them entered the house and danced, and they were all again supplied with beer.

They became very disorderly and used filthy language, and when they were remonstrated with, one of them struck Michael O'Brien with a stone on the forehead, inflicting a deep cut. One of the wedding party produced a gun, but on the suggestion of Sergeant Clancy, he did not use it. The straw boys, after dancing and drinking, were got out of the house, but commenced to wrangle amongst themselves, one of them remarking that they would not leave till they each got ten pints of beer. The sergeant requested them to go away, but one of them made a slash of a graip at him, tearing his greatcoat, while another struck him with a stone on the right side of the head behind the ear, the blow knocking him down and stunning him. The sergeant cried out, "I'm killed! I'm killed!" Witness helped the sergeant to his feet, when the straw boys made a rush at them, one of them sticking a graip in witness's coat. They were overpowered in the presence of the straw boys, who forced them back to the door, slashing the weapons at them all the time, inflicting injuries on the sergeant. Witness escaped a cut on the jaw through the collar of his coat being turned up. Witness and the sergeant sought refuge in the wedding house, and while there the windows were smashed in and the doors battered. One of the wedding party took down a gun and discharged two shots, and these had the effect of chasing the straw boys. The police subsequently went out, and heard some of the defendants say that they were recognised by the girls in the house. . . .[71]

\*   \*   \*

Violence of a different sort occurred shortly after midnight on the morning of 2 May, when there was a serious fire at the Royal Hippodrome in Belfast. The fire, according to *The Evening Mail*

> . . . before it could be extinguished demolished the stage portion of the building and a valuable quantity of scenery and effects. Those who were present at the early stages of the fire state that the flames progressed with remarkable suddenness. There was a sound of crackling, and almost immediately one end of the Hippodrome was involved in flames which penetrated through the glasswork which had covered the stage. It should be stated that in addition to the stock scenery there was last evening before the fire broke out in the Hippodrome the very valuable effects in connection with the revue which was the special feature of the programme during the week, and which, it was stated, in themselves ran into a matter of about £2,000 as regards cost. . . .
>
> The flare of the fire could be seen all over the city, while the crackling of the large beams composing the roof could be heard as far away as Smithfield. As the huge tongue of flame shot up, sparks were carried over the adjoining houses. . . . The fire appeared to be confined principally to the stage, but the outbreak at one period extended slightly to the galleries, where the fire was carried by flying sparks. . . .[72]

\*     \*     \*

Before the war engaged all his attention, the columnist who wrote the 'Things Seen and Heard' column in *The Evening Herald* would sometimes include remarks about theatrical personages. For instance, on 29 June, he noted:

> I came across Mr. William Boyle, the dramatist, who was paying a flying visit to Dublin, at the open-air performance of *Deirdre* on Saturday. He was telling me his whole time at present is taken up with the building of his new home in Louth, but he is picking up types and quaint turns of phrase each day in the hope that when he is settled down in his country-home he may be able to turn them to account in drama, song, or story.
>
> On being asked how he came to write *Dempsy*, he replied: "I first thought what was one of the chief failings of the Irish people, and came to the conclusion it was their love for 'spouting'. Then I ransacked my mind for the greatest lovers of talk I had come across, and hit upon two examples, but

not being able to decide on either, combined the characters of both, and *Dempsy* was the result." [73]

In the same column he quoted from a letter from Seumas O'Brien, the sculptor and author of *Duty*, who was living in San Francisco. O'Brien wrote that he 'would prefer to live at home in Ireland, provided I could pick up a comfortable living there'. A few days later the column printed a chat with Frank Fay who was on a three-weeks vacation from Alexander Marsh's company. Fay was 'full of hopes that some day he may get planted again in Dublin and found a little company of players to give *Hamlet* and other Shakespearean plays in their entirety. This is the dream of his life.' In the same column appeared the author's reminiscence of the young Joyce: 'I remember him as a tall, strange, ungainly-looking youth, who wore his hair long under a soft hat, and with a seven-league-boot style of walking, he swung his arms vigorously to and fro.' [74]

On March 30, T. D. Sullivan, who wrote 'God Save Ireland', died.

On 8 April, James Bernard Fagan, the dramatist, was divorced in London by his wife on the grounds of his desertion and adultery. The suit was undefended.

\* \* \*

Perhaps the most important book published during the year was Maunsel's edition of *Five Plays* by George Fitzmaurice. The following is one of the few reviews of the volume. It appeared in *The Irish Times* and is generally respectful, but one would suspect that Fitzmaurice regarded parts of it as rather stupid.

Unlike many authors, Mr. Fitzmaurice is, in our opinion, superior in his longer dramas. . . . Hence one may come to the conclusion that the development of character, or rather the play of character, as different circumstances affect it from time to time, is well worked out. . . .

The shorter plays do not give the opportunity for such character-drawing. They depend altogether on the situation, so that their success will rest wholly on the truth and novelty of the central idea. *The Pie-Dish* is especially happy in this. . . . *The Magic Glasses*, a story of a half-poetic, half-delusioned youth, whose tragedy is that he lives amongst people who cannot understand his fancies, makes up for its rather whimsical theme by the portrayal of the old reprobate of a witch-doctor, Mr. Quille, and by the fantastic and poetical rhapsodies of poor Jaymoney.

As regards the last piece, *The Dandy Dolls*, we can imagine a company of lunatics conversing in the style and taking part in the seemingly inconsequent narrative employed therein. It is difficult to understand how the author means it to be read, but in print the abusive language of which it is in great part composed is repulsive, and coming at the close of the book, the piece cannot fail to leave a sense of disappointment with the reader. The language of the other pieces is at times strong, but the Kerry peasant has not learned civilisation's veneered phrases, nor has he lost his own rich imaginative vocabulary, of which Mr. Fitzmaurice is himself a master. The people of these plays live: strong, cunning farmers and their wives, whose days are in great part spent in making matches for their children; the moonlighters burning with a passionate longing for justice; and, less often represented, but in whose characterisation the author excels, the match-making professional from the mountains and his compeer, the quack doctor, *Arcades ambo.*[75]

Fitzmaurice joined the British army.

Also during the year Maunsel published Terence J. MacSwiney's five-act play, *The Revolutionist*. L.C. reviewed it in *The Irish Citizen*:

Mr. MacSwiney's work is earnest, sincere and ambitious, but his talent falls short of his aspirations. He has not mastered sufficient realism in dialogue, nor sufficiently convincing portraiture of character. His hero, Hugh O'Neill, is somewhat stiff and stilted; and the great moments of his plot somehow fall flat. The theme is one admirably suited for dramatic presentation — the conflict between the political idealist and the politicians of compromise, of intrigue and of self-seeking. Dublin is the field of this conflict in Mr. Mac-Swiney's play, and Irish Nationalism is the cause with reference to which it is fought out. The fearless and uncompromising "Revolutionist", attacked on all sides, notably by the Church, wears himself out in the endeavour to keep his flag flying, and dies with his mission unfulfilled. The scenes of keen political controversy are among the best in the play; though even here Mr. MacSwiney's vagueness, his reluctance to use definitely the words "Home Rule", "Separation", and the like, keep the puzzled reader in a mood of dissatisfaction at needless obscurity. But the characters of the committee men, and their varying attitudes towards political principles and methods, are well drawn, and apparently from an inside knowledge of what goes on in many political conventicles of little political coteries in Dublin. The "love-interest", to which the author evidently attaches much importance, is the weakest part of the play; he does not understand the modern woman, and his women are mere reproductions of types long antiquated — if they ever had any real existence outside the mind of the "romantic" fictionist. Here is just one flash of insight:

> FOLEY: . . . I admit women are not fitted for politics.
> NORA: Why?
> FOLEY: They jump at conclusions.
> NORA: While the man walks around the conclusion and runs away from it.

But it is only an oasis in a desert of banality. Mr. MacSwiney must try again. The best that can be said of him is that it is worth his while.[76]

\*   \*   \*

Although the war seemed, quite falsely as it turned out, to have distracted the attention of Irishmen from national politics, there was a social as well as a national reason for revolution. Consider, for instance, some facts from a report of the Departmental Committee on Dublin Housing Conditions that was published in May. In Dublin, it was estimated that 229 persons per 1,000 were living in one-room tenements and 194 more per 1,000 in two-room tenements, as opposed to only 23 per 1,000 and 59 per 1,000 in one and two room tenements respectively in Birmingham. Outside of Dublin, the next largest population of one-room tenements in the British Isles was in Finsbury with 148 per 1,000 in one-room tenements. In all, it was estimated that 74,000 people in Dublin lived in one-room tenements, and about 56,000 more in two-room tenements; and this 130,000 people represented 42 per cent of Dublin's citizens. It was small wonder that there was some resistance in Dublin to the British appeals to fight for the rights of small nations.[77]

# 1915

The Abbey had a busy but undistinguished year. Although only about five months were spent in Dublin, the theatre played at the Opera House in Cork, at the Gaiety in Manchester, and in May made an extended visit to the Little Theatre in London. There were many productions, but most were revivals, and only six new pieces were brought out, of which two were one-acts. Of the new plays, St. John Ervine's superb *John Ferguson* was by far the best. However, Lennox Robinson's Emmet play, *The Dreamers*, was a worthy and ambitious effort, and its long cast usefully taxed the resources of the theatre. Lady Gregory's racing melodrama-cum-ghost story, *Shanwalla*, is one of her poorest efforts; and William Crone's Northern play, *The Bargain*, has been justly forgotten. Of the two one-acts, Martin J. McHugh's *The Philosopher* failed to repeat the success of *A Minute's Wait*, and *By Word of Mouth* by two young men, F. C. Moore and W. P. Flanagan, was probably staged because of Wilson's policy of putting on anything even halfway plausible.

But undoubtedly part of the reason for the undistinguished programme was that the theatre had a change of managers during the year when Wilson violently quarrelled with Yeats and was replaced by St. John Ervine.

Nevertheless, the year began harmoniously, as several interesting letters from Wilson to Yeats indicate:

Abbey Theatre, Dublin
18 January 1915

Dear Mr. Yeats,

. . . In Cork I had your letter about Conniffe. He has given me plays to read from time to time, and as you say, he has a distinct grip for dialogue, and I am of opinion that he should be encouraged. As a matter of fact, I have given him what encouragement I could, but his difficulty seems to be an utter want of logic, and each play he has given me, curiously enough, seems to have grown worse in this respect. I have spoken to him since the receipt of your letter, and what I intend doing with him is to go through all the plays he has now, select the best of them, and make him go over and over it until he has licked it into some sort of shape, then I will get it typed and send it to you for criticism. . . .

I had a letter last week from Miss Moloney saying she had returned. I will certainly use her as much as possible. . . .

363

Last week's business in Cork was the best we have ever done there. Our gross receipts were £193.6.4, £40 ahead of last year, making our share £96.13.2, £20 more. . . .

Of course you will have heard by this time that Miss Allgood is now willing to sign her contract with that clause, copy of which you got from Mr. Bailey. She is coming in to-morrow to do so. Sinclair, of course, gets his rise now, too, under our previous agreement made in Coole Park.

Yours very sincerely,

A. PATRICK WILSON

Abbey Theatre, Dublin
25 January 1915

Dear Mr. Yeats,

. . . I am writing to Pearse to-day about that matter of the Theatre. He had it before, I understand, and there is not the slightest likelihood that anyone will be wanting the Theatre for Holy Week, so he may as well have the two dates he asks for. I shall let him have it for the expense and his promise that he does not go shouting it about.

I had the other day the play, *The Bargain*, together with your letter about it. I got it read yesterday, and while I think parts of it are very good, I think the play as a whole is poor. I shall, however, put it on the list in place of *Plough Lifters*, and reserve *Plough Lifters* for the Autumn. I am also finding it necessary to put *The Briery Gap*, Murray's one-act, back for a week or two. The trouble is that O'Donovan, whom I want for it, has such a tremendous part to get off for Robinson's play that it would be impossible for him to get off the two. With regard to this play also, I had a very shaky letter from Murray when he sent back his signed agreement hoping that the play will not be allowed to go on without you seeing a rehearsal of it, thus getting your decision whether it should be risked before the Dublin public. . . .[1]

Yours sincerely,

A. PATRICK WILSON

Abbey Theatre, Dublin
Thursday, 28 Jan. 1915

Dear Mr. Yeats,

Your letter to hand about Ervine's play, etc. tonight. I think it would be a total mistake to entertain Miss O'Neill to play that part. My reasons are many.

First of all, let me say that I would be immensely pleased

were we to have Ervine's play, and I would be delighted if we could come to some compromise, but there are several practical objections to the re-engagement of Miss O'Neill. In the first place, how do we now know she could do it justice? The balance of proof is all on the other side. In any case, her re-engagement could only be a temporary flash-in-the-pan affair. She could never be a permanent fixture with us again and the unsettling influence she would undoubtedly assert would strike at the whole company, and would particularly strike at Miss Allgood. The result would probably be that we would lose Sara Allgood once more, and the temporary little advantage we would have in Miss O'Neill's return would not be worth Sara's loss. My own opinion is that Sara is one of the most easily managed individuals on earth if she can be kept clear of the devilish influence of the O'Neill woman.

Why not Sara herself in the Ervine play? I am at present rehearsing her in Robinson's new play — she is superb. . . .

About *The Bargain*. The curious thing about this play is just this to my mind. Some parts of it are so good, particularly at the beginning of the acts, that the dramatic ineffectiveness of the play as a whole would annoy an audience. Certainly unless my dramatic sense has all gone to pieces, I can't see that it will ever be even a moderate success, but still in spite of that the good bits make the play worth producing, though it were only to act as an object lesson to the author. . . .

Yours sincerely,<br>A. PATRICK WILSON[2]

Despite Wilson's vigorous policy, the Abbey in early 1915 was in financial difficulty. Except for the successful week in Cork, the company played the first three and a half months of the year in Dublin. The programme was varied every week, and there were good houses. On the first night of Robinson's *The Dreamers*, the house was packed, and Wilson wrote Yeats that the box office receipts were £32.[3] Nevertheless, on 3 February, Fred J. Harris, the theatre's accountant, wrote to Yeats to say that the Manager of the Munster and Leinster Bank was inquiring about the theatre's overdraft:

| | |
|---|---|
| Theatre Proper A/C | £186.10.5 overdrawn |
| 1st Company A/C | 67.17.5 to credit.[4] |

The situation was not exactly desperate, as the following list of securities in the Abbey Theatre Fund indicates:

1. £141.14.5 Railway Co. of England, 2½% Deb.
   Stock                                        £85.10.0
2. £585 Gt. S. & W. Railway Co. of Ireland 4%
   Deb. Stock                                   586.0.0
3. £1,143 London & N.W. Railway Co. 3% Perpetual
   Deb. Stock                                   858.0.0
4. £1,116.3.0 Guaranteed 3% Stock (1939) at 80¼  798.0.0
                                               ─────────
                                               £2,327.10.0[5]

But, on the other hand, the theatre's expenses were heavy, and the income from English touring had become negligible, as these figures show:

Net Profit on London Tours
Six weeks, 1914      £21.13. 6
Six weeks, 1913       433.11. 2
Six weeks, 1912     1,323. 5.10
Four weeks, 1911      482. 1. 1[6]

In consequence, Yeats drew up the following statement, probably in March or early April:

### STATEMENT

There seem to be just two possible courses before us.

(1) To carry on until better times come with a reduced Company.

(2) To close down altogether, except for the Theatre and its lets, until better times have come.

Now as to the first course:

I enclose a list of players suggested by Mr. Wilson. Their total salaries amount, as you will see, to £15.15.0 per week. He believes that he could tour them during the summer months, but, in that case, certain additions would have to be made, and one should count the salary list at £21 or £22. He would have, however, to make inquiries as to the possibility of summer touring. I will consider them at the moment as merely nucleus kept together for the autumn. They to a great part consist of players whose salaries having been small . . . are unlikely to have saved much money. Keeping them on would, therefore, mean the smallest amount of hardship.

By another list which I enclose you will see the annual expenses of the Theatre proper, including salary of Shaun Barlow, come to £590. If, therefore, we count the payment of this nucleus Company as dead loss, our expenses for the three months during which we cannot play, would amount to about £147 for the Theatre proper, and £73 for the Company, or in all £220. I am writing on the assumption that Kerrigan will not object to his salary coming down to the sum stated. In the autumn one should be able to make this Company something more than self-supporting even if the war remains at the worst. Wilson suggests our playing fortnightly. He does not think that we would have sufficient new work to play oftener. We would have, of course, the lets of the Theatre, which would be much more valuable, as we shall be using the Theatre less. I must add to the summary of expenditure of £220 a sum of £50 or £60 to be spent on making the large room of the Mechanics Institute suitable for lets. The floor is out of order, but can be put to rights with our labour. During the winter months, I should be inclined to bring over, from time to time, some player to take principal parts for a brief period. No doubt, some of our own people would be available, and there is always Miss Sheddon, or her like. To some extent, we should try and break new ground with the work, and take advantage of the situation and of the smaller number of performances to drop out certain plays. We could do also a greater amount of touring in the provinces.

(2) I will now consider the proposal of closing everything except the Theatre proper.

The advantage would be that we could wait until, as I said, the start of the Home Rule Bill, and then probably get more capital and start on really good conditions. One has, however, to weigh against this the scattering of all our people; the difficulty of forming again a group of trained players, and the hardship to individuals. I hope, therefore, that our analysis of our finance will enable us to take the first course.

Our figures for the last year have proved the necessity of one or other of these courses. I was inclined to think at first that there was just a chance of a successful London Tour and Manchester Tour enabling us to hold on. However, on getting the detailed figures, I gave up this hope. During the last financial year our total loss has been £1,210.13.4. If I deduct from this a loss on the American Tour of £585.5.2 as accidental, I find there has been a loss on the working year of £622.8.2. This is the more serious because we have not made on any quarter of the year's work. Our net loss on the quarter just closed has been £135.5.1, and on the November quarter — the best of the year — £71.16.5. The losses on the previous quarters, which included tours and the summer holidays, were, of course, very much greater. We have failed to make the Theatre in Dublin self-supporting, and as we have played out all our most popular pieces it cannot do much better for some time. If we go on as at present I am afraid we must look forward to a heavier loss during the coming winter reason in Dublin. I have also had to give up hope of a successful London season. I have written to Allan Wade, but from what I can hear, the element that supports us in London is not now going to the theatres. Many of our best supporters are occupied with various war interests. Apart from that, we have always depended so much upon the talk of dinner tables, so far as London is concerned, and the dinner tables have now something more exciting to talk of. I expect, however, we will do fairly in Manchester, as we have not been there for so many years.

I find it difficult to find out exactly what capital we have in reserve. Hanson is in London, and I have only the statement as to the nominal capital, some of which, for instance, was bought at $80\frac{1}{2}$. In the case of the rest of the figures supplied by Dr. Moore, it is not stated at what price the stock was bought. I think, however, the actual sum paid must have been about £1,600. I am referring only to the stock which is at our disposal for general theatrical purposes. The first two figures on the enclosed list refer to stock which is ear-marked for a special purpose. Now, of course, if we sold out, we would get very much less. Our aim should be to try and carry on without selling. Acting upon the advice both of Dr. Moore and Mr. Harris, we have just bought the Mechanics Institute for a sum of £1,200 odd. This money we raise from the Bank. In order that we may do so, we propose to deposit our Leases. I do not know whether that sum exhausts our borrowing powers or not; but I should think not. The purchase of the Mechanics Institute was necessary as if any one else had bought it they could have made our tenancy very difficult, and probably raised our rent. The result of the purchase is a saving of about £20 a year, the percentage on our loan being about £20 less than the rent charged.

As soon as I arrived here and found the seriousness of the financial state, I laid the facts before the Company. I thought that I was bound to do this as they had to consider their own futures. I, however, told them that we could not decide anything until you returned. They seemed inclined to make some offer to us of working for a reduction. I have heard nothing since except that Sinclair has refused to work for any reduction. I am not inclined to press the matter upon them further as I doubt in the absence of a London Tour its being possible to arrange a workable scheme. I believe those who will leave us are those who have saved money or who can find employment in the English Theatre.

Note. In the list of expenses of the Theatre proper, I have put Miss McConaghy down at 30/-. She has offered to work for this reduced salary until better times. She has suggested going altogether, or working for even less, but I think she is an indispensable person.[7]

Wilson's statement about the financial condition of the Theatre was as follows:

(1) The following artists are, in my opinion, essential:

| J. M. Kerrigan | Eithne McGee |
|---|---|
| U. Wright | P. Guiry |
| J. A. O'Rourke | H. Hutchinson |
| S. J. Morgan | K. Drago |

To pay them 25/- per week from the first week in May to the beginning of August would mean the gross total of £130.

(2) In the event of paying full salaries on present contracts up to the time they elapse, the following table shows how much this would cost.

| ARTIST | SALARY PER WEEK | SALARY DUE FROM 1 MAY TO END OF CONTRACT [1 AUG.] |
|---|---|---|
| A. Sinclair | £4. 0. 0 | £36. 0. 0 |
| F. O'Donovan | 3.10. 0 | 31.10. 0 |
| J. M. Kerrigan | 3.10. 0 | 31.10. 0 |
| U. Wright | 3. 0. 0 | 27. 0. 0 |
| J. A. O'Rourke | 3. 0. 0 | 27. 0. 0 |
| S. J. Morgan | 2. 0. 0 | 26. 0. 0 |
| N. Desmond | 2. 5. 0 | 20. 5. 0 |
| E. Magee | 2. 0. 0 | 26. 0. 0 |
| P. Guiry | 1.10. 0 | 13. 0. 0 |
| H. E. Hutchinson | 1. 5. 0 | 12.10. 0 |
| A. Coppinger | 1. 5. 0 | 11. 5. 0 |
| K. Drago | 1. 0. 0 | 9. 0. 0 |
| | | £271.10. 0 |

(3) After careful consideration, I have formed the opinion that to attempt a tour in the Irish provinces before August

would be to court disaster. Say, however, we were going to play the provinces for four weeks, I estimate the expenses at £75 per week at the lowest. They could not be less, but would possibly be more. To take that amount in per week in receipts would be excellent Provincial business at the best of times. We would probably not take more than £50 per week in the summer, if that. I can only see, therefore, a possible loss of anything up to £25 per week. To meet that on a four weeks' tour I would require a capital of £100.

| Some of the General Expenses for Years | 1914 | 1915 |
|---|---|---|
| Salaries | £5,793 | £4,644 |
| Lighting and Heating | 68 | 109 |
| Dramatists | 472 | 898 |
| Stationery and Postage | 28 | 19 |
| Stage Scenery | 134 | 84 |
| Stage Scenery (America) | 69 | |
| Advertising, Printing, &c. | 603 | 638 |
| Costumes | 20 | 55 |
| House Expenses | 8 | 8 |
| Insurances | 62 | 67 |
| U. Wright's A/C. Tours | 81 | 169 |
| Rents | 116 | 88 |
| Rates | 86 | 116 |

The explanation of the rise in dramatists' fees is that during the American Tour of 1914 the dramatists were not paid by us, but in 1915 they were paid by us. The amount of fees paid for America alone being £540.[8]

Beginning on 12 April, the Abbey spent two weeks at the Gaiety Theatre, Manchester. Then the Company returned to play in Dublin for a week and a half, and then towards the end of May went to London for an extended visit at the Little Theatre. In that period, Yeats and Wilson had a ferocious quarrel over Wilson's refusal to rehearse *Deirdre of the Sorrows* for London. Wilson then wrote to Yeats:

14 May 1915

Dear Mr. Yeats,

After the Meeting this morning, it was quite evident there was only one thing left for me to do, and that is to resign my position as Manager of the Abbey Theatre Company. I do so herewith, giving notice to terminate my engagement this day month, 14 June. During that time I will act as Business Manager only, and at the end of the period I must have a signed report from the Auditor upon the books as they leave my charge.

As I do not know Lady Gregory's private address, I enclose a copy of this letter addressed to her and rely upon you handing it to her.

Yours faithfully,

A. PATRICK WILSON[9]

To which the Directors replied:

17 May 1915

Dear Mr. Wilson,

We have to-day received your letter. As you say, it was necessary for you to resign after the Meeting, and we are sorry it is necessary for us to accept your resignation.

We have come to this conclusion, not only because of your attempt, which we feel sure was not premeditated, to stir up the players against their employers, but on other grounds.

You knew perfectly well last year that *Deirdre of the Sorrows* was to be produced this season, and that it was necessary to produce it. You knew when at Easter we talked over plays for London that it was one of the plays put upon the list. You now say it is impossible to produce it during our season, yet, knowing it was to be put on, you did not give it any rehearsals in Dublin or elsewhere. We did not interfere with you as to rehearsals; we told you in good time what were the plays essential for London; and we cannot but look on this as neglect of duty.

We do not think you justified in resigning one part of your business during your last month with us, but as you pleaded possible overwork we do not like to press this matter.

We have found you in many ways a satisfactory and capable Manager, and regret the necessity of parting.

Yours faithfully,

W. B. YEATS

AUGUSTA GREGORY[10]

After the Little Theatre run, some of the players were engaged for their usual appearance at the Coliseum in July. Wilson was still managing this business for the Abbey, but relations were very strained between him and Yeats. However, on 11 July, Wilson could still write in a friendly fashion to Lady Gregory:

I have just had a big new Scotch play of mine taken for Miss Madge MacIntyre, the American Scotch actress, for which I got £100 down from her agent. This unexpected

371

stroke of luck enables me to get married sooner than I expected. It comes off next Saturday but we are not going out of town for the present. It's just possible that I will be crossing to America in the early part of September for the production.[11]

On 14 July, Wilson wrote to Yeats, mentioning that, 'Yesterday I completed negotiations for a new Scotch sketch of mine to go out on the music-halls starting August Bank Holiday', and then mentioning an offer for the Irish Players to play *Duty* for four weeks during the summer in Manchester. Wilson offered to handle the arrangements and to guarantee £10 to the Abbey.[12] Yeats apparently thought that the Theatre was being bilked, and so undoubtedly replied with some heat. This was Wilson's reply:

102 Long Acre, W.C.
19 July 1915

Dear Mr. Yeats,

Thanks for your letter which I presume was written yesterday, Sunday the 18, though it bears no date.

I take it that it is intended as all the reply you propose to make to my last letter to you. This also applies to Lady Gregory's attitude I suppose. I have no comment to make on that aspect — it is entirely your own affair and is at least characteristic.

Your letter as it stands, however, is quite another matter. It has evidently been hastily written and without a due knowledge of the facts. There can be no dismissal. My resignation was made to you some time ago and accepted. Since that occurred an extra arrangement was made verbally with Lady Gregory that I should manage the Coliseum engagement of four weeks. This engagement does not terminate until Saturday 24 July, and even if I was only a charwoman you could not dismiss me without a week's notice. I'm sorry but the whole business tradition of the world is against you, and much more important than that is the fact that my business reputation cannot and will not be allowed to remain at your mercy. My books and other papers will be delivered up just as soon as the Coliseum engagement terminates and my last week's salary of £8 is paid. If you desire them before that, you can seek any legal remedy that is open to you. I had no intention of going to Bristol or Manchester — my engagement did not cover them, but I would have done the ordinary preliminary business as a matter of course. It now falls upon you to do what remains to be done in any way that best suits you in regard to those places, but it does not affect my position regarding the Coliseum engagement.

I am sending on a copy of this letter to Lady Gregory together with the usual cheque for current week's salaries and petty cash to receive her signature.

Yours faithfully,<br>A. PATRICK WILSON[13]

At the same time Wilson wrote to Lady Gregory, 'My conscience regarding the Coliseum is quite clear. For the first time on record so far as that house is concerned, you will have a profit.' [14]

Wilson's refusing to be summarily dismissed impelled Yeats to write to Commissioner Bailey, one of the theatre's financial advisors:

18 Woburn Buildings,<br>Euston Road, W.C.<br>20 July 1915

Dear Mr. Bailey,

I enclose a copy of Wilson's answer. It is a question now of his £8 or a lawyer's letter. I would like your opinion. If he is really nervous about being shown up, it may be just as well not to be in any hurry to set his mind at ease. Till I see Dossy Wright to-day, I will not know what books or papers he has. I should think the case is pretty clear. While acting as our paid representative, he made contracts against our interest, approached our players to make contracts with himself, and that he turned to his own purposes offers that were intended for us. Dossy Wright saw Macleod, the agent, yesterday. They explained that they would be paid in any case. The theatrical habit is that whoever makes an introduction which leads to business, gets a percentage on that business. They introduced Wilson as our representative to the American agent, Hassan, and Wilson arranges a contract in his own interest. That, however, does not affect their percentage. . . .

I have just had a wire from Lady Gregory in these words: "I will come London immediately unless prospects clearing — answer." I have replied "no change", but will write or wire later in the day. I don't like bringing her a journey but I confess it will be a great relief if she comes. Before she arrives, I would be very much obliged if you could get from Harris, information for me on the following subject: I had intended to go to Dublin and get it myself at the end of the week. Last spring, when we considered the question of closing, my recollection is that Harris calculated that our buildings altogether should be worth about £6,000, and that there were mortgageable to the extent of £3,000. When I found that Lady Gregory wanted the Company to come to London, I said at a meeting in the office where you and Harris were present, It is essential that we keep in our hands a sufficient sum to pay the expenses of the building apart from any company being in it for, say, two years, and have a small reserve in addition. We calculated that we would still have this reserve if we lost the sum of £1,200 on working expenses. I remember saying to Lady Gregory, "There now, you have £1,200 to lose." I find now that a very much less loss has apparently exhausted our available funds. I would be very much obliged if you would tell me whether the bank told Harris that they would advance nothing more or that they would only advance a small sum more. . . .[15]

Despite all of these difficulties, the theatre engaged a new manager, St. John Ervine, and opened the autumn season in Dublin as usual.

\* \* \*

On 27 January, Jacques visited the Abbey and reported that he had never seen it so crowded since the 'memorable Horse Show night when *Blanco Posnet* was shown up for the first time. . . . The balcony overflowed into the back stalls. It was a record audience for this theatre, and it was not difficult to understand why.' [16] The reason was not the production of the new one-act play by two young Dublin men, F. C. Moore and W. P. Flanagan, but the return of Sara Allgood to the company.

> The moment the curtain went up on the first act of *Mixed Marriage*, disclosing Miss Allgood busy cutting bread for Rainey's "tay", applause mixed with cheers rumbled through the house, and continued rumbling for several minutes.[17]

The new one-act was, incredibly enough, another American western piece, *a la* Bret Harte. Titled *By Word of Mouth*, this comedy was a simple joke about two swains who paid the local newspaper editor to write love letters for them, not realising that the editor himself had already married the girl. Although *The Irish Times* said that the characters were well drawn and the dialogue breezy, it concluded that the play lacked the 'vigorous invective' of *Blanco Posnet*.[18] Jacques, noting that the inhabitants of the play's Florenceville, U.S.A., all carried six-shooters, remarked that, 'Nothing was killed except twenty minutes.' [19] And *The Irish Citizen* reported that, 'A feeble one-act piece was put on along with *Mixed Marriage*. I have forgotten its name; it is not worth criticising.' [20]

374

Early in February, the Abbey produced a double bill of two popular plays, *The Magnanimous Lover* and *The Country Dressmaker*; and one critic noticed Sinclair's growing tendency to play for laughs:

> *The Country Dressmaker* followed. Readers of *The Irish Citizen* have been already made familiar with its leading features. It was played on this occasion with such spirit and distinction as to almost succeed in rescuing it from mediocrity. Fred O'Donovan, as the professional matchmaker, was a pure joy. The last act is so hopeless that no amount of genius on the part of the actors could redeem it. It was reduced to an absurdity by the grotesque antics of Arthur Sinclair in his efforts to raise a laugh at any expense to the artistic merits of his part. It is distinctly regrettable that the Abbey audience has grown less critical. A few years ago such an exhibition of stupid buffoonery would not have been tolerated. Actors, like a host of greater and lesser mortals, need plenty of wholesome criticism to prevent them from degenerating.[21]

Lennox Robinson's three-act play, *The Dreamers*, which was produced on 10 February, was one of the worthier efforts of the year, but it did not get an enthusiastic press. Indeed, at one point in the opening night there was even some hissing from a small section of the audience. Nevertheless, *The Irish Times* thought that Robinson's picture of the Emmet rebellion was not distorted, even though some 'unpleasant aspects' of it may have been emphasised. The paper's only other criticism was that 'the pruning knife could easily be used with discretion.' The acting, particularly that of O'Donovan as Emmet and that of Kerrigan who played four different roles in the large cast, was admired, as was Wilson's effective production. Mrs. Cruise O'Brien in *The Irish Citizen* was lukewarm in her praise:

> I wonder if Mr. Lennox Robinson was right in making of the life of Robert Emmet a history play rather than a tragedy. That is what he does and does well in *The Dreamers*. . . . It is true that there is much fine work in the putting together of the cumulation of accidents — the unpreparedness of men, the explosion of the arms factory, the drunkenness of the insurgents — all these things which made a great plan fail, which mocked Emmet's dreaming and effort. But suppose Mr. Robinson had taken as the central motif of his tragedy the doubt and struggle in the mind of Emmet as to whether he ought to rise at once, even without Wicklow, or wait, and

375

so to the final tragedy of his mind, when he found his decision wrong in taking the hazard. Mr. Robinson could have given us a fine tragedy. One wanted something of the mind of Emmet and less of the external accidents, except of course Miss Allgood, altogether a charming accident, as Sarah Curran.[23]

Jacques, however, thought the play quite bad:

"There's something wild and unstable with the country; you can't get behind or beyond it." So said one of the stage characters at the Abbey Theatre last night. *The Dreamers* has not helped us to get behind or beyond anything. It is a three-act play about Robert Emmet and Sarah Curran written by Mr. Lennox Robinson. If the author wished us to take his hero seriously, he failed dismally. If he had given us a story of pathos and patriotism only, he might have been interesting, but he introduced porter, and so the play became a thing of love, laughter, and blather.

The historian's story of Emmet's effort is tragedy from first to last — magnificent, pitiful, but always tragedy. The author has chosen one week from a fitful career — 16 July to 23 July of 1803 — and has added one day — the episode of Emmet's arrest in August — and from that period he forms his theme.

He shows us the young rebel fired with enthusiasm about his country, and touched with vanity about his uniform in the cobbler's house at Rathfarnham. He brings Emmet and his sweetheart together under the cobbler's roof. He discovers to us Emmet and his supporters discussing the "rising" in an inn in Thomas Street. To make laughter for the audience seemed the main object of the discussion, for the patriots who were to free Ireland then were as well equipped as the Volunteers are to-day to beat back a German invasion.

Laughter, mingled with hissing, was again the reward of the actor's effort in a scene depicting the Depot in Marshalsea Lane, and the audience repeated its demonstration during and at the close of the scene disclosing the battlers for Ireland's freedom swilling whiskey and mouthing drink-talk in a Thomas Street public-house.

Apart from faults in construction — and they are many — the author made one big mistake in allowing the cobbler's boy, Martin Brady (Mr. U. Wright), to occupy the place of chief dreamer. Emmet was central figure, but one looked past him, the pure-souled boy, to Martin, whose fate was noble, yet so wayside. The King's bootmaker would make an audience gulp when the King would make them tired.

The acting was always and ever sincere as Abbey acting usually is, but the doubling of parts was very confusing. There were thirty-five characters. Abbey actors can play different parts in different plays, but not different parts in the same play — even when the stage is darkened. The elocution of Mr. F. O'Donovan, the sobs and sentiment of Miss Allgood — they were the lovers — the declamation of Mr. Sinclair, the common sense of Mr. Connolly, and the evidence of careful rehearsing by other actors were all admirable, but futile. The play remained a hotch-potch of forced effects.[24]

On 5 April, the Abbey presented a double-bill of two new plays, William Crone's three-act *The Bargain* and Martin J. McHugh's one-act *The Philosopher*. The fullest discussions of both were by W. J. Lawrence in *The Stage*. Of *The Bargain*, he wrote:

> Mr. Crone strikes a new chord in Abbey Theatre dramaturgy, too long obsessed by the demon of morbidity. He may even be said to have formulated a new genre. It is only at the eleventh hour that the seasoned critic suddenly recognises that *The Bargain* is an effectively disguised thesis-play, girding with a single final home-thrust at loveless alliances of a more or less mercenary order and at the intolerable tyranny of parents. Mr. Crone has attained the distinction of enforcing a found moral wholly without didacticism. His play has no apparent seriousness, and yet is deadly in its attack. It is only in the last act that the flavour of the powder comes through the jam. This feat has been accomplished by emulating the methods of the literary impressionist in the avoidance of conventional draughtsmanship and by surrounding the theme with a light-comedy atmosphere. Rarely even in the Abbey has there been experienced such nimbleness of natural and yet consistently vivacious dialogue.
>
> Weary of the drudgery of his unaided labours in his grocery in an Ulster village, William John McComb, a kindly, matter-of-fact, middle-aged widower, discusses his uncared-for state with his son, Tom, a college student, and announces his intention of re-marrying. Negotiations are on foot, but so far from there having been any love-making, the likes or dislikes of the mere girl selected by McComb for his second adventure into matrimony have not been given a passing thought. The industrious, God-fearing grocer is a most eligible candidate, and Andy Simpson views his proposal for his daughter Mary's hand with a favourable eye, and the only matter of moment

377

to determine is the amount of "the fortune". After a scene of adroit fencing between the two bargainers, it is finally settled that McComb is to get £100 with the girl.

The unenviable office of bunco-steerer is left to Mary's mother, an astute, strong-minded, voluble-tongued body, who exercises all the weapons in the feminine armoury to overcome the young girl's repugnance to the match. Mary, as we learn somewhat belatedly in the last act, had already been looking out for herself, and had had some incipient love passages with a youth of her own age. At last, when all other arguments fail, the mother points out to the girl that her brother James was desirous of marrying Annie Harvey, and of bringing her home to the family roof-tree. This could not well be done unless Mary made way for the young couple by making a home for herself. Thus adroitly appealed to on the altruistic side, the young girl sighingly consents to the sacrifice.

But the mother is not playing fair. The devil has not a greater hatred of holy water than she has for this Annie Harvey, a veritable young shrew, who has completely subjugated her loutish son. At the back of her mind she has determined to do all in her power to break off the match. Six months pass. When the last act opens Mary has been for some little time the second Mrs. McComb and begins to realise the tragedy of her situation. It is Sunday morning, and her stepson, Tom, is home for the vacation. About her own age, he is sympathetic towards her through divination of her sorrows. He brings her a letter addressed to her in her maiden name, and in recognising the handwriting knows that it comes from an old fellow-student. Mary puts the letter in the fire unopened, but in a scene admitting of delicate emotional art, when properly acted, reveals her state of mind to the kindhearted Tom. She does not love, but has grown to respect her honest-minded husband.

Diversion is occasioned by the abrupt arrival of Mrs. Simpson, who tells of a terrible row in the Simpson *ménage* through the efforts of the father and mother to break the match between their son and Annie. Finding there will be no peace under the family roof-tree, James has determined to take the woman of his choice to America. But he has no money, and Mrs. Simpson comes post-haste to William John McComb to beg him not to lend any. McComb would not have been hard to persuade; but his young wife, disgusted at her mother's treachery towards herself, and convinced that the tyranny of parents must be defeated, coaxes her husband to lend her brother the passage money. As the curtain falls one arrives at the conviction that May and October have somehow arrived at a compromise and that the future will not be without its sunshine.

Unfortunately, the merits of Mr. Crone's unconventional play were somewhat obscured by uncertainty of touch on the part of the players. Much of the grace and humour of the dialogue was lost in the prevailing flurried and hurried manner of delivery. Mr. Sydney J. Morgan, who rarely errs in this respect and is generally one of the most trustworthy of Abbey actors, did considerable injustice to his own able conception of the hard-working and hard-headed but kindly-hearted grocer by a nervous indecision almost foreign to his temperament. Blemishes such as this will, of course, quickly disappear, but mis-casting cannot be as easily rectified. In the crucial interview in the last act between the young wife and her sympathetic step-son, Miss Cathleen MacCarthy's constitutional impassivity, acting in conjunction with Mr. Philip Guiry's incapacity to wring the necessary emotion out of the situation, deprived the audience of a keen dramatic pleasure. The best acting of the afternoon came from a wholly unexpected quarter. Every allowance could have been made for Miss Helen Moloney had she failed in her portrayal of the shrewd, strong-minded Mrs. Simpson, as she only took up the part a day or so before the production owing to Miss Nora Desmond's regrettable illness. As a matter of fact, however, she succeeded in extracting every ounce of effect out of the part, getting all her lines home with telling effect and humorious acerbity. Miss Eithne Magee, always sound in characterisation, rather over-emphasised the shrewish attributes of Annie Harvey. She should bear in mind that cats do not always reveal their claws. Mr. H. E. Hutchinson, on the other hand, gave an almost faultless rendering of the loutish and taciturn James Simpson.[25]

Of McHugh's *The Philosopher*, which *The Evening Herald* described as amusing, but bordering on the burlesque, Lawrence wrote:

Mr. McHugh's agreeable if somewhat prolix and slow-moving trifle shows much of the ingenuity and humour which marked his first playlet, *A Minute's Wait*, but will scarcely rival that little gem in popularity. Into the bill-hung Market House of Killalad out of the hurly-burly of the fair come three acquaintances, two of them avid with curiosity. News has been circulated that Dan McInerney, a serene-minded local shopkeeper, has been left an immense fortune; and John Magrath and Mickey Donnellan want to hear all about it. Dan has little to tell. Word has come that his Uncle Corny has died in Australia and left him "all he had". Conjuring up a vision of thousands, Dan's friends plan a glorious future for him and see him in their minds' eye married to "a high-up lady". Dan, however, fails to rise to the bait. He has been happy in his little shop and views with suspicion this access of wealth which is to alienate him from his friends and upset his routine. A delightfully humorous colloquy between the trio is interrupted by the surging in of a motley crowd headed by Mr. Sullivan, the auctioneer. The main business on hand is the sale of an adjoining farm of good land, for which Tom Burke and Joe Minogue are the protagonists. Much excitement is caused by the rivalry between the two, so much so that when the biddings seem to have reached a climax and Tom Burke is about to become the purchaser, Dan McInerney, hitherto an interested but unparticipating spectator, loses his head, and offering £1,500, has the farm knocked down to him. A free fight follows, and Sergeant Duffy temporarily clears the Market House. But the highly indignant Tom Burke sturdily returns to abuse Dan for stepping over his head on the matter, only to find himself placated by the frank explanations of the philosophic shopkeeper. Carried away by the excitement of the moment, he had bidden for the fun of the thing, just to keep the ball a-rolling. A compromise is suggested, and they toss for it, head or harp, the best of three. Dan wins, and it is agreed that Tom Burke should give him a profit of £100 on his bid. This is Dan's lucky day. Honan, the solicitor, arrives with the intelligence that he is not his uncle Corny's heir after all, a later will having been found bequeathing the property to another branch of the family. So all is for the best in the best of all possible worlds. £100 the better for his day's "divarsion", Dan accepts his loss of fortune with gladness and goes back contentedly to the routine of his little shop.

Contrary to the experience in *The Bargain*, Mr. McHugh's brightly written little piece lost nothing at the hands of its interpreters. Added to his gifts for humorous characterisation, Mr. Arthur Sinclair has an underlying sincerity of purpose (mostly observable save when he plays serious roles) which made feasible the philosophic contentment of the unambitious Dan McInerney. Seldom have we seen him in a humorous embodiment in which he was so free of all exaggeration. Mr. J. M. Kerrigan, who alone among Abbey actors — and that, too, without gagging — has the capacity of making something out of nothing, aroused intense merriment by his quaint inflexions and quizzical commentaries on the rich man passing through the eye of a needle, as John Magrath. In his scheme of laughter-provoking he was substantially aided and abetted by Mr. O'Rourke in the small part of Michael Donnellan. Mr. Fred O'Donovan conducted the rural auction as if to the manner born, and Mr. Sydney J. Morgan gave a characteristically sturdy interpretation of the determined-minded Tom Burke. It is noteworthy that through the kind offices of some Good Samaritan twenty-five convalescent wounded soldiers from the various Dublin hospitals sat in a row in the stalls throughout the afternoon, and seemingly much enjoyed the performance.[26]

On 8 April, Lady Gregory's three-act *Shanwalla* was first produced, and roundly denounced by everyone. Lawrence called it 'an amazing farrago . . . Boucicault at his worst never concocted anything half so preposterous, and at least his handling was never feeble.' Jacques found that the performance 'has left me limp. . . . The play was written by Lady Gregory. It may have some meaning to convey. . . .' But if so, he failed to discern it, although he commended the heroic earnestness of the actors.[28] The gentlest critique was that of *The Irish Times*, which summarised the plot like this:

The title of the play is the name of a racehorse, and it is around attempts to dope the horse that a powerful drama is built up. It is, however, in its relation to the supernatural that the play presents most novelty, and on the whole, the introductions of a spirit are typified in an acceptable manner, and arrest the attention firmly.

Lawrence Scarry, stableman, is a faithful and devoted, if hot-tempered, servant of Hubert Darcy, owner of Shanwalla, a dark horse. It is the aim of James Brogan and Pat O'Malley to put the horse out of a coming race, and thereby serve their own nefarious ends. Brogan, discovered by Bride Scarry in the act of doctoring Shanwalla's feed, murders her to preserve secrecy. His villainy goes further, and in the dead of night he suggests to Scarry that his master had tempted and murdered Bride Scarry, and prompts the stableman to poison the horse. Scarry is saved from this misdeed by a dream apparition of his spirit wife. Nevertheless, he is accused of the crime, and Brogan endeavours to fasten also the crime of murdering his wife upon him. Bride Scarry the spirit uses Owen Conary, a blind beggar, as a medium to protect her husband in this new trouble, and through his agency Brogan is made to confess the murder and his other misdeeds.

As a drama the play has some strong features, and indeed, it is a matter for consideration whether *Shanwalla*, with alterations of course, would not stand successfully without the introduction of the supernatural element, though the latter provides a niche for the interesting character of the blind beggar. The threatening of Bride Scarry in the first act, and the machinations of Brogan and O'Malley in the second, are powerful scenes. The last act is somewhat weak, the quick change in the general attitude from suspicion of Scarry as a murderer, and the confession of Brogan, strike one as taken in much too light-hearted a way. It is not natural, for instance, that two young girls should remain alone in a room with a man denounced as, and generally believed to be, a murderer. With this exception, one's interest is absorbed fully by the play, and the chief characters are capably portrayed. Kathleen Drago treated the part of Bride Scarry with due care and skill. The character of the blind beggar was a very good piece of work on the part of J. M. Kerrigan. . . .

In response to repeated calls, Lady Gregory appeared on the stage at the end of the performance and bowed her acknowledgements of the good reception accorded the play. . . .[29]

But the most notable approval of the play came from Bernard Shaw:

> Friday, 16 April 1915
> The Shaws are here. They are very easy to entertain, he is so extraordinarily light in hand, a sort of kindly joyousness about him, and they have their motor car so are independent. He says *Shanwalla* the best ghost play he ever saw, and thinks Sinclair *very* fine in it.[30]

The autumn season finally opened on 10 November under a new manager, the Ulster playwright St. John Ervine. Ervine took up his duties on 29 October and was immediately interviewed by the Press:

> "We are hoping that the Shaw play [*O'Flaherty V.C.*] will draw very well," Mr. Ervine said to a representative of *The Evening Telegraph*. "It is said to be very good, and its name is sufficiently indicative of its subject. One thing I would very much like to get," he stated, "would be a play by James Stephens. We want something of his style in the Abbey, and I am sure it would appeal immensely. Then, again, there are

complaints that our repertoire is mostly one of peasant plays — that we are too much devoted to one set of subjects. Well, if somebody will write a good drama of middle-class life in Ireland, one worth producing, I can guarantee that it will be produced in the Abbey."

With regard to the players, Mr. Ervine first mentioned the great success of the English tour in *Duty,* and said that Miss Allgood, who was at present touring in *Peg o' My Heart,* would return to the Abbey probably about Christmas. There were several matters connected with the personnel, he said, which were receiving attention and which were not yet quite settled. Amongst other things, he mentioned the engagement of a new artiste, Miss Close, and said that there were numerous applications to be dealt with and a good deal of promising artistic material to be recruited from for the Abbey. Mr. Sinclair, he said, was not a member of the company at present, and Miss Magee had also severed her association with it.

"We want the support of the public for the theatre," Mr. Ervine concluded. "The Abbey requires everybody associated with it to put his best into the work, and that being done, we hope the public will appreciate it and support our efforts." [31]

The new artist Ervine referred to, Miss Close, was his own wife, and the two new plays he announced for production were Shaw's recruiting play, *O'Flaherty V.C.,* and his own study of Northern life, *John Ferguson.* Shaw's complex but outspoken attitude toward the war had endeared him to practically no one, and the production of his play at the Abbey did not occur. As is usual in Dublin, there were many rumours and speculations about the matter, and on 18 November Ervine wrote this account for the Press:

It is untrue that the play has been suppressed by the military authorities, or that they have made any suggestion to us concerning the play. It is untrue that the play was submitted to the English Censor, and that he made so many cuts in it that Mr. Shaw decided not to have it produced. It is untrue that the play is anti-recruiting or pro-German in character; indeed, Mr. Shaw is anxious to promote recruiting. The legend that he is a pro-German was, of course, invented by penny-three-farthing persons, and is only believed by young ladies and old gentlemen who have never read a word he has written. Mr. Shaw has written an excellent comedy of disillusionment, in which he shows how the war has broadened the mind of an Irish soldier and given him a larger world-sense than he ever had before. The play has been read by a number of Irish and

English gentlemen, some of them officers in his Majesty's forces, and all of them have taken pleasure in reading or listening to the play. I, personally, knew nothing of the report in a Dublin morning paper that the play had been suppressed until two reporters came to interview me on the subject and I informed them of the facts stated above. The reason for the postponement of *O'Flaherty V.C.* is just that we are producing a number of new plays here, for which the rehearsals are of a very heavy nature, and in order not to exhaust the players and to assure that the first performances shall be finished productions instead of monologue by the prompter, I decided to complete the production of my own play, *John Ferguson*, which will be performed on 30 November, and leave Mr. Shaw's until we had more leisure. May I add that the interview with "a prominent member of the Abbey Company", which is reported in one of your contemporaries, is totally untrue. The players, without exception, deny that they have been interviewed by any journalist or reporter on the subject of Mr. Shaw's play.[32]

A clearer picture of what really happened may be pieced together by the following letters:

Ayot St. Lawrence, Welyn, Herts.
8 Nov. 1915

My dear Yeats,

I wrote to Ervine on Sunday, explaining why I committed myself to Sinclair subject to his rejoining the company. Kerrigan is really the only male member of the company who has charm; and if *O'Flaherty* were a romance of illusion, instead of a comedy of disillusion, and ended with the hero's union to a colleen bawn, he would be perfect in it; for he has not only charm but youth. I think his Fenian in *The Rising of the Moon* one of the best things in the repertory. But he lacks variety, and is not a real comedian. People want a happy ending for him; but for Sinclair, who *is* a comedian, they want confusion, disillusion and bathos. It is Kerrigan's tragedy that there is so little romance in the repertory; he is always character-acting, which is a mechanical business; and Sinclair gets all the fat. Writing for Kerrigan, I should have done quite another sort of part. By the way, I'll turn this postcard into a letter, because I want to say that I think Ervine is wrong in clearing the idle members out of the green room. The alternative is the public house; and he will curse the day he drives them there if he carries his plan out. I think the theatre

384

ought to be a club for the company if there is room for them. You have a lot of building next door that you have taken in, haven't you? If a room could be furnished as a reading room & library, with books & papers and cheap teas &c., it would not only avoid this demoralization of loose ends of time in the staff, but act as a substantial addition to the salaries, which are devilish small. Ulster discipline will never do; Ervine will be the first to kick through it himself; and a Utopia that breaks down is ten times worse than an Alsatia that evolves law & order.

I come up to town tomorrow (Tuesday) until the end of the week; but this, of course, requires no answer.

G.B.S.[33]

A few days later Yeats visited Shaw in London. As he subsequently described it to Lady Gregory:

Last week I had a wire from Bailey saying that Shaw's play (*The O'Flaherty*) will have to be changed for another. I went off to Shaw and found him in the middle of lunch. I pointed out that the telegram must mean that the authorities objected to the play. He wired to Bailey who replied that it was the military. Shaw then wrote a detailed letter to Nathan putting the case before him. I should say that my very first sentence had been that it was out of the question our fighting the issue. Shaw I thought was disappointed. He said if Lady Gregory was in London she would fight it, but added afterwards he didn't really want us to act, but thought you would do it out of mischief. I told him that was a misunderstanding of your character. Monday morning I got another letter from Bailey. It was the military authorities and they had threatened to close the theatre; he was arguing the point with the military authorities and with the civil government and was convinced we should be allowed to play it with some cuts. I sent his letter to Shaw who wrote or wired that he would accept any cuts proposed.[34]

10 Adelphi Terrace W.C.
12 Nov. 1915

My dear Yeats,

I got overwhelmed by a mass of business after you left; and the end of it was that I could not write to Bailey nor copy my letter to Nathan, which got posted at Euston at the very last moment.

Plunkett wired that Sir Matthew [Nathan] is at the Under

385

Secretary's Lodge all right. Bailey wired later that the difficulty is not with the castle, but with the military authorities. On the whole, I had rather deal with them than with the Castle. Nathan is a colonel, and will perhaps be as useful on the military as on the civil side.

The line I took was that the suppression of the play will make a most mischievous scandal, because it will be at once assumed that the play is anti-English; that this will be exploited by the Germans and go round the globe; that there will be no performances to refute it; and that a lot of people who regard me as infallible will be prevented from recruiting, shaken in their patriotism &c &c. I enclosed a copy of the play in my letter, and explained that I had not presented it for a licence here because the Lord Chamberlain would not pass the description of the queen, though she herself would like it, and that his refusal would start the same mischief of false reports of my pro-Germanism. I dwelt on the hardship to the starving theatre, and altogether made a strong & quite genuine case for letting the performances proceed.

Ever,

G.B.S.[35]

Abbey Theatre, Dublin
16 November 1915

Dear Yeats,

I have received your various letters, and have been in communication with Bailey. This afternoon I am going to tea with Sir Horace Plunkett to discuss the matter further. The general opinion of those who are acquainted with the play is that it may do a considerable amount of injury to the Theatre — not because of the play itself but because of the mixed element in the audience. Moreover, if there is trouble with the Sinn Féin element — which will come on purpose to make trouble, and will desert us immediately afterwards — Mr. Shaw himself will suffer a further outburst of the silly journalistic hysteria from which he has suffered since the war began. . . .

Sincerely,

ST. JOHN G. ERVINE[36]

Chief Secretary's Office
Dublin Castle
16 November

Dear Mr. Bernard Shaw,

I have now had an opportunity of consulting confidentially on the subject of *O'Flaherty V.C.* Several persons in whose judgment I have confidence and I find they are definitely of opinion that the representation of this play at the present moment would result in demonstrations which could do no good either to the Abbey Theatre, or to the cause that at any rate a large section of Irishmen have made their own. By such demonstrations the fine lesson of the play would be smothered while individual passages would be given a prominence you did not intend for them, with the result that they would wound susceptibilities naturally more tender at this time than at others and be quoted apart from their context to aid propaganda which many of us believe are inflicting injury on Ireland as well as on my country. In these circumstances, I think, and so does General Friend, that the production of the play should be postponed till a time when it will be recording some of the humour and pathos of a past rather than of a present national crisis. I am in a way sorry to have to suggest this as, though it may be presumptuous on my part to say so, I feel strongly that the main idea as you quote it in your letter to me is entirely right, that this war does give to the most thinking of all peasantries the chance of contact with the wider world which will enable them to rise above the hopelessness derived from their old recollections and surroundings.

Yours sincerely,<br>MATTHEW NATHAN[37]

10 Adelphi Terrace, W.C.<br>17 November 1915

My dear Bailey,

I enclose a copy of a letter I have just received. I feel that we should not hesitate for a moment about withdrawing if they demand it; but I still think, now that the play has been announced, that less mischief might be done by the performance of a carefully cut version than by what would appear to the public as suppression in spite of all possible disclaimers. I have written to Sir Matthew in this sense. What do you think yourself?

Yours ever,<br>G. BERNARD SHAW[38]

The rumour that the play had been suppressed was by this time widespread, and so *The Manchester Guardian* asked Shaw to comment on the matter. Shaw said:

The report is extremely inconsiderate because, thanks to the folly of the London Press, the claim which the Germans have been intelligent enough to make that I am what is called a pro-German, has been very widely circulated on the Continent, in America, and even in Morocco. This is not my fault. I can state an unanswerable case against the Germans, but I cannot make the English intelligent enough to see that it is a better case than the kinematograph heroics with which they hope to impress Europe as well as amuse themselves.

Now this silly report will probably be picked up by the Germans, and circulated abroad in the form of a statement that I have written a play which the English Government is suppressing because the poet Shaw has again raised the cry of "Deutschland uber Alles". I therefore appeal to the Press, if they must circulate an unfounded report, at all events to make it clear that the author has no more desire to discourage recruiting in Ireland than the military authorities themselves.

The report, moreover, is absurd, because there is no censorship in Ireland. There are two authorities — the Castle authorities and the military authorities. The Castle authorities have not intervened, and neither I nor the Abbey Street Theatre would think for a moment of producing a play if the military authorities felt that it could do the slightest harm to recruiting or to anything else. As a matter of fact the play, which appeals strongly to the Irishman's spirit of freedom and love of adventure, would, in my opinion, help recruiting rather than otherwise.

But the military authorities will be the judges of this, and there will be no attempt to disregard their wishes should they for any reason prefer that the Abbey Street Theatre should adhere to its original intention to produce the play in America.[39]

But no matter what Shaw could say, the theatre was not, in the face of opposition, going to produce the play. There was to be no new *Blanco Posnet* affair.

On 30 November, the theatre gave the first performance of *John Ferguson*, undoubtedly the finest Irish play of the year. *The Evening Mail* thought it, nevertheless, 'in parts crude and overdrawn', albeit 'powerfully conceived and written'.[40] Jacques in *The Evening Herald* has a review well worth quoting, if for no other reason than its incredible stupidity.

Mr. St. John Ervine is the author of the new play produced last night at the Abbey Theatre. *John Ferguson* is the title and the author labels it a tragedy. It is kind of him to do that. Otherwise it might be mistaken for mere melodrama or something more comical. The theatre was crowded, and the applause tumultuous. The author was "called".

John Ferguson, a Co. Down farmer, has a wife, a son, and a daughter. The farm is mortgaged to one Henry Witherow, a big brutal gombeen man, and the daughter is about to be sold to one James Caesar, a prosperous grocer, who is endowed with much money and no physical courage. This latter bargain is made in the first act. In the second act the daughter is criminally assaulted by Witherow (off the stage), the details of the outrage are made public by the girl herself (on the stage).

In the third act (next morning) we learn that Witherow has been murdered, and the daughter, who comes down to breakfast with Caesar, hears the news with joy. The father hears it with horror. Caesar is arrested for the murder. In the last act the son declares Caesar's innocence and his own guilt of the crime. And the curtain falls on the father reading the Bible while the son goes out to give himself up to the police.

One of the characters says in the course of the play: "Ah, you make me feel sick. I'll go out in the air a while and be quit of you. I'm near stifled in here!" I felt inclined to shout "hear! hear!" and follow his example. His father's constant dull droning preaching from the Scriptures, his sister's whining, his sister's suitor's whinging and blubbering, his mother's hysterics, the atmosphere of morbidity and sanctimoniousness and callousness all made for unreality that would make anyone sick.

The play is constantly striving to be hot, panting, full-blooded realism. It only succeeds in becoming coarse, clear-eyed melodrama saved from positive dullness and pitiful mediocrity by the acting of Messrs. Kerrigan, Morgan, O'Donovan and Guiry. Whatever chance these sincere artists had of giving the necessary touch of cleanliness to foul things was utterly ruined by the casting of the principal female part, that of the outraged daughter. Nothing through the dialogue explained or suggested how she came to be educated away, for her accent all through left the impression that she had been trained far from the hills of Co. Down.[41]

The principal female part was played by Nora Close, Ervine's wife, and W. J. Lawrence, who was an Ulsterman himself and finally quite sympathetic to Ervine, does bear out Jacques and called Mrs. Ervine 'a howling novice' who 'ruined the play'. Otherwise, Lawrence's own notice does much to redress the balance:

Mr. St. John Ervine has signalised his accession to managerial power at the Abbey, the scene of his *début* as a dramatist, by producing there a prose tragedy of very considerable superiority in point of constructiveness and metaphysical subtlety to any of the four plays from his pen already seen at that house, and imbued with a fine spirituality. Few nobler or more pathetic figures have appeared on the modern stage than that of honest old John Ferguson, the simple-minded man, whose Christian faith has so permeated his life that he has charity even for his bitterest wronger, and so convinced him of the beneficent purposefulness of the Almighty that he bears with fortitude and resignation the succession of overwhelming and apparently unjustifiable blows rained by Providence on his unoffending head. Around this finely conceived and firmly drawn character, Mr. Ervine has woven a plot of intensely harrowing human interest. Almost too severe, indeed, is the tension of the last act. Beyond the occasional blemish of jarring literary polish, as in the third act where the old farmer is made to talk of "reaction", the play is flawless. . . .

Uncommon types call for uncommon acting, and *John Ferguson* happily received it. At no first night at the Abbey has one experienced such a combination of histrionic treats and theatrical *tours de force*. One slight blot, however, considerably marred the picture. It was doing a grave injustice to Miss Nora Close, a young actress who has only recently joined the company, to cast her for Hannah Ferguson, a character in all its nuances for which she is physically and temperamentally unfitted. Miss Close's pure and undisguisable English accent and her phlegmatic town-bred air were utterly out of keeping with the daughter of a rugged Co. Down farmer. In a matter of accent she was in only slightly worse case than the rest of the cast, the Abbey players being incapable of dulling their melodious Dublin tones to the flat, chipped diction of the north; but when we get a variety of accents in a play, and none with the true local colour, the result is confusing. Save by delicacy of portraiture, it is difficult to get much effect out of a character of consistent level speaking — the Brutus type — but Mr. Sydney J. Morgan achieved that rare distinction by the consistency of his interpretation and the nobility of his pathos as the high-minded John Ferguson. Occasionally in the Bible-reading passages, Mr. Morgan lacked audibility and impressiveness; but it is difficult to be old and ailing and at the same time elocutionary. Probably this blemish will disappear once the actor gets into his stride. As a necessary foil to the almost saintly old farmer with his selflessness came the opportunism and common human weaknesses born of strong impulsions of the maternal instinct of his wife. Mr. Ervine is never so convincing as in his female types (witness his Mrs. Rainey in *Mixed Marriage*) and he must be congratulated on having to hand an actress of such ample technical accomplishment and so unerring in taste and comprehension as Miss Nora Desmond for his Sarah Ferguson. In the harrowing scene of leavetaking with the son in the last act, Miss Desmond produced a most powerful effect by her whole-souled abandon. In his one brief scene as Henry Witherow, Mr. Arthur Sinclair conveyed the necessary air of ruthless brutality, dominating the stage while he remained. Mr. J. M. Kerrigan had a severe and delicate task in the assumption of the pusilanimous James Caesar; severe because of the little grocer's sudden alternations from effeminate whining and sobbing to manly anger, and of the necessity to make feasible his *penchant* for public self-analysis; delicate because the slightest exaggeration of tone or manner would have dissipated the atmosphere by winning the laugh. Over all these obstacles Mr. Kerrigan bounded with the confident skill of a hurdle-racer, and putting on a spurt at the close, gave a very powerful rendering of Caesar's horrible state of panic when fearing arrest. In the character of Andrew Ferguson, where no opportunities were afforded for *bravura*, Mr. Fred O'Donovan was quietly impressive. Mr. Philip Guiry, an actor who always carries with him an air of cuteness, afforded some relief from the general gloom by his rambling talk as Clutie, the fool, but erred in not showing more frequently, especially in his scene with Andrew in the third act, glimmerings of his mental defectiveness. *John Ferguson* was hailed from first to last by a large and distinguished audience with unmistakable demonstrations of approval, and at the close Mr. Ervine was honoured with a double call.[42]

*John Ferguson* was one of the great successes of the Theatre Guild in New York, and its production there in 1919 afforded Dudley Digges one of his most notable roles as James Caesar.

\* \* \*

At the first of the year, the Irish Theatre moved into its renovated premises in Hardwicke Street. There were some quite able actors who worked for the theatre during the year, among them Frank Fay, Una O'Connor and Mary Walker; nevertheless, the theatre was at best only semi-professional, and most of its recruits were interesting amateurs like the Reddin brothers or Willie Pearse. Indeed, in many ways, the venture was a hearkening back to the days of the Irish National Theatre Society in 1902–1904. Enthusiasm often had to take the place of money, and there are many complaints of insufficient rehearsal and tatty settings.

The finest writing talent that the theatre fostered was that of Eimar O'Duffy. However, after some early attempts at light verse and a handful of plays, O'Duffy's talent was mainly directed to fiction; and at least three of his novels — *The Wasted Island, King Goshawk and the Birds,* and *The Spacious Adventures of the Man in the Street* — are among the finest works of prose fiction that Ireland produced after the war. O'Duffy's own view of the Irish Theatre appears in his light satiric novel, *Printer's Errors.* His hero is an engaging Philistine named Mr. Wolverhampton for whom ' "the theatre" meant Pantomime, Musical Comedy or Farce; he went there "to be amused". . . .' One evening Mr. Wolverhampton attends the Eclectic Theatre and meets a young playwright who seems more or less modelled on O'Duffy:

> The Eclectic Theatre stood in a street which was just one degree better than a slum. It was a very shabby street, with a public-house at the corner and children playing in the gutters. The theatre itself was a large, ugly, rambling old building, erected a hundred and fifty years ago for no one knows what purpose. It had been untenanted for a dozen years before the Eclectic Theatre Company took it; before that it had been a school, and before that a conventicle of some unknown religion.
>
> The Theatre Company was the foundation of a number of amiable gentlemen of artistic inclinations, who wished to form (we quote their own words without professing to understand them) a School of Psychological Drama in Ireland — as if all drama worthy of the name, from Aeschylus to Shakespeare, and from Shakespeare to Synge, were anything else. Of course, what the amiable gentlemen in their foggy intellectualism really meant by psychological drama was drama more or less frankly plagiarised from Ibsen and the Scandinavians and Russians, and as this kind of morbid and unskilled research into not very important ideas and not very common emotions is uninteresting to the sane and logical mind of Ireland, and as dramatists naturally like to have an audience to their plays, the Eclectic Theatre had to rely for its authors upon a few weedy-minded young men who were content to dish out parodies of the Northern dramatists as new and original plays,

or upon the Northern dramatists themselves.

The Eclectic was unlike any theatre Mr. Wolverhampton had ever seen. The audience, conversing in whispers in the dimly-lighted auditorium or waiting silently in fervent anticipation for the rising of the curtain, resembled more a church congregation than any other kind of assembly. About half the hundred odd seats available were empty. Programmes (free) and chocolates were to be had, not from paid menials, but from a number of elegantly-dressed young ladies who served you in an awkward manner calculated to demonstrate conclusively their amateur status. There was no orchestra — as one of the directors put it neatly, at the Eclectic Theatre the play was to be the thing. . . .

In the auditorium, Mr. Wolverhampton espied one familiar face, that of Lucius Loftus, beside whom were two seats, which Lelia and he promptly appropriated. Mr. Loftus greeted them in friendly fashion, and then Mr. Wolverhampton turned to scrutinise the programme.

"*Uncle Vanya* by Anton Tchekoff," he read, "preceded by *The Cock and the Bull*, a psycho-allegorical comedy by Lucius Loftus."

"So the curtain-raiser's by you," he said, turning to the poet.

"Yes," said Loftus, "though I demur to your designation. *The Cock and the Bull* is a play; the curtain-raising business is left to the scene-shifters."

"I didn't know you wrote plays," said F.F. [Mr. Wolverhampton].

"I don't. This is my first."

"What does — er — spiko — what-you-may-call-it mean?" pursued F.F.

"Nothing, so far as I know," replied Loftus. "The play is a mere light-hearted comedy, but if I hadn't called it psychosomething it would never have been accepted by this temple of the muses."

"Well, why didn't you take it to the other theatres?"

"I did. But it was too Irish for the Gaiety, and not Irish enough for the Abbey, so there was nothing else for it but the Eclectic. . . ."

Mr. Wolverhampton enjoyed the play immensely. It was, he declared, the funniest thing he'd ever listened to: far funnier than *Charley's Aunt* or *The Private Secretary*. His hearty laughter rang through the theatre, sounding high above the intellectual chuckles of the rest of the audience. Undeniably these latter were enjoying the crude merriment of the piece, but as they wanted it to be understood that it was the subtler undercurrent of psychological satire supposed to be present that they really enjoyed, they could turn to each other every now and again with knowing looks and say: "There's irony for you", or "Subtle, isn't it" or such-like comment.

"Deep! Deep!" Mr. Cavanagh would mutter every now and again when some particular sally would convey an underlying meaning to his probing brain.

"This is damn good," said a candid gentleman in the seat behind, to his companion. "But I confess I can't see any of those double meanings you promised me."

"Ah!" replied the other appreciatively. "They're there all the same. I'm not sure I see them all myself, but I know they're there. That fellow, Loftus, is a subtle genius, and he wouldn't write a word that hadn't a double significance in it. Why, the whole play is symbolical of some psychological process of which we know nothing. . . ." [43]

When the Irish Theatre opened its doors on 4 January, for the first time on its own premises, it presented a quadruple bill of Chekhov, Villiers de L'isle Adam, an Irish translation of Rutherford Mayne, and the first production of Eimar O'Duffy's *The Phoenix on the Roof*. Jacques remarked:

> The home of the Irish Theatre in Dublin is unpretentious; the aim of the theatre is not. The home is a converted schoolhouse in Hardwicke Street, the aim is to produce drama of ideas. The directors are Messrs. Edward Martyn, Thomas MacDonagh, and Joseph Plunkett. The manager is Mr. John MacDonagh.[44]

In the initial programme, the aims of the theatre were defined as an attempt

> . . . to apply the methods of the Abbey Theatre to an organisation for the encouragement and production of native Irish drama other than the peasant species, and thereby see if by study and perseverance we may similarly create a school of young dramatists who will devote themselves to this particular department. Our plays, both native and translations of foreign masterpieces, shall be those not usually acted by professionals. We will also act plays, co-operating with the Gaelic players, in the Irish language, from which, of course, peasant subjects must not be excluded.[45]

Of the opening night *The Irish Times* reported:

This little theatre has been considerably renovated recently, and further repairs are in progress. When these are completed, it will be fairly comfortable. The gentlemen associated with the management have placed before themselves a high ideal, and even if they do not fully attain it, they will still have done good work in furthering literature and dramatic art in Dublin. During the present week four playlets are being staged, each of which has its own individual merit, and provides many opportunities for good acting. *The Troth*, by Rutherford Mayne, is given in Liam O'Domhnaill's Irish translation. It deals with the bad old days of eviction in the time of the Land League, and was very capably enacted. *The Revolt* is a one-act French play of Villiers de l'Isle Adam, according to Teresa Barclay's translation. When first given in Paris in 1870, it was objected to by the Censor, and withdrawn after three nights. To the translation acted last night the most sensitive could take no objection, and the scene is such as might take place in any home where the ideals of life are replaced by the greed of gold and the desire for gain. *The Phoenix on the Roof* is a satire in one act by Eimar O'Duffy, given for the first time. This young Irish author shows much insight into the Irish character and ingenuity in his satire. The sketch is one of some merit, and proves that something better may sub-sequently be expected from the same writer. *The Swan Song*, by Anton Tchekoff, according to Marian Fell's translation, is a powerful dramatic sketch, showing how an actor of 68, after being forty-five years on the stage, makes the triumph of his career; but, in a subsequent soliloquy, in which selections from *Hamlet*, *Lear*, and *Othello* are recited, he emphasises that success has come too late, and that he has neither home, wife, nor children, or any of the things which really make life worth living. The four pieces were on the whole reasonably well acted by all who took part, and any imperfections appar-ent on the first night can easily be remedied in subsequent performances. The same programme stands good for the week, and the promoters deserve encouragement for the pluckiness of their venture, and are to be congratulated on the success already attained.[46]

*The Irish Citizen* thought this performance more successful than the group's first which had taken place in 1914 in the Little Theatre in O'Connell Street. Of O'Duffy's play, the reviewer wrote:

In *The Phoenix on the Roof*, a delightful satire, it is the woman (charmingly acted by Cathia Ní Cormaic), who from the first has no doubts as to the reality of the ideal, and who persuades her lover to fetch the phoenix egg which for them contains all potentialities of happiness. In this and in Tchekoff's *Swan Song*, the honours of the acting were with John MacDonagh. The Irish Theatre should afford a healthy stimulus to the Abbey Theatre Company, several of whose members were among the scanty first-night audience.[47]

On 12 February, the theatre revived Edward Martyn's *The Dream Physician* for five performances, and for the week of 19 April Thomas MacDonagh's *Pagans* and O'Duffy's *The Walls of Athens* were given first productions. Neither occasioned much comment, but *The Evening Mail* reported:

The Irish Theatre, Hardwicke Street, is developing an interesting branch of Irish drama. The plays produced have been distinctive; there has been no following an outstanding pattern, either in ideas or form.

Last night, the company staged two new plays. *The Walls of Athens*, by Mr. Eimar O'Duffy, is a vigorously written dramatic comedy. It is concerned with the Athenians and the long walls that connected the city with her seaport, the Peiraieus. The play begins in the twenty-seventh and last year of the Peloponnesian war, 405 B.C. Phryne, a vegetable-seller, is the chief character, and the author was fortunate in having so fine an actress as Miss Kathleen MacCormack to interpret the part. Phryne intrigued with consummate skill, prevented the Athenians from surrendering until her supply of vegetables was sold at famine prices, and swayed the Demos with her wily tongue. She plays her unscrupulous game so well that even the Spartan conqueror is forced to leave portion of the wall intact, to provide Phryne of the Walls with an advertisement. The play develops smoothly. At two points the dialogue, which, on the whole, is bright and natural, could be improved. These are minor defects, however, and Mr. O'Duffy is to be congratulated upon a fine piece of work. He has caught some of the atmosphere of antique Greece, and uses it well. The costumes by the Dun Emer Guild, and the scenery by Mr. Jack Morrow, were excellent. Miss MacCormack was beyond criticism; the parts of Theramenes, Cleander, and the armourmaker were also very well portrayed.

Mr. Thomas MacDonagh's *Pagans* is a peculiar play, interesting and elusive in the treatment of a matrimonial *mésalliance*. The author approaches the question from an unusual point of view, and the result might be described as a study in psychology. At times there is a note of confidence, but the problem of incompatibility is, one might say, too successfully depicted. The husband drifts; the wife, despite her declared strength of mind, does not seem to know what should be done; Helen Noble, another passivist lover, provides a hope of possible happiness for two of the distressed trio. Mr. MacDonagh has raised the curtain upon a realistic domestic scene. It is interesting but too fatalistic, too Muscovite, to be pleasant. Miss Una O'Connor, Miss Grace Mac-Cormack, Miss Lelia McMurrough, and Mr. John McDonagh represented the various characters.[48]

On 20 May, the pupils of Patrick Pearse's St. Enda's School performed at the Irish Theatre, doing Pearse's *Iosagán* in Irish and his *The Master* in English. On the same occasion, Pearse addressed the audience briefly on the Irish style of dramatic speaking, 'and referred to the beautiful modulations of voice and the remarkable manner in which the meaning and the poetry of the subject were conveyed by those possessing the genuine old Irish style.' His address was illustrated by the performance for the first time on any stage of the ancient dramatic fragment, *Dunlaing Og agus an Leannan Sidhe*, '. . . the persons represented being Dunlaing, the hero, and his fairy lover'.[49] This fragment was said to have been 'handed down traditionally in County Kerry, and forming part of a long play which was enacted among the people probably up to the forties of the last century'.[50] The performances of the St. Enda's boys in Pearse's plays were admired: '. . . . the boys displayed confidence and ease in their acting, which was devoid of the stiltedness that frequently mars the efforts of youthful performers.'[51]

Late in June, George Moore was in Dublin and wrote a typically Georgian puff for the Irish Theatre's forthcoming production of *Uncle Vanya* during the week of 28 June. He began:

To the Editor of *The Irish Times*

Sir,— It is a long time since you have printed any bit of prose of mine in English or in French, and finding myself in Dublin, I am tempted to send you something lest this visit should seem visionary to me and my friends. . . . My morning was spent with my old friend, Edward Martyn, whom I found in distressful conditions suffering from rheumatic gout. But, despite his swollen foot, he seemed as glad as ever to talk art, and . . . we fell to talking of masterpieces. And it was pleasant to find, after many years of absence, that our preferences were as of yore. Dear Edward admires Tchekoff, and his

397

works please me more than those of any modern writer since Tourguenoff.

Then, after some reflections on how his friend 'Tourguenoff' would have admired 'Tchekoff', and after a longish discussion of *The Cherry Orchard*, Moore continued:

> The Stage Society in London produced this play, and it was hissed, and my object has been for many years to induce the Stage Society to reproduce it, and so great is my desire to see it that there is no reasonable sum I would not pay to see a performance of it.
>
> Another play by Tchekoff is *Uncle Vanya*, and Mr. Edward Martyn will produce it next week. This play was also produced by the Stage Society, but alas, I missed seeing it, and have not yet found time to read it. But all my friends have seen it, and my friends are men for the most part of very fine discrimination; they all tell me they know of nothing as perfect since Ibsen — new forms, new modes of expression, and above all, a beautiful touch. No one ever had a more beautiful touch than Tchekoff, and in the last analysis, art is touch. . . . It would take a great deal indeed, to prevent me from being present at the performance of *Uncle Vanya*.
>
> Yours, etc.
>
> GEORGE MOORE[52]

To O'Duffy's Mr. Wolverhampton, the evening was a rather less pleasant experience:

> If *The Well of the Saints* had been a puzzle to Mr. Wolverhampton, *Uncle Vanya* was sheer chaos. The rise of the curtain disclosed a garden in which a querulous old professor, his discontented young wife, his former wife's absent-minded mother, his maudlin hypochondriac brother-in-law, the latter's ugly niece, a disillusioned vodka-bibbing doctor, and a pock-marked man who had seen better days, sat or strolled about, or wandered off and on, telling each other or thinking aloud how bored they were and what wrecks they had made of their lives. In the whole cast there was only one normal human being — an old peasant woman; all the rest were morbid, self-conscious, perverse, aimless monomaniacs. Someone proclaimed his love for someone's else's wife towards the end of the act, and then, to the tinkle of a guitar, the scene came to a close. There was more talking and soliloquising, with a little drinking thrown in, in the second act. The inaction meandered through Act III, and then suddenly things began to happen.

The doctor kissed the professor's wife, the maudlin uncle shot at the professor, and Mr. Wolverhampton woke up feeling more at home — feeling, in fact, as if he were in the Queen's Theatre. With the fourth act, however, the situation eased. The doctor and the professor's wife kissed again, it is true, but nothing else occurred to break the dialogue; and, with the depature of the bulk of the caste for the city, the play closed with the remainder yawning in their chairs.[52]

The theatre then closed for the summer and did not re-open until 8 November when Martyn's new three-act play, *The Privilege of Place* was performed. *The Evening Mail* did not think the play was up to the standard of *The Heather Field*, a comment which, not without justice, greeted the production of every new Martyn play.

Mr. Martyn has done better work, and we hope his future writing will bear more distinctly the imprint of his undoubted talent. It is not that *Privilege of Place* is worse than many plays which have been "successful"; it is because a higher standard is looked for from his pen that his admirers will experience a slight feeling of disappointment. During the first act it seemed that a most excellent play had been made, but the treatment of the middle and last acts was unsatisfactory. The sentiments expressed at times appeared a little tawdry. Occasionally also a gap in the development of Owen was left unbridged. So much for criticism.

The play will be found very interesting, and there is some brilliant dialogue. The central idea is big; indeed one is reminded of Ibsen and the European school of playwrights, of which he was the founder. Sir Matthew Hort teaches that there are two codes of morals; that place has its privilege. His son yields to the father's stronger will and gives up "foolish ideals". The play deals with the son's development until he emancipates his soul by public avowal of a fraud, by which he had passed an important examination. A picture of what is alleged to be life in a Dublin official's house is presented. The great Scandinavian's influence is again shown in this; but the ruggedness of Ibsen characters needs to be supported by a sense of their sincerity and power. This is missing in *The Privilege of Place*. The aid of the prompter was required too frequently. The first night of a new play by an amateur company is usually accompanied by this blemish. During the week this will disappear and the general effect of the play will be so much improved.

The acting, on the whole, was very good. Miss Lelia MacMurrough entered thoroughly into the spirit of her part, and did it well. Miss Máire Nic Shiubhlaigh and Miss Nell Byrne, both fine actresses, had comparatively small parts. The part of Mark Bodkin, described as an experimentalist in life, was efficiently played by Mr. Charles Power. Mr. John MacDonagh was not so convincing as we expected, but his part was the most difficult. In the first act Mr. J. Derham was clever and interesting, but somewhat dull when Owen reformed. Mr. Kerry Reddin has a good voice and, if a little over-emphasised at times, the part of Uncle Joseph was presented clearly and with considerable histrionic skill. Seán Mac Caoilte played Terence very naturally.[54]

On 27 December, there was another bill of one-acts, including revivals of *The Phoenix on the Roof* and *Swan Song*, and of Padraic O'Conaire's *Bairbre Ruadh* in Irish, and also the first production of John MacDonagh's *Author! Author! The Evening Mail* called MacDonagh's play 'a pleasant satire on peasant plays, peasant authors, and peasant dialogue', and thought it 'cleverly constructed', its humour plentiful and its satire subtle and effective.[55] *The Evening Herald* thought the play 'not of much substance', but amusing and well-received:

> The scene is laid in a "cheap Dublin Hotel" this year. A play called *The Corncrake* has been successfully produced in Dublin, and favourably criticised in the London Press, the authorship having been erroneously ascribed to an addle-pated looking person named John Henry, Knight of Balinafiddle, Co. Cork. An enterprising director of a London theatre entered into a contract with the supposed author for another new play, which he had just written, called *The Mare's Nest*, paying him £200 in respect of royalties. The real author of the plays, however, was Miss Annabella MacElhanney, also of Balinafiddle; and that young lady, who seemed to be engaged to the supposed author, turned up at the crucial moment and effectively asserted her rights, collaring the £200 and the signed contract, and threatening the London theatrical director and the leading actor of the Dublin theatre where *The Corncrake* was produced, who was aware of the real author of both plays, as a pair of swindlers.[56]

\*     \*     \*

400

In October, a new play, *Driftwood*, from Seumas O'Kelly appeared, but it received its initial performance at Miss Horniman's theatre in Manchester.

At the Gaiety Theatre, Manchester, there was a very welcome break in the succession of middle-aged plays with which we have been regaled of late (says *The Manchester Courier*). And not only was this the first appearance of a new play, *Driftwood*, but this fresh arrival gave one almost all the sensations that a good play should give. There was surprise, stimulation, humour, illumination, hint of tragedy, and taken as a whole, we had a cutting though kindly commentary on life as it is written and as it is lived.

The curtain rose on what appeared to be a potted and highly varnished version of *A Doll's House*. There was the conventional setting, evening, full dress; the wife, clad in black velvet, hatless, trailing a filmy cloak after her, the accompaniment of much luminous rhetoric, about to depart into the night. But just as you are beginning to get rather worried about the unreality of it all, the surprise comes. Perhaps it would be unfair to the audiences which are still to enjoy this surprise to reveal to them the nature of it, but you are very soon made aware that Mr. Seumas O'Kelly is no chicken at the playwriting business, nor is he under any delusions as to how people do act in real life when confronted with the matrimonial upheavals that face the couple in *Driftwood*.[57]

\*　　\*　　\*

A superb new commercial house, the Coliseum, was opened in Dublin on Easter Monday.

The building, which is situated at the back of the G.P.O., and consequently right in the city's main artery, runs from Henry Street, where the main entrance, with its imposing neo-Grec façade, is directly opposite Moore Street, to Prince's Street, and has taken twelve months to erect. Planned for luxury comfort and safety and replete with every accommodation and appurtenance, it may be said to be the last word in theatre construction. The architect was Mr. Bertie Crewe, who has been responsible for over sixty similar buildings in Great Britain and on the Continent, and has designed this building in collaboration with Mr. F. Bergin, the well-known Dublin architect.

Within the past few weeks the building has undergone a

transformation so rapid and thorough as to almost take one's breath away. Seating accommodation is provided for 3,000, and so ample are the emergency exits that the house could be cleared in three minutes. There are 400 stall tip-up seats, sumptuously upholstered, and with plenty of knee-space between, the carpeting being rich blue pile, and the draperies in old rose to harmonise with the cream and gold decoration. The stalls and circle patrons have spacious waiting foyers and there are 600 circle arm-chairs.

The biograph chamber is so designed that it will beautify, not mar the general scheme. There are eight boxes approached from the circle; and the pit and gallery approaches are in Prince's Street, the accommodation being for 800 patrons. Spacious saloon and ample cloak, etc., room has been provided, every fitting being of the most modern type. There is not a single column to obstruct the "sight lines". . . .

The stage is one of the largest ever constructed, being forty feet deep and eighty feet wide, and can effectively accommodate the largest revues and spectacular shows on tour. A portion of the stage floor, concealing a tank, can be easily removed for water-shows.

Messrs. H. and J. Martin Ltd., were the contractors, and Mr. W. Martin was clerk of works. It was announced in *The Dublin Gazette* last night that by Letters Patent authority had been granted to establish and keep for twenty-one years "a theatre or playhouse in Dublin to be known as the Coliseum Theatre".[58]

However, the owners were only able to keep the theatre open for one year. One year later, to the day, the Easter Rising commenced, when around the corner in O'Connell Street, Pearse read the Easter Proclamation. The Coliseum, situated right behind the General Post Office, was destroyed in the general holocaust in O'Connell Street.

Dramatically, the loss was not great, for the theatre's offerings were a series of mainly unmemorable variety programmes, among which were sometimes interspersed short dramatic skits or sketches. Also during the year, the Empire was redecorated and passed into the hands of Barney Armstrong, but the usual repertoire continued unchanged.

In one way, the commercial stage was losing ground to the cinema; and also the war, rising costs, and a lengthy dispute with the Dublin Steam Packet Company about the transportation of scenery and effects from England to Dublin, made it difficult for the Gaiety and the Royal to book the best attractions. Some kinds of plays, such as the spectacular melodrama, still popular at London's Drury Lane, almost ceased to appear in Ireland. The one instance of an expensively mounted spectacle which did appear in Dublin during the year was a touring company of *Sealed Orders*, the patriotic naval play which had run for three years in Drury Lane and which depended entirely on its effects, such as 'an illuminated ball on a super-Dreadnought, the destruction of a Zeppelin by gunfire, a hand-to-hand struggle in mid-air, kidnapping in a motor, rescue from the ocean . . . and other spectacular depictures calling for the use of motors, airships, searchlights, explosives and other strange stage mechanisms.' (The above description, incidentally, concludes by noting that the play 'is essentially a warlike one'.[59]) However, if this sort of thing is to be effective, it must be done with great smoothness, and conditions of the time made smoothness impossible. In this instance, the effects were ineffective:

> Apart from those who delight to honour the spectacular only in drama, I greatly fear that the audiences of the week will find in *Sealed Orders* much that is not only unreal but boring, much too that will constrain them to laughter if not to tears. In the first place it is quite outside the bounds of reason to expect an audience to sit down to a placid contemplation of a play with over forty characters and fourteen scenes, on the last of which the curtain did not descend until 11.20. The play as it stands speaks trumpet-tongued of the advantages of drama twice nightly. This represents the extent to which the play might be boiled down without any disadvantage to the plot or its development. The constant changing of scene — such an objectionable feature of this type of melodrama — produces nothing but irritation in the mind of the audience, which finds mental concentration an impossibility, as it is being whisked from scene to scene in a manner which produces nothing but bewilderment. It is very rarely, too, that the sensational mechanical features which are advertised as forming such an important part of these productions can be adequately represented. Of these last night there were many; but only one might be said to have been a success spectacularly — the robbery at the diamond merchants by burglars, who made an entry through the floor of the room above. This, of course, was quite within the mechanical capacity of the theatre, but the same cannot be said of the business with the airship in the last act, which was hopelessly

unrealistic. I have often wondered, too, why melodramatic actors find it necessary to shout the most ordinary dialogue. Last night I discovered the secret. It is in order that their words may be heard above the din of changing scenery at the back. Notwithstanding the best vocal efforts of the artistes much of the dialogue was lost in the pandemonium which reigned almost throughout the whole performance. A noise suggestive of belated carpentry repairs is not the best incentive to a dispassionate study of the drama.[60]

The movies could do it better, and it cost little to transport a can of film. Nevertheless, the melodrama with a plethora of exciting incidents, and perhaps a small spectacle which could be transported by a second-class touring company, continued to flourish at the Queen's, and the occasional spectacular one-act still toured the music-halls. For instance, in July the Coliseum included on its bill a playlet called *The Burning Forest* which depicted 'with entirely realistic effect one of the many perils that beset the life of settlers out West. Flames are seen spurting and trees falling, whilst a railway train rushes through the blazing mass. It is worthy of note that this great spectacle is presented by means of skilful electrical contrivances, and that not a spark of real fire is used.' [61] Also, during the week of 15 August, the Coliseum presented a revue that featured a water spectacle entitled *Tronville on Sea*, and that involved filling the stage tank with 50,000 gallons of water for the bathing belles to disport in.[62]

The growing popularity of films even affected to some extent what people saw in the theatre. The Charlie Chaplin craze came to rival the Tango craze, and innumerable Chaplin imitators appeared in the music-halls. This was particularly evident in the revue *Charlie Chaplin Mad* which promised that patrons of the Coliseum during the week of 27 September would see 'A Stage full of Charlie Chaplins', including 'The only Charlie Chaplin Girl Extant'. The legitimate theatre also tried to exploit the new medium, and the Royal and the Gaiety booked English companies in plays called *The Cinema Star* and *The Girl on the Film*. In *The Girl on the Film*, one scene purported to show an actual film being shot: '. . . acted before the camera just as it is portrayed on the stage in real life. . . . To add to the interest the film which the audience had watched being taken is actually displayed to them in the last act.' [63]

Little of Irish interest played at the commercial houses, but on 11 October there appeared at the Gaiety an Irish-American comedy, *Peg o' My Heart*, by J. Hartley Manners, which had already been a great success in London and New York. The American production had starred Laurette Taylor who, many years later, was to perform memorably as the mother in Tennessee Williams's *The Glass Menagerie*. In the English touring company, her part was played by Sara Allgood, and of her performance Jacques wrote effusively:

> You rarely hear cheers at the Gaiety — loud, lusty hurrahs. We heard cheers last night at the Gaiety. Such cheers as did the heart good. The public at last got something worthwhile, something topical, something Irish, something that brought the freshness of our mountain breezes to the theatre. *Peg o' Me Heart* — I write it as it is spoken, not spelt — is a Hartley-Manners's modern comedy, and a heartly welcome comedy of manners. There's a human element underlying the comedy; there are international lessons to be learnt from it. . . . The play we saw last night is the philosophy of optimism. . . .
>
> Well, Sara Allgood was that girl — Sara Allgood run loose, sliding on the carpets, jumping on the chairs, causing pandemonium in Regal Villa and giving her audience that pain in the face that follows continuous laughter. But Sara must practice the laugh. That sudden "bark" that explodes from her every time she is highly amused sounds unnatural. It's not a bit like the jolly laugh of our Abbey Theatre Sara. And does she not overdo the gawky moments a little bit? After one month at Regal Villa she should be able to move without sprawling. We don't want our Peg to look such a shocking fright all the time. As for the rest she makes Peg the fiery little Fenian, Peg the child philosopher, Peg the pure, Peg the picture of passionate pleading, Peg "the playboy", Peg the pathetic — she makes this Peg the most charming conception of Irish girlhood ever presented on our stage. Peg of her father's heart is Peg of all our hearts.[64]

The play is a piece of commercial stage-Irish hokum, but hokum with even still a residue of vitality. In the Spring of 1977, camp versions of the play were running both in Dublin and off Broadway in New York. However, the lingering interest in this 1915 production lies not in the play itself, but in its Irish reception. Peg was basically a female Handy-Andy, or indeed, a sister to George A. Birmingham's Mary Ann, the servant girl of *General John Regan*. But in this instance the ludicrous Irish girl occasioned no patriotic protests, but merely genial delight.

The touring companies which visited the Queen's were ever receptive to the interests of the audience, and so included among their usual subjects of cowboys, detectives, long-suffering mothers, and innocent Lancashire mill girls, a rash of plays about the war — among them such 'powerful military dramas' as *Dick the Trumpeter, It's a Long Way to Tipperary, Boys of the Bulldog Breed, A Son of Belgium,* and *The Son of a Soldier.* P. J. Bourke, whose company usually visited the Queen's once or twice a year, rented the Abbey in 1915 for the first production of his patriotic Irish melodrama, *For the Land She Loved.* Usually these neo-Boucicault melodramas were accorded scant attention in the Press, but on this occasion W. J. Lawrence reviewed the play at length:

For sheer irony of circumstances, an Irish drama of the old, illogical, and cheaply patriotic order, which the Abbey Theatre was instituted to kill, has had its first production at that theatre. Barring that it has few glints of relieving humour, *For the Land She Loved* is just the sort of play that the late Hubert O'Grady would have delighted in taking round the provinces. It has all the picturesque exteriority, all the bustle and movement, and all the appalling inconsistency which marked the old school of Irish melodrama. Seemingly for that sort of play there is still a considerable public. Round about the pathetically true story of Betsy Gray, the Ulster Joan of Arc of '98, who laid down her life on the gory battlefield of Ballynahinch, Mr. P. J. Bourke has wound a stirring plot all compact of melodramatic criss-cross and the perversity of passion. Lady Lucy Nugent (whence her title?), daughter of General Sir John Nugent, commander in Ireland of the British Forces, has conceived a devouring passion for the gallant Munro, leader of the rebels in the North, but Munro is steadfast in his affection for Betsy Gray, the daughter of Squire Gray, "the Lord Lieutenant of County Down", and all the fires in Lady Lucy's breast turn to hate. In her frenzy she lends a willing ear to the machinations of Colonel Johnston, an English officer, who is the arch-villain of the piece, and who, for purely mercenary reasons, is desirous to espouse the unhappy Betsy Gray. During an attempt to arrest General Munro whilst he is visiting the forge of Matt McGrath, a pike-making blacksmith, Squire Gray is shot dead in a surreptitious way by Lady Lucy, and the blame of the deed fastened on the rebel leader. But, thanks to the good offices of the loving Betsy Gray, who manages to get the charges extracted from his guards' muskets, Munro escapes and contrives to get on board a French schooner lying in Belfast lough. A stirring scene ensues when the schooner is chased and fired at unavailingly by a British sloop-of-war. The whole of the fourth act is devoted to the depiction of various episodes in the momentous battle of Ballynahinch, and here and there we get affecting glimpses of the true story of the ill-starred Betsy Gray. After successfully storming the town, the rebels mis-comprehend a bugle-call of retreat sounded by the British forces, and thinking their antagonists have received reinforce- ments, fly for their lives. In vain does Betsy Gray, who has led on the insurgents, strive to rally them. Her brother George is killed; she is herself assailed by the infuriated Lady Lucy Nugent, and a fight with knives between the two women ensues, in the midst of which the loyalist leader's daughter is killed by a chance shot. Poor Betsy herself meets her fate by rushing in between the clashing swords of her lover, Munro, and a redoubtable English officer. The day is lost.

Although there were some signs of insufficient rehearsal towards the close — sundry haltings which slackened the tension of the cumulative interest of the battle scenes — the acting on the whole was on a much higher plane of merit than the play. First honours went to Peggy Courtney for her richly sympathetic and, at times, forcible renderings of the ill-starred Betsy Gray. Aided and abetted by the quietly im-pressive acting of John Connolly as the gallant Munro, Miss Courtney, by a plausible sincerity of method, accomplished the difficult feat of keeping the play and its plot in occasional touch with the possible. Kitty Carrickford, whom Nature has endowed with a finely-moulded figure, and who has the gift of picturesque dressing, gave a full-flavoured, unabashed impersonation of the melodramatically-conceived Lady Lucy Nugent, and while undeniably effective in a conventional way, was a trifle disposed to force the note. P. J. Bourke, the author of the play, merits commendation for the phlegm and restraint with which he depicted the unblushing villainies of the ruthless Colonel Johnston. Our only plaint is that he somewhat over-dressed the part, being much more gorgeous in array than the surrounding English officers of considerably higher rank. A few of the other players showed capacity much beyond the demands of their parts, notably M. Carolan, who found little to exercise his gifts of easy natural humour upon in the some-what hazily outlined Dermot McMahon, Squire Gray's man-servant. Much the same remark applies to their claws. Mr. H. E. Hutchinson, on the other hand, gave an almost faultless rendering of the loutish and taciturn James Simpson.[65]

* * *

407

There continued during the year a good deal of criticism of the moral tone of public entertainment, particularly the offerings of the music-halls and cinemas. A typical criticism of the music-hall appears in this letter from 'Citizen':

> Where will this kind of thing end? What will it lead to? What will be the moral condition and reputation of the people of Dublin when they are thoroughly accustomed to performances of this kind? Questions like these were asked as a friend and myself left a Dublin music-hall after witnessing a "Revue" performance very recently. . . .
> From the point of view of the audience these shows are doubly objectionable. First, they are demoralising, and if they are allowed to go on unchecked it is impossible that a high standard of morality can continue to be maintained in our city. Any noodle can make double-meaning and dirty jokes, and a show girl requires no ability and no accomplishment except a willingness to allow herself to be exhibited in a more or less nude condition. . . .[66]

At the same time, that vigilant defender of the public's morals, William Larkin, continued his crusade. One instance occurred in September when the Bohemian Picture House in Phibsborough was showing a film attributed to C. Haddon Chambers and entitled *A Modern Magdalen*. Larkin arose during the performance to shout, 'It is time we had an Irish Censor Board', and this caused 'the audience to rise from their seats and a general stampede amongst them, and when asked to desist by the manager [Larkin] repeated the above words while leaving the theatre. He was also charged with obstructing the entrance to the theatre by making a speech from the steps outside. . . .'[67] After several appearances in court, Larkin was eventually fined five shillings.

\*　　\*　　\*

In May, *The Evening Herald* reported that a letter had been received from Count Markievicz who

> . . . is at present in hospital at Lemberg, recovering from typhus fever. At the outbreak of the war he joined his old Hussar regiment at Achtynsky, and saw severe fighting. He was in the Carpathian mountains, where he had some terrible experiences. The snow at times, he relates, was four feet deep, and under such conditions the soldiers had to advance. At the beginning of the war he contracted pneumonia, and in an

engagement was wounded in the side. He was taken into a hospital at Lemberg suffering from typhus, and is now convalescent. He is to return to his regiment in August. According to a letter received this morning, he has not yet recovered the use of his left arm.[68]

And, of course, much worse news was to come for Ireland and its theatre.

# Appendix I :

## The Abbey Company in America, 1911–1912

Between 1911 and 1912, the Abbey company made three extended tours to North America. The first tour lasted about five and a half months and received wide publicity because of the Irish-American opposition to Synge's *Playboy*. In New York, there was a rowdy disturbance in the theatre when the play was first performed, and in Philadelphia its actors were arrested. The second and third tours were peaceful, and the company was greeted with considerable critical acclaim, if not with overwhelming box office receipts.

The first tour is treated separately here in some detail because its dramatic events are of significance for the theatrical history of both Ireland and the United States. However, that significance goes well beyond the exciting contemporary events of theatre riots, court cases and newspaper controversy that are detailed below. The lasting significance of the tours is their honing of American dramatic taste. Influence is impossible to gauge precisely, but it would certainly seem unarguable that the Abbey example was a major factor in changing the nature and quality of the American drama.

\*     \*     \*

Even before the Abbey players arrived in America, there were signs that their tour would, in one way or another, arouse controversy. In July, *The New York Times* editorialised:

> The announcement that the players of the Irish National Theatre, under the guidance of William Butler Yeats and Lady Gregory, will visit the United States next Autumn is most interesting. As they represent an idea and also an ideal, we hope they will be cordially received, but we have not noticed that the theatrical taste of our people had been tending largely toward the poetical, the mystical, the subtly humorous, or the obscure. . . . It was a complaint of the late Edward Harrigan that the kind of Irish play most popular with Irish Americans is the one in which an Irishman in a green wig drives a nail into the head of an Irishman in a pink wig. . . . We should feel surer of Irish American support of the Irish National players if the plays were to be of the old-fashioned, frankly sentimental sort like *The Shaughraun* and *The Colleen Bawn*.[1]

Presently W. B. Yeats issued a rebuttal calculated to bring spectators into the theatre, but unfortunately not calculated to ally the patriotic suspicions of Irish-Americans:

> In your issue of July 14 [*sic*] there is a sympathetic article upon the forthcoming visit of the Irish players to the United States. There is, however, a sentence which would lead to misunderstanding, and it may be to the practical injury of our enterprise. You imply that our plays are "poetic", "mystical", 'subtly humorous", and "obscure". This impression has perhaps arisen from my being Managing Director of the theatre, and a poet (Are not all poets supposed to be mystical and obscure?) The artisans, clerks, shopboys, and shopgirls who crowd our pit and gallery, and have been the main support of our movement for years, would not accept your impression. An intellectual movement in Ireland has to begin with the classes or the masses that it may win both in the end, and our work has begun among the masses. We are no dillettante theatre appealing to a few educated and leisured men and women. We have moved our audiences to riot (Have we not been under police protection?), to enthusiasm, and to laughter, but we have never played to indifferent curiosity — that is, "the subtly humorous". Synge's intellect was subtle because it was profound, but his laughter was as riotous as that of Shakespeare or Molière or Aristophanes; and Lady Gregory's little comedies are at this moment being played very successfully by some of our players during their holidays to music-hall audiences in England.[2]

After that overture, the Abbey company arrived in Boston in the last week of September to open what was initially meant to be a two-week engagement at the Plymouth Theatre. The company had been preceded by considerable agitation in the Irish-American press. As Edward Abood mildly put it, 'The Irish-Americans lacked critical detachment.'

> Their writing was emotionally charged and generally abusive. They referred to the Irish dramatists as "neurotic, decadent, and non-Gaelic" disciples of Zola, and to the Irish plays as "hybrid abortions"; they compared the Irish Players to a "hyena or carrion crow which prowls about a battlefield" and to "vermin that feed upon the corpses found there"; they denounced the company as a "shameless and mercenary crew who are coining money by catering to a prurient curiosity and malignant bigotry. . . ."[3]

411

There was a very good deal of such fustian during the company's stay in America, and there was even the suggestion made that the entire project was financed by the English Tory party as a method of discrediting the Irish character and thereby hindering the passage of the Home Rule bill.[4] All of this Irish brouhaha led to a peculiarly American phenomenon, which is still recognizable in American Supreme Court obscenity rulings — the municipal judgment.

Approached by delegates from various Irish-American patriotic societies, Mayor Fitzgerald of Boston sent his secretary Mr. Leahy to evaluate *The Playboy*. Leahy's report was a hearteningly judicious statement which basically concluded that 'The play is simply a wild extravaganza, to be taken as we take Aristophanes, and characterized by the same extremes of delineation.' Appended to Leahy's report was a note stating that the Mayor and Police Commissioner were at the first *Playboy* performance and saw no reason for any portion of the play to be censored. As Yeats noted in *The New York Times*: 'As to the opposition in Boston, it is the opposition of individuals and not of organizations. Lady Gregory is to be entertained next Sunday night by a branch of the Gaelic Society in Boston, and we have been in receipt of many congratulatory letters from prominent Irishmen of that city.' Of the Gaelic League reception, Lady Gregory wrote, 'The League presented me with a big bouquet of daffodils, and the President came back and told me: "Whoever is against you, the Gaelic League is with you." '

The Boston engagement seemed to be a total victory for the theatre over its critics, and the productions were so enjoyed and admired that the run was extended from two to five weeks. Yeats, who had returned to Dublin, was interviewed by *The Irish Times*, and said that:

> Our American success has surpassed all our expectations. Our engagement was to the end of December, with a possibility of waiting until the end of May. The syndicate is now trying to persuade us to stay till May, but our players feel that they should return to Dublin, and carry on their work here, notwithstanding the monetary loss. They will probably remain in the States until the end of February. . . . Our greatest successes up to this have been *The Well of the Saints*, which has never had a reception approaching its reception in Boston, *Blanco Posnet* and *The Playboy of the Western World*. I am speaking, of course, only of the long plays. Lady Gregory's little comedies have delighted everybody, but one cannot measure

412

their success in actual drawing power, as owing to their short-ness they are never the main piece of an evening.[5]

On 9 October, part of the programme was the first and apparently the only Abbey production of Johanna Redmond's *Falsely True*. As historians have never heretofore noted that this play was produced by the Abbey, we might note briefly its initial reception. *The Boston Globe* thought the piece had 'a graphic, pitiful realism' and compelled 'the absorbed and sympathetic interest of the audience'. *The Boston Journal* thought it 'a gloomy sort of appetizer, and *The Boston Evening Transcript* in the only critique of any length and substance concluded flatly that 'Miss Redmond is no dramatist.' One can only surmise that the theatre's reasons for staging the play were more politic than aesthetic.[6]

After the heady Boston success, the company made its way circuitously to New York city, with brief performances on the way in Providence, Rhode Island (30 October–1 November), Lowell, Massachussetts (4 November), New Haven, Connecticut (6–7 November), and Washington, D.C. (13–18 November). In New Haven, the Police Commissioner, acting for the Mayor, attended a rehearsal of what he thought was *The Playboy*, and departed requiring the suppression of only a few phrases. Actually, he had seen rehearsals of *Blanco Posnet* and of *The Image*.

The tour thus far had encountered little significant opposition, but on 9 October *The New York Times* had reported a meeting which was both amusing and ominous:

> At a meeting of the United Irish-American societies, held last night at the Irish American Athletic Club, 110 East Fifty-ninth Street, resolutions were passed condemning the play by G. [*sic*] N. Synge, *The Plowboy* [*sic*] *of the Western World*, which is announced to be presented here by the Irish players now appearing in Boston. The resolutions say that the play is immoral and not true to Irish character, and that it makes a hero of a parasite [*sic*]. At the meeting last night it was said that an effort would be made to prevent the production of the play in New York.[7]

The company arrived in New York on 19 November, to open a six-week engagement, from 19 November to 30 December, at the Maxine Elliott Theatre. Lady Gregory, interviewed at her hotel, the Algonquin, attempted to minimize the criticism of the repertoire and to placate the critics:

> She is a jolly, pleasant-faced woman, and full of pride in her grandchildren. . . . The opposition shown to Synge's drama,

413

*The Playboy of the Western World*, in Boston and in other places has been due, according to Lady Gregory, to a misunderstanding of Synge's purpose. Even those who found fault with its subject, and felt that the play did not give a real picture of Irish life, were still of the opinion that it was good drama. . . . The troubles the players had when they first appeared in Dublin, said Lady Gregory, have made opposition received here seem quite natural. They are used to being in hot water. The action taken by various Irish societies in condemning plays, she believed, was due altogether to misunderstandings, and to something that might be called "race sensitiveness".[8]

The focal point of trouble, *The Playboy*, was not on the first week's bill. It was scheduled for its first New York performance on 27 November. On the morning of 27 November, a lengthy diatribe by Seumas MacManus appeared in the press, condemning not only *The Playboy*, but also some of the other plays, the policy of the theatre, and Yeats himself:

> But two qualities I have never set down for our people, because these two qualities I never discovered among them, and they are vulgarity and immodesty. Yet in *The Playboy* is shown us a simple Irish maiden of the remote coast, speaking in language that I feel confident very few girls of the street in New York or Chicago would bring themselves to use in ordinary conversation. Moreover, *The Playboy*, with which New York is to be regaled — that is, if the temper of the most Irish of Irish societies in America will permit — pictures these modest Irish maidens as tumbling over one another to win a blackguard whose fascination is that he murdered his father, or is supposed to have murdered him."

> Mr. MacManus said that it is a patriotic instinct in the Irish to side with anyone whom English law is against. . . . "But if there was one kind of crime that horrified our people and turned them in terror from the criminal, it was that almost unheard-of kind, parricide and the like. And apart from the gross immodesty and repulsive vulgarity which the Irish colleen stands for in this play, I know of no other viler libel that could be put upon her than, as in the play, to show her throwing herself at the head of a scoundrel who believed he had murdered his father — throwing herself at him because he was now her ideal hero."

MacManus also commented disparagingly about some unidentified other plays in the company's repertoire:

I have only spoken on *The Playboy of the Western World* as a particularly offensive play. There are one or two others, where, following the new idea of creating a sensation to help out drama, the very qualities that are not to be found in Ireland are chosen to set against an Irish background and clothed with an Irish atmosphere, and put forth to give some fascinating to that large and growing class of innocents, who, harmlessly thinking themselves thinkers, consider it a religious duty to shock and be shocked in a small way.

MacManus finally concluded by arguing that Yeats had sold out to the English:

Mr. Yeats, a young, strong, healthy man, with his beautiful mind and his genius, worth to Ireland ten thousand of us little mortals, was in the past year offered a pension by the British Government, and accepted it. Ireland has lost Yeats: Yeats has lost Ireland. There's no lover of Ireland but sorrows for both.[9]

MacManus was the Donegal writer whose best work was probably his excellent versions of folk-tales and fairy-tales. He had married Ethna Carberry, the poetess, and after her death he lived much of his long life in America. Readers of Volume II of this history may remember that the Irish National Theatre Society had produced one of his one-acts as an early offering, and that fact may have been in Lady Gregory's mind when she described him, after this outburst, as 'Shame-Us MacManus'.

Undoubtedly the long MacManus story gave fuel to the opposition that evening. After the evening's performance at the Maxine Elliott Theatre, Reuters News Service cabled this short account which appeared in *The Irish Times*:

The production by Lady Gregory's Irish players of *The Playboy of the Western World* led to a riot at Maxine Elliott's Theatre last night. Potatoes and eggs were hurled at the stage, and several actors were struck. The police were called in, and when a dozen of the disturbers had been arrested order was restored.

The Irish players announce that they will continue to act *The Playboy of the Western World*, depending upon an increased force of police to maintain order. The prisoners arrested yesterday evening are Irish-Americans, and it is understood that they made a demonstration because they regarded the play as a reflection upon the Irish character.[10]

A fuller, more accurate account appeared in *The New York Times*. This account makes it clear that the disturbance was hardly of riot proportions. The show did go on, albeit with police in the house, after theatre employees had squelched most of the trouble. The difficulties began as soon as Fred O'Donovan, who played Christy, spoke the words, 'I killed my father a week and a half ago for the likes of that':

Instantly voices began to call from all over the theatre: "Shame! Shame!"

A potato swept through the air from the gallery and smashed against the wings. Then came a shower of vegetables that rattled against the scenery and made the actors duck their heads and fly behind the stage setting for shelter.

A potato struck Miss Magee, and she, Irish like, drew herself up and glared defiance. Men were rising in the balcony and crying to stop the performance. In the orchestra several men stood up and shook their fists.

"Go on with the play," came an order from the stage manager, and the players took their places and began again to speak their lines.

The tumult broke out more violently than before, and more vegetables came sailing through the air and rolled about the stage. Then began the fall of soft cubes that broke up as they hit the stage. At first these filled the men and women in the audience and on the stage with fear for only the disturbers knew what they were.

Soon all knew. They were capsules filled with asafoetida, and their odour was suffocating and most revolting.

One of the theatre employees had run to the street to ask for police protection at the outset of the disturbance, but the response was so slow that the ushers and the door-tenders raced up the stairs and threw themselves into a knot of men who were standing and yelling "Shame!"

The employees grabbed these men and began hustling them towards the doors. Every one they got there was thrown out and followed until he became a rolling ball that thumped and thumped down the stairs. On the lower floor a big man caught them and threw them out without bothering to open the swinging doors first. . . . Men were rolling down the stairs and yelling out that they were being outraged and would have the law on somebody. Up the stairs ran half a dozen policemen. If they hesitated at the outset to take a hand in the row, they seemed to be anxious to make up for it now. No questions were asked, but they reached for every man who was on his feet and dragged him to the stairs, where willing hands helped him to the street.[11]

During the excitement, Lady Gregory remarked to reporters:

I wish the men who threw the things on the stage had taken better aim, for I can't believe that they intended to hit anybody. Miss Magee would have been injured if her thick hair had not protected her. She was struck on the head. . . . The play was first produced in January, 1907, in Dublin, but we had no trouble like this. The police put a stop to it. The second time it was put on in Dublin the disturbers were put out right at the beginning. We had some trouble in Boston and in Providence, but nothing like this.[12]

The final act of the evening occurred in Police Night Court. Trouble seemed to have been anticipated, for two attorneys were there to appear for the ten people who had been arrested. The hearing concerned itself with the nature of 'decent bounds' for expressing criticism, Magistrate Corrigan holding the view that the legal limits of protest precluded rowdy behaviour. Three of the defendants were released without penalty, and most of the others were fined from two to five dollars. One Shean O'Callaghan was fined ten dollars for throwing eggs from the balcony, and a witness against him was a Miss Emmet who alleged that she was a niece of Robert Emmet.

*The New York Times* gave both play and players an excellent notice, and the paper also commented sensibly on the affair in a leading article:

If the Arabs in New York should throw rotten eggs on the stage and abuse the actors because they felt that the realistic picture of proceedings in the Oriental dance house in *The Garden of Allah* was a reflection on the character of their race, New Yorkers would conclude that things had come to a pretty pass. Our theatre, such as it is (and there is plenty of it), is free. So long as the dramatists and actors avoid sedition and filth the authorities do not interfere with them. One of Shaw's plays was rather foolishly suppressed by order of a well-meaning Police Commissioner, but as few desired to see it little harm was done. Americans are prejudiced against hissing in the theatre. They have an idea that if one does not like a play he should either endure it in silence or go home. Others in the audience may like it, and we are rather particular here about the feelings of others. Our Irish-American fellow-

417

citizens should bear that fact in mind.

The row about *The Playboy of the Western World* is peculiarly Irish. Synge was a poet, and the aim and quality of his play are poetical. It is an outcome of the Gaelic movement, a small but genuine literary revival in Ireland which has interested scholars the world over. We need not discuss further the quality of the play or its motive, for all that has been done. Nobody doubts that the purpose of the Abbey Theatre and its players is wholly artistic. The skill of the actors is somewhat deficient, but they are at their best in this queer, partly droll, partly pathetic piece by the dead poet. Naturally a large number of playgoers hereabout have been anxious to see the performance. But a few quarrelsome Irish patriots, who claim American citizenship, though obviously they do not value it, declare that the posture of events, the characterization, and some of the text of *The Playboy* misrepresent Ireland, which they hold to be a land devoid of crime and violence, free from evil passions, and full of brotherly love and virtue. So the patriots invade the theatre, pelt the actors with missiles, and try to howl down the performance. Whereupon Irish-American policemen arrest them, and arraign them before an Irish-American Magistrate while the performance proceeds.

The delightful Hibernianism of it all is obvious, but the incident may not be dismissed as a joke. Even if the Irish players are employed by the British Government to create ill feeling against Ireland, which is one of the preposterous assertions of their Irish opponents, they have a right to a fair hearing in our theatre. But everybody knows that they are merely a band of enthusiasts working with a will to upbuild a national drama. The argument of the malcontents is not reasonable. They may object as strongly as they please to what they consider a false picture of Irish life, but as it was drawn by an Irishman, and is presented by Irish actors, under the most distinguished Irish auspices, it is possible that their objection is unreasonable. They must not be permitted, however, to turn any theatrical performance into a Donnybrook Fair.

New Englanders might as well become riotous over the portrayal of the brutal father in *Shore Acres*. Frenchmen in America might violently interrupt performances of French plays which depict immoral conditions in French society; Germans might prevent the production here of such plays as *Die Ehre*. But that is not to the point. There is a new and hopeful political movement in Ireland, which has all our

418

sympathy, and some of its adherents, who seem to lack literary appreciation and artistic sense, feel that Irish character has been belittled in literature and the drama, and that the time has come to correct the world's erroneous impression of their country. These particular adherents, however, have gone about the business in a way that will strike the world as particularly Irish, and by their violence, their insult to un-offending persons, their interference with the pleasure and business of others, have helped to justify the portrayal of ruffianism in the play. Synge's *Playboy* may or may not misrepresent the character of the Western Irish peasantry, but it is quite clear that the howlers and egg-throwers have grossly misrepresented the great body of law-abiding American citizens of Irish birth and descent.[13]

On the day after the disturbance, some prominent Irish-Americans went to City Hall to protest against further performances. A leader of the group was James Mark Sullivan who was to found the Irish Film Company.

Something approaching normalcy returned for the second night's performance which was attended by the mayor's official representative, Chief Magistrate McAdoo, and by Theodore Roosevelt. As *The New York Times* reported:

Hisses, sneezes, and groans contended with right good-natured laughter and applause at the second night's performance of *The Playboy of the Western World*. . . . No punishment was meted out to those who applauded the play, but six of those who made noisy demonstrations of disapproval were collared at various stages of the performance and thrust unceremoniously out of the balcony and gallery, bundled thumping down the stairs, and shoved by plain clothes members of the strong-arm squad into the street. . . .[14]

Although milder, the protest appears to have been organized and began during the performance of Lady Gregory's *Gaol Gate*:

Immediately there arose at various points in the balcony and gallery an epidemic of sneezing, complicated in many instances by a dangerous bronchial cough. Sneezing and coughing, not being in the ordinary list of crimes or misdemeanours, the detectives stationed in the audience at first were puzzled as to what treatment to accord it. Capt. McElroy and three of his men finally solved it by collaring one cough-racked man. . . . A woman companion joined in the protest. . . . " 'Tis a shame!" she cried. "They can manifest their approval, but

419

are arrested for showing disapproval!" [15]

Another leading article appeared in the *Times* on the following day, and this one made some salutary points that not even the most embattled defenders of the play had made in Ireland:

> Not much of the criticism directed against *The Playboy of the Western World* is articulate, but such of it as has appealed to the reason more directly than by throwing eggs, potatoes, bread crusts, and malodorous drugs, all simmers down to one often-repeated statement — the play presents the Irish peasant in a false light.
>
> Well, suppose it does? Why not? Who or what, in the name of history, of common sense, and of all the gods, male and female, is the Irish peasant that he shouldn't be presented in any light that any literary man, romancer or dramatist as the case may be, wants to present him? Who or what is the Irish peasant — or peer, for that matter — that he should escape the common lot of mortals, which is to supply "material" out of which stories and plays are made. . . . In a false light indeed! It is not to the falseness of the light in which Synge may or may not have presented the Irish peasant that these disturbers of the peace object. Never a one of them raised a single yelp, or even a single whine, while through innumerable years the Irish peasant has been presented in the falsest possible light — that of a knee-breech hero in a tailed coat, whose entire life is spent in singing sentimental songs, rescuing persecuted heroines from the deep pool below the waterfall and administering corporal punishment to British villains with a mortgage on the old farm. . . . All that was as false as it could possibly be. . . . But it was also flattery, and therefore it was received with smiling contentment, or the higher tribute of happy tears, by exactly the sort of people who are now putting so much of professional heat into their absurd resentment of a play that doesn't minister to their racial illusions and conceits. . . . Who is to say what vices, weaknesses, and imbecilities are not to be found in or around a miserable, low-down drinking-place, even in Ireland? And if a genius discovers and reveals poetry and humour even there, is it his fitting reward to be lynched as a traitor and liar? [16]

A news story in the same issue of *The Times* noted that Chief Magistrate William McAdoo, who had seen most of the Abbey plays thus far presented in New York, as well as most plays presented in recent years in New York which were thought to be objectionable, was unable to find anything offensive in *The Playboy*. On this third performance of the play on Wednesday night, there were no more hisses, and much laughter and applause.

The only other troubling incident during the New York run was a report in *The Gaelic American* that the actresses were dissatisfied. The actresses, who included Sara Allgood, Eithne Magee, Máire Nic Shiubhlaigh, Eileen O'Doherty, and the young English actress Cathleen Nesbitt,[17] immediately sent the following rejoinder to *The New York Post*:

> Certain statements have been made in the *Gaelic American* of to-day's date, which we, the players concerned, wish to contradict.
> 1. "There has been trouble about the contracts, and the trouble was about *The Playboy*."
> We have all signed a contract to stay on in America for a month beyond the time agreed, that is, we stay till the end of February, instead of the end of January. We were left absolutely free by the directors to stay, or not stay, this extra month, though they refused to accept Messrs. Liebler's proposal that we should stay through the entire spring.
> 2. "Some of the girls objected to the production of *The Playboy*, and refused to appear in it. They appealed to Lady Gregory, but their appeals fell on a heart of stone."
> We are all the girls who appeared in *The Playboy*, and we did not make any appeal to Lady Gregory, or anyone else.
> 3. "They don't get their wages; they are working on tick."
> We are paid regularly on the Friday of each week our weekly salary. The third share of profits, which such of us as are regular members of the company will receive, and which already amounts to a considerable sum, will not be divided until after our return to Ireland.[18]

The company ended its New York engagement at the end of December, and during the first week of January played one-night stands in six towns, among them Reading, Pennsylvania, and Johnstown, Pennsylvania.

On 8 January, the company opened a two-week stand at the Adelphi Theatre in Philadelphia. The opening performance was a triple bill of *Blanco Posnet*, *The Building Fund* and *The Rising of the Moon*. A typical review was that of *The Philadelphia Evening Bulletin* which remarked that Shaw had 'no conception of an American mining camp, and the Western atmosphere is as strange to the Irish Players as to Shaw himself'. The other performances for the week received high praise for both the quality of the plays and of the playing.

On 15 January, however, the company presented *The Playboy* for the first time in Philadelphia, and the newspaper headlines on the following days read 'Halt Performance of Playboy with Hoots and Yells — Riot at Adelphi Theatre' and '13 Are Arrested Accused of Riot at Irish Drama'.

In actuality, fifty plain-clothes policemen had been stationed in the audience for the 15 January performance; and the disturbers — twenty-nine in all — were so quickly ejected that they hardly caused a commotion:

> Fashionably attired men and women turned or arose from their seats and applauded as the police ejected the disturbers . . . and, after the play had been interrupted for several minutes, order was restored and the production went on smoothly.[19]

*The Playboy* was repeated on 16 January, and disturbances were more forceful. Missiles such as eggs and pie were hurled, the play was halted for fully five minutes, and fourteen people were arrested. One droll vignette was recorded by *The Philadelphia Evening Bulletin*:

> An amusing incident occurred during the evictions. One of the spectators had come to the theatre with the intention of making things as uncomfortable as possible for the players and other spectators by means of rotten eggs. His pockets bulged with them but before he threw any the lure of oratory seized him. He arose to his feet to begin a harangue and was promptly collared by two cops, who firmly, but by no means gently, dragged him from his seat. In the course of his egress the eggs were mostly smashed in his pockets and the atmosphere around him was filled with laughs and a decidedly unpleasant odour.[20]

Among those ejected on the first night was a liquor wholesaler named Joseph McGarrity who had strong ideas about the true nature of Ireland and who found the play both 'a gross misrepresentation of Irish life' and 'immoral and blasphemous almost from start to finish'. Nevertheless, he announced that he intended to bring suit against the theatre management for forcing him to leave the house.[21] McGarrity's denunciations were echoed more or less vehemently by several other patrons, and these people may not have been uncharacteristic. For instance, an article in the 19 January *Evening Bulletin* seriously argued that basketball was bad for morals. In some respects, the City of Brotherly Love seems to have been as straitlaced as the City of the Ford of the Hurdles.

On 16 January, Mayor Blankenburg met with a delegation of representatives of various local Irish organizations and politely denied their request that he forbid further performances of *The Playboy*. The mayor said that his office had made a careful investigation of the play even before the company's arrival. His secretary, Cyrus D. Foss, had been in touch with authorities in other American cities where the play had been performed, to determine whether it had been found objectionable. 'The mayor told the delegation yesterday that he would be establishing a remarkable precedent if he should order the play to be suppressed, and that having received assurances from many sources that there was really nothing objectionable in it he would not interfere with its production.' [22] Editorials in the next day's papers supported the major's judgment and affirmed the right of audiences to view the play. 'If you don't like a play,' wrote the *Inquirer*, 'keep away from it. . . . But once in a theatre, one should and must conduct oneself in an orderly manner and with a due regard for the rights of others.'

Joseph McGarrity, however, was not yet finished. He pressed charges against the company under the 1911 McNichol Act, a Pennsylvania law intended to 'prohibit the presentation of lascivious, sacrilegious, obscene, indecent plays, or plays of an immoral nature or character, or such as might tend to corrupt morals.' Oddly enough, the act was originally intended to halt the presentation of *La Samarataine* with Sarah Bernhardt. The act provided for a fine of up to $1,000, or imprisonment for one year, or both.

The sequence of events went like this. On 17 January, warrants were sworn out for the arrest of the players, but a bail of $5,000 was immediately posted, and so the warrants were never physically served. That night the play was repeated with 'Phalanxes of policemen and plain-clothes men' in the theatre. One protestor was removed, but 'No other untoward incident clouded the appreciation, often enthusiastically expressed, of an audience that sat in unmistakable enjoyment. . . . "I don't see what's the matter with this show", was the opinion most commonly expressed.' [23]

At nine the next morning, the players appeared at Magistrate Carey's office, as also did the accusers, among whom were McGarrity, his brother Peter who was a priest, and another priest named James T. Higgins. Agreement was then reached that a writ of *habeas corpus* would be sought, with the hearing on that petition to begin at three o'clock before Judge Carr at City Hall. McGarrity and his group were represented by William A. Gray, assisted by

423

Assistant District Attorney Fox. The Abbey players were represented by William H. Redheffer, Jr., Howard H. Yocum and Charles Biddle from Philadelphia, and by John Quinn sitting in as Lady Gregory's personal representative.

The court hearing seems absurd today, and it may have seemed so to the press at the time. The *North American* of 20 January wrote of:

> . . . the unadvertised comedy participated in by The Irish Players yesterday afternoon, at a matinee performance held in Judge Carr's room in the quarter sessions court. . . .

William A. Gray represented Joseph McGarrity, the liquor leader, who has taken principal part in the prosecution of the actors. He was aided at times by Assistant District Attorney Fox on behalf of the commonwealth, although the latter's choice in calling Director Porter to give testimony caused Mr. Gray both surprise and embarrassment. Inasmuch as Mr. Porter said there was nothing in the piece to offend the most devout and reverent of women. He said he had attended the theatre with his wife and that neither of them was "shocked"; on the contrary, distinctly pleased.

After a brief prologue by Mr. Fox, in which he informed Judge Carr that the case was brought under the act of 1911, fathered by Contractor James P. McNichol, the curtain was rung up on the first act of the little comedy, which had had no rehearsal.

The scene showed a courtroom, crowded to the doors. Arraigned before the bar were eleven actors. The learned judge sat upon his bench, and the jury inspected the fresh and piquant faces of the lassies from Erin, who were accused of participating in a lewd and blasphemous play.

Mr. Gray called Joseph McGarrity to the stand. In all seriousness and sincerity the witness testified that, in his opinion, the *Playboy* was a wicked piece and that he thought he had a perfect right to show his disapproval by protesting. He was questioned by Judge Carr as to the reason why he did not leave the theatre before he was ejected, if he thought the play was bad. He could give no adequate reply.

"How old are you?" said Judge Carr.

"Thirty-seven."

"And you are experienced in city life and customs?" was the query of the court.

"Your honour," interjected Mr. Gray, "we are not concerned with anything except whether the play is a violation of the law."

424

"I know that," replied the judge, "but I wanted to find out from this witness his opinion, from his valuable judgment," and he ordered McGarrity to testify further.

John J. Carr, of 2419 Carpenter Street, was the next witness called by Mr. Gray. He recited several lines from the play and said he thought they were sacrilegious. The judge asked him whether the play was a tragedy or a comedy.

Carr declared that it was a travesty, and said he believed "Synge was sorry he had written it after he had seen it produced". Father P. J. McGarrity, assistant rector of St. Monica's Church, was then called. He swore he had witnessed the whole performance and had read the book of the play.

"First of all," he said, "I object to it because it is degrading, as it holds a parricide up to admiration."

"But the father was not murdered, was he?" asked Judge Carr.

"Yes, so far as the public and the actors are concerned."

"But there has to be a plot," continued the court. "What would a play be without a plot?"

The audience broke into appreciative titters. Silence was restored by the tipstaves. Father McGarrity continued his testimony by saying that the comedy was blasphemous, because of the continued and profane use of the word "God". He asserted that the play was a travesty on the sacrament of matrimony and branded it as an indecent production for young people to witness who had not been informed of its purpose.

Just at this point Mr. Quinn stepped into the centre of the stage, and he and Father McGarrity had a lively tilt of characteristic Irish badinage. Mr. Quinn asked the young priest, who said he had lived in Ireland nearly all his life, if he would swear upon his oath that the first act of the *Playboy* was immoral. The priest then admitted that the play was immoral by innuendo only.

He showed his ignorance of colloquial Irish expressions when he declared that the Name was not commonly used among the peasantry in salutation, or for the purpose of expressing surprise, favour or indignation. He later admitted this on cross-examination.

The Rev. James T. Higgins, another priest, who lives in Chester Avenue near Fifty-seventh Street, said that in his opinion the play was objectionable for three reasons: glorification of crime, innuendoes of a licentious nature, and profanity. He stated that when the Playboy asserts he has murdered his father, the other members of the company, instead of regarding him as a monster, take him to their hearts and make a hero of him, and that his acceptability to the girl in the case rests solely on the account of his recital of his bloodthirsty deed.

"But didn't everybody in the theatre seem to take it as a joke?" interposed the court.

"No, they accepted it as it was presented by the actors," replied Father Higgins.

Mr. Gray then read passages from the book, declaring that it had been expurgated to make it presentable on the American stage. Frederick O'Donovan, one of the company who takes the part of the Playboy, testified that productions of the play had been made in Dublin, Belfast, Cork, London, Oxford, Cambridge, Harrogate, Boston, New York, New Haven and Providence without causing any public disturbance except in New York, and without any criminal prosecution being brought anywhere.

It was pointed out to the court by Mr. Gray that Pennsylvania is the only state having a statute preventing immoral or sacrilegious plays and that this was of so recent a date that neither side could argue that other plays of a much more objectionable nature than this had been permitted without hindrance.

Mr. Biddle and Mr. Quinn then summed up their arguments, in which the court concurred openly. The New York lawyer paid a tribute to Philadelphia concerning the testimony of Director [of Public Saftey] Porter. He said: "Philadelphia ought to be proud of the manhood displayed by such a witness. He stood before the court and testified that he and his wife had witnessed the performance, and that neither was displeased by any exhibition of immorality.[24]

"I say that any man who takes a lascivious meaning out of any of the lines of the play, or who declares that the piece is in any way improper, must have a depraved and abnormal mind.

"I am ashamed that such men could come here and insult womanhood with their views. The American people are too good a judge of the Irish race to agree with them."

The court then took the case under advertisement, reserving decision, counsel agreeing, under his advice, to allow the company to renew the bail bond of $5,000.

When the last lines in the little comedy had been spoken, the curtain rang down and the courtroom cleared of the public, the players heaved sighs of relief.

426

Miss Eithne Magee, the heroine of the piece, said she had never had so much fun in her life, and Lady Gregory candidly admitted that there was material for another bit of play-writing in the afternoon's events.[25]

The incident occasioned considerable public debate in Philadelphia, and the news of the arrest reached London where Bernard Shaw remarked:

"This occurrence is too ordinary to excite comment. All decent people are arrested in the United States. That is the reason why we have refused all invitations to go there.

"Besides, who am I that I should question Philadelphia's right to make itself ridiculous?" [26]

In the meantime, the company quietly played out the rest of the week to sympathetic and appreciative audiences, and then departed for Chicago with stops along the way at Pittsburgh, Indianapolis and probably other cities. Back in Philadelphia on 23 January, Judge Carr granted the petition for the writ of *habeas corpus*, in effect discharging the players without comment.

The company opened at the Grand Opera House in Chicago on 5 February and played there uneventfully until 2 March. During the four weeks, thirty-five performances of eighteen plays were presented. There were the usual attempts by Irish-Americans to secure official censure of *The Playboy*, but Mayor Harrison simply found the whole matter stupid, and the play was performed for a week without incident. Lady Gregory did receive a semi-literate threatening letter, with a crude sketch of a pistol and a coffin, but she was also greeted by the following sonnet by P.S.W., which appeared in a local paper.

Long be it ere to its last anchorage.
   Thy oaken keel, O "Fighting Temeraire",
   Shall forth beyond the busy harbour fare;
Still mayest thou the battle royal wage
To show a people to itself: to gauge
   The depth and quality peculiar there;
   Of its humanity to catch the air
And croon its plaintiveness upon the stage.

Nay, great and simple seer of Erin's seers,
   How we rejoice that thou wouldst not remain
Beside thy hearth, bemoaning useless years,
   But hear'st with inner ear the rhythmic strain
Of Ireland's mystic, overburdened heart,
Nor didst refuse to play thy noble part![27]

427

Financially the month in Chicago was a disappointment. As the critic Percy Hammond wrote:

> The visit of the Abbey Theatre players has inspired controversy, if not attendance. . . . The engagement has been for Chicago a fine experience. Chicago doesn't know it. . . . After the first sensation over Synge's *The Playboy of the Western World* we paid very little attention to our interesting guests. The Irish were offended deeply enough by that one play of the repertory to punish the enterprise by remaining away from them all. The playgoing members of the Drama League displayed a lamentable indifference. . . . And the remainder of the public, save for a few enthusiasts who went repeatedly, did not like the strange fare and stubbornly turned their backs on it.[28]

On 3 March, the company left Chicago, and on 5 March reached Boston by train. In Boston the players performed a matinee, and then travelled to New York where they sailed early on the morning of 6 March on the *Campania*. *The New York World* noted that 'They presented John A. Quinn, the lawyer who got them out of difficulties in Philadelphia, with a loving cup just before they sailed'.

\*     \*     \*

Apart from the patriotic and vehement Irish-American reaction to *The Playboy*, the Abbey company startled the new world in other ways — in the nature of its plays and in the quality of its acting. Irish plays and players had long been popular on the American stage, and the theatrical view Americans had of Ireland was best expressed in the plays and acting of Dion Boucicault. Boucicault had died in New York in 1890, and the last article which he wrote referred to the plays of Ibsen and noted that a new theatrical era was dawning. However, in 1911, twenty-one years after Boucicault's death, that era had not yet arrived; and the American drama had progressed no further towards reality than a character in a Clyde Fitch play exclaiming 'God damn!'.

Actually in 1911, there was little or nothing in the American drama to compare with the best plays in the Irish repertoire. The Boucicault version of *Rip Van Winkle*, played for years with enormous success by Joe Jefferson, had all of the racy theatrical elements of Boucicault's best Irish plays, but it was, like them, a theatre piece that made few claims to being dramatic literature. The theatrical confessions of David Belasco, such as *The Girl of the Golden West*, were staged with impressive realism, but had no more reality and much less literary merit than the best of Boucicault. Before the First World War, Clyde Fitch and Langdon Mitchell had probably the strongest claims to literary merit, and Mitchell's *The New York Idea* has been revived with some success. However, the wit of Mitchell is but a pale carbon of that in the high comedies of Congreve, Sheridan or Wilde. The poetic drama, then as now, was little written and seldom performed. The leading poetic dramatists were William Vaughn Moody and Percy Mackaye whose works are justly forgotten today, and whose only works really to succeed on the stage were written in prose.

In short, the pre World War I American drama had little relevance either to the art of the theatre or to actuality. A typical 'serious' play would be a comic melodrama, which was patterned on such pieces as *The Poor of New York* or *The Octoroon* which Boucicault and other craftsmanlike hacks churned out in the middle of the nineteenth century, and which George M. Cohan and many others were currently writing. If there was any development in the comic melodrama from the middle of the nineteenth to the early years of this century, it was probably in the increased tightening up of the plot, a change due in part to the example of the well-made play of Scribe and Sardou. Indeed, in such entertainments plot was almost everything, and the audience was hurtled from one exciting event to others increasingly more exciting and finally to some overwhelming climax, some 'punch' scene. Within this tightly rigorous structure, there was little opportunity for the presentation of thickly drawn or original characters, while the dialogue was generally as flat and functional as that of most film entertainments to-day.

The Irish plays of Synge and Lady Gregory were to the most sophisticated American audiences a revelation of what the power and beauty of words could accomplish, while the plots remained for the most part relatively flimsy. Yeats's plays, which made much less of an impact, were considered all words and no plot; but the plays of Ervine, Murray and Robinson, which were generally well plotted, were also admired for their language.

Many of these plays were also a revelation because they seemed truly to be grappling with reality. After *The Playboy*, probably the most admired piece in the repertoire was St. John Ervine's *Mixed Marriage* (and a decade or so later it was Ervine's *John Ferguson* and *Jane Clegg* that were the financial saving of the then *avant garde* Theatre Guild). A play like *Mixed Marriage* or *The Magnanimous Lover*, like *Birthright* or *Maurice Harte*, or like *Crossroads* or *Patriots* seemed to the best American audiences a much truer depiction of reality than did breezy American entertainments like *Secret Service* or *Seven Keys to Baldpate*. As one commentator on the American drama put it:

> The result of this practical necessity for striking plays has been to change the whole outlook of the American playwright. The observation of life except in its most vulgar, degraded or criminal phase has ceased to interest him. He has been taught that the public will not turn into the doors of a theatre that has anything so little out of the ordinary to claim its attention.[29]

In other words, the American drama in 1911 was basically a simplistic, lurid commercial entertainment with its roots far back in the nineteenth century. The Irish plays, on the other hand, were seen like this:

> They are audacious enough, these Players, to believe that the theatre should have some relation to the thought of the society that is called upon to support it. . . . What is attractive in these players is the revelation that they give of Irish life and character, life and character wonderfully unlike the [American] fustian that has been served up for many years to the present puzzlement of a public which sees something quite unlike anything it was prepared for.[30]

A few of the Irish plays, such as *Mixed Marriage* and *Birthright*, were thought to veer away from tragedy into melodrama, but the melodrama was not that simple and specious kind which has given the genre a bad name. Some of the other plays, particularly *Riders to the Sea* and *The Playboy*, were greeted as poetic masterpieces, and many of the comedies were thought as true to nature as they were delightful. To a small, discerning and influential segment of the audience, the Irish plays were indeed a revelation.

In 1903 the acting of the Irish players had created a sensation among London critics because of its intense naturalness. By and large, the acting made that same impression in America in 1911, and for the same reasons. There were two main traditions of acting at the time on the American stage. One was the stylized histrionics inherited from the nineteenth century and earlier. In this school, gesture, expression, movement and intonation were large, fixed and conventional. Such playing had evolved partly from the stylization of acting the classics, such as Shakespeare, and partly from having to play in large, ill-lit theatres. In such a situation, if a gesture or a facial expression were to register in the back row of the gods, it had to be much larger than life. Also, if the words were to be easily caught, they had to be spoken with a sonorous and even finicky articulation. Boucicault wrote in *The Art of*

430

*Acting* that he tried to pronounce not only every syllable but 'as far as I can every consonant'. Playgoers over the years had become used to this convention, but obviously its techniques were quite inappropriate for a contemporary realistic play. Old turn-of-the-century theatrical posters reveal the actors in what to us seem incredibly stilted postures; and such acting can be seen in many of the early silent films. (See, for instance, the extraordinary broadness of Lionel Barrymore in Henry Irving's old part of Mathias in the film of *The Bells*; or see the incredibly stylized acting of Nazimova in the silent film version of Wilde's *Salomé*.)

The second school of acting in America revolved around the star system and typecasting, and in many respects resembled the movie acting of the 1930s and 1940s. The great stars of the day, such as Ethel Barrymore, George M. Cohan, H. B. Warner, or Otis Skinner, played themselves. Each role was a projection of the star's personality, much as in the movies Clark Gable was always Clark Gable and John Wayne was always John Wayne. Such 'acting' never really varied from part to part, for the star was always doing the same thing, being himself. Clark Gable as Rhett Butler is indistinguishable from Clark Gable as Parnell.

In the star system, little attention is paid to the supporting players. On the stage, as later in the movies, the supporting players were cast for their types. Minor roles were typified, not individualized, and so reality on the stage was cast at one yet further remove.

In every way, the Abbey players contrasted with these styles of acting. Instead of stylized histrionics, there was such lack of movement, quietness of gesture, and evenness of tone, that what happened in the Abbey plays seemed startlingly real. Also, there were no star actors among the Abbey players. Critics began to notice Sara Allgood and Arthur Sinclair particularly, but were sometimes likely to see them cast in quite different or even in minor roles. Indeed, one of the delights of the Irish company for American critics was how the actors portrayed such a great variety of well-differentiated parts. One report issued by the theatre noted that Sinclair could play 78 roles on short notice, Sara Allgood 65, Fred O'Donovan 57, Sidney Morgan 56, Udolphus Wright 32, J. A. O'Rourke 67, and Eileen O'Doherty 37.[31] Such figures would have seemed incredible to most actors on the commercial stage in 1911; they would also seem incredible to present-day Abbey actors.

The Abbey acting, impressive as it was, was not uniformly eulogized.[32] Certain effects were seen as quite entirely outside of the actors' range. The affectation of Western American accents for *Blanco Posnet* was justly regarded as a ludicrous failure. The speaking of Yeats's verse by most of the actors other than Sara

Allgood was thought awkward and uninspired. The nasal brogue of J. A. O'Rourke, which had so irritated Miss Horniman, was an especial distraction in the Yeats plays. Also, the actors were thought to be better generally in the quiet moments of the more realistic plays than they were in the intense moments of the more poetic ones. Many critics, in short, thought both poetic speech and big moments a bit beyond the capacity of the actors' technique.[33]

In the main, however, the acting was about the first thorough example of realistic ensemble playing to be seen on the modern American stage. It was, in other words, about the first example seen of a form of the new technique practised by Antoine and by Stanislavsky, and that was to become the reigning acting convention of the twentieth century. As a technique, it opened up new possibilities for effects, just as its appropriate Irish plays opened up new vistas for truth to replace the stylized simplicities of the nineteenth-century drama.

The Chicago critic Percy Hammond wrote perceptively of much of this:

> Besides the disastrous impression bruited about that the Irish players represented a "highbrow" entertainment, and thus could not possibly be a good "show", they did, in fact, lack one of the qualities which the American theatregoer demands. They and some of their plays lacked what we call "action". What they gave in place of it was a quality which very few American actors can, and fewer still dare indulge in, though it is one of the highest virtues of artistic expression in any medium: repose. . . .
>
> But if "highbrow" means removed from the comprehension and sympathy of the average man, there was nothing "highbrow" about the Irish season. The simplicity and sincerity of the acting brought every effect easily to the audience, and the plays, with the exception of *The Shadow of the Glen*, and perhaps *Kathleen ni Houlihan*, were simple and direct appeals to our humour or our feeling. Excellent farce kept close to human nature and gripping drama commend these plays to every healthy dramatic appetite.
>
> The rock the Abbey players split on in our fair city is the paradox that American theatregoers want realism in the theatre rather than reality. That is, we want what we call realism, which is of all things the most unreal. If there is a stage telephone in the room we call that realism. If we hear the whir of an elevator and the familiar click of its gate, we call that realism. If we have an orchard with papier mâché

apples or an electric cataract or a shower of real water, we call that realism. Mr. Belasco is a "realist" and, ravished by his legerdemain, we accept the falsest of plays and the most unlifelike of acting. . . .

But to our playgoing taste they were tame and slow. Neither in the plays, nor in the stage management, nor in the acting were there any tricks. We don't care for that sort of thing. So much the worse, for the American dramatist who wishes to write honestly and courageously about life, and for the actor and producer who try to make the theatre a place to enjoy an art.[34]

And, finally, one of the company's biggest boosters, Theodore Roosevelt, wrote intelligently of the significance of the first tour for the American drama:

In the Abbey Theatre Lady Gregory and those associated with her . . . have not only made an extraordinary contribution to the sum of Irish literary and artistic achievement, but have done more for the drama than has been accomplished in any other nation of recent years. . . . The Irish plays are of some importance because they spring from the soil and deal with Irish things, the familiar home things which the writers really knew. They are not English or French; they are Irish. In exactly the same way, any work of the kind done here, which is really worth doing, will be done by Americans who deal with the American life with which they are familiar. . . . This will not lessen the broad human element in the work; it will increase it. These Irish plays appeal now to all mankind as they would never appeal if they had attempted to be flaccidly cosmopolitan; they are vital and human, and therefore appeal to all humanity, just because those who wrote them wrote from the heart about their own people, and their own feelings, their own good and bad traits, their own vital national interests and traditions and history. . . . Our American writers, artists, dramatists, must all learn the same lesson until it becomes instinctive with them, and with the American public. . . . When that day comes, we shall understand why a huge ornate Italian villa or French chateau or make-believe castle, or, in short, any mere inappropriate copy of some building some-where else, is a ridiculous feature in an American landscape . . . we shall use statues of such a typical American beast as the bison . . . to flank the approach to a building like the New York library. . . .[35]

433

This was a lesson that the American theatre rather quickly learned. The initial Abbey impact was summed up by John Quinn:

> Not only have the New York daily papers devoted columns to the work of the company throughout its stay here, giving elaborate reviews of their work, and interviews with Lady Gregory and others, but many magazines have an appreciative and complimentary articles . . . among others, the *Yale Review, The Harvard Monthly, Collier's Weekly, The Nation* (two notices), *The New York Dramatic Mirror* (five notices), *Metropolitan Magazine, Munsey's Magazine, The Craftsman, Life, Harper's Weekly.* . . .
>
> Our universities and colleges have shown the liveliest interest in the Irish dramatic movement. The professors have lectured upon the plays, and the plays have been studied in the college classes, and the students have been advised to read them and see the players.[36]

The Irish lesson was indeed learned quickly. Professor Baker's 47 Workshop at Harvard was training such new dramatists as O'Neill, Behrman and Barry. The Washington Square Players, which grew into the Theatre Guild, became active. The Provincetown Playhouse commenced operations. In 1914, the first really modern American dramatist, Elmer Rice, had his first Broadway production. A few seasons later, during another Rice play, the actor Richard Bennett gave some matinee productions to *Beyond the Horizon*, and that was Eugene O'Neill's first Broadway production. After World War I, new and talented and quite modern and utterly American dramatists seemed to appear in profusion — Anderson and Stallings, Barry, Behrman, Howard, Sherwood, Kingsley, Odets, Hellman, Saroyan.

The war, of course, interrupted the Abbey's tours to America, but the company returned several times between 1921 and 1938. Their great new plays were the early works of Seán O'Casey, and there was nothing in the rest of their repertoire that was so good. Most of the new dramatists had nothing to teach the Americans. There were good actors in the tours between the two wars, but there was also a deal of bad acting. After listening to the poor diction of the theatre's chief comic actor, and after watching the mugging of the theatre's chief comic actress, the ever-astute George Jean Nathan headed one of his critiques with the line 'Erin Go Blah'. It was now the American theatre which could give lessons to the Irish.

# Appendix II : An interview with Michael Conniffe
Conducted by Robert Hogan

I was born on the island of Tawin, that's joined to the mainland by a bridge. It's called an island, but it's a peninsula jutting out into Galway Bay. I'd a cousin, Dr. Seumas O'Beirne, that qualified as a doctor in Tawin, and he was a Gaelic enthusiast, mad enthusiast for the language, and he wrote a bi-lingual play called *An Doctúir, The Doctor*, and he passed it among the villagers of the island, of whom I was one. He conducted the rehearsals himself, and eventually he set up a stage in the hall on Tawin, and he invited two critics of his, Dr. Tommy Walsh of Galway and his intended Mrs., Miss Molly Weldon, and the players gave a performance in the hall. Straightaway the critics demanded it should be brought to the town hall of Galway. Now that was 1902. 1902, think of that. We went to the town hall of Galway with the play, and we got a marvellous reception. In other words, in theatrical parlance, we pulled down the house. But there was a kind of spleen that a play coming from a Gaelic village was half English. But finally at the fall of the curtain, we had a wonderful reception. Dr. O'Beirne, the author, went to the front of the hall, and he said, 'We're going to produce this play again and again, and we'll force it down the throats of the shoneens.' That got marvellous applause.

Now we went home, and our next tour was to Dublin on 14, 15 and 16 November 1903, when we played for three nights in the Banba Hall, the Grocers' Assistants Hall in Parnell Square, and we got a tremendous reception from the Press and all in Dublin. Now our next move was — the Gaelic League in Dublin invited us to play for the Oireachtas in the Rotunda, Dublin, 1904, and we played there for a week. There was another company there. Cathal McGarvey had it. It was a play called *Seaghan na Scuab*.

We got another invitation in Dublin at the same time. There was a lady, a Gaelic enthusiast lady, living out in Blackrock, called Mrs. Clarke, and she invited the company out to give a performance. Now the company left Tawin that morning to catch the half-past-six train eight miles from their village in Oranmore. We went to Dublin, went out to Mrs. Clake, gave a performance in it, and came back and gave a performance in Dublin that same night. And we were on our feet from — oh, say from three to four o'clock that morning until that night. Now the *Seaghan na Scuab* play was the first. At the Rotunda it was played the first that night, with the result that we had to be one hundred per cent perfection itself to keep the house going — and we didn't start till ten o'clock. And we kept the house going to such an extent that the final curtain didn't come down till eleven o'clock that night, it was such a terrific success. We got curtain call after curtain call, after the final curtain. . . .

Now we left and we went home, and Galway clamoured out for a performance. So we played in a place called the Racquet Court in Galway, that's now the Court Theatre. And that's the first place that we met that noble gentleman and patriot, Sir Roger Casement. Sir Roger Casement was so full of enthusiasm for the players that he joined them the next day on the sidecars into the village of Tawin fourteen miles away, and travelled on the sidecars with us. And the countryside applauded. . . .

Now some time later, 1912, I saw where there was a school of acting opened at the Abbey in Dublin under the charge of Nugent Monck of Norwich. I took an excursion ticket from Oranmore, return for 2/6, but I didn't need a return. Shows you how cheap fares were at that time — 2/6 from Oranmore to Dublin and back. So I went to Dublin, but I had no intention of returning. I went down and I entered my name in the School of Acting at the Abbey Theatre. There were about over sixty students at the Abbey, but I was a half-professional already. Of course, the Number One Company was in America. At the end of the school, Mr. Monck produced two plays or three by the School of Acting pupils. A peculiar thing about it was that one of them was *The Marriage* by Douglas Hyde. It was a play where Raftery, the fiddler, the old poet, comes into it; and I was given the part of Raftery the poet. We pulled down the house with me performance, and the papers come out the next day with big headlines about the success of the Abbey Players, the Number Two Company, the pupils. So the leading critic, Jacques, of *The Freeman's Journal*, gave a wonderful report for us.

HOGAN: I've read that.

CONNIFFE: You have? Well, Lord and God above. And a gentleman named Timothy Holloway —

HOGAN: Joseph Holloway.

CONNIFFE: Joseph Holloway! Ah God, you have them all, you have them all. So Mr. Yeats and Lady Gregory came back from the tour in America, and they inquired about the company, the school, and how they were getting on. And they were shown the critiques, and shown how Michael Conniffe from Galway got such great praise in all things. And then Lady Gregory immediately jumped for me, and put me — I being a West of Ireland man — put me in the leading parts in her own plays. *Hyacinth Halvey* was one of them, and the next part was in *Spreading the News*. I had

436

the leading part in that — what was it called? I'll have it now in a minute. . . . And the next was *The Workhouse Ward*. Oh, I had to play all Lady Gregory's chief parts, with the result that I immediately got a contract from the Abbey Theatre, and was held there, and was joined to the Number One Company.

I played all Synge's plays, and I played T. C. Murray's. And Yeats's plays, *The Hour Glass*. . . . And *Kinship*. Well now, I couldn't tell you a lot about *Kinship*. It's so long ago. I couldn't even quote for you. I could quote from any of the other plays probably. I remember *Kinship* now. It was a big play by J. Bernard MacCarthy. My brother now, he was in the Abbey then—he's dead since, God rest him — he played in *Kinship* also. And so did Barry Fitzgerald. I was the first that ever made up Barry Fitzgerald's face when he came into the Abbey, I was. I saw him play for five shillings, five shillings they got for going on in a crowd. He smoked a burned-out pipe, no cigarettes, always a burned-out pipe. And I was the first ever made up Maureen Delany's features. She was in the School of Acting. Oh, they thought I was a genius.

I was in *The Magic Glasses*, by George Fitzmaurice. And Charlie Power was in it. Charlie Power, he's dead. He became Judge Wyse Power at the turn of the Government. His mother, God rest her, she had a restaurant down in Henry Street. And I was a great friends with Padraic Pearse and Willy: They brought an Irish play — I think it was *Iosagán* — into the theatre one time to play it. I had Irish as good as themselves. . . . Well, is there any other thing? Put me any question you want.

HOGAN: Did you know A. Patrick Wilson?

CONNIFFE: A. P. Wilson, why he was our manager, a very good manager, but of course he was Scotch. He got round Lady Gregory anyway, and he got the management of the theatre. But he left it after a short while. I was a pupil of his. He tried to act some plays, but he couldn't act. He wasn't an actor, and he wasn't for Irish drama.

HOGAN: He did write an Irish play —

CONNIFFE: Called *The Slough*. I played in it. It was about the 1913 strike in Dublin. 'Twas a tough time. I was in Dublin at the time, and on a Saturday night, before what they call Bloody Sunday, Helena Moloney and meself were playing in *The Mineral Workers*. I was Ned Mulroy, and she was Mrs. Mulroy, and during the play, over the fireside during our pauses, what were we discussing but Jim Larkin's coming escapade in the Imperial Hotel.

HOGAN: So many of these plays are just lost, were never published.

I don't suppose you ever kept any scripts?

CONNIFFE: Oh sure, I had all those scripts. I had a lot of material, but when I changed from the West of Ireland to up here I discarded a whole lot of stuff, valuable stuff. I was leaving the theatrical atmosphere. I burned them, the whole lot. Often thought of it since.

HOGAN: Did you know Seumas O'Kelly?

CONNIFFE: The author of *The Bribe*.

HOGAN: I believe you played the pauper in *The Bribe*, and got a big hand of applause when you went off the stage.

CONNIFFE: You said the truth. By God, you have it all.

HOGAN: Did you know O'Kelly?

CONNIFFE: I met him only once, I did. I did meet George Bernard Shaw. He came up in the Green Room himself, and Sir Hugh Lane before Sir Hugh was drowned, and Commissioner Bailey — the three of them were up in the Green Room.

HOGAN: Were you in *The Lord Mayor*?

CONNIFFE: I was in *The Lord Mayor*, of course. Seán Connolly was a good actor.

HOGAN: Did you meet the author?

CONNIFFE: Edward McNulty. I did. I met him. He was very nice. He wrote another play after that, at the time of the start of the war. It was turned down, the Abbey turned it down. Oh, he used to come round and shake hands with the actors. But the most popular plays were Boyle's plays. They were pure good stuff. *The Building Fund* was one of them, and *The Eloquent Dempsy*.

HOGAN: What was Nugent Monck like?

CONNIFFE: I tell you, he was for the old mystic plays, the morality plays. He made a speech one night, and he told the audience that he wanted to produce morality plays. And there was a gentleman there by the name of — ah, I think it was Lawrence.

HOGAN: W. J. Lawrence.

CONNIFFE: By God, you have it all. W. J. Lawrence, and he says, 'You mustn't produce such plays. This theatre is for the Irish theatre, and we don't have mystic plays.'

But we did produce one or two mystic plays. And I was also in Yeats's *Countess Cathleen*. Which reminds me, here's an incident I will tell you, and it's worthy of recording. We were playing in the Court Theatre in London — no, it was the Strand. We played in the Court and in the Prince of Wales, but this time it was the

438

Strand. We were going to play this time Mr. Yeats's *Hour Glass*, and I had never played in it in me life. Mr. Sinclair, he went sick at the first rehearsal, and he had the biggest part in the whole performance.

HOGAN: The Wise Man?

CONNIFFE: That's right, the same. And Lady Gregory says, 'Well, we'll give the part to the quick study of the Abbey Theatre, Mr. Conniffe.'

Well, I was given the play. I hadn't even seen it. I was given the play, and in two days' time there was a rehearsal called. So I went home, and what I did — I learned it by eyesight. You can learn by eyesight, and you can learn by memory. I had to learn fast. You keep writing the play that appears before your eyes always. I wrote that play I suppose ten times out in a copy book. I did certainly, and I used to have the script behind me back, and I walking the streets of London, saying it over and never looking behind.

So I turned up to rehearsal, and the first thing that Yeats said was, 'Mr. Conniffe, you have a whole knowledge of the part. You're better than those who are always playing in it.'

I said, 'I hope I will have the part.'

So the performance came on two days after that. And I ever remember Joe Kerrigan says to me — he was playing one part and I another — 'Are you nervous, Mick?'

'No,' I said, 'only of me lines.'

Lady Gregory and Yeats were out there in the box-office.

So the curtain came down, and we got tremendous applause, and we went off to the dressing room. And Yeats left the box office, left Lady Gregory there, and came off up the whole way through the theatre, through the stairs, into the dressing room, and came in and shook hands with me.

'Mr. Conniffe, I offer you my heartiest congratulations. Congratulations! You made a marvellous performance, a marvellous performance!' And he left.

And Sydney Morgan turned to me and says, 'As long as I'm connected with the theatre that's what I have never known Yeats to do, to come and congratulate anyone on the performance of his plays.'

But he done that now.

HOGAN: Tell me about some of the people you acted with.

CONNIFFE: Well, of all the actors that ever acted at the Abbey Theatre, there was one outstanding, and that was Arthur Sinclair in the Number One Company, on the gentlemen's side. And on the ladies' side, of course, there was Sally Allgood. She was the leader of the ladies' side. But Arthur Sinclair was an outstanding performer, an outstanding artist altogether. He broke away from the theatre on the Lane pictures, I think. A gallery there was to be built, am I right? There was a gallery to be built for the Lane pictures, and the Abbey gave performances for to raise money, and with the result that when the gallery wasn't built, the players demanded their money. There was a crux there. They broke with Yeats and with Lady Gregory, and they got their money. And Sinclair set up a company himself, the Irish Players, and I joined him. I did. I joined him, and we toured the country. The last time I played with him was in November 1919, in the Opera House, Cork.

Now at that time I was a sworn member of the Irish Republican Brotherhood. I was a wild mad enthusiast for freedom, and there was an order given from general headquarters that I was to cancel my tour with Sinclair. I had a contract signed to tour with Arthur Sinclair for three years. We were to go to London for three months. We were to go from there to New York, New York to Chicago, then to Montreal, from there on to South Africa, New Zealand, Australia, and back again to London. It would take us three years to do it, and I cancelled it all. I had my contract signed at 25 guineas a week, and travel expenses paid. I was a wild young mad enthusiast, that's what I was. So I shook hands with the company on the night of November — I forget the date — it was November, 1919. And I said, 'It's duty's call, I must obey.'

Well, Arthur Sinclair wrote to me afterwards to come back and join him because he could get nobody more. But I was so mad I tore the letter. I wish I had that letter to-day. And I stayed as an I.R.A. officer till the night of the truce.

I did a lot of other things for charity after that. . . .

HOGAN: What were you best in? Country roles?

CONNIFFE: Country roles. They were natural to me. I was an outstanding comedian in country roles. I held the city of Dublin in the hollow of me hand. I did, one time. I could walk on the stage, and the moment I started me personality alone had the whole house roaring.

HOGAN: What was your best part?

CONNIFFE: I used to get a tremendous applause in a play called *Birthright*, T. C. Murray's play. And now I'm going to tell you a funny thing, and it's God's Gospel Truth. We had a company in Galway. It was the time of the Civil War, and we were raising funds for the destitute, and we were going to play in Loughrea. And you know in the play where the two brothers — one kills the other? Well, I had Frank Connors of Galway — he's dead since, God rest him — do a part. And I was playing Hughie, the principal part. And of course we had the stage all set. We had the table and a big basin of delph on the table, and the delph already broken. And it came to the row, and I went over to the table. I first struck the candle against the ground and quenched it. There was no light. Then I got the table and turned it upside down and round and round.

But what happened? It's hard to believe it. The light was switched on in the theatre, and the people started to leave. They thought it was a real row.

Now, what happened. Seán knocks Hughie down on the hearthstone, and he's beatin' his head against the thing, and with his boots he's striking on the hearthstone to make a knocking noise for the head, you understand me? Frank Connors says to me, 'Mr. Conniffe,' he says, 'the lights are on, and the people are leaving the theatre. What are we to do at all?'

'Rise up,' I says, 'from killin' me, and walk to the front of the theatre, and tell the management please put out the light, and have the audience come back in and take their place.'

So he had to rise up, and go out and make a speech, and tell them to come back, that it was still a play. So they came back, they did. Now you never heard of that before. Well, that's as sure as God'll judge me. They had to come back, and we had to repeat the killing. So when the curtain came down finally, the company got tremendous applause. It was the most genuine bit of acting I was ever in. . . .

Oh, there wasn't a more popular artist in the Abbey Theatre than what I was, because I was a natural artist. I hadn't to try to put on acting at all. I was myself. I didn't have to act because it was in me natural. I had only to go out and say the words because I was a countryman, and they were all country plays. You follow me. They were all country plays, and the town's personnel found it difficult to play them, because they couldn't interpret like a countryman could. . . .

Oh, there's no man alive to-day could tell you more about the Abbey Theatre than what I could.

*　　*　　*

Michael Conniffe died in the Spring of 1979.

441

# Appendix III :

## Anglo-Irish Drama, *a checklist* 1910–1915

This list attempts to give the date of first publication, the date of first production, and the original cast of the most significant plays of the Irish theatre during these years. It includes only the most important plays written in the Irish language, and it omits plays which lack any tincture of literary or theatrical or historical merit.

The plays are listed chronologically by date of first production. When the plays were not produced or when the production date is uncertain, they are listed by the date of their first publication. The cast lists, whenever possible, are based upon the original programmes, rather than upon the sometimes variant cast lists to be found in the books of some published plays. Often, neither programme nor published book was available, and in such cases the cast lists have been formed by a comparison of available newspaper accounts.

Some details in the checklists of previous volumes of this history have occasioned queries by individuals who have noted discrepancies between our information and that of previous historians. The purpose of the checklist is, of course, to provide a mass of accurate factual data; and so, when James Kilroy and I discovered an inaccuracy in another historian, we simply silently corrected the error. In this checklist, however, I have footnoted some such errors and some of my own uncertainties. My motive is not a desire to denigrate the work of previous writers, for which I usually have an admiration approaching awe. Nevertheless, a checklist of this nature offers the possibility for endless error. Nothing, I have discovered, is so difficult to establish as a simple fact, and I trust that future historians will correct, either silently or loudly, whatever errors have crept into the present work.

After the initial bibliographical listing of a frequently cited book, I have, for reasons of space, given a short title listing in subsequent citations.

From time to time, the names of some actors vary in their form or spelling. Unless there has been an obvious misprint in the original sources, I have retained whatever form the actor used on the occasion.

442

# 1910

## J. M. SYNGE

*Deirdre of the Sorrows*
a Play in Three Acts.
First produced: 13 January 1910,
by the Irish National Theatre
Society, at the Abbey Theatre,
Dublin.

CAST

| | |
|---|---|
| Lavarcham | Sara Allgood |
| Old Woman | Eileen O'Doherty |
| Owen | J. A. O'Rourke |
| Conchubor | Arthur Sinclair |
| Fergus | Sydney J. Morgan |
| Deirdre | Máire O'Neill |
| Naisi | Fred O'Donovan |
| Ainnle | J. M. Kerrigan |
| Ardan | John Carrick |
| Soldiers | Ambrose Power, |
| | Harry Young |

Directed by Máire O'Neill
and W. B. Yeats
Incidental Music composed by
John F. Larchet
First published: Churchtown:
Cuala Press, 1910; reprinted in J.
M. Synge, *Collected Works*, Vol.
IV, *Plays*, Book II, ed. Ann
Saddlemyer (London: Oxford
University Press, 1968).

## LENNOX ROBINSON

*The Cross Roads*
a Play in Two Acts (revised version with the prologue omitted).
First produced: 3 February 1910,
by the Irish National Theatre
Society, at the Abbey Theatre,
Dublin.
This revised version apparently
unpublished.

## W. B. YEATS

*The Green Helmet*
a Play in Ballad Metre in One Act,
based on *The Golden Helmet*.
First produced: 10 February 1910,
by the Irish National Theatre
Society, at the Abbey Theatre,
Dublin.

CAST

| | |
|---|---|
| Cuchulain | J. M. Kerrigan |
| Conall | Arthur Sinclair |
| Leagaire | Fred O'Donovan |
| Laeg | Sydney J. Morgan |
| Emer | Sara Allgood |
| Conal's Wife | Máire O'Neill |
| Laegaire's Wife | Eithne Magee |

| | |
|---|---|
| Red Man | Ambrose Power |
| Scullions, Horse Boys, and | |
| Blackmen | Eric Gorman, J. A. |
| | O'Rourke, John Carrick, |
| | F. R. Harford, T. Moloney, |
| | T. Durkin, P. Byrne |

First published: Churchtown, Dun-
drum: The Cuala Press, 1910;
reprinted in *The Variorum Edition
of the Plays of W. B. Yeats*, ed.
Russell K. Alspach and Catherine
C. Alspach (London: Macmillan,
1966; New York: Macmillan,
1966).

## KATHLEEN FITZPATRICK

*Expiation*
a Tragedy in One Act.
First produced: 18 February 1910,
by the Theatre of Ireland, at the
Molesworth Hall, Dublin.

CAST

| | |
|---|---|
| Philip Courteney | J. M. Carré |
| Catherine Courteney | |
| | Nora Fitzpatrick |

Directed by Fred Morrow
Unpublished.

## CHARLES MACKLIN

*The True Born Irishman*
an 18th Century Comedy in
Two Acts.
First produced by the Theatre of
Ireland: 18 February 1910, at the
Molesworth Hall, Dublin.

CAST

| | |
|---|---|
| Murrough O'Dogherty (played in 1763 by Macklin at the first per-formance in Crow Street, Dublin) | George Nesbitt |
| Councillor Hamilton A. H. Gordon | |
| Count Mushroom | J. M. Carré |
| Pat Fitzmongrel George Fitzgerald | |
| Major Gamble | Luke Kileen |
| John | C. S. Power |
| Mrs. O'Dogherty | Mary Delane |
| Katty Farrell | Cátia Nic Cormac |
| Lady Kinnegad | |
| | P. Ní Pluinghchéad |
| Lady Bab Frightful | |
| | Nora Fitzpatrick |
| Mrs. Jolly | Gráine Nic Cormac |
| Mrs. Gazette | |
| | Máire Ní Pluinghchéad |

Directed by Fred Morrow
First published: Dublin, 1783;
reprinted in *Four Comedies*, ed.
J. O. Bartley (London: Sidgwick
and Jackson, [1968]).

443

## CARLO GOLDONI
*Mirandolina*
Translated and adapted from *La Locandiera* by Lady Gregory, a Comedy in Three Acts.
First produced: 24 February 1910, by the Irish National Theatre Society, at the Abbey Theatre, Dublin.

CAST

Captain Ripafratta
Fred O'Donovan
Marquis of Forlipopli
Arthur Sinclair
Count of Albafiorita
J. M. Kerrigan
Mirandolina      Máire O'Neill
Ortensia      Eileen O'Doherty
Dejanira      Eithne Magee
Fabrizio      J. A. O'Rourke
The Captain's Servant
Sydney J. Morgan
First separately published: London & New York: Putnam, 1924; reprinted in *The Translations and Adaptations of Lady Gregory, Being the Fourth Volume of the Collected Plays*, ed. Ann Saddlemyer (Gerrards Cross, Buckinghamshire: Colin Smythe, 1970).

## LADY GREGORY
*The Travelling Man*
a Miracle Play in One Act.
First produced: 3 March 1910,* by the Irish National Theatre Society, at the Abbey Theatre, Dublin.

CAST

A Mother      Sara Allgood
A Child      Elinor Moore
A Travelling Man
Fred O'Donovan
First published: in *Seven Short Plays* (Dublin: Maunsel, 1909), reprinted in *The Wonder and Supernatural Plays of Lady Gregory, Being the Third Volume of the Collected Plays*, ed. Ann Saddlemyer (Gerrards Cross, Buckinghamshire: Colin Smythe, 1970).

## RUTHERFORD MAYNE
(Samuel J. Waddell)
*Captain of the Hosts*
a Play in Three Acts.

First produced: 8 March 1910, by the Ulster Literary Theatre, at the Grand Opera House, Belfast.

CAST

Neil Gallina      Ross Canmer
Barbara McDonald
Seveen Canmer
Billy Baird      Charles Kerr
Thomas      J. M. Harding
Flapper McKeown
Gerald MacNamara
Herbert Young  Jackson Graham
Annie      Helena Cairns
Mrs. McKee  Margaret O'Gorman
Jamesy McCloy  Alan Whitley
Hughey Thompson  G. A. Charters
Unpublished.

## SIR SAMUEL FERGUSON
*The Naming of Cuchulain*
a Dramatic Poem.
First produced: 9 March 1910, by the Ulster Literary Theatre, at the Grand Opera House, Belfast, on the occasion of the Ferguson Centenary.

CAST

Cathbad      Joseph Campbell
Conor      Charles Kerr
Setanta      Frederick Cairns
Cullan      Ross Canmer
Fergus      P. Carey
Published in *Lays of the Red Branch* (London: T. Fisher Unwin & Dublin: Sealy, Bryers & Walker, 1898); reprinted in *Poems of Sir Samuel Ferguson* (Dublin: Phoenix Publishing Co., [1916]).

## SEUMAS O'KELLY
*The Home-Coming*
a Play in One Act.
First produced: 28 March 1910, by the Theatre of Ireland, at the Molesworth Hall, Dublin.

CAST

Mrs. Ford  Máire Nic Shiubhlaigh
Donagh Ford      John Connolly
Hugh Deely      Charles Power
Agnes Deely  Una Nic Shiubhlaigh
First published: in *Sinn Féin*, 28 August 1909; reprinted in *Three Plays* (Dublin: M. H. Gill, 1912) and in *Waysiders* (Dublin: Talbot [1917]).

*Saddlemyer incorrectly lists 2 March 1910.

## J. O'E*

*The Spurious Sovereign, or Nailed
to the Counter*
a Burlesque-Melodrama in a
Prologue and Four Acts.
First produced: 28 March 1910,
by the Theatre of Ireland, at the
Molesworth Hall, Dublin.

CAST

Kropotkin     Una Nic Shiubhlaigh
Prince Robert          Luke Kileen
Prince William
              Seaghan MacMurchada
The A. B. Pirate
              P. MacShiubhlaigh
The Icelander        Stephen James
                     (James Stephens)
Also with Charles Power, U. Ro-
berts, C. Brady, George Fitzgerald,
Seumas James, Samuel James, and
M. Carolan .
Unpublished.

## SIGNOR ESPOSITO and DOUGLAS HYDE

*The Tinker and the Fairy*
an Operetta in One Act, music by
Esposito and libretto from the play
by Hyde.
First produced: 29 March 1910,
by the Dublin Amateur Operatic
Society.

CAST

The Fairy           Nettie Edwards
A Youth             Thomas Collins
The Tinker          John C. Crowner

## P. H. PEARSE

*Iosagán*
a Play in One Act.
First produced: 5 February at St.
Enda's School, Rathfarnham; first
public production: 9 April 1910,
by St. Enda's School, at the Abbey
Theatre, Dublin.

CAST

| Sean-Mhaitias | Patrick Conroy |
| Cuimin | Conor MacGinley |
| Cóilín | Thomas Power |
| Pádraic | Frank Dowling |
| Darach | John Power |
| Briocán | Brian MacNeill |
| Máirtín | Niall MacNeill |
| Eoghan | Matthew O'Kelly |
| Feichín | Joseph Buckley |
| Other Boys | Turlough MacNeill, |
| | Frederick Holden, |
| | Dermot MacCarthy |
| Men | Colm Naughton, |
| | Stephen McDermott |
| Women | Eileen Colum, |
| | Susan Colum |
| An Sagart | Joseph Fagan |
| Iosagán | Eunan MacGinley |

First published: in *An Macaomh*,
Christmas 1909; reprinted in *Plays,
Stories, Poems* (Dublin: Phoenix
Publishing Co., 1917).

## PADRAIC COLUM

*The Destruction of the Hostel*
a Play in One Act.*
First produced: 5 February 1910
at St. Enda's School, Rathfarnham;
first public production: 9 April
1910, at the Abbey Theatre,
Dublin.

CAST

| Lomna Druth | Eamonn Bulfin |
| Ferrogain | Desmond Ryan |
| Fergabar | Maurice Fraher |
| Ingcel, a British Outlaw | |
| | Sorley MacGarvey |
| Maine Honeymouth | Denis Gwynn |
| Conall Cernach | Frank Connolly |
| Cormac Condloingeas | |
| | Donal O'Connor |
| Bricriu | Eamonn Nolan |
| Mac Cecht | Vincent O'Doherty |
| Ni-Fri-Fliath | Richard O'Rahilly |
| The Three Red Pipers from | |
| the Elf-Mounds | |

*To take a guess, 'J. O'E' is either Gerald MacNamara or James Stephens,
both of whom were connected with the theatre, MacNamara by his brother,
Fred Morrow, and Stephens as an occasional actor. The piece seems rather
more in MacNamara's vein, although it should be noted that Stephens was
a member of the cast.

*Colum's programme note reads: 'The dramatic version of "The Destruc-
tion of Da Derga's Hostel" is based on the translation by Whitley Stokes,
published in the *Revue Celtique*, Vol. 22. In many of the speeches the
actual words of the saga as translated by Stokes have been used. Something
has also been taken from Ferguson's fine poem "Conary".'

Frederick O'Doherty,
Milo MacGarry,
John Dowling
First published: in *An Macaomh*,
Christmas 1910; first book publication in *A Boy in Eirinn* (New
York: E. P. Dutton, 1913).

## THOMAS KING MOYLAN
*The Naboclish*
a Comedy in Two Acts.
First produced: 31 May 1910, by
the Students' Union of the Metropolitan School of Art, at the
Abbey Theatre, Dublin.

CAST

Jerry Cullinan        Austin Molloy
Molly                 Julie Hayden
Pat Carmody,
  a car driver        James Golden
George Herbert Chantilly
  Smith               Harry Clarke
Matty Moroney,
  a Shoemaker    Dinny O'Meagher
Mick Considine,
  a Publican          R. J. Long
Jamesy Linnane,
  a Blacksmith        A. Nolan
First published: in *The Naboclish
and Uncle Pat* (Dublin: James
Duffy, 1913).

## CASIMIR DUNIN MARKEVICZ
*The Memory of the Dead*
a Romantic Drama of '98
in Three Acts.
First produced: 14 April 1910,
by the Independent Dramatic
Company, at the Abbey Theatre,
Dublin.

CAST

Michael Doyle    Seaghan Connolly
Colonel Charort       J. M. Carré
James McGowan    Edward Keegan
Father Moran        P. MacCartan
Stephen O'Dowd      M. Carolan
English Officer   Mervyn Colomb
Dermod O'Dowd     George Nesbit
Brigid             Honor Lavelle
Norah    Constance de Markievicz
First published: Dublin: The
Tower Press, 1910.

## CASIMIR DUNIN MARKIEVICZ
*Mary*

a Comedy in Four Acts.
First produced: 15 April 1910, by
the Independent Dramatic Company, at the Abbey Theatre,
Dublin.

CAST

Plaid, a 'Parlour'
                  Una Nic Shiubhlaigh
Mr. Brown, a Stockbroker
                     George Nesbit
Mrs. White           Mary O'Hea
Mr. White, an Agent  C. Atkinson
Mr. John White, his brother
                     P. J. O'Hara
Miss Green, their First
  Cousin          Nora Fitzpatrick
Mr. Black, a Philosopher
                     R. M. Tweedy
Mr. Smythe, a friend of the
  White family       J. M. Carré
Mrs. Black Máire Nic Shiubhlaigh
Unpublished.

## PADRAIC COLUM
*Thomas Muskerry*
a Play in Three Acts.
First produced: 5 May 1910, at
the Abbey Theatre, Dublin.*

CAST

Christy Clarke          U. Wright
Felix Tournour    Sydney J. Morgan
Myles Gorman    Fred O'Donovan
Thomas Muskerry   Arthur Sinclair
Albert Crilly        Eric Gorman
Crofton Crilly      J. M. Kerrigan
Mrs. Crilly          Sara Allgood
Anna Crilly          Máire O'Neill
James Scollard     J. A. O'Rourke
Mickie Cripes        F. R. Harford
                     (Fred Rowland)
Thomas Shanley     Ambrose Power
An Old Man         J. M. Kerrigan
  Directed by S. L. Robinson
First published: Dublin: Maunsel,
1910; revised, in *Three Plays*
(Dublin: Figgis, 1963).

## E. K. WORTHINGTON
*The Burden*
a Tragedy in One Act.
First produced: 11 May 1910, by
the Cork Dramatic Society, at the
Dun Theatre, Cork.

CAST

Din Kaedach, a Publican
                     C. B. Ronayne
Shawn Roe, a Fisherman J. Gilley

*MacNamara incorrectly lists 12 May.

446

Dan Rorke, a Miner    C. O'Leary
Cosby Dunne, a Miner
                      P. O'Leary
Mike Mescall, a Labourer
                      M. W. Good
Rafferty, a Fiddler    E. O'Shea
Máire, his Daughter
                   Miss M. Murray
No record of publication.

## CON O'LEARY
*Struck*
a Comedy in One Act.
First produced: 11 May 1910, by
the Cork Dramatic Society, at the
Dun Theatre, Cork.

CAST

Corny Mullane         P. O'Leary
Mrs. O'Driscoll, his daughter
                      Daisy Gilley
Her sons:
  Tim
  Denis
Annie Murphy          Lillie Gilley
Sergeant            C. B. Ronayne
Perrott, a House Agent
                 E. K. Worthington
No record of publication.

## ROBERT O'DWYER and
## REV. THOMAS O'KELLY
*Eithne*
an Opera, music by O'Dwyer and
libretto by O'Kelly
First produced: 16 May 1910, at
the Gaiety Theatre, Dublin, with
Joseph O'Mara, William Dever,
chorus and orchestra.

## MARY COSTELLO
*The Coming of Aideen*
a Play in One Act.
First produced: 18 May 1910, by
the Irish Theatrical Club, at 40
Upper O'Connell Street, Dublin.

CAST

Aylmer Fitzgerald  George Nesbitt
Mary Martin         Deena Tyrrell
Aideen             Miss O'Meara
Kate Ann             Vera Blood
Patrick Scully
                 St. Laurence Tyrrell
No record of publication.

## MARY COSTELLO
*The Gods at Play*
a Play in One Act.

First produced: 18 May 1910, by
the Irish Theatrical Club, at 40
Upper O'Connell Street, Dublin.

CAST

Aubrey             Miss Campbell
Marie               Sheela Tobin
Also with Miss Wogan-Browne
and W. F. Casey.
No record of publication.

## S. L. ROBINSON
*Harvest*
a Play in Three Acts.
First produced: 19 May 1910, at
the Abbey Theatre, Dublin.

CAST

Jack Hurley      Fred O'Donovan
Mildred, married to Jack
                    Sara Allgood
Bridget Twomey, a neighbour
                 Eileen O'Doherty
Maggie Hannigan    Eithne Magee
Timothy Hurley   J. A. O'Rourke
Maurice Hurley    J. M. Kerrigan
William Lordan, a retired
  schoolmaster    Arthur Sinclair
Mary Hurley        Máire O'Neill
  Directed by S. L. Robinson
First published: in *Two Plays:
Harvest and The Clancy Name*
(Dublin: Maunsel, 1911).

## M. B. PEARSE
*The Message*
a Play in One Act and an
Epilogue.
First produced: 28 May 1910, by
the Leinster Stage Society, at the
Abbey Theatre, Dublin.

CAST

Donal              William Pearse
Shaun               Fred. Holden
Tadhg            Morgan O'Friel
A Neighbour           J. Doran
Máire               Julie Hayden
Noreen           Maureen Nugent
Cathleen            Ella Delaney
Lady Rivers    Miss M. Anderson
Mona Fitzgerald  Mary Fitzgerald
No record of publication.

## R. J. RAY (Robert J. Brophy)
*The Casting-Out of Martin Whelan*
a Play in Three Acts.
First produced: 29 September
1910, at the Abbey Theatre,
Dublin.

CAST

Mrs. Kirby          Sara Allgood
William Kirby, her son
                    Fred Harford
James Kirby, his father
          Sydney J. Morgan
Ned Mooney, a pig-buyer
          Arthur Sinclair
Peter Barton, a farmer
          J. M. Kerrigan
Ellen Barton, his daughter
          Máire O'Neill
Martin Whelan, an Australian
          Fred O'Donovan
Mrs. Pender, a servant
          Eileen O'Doherty
Mikeen Whip-the-Wind,
a fool          J. A. O'Rourke
Denis Barton Brinsley MacNamara
Peasants Eric Gorman, U. Wright,
     J. H. Dunne, R. Jameson,
                    Harry Young
     Directed by R. J. Ray
Unpublished.

T. C. MURRAY
*Birthright*
a Play in Two Acts.
First produced: 27 October 1910,
at the Abbey Theatre, Dublin.

CAST

Dan Hegarty     J. A. O'Rourke
Maura Morrissey
          Eileen O'Doherty
Bat Morrissey Sydney J. Morgan
Frank Harrington, a
schoolmaster     J. M. Kerrigan
Shane Morrissey  Arthur Sinclair
Hugh Morrissey Fred O'Donovan
     Directed by T. C. Murray
First published: Dublin: Maunsel,
1911.

T. J. MacSWINEY
*The Last Warriors of Coole*
a Hero Play in One Act.
First produced: 2 November 1910,
by the Cork Dramatic Society, at
the Dun Theatre, Cork.

CAST

Crimal, brother of Coole
          E. O'Shea
Warriors of Crimal:
   Fergor        Con O'Leary
   Bascell       T. O'Hea
   Fial          C. B. Ronayne
   Aenvar        P. O'Leary

Fionn, son of Coole, Saviour
   of his people     J. Gilley
   Stage Manager — J. Gilley
Unpublished.

LADY GREGORY
*The Full Moon*
a Comedy in One Act.
First produced: 10 November
1910, at the Abbey Theatre,
Dublin.

CAST

Bartley Fallon    Arthur Sinclair
Shawn Early     J. A. O'Rourke
Hyacinth Halvey
          Fred O'Donovan
Mrs. Broderick    Sara Allgood
Peter Tannian  Sydney J. Morgan
Miss Joyce      Eileen O'Doherty
Cracked Mary     Máire O'Neill
Davideen, an innocent, her
   brother       J. M. Kerrigan
     Directed by Lady Gregory
First published: By the author at
the Abbey Theatre, 1911; reprinted
in *Collected Plays*, Vol. III (Ger-
rards Cross, Buckinghamshire:
Colin Smythe, 1970).

SEUMAS O'KELLY
*The Shuiler's Child*
First production by the Abbey
Company: 24 November 1910.

CAST

Tim O'Halloran
          Sydney J. Morgan
Mrs. Finnessy  Sheila O'Sullivan
Nannie O'Hea   Eileen O'Doherty
Phil Woods      Felix Hughes
Moll Woods, a Shuiler
          Máire Nic Shiubhlaigh
Miss Cecilia Stoney  Eithne Magee
Andy O'Hea     Fred O'Donovan
First published: Dublin: Maunsel,
1909.

LADY GREGORY
*Coats*
a Comedy in One Act.
First production: 12 December
1910, at the Abbey Theatre,
Dublin.*

CAST

Hazel, editor of *Champion*
          J. M. Kerrigan
Mineog, editor of *Tribune*
          Arthur Sinclair

*Robinson, MacNamara and Saddlemyer incorrectly list 1 December.

448

John, a waiter    J. A. O'Rourke
First published: in *New Comedies*
(New York and London: Putnam,
1913); reprinted in *Collected Plays,*
Vol. I (Gerrards Cross, Bucking-
hamshire: Colin Smythe, 1970).

### T. J. MacSWINEY
*The Holocaust*
a Tragedy in One Act.
First produced: 27 December
1910, by the Cork Dramatic Society, at the Dun Theatre, Cork.

CAST

Mike Mahony    C. B. Ronayne
Polly Mahony    Daisy Gilley
Father Cahill    E. O'Shea
Dr. Condon    J. Flynn
Child
    Stage Manager — J. Gilley
Unpublished.

## 1911

### DOUGLAS HYDE
*A Nativity Play*
a Play in One Act, translated from
the Irish by Lady Gregory.
First produced: 5 January 1911,
at the Abbey Theatre, Dublin.

CAST

First Woman    Sara Allgood
Second Woman    Máire O'Neill
Kings  Fred O'Donovan, Ambrose
        Power, J. M. Kerrigan
Shepherds    Arthur Sinclair, J. A.
        O'Rourke, Eric Gorman
Saint Joseph    Sydney J. Morgan
Mary Mother
        Máire Nic Shiubhlaigh
Directed by S. L. Robinson
Set design by Robert Gregory
First published: in *Poets and
Dreamers* by Lady Gregory (Dub-
lin: Hodges Figgis, 1903 and Lon-
don: John Murray, 1903); re-
printed by Colin Smythe, 1974.

### LADY GREGORY
*The Deliverer*
a Tragic Comedy in One Act.
First produced: 12 January 1911,

at the Abbey Theatre, Dublin.

CAST

Dan    Arthur Sinclair
Ard    Fred O'Donovan
Malachi    J. A. O'Rourke
Dan's Wife    Máire O'Neill
Malachi's Wife    Sara Allgood
Ard's Wife  Máire Nic Shiubhlaigh
A Steward    Sydney J. Morgan
King's Nursling    J. M. Kerrigan
An Officer    Brinsley MacNamara
Directed by Lady Gregory
Lighting and arrangement of
Craig Screens by W. B. Yeats
Costumes designed by
        Gordon Craig
First published: in *Irish Folk-
History Plays,* Second Series (New
York and London: Putnam, 1912);
reprinted in *Collected Plays,* Vol.
II (Gerrards Cross, Buckingham-
shire: Colin Smythe, 1970).

### LORD DUNSANY
*King Argimenes and the
Unknown Warrior*
a Play in Two Acts.
First produced: 26 January 1911,
at the Abbey Theatre, Dublin.

CAST

King Argimenes  Fred O'Donovan
Zarb    J. M. Kerrigan
An Old Slave    Fred Harford
A Young Slave
        Brinsley MacNamara
A Prophet    J. A. O'Rourke
The King's Overseer
        Ambrose Power
King Darniak    Arthur Sinclair
Queen Atharlia    Sara Allgood
Queen Oxara    Maeve O'Donnell
Queen Cahafra    Máire O'Neill
Queen Tragolind
        Máire Nic Shiubhlaigh
The Idol Guard
        Sydney J. Morgan
The Servant of the King's
Dog    Eric Gorman
An Attendant    R. V. Jamieson*
Directed by S. L. Robinson†
First published: in *Five Plays*
(London: Grant Richards, 1914;
New York: Mitchell Kennerley,
1914).

*This spelling is from the original Abbey programme; Robinson, however,
has 'R. V. Jameson'.

†Robinson cites himself as director; Bierstadt has Nugent Monck directing,
and also designing set and costumes.

## W. B. YEATS
*The Land of Heart's Desire*
a Play in One Act.
First production by the Abbey
Company: 16 February 1911.

CAST

Bridget Bruin   Eileen O'Doherty
Shawn Bruin   Fred O'Donovan
Maurteen Bruin   J. M. Kerrigan
Father Hart   Arthur Sinclair
Máire Bruin   Sara Allgood
A Faery   Máire O'Neill
Directed by S. L. Robinson
First published: London: T. Fisher
Unwin, 1894; reprinted in *The
Variorum Plays*, 1966.

## T. C. MURRAY
*Birthright*, revised version.
First produced: 16 February 1911,
at the Abbey Theatre, Dublin.

## M. B. PEARSE
*The Cricket on the Hearth*
adapted from Dickens.
First produced: 23 February 1911,
by the Leinster Stage Society, at
the Abbey Theatre, Dublin.

CAST

John Perrybingle   William Pearse
Dot   Mary Fitzgerald
Caleb Plummer
   Fred A. MacDonald
Bertha   M. Anderson
Tackleton   Edwin P. Lewis
May Fielding   Ella Delaney
A Stranger   Morgan O'Friel
Directed by M. B. Pearse
Unpublished.

## MORGAN O'FRIEL
*The Skull*
a Farce in One Act.
First produced: 23 February 1911,
by the Leinster Stage Society, at
the Abbey Theatre, Dublin.

CAST

William James Dougherty
   Fred A. MacDonald
Maggi Ann   Mary Fitzgerald
Master McIlwee   William Pearse
Sergeant Reilly, R.I.C.
   Andrew Nowlan
Directed by Morgan O'Friel
Unpublished.

## BRIAN MacCARTHY
*Down in Kerry*

a Play in One Act.
First produced: 28 February 1911,
by the Uí Breasail Amateur
Dramatic Society, at the Abbey
Theatre, Dublin.
Unpublished.

## JOHANNA REDMOND
*Falsely True*
a Play in One Act.
First produced: 6 March 1911, at
the Palace Theatre, London.

CAST

Moran   W. G. Fay
Mary   Sara Allgood
Shaun   Fred O'Donovan
Directed by W. G. Fay
First and only Abbey production:
9 October 1911, at the Plymouth
Theatre, Boston.

CAST

Moran   ?
Mary   Sara Allgood
Shaun   Fred O'Donovan
Unpublished.

## ST. JOHN ERVINE
*Mixed Marriage*
a Play in Four Acts.
First produced: 30 March 1911,
at the Abbey Theatre, Dublin.

CAST

John Rainey   Arthur Sinclair
Mrs. Rainey   Máire O'Neill
Tom Rainey   U. Wright
Nora Murray
   Máire Nic Shiubhlaigh
Hugh Rainey   J. M. Kerrigan
Michael O'Hara   J. A. O'Rourke
Directed by Lennox Robinson
First published: Dublin: Maunsel,
1911.

## P. H. PEARSE
*The Passion Play* (*An Páis*)
a Play in Three Acts.
First produced: 7 April 1911, by
the pupils of St. Enda's School,
at the Abbey Theatre, Dublin.
Unpublished.

## T. J. MacSWINEY
*Manners Masketh Man*
a Comedy in One Act.
First produced: 19 April 1911, by
the Cork Dramatic Society, at the
Dún Theatre, Cork.

Paddy Brennan      J. Flynn
Molly      Miss D. Gilley
Nora      Miss L. Gilley
Eva Moore    Miss M. Moynihan
Miss Sarah Mullins
         Miss B. Duggan
Stage Manager — C. B. Ronayne
Unpublished.

## DANIEL CORKERY
*The Onus of Ownership*
a Comedy in One Act.
First produced: 19 April 1911, by
the Cork Dramatic Society, at the
Dún Theatre, Cork.

CAST

Jeremiah Farrell    C. B. Ronayne
Kate Farrell    Miss M. Moynihan
Mrs. Casey    Miss D. Gilley
Paddy      T. O'Hea
Mrs. Dorgan    Miss B. Duggan
Johnnyboy    J. Scannell
Mikus    P. K. K. Lynch
Stage Manager — C. B. Ronayne
Unpublished.

## DANIEL CORKERY
*Epilogue*
First produced: 18 May 1911, by
the Cork Dramatic Society, at the
Dún Theatre, Cork.
Unpublished.

## JOHANNA REDMOND
*Honor's Choice*
a Comedietta of Irish Rural Life
in One Act.
First produced: 26 June 1911, by
the Irish Theatre and National
Stage Company, at the Queen's
Theatre, Dublin.

CAST

Morough    Jack Little
Phelim    George Larchet
Widow Kelly    Miss N. Black
Honor    Miss K. Drago
Unpublished.

## JOHANNA REDMOND
*The Best of a Bad Bargain*
a Play in One Act.
First produced: 26 July 1911, by
Mrs. Mouillot, at the Gaiety
Theatre, Dublin.

CAST

Ben Brusnahan    Charles Macdona
Mary Sheehan    Mrs. Mouillot

Jerry O'Rourke    Arthur Eldred
Unpublished.

## WILLIAM BOYLE
*The Love Charm*
a Farce in One Act.
First produced: 4 September 1911,
at the W. A. Henderson Benefit
Performance, at the Abbey Theatre, Dublin.

CAST

Terence Tracy    Arthur Sinclair
Patsy Ward    Fred O'Donovan
Betty Cronin    Nora Desmond
Ann Cronin    Sara Allgood
Unpublished.

## MARY COSTELLO
*The Coming of Aideen*
a Comedy in One Act.
First produced: 4 September 1911,
by the Irish Theatre and National
Stage Company, at the Queen's
Theatre, Dublin.
Unpublished.

## JOHANNA REDMOND
*Pro Patria*
a Play in One Act.
First produced: 4 September 1911,
by the Irish Theatre and National
Stage Company, at the Queen's
Theatre, Dublin.

CAST

Sarah Kelly    Kathleen Drago
Mrs. Kelly    Helena Moloney
Peter Kelly    H. Hutchinson
Michael Dwyer    F. J. Bridgeman
John    Bob Arthur
An English Officer    Harry Kildare
Spy    Jack Little
     Directed by J. M. Carré
Unpublished.

## J. MALACHI MULDOON
*A Hospital Ward*
a Drama in One Act.
First produced: 4 September 1911,
by the Irish Theatre and National
Stage Company, at the Queen's
Theatre, Dublin.

CAST

Eileen    Miss D. Manners
Miss Desmond    Violet McGuinness
Nurse    Nettie Neville
Shaun    Jack Little
House Surgeon    H. Hutchinson
Priest    M. Flynn
Unpublished.

## P. KEHOE

*When Wexford Rose*
a Play in One Act.
First produced: 13 November
1911, at the Queen's Theatre,
Dublin.
The cast included Lincoln Cal-
thrope, Jack Little, Joe Birdman,
Gerald Desmond, Harry Hutchinson, Madame Luise Grafton, Miss
D. Manners. This was a curtain
raiser to *A Daughter of Ireland*
by G. J. Hurson, apparently produced earlier in the North.
First published: Enniscorthy: Echo
Printing & Publishing Co., [1911].

## ANON.

*The Interlude of Youth*
(*Mundus et Infans*)
a Medieval Morality.
First production by the Abbey
Company: 16 November 1911, by
the Abbey School of Acting, at
the Abbey Theatre, Dublin.

CAST

| | |
|---|---|
| Charity | Belle Johnston |
| Youth | Nugent Monck |
| Riot | Jack Martin |
| Pride | Charles Power |
| Luxury | Nora Desmond |
| Humility | Violet McCarthy |

Directed by Nugent Monck
Dresses designed by Jennie Moore

## DOUGLAS HYDE

*The Marriage (An Posadh)*
a Play in One Act, translated from
the Irish by Lady Gregory.
First production by the Abbey
Company: 16 November 1911, by
the Abbey School of Acting, at
the Abbey Theatre, Dublin.

CAST

| | |
|---|---|
| Martin | Charles Power |
| Mary | F. M. Salkeld |
| Blind Fiddler | Michael Conniffe |
| Old Farmer | A. Patrick Wilson |
| Middle-Aged Woman | R. Leech |
| Fair Young Man | W. J. Manser |
| Grey-Haired Man | J. McCabe |
| Two Girls | Mona Shiel, M. Perolze |
| Young Man | J. R. Burke |
| Miser | Patrick Murphy |

Directed by Nugent Monck
First published: in *Poets and
Dreamers* by Lady Gregory (Dub-
lin: Hodges, Figgis; London: John
Murray, 1903.

## JAMES STEPHENS

*The Marriage of Julia Elizabeth*
a Comedy in One Act.
First produced: 17 November
1911, by the Theatre of Ireland,
at the Hardwicke Street Hall,
Dublin.

CAST

| | |
|---|---|
| Mrs. O'Reilly | Kitty McCormack |
| Mr. O'Reilly | Fred Jeffs |
| Mr. O'Grady | Cyril Keogh |

Directed by Fred Morrow
Scenery and Lighting by
Norman Morrow
First published: New York: Cros-
by Gaige, 1929, in a limited signed
edition of 861 copies.

## ANON.

*The Second Shepherd's Play*
a Medieval Morality.
First production by the Abbey
Company: 23 November 1911, by
the Abbey School of Acting, at
the Abbey Theatre, Dublin.

CAST

| | |
|---|---|
| First Shepherd | S. Grenville Darling |
| Second Shepherd | George St. John |
| Third Shepherd | Farrell Pelly |
| Mac | A. Patrick Wilson |
| Gabriel | W. J. Manser |
| Gill | Mary Roberts |

Directed by Nugent Monck

## MOLLY F. SCOTT

*Charity*
a Play in One Act.
First produced: 4 December 1911,
by the Ulster Literary Theatre, at
the Grand Opera House, Belfast.

CAST

| | |
|---|---|
| Timothy Tracy | Arthur Malcolm |
| Farmer Flanagan | J. M. Harding |
| Mrs. Flanagan | Margaret O'Gorman |
| Maggie Harty | Kathleen Lawrence |
| Kate | Mary Crothers |
| Mrs. Donovan | Marion Crimmins |

Also with C. K. Ayre and Walter
Kennedy.
Unpublished.

## RUTHERFORD MAYNE

*Red Turf*
a Play in One Act.
First produced: 5 December 1911,
by the Ulster Literary Theatre, at
the Grand Opera House, Belfast.

Martin Burke        Joseph Campbell
Mary Burke          Josephine Mayne
Michael Flanagan    Ross Canmer
Michael Flanagan the Younger
                    C. K. Ayre
John Heffernan      J. M. Harding
Produced also: 7 December 1911,
by the Abbey School of Acting, at
the Abbey Theatre, Dublin.

CAST

Martin Burke        J. R. Burke
Mary Burke          Máire O'Neill
Michael Flanagan    Patrick Murphy
Michael Flanagan the Younger
                    Charles Power
John Heffernan      Farrell Pelly
Directed by Nugent Monck with
the assistance of Máire O'Neill
First published: in *The Drone
and Other Plays* (Dublin: Maunsel, 1912).

## WILLIAM PAUL
*The Jerrybuilders*
a Play in One Act.
First produced: 5 December 1911,
by the Ulster Literary Theatre, at
the Grand Opera House, Belfast.

CAST

Mary Crichton       Eveleen Fitzgerald
Ada Kelly           Kathleen Lawrence
Eva Grainger        Marion Crimmins
Eileen              Miss Kelso
Miss Beggs          Mary Crothers
Rev. Joseph McCurdy
                    Gerald MacNamara
Robert Grainger     Ross Canmer
Howard Grainger     Norman Gray
Hugh Rowan          Walter Kennedy
The Country Doctor
                    Francis Dornan
Unpublished.

## T. J. MacSWINEY
*The Wooing of Emer*
a Play in Three Acts.
First produced: 6 December 1911,
by the Cork Dramatic Society, at
the Dún Theatre, Cork.

CAST

Cuchullain          T. O'Hea
Laeg                J. Flynn
Forgal              J. MacSwiney
Colla               P. J. K. Lynch
Conn                J. Scannell
Emer                Miss D. Gilley
Ita                 Miss M. Murray

1st Guard           C. Foley
2nd Guard           T. Doherty
3rd Guard           P. O'Leary
Wounded Warrior     C. Ronayne
Guards and Warriors
Stage Manager — P. O'Leary
Unpublished.

## GEORGE A. BIRMINGHAM
(Canon J. O. Hannay)
*Eleanor's Enterprise*
a Comedy in Three Acts.
First produced: 11 December, by
the Independent Theatre Company, at the Gaiety Theatre,
Dublin.

CAST

Lord Kilbarron      George Nesbitt
The Archdeacon of Barna
                    Eric Gorman
Dr. Reilly          G. P. Quill
Paudeen Finnegan    J. Connolly
Butler              Mr. Fitzherbert
Sergeant, R.I.C.    Mr. Stockley
Constable, R.I.C.   Mr. G. Moore
Lady Kilbarron      Violet Mervyn
Eleanor Maxwell
    Mme. Constance de Markievicz
Marion Ashley       Eleanor Moore
Mrs. Finnegan       Helena Moloney
Housemaid           Miss de Vere
Cook                Miss Fairfax
        Directed by
    Casimir Dunin Markievicz
Unpublished.
A revised version with the title of
*Send for Dr. O'Grady* was produced in July, 1923, at the Criterion Theatre, London.

## CASIMIR DUNIN MARKIEVICZ
*Rival Stars*
a Drama of Parisian life in
probably Three Acts.
First produced: 12 December
1911, by the Independent Theatre
Company, at the Gaiety Theatre,
Dublin.

CAST

Robert Ellis        John Raeburn
Rene Dupuis         Patrick Quill
Roy Goldberg        Eric Gorman
John Maxwell        V. Justice
Mr. Hayes           G. Fitzgerald
A Beggar            Mr. Lytton
Mary             Miss N. Fitzpatrick
Amy Webster         Violet Mervyn
Dagna Ellis

Mme. Constance de Markievicz
Directed by
Casimir Dunin Markievicz

## JANE BARLOW
*A Bunch of Lavender*
a Play in Two Scenes.
First produced: 18 December 1911,
by the Theatre of Ireland, at the
Hardwicke Street Hall, Dublin.

CAST

| | |
|---|---|
| Fergus McDonough | Crawford Neil |
| Murtagh Regan | Frank Walker |
| Lance Fitzalleyne | G. Jackson |
| Mrs. Helen O'Neill | Norah Hague |
| Eileen O'Neill | Gipsy Walker |
| Teresa Finucane | Mary Delane |

No record of publication.

## WATTY COX
*The Widow Dempsey's Funeral*
Condensed into Two Scenes by
J. Crawford-Neil.
First produced: 18 December 1911,
by the Theatre of Ireland, at the
Hardwicke Street Hall, Dublin.

CAST

| | |
|---|---|
| Dan Flattery | Fred Jeffs |
| O'Regan | Jack Morrow |
| Mr. Pat Maley | Mr. Keogh |
| Mrs. Artichoke | |
| | Miss K. McCormick |
| Mrs. B. Maley | Miss Foley |
| Biddy | Miss Taaffe |

Unpublished in this form.

## M. B. PEARSE
*The Good People*
a Comedy in One Act.
First produced: 26 December 1911,
by the Leinster Stage Society, at
the Abbey Theatre, Dublin.

CAST

| | |
|---|---|
| Honor | Mary Fitzgerald |
| Fan | M. Jubb |
| The Fairy of the Thorn | |
| | Eileen O'Donahoe |
| Larry | William Pearse |

Unpublished.

## SEAMUS O'HERAN
*For a Lady's Sake*
an Unfinished Play in One Act.
First produced: 26 December 1911,
by the Leinster Stage Society, at
the Abbey Theatre, Dublin.

CAST

| | |
|---|---|
| Victor Delane | Fred Loco |
| Edith | Florence Lehane |
| Stage Manager | Samuel Lyons |
| Acting Manager | Marcus O'Neill |

Unpublished.

# 1912

## ANON.
*The Annunciation*
a Medieval Mystery Play.
First production by the Abbey
Company: 4 January 1912, by the
Abbey School of Acting, at the
Abbey Theatre, Dublin.

CAST

| | |
|---|---|
| Mary | Nell Byrne |
| | (Blanaid Salkeld) |
| St. Joseph | Nugent Monck |
| Gabriel | Charles Power |

Directed by Nugent Monck

## ANON.
*The Flight into Egypt*
a Medieval Mystery Play.
First production by the Abbey
Company: 4 January 1912, by the
Abbey School of Acting, at the
Abbey Theatre, Dublin.

CAST

| | |
|---|---|
| Mary | Nell Byrne |
| St. Joseph | Nugent Monck |
| Gabriel | Charles Power |

Directed By Nugent Monck

## LADY GREGORY
*MacDaragh's Wife*
(later called *McDonough's Wife*)
a Play in One Act.
First produced: 11 January 1912,
by the Abbey School of Acting, at
the Abbey Theatre, Dublin.

CAST

| | |
|---|---|
| First Hag | Mary Roberts |
| Second Hag | Helena Moloney |
| MacDaragh | Philip Guiry |
| Sheep-shearers | Messrs. Michael |

Conniffe, George St. John,
Farrell Pelly, Patrick Murphy,
A. P. Wilson, J. R. Burke.
Directed by Nugent Monck
First published: in *New Comedies*
(London & New York: Putnam's,
1913); rpr. in *Collected Plays*,
Vol. II.

## EVA GORE-BOOTH

*Unseen Kings*
a Mythological Verse Play in
One Act.
First produced: 25 January 1912,
by the Independent Theatre Company, at the Abbey Theatre,
Dublin.

CAST

| | |
|---|---|
| Cuchulain | Patrick Quill |
| Cathvah | George Fitzgerald |
| A Bard | Breffni O'Rourke |
| Niamh | Violet Mervyn |
| Eineen | Helena Moloney |
| A Stranger | |
| | Mme. Constance de Markievicz |
| First Singer | Nettie Edwards |
| Second Singer | Eileen Furlong |

Directed by
Casimir Dunin Markievicz
Music by Prof. Max Mayer
First published: in *Poems of Eva
Gore-Booth* (London: Longman's,
Green, 1929).

## EDWARD MARTYN

*Grangecolman*
a Domestic Drama in Three Acts.
First produced: 25 January 1912,
by the Independent Theatre
Company, at the Abbey Theatre,
Dublin.

CAST

| | |
|---|---|
| Michael Colman | George Fitzgerald |
| Lucius Devlin | Patrick Quill |
| Horan | Robert V. Justice |
| Clare Farquhar | Edith Dodd |
| Catherine Devlin | |
| | Mme. Constance de Markievicz |

Directed by
Casimir Dunin Markievicz
First published: Dublin: Maun-
sel, 1912.

## JOHANNA REDMOND

*Leap Year*
a Play in One Act.
First produced: 4 February 1912,
at the Aughrim National School.

CAST

| | |
|---|---|
| Mona Carey | Johanna Redmond |
| Cathal O'Connor | |
| | Murrough Barry O'Brien |

Unpublished.
Later revised as *Leap Year in the
West* and performed on 18 March
1912, by the Pioneer Club at the
St. Francis Xavier Hall, Dublin.

## DOUGLAS HYDE

*An Tincéar agus an t-Sidheóg*
(*The Tinker and the Fairy*)
First production by the Abbey
School of Acting, at the Abbey
Theatre, Dublin.

CAST

| | |
|---|---|
| An t-Sidheóg | Nell Ní Bhrion |
| An Tincéar | Cathal Paor |
| Fear Og | Micheál Ua Coinnibh |
| Feilmeóir | Philip MacGaoraidh |
| Bean Og | Una Ní Conochubhar |
| Sidheógha | Una Nic Shiubhlaigh, |

G. Ní Muiris, Máire Ní hAodha,
M. Ní Ghallcobhair, E. Ní
Cathmhaoil, C. Ní Riain, Una
Ní Leigh, Mildred Connmhaigh,
T. Bairéad, F. Peallaí, A.
Mistéal, A. P. Mac Liam,
H. Hutchinson, S. Mac Eoin
Directed by Nugent Monck

## NORAH FITZPATRICK

(Mrs. O'Hara)
*The Dangerous Age*
a Play in One Act.
First produced: 19 February 1912,
by the Independent Theatre Company, at the Abbey Theatre,
Dublin.

CAST

| | |
|---|---|
| Jack Burns, a London Barrister | |
| | P. J. O'Hara |
| Mary, his Wife | Violet Mervyn |
| Matilda Strongbow, a | |
| Suffragette | Norah Fitzpatrick |
| Jane, the maid | Miss G. McCormac |

Unpublished.

## ANON.

*The Worlde and the Chylde* (The
Interlude of *Mundus and Infans*)
a Sixteenth Century Morality Play,
edited by Nugent Monck.
First production by the Abbey
Company: 29 February 1912, by
the Abbey Theatre School of Acting, at the Abbey Theatre, Dublin.

CAST

| | |
|---|---|
| The World | Patrick Murphy |
| The Mother | Una Nic Shiubhlaigh |
| The Child | Master Felix Hughes |
| Manhood | Nugent Monck |
| Conscience | A. Patrick Wilson |
| Folly | Philip Guiry |
| Perseverance | Charles Power |
| Pride | Ethel Fletcher |
| Covetousness | Maidha Gallagher |

| Wrath | Kathleen O'Brien |
|---|---|
| Envy | Mary Roberts |
| Indolence | Nell Byrne |
| Gluttony | Miss G. Laird |
| Luxury | Miss Mona O'Beirne |
| Page | Miss P. Goodwin |

Directed by Nugent Monck

## L. McMANUS

*O'Donnell's Cross*
a Play in One Act.
First produced: Possibly on 18 March 1912, by the Pioneer Dramatic Club, at St. Francis Xavier's Hall, Dublin.
Unpublished.

## WILLIAM BOYLE

*Family Failing*
a Comedy in Three Acts.
First produced: 28 March 1912, by the Abbey Company, at the Abbey Theatre, Dublin.

### CAST

| Dominic Donnelly | Arthur Sinclair |
|---|---|
| Joe Donnelly | Sydney J. Morgan |
| Robert Donnelly | Fred O'Donovan |
| Tom Carragher | J. M. Kerrigan |
| Francy Niel | M. J. Dolan |
| Maria Donnelly | Eileen O'Doherty |
| Mrs. Carragher | Cathleen Nesbitt |
| Nelty | Kathleen Drago |

Directed by Lennox Robinson
First published: Dublin: Gill, 1912.

## D. P. LUCEY

*The Passing of 'Miah*
a Comedy in One Act.
First produced: 10 April 1912, by the Cork Dramatic Society, at the Dun Theatre, Queen Street, Cork.
Unpublished.

## LENNOX ROBINSON

*Patriots*
a Play in Three Acts.
First produced: 11 April 1912, by the Abbey Company, at the Abbey Theatre, Dublin.

### CAST

| James O'Mahoney | |
|---|---|
| | Sydney J. Morgan |
| Ann Nugent | Sara Allgood |
| Rose Nugent, her child | |
| | Kathleen Drago |
| Mrs. Sullivan | Eileen O'Doherty |
| Ann's brothers: | |
| Bob | Arthur Sinclair |

| Harry | J. A. O'Rourke |
|---|---|
| Willie Sullivan | Charles Power |
| James Nugent | Fred O'Donovan |
| Father Kearney | J. M. Kerrigan |
| Dan Sullivan | Philip Guiry |
| Jim Powell | J. M. Kerrigan |
| Two Young Men | U. Wright, Philip Guiry |

Directed by Lennox Robinson
First published: Dublin: Maunsel, 1912.

## JOSEPH CAMPBELL

*Judgment*
a Play in Two Acts.
First produced: 15 April 1912, by the Abbey Theatre's Second Company, at the Abbey Theatre, Dublin.

### CAST

| Owen Ban | H. E. Hutchinson |
|---|---|
| Nabla, his wife | Nell Byrne |
| John Gilla Carr | J. G. St. John |
| Parry Cam Aosta, a very old man | Philip Guiry |
| Colum Johnston | A. P. Wilson |
| Peter MacManus | T. Barrett |
| Kate Kinsella, a midwife | Mona O'Beirne |
| Peg Straw, a strolling woman | Mary Galway |
| The Stranger | G. R. Burke |
| Father John | Charles Power |

In the published text, Patcheen, a boy, and Other Men and Women are listed in the Cast.
Directed by Lennox Robinson
First published: Dublin & London: Maunsel, 1912.

## THOMAS MacDONAGH

*Metempsychosis, or a Mad World*
a Play in One Act.
First produced: 18 April 1912, by the Theatre of Ireland, at the Hardwicke Street Hall, Dublin.

### CAST

| Earl Winton-Winton de Winton | |
|---|---|
| | Crawford Neill |
| The Stranger | Robert Eaton |
| Lady Winton-Winton de Winton | |
| | Moire Walker |
| Gladys | Gipsy Walker |

First separate publication: [Dublin: Reprinted from *The Irish Review* (Feb., 1912), 1912.]

## W. B. YEATS

*Kathleen Ni Houlihan*
a Play in One Act, translated into

Irish by Rev. Thomas O'Kelly.
First produced: 2 May 1912, by
the Theatre of Ireland, at the
Hardwicke Street Hall, Dublin.

CAST

Peadar O Giollarain
                    Shaun Cavanagh
An t-Shan Bhean Bhocht
                    Máire Nic Shiubhlaigh
And others.

## PADRAIG O SEAGHDHA

*An Gliocas*
a Bilingual Play in One Act.
First produced: 2 May 1912, by
the Theatre of Ireland, at the
Hardwicke Street Hall, Dublin.

CAST

A Pensions Officer    H. Nicholls
A County Councillor
                    Shaun Cavanagh
And others.
Unpublished.

## FRANCIS MACNAMARA

*The Schemers*
a Play in One Act.
First produced: 18 May 1912, by
the Theatre in Eyre [*sic*], at the
Crosby Hall, More's Garden,
Chelsea, London.
No record of publication.

## P. H. PEARSE

*An Rí (The King)*
a Pageant Play.
First produced: 15 June 1912, by
the pupils of St. Enda's, at St.
Enda's College, Rathfarnham.
Irish version first published: in
*An Macaomh*, II (May, 1913);
both Irish and English versions
in *Collected Works* (Dublin:
Phoenix Pub., 1917).

## T. C. MURRAY

*Maurice Harte*
a Play in Two Acts.
First produced: 20 June 1912, by
the Abbey Company, at the Royal
Court Theatre, London.

CAST

| | |
|---|---|
| Mrs. O'Connor | Eileen O'Doherty |
| Ellen Harte | Sara Allgood |
| Maurice Harte | Fred O'Donovan |
| Father Mangan | Sydney J. Morgan |
| Michael Harte | Arthur Sinclair |

| | |
|---|---|
| Owen Harte | J. A. O'Rourke |
| Peter Mangan | U. Wright |

Directed by Lennox Robinson
First published: Dublin: Maunsel,
1912.
First produced at the Abbey
Theatre on 12 September 1912.

## VICTOR O'D. POWER

*The Ordeal of David*
A Play in Three Acts.
First produced: 1 July 1912, by
the Theatre of Ireland, at the
Hardwicke Street Hall, Dublin.
Unpublished. Apparently this is an
early version of the author's later
*David Mahony*.

## LADY GREGORY

*The Bogie Men*
a Comedy in One Act.
First produced: 4 July 1912, by
the Abbey Players, at the Royal
Court Theatre, London.

CAST

Chimney Sweeps:

| | |
|---|---|
| Taig O'Harragha | J. M. Kerrigan |
| Darby Melody | J. A. O'Rourke |

Directed by Lennox Robinson
First published: in *New Comedies*
(New York & London: Putnam's,
1913); rev. & rpr. in *Collected
Plays*, Vol. I.

## S. R. DAY

*Out of the Deep Shadow*
a Play in One Act.
First produced: 30 September 1912,
by the Independent Theatre Company, at the Gaiety Theatre,
Dublin.
Unpublished.

## ST. JOHN G. ERVINE

*The Magnanimous Lover*
a Play in One Act.
First produced: 17 October 1912,
by the Abbey Players, at the
Abbey Theatre, Dublin.

CAST

| | |
|---|---|
| Samuel Hinde | J. A. O'Rourke |
| Henry Hinde | J. M. Kerrigan |
| William Cather | Sydney J. Morgan |
| Mrs. Cather | Mona O'Beirne |
| Maggie Cather | Máire O'Neill |

Directed by Lennox Robinson
First published: Dublin: Maunsel,
1912.

## W. B. YEATS

*The Hour Glass*
a New Version of the One-Act
Morality Play.
First produced: 21 November 1912,
by the Abbey Theatre's Second
Company, at the Abbey Theatre,
Dublin.

CAST

| | |
|---|---|
| The Wise Man | Nugent Monck |
| Teague the Fool | J. A. O'Rourke |
| The Angel | Mona Beirne |
| Wife | Eileen O'Doherty |
| Child | Kathleen Drago |
| Pupils | Messrs. Eric Gorman, |

Charles Power, Fred Harford,
Michael Dolan, T. Barrett,
Desmond Fitzgerald and T. Healy
Directed by Nugent Monck

## LADY GREGORY

*Damer's Gold*
a Comedy in Two Acts
First produced: 21 November
1912, by the Abbey Players, at the
Abbey Theatre, Dublin.

CAST

| | |
|---|---|
| Delia Hessian | Sara Allgood |
| Staffy Kirwan, her brother | |
| | Sydney J. Morgan |
| Ralph Hessian, Delia's husband | |
| | J. M. Kerrigan |
| Patrick Kirwan (called Damer), | |
| Delia's and Staffy's brother | |
| | Arthur Sinclair |
| Simon Niland, their nephew | |
| | U. Wright |

Directed by Lennox Robinson
First published: in *New Comedies*
(New York & London: Putnam's,
1913); rpr. in *Collected Plays*,
Vol. I.

## J. BERNARD MacCARTHY

*The Dream Market*
a Play in One Act.
First produced: 21 November 1912,
by the Dramatic Society of the
I.C.I.C.Y.M.A., in Cork.

CAST

| | |
|---|---|
| Allan Moore | T. Horne |
| Mrs. Moore, his mother | |
| | Dora Ingle |
| Kathleen Ryan | |
| | Olive Brooke Hughes |
| Iris Cairnham | E. M. Bridges |
| Captain Gainford | F. W. Thompson |

No record of publication.

## DANIEL CORKERY

*Israel's Incense*
a Play in Three Acts
and a Prologue.
First produced: 2 December 1912,
by the Cork Dramatic Society, at
the Opera House, Cork.

CAST

| | |
|---|---|
| Tetha, the King | Con O'Leary |
| Keltar, the Keeper of his | |
| Annals | J. Flynn |
| Fanla, the King's Counsellor | |
| | P. J. K. Lynch |
| Cormac, the King's Counsellor | |
| | P. J. K. Lynch |
| Alova, the Queen | M. O'Connell |
| Eeving, a Singing Maiden | |
| | Miss L. Desmond |
| Findmor, a Singing Maiden | |
| | Miss N. O'Brien |
| Fohnam, the Sculptor | T. O'Hea |
| Connud, his Gilly | C. Foley |
| Ivor | P. Mulcahy |
| Delbay | P. O'Connell |
| Sailor | C. Perrott |

Also Guards, Voices, Sailors, etc.
Stage Manager — Charles Perrott
Dresses designed by
Daniel Corkery
First published: in a revised ver-
sion under the title of *Fohnam
the Sculptor* (Newark, Delaware:
Proscenium Press, 1973).

## CON O'LEARY

*The Crossing*
a Tragedy in One Act.
First produced: 3 December 1912,
by the Cork Dramatic Society, at
the Opera House, Cork.

CAST

| | |
|---|---|
| William Fenton | J. Flynn |
| Mary the Roads | Miss M. O'Connell |
| Mathew the Rhymes | P. J. K. Lynch |
| Thomas Fenton | T. O'Hea |

Stage Manager — Charles Perrott
Unpublished.

## JOHN F. LYONS

*Drift*
a Tragedy in One Act.
First produced: 3 December 1912,
by the Cork Dramatic Society, at
the Opera House, Cork.

CAST

| | |
|---|---|
| Mrs. Downey | Miss M. O'Connell |
| Mary, his daughter | |
| | Miss L. Desmond |

Shawn, her son       T. O'Hea
Donal O'Neill       P. J. K. Lynch
Ned Corcoran, a postman   J. Flynn
Stage Manager — Charles Perrott
Unpublished.

## MISS M. F. SCOTT

*Family Rights*
a Play in One Act.
First produced: 9 December 1912,
by the Ulster Theatre, at the
Grand Opera House, Belfast.

CAST

Mrs. Rooney       Peggy McCurdy
Mrs. Fogarty       Miss M. Crother
Dan Fogarty       J. M. Harding
John Rooney       G. A. Charters
Unpublished.

## WILLIAM PAUL

*Sweeping the Country*
a Comedy in Two Acts.
First produced: 10 December 1912,
by the Ulster Theatre, at the
Grand Opera House, Belfast.

CAST

James McKay, J.P., Chairman of
  the Oldtown Town
  Council       Gerald MacNamara
Mrs. McKay, his wife
            Eveleen Fitzgerald
Molly       Kathleen Lawrence
Arthur Vincent of Dublin
            Jackson Grahame
Charley Moore       C. J. Abbey
Andy Cunningham   J. M. Harding
Paddy Doyle       Alan Whitley
Albert Barr       John Field
Mrs. Gray       Mary Crothers
    Directed by J. F. Magee
Unpublished.

## GERALD MacNAMARA

(Harry Morrow)
*Thompson in Tír-na-nOg*
a Comedy in One Act.
First produced: 9 December 1912,
by the Ulster Theatre, at the
Grand Opera House, Belfast.

CAST

High King of Tír na nOg
            Jackson Grahame
Finn       Norman Gray
Angus       C. J. Abbey
Cuchulain       C. K. Ayre
Conan       Charles W. Wilson
Maeve       Kathleen Lawrence
Grania       Eveleen Fitzgerald

Thompson of Scarva  J. M. Harding
    Directed by J. F. Magee
First published: Dublin: Talbot
Press, [1912].

## MARY COSTELLO

*The Gods at Play*
a Play in One Act.
First produced: Probably on 13
December 1912, by amateurs at
the Abbey Theatre, Dublin, with
Breffni O'Rourke in the cast.
Unpublished.

## PADRAIC COLUM

*The Shepherd's Play*
Being the Wakefield Second Shep-
herd's Play, translated into terms
of Irish Peasant life, on the sug-
gestion of W. B. Yeats, in One Act.
No record of production.
First published: in *Sinn Féin* (21
December 1912), pp. 2–3.

## E. HAMILTON MOORE

*A Little Christmas Miracle*
a Play in One Act.
First produced: 26 December 1912,
by the Abbey Theatre's Second
Company, at the Abbey Theatre,
Dublin.

CAST

Daniel Byrne       Philip Guiry
Michael O'Halloran
            Patrick Murphy
Larry Sullivan   Michael Conniffe
The Captain       Farrell Pelly
Bridget Cassidy   Helen Moloney
The Strange Woman   Nell Byrne
    Directed by Lennox Robinson
Unpublished.

## A. PATRICK WILSON

*Victims*
a Play in One Act.
First produced: 26 December 1912,
by the Irish Workers Dramatic
Club, at Liberty Hall, Dublin.

CAST

Jack Nolan       A. Patrick Wilson
Anne Nolan       Delia Larkin
George Purcell       Denis Greghan
James Quinn       James Smith
First published: in *Victims and
Poached*. [Dublin: Irish Transport
and General Workers' Union, ca.
1912.]

459

# 1913

### REV. J. M. COSTELLO
*The Return of Columbkille*
First produced: 7 January 1913, by the Irish Historical Players, at St. Francis Xavier's Hall, Dublin. Unpublished.

### GEORGE A. BIRMINGHAM
*General John Regan*
a Play in Three Acts.
First produced: 9 January 1913, at the Apollo Theatre, London.

CAST

Dr. Lucius O'Grady
Charles Hawtrey
Timothy Doyle    Leonard Boyne
Major Kent    Frank Stoney
Thaddeus Golligher    W. G. Fay
Horace P. Billing    Henry Wenman
C. Gregg    J. R. Tozer
Sergeant Colgan, R.I.C.
Patrick Quill
Tom Kerrigan    Bernard Crosby
Rev. Father McCormack
Edmund Gurney
Lord Alfred Blakeney
A. Vane Tempest
Mrs. de Courcy    Gladys ffolliot
Mrs. Gregg    Dorothy O'Neill
Mary Ellen    Cathleen Nesbitt
First published: London: Allen & Unwin, [1933], based on Birmingham's 1913 novel.

### G. SIDNEY PATERNOSTER
*The Dean of St. Patrick's*
a Play in Four Acts.
First produced: 23 January 1913, by the Abbey Theatre's Second Company, at the Abbey Theatre, Dublin.

CAST

Patrick    Michael Conniffe
Sweetheart    Helena Moloney
Mistress Esther Johnston
Nell Byrne
Mrs. Dingley    Nora Desmond
Dr. Jonathan Swift   Patrick Murphy
His Grace, the Archbishop of
Dublin    George St. John
Mr. Joseph Addison    Farrell Pelly
Mrs. Van Homrigh   Ettie Fletcher
Mistress Anne Long
Una O'Connor
Mistress Hester Van Homrigh
Ann Coppinger

Mrs. Touchet    Nell Stewart
First Lady    Kathleen O'Brien
Second Lady    Betty King
Henry St. John, Viscount
Bolingbroke    Philip Guiry
Royal Servant    Thomas Barry
Mr. Congreve   A. Patrick Wilson
His Grace, the Duke of
Ormond    Charles Power
Dr. John Arbuthnot   Eric Gorman
Robert Harley, Earl of Oxford
Seán Connolly
Directed by Lennox Robinson
Unpublished.

### J. BERNARD MacCARTHY
*The Men in Possession*
a Comedy in One Act.
First produced: 29 January 1913, by the Cork Dramatic Society, at the Dún Theatre, Cork.

CAST

Mike Clancy    C. Foley
Mrs. Clancy   Miss L. Desmond
Members of the local dramatic
society    J. Scanlon and
P. J. O'Connell
Bailiffs    P. J. K. Lynch and
Mr. Gilhooly
Ellie Clancy   Miss M. Carroll
First published: as a farce in Three Acts, Dublin: M. H. Gill, 1922.

### J. BERNARD MacCARTHY
*Wrecked*
a Tragedy in One Act.
First produced: 29 January 1913, by the Cork Dramatic Society, at the Dún Theatre, Cork.

CAST

Shaun Bourke   P. J. K. Lynch
Mrs. Bourke   Miss L. Desmond
Mikeen Farrell    J. Flynn
Mary Doyle   Miss G. Howard
First published: Dublin: M. H. Gill, 1922.

### IRA ALLEN
*The Bailiff of Ballyfoyle*
a Melodrama in Four Acts.
First produced: Probably on 17 February 1913, by Ira Allen's Company, at the Queen's Theatre, Dublin.

CAST

Lord Hardman    Leo Strong
Lady Evelyn    May Murnane

Michael Rooney Ira Allen
Fergus O'Mara Peter Judge
Mark Daly Conn Conroy
And others.
Unpublished.

## DARRELL FIGGIS

*Queen Tara*
a Verse Play in Three Acts.
First produced: 25 February 1913,
by the F. R. Benson Company, at
the Gaiety Theatre, Dublin.

CAST

Julian, King of Illyricum
Henry Herbert
Queen Tara Gladys Vanderzee
Serge Horace Braham
Peter H. Pardoe Woodman
Antony John Cairns
Stephen Charles Warburton
Brabo Duncan Yarrow
Lyof Basil Rathbone
Hagen Edmund Sulley
Cathna Miss Miller
A Page Muriel Dawn
First published: London: J. M.
Dent, 1913.

## P. J. BOURKE

*When Wexford Rose*
a Patriotic Melodrama in
Four Acts.
First produced: Possibly on 3
March 1913, by P. J. Bourke's
No. 1 Company, at the Queen's
Theatre, Dublin.

CAST

Ned Traynor Mathew Carolan
Kitty Cassidy Lily Roberts
Donal Don O'Byrne
George Lawrence
Grace Bassett Louie Colclough
Mary Doyle Violet Gore
Biddy Dolan Connie Campbell
Colonel Needham P. J. Bourke
Father John Murphy Alex Dare
General Holt William Rollins
And others.
Directed by P. J. Bourke
Unpublished.

## VICTOR O'D. POWER

*The Peril of Sheila*
a Romantic Play in Four Acts.
First discovered performance: 12
March 1913, by the O'Brien and
Ireland Company, at the Opera
House, Cork.

CAST

Donach Dubh ('Maurice
Desmond') Wilfred Short
Sheila O'Mahony Elsie Chapin
Timothy Casey H. Ireland
The Unknown Woman
Laura Lawson
Sheila's Aunt Maude Barnes
Nora Burke Edna Vere
Andy Sullivan James O'Brien
Maurice John Desmond
J. C. Wilton
And others.
Unpublished.

## JOHN GUINAN

*The Cuckoo's Nest*
a Comedy of Contemporary Irish
Life in Three Acts.
First produced: 13 March 1913,
by the Abbey Theatre's Second
Company, at the Abbey Theatre,
Dublin.

CAST

Phil Dolan Michael Conniffe
Luke Muldowney Philip Guiry
Hugh Loughnane Farrell Pelly
Nancy Kennedy Helena Moloney
Nora Flanagan Peggy Buttimer
Peg Galvin Nell Stewart
Directed by Lennox Robinson
First published: Dublin: Gill, 1933.

## P. J. BOURKE

*The Northern Insurgents,*
*or Ulster in 1798*
a Patriotic Melodrama
in Four Acts.
First produced: Possibly on 17
March 1913, by P. J. Bourke's
No. 1 Company, at the Queen's
Theatre, Dublin.

CAST

Maurice St. Clair Alexander Dare
Neil Ward, a United Irishman
George Lawrence
Major Fox, Town Mayor of
Belfast P. J. Bourke
Una St. Clair Louise Colclough
James Hughes Felix O'Brien
Nora McIlroy Lily Roberts
Also with J. J. Sullivan, Arthur
Roberts, William Rollins, Robert
Hardinge, M. Carolan, H. Fergu-
son, Denis Grogan, Alice Beau-
mont, Violet Gore, and Connie
Campbell.
Directed by P. J. Bourke
Unpublished.

R. G. WALSHE

*Knocknagow*
an Adaptation of the novel
by C. J. Kickham.
First produced: Possibly on 24
March 1913, by the Pioneer
Dramatic Society, at St. Francis
Xavier's Hall, Dublin.

CAST

| | |
|---|---|
| Nora Lahy | Annie Hayden |
| Phil Lahy | M. Harmon |
| The Flute Player | Jas. M. Duffy |
| Father Hannigan | Jas. Delany |
| Captain Butler | Lewis Anthony |
| The Land Agent | P. J. Dillon |
| Mrs. Lahy | Marie Sweeney |
| The Tailor's Son | A. Bonass |
| '98 Veteran | W. J. Buckley |
| Evicted Tenant | Raymond Murphy |
| Bailiffs | Jas. A. Dillon and |
| | F. Bonass |

Phil's grand-daughter
Miss F. Leavy
Peg Brady     Miss M. J. Kennedy
Produced by W. Walshe
First published: Dublin: Duffy,
1931.

LADY GREGORY

*Galway Races**
a Comedy in One Act.
First produced: 24 March 1913,
by the Abbey Theatre, at the Plymouth Theatre, Boston.

CAST

| | |
|---|---|
| Michelin | J. M. Kerrigan |
| Julia | Sara Allgood |
| Steve Roland | M. J. Dolan† |

First separate publication: London
and New York: Putnam's, 1926,
in the version called *On the Race-
course*; rpr in Collected Plays,
Vol. I.

PADRAIC COLUM

*The Betrayal*
a Play in One Act.
First produced: 7 April 1913, by
B. Iden Payne's Company, at the
Theatre Royal, Manchester. The
only Irishman in the cast was

Joseph A. (later J. Augustus)
Keogh, as the innkeeper.
Directed by B. Iden Payne

CHARLES PENDER

*The Ghost*
a Play in One Act.
First produced: 7 April 1913, at
the Concert for Pauline Elsner, at
the Abbey Theatre, Dublin.

CAST

| | |
|---|---|
| Horace Overend | S. W. Maddock |
| Frank Wakely | J. G. Butt |
| Ethel Desmond | Eleanor Story |
| Peter | Robert V. Justice |

Directed by Mary O'Hea
Unpublished.

GERTRUDE ROBINS

*The Home-Coming*
a Play in One Act.
First produced: 10 April 1913, by
the Abbey Theatre's Second
Company, at the Abbey Theatre,
Dublin.

CAST

| | |
|---|---|
| Ivan Loweski | Philip Guiry |
| Stefan | Seán Connolly |
| Paul Loweski | Farrell Pelly |
| Catherine Loweski | |
| | Helena Moloney |

Directed by Lennox Robinson
Unpublished.

S. R. DAY and G. D. CUMMINS

*Broken Faith*
a Play in Two Acts.
First produced: 24 April 1913, by
the Abbey's Second Company, at
the Abbey Theatre, Dublin.

CAST

| | |
|---|---|
| Mrs. Gara | Una O'Connor |
| Bridget Gara, her daughter- | |
| in-law | Nora Desmond |
| Dan Hourihan | Michael Conniffe |
| Michael Gara | Farrell Pelly |
| Mikeen | Laurence Byrne |
| Timothy Coll | Philip Guiry |
| A Policeman | Charles Power |

Directed by Lennox Robinson
No record of publication.

*This Lady Gregory premiere seems to have gone unnoticed by historians;
the story, however, appears to be merely another version of the story of
*Twenty-Five* or *On the Race-course*.

†All of the Boston papers cite a Mr. Doran in the cast. There was no such
actor with the company, and we have assumed there was a misprint in the
programme, and the actor intended was M. J. Dolan.

462

## GEORGE FITZMAURICE
*The Magic Glasses*
a Play in One Act.
First produced: 24 April 1913, by
the Abbey's Second Company, at
the Abbey Theatre, Dublin.

CAST

Maineen Shanahan
    Helena Moloney
Padden Shanahan George St. John
Mr. Quille   Philip Guiry
Jaymoney Shanahan
    Charles Power
Aunt Jug  Una O'Connor
Aunt Mary  E. Stewart
 Directed by Lennox Robinson
First published: in *Five Plays*
(London and Dublin: Maunsel,
1914); rpr. in *The Plays of George
Fitzmaurice*, Vol. I (Dublin:
1967).

## RABRINDRANATH TAGORE
*The Post Office*
a Play in Two Acts, translated
by Devabrata Mukerjee.
First produced by the Abbey
Theatre: 17 May 1913, at the
Abbey Theatre, Dublin.

CAST

Madhav   Philip Guiry
Doctor   Charles Power
Gaffer   Michael Conniffe
Amal, Madhav's adopted child
    Lilian Jago
Dairyman   Farrell Pelly
Watchman H. E. Hutchinson
Headman  James Duffy
Sudha   Nell Stewart
Boys Desmond Murphy, Owen
  Clarke, Horace Jennings
King's Herald Thomas Barrett
King's Physician Seán Connolly
 Directed by Lennox Robinson
The Scene, composed of Gordon
Craig screens, arranged by
   J. F. Barlow
First published in Ireland: Dun-
drum: Cuala Press, 1914.

## FLORENCE EATON
*Playing with Fire*
a Miracle Play in Four Acts
and an Epilogue.
First produced: 27 May 1913, by
amateurs, at the Abbey Theatre,

Dublin. The Cast included Máire
Nic Shiubhlaigh, Betty King, Miss
Fletcher, Maeve Jackson, and
Florrie Ryan.
Unpublished.

## R. J. RAY (Robert J. Brophy)
*The Gombeen Man*
a Play in Three Acts.
First produced: 30 June 1913, by
the Abbey Company, at the Royal
Court Theatre, London.

CAST

Michael Myers J. M. Kerrigan
Richard Kiniry Fred O'Donovan
Roger Connors J. A. O'Rourke
William Naughton Philip Guiry
Mrs. Naughton Eileen O'Doherty
Stephen Kiniry, a Gombeen
 Man  Arthur Sinclair
Martin Shinnick Sydney J. Morgan
Mrs. Kiniry  Sara Allgood
 Directed by Lennox Robinson
Unpublished.

## IRA ALLEN
*Father Murphy, or the Hero of
Tullow*
a Patriotic Melodrama in
probably Four Acts.
Produced (not necessarily for the
first time): 21 July 1913, by Ira
Allen, at the Queen's Theatre,
Dublin.

CAST

Father Murphy  Ira Allen
Grace Gallagher May Murnane
Gallagher  Philip Murphy
Edmund Ryan  Leo Strong
Felix Horsley Patrick Murphy
Peggy O'Neill Madeline Hunt
Tim Hogan  Frank Delaney
Some Boys of Ballyvogue
  T. Keely, Michael Whelan
Mother Hogan Cecilia Conroy
English Officers J. W. Bostock,
  Peter Judge, John Walsh
  Directed by Ira Allen
Unpublished.

## T. C. MURRAY
*Sovereign Love**
a Comedy in One Act.
First produced: 11 September
1913, by the Abbey Company, at
the Abbey Theatre, Dublin.

**Sovereign Love* is a revision of Murray's *The Wheel o' Fortune*, which
had been first presented by the Cork Dramatic Society.

Donal Kearney, a farmer
                  J. M. Kerrigan
His daughters:
  Ellen          Ann Coppinger
  Katty         Eithne Magee
Maurice O'Brien     Philip Guiry
Mrs. Hickey   Helena Moloney
Charles O'Donnell
             Sydney J. Morgan
David, his son    Charles Power
Tom Daly    Michael Conniffe
Andy Hyde, a returned Yank
               Farrell Pelly
  Directed by Lennox Robinson
First published: in *Spring ana Other Plays* (Dublin: Talbot Press, 1917).

## JOSEPH CONNOLLY
*The Mine Land*
a Comedy in Three Acts.
First produced: 2 October 1913, by the Abbey's Second Company, at the Abbey Theatre, Dublin.

Matta Lynn    Sydney J. Morgan
Jane Lynn, his wife  Una O'Connor
Barney O'Hara    Philip Guiry
Burnett, president of the Geological Society    Charles Power
Members of the Geological Society:
  Lavelle    H. E. Hutchinson
  Hardy     George St. John
Annie McKendry   Eithne Magee
Alec Liddell     Farrell Pelly
William Liddell  H. E. Hutchinson
Charlie McCrea   Seán Connolly
  Directed by Lennox Robinson
No record of publication.

## GEORGE BERNARD SHAW
*John Bull's Other Island*
a Play in Four Acts.
First production by an Irish Company: 6 October 1913, by the Dublin Repertory Theatre, at the Gaiety Theatre, Dublin.*

Tom Broadbent  S. W. Maddock
Larry Doyle     Earle Grey
Nora Reilly  Flora MacDonnell
Aunt Judy      Nell Byrne

Barney Doran   Fred A. Jeffs
Father Keegan  G. H. Fitzgerald
Father Dempsey  Dermot Dignam
Matt Haffigan   Evelyn Ashley
Corney Doyle  Raymond Molloy
Hodson      J. M. S. Carré
Patsy Farrell   Gerald Doyle
Tim Haffigan  Valentine Roberts
  Directed by Evelyn Ashley
First published: London: Constable, 1907.

## S. R. DAY
*Toilers*
a Play in One Act.
First produced: 6 October 1913, by the Irishwomen's Reform League, at Sackville Hall, Dublin.
  Directed by Una O'Connor
No record of publication.

## MRS. BART KENNEDY
*My Lord*
a Play in One Act.
First produced: 16 October 1913, by the Abbey Company, at the Abbey Theatre, Dublin.

My Lord     Arthur Sinclair
Dermot, an old huntsman,
  My Lord's foster-
  brother    J. A. O'Rourke
Tenants:
  Curran      Philip Guiry
  O'Grady  Sydney J. Morgan
  Malone    J. M. Kerrigan
Nurse    Helena Moloney
Other tenants
  Directed by Lennox Robinson
No record of publication.

## ST. JOHN ERVINE
*The Critics, or a New Play at the Abbey Theatre*
Being a Little Morality for the Press in One Act.
First produced: 20 November 1913, by the Abbey Company, at the Abbey Theatre, Dublin.

Dramatic Critics:
  Mr. Barbary   J. M. Kerrigan
  Mr. Quacks  Fred O'Donovan
  Mr. Quartz  Sydney J. Morgan

*This play had been written at Yeats's request for the Abbey, but had not been produced as W. G. Fay felt that he could not cast it adequately. Its first production was on 1 November 1904, by Vedrenne and Barker, at the Royal Court Theatre, London.

Mr. Bawlawney    Arthur Sinclair
An Attendant    H. E. Hutchinson
Directed by Lennox Robinson
First published: in *Four Irish
Plays* (London & Dublin: Maunsel, 1914).

## LYNN DOYLE
(Leslie A. Montgomery)
*Love and Land**
a Comedy in Four Acts.
First produced: 24 November 1913,
by the Ulster Theatre, at the
Grand Opera House, Belfast.

CAST

| | |
|---|---|
| Peter O'Hare | J. G. Abbey |
| Mary O'Connor | Marion Crimmins |
| Rose Dorrian | Mary Crothers |
| Brian O'Connor | Joseph Roney |
| Thomas Dorrian | Charles K. Ayre |
| Widow Doherty | |
| | Margaret O'Gorman |
| Pat Murphy | Robert Gorman |
| Hughey Rogan | Rutherford Mayne |
| Billy Rourke | Laurence M. Larnon |

Directed by Fred. Mecredy
First published: Dublin: Talbot
Press, [1927].

## RUTHERFORD MAYNE
*If!*
a Farce in Three Acts.
First produced: 25 November
1913, by the Ulster Theatre, at
the Grand Opera House, Belfast.

CAST

| | |
|---|---|
| Colonel Sylvester | |
| | Rutherford Mayne |
| Tom, the waiter | |
| | Gerald MacNamara |
| Higgs | Herbert Grant |
| Mrs. West | Rose McQuillan |
| Politicians | Charles K. Ayre, |
| | John Field |
| Engineer | Norman Gray |
| Forbes | Jackson Grahame |
| Eckerstein | Frederick Mears |
| Robinson | Donald McKay |
| Mahaffy | Lawrence McLarnon |
| Forsythe | William Murray |
| Smythe | Philip Doyle |
| McAlpine | J. G. Abbey |
| Joe | Joseph Roney |
| Annie West | Kathleen Lawrence |
| Lily West | Mary Magee |
| Dorothy Manners | |
| | Josephine Mayne |

Mrs. Bradbury    Marion Crimmins
Directed by Fred Mecredy
Unpublished.

## MARY COSTELLO
*A Bad Quarter of an Hour*
a Play in One Act.
First produced: 1 December 1913,
by the Countess of Roden's Company, at the Gaiety Theatre,
Dublin.

CAST

| | |
|---|---|
| Mrs. Murphy | |
| Kitty Clark | |
| | Mrs. Peronett Thompson |
| Maud Grosvenor | Deena Tyrrell |
| Capt. Head | Charles Walters |
| Mike | |
| Capt. Grosvenor | |
| | Col. Malcolm Moore |

No record of publication.

## ALICE MAYE FINNY
*A Local Demon*
a Play in One Act.
First produced: 1 December 1913,
by the Countess of Roden's Company, at the Gaiety Theatre,
Dublin.

CAST

| | |
|---|---|
| Mrs. Devany | Ann Coppinger |
| Michael Goram | W. Henry |
| Dr. Wilson | Dr. Fisher |
| Denis Kanavan | R. V. Justice |
| Mrs. Clancy | Edith Dodd |
| Biddy Clancy | Elsie Hughes |

No record of publication.

## SEUMAS O'BRIEN
*Duty*
a Comedy in One Act.
First produced: 16 December
1913, by the Abbey Company, at
the Abbey Theatre, Dublin.

CAST

| | |
|---|---|
| Padna Sweeny | J. A. O'Rourke |
| Micus Goggin | J. M. Kerrigan |
| Mrs. Cotter | Una O'Connor |
| Head Constable Mulligan, R.I.C. | |
| | Fred O'Donovan |
| Constable Huggins, R.I.C. | |
| | Sydney J. Morgan |

Directed by Lennox Robinson
First published: in *Duty and
Other Irish Comedies* (Boston:
Little, Brown, 1916).

*The play was later presented in London with the title of *Preserving Pat.*

## SEUMAS O'KELLY

*The Bribe*
a Play in Three Acts.
First produced: 18 December 1913, by the Abbey Company, at the Abbey Theatre, Dublin.

CAST

Mrs. Diamond    Nora Desmond
Mary Kirwan    Kathleen Drago
Mrs. Kirwan    Eileen O'Doherty
John Kirwan    Arthur Sinclair
Dr. Luke Diamond
     Fred O'Donovan
Dr. Power O'Connor
     Sydney J. Morgan
Dr. Jack Power O'Connor
     Philip Guiry
Mr. Toomey    H. E. Hutchinson
A Pauper    Michael Conniffe
Mrs. Cooney    Eithne Magee
Poor Law Guardians
   J. M. Kerrigan, J. A. O'Rourke,
   U. Wright, A. Patrick Wilson,
     Farrell Pelly, etc.
Directed by Lennox Robinson
First published: Dublin: Maunsel, 1914.

# 1914

## GEORGE A. BIRMINGHAM

*General John Regan*
a Play in Three Acts.
First production in Ireland: 26 January 1914, by W. Payne Seddon's Company, at the Kilkenny Theatre, Kilkenny.*

CAST

Doctor Lucius O'Grady
     R. Ivor Barry
Timothy Doyle
     John S. Chamberlain
Major Kent    Gerald Mirrielees
Thaddeus Golligher   J. M. Dolan†
Horace P. Billing   Hubert Barwell
C. Cregg, District Inspector, R.I.C.
     Tom O'Brien
Sergeant Colgan, R.I.C.   G. West
Constable Moriarty, R.I.C.
     H. Sinclair
Rev. Father McCormack
     George Flood
Lord Alfred Blakeney
     Nevill Graham

Mrs. de Courcy    Gertrude Le Sage
Mrs. Gregg    Eily O'Dempsey
Mary Ellen    Charity Wynne
First published: London: Allen & Unwin, [1933].

## VICTOR O'D POWER

*David Mahony*
a Play in Three Acts.
First produced: 29 January 1914, by the Abbey's Second Company, at the Abbey Theatre, Dublin.

CAST

Norrie Burke    Eithne Magee
Peggy Hegarty    Kathleen Drago
David Mahony   H. E. Hutchinson
Flurry Mahony    Philip Guiry
The Widow Mahony
     Nora Desmond
   Directed by Lennox Robinson
No record of publication.

## RUTHERFORD MAYNE

*Evening*
a Co. Down Playlet in One Act.
First produced: 2 March 1914, by the Ulster Theatre, at the Grand Opera House, Belfast.
The cast included Rose McQuillan, Jackson Grahame, Walter Kennedy, and Frederick Mears.
First published: in *The Lady of the House* (Christmas Number, 1913), pp. 43–44.

## ST. JOHN ERVINE

*The Orangeman*
a Comedy in One Act.
First produced: 13 March 1914, by the Abbey's Second Company, at the Abbey Theatre, Dublin.

CAST

John McClurg   A. Patrick Wilson
Jessie McClurg
     Cathleen MacCarthy
Andy Haneron    Seán Connolly
Tom McClurg    Thomas O'Neill
   Directed by A. Patrick Wilson
First published: in *Four Irish Plays* (London and Dublin: Maunsel, 1914).

## EDWARD McNULTY

*The Lord Mayor*
a Comedy in Three Acts.

*First produced in Dublin on 16 February 1914, by Leonard Boyne's London Company, with Boyne as Dr. O'Grady.
†Apparently M. J. Dolan.

First produced: 13 March 1914,
by the Abbey's Second Company,
at the Abbey Theatre, Dublin.

CAST

Charwomen:
Mrs. Murphy    Sheila O'Sullivan
Mrs. Moloney    Maura O'Byrne
Gaffney, a solicitor
Reginald Montgomery
Kelly, his clerk    Michael Hayes
O'Brien, an ironmonger,
afterwards Lord Mayor
Seán Connolly
Mrs. O'Brien, his wife
Maureen Delany
Moira O'Brien, his daughter
Cathleen MacCarthy
Creditors:
Scanlon    Michael Conniffe
Doherty    Edward Reardon
Mrs. Moran    Ethel Fletcher
Mr. Butterfield    Arthur Shields
Lackey    Thomas O'Neill
Creditors    John Conniffe,
J. McEentee, T. L. Christopher,
George Harold
Directed by A. Patrick Wilson
First published: Dublin & London: Maunsel, 1917.

ANNIE J. W. LLOYD

*A Question of Honour*
a Tragedy in One Act.
First produced: 27 March 1914,
by 'a company of well-known
amateurs', at the Abbey Theatre,
Dublin.
The cast included Cecil Robinson,
F. Edwards, Mrs. T. Kirkwood-
Hackett, Miss Haggie Campbell,
and Edward Moor.
No record of publication.

CRUISE O'BRIEN

*Candidates*
a Comedy in Three Acts.
First produced: 27 March 1914,
by 'a company of well-known
amateurs', at the Abbey Theatre,
Dublin.

CAST

Sir Dighton Stimant
Cruise O'Brien
Thomas Blake    William Mervyn
Mrs. Blake    Katherine O'Brien
Peggy Clohissey    Patricia Nally
Patrick Hennessy    F. Edwards

Jack Blake    W. Patrick Hone
Viola Stinmut    Haggie Campbell
Lady Stinmut    Isa M. Macnie
Joe Hines    Stuart Harris
John Forbes    Cecil Robinson
Bella Stinmut    Helen Frith
A butler    C. U. Spadaccini
No record of publication.

J. BERNARD MacCARTHY

*Kinship*
a Tragedy in One Act.
First produced: 2 April 1914, by
the Abbey's Second Company, at
the Abbey Theatre, Dublin.

CAST

The Widow Connell    Nora Shannon
Hugh Connell    Seán Connolly
Mike Connell    Shawn Joyce
(John Conniffe)
Bride Cassidy    Cathleen MacCarthy
Jim Twomey    Michael Conniffe
Sergeant Desmond    Brick Noels
Directed by A. Patrick Wilson*
First published: Dublin: Gill,
[1936].

A. PATRICK WILSON

*The Cobbler*
a Play in One Act.
First produced: 13 April 1914, by
the Abbey's Second Company, at
the Abbey Theatre, Dublin.

CAST

A Cobbler    A. Patrick Wilson
A Ploughman    Seán Connolly
A Farmer    Thomas O'Neill
A Village Gossip
Cathleen MacCarthy
A Schoolmaster    Arthur Shields
A Schoolboy    Felix Hughes
Directed by A. Patrick Wilson
Unpublished.

FRANCIS SHEEHY-
SKEFFINGTON

*The Prodigal Daughter*
a Comedy in One Act.
First produced: 24 April 1914,
under the auspices of the Irish
Woman's Franchise League, at the
Molesworth Hall, Dublin.

CAST

Michael Considine, P.L.G.,
R.C.G., Grocer & Publican
A. L. Shields

*The cast list in the published play cites Lennox Robinson as the director.

467

Margaret Considine, his wife
Máire Walker
Tommy Considine, their son
John Downes
Lily Considine, their daughter
Katharine O'Brien
Maggie Rafferty, their daughter
Patricia Lally
Dr. Athur Rafferty, Maggie's
husband                 Robert Ryan
Fr. Phil O'Sullivan Fred Harford
Sarah O'Brien, a servant
Máire Perolze
First published: Dublin: Manico,
[1914].

## P. J. BOURKE

*For Ireland's Liberty*
Produced (not necessarily for the
first time): 11 May 1914, by P. J.
Bourke's No. 1 Company, at the
Queen's Theatre, Dublin.

CAST

The Wild Rose of Lough Gill
Peggy Courtenay
Noreen O'Regan      Lily Roberts
Also with P. J. Bourke, F. J.
McCormack (Peter Judge), F.
Healy, Hubert Cecil, Alice Beau-
mont, D. F. Grogan, Alexander
Dare, Felix O'Brien and others.
Directed by P. J. Bourke
Incidental music composed by
F. L. Baynton
Unpublished.

## H. B. O'HANLON

*Her Second Chance*
a Play in One Act.
First produced: 19 May 1914, by
the St. Mary's College (Rathmines)
Literary and Dramatic Society, at
the Abbey Theatre, Dublin.

CAST

Callaghan         J. B. Magennis
Sidney Wainford   P. J. Hayden
Sparkles          F. Purcell
Directed by James C. O'Brien
No record of publication.

## J. BERNARD MacCARTHY

*The Supplanter*
a Play in Three Acts.
First produced: 4 June 1914, by
the Abbey Company, at the Royal
Court Theatre, London.

CAST

Mrs. Keegan*      Eileen O'Doherty
Phil Keegan       Fred O'Donovan
Ellie Cassidy     Eithne Magee
John O'Connor     Sydney J. Morgan
Widow Flynn†      Ann Coppinger
Pad Saunders      Philip Guiry
Directed by Lennox Robinson
First published: with the title
*Master of the House* (Dublin:
Gill, 1950?).

## MARTIN J. McHUGH

*A Minute's Wait*
a Comedy in One Act.
First produced: 27 August 1914,
by the Abbey Company, at the
Abbey Theatre, Dublin.

CAST

Barney Domigan    Arthur Sinclair
Christy Domigan   Philip Guiry
Mrs. Falsey       Nora Desmond
Mary Ann McMahon
Eithne Magee
Andy Rourke       Fred O'Donovan
Pat Morrissey     J. A. O'Rourke
Jim O'Brien       Sydney J. Morgan
Tom Kinsella      J. M. Kerrigan
Mrs. Kinsella     Ann Coppinger
And others.
Directed by A. Patrick Wilson
First published: Dublin: James
Duffy, 1918.

## R. A. CHRISTIE

*The Dark Hour*
a Comedy in One Act.
First produced: 9 September 1914,
by the Abbey Company, at the
Abbey Theatre, Dublin.

CAST

William Finlay    J. M. Kerrigan
Jane Finlay       Nora Desmond
Samuel James Finlay
H. E. Hutchinson
Willie Davis      Philip Guiry
Mary Davis        Eithne Magee
Rachael‡ McDowell
Ann Coppinger
Wandering Danny
Sydney J. Morgan
Directed by A. Patrick Wilson
First published: Belfast: H. R.
Carter, 1950.

*Called in the published version Mrs. O'Connor.
†Called in the published version Judy Flynn.
‡Rachell in the published version.

468

## CON O'LEARY

*The Crossing*
a Play in One Act.
First produced: 23 September 1914, by the Abbey Company, at the Abbey Theatre, Dublin.

CAST

| | |
|---|---|
| William Fenton | Arthur Sinclair |
| Mary the Roads | Nora Desmond |
| Matthew the Rhymes | |
| | J. M. Kerrigan |
| Thomas Fenton | Fred O'Donovan |

Directed by A. Patrick Wilson
No record of publication.

## WALTER RIDDALL

*The Prodigal*
a Play in Four Acts.
First produced: 30 September 1914, by the Abbey Company, at the Abbey Theatre, Dublin.

CAST

| | |
|---|---|
| Samuel Walker | Arthur Sinclair |
| Sarah Walker | Nora Desmond |
| Helen Walker | Eithne Magee |
| George Walker | H. E. Hutchinson |
| Stanley Walker | Fred O'Donovan |
| Rev. Hugh Chapman | Philip Guiry |
| Billy Bradley | J. M. Kerrigan |
| Lizzie Bradley | Kathleen Drago |
| John Evans | Sydney J. Morgan |
| Maggie | Ann Coppinger |

Directed by A. Patrick Wilson
Unpublished.

## A. PATRICK WILSON

*A Call to Arms*
a Play in One Act.
First produced: 12 October 1914, at a Benefit for the Soldiers' and Sailors' Families Association, at the Abbey Theatre, Dublin.

CAST

| | |
|---|---|
| The Old Man | Arthur Sinclair |
| The Missus | Nora Desmond |

Also with Eithne Magee and Fred O'Donovan.
Unpublished.

## F. JAY (F. J. LITTLE)

*The Cobweb*
a Play in One Act.
First produced: 13 October 1914, by the Abbey Company, at the Abbey Theatre, Dublin.

CAST

| | |
|---|---|
| Secretary Cooke | Arthur Sinclair |
| Kate Caraher | Eithne Magee |
| Eustace Hyme | Philip Guiry |
| Leonard McNally | Seán Connolly |
| Dr. Trevor | Eric Gorman |
| Slippoon | H. E. Hutchinson |
| Pinlock | Michael Conniffe |

Directed by A. Patrick Wilson
Unpublished.

## W. P. RYAN

*The Jug of Sorrow*
a Comedy in One Act.
First produced: 30 October 1914, by the Abbey Company, at the Abbey Theatre, Dublin.

CAST

| | |
|---|---|
| Patsy | Sydney J. Morgan |
| Syve | Ann Coppinger |
| Peg | Kathleen Drago |
| Donal | Philip Guiry |
| Seumas | J. M. Kerrigan |
| Nora | Eithne Magee |
| Father Eamonn | Fred O'Donovan |

Directed by A. Patrick Wilson
Unpublished.

## EDWARD MARTYN

*The Dream Physician*
a Comedy in Four Acts.
First produced: 2 November 1914, by the Irish Theatre, at the Hardwicke Street Hall, Dublin.

CAST

| | |
|---|---|
| Colonel Gerrard | Eric Gorman |
| Otho | Richard Sheridan |
| Audrey | Una O'Connor |
| Shane Lester | J. B. Magennis |
| Stephen | G. H. Fitzgerald |
| Sister Farnan | |
| | Máire Nic Shiubhlaigh |
| George Augustus Moon | |
| | John MacDonagh |
| Birdie Whelan | Helen Bronsky |
| Beau Brummell | J. M. S. Carré |

Directed by John MacDonagh
First published: Dublin: Talbot Press, 1917?

## A. PATRICK WILSON

*The Slough*
a Play in Three Acts.
First produced: 3 November 1914, by the Abbey Company, at the Abbey Theatre, Dublin.

CAST

| | |
|---|---|
| Peter Hanlon | Arthur Sinclair |
| Mary Hanlon | Maura O'Byrne |
| Annie Hanlon | Kathleen Drago |
| Peg Hanlon | Eithne Magee |
| Jack Hanlon | Philip Guiry |

Edward Kelly           H. E. Hutchinson
Margaret Kelly         Nora Desmond
Tom Robinson           Fred O'Donovan
Jake Allen             A. Patrick Wilson
Joe Moran              J. F. Barlow
Jim Crocker            Sydney J. Morgan
Tim Daly               J. A. O'Rourke
Bill Nolan             J. M. Kerrigan
Pete Riley             Michael Conniffe
Matt Taylor            Thomas O'Neill
    Directed by A. Patrick Wilson
Unpublished.


GEORGE BERNARD SHAW

*Mrs. Warren's Profession*
a Play in Three Acts.
First public production: 16 No-
vember 1914, by the Dublin
Repertory Theatre, at the Little
Theatre, 40 Upper Sackville Street,
Dublin.

CAST

Mrs. Warren           Flora MacDonnell
Vivie Warren          Una O'Connor
Praed                 J. M. S. Carré
Sir George Crofts     Ernest Lewis
Rev. Sam Gardiner
                      G. H. Fitzgerald
Frank Gardiner        Arthur Orrett
    Directed by Evelyn Ashley


P. J. BOURKE

*In Dark '98*
a Patriotic Melodrama
Produced (not necessarily for the
first time): 7 December 1914, by
P. J. Bourke's No. 1 Company, at
the Queen's Theatre, Dublin.

CAST

Wolfe Tone            J. F. Nevin
Sir Trevor Mortimer   P. J. Bourke
Redmond Barrington, United
    Irishman          Mr. Sullivan
Admiral Bompart       Alexander Dare
Eugene Lefevre        F. J. McCormack
Helen Barrington      Peggy Courtney
Nora O'Brien          Miss Roberts
    Directed by P. J. Bourke
Unpublished.


RICHARD BRINSLEY
SHERIDAN

*The Critic*
a Comedy in Three Acts.
First production by the Abbey
Company: 26 December 1914, at
the Abbey Theatre, Dublin.

CAST

Mr. Puff              Arthur Sinclair
Mr. Dangle            Fred O'Donovan
Mr. Sneer             Philip Guiry
Sir Fretful Plagiary  J. M. Kerrigan
Mrs. Dangle           Nora Desmond
Signor Pasticcio Ritornello
                      Eric Gorman
The Singers    The Rafter brothers
The Prompter   H. E. Hutchinson
The Master Carpenter  J. F. Barlow
Assistant Carpenter
                      Thomas O'Neill
The Property Man
                      George St. John

CHARACTERS OF THE TRAGEDY

Lord Burleigh         J. R. St. Rich
Governor of Tilbury Fort
                      Sydney J. Morgan
Earl of Leicester     Seán Connolly
Sir Christopher Hatton
                      J. H. Dunne
Sir Walter Raleigh    J. A. O'Rourke
Master of the Horse   U. Wright
Don Ferolo Whiskerandos
                      J. M. Kerrigan
Beefeater             Michael Conniffe
Justice               Edward Reardon
Son                   Charles Power
Constable             Arthur Shields
Justice's Lady        Maureen Delany
Tilburina             Ann Coppinger
Confidante            Sheila O'Sullivan
First Niece           Eithne Magee
Second Niece
                      Cathleen MacCarthy
First Sentinel        J. Eustace
Second Sentinel       W. Shields
                  ('Barry Fitzgerald')
    Directed by A. Patrick Wilson


# 1915

F. C. MOORE and
W. P. FLANAGAN

*By Word of Mouth*
a Comedy in One Act.
First produced: 27 January 1915,
by the Abbey Company, at the
Abbey Theatre, Dublin.

CAST

Cyranus P. Blaine   J. M. Kerrigan
Hank Morgan         Sydney J. Morgan
Deacon Ezra Simmons
                    Arthur Sinclair
Fidelia             Ann Coppinger
    Directed by A. Patrick Wilson
Unpublished.

HELEN WADDELL
*The Spoiled Buddha*
a Play of Japan in Two Acts.
First produced: 1 February 1915,
by the Ulster Theatre, at the
Grand Opera House, Belfast.

CAST

| | |
|---|---|
| The Buddha | Rutherford Mayne |
| Binzuru | Gerald MacNamara |
| Daruma | Jackson Grahame |

Also with Norman Gray.
First published: Dublin: Talbot;
London: T. Fisher Unwin, 1919.

SHAN F. BULLOCK
*Snowdrop Jane*
A Comedy in Three Acts, adapted
from his novel *The Squireen*. First
produced: 2 February 1915, by
the Ulster Theatre, at the Grand
Opera House, Belfast.

CAST

| | |
|---|---|
| Jane Fallon | Josephine Mayne |
| Martin Hynes | Jackson Grahame |
| Bashful Lover | J. M. Harding |
| Ned Noble | Walter Kennedy |
| Fallon | Robert Gorman |
| Mrs. Hynes | Mary Crothers |
| Mary Trant | Rose McQuillan |

No record of publication; Bullock's novel, *The Squireen*, was
published in London by Methuen
in 1903.

LENNOX ROBINSON
*The Dreamers*
a Play in Three Acts.
First produced: 10 February 1915,
by the Abbey Company, at the
Abbey Theatre, Dublin.

CAST

| | |
|---|---|
| John Brady | Arthur Sinclair |
| Robert Brady | A. Patrick Wilson |
| Martin Brady | U. Wright |
| Robert Emmet | Fred O'Donovan |
| Lacey | Eric Gorman |
| Sarah Curran | Sara Allgood |
| Henry Howley | J. M. Kerrigan |
| Thomas Freyne | James Smith |
| McCartney | Seán Connolly |
| Hannay | H. E. Hutchinson |
| Morrissey | J. M. Kerrigan |
| Treanaghan | Philip Guiry |
| Peter Freyne | George St. John |
| Roche | J. A. O'Rourke |
| Mulligan | William Shields |
| Julia | Kathleen Drago |
| Jerry | Thomas O'Neill |
| Peter Flynn | Sydney J. Morgan |

| | |
|---|---|
| Felix Rourke | J. M. Kerrigan |
| Larry | |
| Con | Seán Connolly |
| Mickey | Michael Conniffe |
| Kate | Sheila O'Sullivan |
| Mary | Cathleen MacCarthy |
| Quigley | Eric Gorman |
| Phillips | Fred Harford |
| Mike | J. A. O'Rourke |
| Mangan | Seán Connolly |
| Mrs. Dillon | Ann Coppinger |
| Mrs. Palmer | Helena Moloney |
| Jane Curran | Nora Desmond |
| Major Sirr | Philip Guiry |
| Jones | H. E. Hutchinson |
| Other Men | Arthur Shields, |

Edward Reardon, Jack Dunne
Directed by A. Patrick Wilson
First published: Dublin: Maunsel,
1915.

WILLIAM CRONE
*The Bargain*
a Play in Three Acts.
First produced: 5 April 1915, by
the Abbey Company, at the Abbey
Theatre, Dublin.

CAST

| | |
|---|---|
| William John McComb | |
| | Sydney J. Morgan |
| Tom McComb | Philip Guiry |
| Andy Simpson | J. A. O'Rourke |
| Mary Simpson | |
| | Cathleen MacCarthy |
| Jane Simpson | Helena Moloney |
| James Simpson | H. E. Hutchinson |
| Annie Harvey | Eithne Magee |
| Sarah | Kathleen Drago |

Directed by A. Patrick Wilson
Unpublished.

MARTIN J. McHUGH
*The Philosopher*
a Comedy in One Act.
First produced: 5 April 1915, by
the Abbey Company, at the Abbey
Theatre, Dublin.

CAST

| | |
|---|---|
| Dan McInerney, a shopkeeper | |
| | Arthur Sinclair |
| Michael Donnellan, his friend | |
| | J. A. O'Rourke |
| John Magrath | J. M. Kerrigan |
| Mr. Honan, solicitor | |
| | Seán Connolly |
| Mr. Sullivan, auctioneer | |
| | Fred O'Donovan |
| Tom Burke | Sydney J. Morgan |
| Joe Minogue | H. E. Hutchinson |
| Sergeant Duffy, R.I.C. | Philip Guiry |

Directed by A. Patrick Wilson
First published: Dublin: Duffy,
1918.

## LADY GREGORY
*Shanwalla*
a Play in Three Acts.
First produced: 8 April 1915, by
the Abbey Company, at the Abbey
Theatre, Dublin.

CAST

Lawrence Scarry, a stableman
H. E. Hutchinson
Hubert Darcy, his master
Sydney J. Morgan
Bride Scarry, his wife
Kathleen Drago
Owen Conery, a blind beggar
J. M. Kerrigan
Pat O'Malley       Fred O'Donovan
James Brogan       Arthur Sinclair
First Girl         Eithne Magee
Second Girl        Ann Coppinger
Head Constable     J. A. O'Rourke
First Policeman    Michael Conniffe
Second Policeman   Philip Guiry
A Boy              Thomas O'Neill
    Directed by A. Patrick Wilson
First published: in *The Image
and Other Plays* (London: Put-
nam's, 1922); rev. & rpr. in *Col-
lected Plays*, Vol. III.

## EIMAR O'DUFFY
*The Walls of Athens*
a Comedy in One Act.
First produced: 19 April 1915, by
the Irish Theatre, at the Hardwicke Street Hall, Dublin.

CAST

Phryne       Kathleen MacCormack
And others.
    Directed by John MacDonagh
Costumes by the Dun Emer Guild
    Scenery by Jack Morrow
First published: Dublin: *The
Irish Review*, 1914.

## THOMAS MacDONAGH
*Pagans*
a Modern Play in Two
Conversations.
First produced: 19 April 1915, by
the Irish Theatre, at the Hardwicke Street Hall, Dublin.

CAST

Frances Fitzmaurice
Una O'Connor
Sarah Churchill

Grace MacCormack
Helen Noble    Lelia MacMurrogh
John Fitzmaurice
John MacDonagh
First published: Dublin: Talbot
Press, 1920.

## EDWARD MARTYN
*The Privilege of Place*
a Play in Three Acts.
First produced: 8 November 1915,
by the Irish Theatre, at the Hardwicke Street Hall, Dublin.

CAST

Sir Matthew Hort, K.C.V.O.
John MacDonagh
Lady Hort (Jane), his wife
Lelia MacMurrogh
Owen, their son    J. Derham
Sheela, their daughter
Máire Nic Shiubhlaigh
Joseph O'Hagan, brother of
Lady Hort      Kerry Reddin
Mark Bodkin, an experimentalist
in Public Life    Charles Power
Peter O'Keeffe     Eric Gorman
Maggie, his daughter Nell Byrne
Terence, his son   Seán Mac Caoilte
Aloysius Fogarty, Constable
in the R.I.C.       Peter Judge
                ('F. J. McCormick')
An Elderly Gentleman
Norman Reddin
    Directed by John MacDonagh

## P. J. BOURKE
*For the Land She Loved*
a Patriotic Melodrama.
First produced: 15 November
1915, by P. J. Bourke's No. 1
Company, at the Abbey Theatre,
Dublin.

CAST

Lady Nugent     Kitty Carrickford
Betsey Gray     Peggy Courtney
Munro           John Connolly
Col. Johnston   P. J. Bourke
Dermot McMahon  M. Carolan
James Simpson   H. E. Hutchinson
And others.
    Directed by P. J. Bourke
Unpublished.

## ST. JOHN ERVINE
*John Ferguson*
a Play in Four Acts.
First produced: 30 November
1915, by the Abbey Company, at
the Abbey Theatre, Dublin.

CAST

John Ferguson, a farmer
             Sydney J. Morgan
Sarah Ferguson, his wife
             Nora Desmond
Hannah Ferguson, his daughter
             Nora Close
James Caesar, a grocer
             J. M. Kerrigan
Henry Witherow, a miller
             Arthur Sinclair
Sam Mawhinney, a postman
             J. A. O'Rourke
'Clutie' John Magrath, a beggar
             Philip Guiry
Andreas Ferguson, John Fer-
    guson's son    Fred O'Donovan
Sergeant Kernaghan, R.I.C.
             H. E. Hutchinson
Two Constables    Arthur Shields,
             D. Kelly
    Directed by St. John Ervine
First published: Dublin & Lon-
don: Maunsel, 1915.

JOHN MacDONAGH

*Author! Author!*
a Satire on Peasant Plays
in One Act.
First produced: 27 December
1915, by the Irish Theatre, at the
Hardwicke Street Hall, Dublin.
The Cast included John MacDon-
agh, Kerry Reddin, John Denham,
Nell Byrne, and Mr. Walsh.
    Directed by John MacDonagh
First published: in *The Dublin
Magazine*, Vol. I, No. 7 (1924).


P. KEHOE

*Ireland First!*
a Play in One Act.
Production uncertain.
First published: Dublin: Gill,
1915.

473

# Notes

## 1910

1  I, 'The Cross Image', *Sinn Féin* (9 July 1910), p. 3.
2  Abbey Theatre programme contained in W. A. Henderson scrapbook, Ms. 1733, National Library of Ireland.
3  *Joseph Holloway's Abbey Theatre*, eds. R. Hogan and M. J. O'Neill (Carbondale: Southern Illinois University Press, 1967).
4  [W. J. Lawrence], 'Provincial Productions', *The Stage* (20 January 1910); also contained in Henderson, Ms. 1733, p. 6.
5  Ashley Dukes, 'Drama', *The New Age* (16 June 1910); also contained in Henderson, Ms. 1733, p. 141.
6  J. T. Grein, 'Premieres of the Week', *The Sunday Times* (5 June 1910); also contained in Henderson, Ms. 1733, p. 137.
7  William Archer, 'The Drama', *The Nation* (4 June 1910), pp. 346–347.
8  'The Abbey Theatre', *The Freeman's Journal* (4 February 1910); also contained in Henderson, Ms. 1733, p. 15.
9  J. H. Cox, 'The Story of a Helmet', *The Irish Independent* (11 February 1910); also contained in Henderson, Ms. 1733, p. 27.
10  'The Grey Mullet' is a reference to one of the year's more entertaining exchanges of correspondence in *The Irish Times*. Early in the year George Moore wrote a long, apparently sincere letter to the paper, advocating that the diet of the Irish be improved by the addition of a fish known as the grey mullet, and listing instances of his own gastronomic enjoyment of the fish. This letter sparked off a long series of rejoinders which included recipes and various more or less knowledgeable information about the habits of the fish. Shaw's boyhood friend, the playwright and novelist Edward McNulty, wrote that he doubted the existence of such a fish and noted that its initials were the same as George Moore's. Susan Mitchell, the satiric poet, contributed a poem on the subject, 'George Moore and his Grey Mullet'.
11  Padraic Colum, 'A Topical Play by Mr. W. B. Yeats', *The Manchester Guardian* (14 February 1910); also contained in Henderson, Ms. 1733, p. 27.
12  G. H. Mair, 'In the Abbey Theatre', *The Manchester Guardian* (25 February 1910); also contained in Henderson, Ms. 1733, p. 28.
13  Jack Point, 'A Miracle Play at the Abbey', *The Evening Herald* (4 March 1910); also contained in Henderson, Ms. 1733, p. 35.
14  Jacques, 'A Workhouse Drama', *The Irish Independent* (6 May 1910); also contained in Henderson, Ms. 1733, p. 86.
15  Thomas M. Kettle, 'Padraic Colum's Play', *The Irish Independent* (7 May 1910); also contained in Henderson, Ms. 1733, p. 86.
16  Imaal, 'Thomas Muskerry', *The Leader* (14 May 1910); also contained in Henderson, Ms. 1733, pp. 91–92.
17  Ella Young, ' "Thomas Muskerry" in Court', *Sinn Féin* (9 July 1910), also contained in Henderson, Ms. 1733, p. 180.
18  X, 'Muskerryism', *Sinn Féin* (16 July 1910), p. 3.
19  Padraic Colum, 'Muskerryism — A Reply to "X" ', *Sinn Féin* (23 July 1910), p. 3.
20  Colum had recently written an Arabian play called *The Desert* and submitted it unsuccessfully to an English manager. When later the manager produced Edward Knoblauch's very successful *Kismet*, Colum charged that he had been plagiarised, and he and his friend Kettle

made an issue of the matter in the Press. Indeed, Colum was so disturbed by the production of *Kismet* that he financed the publication of his own play. Many years and several revisions later, Colum's play was produced by the Dublin Gate Theatre under the title of *Mogu of the Desert*.

21  Jacques, 'Beneath Criticism', *The Irish Independent* (20 May 1910); contained in Henderson, Ms. 1733, p. 104.

22  'An Outside Criticism', *The Evening Telegraph* (20 May 1910); also contained in Henderson, Ms. 1733, p. 106.

23  'New Play at the Abbey', *The Irish Times* (20 May 1910), p. 5.

24  These passages are excerpted from pp. 66–100 of Brinsley MacNamara's *In Clay and in Bronze* (New York: Brentano's, 1920).

25  'The Casting Out of Martin Whelan', *The Irish Times* (30 September 1910), p. 8.

26  [W. J. Lawrence], 'Provincial Productions', *The Stage* (6 October 1910); also contained in Henderson, Ms. 1733, p. 262.

27  'New Play at the Abbey', *The Leader* (8 October 1910); also contained in Henderson, Ms. 1733, pp. 260–261.

28  Letter of R. J. Ray to W. A. Henderson, dated 7 October 1910, and contained in Henderson, Ms. 1733.

29  'A New Play at the Abbey', *The Freeman's Journal* (28 October 1910); also contained in Henderson, Ms. 1733, p. 278.

30  Jacques, 'An Abbey Tragedy', *The Irish Independent* (28 October 1910); also contained in Henderson, Ms. 1733, p. 279.

31  C, 'A New Irish Comedy', *The Manchester Guardian* (15 November 1910); also contained in Henderson, Ms. 1733, p. 289.

32  Jacques, 'At the Abbey', *The Irish Independent* (11 November 1910); also contained in Henderson, Ms. 1733, p. 289.

33  'Abbey Theatre', *The Irish Times* (11 November 1910), p. 8.

34  An Philibin [J. H. Pollock], 'Birthright', *The National Student* (November, 1910), p. 56.

35  H.F., 'At the Abbey Theatre', *Sinn Féin* (14 May 1910), p. 2.

36  Letter of Lennox Robinson to W. B. Yeats, dated 31 January 1911, and contained in Manuscript file 13,068 (23), National Library of Ireland.

37  The original series of telegrams is also contained in Manuscript file 13,068 (23), National Library of Ireland, as is Robinson's letter of 7 May to Lady Gregory.

38  *Ibid.*

39  'Miss Horniman and the Abbey Theatre', *The Irish Times* (13 May 1910), p. 7.

40  Letter of W. A. Henderson to W. B. Yeats, dated 16 May 1910, and contained in Manuscript file 13,068 (23), National Library of Ireland.

41  'Miss Horniman, M.A.', *The Referee* (21 August 1910).

42  Contained in Henderson scrapbook, Ms. 1733, National Library of Ireland.

43  Miss Horniman at this point added a footnote to the document: '*No*, the leases will be taken over from me, *not* bought.The annex which is part of the Abbey Theatre and one house and shop in Abbey Street, bringing in £70 per annum cost £1,428. These two properties I will sell for the sum I gave for them and I will hand over everything else for nothing.'

44  Make clear that you are not going to have a brigade of infantry for staff. Engaging better than hiring. Miss Horniman's note.

475

45 Why a *man*? You have taken female help from Lady Gregory and from me and now despise it publicly. Better to put 'For' instead of 'we' before 'ourselves'. Miss Horniman's note.

46 'seem' and 'leaves' in one sentence appear to be shakey in grammar to me. Miss Horniman's note.

47 Yeats actually wrote erroneously '1908'.

48 Contained in Manuscript file 13,068 (3), National Library of Ireland.

49 'Irish National Theatre', *The Irish Times* (16 June 1910), p. 7.

50 Ford Madox Hueffer (later Ford) wrote a long letter to *The Star* on 17 June about the plight of the Abbey, in which he said in part:

> As to the artistic merits of the productions of the Irish Theatre, no doubt the management would wish modestly to dissociate themselves from my somewhat extreme views. But I am not exaggerating if I say that I have this morning looked down the list of play-bills in my morning paper without perceiving the name of any single new play that could move me to the slightest thrill of curiosity. The only theatre to which in this warm weather I could nerve myself to go would be to the Court — and to the Court because the Irish Company is there performing. This is a rash and sweeping statement — but let it stand as representing the amount of emotion that can be aroused in a very hardened play-goer by these players.
>
> I don't think there has been anything like it in the world, and for myself, I wish we could apply for writs *no exeat regno* against Lady Gregory and Mr. Yeats and all the members of their company. I don't want them to go back to Ireland, I want them to stop here. . . .

Contained in Henderson scrapbook, Ms. 1733, National Library of Ireland.

51 'The Irish National Theatre', *The Irish Times* (25 June 1910), p. 7.

52 'Abbey Theatre', *The Irish Times* (28 October 1910), p. 7. It is interesting to note on p. 284 of Henderson's scrapbook for 1910 (Ms. 1733, National Library of Ireland) that among the subscribers to the Endowment Fund were Lord Dunsany who pledged £300, Wilfrid Scawen Blunt who pledged £50, J. M. Barrie who pledged £10, and Dr. Oliver Gogarty who pledged five guineas.

53 'Lady Gregory "At Home" at the Abbey Theatre', *The Irish Times* (22 November 1910), p. 8.

54 Actually, on 29 November, the following disclaimer from Æ appeared in the Press:

> Sir, — It appears from your report of the application of Lady Gregory and Mr. Yeats for a new patent for the Abbey Theatre that Mr. Dudley White mentioned my name in connection with the Theatre of Ireland. Though I am in sympathy with the general work of this Society, I wish to say that I am not a member, nor have I ever been a member; and I have given no person permission to use my name in any way in connection with its application for right to act in the Abbey Theatre. Yours, etc.,
>
> GEO. W. RUSSELL

From *The Irish Times* (29 November 1910), p. 9.

55 'Abbey Theatre', *The Irish Times* (28 November 1910), p. 5.

56 'The Tragic Theatre', *The Irish Times* (9 February 1910); also contained in Henderson, Ms. 1733, p. 21.

57  'The Theatre in Ireland', *The Evening Telegraph* (4 March 1910); also contained in Henderson, Ms. 1733, p. 21.

58  In a leading article on 4 March, *The Irish Times*, for instance, wrote of Yeats:

> The Ireland which he sees in his visions would never create a theatre or produce a literature. The really great poets have always kept in close touch with the hard facts of life. They have left us documents in which we may read the work and genius of their times. In the 'organised conception' which Mr. Yeats despises lies Ireland's only hope of evolving a true national life and a great national character. It is these things thus evolved — and not Mr. Yeats, *bombinans in vacuo* — that will lay the foundations of an Irish renaissance in literature and art.

From the other side of the political spectrum, Arthur Griffith in *Sinn Féin* reached similar conclusions:

> The man who wrote and thought as Mr. Yeats wrote in 1886 is a loss to the nation while his eyes are shut. Once upon a time George Faulkner, the Dublin printer, waited upon Dean Swift in foppish attire, and the Dean pretended not to recognise him. Later he waited on him attired as became him, whereupon the Dean, shaking him heartily by the hand, bade him welcome. "Here came a fop, George, a while ago pretending to be you," said the Dean, "but, egad, I sent him packing about his business." There is a bundle of affectations and vanities waiting upon Ireland now pretending to be W. B. Yeats, and much astonished that Ireland will not recognise it. But these vanities and affectations are not the man from whom we have quoted, and when that man waits on Ireland again, as we trust he soon will, Ireland will receive him as the Dean did Faulkner with a welcome and "Here was a fop, Yeats, awhile ago pretending to be you, but, egad, I sent him packing about his business." Also contained in Henderson, Ms. 1733, p. 25.

59  My reference for this quotation has been lost in the mail; and although I have been unable to rediscover my source, I have decided to let the quotation stand. R.H.

60  'The Fantastic Irishman', *The Irish Independent* (12 March 1910), p. 5.

61  [Arthur Griffith], 'This Week', *Sinn Féin* (19 March 1910), p. 1.

62  'Irish National Drama', *Cambridge Daily News* (25 May 1910); also contained in Henderson, Ms. 1733, p. 122.

63  'Mr. Yeats's New Play', *The Daily News* (9 July 1910); also contained in Henderson, Ms. 1733, p. 212.

64  'Mr. W. B. Yeats on Irish Literature', *The Manchester Guardian* (15 November 1910); also contained in Henderson, Ms. 1733, p. 271.

65  'The People's Vision', *The Irish Nation* (26 November 1910); also contained in Henderson, Ms. 1733, p. 303.

66  'Irish Ideas', *The Irish Nation* (26 February 1910).

67  'Theatre of Ireland', *The Irish Times* (29 March 1910), p. 6.

68  [Arthur Griffith], 'This Week', *Sinn Féin* (Easter Week, 1910), p. 1.

69  *Ibid.*

70  'New Play by Count Markievicz', *The Irish Times* (15 April 1910), p. 3.

71  'Abbey Theatre', *The Irish Times* (16 April 1910), p. 7.

72  'Dublin Amateur Operatic Society', *The Irish Times* (30 March 1910), p. 7.

73 'Irish Opera at the Gaiety Theatre', *The Irish Times* (17 May 1910), p. 5.
74 'Sgoil Eanna Players', *An Claideamh Soluis* (16 April 1910), p. 8.
75 'Amateurs at the Abbey Theatre', *The Irish Times* (1 June 1910), p. 8.
76 'The Oireachtas', *An Claideamh Soluis* (21 May 1910), p. 8.
77 'Public Amusements', *The Irish Times* (11 October 1910), p. 8.
78 'Plays and Players', *The Weekly Freeman's Journal* (15 October 1910), p. 15.
79 'Grand Opera House', *The Northern Whig* (9 March 1910), p. 12.
80 'Cork Dramatic Society', *The Cork Constitution* (12 May 1910), p. 7.
81 'Music and the Drama', *The Cork Tattler* (May 1910), contained in Daniel Corkery's papers, University College, Cork.
82 'Cork Dramatic Society', *The Cork Constitution* (3 November 1910), p. 6.
83 Daniel Corkery, 'Terence MacSwiney: Lord Mayor of Cork', *Studies* (December, 1920), pp. 516–517.
84 'Cork Dramatic Society', *The Cork Constitution* (28 December 1910), p. 6.
85 Imaal, 'Cork Plays and Players', *The Leader* (14 January 1911), p. 538.

# 1911

1 'The Abbey Theatre', *The Evening Telegraph* (4 May 1911); also contained in Henderson, Ms. 1734, p. 123.

2 Ms. 13,068 (23), National Library of Ireland.

3 *Ibid.*

4 *Ibid.*

5 J.H.C., 'An Abbey Mystery', *The Irish Independent* (6 January 1911), p. 5.

6 'Abbey Theatre', *The Irish Times* (6 January 1911), p. 4.

7 'Abbey Theatre', *The Evening Telegraph* (9 January 1911); also contained in Hendreson, Ms. 1734, p. 5.

8 'The Abbey Theatre', *The Evening Mail* (9 January 1911); also contained in Henderson, Ms. 1734, p. 6.

9 A reference to St. John Ervine's *Mixed Marriage.*

10 'Stage Lighting', *The Pall Mall Gazette* (13 January 1911); also contained in Henderson, Ms. 1734, p. 14.

11 *Ibid.*

12 'The Deliverer at the Abbey', *The Freeman's Journal* (13 January 1911); also contained in Henderson, Ms. 1734, p. 7.

13 'Abbey Theatre', *The Irish Times* (13 January 1911), p. 8.

14 'The Abbey Theatre', *The Irish Times* (14 January 1911); also contained in Henderson, Ms. 1734.

15 'In New Guise', *The Irish Independent* (13 January 1911), p. 7.

16 'A New Play at the Abbey', *The Freeman's Journal* (27 January 1911); also contained in Henderson, Ms. 1734, p. 23.

17 [W. J. Lawrence], 'Provincial Productions', *The Stage* (February, 1911); also contained in Henderson, Ms. 1734, p. 25.

18 'The Abbey Theatre', *The Irish Times* (4 February 1911), p. 7.

19 'Mr. W. B. Yeats on the Art of the Minstrel', *The Irish Times* (6 February 1911), p. 7.

20 'From "The Times" of To-Day', *The Irish Times* (17 February 1911), p. 5.

21 'Tragic Recitation', *The Chronicle* (London), (17 February 1911); also contained in Henderson, Ms. 1734, p. 27.

22 'Joe Sandes was also a theatrical agent and promoter, co-founder of the Brisan Opera Company which Blazes Boylan might have adorned. He happens to have been connected by marriage with my mother's family, and ledgers of his in my possession are a mine of information about Dublin theatre costings in the first quarter of this century.' Ria Mooney's note.

23 Miss Mooney is undoubtedly wrong, for by 1911 Norreys Connell had left the theatre. The little man she refers to could not, of course, have been the very tall Lennox Robinson who directed the play, but it may have been Nugent Monck who had been hired to form a School of Acting at the Abbey when the company went on the first American tour.

24 Ria Mooney, *Players and the Painted Stage*, an unpublished manuscript, edited by Val Mulkerns.

25 'The Land of Heart's Desire at the Abbey', *The Freeman's Journal* (17 February 1911); also contained in Henderson, Ms. 1734, p. 32.

26 'The Abbey Theatre', *The Daily Express* (17 February 1911); also contained in Henderson, Ms. 1734, p. 31.

27 W. Hillox, 'Abbey Theatre', *The Irish Times* (8 March 1911), p. 6.

28  'Ulster Humour', *The Pall Mall Gazette* (31 March 1911); also contained in Henderson, Ms. 1734, p. 97.
29  J. H. Cox, 'Prejudice Deeper Than Reason', *The Irish Independent* (31 March 1911), p. 5.
30  'New Play at the Abbey Theatre', *The Irish Times* (31 March 1911), p. 7.
31  *Ibid.*
32  'A New Play at the Abbey', *The Freeman's Journal* (31 March 1911); also contained in Henderson, Ms. 1734, p. 97.
33  F. Sheehy Skeffington, 'Drama', *The New Age* (6 April 1911), pp. 547–548.
34  Padraic Colum, 'New Play at the Abbey Theatre', *The Manchester Guardian* (4 April 1911), p. 9.
35  Henderson, Ms. 1734, p. 143.
36  'The Irish National Theatre', *The Pall Mall Gazette* (9 June 1911); also contained in Henderson, Ms. 1734, p. 165.
37  P.J., 'The Irish Players', *The Saturday Review* (10 June 1911), pp. 706–707.
38  Robert Lynd, 'The Drama', *The Daily News and Leader* (June 1911), p. 183.
39  'The Court Theatre', *The Academy* (10 June 1911), pp. 723–724.
40  'The Theatre', *The Academy* (24 June 1911), pp. 785–786.
41  'The Abbey Players', *The Evening Telegraph* (26 June 1911); also contained in Henderson, Ms. 1734, p. 188.
42  'The Abbey Theatre', *The Evening Telegraph* (28 June 1911); also contained in Henderson, Ms. 1734, p. 188.
43  'Abbey Players', *The Evening Mail* (6 July 1911), p. 5.
44  'Public Amusements, Abbey Theatre', *The Irish Times* (5 September 1911), p. 5; 'Benefit Performance at the Abbey', *The Daily Express* (5 September 1911).
45  Letter from William Boyle to W. A. Henderson, dated 8 September 1911, contained in Henderson, Ms. 1734.
46  'Mr. Yeats on the Abbey Theatre', *The Irish Times* (9 September 1911), p. 8.
47  'Abbey Theatre', *The Irish Times* (30 September 1911), p. 8.
48  'The Playboy Again', *The Irish Times* (31 October 1911), p. 4.
49  'The Abbey Theatre', *The Evening Telegraph* (24 November 1911); also contained in Henderson, Ms. 1734, p. 258.
50  In his scrapbooks contained in the National Library of Ireland, Lawrence identifies himself as the culprit, and this identification is corroborated by Michael Conniffe in Appendix II.
51  'The Abbey Theatre', *The Evening Telegraph* (24 November 1911); also contained in Henderson, Ms. 1734, p. 258.
52  Jack Point, 'Abbey Theatre Pupils', *The Evening Herald* (8 December 1911); also contained in Henderson, Ms. 1734, p. 264.
53  Jacques, 'Just Like the Abbey', *The Irish Independent* (8 December 1911); also contained in Henderson, Ms. 1734, p. 263.
54  Quoted in Liam Miller, *The Noble Drama of W. B. Yeats* (Dublin: Dolmen Press, 1977), p. 171.
55  Jacques, 'Things Theatrical', *The Irish Independent* (15 December 1911); also contained in Henderson, Ms. 1734, p. 266.
56  'Abbey Theatre', *The Irish Times* (15 December 1911), p. 8.
57  'The Abbey Theatre Repertory', *The Irish Times* (19 December 1911), p. 8.

58 Victor O'D. Power, 'The Playboy of the Western World', *The Evening Telegraph* (8 May 1911); also contained in Henderson, Ms. 1734, p. 125.
59 F.R. [Fred Ryan], 'The Abbey Theatre', *The Evening Telegraph* (13 May 1911); also contained in Henderson, Ms. 1734, p. 126.
60 Padraic Colm [*sic*], 'The Irish Peasant', *The Evening Telegraph* (20 May 1911); also contained in Henderson, Ms. 1734, p. 128.
61 Fred Ryan, 'The Irish Peasant and the Abbey Dramatists', *The Evening Telegraph* (3 June 1911), p. 4. Somewhat relevant to this debate was the following account from another newspaper:

> While many people know in a vague way that there has been lately a general revival in the literature and folklore of early Christian Ireland, few know that within fifteen or twenty miles of Boston there is a colony of nearly 1,000 natives of the Aran Islands, off the Irish Atlantic coast, many of whom speak Gaelic, and not a few of whom are able to transcribe the characters of a language which was a medium of Christian civilisation as early as the fifth century of the Christian era.
>
> The writer of the article, together with a [Boston] *Globe* artist, went to Woburn recently to see Patrick McDonough, a native Aran Islander, who is employed at Arlington gas works. Asked about Gaelic, he said:
>
> "It's been a long while since I wrote in Gaelic, but I speak it still. In the old days in Killrona I used to write it the same as I spoke it, and it was at my house that John McNeil, and Synge, and Lady Gregory would be coming to stay now and then, and pick up the words. Around about the country they would go every day learning words from the neighbours, and then at nights they would be asking the meaning of the same, setting it down in writing. They were all writing books, and Lady Gregory learned very fast. The second time she came she learned to understand all that would be said to her in Irish, and pleased she was. And Synge? Why he hunted for the old stories and legends all about Killrona, setting 'em down on bits of paper as he heard them. All the old people got to know him, and she too, round about the village. Many a tale they heard, I'm thinking.
>
> "It was when I was a boy that they began digging in the islands among the ruins and the graves." Here he paused for a moment. "Did I see them at work?" he continued. " 'Twas from a mound I saw them take a skeleton of a woman that measured seven feet long. A race of giants? Yes, that's what they say. And that's what you can read in the old Gaelic tales and songs that are translated and kept in Dublin. John McNeil! 'Twas him that started them coming over to the islands to study the old Irish language. Since then there's been many there. Mr. Yeats and Mr. Synge and Lady Gregory stayed at my house in Killrona, and they left their pictures with us when they went away. Good scholars they were too, learning very fast."

'Aran Islanders Abroad', *The Irish Independent* (15 April 1911).
62 'Platform and Stage', *The Irish Times* (11 November 1911), and nearly a direct quotation from a Theatre of Ireland brochure, contained in Henderson, Ms. 1734, p. 260.
63 'The Theatre of Ireland', *The Irish Times* (20 November 1911), p. 6.
64 'Irish Plays', *The Stage* (23 November 1911); also contained in Henderson, Ms. 1734, p. 261.

65 'The Theatre of Ireland', *The Irish Times* (20 November 1911), p. 6.
66 Gipsy Walker, the sister of Máire Nic Shiubhlaigh.
67 'Theatre of Ireland', *The Irish Times* (19 December 1911); also contained in Henderson, Ms. 1734, p. 278.
68 [W. J. Lawrence], 'Irish Productions', *The Stage* (21 December 1911); also contained in Henderson, Ms. 1734, p. 280.
69 'Miss Johanna Redmond's Play', *The Pall Mall Gazette* (7 March 1911); also contained in Henderson, Ms. 1734, p. 35.
70 Letter of W. F. Casey to W. A. Henderson, undated but written in late March or early April from London, contained in Henderson, Ms. 1734.
71 Jacques, 'Falsely True', *The Irish Independent* (18 April 1911); also contained in Henderson, Ms. 1734, p. 115.
72 'The Theatre', *The Academy* (16 December 1911); also contained in Henderson, Ms. 1734, p. 245.
73 The growing popularity of the film may be attested to by the following leading article from a Dublin newspaper:

> The cinematograph has evidently come to stay. Most of us expected that the boom of the "picture-hall" would soon share the fate of most of the skating-rinks. . . . The improvements and emendations which cinematography has undergone . . . are among the marvels of this marvellous age of ours. The advent of colours, in the place of black and white, figures among the most recent innovations, while at an entertainment which is at present being given in Vienna the figures appearing on the screen are shown in relief. The cinematograph show is now an established fact, and, as such, calls for impartial criticism. . . . The great danger of the cinematograph show is that it may cause the public to lose its true perspective of the value of entertainments which call for no mental effort. An amusement which serves no higher purpose than to pass the time is not an entertainment in the true sense. That it panders to this inclination is the gravest charge which can be levelled against the cinematograph.

'The Cinematograph', *The Irish Times* (27 December 1911), p. 4.
74 'Gaiety Theatre', *The Irish Times* (27 July 1911), p. 7.
75 Jacques, 'A Stage Meldon', *The Irish Independent* (12 December 1911); also contained in Henderson, Ms. 1734, p. 273.
76 Jacques, 'Rival Stars at the Gaiety', *The Irish Independent* (13 December 1911); also contained in Henderson, Ms. 1734, p. 276.
77 'Gaiety Theatre', *The Irish Times* (13 December 1911), p. 7.
78 'Mr. Frederick Mouillot', *The Irish Times* (5 August 1911), p. 7.
79 'Public Amusements', *The Irish Times* (14 November 1911), p. 5.
80 'Abbey Theatre', *The Irish Times* (27 December 1911), p. 6.
81 'Triple Bill at the Abbey Theatre', *The Irish Times* (1 March 1911), p. 9.
82 'Passion Play in Dublin', *The Irish Times* (3 April 1911), p. 6.
83 F. R. Goff, 'Passion Play in Dublin', *The Irish Times* (6 April 1911), p. 6.
84 P. H. Pearse, 'The Passion Play in Dublin', *The Irish Times* (7 April 1911), p. 5.
85 'Passion Play at the Abbey Theatre', *The Irish Times* (8 April 1911), p. 8.
86 'Irish Theatre and National Stage Company', *The Irish Times* (5 September 1911), p. 5.

87 [W. J. Lawrence], 'Irish Plays', *The Stage* (7 September 1911); also contained in Henderson, Ms. 1734, p. 231.
88 'Grand Opera House', *The Northern Whig* (5 December 1911), p. 10.
89 'Grand Opera House', *The Northern Whig* (6 December 1911), p. 9.
90 Quoted in Sam Hanna Bell, *The Theatre in Ulster* (Dublin: Gill & Macmillan, 1972), p. 39.
91 *Ibid.*, p. 40.
92 'Cork Dramatic Society', *The Cork Constitution* (20 April 1911), p. 10.
93 Tom Jones [Mrs. Brooke Hughes], 'Literary Gossip', *The Cork Tatler* (27 May 1911); 'Cork Dramatic Society', *The Cork Constitution* (19 May 1911), p. 10.
94 'Cork Dramatic Society', *The Cork Constitution* (7 December 1911), p. 7.

# 1912

1 'Mystery Plays at the Abbey Theatre', *The Evening Telegraph* (5 January 1912), p. 4.

2 W. J. Lawrence, 'The Abbey Theatre: Its History and Mystery', *The Weekly Freeman* (7 December 1912), p. 11.

3 Letter of W. B. Yeats to Lady Gregory, dated 7 January 1912. Ms. 18,721, National Library of Ireland.

4 Letter of W. B. Yeats to Lady Gregory, dated 11 January 1912. Ms. 18,721, National Library of Ireland.

5 Letter of W. B. Yeats to Lady Gregory, dated 7 January 1912. Ms. 18,721, National Library of Ireland.

6 Letter of W. B. Yeats to Lady Gregory, dated 11 January 1912. Ms. 18,721, National Library of Ireland.

7 'The Abbey Theatre — New Play by Lady Gregory', *The Evening Telegraph* (12 January 1912), p. 2.

8 [W. J. Lawrence], 'An Irish Play', *The Stage* (18 January 1912), p. 22.

9 *Ibid.*

10 'The Abbey Theatre — New Play by Lady Gregory', *The Evening Telegraph* (12 January 1912), p. 2.

11 Jacques, 'An Abbey Theatre "Discovery"', *The Irish Independent* (12 January 1912).

12 'Abbey Theatre', *The Irish Times* (11 January 1912), p. 7.

13 Letter of W. B. Yeats to Lady Gregory, dated 21 January 1912. Ms. 18,721, National Library of Ireland.

14 J.P.M., 'The School of Acting', *The Evening Telegraph* (20 January 1912), p. 5.

15 Mise, 'Hill-Talk', *Sinn Féin* (10 February 1912), p. 2.

16 Letter of W. B. Yeats to Lady Gregory, dated 13 February 1912. Ms. 18,721, National Library of Ireland.

17 W. J. Lawrence, 'The Abbey Theatre: Its History and Mystery', *The Weekly Freeman* (7 December 1912), p. 11.

18 'The Abbey Theatre — Plays in English and Irish', *The Evening Telegraph* (16 February 1912), p. 6.

19 'Abbey Theatre', *The Irish Times* (16 February 1912), p. 8.

20 Letter of W. B. Yeats to Lady Gregory, dated 11 January 1912. Ms. 18,721, National Library of Ireland.

21 Letter of W. B. Yeats to Lady Gregory, dated 9 February 1912. Ms. 18,721, National Library of Ireland.

22 Letter of W. B. Yeats to Lady Gregory, dated 18 March 1912. Ms. 18,721, National Library of Ireland.

23 Letter of W. B. Yeats to Lady Gregory, dated 15 February 1912. Ms. 18,721, National Library of Ireland.

24 Alice Milligan, 'Native Drama', *The Irish Independent* (13 March 1912), p. 4.

25 P. S. O'Hegarty, 'Art and the Nation', *Irish Freedom* (May 1912), p. 2.

26 'Abbey School of Acting', *The Evening Herald* (1 March 1912), p. 5.

27 [W. J. Lawrence], 'The Worlde and the Chylde', *The Stage* (7 March 1912), p. 24.

28 Jacques, 'The U.S. A-bbey Players', *The Irish Independent* (15 March 1912), p. 4.

29 *Ibid.*

30 'The Abbey Players' Return', *The Freeman's Journal* (15 March 1912), p. 7.

31 [W. J. Lawrence], 'Irish Productions', *The Stage* (11 April 1912), p. 14.
32 'New Play at the Abbey Theatre', *The Irish Times* (29 March 1912), p. 5.
33 Padraic Colum, 'A New Play at the Abbey Theatre', *The Manchester Guardian* (30 March 1912), p. 8.
34 Letter of W. B. Yeats to Lady Gregory, dated 18 March 1912. Ms. 18,721, National Library of Ireland.
35 Letter of Arthur Sinclair to Joseph Holloway, dated 1 April 1912. Ms. 13,267, National Library of Ireland.
36 Letter of William Boyle to Joseph Holloway, dated 31 March 1912. Ms. 13,267, National Library of Ireland.
37 *Ibid.*
38 *Ibid.*
39 Letter of Frank Fay to Joseph Holloway, dated 1912. Ms. 13,267, National Library of Ireland.
40 'New Play at the Abbey Theatre', *The Irish Times* (29 March 1912), p. 5; and Padraic Colum, 'A New Play at the Abbey Theatre', *The Manchester Guardian* (30 March 1912), p. 8.
41 [W. J. Lawrence], 'Irish Productions', *The Stage* (11 April 1912), p. 14.
42 Letter of William Boyle to Joseph Holloway, dated 15 April 1912. Ms. 13,267, National Library of Ireland.
43 Letter of William Boyle to Joseph Holloway, dated 2 November 1912. Ms. 13,267, National Library of Ireland.
44 Jack Point, 'Patriots', *The Evening Herald* (12 April 1912), p. 2.
45 'Abbey Theatre', *The Daily Express* (12 April 1912), p. 12.
46 Lennox Robinson, *Curtain Up* (London: Michael Joseph, 1942), p. 43.
47 J.P.M., 'New Play at the Abbey Theatre', *The Evening Telegraph* (12 April 1912), p. 4.
48 Letter of Miss Byrne to W. B. Yeats, dated 15 April 1912. Ms. 18,722, National Library of Ireland.
49 Jacques, ' "Patriots" at the Abbey', *The Irish Independent* (12 April 1912), p. 10.
50 [W. J. Lawrence], 'Irish Productions', *The Stage* (18 April 1912), p. 16.
51 Letter of W. B. Yeats to Joseph Campbell, dated 26 July 1911. Private collection of Flann Campbell.
52 Letter of Joseph Campbell to Lennox Robinson, undated (probably 19 or 20 March 1912). Private collection of Flann Campbell.
53 Letter of Lennox Robinson to Joseph Campbell, dated 16 March 1912. Private collection of Flann Campbell.
54 Letter of Lennox Robinson to Joseph Campbell, dated 18 March 1912. Private collection of Flann Campbell.
55 Letter of Joseph Campbell to Lennox Robinson, undated (probably 19 or 20 March 1912). Private collection of Flann Campbell.
56 Letter of W. B. Yeats to Lady Gregory, dated 21 March 1912. Ms. 18,722, National Library of Ireland.
57 Letter of Lennox Robinson to Joseph Campbell, dated 11 April 1912. Private collection of Flann Campbell.
58 [W. J. Lawrence], 'Irish Production', *The Stage* (18 April 1912), p. 16.
59 *Ibid.*
60 'Abbey Theatre', *The Irish Times* (16 April 1912), p. 10; and J. H. Cox, 'New Abbey Play', *The Irish Independent* (16 April 1912), p. 4.
61 Letter of W. B. Yeats to Joseph Campbell, dated 6 May 1912. Private collection of Flann Campbell.

62 Letter of W. B. Yeats to Joseph Campbell, dated 29 April 1912. Private collection of Flann Campbell.

63 Letter of Joseph Campbell to Whitford Kane, dated 9 May 1912. Whitford Kane papers, New York Public Library.

64 Letter of W. B. Yeats to Lady Gregory, dated 14 April 1912. Ms. 18,722, National Library of Ireland.

65 *Ibid.*

66 'Amusements — Grand Opera House', *The Belfast News-Letter* (30 April 1912), p. 9; 'The Irish Players at Kelly's Theatre', *The Liverpool Post and Mercury* (7 May 1912), p. 7; G.B., 'Kelly's Theatre — The Irish Players', *The Liverpool Courier* (7 May 1912), p. 8; 'Royalty Theatre — "The Irish Players" ', *The Glasgow Herald* (24 May 1912), p. 8; 'Court Theatre — Irish Players', *The Daily Telegraph* (4 June 1912), p. 9; E. A. Baughan, 'Two Repertory Theatres', *The Daily News and Leader* (8 June 1912), p. 6; E.F.S., 'Scenery and the Irish Plays', *The Westminster Gazette* (22 June 1912), p. 3.

67 W. F. Casey, 'The Irish Players', *The Daily Chronicle* (17 June 1912), p. 4.

68 *Ibid.*

69 Letter of T. C. Murray to Joseph Holloway, dated 17 March 1912. Ms. 13,267, National Library of Ireland.

70 Letter of T. C. Murray to Joseph Holloway, dated 17 June 1912. Ms. 13, 267, National Library of Ireland.

71 Letter of Lady Gregory to John Quinn, dated 26 June 1912. John Quinn Memorial Collection, New York Public Library.

72 E.F.S., ' "Maurice Harte" by The Irish Theatre', *The Westminster Gazette* (21 June 1912), p. 3.

73 D. L. Kelleher, 'Two Irish Playwrights', *The Evening Telegraph* (19 August 1912), p. 5.

74 See, for instance, 'Maurice Harte', *The Irish Independent* (21 June 1912), p. 4.

75 See, for instance, 'Irish National Theatre', *The Morning Post* (21 June 1912), p. 8.

76 Letter of T. C. Murray to Joseph Holloway, dated 27 June 1912. Ms. 13,267, National Library of Ireland.

77 See, for instance, 'A New Irish Play', *The Yorkshire Post* (21 June 1912), p. 6; 'Court Theatre', *The Globe* (21 June 1912), p. 4; 'Eerie New Irish Play', *The Standard* (21 June 1912), p. 8; H. de S., 'Court Theatre', *The Star* (21 June 1912), p. 2.

78 Letter of T. C. Murray to W. A. Henderson, dated 26 January 1913. Private collection of Richard Burnham.

79 Letter of Lady Gregory to John Quinn, dated 26 June 1912. John Quinn Memorial Collection, New York Public Library.

80 Bookman, 'New Forces in Irish Drama', *The Northern Whig* (22 June 1912), p. 10.

81 Mordred, 'Irish Plays at the Court', *The Referee* (14 July 1912), p. 2.

82 'The Bogie Men', *The Pall Mall Gazette* (9 July 1912), p. 5.

83 'Court Theatre', *The Globe* (9 July 1912), p. 10.

84 *The Comedies of Lady Gregory*, ed. Ann Saddlemyer (Gerrards Cross: Colin Smythe, 1970), p. viii. The National Library of Ireland possesses a prompt copy of *The Bogie Men*, dated July, 1912, which was used by J. A. O'Rourke and which also contains several deletions and additions.

85 H. de S., 'Court Theatre', *The Star* (12 July 1912), p. 4.

86  'Mr. W. B. Yeats's Play', *The Pall Mall Gazette* (12 July 1912), p. 5.
87  See, for instance, 'Abbey Theatre', *The Daily Express* (27 September 1912), p. 7; and J.P.M., 'The Abbey Theatre', *The Evening Telegraph* (27 September 1912), p. 2.
88  Jacques, 'An Abbeyesque Ulster', *The Irish Independent* (27 August 1912), p. 4.
89  Letter of W. B. Yeats to Lady Gregory, dated 6 November 1912. Ms. 18,723, National Library of Ireland.
90  See, for instance, 'Abbey Players at Doneraile', *The Irish Times* (15 and 16 November 1912), p. 8.
91  'Abbey Players at Doneraile', *The Irish Times* (15 November 1912), p. 8.
92  'The Dramatic Revival', *The Evening Telegraph* (21 November 1912), p. 3.
93  'Abbey Theatre', *The Irish Times* (18 October 1912), p. 8.
94  Jack Point, 'An Abbey Shocker', *The Evening Herald* (18 October 1912), p. 4.
95  Jacques, 'Censor, Please', *The Irish Independent* (18 October 1912), p. 6.
96  [W. J. Lawrence], 'Irish Productions', *The Stage* (24 October 1912), p. 24.
97  Letter of St. John Ervine to W. J. Lawrence, dated 24 October 1912. Ms. 4,299, Vol. 8, National Library of Ireland.
98  St. John Ervine, 'The Magnanimous Lover', *The Irish Times* (22 October 1912), p. 5.
99  Letter of William Boyle to Joseph Holloway, dated 2 November 1912. Ms. 13,267, National Library of Ireland.
100  Letter to the Editor, 'The Magnanimous Lover', *The Irish Times* (23 October 1912), p. 9.
101  Letter of Lady Gregory to John Quinn, dated 22 October 1912. John Quinn Memorial Collection, New York Public Library.
102  'The Abbey Theatre', *The Freeman's Journal* (22 November 1912), p. 9.
103  Jacques, 'Two New Productions', *The Irish Independent* (22 November 1912), p. 4.
104  *Ibid.*
105  [W. J. Lawrence], 'Irish Productions', *The Stage* (28 November 1912), p. 25.
106  James Flannery, *W. B. Yeats and the Idea of a Theatre* (New Haven: Yale University Press, 1976), p. 307.
107  Letter of Frank Fay to W. J. Lawrence, dated 1912. Ms. 10,952, National Library of Ireland.
108  [W. J. Lawrence], 'Irish Productions', *The Stage* (28 November 1912), p. 25.
109  *Ibid.*
110  Letter of Lily Yeats to John Quinn, dated 25 November 1912. John Quinn Memorial Collection, New York Public Library.
111  Letter of Lennox Robinson to Lady Gregory, n.d. (Christmas, 1912?). Berg Collection, New York Public Library.
112  W. J. Lawrence, 'Irish Production', *The Stage* (2 January 1913), p. 31.
113  Ernest A. Boyd, 'The Irish National Theatre', *The Irish Times* (27 December 1912), p. 5.
114  See, for instance, Ellen Duncan's letter on 'The Irish National Theatre', *The Irish Times* (28 December 1912), p. 9, and E. J. Finlan's letter on

'The Irish National Theatre', *The Irish Times* (30 December 1912), p. 9.

115 Lennox Robinson, 'The Irish National Theatre', *The Irish Times* 1 January 1913), p. 9.

116 Constance de Markievicz, 'The Irish National Theatre', *The Irish Times* (1 January 1913), p. 9.

117 Joseph Holloway, 'The Irish National Theatre', *The Irish Times* (3 January 1913), p. 5.

118 Ernest A. Boyd, 'The Irish National Theatre', *The Irish Times* (4 January 1913), p. 8.

119 Constance de Markievicz, 'The Irish National Theatre', *The Evening Irish Times* (6 January 1913), p. 10; Ernest A. Boyd, 'The Irish National Theatre', *The Evening Irish Times* (7 January 1913), p. 8.

120 'The Independent Theatre Company', *The Evening Telegraph* (26 January 1912), p. 2.

121 [W. J. Lawrence], 'Irish Productions', *The Stage* (1 February 1912), p. 22.

122 Edward Martyn, 'The Lady from the Sea', *The Irish Times* (30 November 1912), p. 9.

123 Jacques, 'Two New Plays', *The Irish Independent* (26 January 1912), p. 4.

124 'Irish Ireland / Mr. Martyn's New Play', *Sinn Féin* (3 February 1912), p. 1.

125 'The Independent Theatre Company', *The Evening Telegraph* (26 January 1912), p. 2.

126 Jacques, 'Two New Plays', *The Irish Independent* (26 January 1912), p. 4.

127 [W. J. Lawrence], 'Irish Production', *The Stage* (1 February 1912), p. 22.

128 Jack Point, 'Amateurs at the Abbey', *The Evening Herald* (20 February 1912), p. 2.

129 'The Theatre of Ireland', *The Freeman's Journal* (19 April 1912), p. 5.

130 Jacques, 'The Theatre of Ireland', *The Irish Independent* (19 April 1912), p. 4.

131 [W. J. Lawrence], 'Irish Production', *The Stage* (25 April 1912), p. 16.

132 'Theatre of Ireland', *The Irish Times* (2 July 1912), p. 5.

133 Jack Point, 'Theatre of Ireland — A New Dramatist', *The Evening Herald* (2 July 1912), p. 4.

134 'The Theatre of Ireland', *The Evening Telegraph* (2 July 1912), p. 2.

135 Letter of Thomas MacDonagh to Frank Fay, dated 28 May 1912. Ms. 10,952, National Library of Ireland.

136 *Ibid.*

137 Letter of Thomas MacDonagh to Frank Fay, undated. Ms. 10,952, National Library of Ireland.

138 'New Play', *The Evening Telegraph* (8 February 1912), p. 2.

139 'The "Pioneer" Club', *The Evening Telegraph* (19 March 1912), p. 2.

140 'New Play by Miss J. Redmond', *The Irish Independent* (19 March 1912), p. 4.

141 'The "Pioneer" Club', *The Evening Telegraph* (19 March 1912), p. 3.

142 'Pioneer Dramatic Club', *The Irish Times* (19 March 1912), p. 7.

143 'Dublin Happenings', *The Evening Herald* (17 June 1912), p. 5.

144 'St. Enda's College', *The Irish Times* (17 June 1912), p. 8.

145 Joseph A. Keogh, 'Can Dublin Support a Repertory Theatre?' *The Irish Times* (25 October 1912), p. 10.

146 'Repertory Theatres', *The Irish Times* (25 October 1912), p. 6; and G. H. Taylor, 'A Repertory Theatre for Dublin', *The Irish Times* (November 1912), p. 9.

147 Ireland's Eye, 'The Music Hall', *The Irish Independent* (19 September 1912), p. 4.

148 H.M.W., 'The Ulster Players', *The Pall Mall Gazette* (2 February p. 5.

149 'The Ulster Players', *The Pall Mall Gazette* (6 February 1912), p. 5.

150 'Royalty Theatre', *The London Times* (7 February 1912), p. 10.

151 Frances, 'Five O'Clock Tea Talk', *T.P.'s Weekly* (16 February 1912), p. 214.

152 'Grand Opera House', *The Northern Whig* (10 December 1912), p. 3.

153 *Ibid.*

154 *Ibid.*

155 *Ibid.*

156 *Ibid.*

157 'Amusements — Grand Opera House', *The Belfast News-Letter* (10 December 1912), p. 4.

158 'Ulster Literary Theatre', *The Belfast News-Letter* (11 December 1912), p. 10.

159 'Cork Dramatic Society', *The Cork Examiner* (12 April 1912), p. 12.

160 'Opera House', *The Cork Constitution* (3 December 1912), p. 8.

161 R.T.O.B., 'Opera House', *Cork Free Press* (3 December 1912), p. 6.

162 'Opera House', *The Cork Constitution* (4 December 1912), p. 6.

163 R.T.O.B., 'Opera House', *Cork Free Press* (4 December 1912), p. 8.

164 *Ibid.*

165 'Opera House', *The Cork Constitution* (4 December 1912), p. 6.

166 'Three Original Plays', *The Cork Constitution* (22 November 1912), p. 8.

# 1913

1 For Yeats's opinion of the strike, see his exchange with the Lord Mayor at a Peace Meeting in the Mansion House on 27 October. It is reported in 'Poet and the Crisis', *The Evening Herald* (28 October 1913), p. 5.

2 Joseph Holloway, 'The "Playboy" in Canada', *The Evening Herald* (12 February 1913), p. 4.

3 Joseph Holloway, 'The Abbey Players and their Reception in New York', *The Evening Herald* (28 February 1913), p. 5.

4 Joseph Holloway, 'Galway Races', *The Evening Herald* (8 April 1913), p. 1.

5 Nevertheless, *The Evening Herald* did catch Kerrigan long enough to elicit the opinion that the American audience 'had not the same subtle sense of humour as the Dublin playgoer, who always saw, and often anticipated, the ludicrous. For instance, he said, any Dublin playgoer would see that *Kathleen ni Houlihan* was a symbolic play, and could not possibly commit the mistake made by the American critic, who, in his paper, solemnly stated that the play dealt with the "tragic history of an old woman who had lost her 'lovely green fields', and had gone insane as a consequence".' *The Evening Herald* (1 May 1913), p. 1.

6 Eugene Monk is apparently Nugent Monck, and the Mr. Doran mentioned by the Boston papers as appearing in *Galway Races* is probably M. J. Dolan.

7 'Across the Pond', *The Evening Mail* (1 May 1913), p. 6.

8 *Bunty Pulls the Strings*, a popular Scottish play by Graham Moffat, who remarked in an interview:

> Well, it was like this. I had an opportunity of seeing the Irish players in Glasgow. I was very much interested, and it seemed to me that something of the same sort should be done for Scotland. . . .
>
> I think it but right that I should acknowledge the debt I owe to the Irish players, he continued. My work only differs from theirs in so much as the Scottish race differs from the Irish. If someone came forward and wrote plays about the Gaelic people in the North of Scotland these plays would be practically the same as the Irish plays. . . .

From 'A Scrape o' the Pen', by W.M.M., *The Evening Mail* (10 March 1913), p. 2.

9 From the Berg Collection, New York Public Library.

10 As knowledgable critics have surmised that G. Sidney Paternoster was a pseudonym, it seems appropriate to quote a letter from him to Yeats:

'Truth' Buildings
Carteret Street
Queen Anne's Gate
London, S.W.
23 Oct. 1912

Dear Sir — Very many thanks for your letter. I am indeed both delighted and flattered by your kindly appreciation of my play and I scarcely need add how sincerely I hope that no insuperable difficulty will be found to stand in the way of its production. . . .

You will not find me one of those sensitive authors who are unwilling to recognise the usefulness and the necessity for the use of the blue pencil, and it will give me the greatest pleasure to discuss the matter with you when you are again in London.

Faithfully yours,

G. SIDNEY PATERNOSTER

From Ms. 13,068 (15), National Library of Ireland.

11 'New Play at the Abbey Theatre', *The Irish Times* (January 1913), p. 5.
12 H, 'The Citizen at the Play', *The Irish Citizen* (1 February 1913), p. 294.
13 'Abbey Theatre', *The Evening Irish Times* (21 February 1913), p. 8.
14 Jack Point, 'Foreign Play at the Abbey', *The Evening Herald* (21 February 1913), p. 7.
15 S Mac O, 'The Citizen at the Play', *The Irish Citizen* (1 March 1913), p. 325.
16 S, 'The Citizen at the Play', *The Irish Citizen* (12 April 1913), p. 370.
17 As a guess, one would suggest that Lennox Robinson played the part.
18 'Abbey Theatre', *The Evening Irish Times* (7 March 1913), p. 8.
19 Jack Point, 'There Are Crimes and Crimes', *The Evening Herald* (7 March 1913), p. 6.
20 Jack Point, 'The Cuckoo's Nest', *The Evening Herald* (14 March 1913), p. 5.
21 'The Abbey Theatre', *The Irish Times* (14 March 1913), p. 5.
22 H, 'The Citizen at the Play', *The Irish Citizen* (22 March 1913), p. 347.
23 Jack Point, 'The Abbey Theatre', *The Evening Herald* (11 April 1913), p. 7.
24 P, 'The Citizen at the Play', *The Irish Citizen* (19 April 1913), p. 379.
25 Jack Point, 'Another Strindberg Play', *The Evening Herald* (18 April 1913), p. 4.
26 S. Mac O, 'The Citizen at the Play', *The Irish Citizen* (26 April 1913), p. 386.
27 I.R., 'The Citizen at the Play', *The Irish Citizen* (8 November 1913), p. 198.
28 F, 'The Citizen at the Play', *The Irish Citizen* (3 May 1913), p. 397.
29 Jack Point, 'Two New Plays', *The Evening Herald* (25 April 1913), p. 4.
30 The Berg Collection, New York Public Library.
31 Ms. 13,068 (27), National Library of Ireland.
32 Ms. 13,068 (15), National Library of Ireland.
33 *Ibid.*
34 'The Gombeen Man', *The Evening Irish Times* (1 July 1913), p. 5.
35 'The Abbey Theatre', *The Evening Irish Times* (13 November 1913), p. 9.
36 Jack Point, 'New Abbey Play', *The Evening Herald* (12 November 1913), p. 4.
37 Quoted in 'The Abbey Players', *The Dublin Evening Mail* (14 July 1913), p. 2.
38 Quoted in 'Irish Dramatists Active' by Joseph Holloway, *The Evening Herald* (2 May 1913), p. 2.
39 Jack Point, 'At the Abbey', *The Evening Herald* (12 September 1913), p. 4.
40 'Abbey Theatre', *The Evening Irish Times* (3 October 1913), p. 4; 'The Citizen at the Play', *The Irish Citizen* (11 October 1913), p. 166.
41 The derogatory reference is to Ervine's *The Magnanimous Lover.*

42  Jack Point, 'New Northern Comedy', *The Evening Herald* (3 October p. 3.
43  Joan, 'The Citizen at the Play', *The Irish Citizen* (25 October 1913), p. 182.
44  'The Abbey Theatre', *The Evening Irish Times* (17 October 1913), p. 6.
45  'New Play at the Abbey Theatre', *The Evening Irish Times* (21 November 1913), p. 5.
46  Jack Point, 'New Abbey Play', *The Evening Herald* (21 November 1913), p. 5.
47  Joan, 'The Citizen at the Play', *The Irish Citizen* (29 November 1913), p. 223.
48  'New Abbey Play', *The Evening Herald* (17 December 1913), p. 5.
49  'The Abbey Theatre', *The Evening Irish Times* (17 December 1913), p. 7.
50  *Ibid.*
51  'The Abbey Theatre', *The Evening Irish Times* (19 December 1913), p. 6.
52  H.R.W., 'Music and the Drama', *The Dublin Evening Mail* (22 December 1913), p. 2.
53  W. A. Henderson, 'The Success of Mr. Kerrigan', *The Evening Herald* (26 April 1913), p. 6.
54  W. A. Henderson, 'Ireland's Greatest Comedian', *The Evening Herald* (17 May 1913), p. 6.
55  Quoted in 'The Abbey Plays', *The Evening Herald* (11 August 1913), p. 5.
56  Quoted in 'The Decadence of the Abbey', *The Evening Herald* (19 July 1913), p. 6.
57  *Ibid.*
58  Quoted in 'Irish Players in London', *The Evening Herald* (21 June 1913), p. 8.
59  *Ibid.*
60  Quoted in 'The Irish Players', *The Evening Herald* (14 July 1913), p. 2.
61  'The Abbey', *The Weekly Freeman* (18 October 1913), p. 14.
62  'Abbey Drama Criticised', *The Evening Herald* (8 January 1913), p. 8.
63  'Johnson', *The Evening Herald* (25 August 1913), p. 4.
64  Something of the public moral temper of the times might be suggested by the following brouhaha:

The normally serene career of the Feis Ceoil Association has been subjected to a temporary jolt by an incident which has led to the resignation of two prominent members of the Committee, and the withdrawal of certain choirs from competition. Among the test themes selected for the chief choir competition — that for mixed choirs (35 voices) — is a madrigal entitled "Camella Fair", by Thos. Bateson, a composition which dates from as far back as the seventeenth century. This madrigal consists of eight crudely constructed lines, the wording of which is as follows:

> Camella fair tripped o'er the plain,
> I followed quickly after;
> Have overtaken her I would fain,
> And kiss her when I caught her.
> Hope being past her to obtain,
> "Camella," loud I call.
> She answered, with great disdain:
> "I will not kiss at all."

492

Objection, we understand, was taken at an early stage by a section of the Committee to the words of this theme, as being unsuitable for practice amongst mixed choirs. Representations to that effect were laid before the Executive Committee of the Feis Ceoil, and the suggestion was made that an alternative piece should be allowed. These representations apparently did not lead to any satisfactory arrangement, and as a result, two well-known members of the Executive Committee — Very Rev. Canon Pettit, P.P., and Rev. George O'Neill, s.J. — have resigned their membership of the Committee. It is also announced that, for the same cause, certain Dublin choirs which had intended entering for the Feis this year, have decided not to enter, amongst them being the choirs attached to St. Peter's Church, Phibsborough, and the Fairview Schools. . . ['Feis Ceoil Competitions', *The Evening Irish Times* (13 March 1913), p. 6.]

Among the public reactions to this tempest in a teapot is an eminently sane letter signed 'G.A.B.'. In fact, the letter is so sensible, good-humoured and witty that one must suspect 'G.A.B.' is none other than Canon Hannay who, as a Protestant clergyman, could hardly in this instance use his well-known pseudonym of George A. Birmingham.

Sir, — Let us honour the names of Canon Pettit and Father O'Neill, s.J. Let us honour, if we can find them out, the names of the members of the choirs who have joined in this noble protest. Let us pronounce a solemn national anathema on the rest of the Committee of the Feis Ceoil. It was high time that some steps were taken to safeguard the morals of our people. Sir, I have read hundreds, nay, thousands, of books in which the word occurs. I have heard songs in which it was repeated again and again. I have seen — I hesitate to mention this, but it is quite true — I have seen the thing actually done, or a colourable imitation of it presented to the audience by actors on the stage. What results can such familiarity with a disgusting idea produce? Need the question be asked? There is, and can be, but one answer to it. Our young men will sooner or later perpetrate the act. Our young women will, in the horrible language of the French proverb, "hold the cheek". Nay, more. The practise will penetrate into the home. The purity of the marriage tie will be violated. Husbands and wives, long accustomed to see the word in print before their eyes will, when they think that no one is looking at them, k . . s each other. We have our literary Vigilance Committees. What are they doing? Are they awake? It is all very well to protest against the reporting of divorce cases in newspapers. But what is it which leads to divorce? Sir, it is k . . . ing. Let us no longer waste our time in attacking the symptoms of evil. Let us trace it to its source, and check it there. The word must be erased from every printed page, and from the script of every song. Cannot we substitute something innocuous for it whenever it appears? Take the madrigal which has been the fortunate occasion of our moral awakening. To the honour of Camella, we must admit that she refused firmly to submit to the degradation threatened; but, alas, she was not ashamed to speak the word, and we tremble to think what may have occurred later on in her life. How much nicer in every way the song would have been if it had run to us:

493

Camella fair tripped o'er the plain,
 I followed quickly after:
Have overtaken her I would fain,
 And shake hands when I caught her.
Hope being past her to obtain,
 "Please, Miss Camella," I call.
She answered with great disdain:
 "I do not want to shake hands with you,
  or even to bow to you in the street,
  or recognise you in any way at all."

Nobody could possibly be injured by that version. And there is no real difficulty about treating all literature in the same way. —

Yours,

G.A.B.

["Letters to the Editor", *The Evening Irish Times* (15 March 1913, p. 7.]

A few days later another genial antidote appeared in the form of a poem by S.L.M., entitled 'The Kiss That Once'. In part it reads:

The kiss that once through Christendom
 A kindly feeling spread
Is now for relatives, or those
 Towards matrimony led.
A universal custom once,
 Enjoinèd by St. Paul,
It's come to this, the girls won't kiss —
 They will not kiss at all.

['The Kiss That Once', *The Evening Irish Times* (19 March 1913), p. 9.]
The initials, 'S.L.M.' mask, of course, the gently chiding pen of Susan L. Mitchell. This instance seems now a particularly absurd one, but the historian cannot go through accounts of the period without feeling that the simple good sense of G.A.B. and S.L.M. was still a minority opinion.

65   'Abbey Players in England', *The Evening Herald* (27 November 1913), p. 3.
66   'Police and the Playboy', *The Evening Herald* (5 December 1913), p. 2.
67   Ms. 13,068 (16), National Library of Ireland.
68   'The Theatre and Beauty', *The Evening Irish Times* (19 March 1913), p. 5.
69   'The Poetry of Rabindranath Tagore', *The Evening Irish Times* (24 March 1913), p. 11.
70   'Municipal Art Gallery', *The Evening Irish Times* (12 April 1913), p. 7.
71   'Municipal Art Gallery', *The Evening Irish Times* (10 May 1913), pp. 7–8.
72   Alfred Esmore, 'The Ulster Literary Theatre', *The Lady in the House* (15 November 1913), pp. 55–56, 58.
73   'Ulster Players in Dublin', *The Dublin Evening Mail* (1 February 1913), p. 6.
74   F, 'The Citizen at the Play', *The Irish Citizen* (8 February 1913), p. 301.
75   Jack Point, 'The Ulster Players', *The Evening Herald* (1 February 1913), p. 5.
76   'Countess Plunkett and her Son's Plays', *The Dublin Evening Mail* (22 May 1913), p. 6.

77  [D. P. Moran], 'Drama in Irish', *The Leader* (10 May 1913), p. 298.
78  Gaedheal, 'The Irish Festival at the Abbey', *The Leader* (22 November 1913), p. 356.
79  H.R.W., 'Music and the Drama', *The Dublin Evening Mail* (29 December 1913), p. 2.
80  'Drama in Dublin', *The Dublin Evening Mail* (11 July 1913), p. 3.
81  Jack Point, 'The Benson Company', *The Evening Herald* (26 February 1913), p. 5.
82  H.R.W., 'Queen Tara', *The Dublin Evening Mail* (26 February 1913), p. 7.
83  There is no very full account of Mary Costello's *A Bad Quarter of an Hour* or of Alice May Finny's *A Local Demon*. Both were comic sketches, the first set in the waiting room of a railway station, and the second in a doctor's dispensary. One journal described Miss Costello's play as having 'quite an exhaustless fund of humour' and Miss Finny's as having 'a good deal of racy humour'. 'The Gaiety Theatre', *The Weekly Freeman* (6 December 1913), p. 15. One suspects that these views were the gentle ones often accorded to amateur work.
84  'Count Markievicz', *The Dublin Evening Mail* (20 May 1913), p. 2.
85  S. W. Maddock, 'Dublin Repertory Theatre', *The Dublin Evening Mail* (22 May 1913), p. 3.
86  Casimir Dunin Markievicz, 'The Conduct of the Police', *The Evening Irish Times* (1 September 1913), p. 7, reprints the count's remarks on Bloody Sunday. His account of the dispute with Ashley appears in 'Count Markievicz and the Repertory Theatre', *The Evening Irish Times* (13 November 1913), p. 9.
87  'Count Markievicz Gives Up his Dublin Home', *The Evening Herald* (12 December 1913), p. 1.
88  'The Mormon Peril', *The Dublin Evening Mail* (25 February 1913), p. 3.
89  'Queen's Theatre', *The Dublin Evening Mail* (15 July 1913), p. 7.
90  'In Dark '98 at the Queen's', *The Weekly Freeman* (29 November 1913), p. 12.
91  'The Empire', *The Dublin Evening Mail* (14 October 1913), p. 3.
92  H.R.W., 'Music and the Drama', *The Dublin Evening Mail* (8 September 1913), p. 5.
93  'Theatre Bomb', *The Dublin Evening Mail* (19 May 1913), p. 5.
94  'A Lunatic's Jump', *The Dublin Evening Mail* (4 August 1913), p. 2. But, however turbulent the theatrical year may have been in Ireland, it produced nothing quite so alarming as what happened in Paris on 26 January:

> A panic occurred in a theatre in the Belleville quarter last night, owing to a lioness, which took part in the performance, escaping and jumping over the heads of the orchestra into a private box. The door of the latter, fortunately, being open, the lioness made her way into the manager's room, whence she was promptly restored to her cage by her tamer. In the stampede which occurred among the audience a number of women fainted, and several persons were slightly injured, but none seriously.

['Escape of a Lioness in a Theatre', *The Evening Irish Times* (27 January 1913), p. 7.]

Or, indeed, as happened in Berlin on 17 December:

> An amazing incident took place before the fashionable audience

assembled for the performance of *Lohengrin* at the Royal Opera last night. While the third act was in progress an unclothed man suddenly burst into the stalls from a side entrance. Making his way to the orchestra, he climbed over the barrier separating the musicians from the stalls, and standing up, began to go through the motions of conducting the orchestra. There was much excitement among the audience. ['Opera House Scene', *The Evening Irish Times* (19 December 1913), p. 1.]

95  'National Drama for Country Districts', *The Weekly Freeman* (7 June 1913), p. 5.

96  'A Western Playboy', *The Weekly Freeman* (24 May 1913), p. 1.

97  Joseph Holloway, 'Agnes Robertson', *The Evening Herald* (11 January 1913), p. 8.

98  Quoted in 'An Irish Rationalist', *The Evening Herald* (12 April 1913), p. 8.

99  'Mr. James H. Cousins', *The Dublin Evening Mail* (28 February 1913), p. 3.

100  'The Cousins Presentation', *The Irish Citizen* (7 June 1913), pp. 20–21.

101  'The Cousins Presentation', *The Irish Citizen* (14 June 1913), p. 27.

102  Joseph A. Keogh, under the name of J. Augustus Keogh, was to become in a few years the manager of the Abbey Theatre.

103  Joseph Holloway, 'The Betrayal', *The Evening Herald* (16 April 1913), p. 7.

104  'National Drama', *The Evening Irish Times* (29 March 1913), p. 9.

105  Quoted in 'General John Regan', *The Evening Herald* (10 January 1913), p. 2.

# 1914

1   In his novel, *Rogues and Vagabonds*, Compton MacKenzie describes a company obviously based on his father's as a 'very pleasant, old-fashioned company which is more like a family party than anything else'.

2   J.S., 'The Dublin Repertory Theatre', *The Evening Mail* (19 May 1914), p. 7.

3   'The Queen's Theatre', *The Irish Times* (12 May 1914), p. 5.

4   'The Posters', *The Evening Herald* (9 December 1914), p. 1.

5   'General John Regan', *The Evening Herald* (27 January 1914), p. 3.

6   'General John Regan', *The Evening Herald* (31 January 1914), p. 7.

7   'Play Riot', *The Evening Mail* (18 July 1914), p. 5.

8   'Comedy', *The Evening Herald* (7 February 1914), p. 1.

9   'The Western Athens', *The Irish Times* (7 February 1914), p. 6.

10   'Gaiety Theatre', *The Irish Times* (23 February 1914), p. 6.

11   'Who's the Lady?', *The Irish Times* (4 March 1914), p. 8.

12   'Disturbances in Theatres', *The Irish Times* (5 March 1914), p. 4.

13   'David Mahony', *The Evening Herald* (29 January 1914), p. 5.

14   Jack Point, 'At the Abbey', *The Evening Herald* (30 January 1914), p. 4.

15   'Abbey Players' Bad Time', *The Evening Herald* (23 February 1914), p. 2.

16   'A Gigantic Wave', *The Evening Herald* (23 February 1914), p. 2.

17   'Abbey Company in Chicago', quoted from *The New York Times* in *The Evening Herald* (5 March 1914), p. 5.

18   James O'Donnell Bennett, quoted in 'Abbey Company in Chicago', *The Evening Herald* (9 March 1914), p. 5.

19   *Ibid.*

20   'Return of the Abbey Players', *The Evening Herald* (7 May 1914), p. 6.

21   H.R.W., 'New Abbey Plays by New Players', *The Evening Mail* (14 March 1914), p. 2.

22   'The Abbey Theatre', *The Irish Times* (16 March 1914), p. 5.

23   Jack Point, 'The Corporation Caricatured', *The Evening Herald* (14 March 1914), p. 2.

24   From the Berg Collection, New York Public Library.

25   'Abbey Theatre', *The Irish Times* (3 April 1914), p. 8.

26   K, 'The Citizen at the Play', *The Irish Citizen* (11 April 1914), p. 370.

27   J. Bernard MacCarthy, *Kinship* (Dublin: M. H. Gill, [1936]), pp. 26–27.

28   J. Bernard MacCarthy, *The Man for Mannarue* (Dublin: M. H. Gill, [1936]), pp. iii–iv.

29   Con, 'The Citizen at the Abbey', *The Irish Citizen* (26 September 1914), p. 147.

30   'Abbey Theatre', *The Irish Times* (14 April 1914), p. 3.

31   'Abbey Theatre', *The Evening Mail* (14 April 1914), p. 3.

32   'Abbey Theatre', *The Irish Times* (4 September 1914), p. 7.

33   Jack Point, 'New Abbey Play', *The Evening Herald* (4 September 1914), p. 2.

34   Joan, 'The Citizen at the Play', *The Irish Citizen* (12 September 1914), p. 134.

35   [W. J. Lawrence], 'A Minute's Wait', *The Stage* (3 September 1914).

36   Joan, 'The Citizen at the Abbey', *The Irish Citizen* (19 September 1914), p. 138.

37   [W. J. Lawrence], 'The Dark Hour', *The Stage* (17 September 1914).

38   Jack Point, 'New Play at the Abbey Theatre', *The Evening Herald*

(24 September 1914), p. 3. Joan, 'The Citizen at the Abbey', *The Irish Citizen* (3 October 1914), p. 155.

39  [W. J. Lawrence], 'The Crossing', *The Stage* (8 October 1914).
40  'Abbey Theatre', *The Irish Times* (24 September 1914), p. 7.
41  Joan, 'The Citizen at the Play', *The Irish Citizen* (10 October 1914), p. 166.
42  'Abbey Theatre', *The Irish Times* (1 October 1914), p. 6.
43  'The Cobweb', *The Evening Herald* (14 October 1914), p. 2.
44  [W. J. Lawrence], 'The Cobweb', *The Stage* (22 October 1914).
45  Arthur Sinclair, letter to W. J. Lawrence, written from the Abbey Theatre, dated 23 October 1914, and contained in Lawrence's scrapbooks in the National Library of Ireland.
46  For instance, M.E., a commentator in *The Irish Citizen*, wondered, 'Is it heresy to criticise Arthur Sinclair? His misery is rather too jovial! Why cut capers? . . . professional mannerisms and stage-gags tend to take the place of the earlier manner.' 'The Citizen at the Abbey', *The Irish Citizen* (31 October 1914), p. 190.
47  J, 'The Jug of Sorrow', *The Evening Herald* (21 October 1914), p. 2.
48  M.E., 'The Citizen at the Abbey', *The Irish Citizen* (28 November 1914), p. 222.
49  The controversy has been most recently reprinted in *The Letters of Seán O'Casey*, ed. David Krause (London: Macmillan, 1975).
50  'Abbey Theatre', *The Irish Times* (4 November 1914), p. 6.
51  Jacques, 'Really Drama', *The Evening Herald* (4 November 1914), p. 2.
52  The reference is to Suzanne R. Day who subsequently wrote some Abbey plays with Geraldine Cummins.
53  F, 'The Citizen at the Play', *The Irish Citizen* (7 November 1914), p. 194.
54  'Abbey Theatre', *The Irish Times* (28 December 1914), p. 7.
55  Jack Point, 'The Ulster Theatre', *The Evening Herald* (2 May 1914), p. 8.
56  J.S., 'Ulster Players', *The Evening Mail* (15 December 1914), p. 5.
57  'The Gaiety Theatre', *The Irish Times* (17 December 1914), p. 7.
58  'New Play at the Gaiety Theatre', *The Irish Times* (17 December 1914), p. 3.
59  Jack Point, 'A New Irish Theatre', *The Evening Herald* (3 November 1914), p. 4.
60  'The Irish Theatre', *The Irish Times* (3 November 1914), p. 3.
61  F, 'The Citizen at the Play', *The Irish Citizen* (7 November 1914), p. 194.
62  Jacques, 'Mrs. Warren's Profession', *The Evening Herald* (17 November 1914), p. 3.
63  'Abbey Theatre', *The Evening Mail* (28 March 1914), p. 2.
64  'Two New Plays at the Abbey Theatre', *The Irish Times* (28 March 1914), p. 8.
65  'Abbey Theatre', *The Evening Mail* (28 March 1914), p. 2.
66  'The Citizen at the Play', *The Irish Citizen* (4 April 1914), p. 365.
67  M.G., 'The Citizen at the Play', *The Irish Citizen* (2 May 1914), p. 395.
68  'St. Mary's College', *The Evening Herald* (20 May 1914), p. 6.
69  K.S.C. O'B., 'Æ's Deirdre', *The Irish Citizen* (4 July 1914), p. 53.
70  'Abbey Entertainment', *The Evening Herald* (13 October 1914), p. 3.
71  'Straw Boys at a Western Wedding', *The Evening Mail* (21 February 1914), p. 5.

72  'Big Blaze', *The Evening Mail* (2 May 1914), p. 5.
73  The Man about Town, 'Things Seen and Heard', *The Evening Herald* (29 June 1914), p. 5.
74  The Man about Town, 'Things Seen and Heard', *The Evening Herald* (1 July 1914), p. 2.
75  'Irish Drama', *The Irish Times* (30 October 1914), p. 7.
76  L.C., 'The Revolutionist', *The Irish Citizen* (29 August 1914), p. 115.
77  'Dublin's Death Rate', *The Irish Times* (23 May 1914), p. 8.

# 1915

1 All of these letters are from Ms. 13,068 (17), National Library of Ireland.
2 *Ibid.*
3 *Ibid.*
4 *Ibid.*
5 *Ibid.*
6 *Ibid.*
7 *Ibid.*
8 *Ibid.*
9 The Berg Collection, New York Public Library.
10 *Ibid.*
11 Ms. 13,068 (17), National Library of Ireland.
12 *Ibid.*
13 *Ibid.*
14 *Ibid.*
15 *Ibid.*
16 Jacques, 'Popular Irish Actress', *The Evening Herald* (28 January 1915), p. 5.
17 *Ibid.*
18 'Abbey Theatre', *The Irish Times* (28 January 1915), p. 3.
19 Jacques, 'Popular Irish Actress', *The Evening Herald* (28 January 1915), p. 5.
20 F, 'The Citizen at the Abbey', *The Irish Citizen* (6 February 1915), p. 291.
21 M.K.C., 'The Citizen at the Abbey', *The Irish Citizen* (13 February 1915).
22 'Abbey Theatre', *The Irish Times* (11 February 1915), p. 6.
23 K.S. O'B., 'The Citizen at the Play', *The Irish Citizen* (20 February 1915), p. 311.
24 Jacques, 'The Dreamers', *The Evening Herald* (11 February 1915), p. 2.
25 [W. J. Lawrence], 'The Bargain', *The Stage* (8 April 1915).
26 [W. J. Lawrence], 'The Philosopher', *The Stage* (8 April 1915).
27 [W. J. Lawrence], 'Shanwalla', *The Stage* (15 April 1915).
28 Jacques, 'Shanwalla', *The Evening Herald* (9 April 1915), p. 2.
29 'Abbey Theatre', *The Irish Times* (8 April 1915), p. 8.
30 Berg Collection, New York Public Library. A few days later in a letter to Yeats also contained in the Berg Collection, Lady Gregory wrote:

> Thursday, 25th. G.B.S. came in to photograph me ten minutes ago at my writing table, and I said it was one of life's ironies that I who had done so much literary work should be photographed writing, as I was, to a kitchen-maid! Then just after I had begun this letter he took another and said we must offer a prize to who-ever could guess by the expression whether I was writing to the kitchen-maid or to you!

31 'Abbey Theatre', *The Weekly Freeman* (30 October 1915), p. 4.
32 St. John G. Ervine, 'O'Flaherty, v.c.', *The Evening Herald* (19 November 1915), p. 5.
33 Ms. 13,068 (26), National Library of Ireland.
34 Berg Collection, New York Public Library.
35 Ms. 13,068 (26), National Library of Ireland.
36 Ms. 13,068 (17), National Library of Ireland.

37   Ms. 13,068 (26), National Library of Ireland.
38   *Ibid.*
39   Quoted in 'Mr. Bernard Shaw and His New Play', *The Weekly Freeman* (20 November 1915), p. 11.
40   'The Abbey Theatre', *The Evening Mail* (1 December 1915), p. 5.
41   Jacques, 'New Play', *The Evening Herald* (1 December 1915), p. 5.
42   A note appended to the review in Lawrence's notebooks, which are housed in the National Library of Ireland, is the source for Lawrence's remark that Nora Close was 'a howling novice'. The review itself was published in *The Stage* (16 December 1915).
43   Eimar O'Duffy, *Printer's Errors* (Dublin: Martin Lester & London: Leonard Parsons, n.d.), pp. 63–66.
44   Jacques, 'Dramatic Novelties', *The Evening Herald* (5 January 1915), p. 2.
45   Contained in an unsorted collection of the Holloway papers in the National Library of Ireland.
46   'The Irish Theatre, Hardwicke Street', *The Irish Times* (5 January 1915), p. 3.
47   F, 'The Citizen at the Play', *The Irish Citizen* (9 January 1915), p. 263.
48   'The Irish Theatre', *The Evening Mail* (20 April 1915), p. 5.
49   'Miracle Plays at the Irish Theatre', *The Irish Times* (21 May 1915), p. 7.
50   'Platform and Stage', *The Irish Times* (15 May 1915), p. 4.
51   'Miracle Plays at the Irish Theatre', *The Irish Times* (21 May 1915), p. 7. In 1915, the influence of the Irish drama reached to India, and Pearse received a letter written on behalf of the Bengali poet, Rabindranath Tagore:

> The poet, Rabindranath Tagore, has asked me to write to you and tell you what a very great joy and happiness your play *An Rí* has been to him. A copy was sent to him, and he came to me with joy written in every line of his face. "Here is the very thing," he cried, "I have been longing for in my school for boys. You must get them to act it, and we will have it at our festival, along with a Bengali play of mine." The Bengali play was not yet written, but he sat down to write it, and it has proved one of the most beautiful of all his dramas. It is called *The Spring Festival*, and relates how the company that lost its way and became conventional and old, finds the springtime of its own youth again through a blind singer, who leads them, by following his own songs, wherever they lead. . . . It will be a pleasure to you to think that your Irish play was acted along with his at our festival. If the poet translates his own play into English it would be a joy to us if you were able to act it at St. Enda's.
>
> We want to act *An Rí* again next year. I wanted also to ask you for permission to adapt it for a Reader I am preparing for Indian boys. It appeals so wonderfully to Indian boys. . . .
>
> We acted the play in the Indian moonlight on an open-air stage, the people seated on the ground, and we wore Bengali dresses. It was most impressive.

   'A St. Enda's Play in Bengal', *The Dublin Evening Mail* (2 September 1915), p. 6.
52   'Uncle Vanya', *The Irish Times* (24 June 1915), p. 6.
53   Eimar O'Duffy, *Printer's Errors*, p. 67.

54  J.E.L., 'The Irish Theatre', *The Evening Mail* (9 November 1915), p. 5.
55  'The Irish Theatre', *The Evening Mail* (30 December 1915), p. 5.
56  'Irish Theatre', *The Evening Herald* (28 December 1915), p. 2.
57  'Irish Dramatist', *The Evening Herald* (13 October 1915), p. 4.
58  'Dublin's New Theatre', *The Evening Herald* (3 April 1915), p. 5.
59  'Gaiety Theatre', *The Dublin Evening Mail* (23 October 1915), p. 6.
60  J.S., 'Gaiety Theatre', *The Evening Mail* (27 October 1915), p. 6.
61  'The Coliseum', *The Evening Mail* (24 July 1915), p. 6.
62  'The Coliseum', *The Evening Mail* (14 August 1915), p. 5.
63  'The Gaiety Theatre', *The Evening Mail* (6 March 1915), p. 3.
64  Jacques, 'Things Seen and Heard', *The Evening Herald* (12 October 1915), p. 4.
65  [W. J. Lawrence], 'For the Land She Loved', *The Stage* (8 April 1915).
66  Citizen, 'Dublin Music Halls', *The Evening Herald* (9 June 1915), p. 2.
67  'Scene in a City Cinema', *The Evening Mail* (22 September 1915), p. 5.
68  'Count Markievicz', *The Evening Herald* (15 May 1915), p. 2.

# Notes to Appendix I

1  *The New York Times*, 15 July 1911.
2  W. B. Yeats, Letter to the Editor, *The New York Times*, 9 August 1911.
3  Edward Abood. *The Reception of the Abbey Theatre in America, 1911–1914*. University of Chicago, unpublished doctoral dissertation, 1962. Abood's discussion is well researched and quite informative, and has been of much use in the writing of this Appendix.
4  Abood, p. 9. Quoted from *Irish World*, 11 November, p. 7.
5  W. B. Yeats, interviewed in *The Irish Times*, 31 October 1911, p. 4.
6  All quotations from Boston papers of 10 October 1911.
7  *The New York Times*, 9 October 1911.
8  *Ibid.*, 20 November 1911.
9  *Ibid.*, 27 November 1911.
10  *The Irish Times*, 29 November 1911, p. 7.
11  'Riot in Theatre Over an Irish Play', *The New York Times*, 28 November 1911.
12.  *Ibid.*
13  'The "Playboy" Row', *The New York Times*, 29 November 1911, p. 10, cols. 3–4.
14  *Ibid.*, 29 November 1911.
15  *Ibid.*
16  'Falsity Not the Grievance', *The New York Times*, 30 November 1911.
17  Cathleen Nesbitt's charming reminiscences of the first American tour are printed in Chapter Four, 'The Irish Player', of her autobiography *A Little Love and Good Company* (London: Faber & Faber, 1975), pp. 51–56. In this chapter, Miss Nesbitt relates how she was, although a young English actress, hired as an understudy for the tour.
18  Quoted in *The Irish Times*, 18 December 1911.
19  'Halt Performance of Playboy', *The Philadelphia Inquirer*, 16 January 1912.
20  'Irish Play Halted by More Disorder', *The Philadelphia Evening Bulletin*, 17 January 1912.
21  'Disturbers Held for Theatre Row', *The Philadelphia Evening Bulletin*, 16 January 1912.
22  *The Philadelphia Inquirer*, 17 January 1912.
23  *North American*, 18 January 1912.
24  *The Philadelphia Inquirer* of 20 January 1912 contains an expanded version of this testimony:
    'Well, your honour,' the Director replied, 'I may have an unusually perverted mind, but I didn't see anything indecent, sacrilegious or immoral in the whole show.'
    'You took your wife with you?' the judge asked. 'Was she shocked? Were her sensibilities in any way affected?'
    'No, sir,' Director Porter replied.
25  'Irish Players Appear for A "Court Comedy"; No Decision', *North American*, 20 January 1912.
26  *The Philadelphia Public Ledger*, 19 January 1912.
27  P.S.W.'s poem, 'The Fighting Temeraire' first appeared in *The Chicago Daily Tribune*, 12 February 1912.
28  Percy Hammond, 'Affairs of the Theatre', *Chicago Sunday Tribune*, 3 March 1912.
29  *The New York Sun*, 24 December 1911, p. 6.
30  *The New York Tribune*, 12 December 1911, p. 7.

31  *Ibid.*, 24 December 1911, pt. 5, p. 6.
32  Neither was the Abbey acting always accurately assessed. There were critics, for instance, who admired the accents of the players in Ervine's *Mixed Marriage*. According to that redoubtable Belfastman, W. J. Lawrence, however, practically none of the actors could manage a plausible Belfast accent.
33  Perhaps a note is germane here about the teaching of Frank Fay. With his brother, W. G. Fay, Frank Fay has been credited with creating the Abbey style of acting. It is certainly true that Fay was receptive in 1900 to what was new in the theatre (see, for instance, his collected theatre pieces, *Towards a National Theatre*), and that he knew of Andre Antoine and Ole Bull. However, he had only *seen* Coquelin. What the Fays contributed to an Abbey style was, in the most general sense, what Stanislavsky contributed to the Moscow Arts Theatre — this was not a Method but Methodicalness. The brothers, particularly W.G., worked for a complete ensemble of realistic natural acting, of truth to nature based upon real observation in the peasant plays, and of an anti-conventional theatricalism. This last was a lesson they learned early. In the original production of *Cathleen ni Houlihan*, W. G. Fay's conventional comic acting got laughs that threw off the entire effect of the play, and he very quickly remedied the matter by underplaying, by doing less. In other words, W. G. Fay quickly learned the value of ensemble playing and of simplicity.

With Frank Fay, the situation was somewhat different. He was most noted as an effective speaker of Yeats's poetry and as an elocutionary coach. However, after he left the Abbey, he pursued his own bent which was to Shakespearean acting. His own acting style and his own teaching became more old-fashioned and his speaking more mannered and pedantic. The generations of actors who studied under Fay learned distinctness of articulation, but they did not learn modern acting. The clearly articulated but monotonous whine of one or two actresses of the recent past may be a product of the teaching of this ultimately reactionary pioneer.
34  Percy Hammond, 'Affairs of the Theatre', *Chicago Sunday Tribune*, 3 March 1912.
35  Theodore Roosevelt, *Outlook*, 16 December 1911; reprinted in *The Irish Times*, 30 December 1911, p. 6.
36  John Quinn, Letter to the Editor, *The Irish Times*, 31 January 1912.

# Index

505

507

Campbell, Mrs. Patrick, 73, 149.
*The Canavans* (Lady Gregory), 177, 193, 240.
*Candida* (G. B. Shaw), 225.
*Candidates* (C. O'Brien), 353-354.
Canmer, Ross (John P. Campbell), 91.
Canmer, Seveen (Josephine Campbell), 91.
*The Captain of the Hosts* (R. Mayne), 89-91.
Carberry, Ethna, 415.
Carleton, William, 30.
*Carmen* (opera), 312.
Carolan, M., 82, 407.
Carr, John J., 425.
Carr, Judge, 423, 424-426, 427.
Carré, J. M., 79, 82, 351, 353.
Carrickford, Kitty, 407.
Carroll, Paul Vincent, 121, 244.
Carson, Sir Edward, 202.
Carter, Miss (?), 174-175.
Casement, Sir Roger, 311, 436.
Casey, W. F., 212, 214, 240, 266. Quoted, 149, 190-191.
Castellana Opera Company, 150.
*The Casting Out of Martin Whelan* (R. J. Ray), 35, 42-45, 49, 129, 239, 240, 252.
*The Cattle Thief* (melodrama), 301.
Censorship, theatrical, 313, 330, 352-353, 383-388, 395, 408, 412, 417-419, 423-427.
Chambers, C. Haddon, 408.
Chaplin, Charlie, 404.
*Charlie Chaplin Mad* (revue), 404.
*Charity* (M. F. Scott), 161-162.
*Charley's Aunt* (B. Thomas), 150, 293, 393.
Charters, G. A., 230.
Chase, Pauline, 292.
Chekhov, Anton, 393, 394, 395, 396, 397-399.
*The Cherry Orchard* (A. Chekhov), 398.
Chester cycle, 176.
Chicago, Illinois, 427-428.
*The Chocolate Soldier* (O. Straus), 150, 290, 292.
Christie, R. A., 334-336.
*The Cinema Star*, 404.
Cinema Theatre, Galway, 314.
*An Claidheamh Soluis*, 69, 86. Quoted, 84-85.
Clarke, Austin, 120.
Close, Nora (Mrs. St. John Ervine), 383, 389, 390.
An Cluithcheóirí, 240, 288.
*Coats* (Lady Gregory), 49, 112, 214.
*The Cobbler* (A. P. Wilson), 329-330.
*The Cobweb* ('F. Jay'), 338-341.
Cockran, W. Bourke, 242, 284.
Cohan, George M., 429, 431.
The Coliseum Theatre, Dublin, 401-402, 404.
The Coliseum Theatre, London, 267, 272, 308, 340, 371, 372, 373.
*The Colleen Bawn* (D. Boucicault), 410.
*Collier's Weekly*, 434.

509

Cummins, Geraldine D., 239, 240, 250-251.
Curran, Sarah, 376.
*Curtain Up* (L. Robinson), 188.
The *Cymric* (ship), 242, 243.

*The Daily Chronicle* (London), 149.
*The Daily Express*, 133, 184. Quoted, 119.
*The Daily News and Leader* (London). Quoted, 128, 271-272, 273.
*Damer's Gold* (Lady Gregory), 203, 205-206, 214, 240.
*Dana*, 306.
*The Dancing Mistress* (musical), 292.
*The Dandy Dolls* (G. Fitzmaurice), 120, 251, 360.
*The Dangerous Age* (N. Fitzpatrick), 219.
Dante, 235.
*The Dark Hour* (R. A. Christie), 334-336.
*A Daughter of Ireland* (G. J. Hurson), 87, 156, 159.
*The Daughter of the Regiment* (opera), 312.
*David Mahony* (V. O'D. Power), 319-320.
Davis, Thomas, 75.
Day, J., 64, 65.
Day, Suzanne R., 239, 240, 250-251, 308, 345.
Dean, Basil, 277.
*The Dean of St. Patrick's* (G. S. Paternoster), 239, 240, 244-245.
*Deirdre* (Æ), 356, 358.
*Deirdre* (W. B. Yeats), 72, 112-113, 133, 193, 265.
*Deirdre of the Sorrows* (J. M. Synge), 18-22, 77, 370, 371.
Delany, Maureen, 325, 345, 437.
*The Deliverer* (Lady Gregory), 101, 103, 104-105, 106, 108, 109, 110.
Derham, J., 400.
*Dervorgilla* (Lady Gregory), 136, 174, 239.
Desmond, Miss L., 234, 237.
Desmond, Nora, 174, 198, 245, 333, 336, 337, 338, 344, 345, 346, 356, 369, 379, 391.
*The Destruction of the Hostel* (P. Colum), 84.
Dever, William, 84.
de Vere, Aubrey, 60.
Devereux, William, 88.
*The Devil's Disciple* (G. B. Shaw), 296.
*Dick the Trumpeter* (melodrama), 406.
Digges, Dudley, 308, 391.
*The Doctor in Spite of Himself* (Lady Gregory/Molière), 265.
*An Doctúir/The Doctor* (S. O'Beirne), 435.
Dodd, Edith, 216.
Dolan, Michael J., 206, 242, 243.
*The Dollar Princess* (musical), 292.
*A Doll's House* (H. Ibsen), 31, 401.
Doran, Mr. See M. J. Dolan.
Dostoyevsky, Fyodor, 32.
*Down in Kerry* (B. MacCarthy), 157.
Downing, Denis J. ('Doctor Dick'), 264.
Doyle, Sir Arthur Conan, 88.
D'Oyly Carte Company, 88, 150, 293.
Doyle, Lynn (Leslie Montgomery), 347-348.
Drago, Kathleen, 160, 186, 206, 243, 332, 338, 342, 344, 345, 369, 382.

511

Quoted, 201-202, 269-271, 327, 382-383, 383-384, 386.

515

*The House of Temperley* (A. C. Doyle), 88.
Housing conditions in Dublin, 361.
Howard, Sidney, 434.
Hueffer, Ford Madox (Ford), 59.
Hughes, Mrs. Brooke, 166.
Hughes, Charles, 316, 318.
Hughes, Felix, 106, 179, 330.
Hughes, Oliver Brooke, 238.
Hughes, Thomas, 316.
Hugo, Victor, 309.
*Hullo Rag-Time* (musical), 292.
Hurson, George J., 87, 156, 159.
Hutchinson, H. E., 198, 206, 261, 338, 369, 379, 407.
Hutchinson, Percy, 293.
*Hyacinth Halvey* (Lady Gregory), 21, 62, 198, 214, 239, 240, 243-244, 436.
Hyde, Douglas, 84-85, 98-100, 108, 135, 136, 176, 239, 240, 308, 436. Quoted, 66.
Ibsen, Henrik, 29, 30, 31, 76, 94, 103, 132, 150, 216, 217, 225, 246, 297, 392, 399, 428.
*Ibsen, 1828-1906* (Ossip-Laurié), 31.
I.C.I.C.Y.M.A. Dramatic Society, 237-238.
*If!* (R. Mayne), 348-349.
'Imaal'. Quoted, 27-28, 95.
*The Image* (Lady Gregory), 413.
*In Clay and in Bronze* (B. MacNamara). Quoted, 35-41.
*In Dark '98* (P. J. Bourke), 302, 313.
*In the Shadow of the Glen* (J. M. Synge), 16, 129, 132, 135, 136, 140, 169, 180, 211, 214, 239, 240, 266, 432.
Independent Dramatic Company, 10, 78, 80-82, 152-155, 216-219, 296.
Indianapolis, Indiana, 427.
*The Inferno* (Dante), 27, 235.
Ingle, Dora, 238.
*Interior* (M. Maeterlinck), 170.
*The Interlude of Youth* (Anon.), 135, 136.
Iona Players, 223.
*Iosagán* (P. H. Pearse), 84-85, 397, 437.
*Ireland's Own*, 320.
Irish Animated Picture Company, 150.
*The Irish Citizen*, 250, 261, 306, 329, 334, 336, 352. Quoted, 245, 246-247, 249, 250, 258, 259, 286, 328, 331-332, 337, 344-345, 346-347, 351-352, 354-355, 374, 375-376, 395-396.
*The Irish Independent*, 116, 188, 217. Quoted, 23-24, 27, 33, 47, 47-48, 99, 121, 137, 174, 219, 223, 226.
*The Irish Nation*, 55. Quoted, 79.
*Irish Plays and Playwrights* (C. Weygandt), 310.
Irish Republican Army, 440.
Irish Republican Brotherhood, 440.
*The Irish Review*, 219, 221.
The Irish Theatre and National Stage Society, 159-161.
Irish Theatre in Hardwicke Street, 10, 221-223, 287-288, 349-352, 391-400.
The Irish Theatrical Club, 85, 274.
*The Irish Times*, 19, 26, 69, 88, 112, 121, 133, 146, 157, 177, 183, 188, 200, 201, 202, 221, 223, 224, 226, 258, 259, 261, 326, 329, 330, 348, 374, 375, 394, 397, 415. Quoted, 34-35, 42-44, 48-49, 59-62, 62-64, 65-66, 79,

81-82, 82-83, 85, 87-88, 99-100, 106-110, 113, 120, 122, 138-139, 145-146, 147-148, 151-152, 154-155, 155-156, 156, 157, 158-159, 159-160, 174, 181, 198, 224, 244-245, 246, 247-248, 248, 255-256, 260, 262, 263, 298-300, 312-313, 318, 319, 336-337, 337-338, 342-343, 346, 349, 351, 353-354, 359-360, 381-382, 395.

Irish Volunteers, 311, 376.
Irish Women's Franchise League, 354.
Irving, H. B., 87, 150.
Irving, Sir Hentry, 102, 431.
Irving, Laurence, 290.
*Israel's Incense* (D. Corkery), 234-235.
*It's a Long Way to Tipperary* (melodrama), 406.
Iveagh, Viscount, 62.

'Jack Point', 137, 184, 200, 221, 246, 249, 251, 256, 285, 336, 349. Quoted, 26, 219, 248, 250, 257-258, 258-259, 260-261, 286-287, 293-294, 320, 326, 330-331, 347-348, 350.
*The Jackdaw* (Lady Gregory), 191, 214.
'Jacques', 138, 180, 436. Quoted, 27, 33, 47, 47-48, 109-110, 137, 149, 152-154, 174, 180, 186, 197-198, 200, 203, 217, 217-218, 219, 341-342, 343-344, 374, 376-377, 381, 394, 405.
Jago, Lilian, 246, 247.
James, Stephen. See James Stephens.
*Jane Clegg* (St. J. Ervine), 249.
'Jay, F', (F. J. Little), 338-341.
Jeffs, Fred A., 146.
*The Jerrybuilders* (W. Paul), 162, 163-164, 285.
*Jim the Penman*, 293.
'Joan', 261. Quoted, 331-332, 334, 336.
*John Bull's Other Island* (G. B. Shaw), 71, 139, 152, 226, 270, 296.
*John Ferguson* (St. J. Ervine), 326-327, 363, 364-365, 383, 384, 388-391, 429.
Johnson, Jack, 274-275.
Johnston, Denis, 244.
Johnstown, Pennsylvania, 421.
Jones, T. Arthur, 301.
Joyce, James, 313, 350, 359.
Judge, Peter. See 'F. J. McCormick'.
*Judgment* (J. Campbell), 186-189.
*The Jug of Sorrow* (W. P. Ryan), 341-342.
*Justice* (J. Galsworthy), 225.

Kane, Whitford, 164-165, 189, 226.
*Kathleen ni Houlihan* (W. B. Yeats and Lady Gregory), 16, 118, 198, 199, 214, 239, 240, 288, 337, 346, 432.
Kearney, Peadar, 87.
Keegan, Edward, 82.
Kehoe, P., 156.
Kelleher, D. L. Quoted, 192.
*The Kelly Gang* (melodrama), 199.
Kelly's Theatre, Liverpool, 124, 164.
Kennedy, Mrs. Bart, 240, 259-260.
Kennedy, Walter, 349.
Keogh, J. Augustus, 308. Quoted, 224-226.
Keogh, Joseph A. See J. Augustus Keogh.

517

519

522

526

530